Drugs and Crime

Drugs and Crime

Edited by
Michael Tonry and
James Q. Wilson

Crime and Justice
A Review of Research
Edited by Michael Tonry and Norval Morris
with the Support of The National Institute of Justice

VOLUME 13

The University of Chicago Press, Chicago and London

This volume was prepared under Grant Number 86-IJ-CX-0032 awarded to the Castine Research Corporation by the National Institute of Justice, U.S. Department of Justice, under the Omnibus Crime Control and Safe Streets Act of 1968 as amended. Points of view or opinions expressed in this volume are those of the editors or authors and do not necessarily represent the official position or policies of the U.S. Department of Justice.

The University of Chicago Press, Chicago 60637
The University of Chicago Press, Ltd., London

© 1990 by The University of Chicago
All rights reserved. Published 1990
Printed in the United States of America

ISSN: 0192-3234

ISBN: 0-226-80810-6
95 94 93 92 91 90   5 4 3 2 1

ISBN 0-226-80811-4
95 94 93 92 91 90   5 4 3 2 1

LCN: 80-642217

Library of Congress Cataloging-in-Publication Data

Drugs and crime / edited by Michael Tonry and James Q. Wilson.
        p.   cm.—(Crime and justice. ISSN 0192-3234; v. 13)
    ISBN 0-226-80810-6 (alk. paper): $40.00
    1. Narcotics and crime—United States. 2. Narcotics, Control of—United States. I. Tonry, Michael H. II. Wilson, James Q. III. Series: Crime and justice (Chicago, Ill.): v. 13.
HV6001.C672   vol. 13
[HV5825]
364 s—dc20
[364.2'4]   90-10825
                                                                      CIP

The paper used in this publication meets the minimum requirements of American National Standard for Information Sciences—Permanence of Paper for Printed Library Materials, ANSI Z39.48-1984. ♾

Contents

Dedication

To the
memory of
John Kaplan,
who taught us
to think more
clearly about
so many things

Preface

"Drugs and Crime" has been promoted to the top of the nation's public policy agenda. Federal funding for drug law enforcement and for drug abuse education, prevention, and treatment programs has increased substantially. For the first time in our history a federal "drug czar" has been appointed. Another "war on drugs" has been launched. Old taboos against the use of military forces in interdiction of drug smuggling have been set aside. Record levels of prison crowding and of rates of increase in prison populations are being driven by the effects of toughened drug laws and longer sentences in drug cases. A military incursion into Panama was precipitated in part by General Noriega's role as a symbol of links between political corruption and drug trafficking.

Though most of these signs of heightened public concern about drug abuse and the links between drug abuse and criminality date to 1988–90, it has been clear since the early 1980s that drug abuse and related social problems would steadily rise in public awareness and political consciousness. And so it was that the National Institute of Justice more than three years ago launched this volume, charging the editors to invite the most distinguished American scholars of various facets of knowledge relating to drugs and crime to prepare review essays summarizing what is known and what needs to be known about their respective subjects.

This is the fourth in a series of thematic volumes published as part of *Crime and Justice—a Review of Research*. *Communities and Crime*, edited by Albert J. Reiss, Jr., and Michael Tonry, *Prediction and Classification*, edited by Don M. Gottfredson and Michael Tonry, and *Family Violence*, edited by Lloyd Ohlin and Michael Tonry, are its predecessors. Like each of these earlier volumes, *Drugs and Crime* draws on the views, advice, and talents of a wide range of leading scholars. A planning meeting consisting of the editors and Douglas Anglin, Paul Goldstein, Bernard Gropper, George Speckart, and Eric Wish was held in Los Angeles in the spring of 1987. Successive proposed outlines for the volume were circulated among the members of the editorial board of *Crime and Justice;* they are identified elsewhere in this volume. Essays were commissioned in due course, and first drafts were discussed at a meeting held in Washington, D.C., in 1988. Discussions, while friendly, were uninhibited, and most of the essays were substantially recast in the meeting's aftermath. In addition to the writers included in this book, those in attendance included Alfred Blumstein, Richard Clayton, Philip Cook, George DeLeon, Paul Goldstein, Steven Gust, Leon Hunt, Nicholas Kozel, Douglas Lipton, David Musto, Lloyd Ohlin, Albert J. Reiss, Jr., Peter Reuter, Beatrice Rouse, Hon. James K. Stewart, Frank Tims, and Richard Will. Finally, each manuscript was sent to as many as four expert referees who provided written critical commentaries on them, which, augmented by the editors' requests, were delivered to the writers as the bases for preparation of subsequent drafts.

Neither *Crime and Justice* nor this volume would exist without the financial support and encouragement of the National Institute of Justice, particularly its director, James K. Stewart. Bernard Gropper, who manages NIJ's research program on drugs, alcohol, and crime; Mary Graham, who oversees all things having to do with *Crime and Justice;* and Paul Cascarano, NIJ's assistant director and the person who first proposed creation of *Crime and Justice,* have helped us at each step.

We hope that *Drugs and Crime* provides a comprehensive review of social science research on the interactions between drug use and criminality in the United States. At minimum, this volume has the value of novelty; no other book takes on so immodest a task. Whether we have succeeded in distilling the best of current research in a form that is up-to-date, authoritative, comprehensive, and readable is for others to decide.

"Drugs and Crime" will remain a pressing American social problem for years to come. May this volume contribute in some small way to better illumination of the complexities encompassed in the phrase "drugs and crime."

Michael Tonry
James Q. Wilson

Michael Tonry

Research on Drugs and Crime

Drugs and Crime aims to provide a comprehensive overview of the current state of research on interactions between crime and drug abuse. Drug-law enforcement, drug-abuse treatment, and drug-abuse prevention are the troika of public policy strategies for dealing with drugs and crime, and this volume addresses each. Concerning law enforcement, Mark Kleiman and Kerry Smith survey research and systematic knowledge on the effects of alternate local drug-law-enforcement strategies (there is not much research) and comment on widespread, but seldom evaluated, alternate strategies adopted by American police departments; Mark Moore discusses law-enforcement strategies concerned with the upper reaches of drug distribution, interdiction of illicit drugs at our borders, and source-country strategies to discourage cultivation of coca, opium, and marijuana. Concerning treatment, Douglas Anglin and Yih-Ing Hser survey what is known about the effectiveness of the major drug-treatment modalities in relation to their effects on contemporaneous and later drug use and on contemporaneous and later crime. Concerning prevention, Gilbert Botvin surveys what is known about the effectiveness of drug education programs in school.

The social problems associated with drugs and crime extend, however, far beyond the law-enforcement agencies and the treatment and prevention programs that constitute the primary governmental responses to drug abuse. Drug abuse and drug trafficking are inextricably related to the deterioration of inner-city sections of many cities, to heightened levels of violence within the drug markets, and to a variety

Michael Tonry is managing editor of *Crime and Justice: A Review of Research*.

1

of social and personal pathologies. Accordingly, this volume also addresses many of those issues. Bruce Johnson and his colleagues provide a powerful, albeit depressing, depiction of the effects of drug trafficking on the quality of life in minority inner-city areas of large American cities. Jeffrey Fagan reviews a wide range of scholarly literatures to determine whether they offer guidance on the effects of drug ingestion on aggression. Eric Wish and Bernard Gropper review both the technology and the uses of drug testing, particularly urinalysis, within the criminal justice system. Jan and Marcia Chaiken survey findings of large-scale quantitative research on the interactions between drug use and criminality—does participation in one lead to the other, and if so, which comes first? If violence is "hard" crime, Dana Hunt surveys facets of the "soft" crime associated with drug use: notably drug trafficking and prostitution. Finally, James Q. Wilson reviews the arguments for and against "legalization" and comments on the implications of the other essays in this volume.

Read together, these essays reveal both that much more is known about their subjects than was true ten years ago and that much less is known than could and should be. Although the volume of research on these subjects has increased significantly in recent years, in absolute terms, drugs and crime research is a minor scholarly activity and is poorly funded. The literature is scant, much of it is fugitive, the research community is fragmented, and too much of the research is poor in quality and weak in design.

One striking feature of research on drug policy is its scantiness. On a number of central questions, very little systematic knowledge is available from methodologically rigorous research. For example, there have been only a couple of modest evaluations of the effectiveness of alternate local drug-law-enforcement strategies, as the essay by Kleiman and Smith demonstrates; police officials have only intuition and experience to guide them, and these leads are too often fallible. On the effects and effectiveness of interdiction strategies for keeping drugs from our shores, the literature is even smaller. Even on the effectiveness of drug treatment, a subject in which the National Institute on Drug Abuse has invested hundreds of millions of dollars, we know only a small part of what we need to know. The major modalities "work," if by that word one means not that instant miracle cures are possible but that sustained treatment efforts over time, generally after a series of relapses in drug use, criminality, or both, can, in a significant proportion of cases, help people reclaim their lives. However, next to nothing is known about criteria for matching drug abusers to the treatment programs most likely to benefit them, and only a little is known about the program characteristics that make one drug-treatment program more successful than another of the same type.

Too much of the literature on drugs and crime is fugitive. Much research on drugs is carried out by private-sector research firms, independent research agencies, and nontenured university-affiliated researchers on "soft-money" jobs; all are dependent on a steady flow of grant awards for their economic survival. As a result, when a major project is finished and the final report is delivered to the funding agency, researchers must often turn to the next project. The researchers often do not have time or money to recast their work into scholarly articles or into books. The reports too often are not published by the government agencies or foundations that sponsored them. Instead, they add to the accumulation of documents on the shelves of government and foundation research administrators and circulate privately among the narrow research community most centrally interested in the report's subject or among researchers personally known by the report's author. Some research firms, like the RAND Corporation, publish many of the reports prepared by affiliated scholars, but these, too, circulate in small numbers and to limited audiences.

In the life of any drug-using offender, the effectiveness or ineffectiveness of prevention programs, of treatment programs, and of law-enforcement strategies plays each its role in determining his or her destiny. Drug abuse generates a complex of interconnected human problems, social processes, and governmental initiatives. The goals and effects of treatment intervention and law-enforcement efforts are inherently interconnected, but in the knowledge community there is little interaction. Thus, education specialists and psychologists study education and prevention programs, survey researchers chart patterns of use, economists and public policy scholars study law-enforcement efforts, medical and related researchers study treatment, sociologists and anthropologists study the ethnography of drug use, and a diversity of scholars study behavioral, biological, and psychopharmacological effects of drug use.

This fragmentation of effort exacerbates the inefficiencies that result from fugitive literatures. Many of the fruits of serious research efforts, whatever their focus, are published only in specialized journals that are unfamiliar (often unknown) to nonspecialists, are published by government agencies and made available to the agency's constituency of policymakers and researchers, or are never published at all. Much of the work financed by the National Institute on Drug Abuse (NIDA), for example, is published by the National Institute on Drug Abuse. Because NIDA is part of the U.S. Department of Health and Human Services and has drug treatment as its primary goal, its work is well known among medical and related researchers and treatment administrators and evaluators but is not widely known by other scholars.

Taking these consequences of fragmentation together—the specialized nature of much drug research and the journals in which it is published, the policy of government agencies to publish the fruits of their own work for the benefit of their own research communities, and the nonpublication of much important work—it is not easy for journalists, public officials, or nonspecialist researchers to find out what has been done or what has been learned.

A fourth property of the drug literature is that much of it—though by no means all—is scientifically weak. Though countless trees have been pulped to provide the paper for hundreds or thousands of treatment evaluation studies, the number in which rigorous research designs were employed and in which the experimental treatment was faithfully implemented can be counted on the fingers of two hands. The literature on the effects of prevention and educational programs is, almost by definition, not rigorous. Thus, as several of the essays in this volume illustrate, researchers and policy analysts must look for inferences and glimmers of insight, rather than for robust, methodologically sound conclusions.

For all those limitations, however, existing research teaches much more about drugs, drug use, and interactions between drugs and crime than was known fifteen years ago. Sometimes, mythology has been shown to be just that. We have learned that there is no inexorable connection between drug use and criminality. Many users of illicit drugs commit no other crimes. Many criminals do not use illicit drugs. Although the National Institute of Justice's Drug Use Forecasting system (see Wish and Gropper, in this volume) instructs that large percentages of arrested felons, as many as 90 percent in some places at some times, test positive for drug use, there is no clear progression from drug use to crime, or from crime to drug use. Sometimes drug use comes first, sometimes criminality comes first; both are powerfully associated with a deviant lifestyle in which each is common.

Drug-policy research reminds us that life is more complicated than we might wish, and that we must ask better questions. Drug treatment provides an illustration of areas in which we have learned to ask better questions. Treatment "works" if that word is not understood to mean that drug abusers are "cured" as a result of a single treatment episode or series of treatment episodes. Sometimes that happens. By that measure, however, most drug-treatment programs fail for most of their patients. Treatment administrators and evaluators, however, no longer think in simplistic, cured-or-not-cured terms, but instead view drug dependence as a chronic condition in which most clients will relapse; a successful long-term outcome will often involve a series of alternating treatments, failures, additional treatments, additional failures, and so on, culminating eventually for many in a pattern of life that is free from both drug dependence and criminality.

Recent research has generated a number of important insights for policymakers. Two, on the causal relation between drug use and criminality and on the effectiveness of treatment programs, have been mentioned. There are others:

- The National Institute of Justice's Drug Use Forecasting system has shown that levels of drug use among persons arrested for felonies are very much higher than was generally believed; in many cities, 50–85 percent of arrestees test positive for drug use (National Institute of Justice 1989).

- Representative national surveys of self-reported drug use (National Institute on Drug Abuse 1989) and representative surveys of self-reported drug use by high school and college students and young adults (Johnston, O'Malley, and Bachman 1988; U.S. Department of Health and Human Services 1989) show that use of cocaine, heroin, and marijuana is declining substantially among most segments of the U.S. population.

- A sizable number of treatment evaluations (summarized in Anglin and Hser, in this volume) indicate that the length of time a drug abuser is in treatment is the single best predictor of a successful outcome.

- A number of ethnographic and longitudinal studies of drug-abusing criminals (summarized in Chaiken and Chaiken, in this volume) demonstrate that among persons who are both high-rate drug users and high-rate offenders, high levels of drug

use are associated with high levels of crime, and low levels of
drug use are associated with low levels of crime.

Research has thus provided important insights for the making of
drug policy and can continue to do so, and do more, in the future.
However, just as drug policy analysts must recognize the complexity of
the problems that they face, that there are no quick fixes, that meaningful changes in American social attitudes toward drug use will involve
long-term processes of moral education and value reinforcement, so the
research enterprise requires a recognition that the accumulation of
knowledge is a slow, gradual, and frustrating business, that current
levels of funding are both insufficient and unstable, and that substantial
advances in knowledge will require that stable, long-term funding become available.

Researchers, of course, always want more and more stable funding,
more and better research; concerning drug research, however, researchers do not stand alone. Many practitioners also recognize a need
for increased investment in both basic and evaluation research on drug
issues. Transient political pressures result in fitful appropriations of
large sums of money for operating agencies, often without adequate
acknowledgment of the need to build institutions slowly, to develop
human resources, and to provide stability of funding and long-term
security to people making career choices. These problems affect operating agencies concerned with drug policy and they affect research on
drug policy. One hundred million dollars a year for eight years for
states to bolster state drug-law-enforcement efforts, for example, assuming the funds are used as intended, is likelier to have a long-term
payoff than $800 million in one year and nothing for the ensuing seven.
And so it is with research.

Research, however, has an additional problem; it tends to be assigned low funding priority compared with needs for funds for operating agencies. Large sums of money are often appropriated by government for operating agencies, without adequate provision even for
evaluation research that, in the long term, can indicate whether the
additional funds made any short- or long-term difference, and whether
new practices, institutions, or policies established with those new funds
are more, less, or equally effective as the programs they supplanted.

Some years ago, the National Institute of Justice and the National
Academy of Sciences sponsored a workshop on drugs and crime research for practitioners and assembled a sizable group of leading state

and local drug-law-enforcement officials. After two days of discussions of current research findings, it became apparent that public officials were as skeptical of large-scale, short-term funding initiatives as were researchers and that those officials recognized the need to set aside federal drug monies to support the basic and evaluation research that has taught us much of what we now know. The introduction to the proceedings volume for that conference summarized their views:

> Widespread concern was expressed by practitioners and researchers alike that the substantial funds appropriated by the Congress in 1986 for drug law enforcement, drug treatment, and drug abuse education might be spent without adequate provision for monitoring the initiatives supported by those funds or for assessing their impact. . . . Participants in the workshop were particularly concerned that large amounts of federal money may be wasted on transient intervention programs formulated as a response to the availability of federal monies, surviving only while those monies remain available, and leaving no legacy in the form of improved policy or increased knowledge. Short-term appropriations, even of substantial funds, are not likely to have lasting effects either programmatically or in terms of knowledge of how most effectively to carry out drug law enforcement, drug treatment, and drug education programs. Long-term commitments of funds are needed to encourage and support collaborative efforts by practitioners and researchers in the criminal justice and treatment communities, to identify promising approaches, to test their impact, and, over time, to tailor them to meet special needs. [Roth, Tonry, and Morris 1987, pp. 18–19]

In similar vein, James Q. Wilson observes in this volume's concluding essay: "I have watched several 'wars on drugs' declared over the last three decades. The wars typically begin with the statement that the time for studies is past and the time for action has come. 'We know what to do; let's get on with it.' In fact, we do not know what to do in any comprehensive way, and the need for research is never more urgent than at the beginning of a 'war.' That is because every past war has led, after brief gains, to final defeat. And so we condemn another generation to risk."

Social science research on drug policy issues, for all the impediments that confront it, offers some solid information on which informed public policy can be based. Well-conceived and adequately funded programs of drug policy research in the 1990s could add important new insights for the future.

REFERENCES

Anglin, M. Douglas, and Yih-Ing Hser. In this volume. "Treatment of Drug Abuse."

Botvin, Gilbert J. In this volume. "Substance Abuse Prevention: Theory, Practice, and Effectiveness."

Chaiken, Jan M., and Marcia R. Chaiken. In this volume. "Drugs and Predatory Crime."

Fagan, Jeffrey A. In this volume. "Intoxication and Aggression."

Hunt, Dana. In this volume. "Drugs and Consensual Crime: Drug Dealing and Prostitution."

Johnson, Bruce D., Terry Williams, Kojo A. Dei, and Harry Sanabria. In this volume. "Drug Abuse in the Inner City: Impact on Hard Drug Users and the Community."

Johnston, Lloyd D., Patrick M. O'Malley, and Jerald G. Bachman. 1988. *Illicit Drug Use, Smoking, and Drinking by America's High School Students, College Students, and Young Adults, 1975–1987*. ADM 89-1602. Rockville, Md.: U.S. Department of Health and Human Services, National Institute on Drug Abuse.

Kleiman, Mark A. R., and Kerry D. Smith. In this volume. "State and Local Drug Enforcement: In Search of a Strategy."

Moore, Mark H. In this volume. "Supply Reduction and Drug Law Enforcement."

National Institute on Drug Abuse. 1989. *National Household Survey on Drug Abuse: 1988 Population Estimates*. Rockville, Md.: U.S. Department of Health and Human Services, National Institute on Drug Abuse.

Roth, Jeffrey A., Michael Tonry, and Norval Morris, eds. 1987. *Drugs and Crime: Workshop Proceedings*. Washington, D.C.: National Research Council, Commission on Behavioral and Social Sciences and Education.

U.S. Department of Health and Human Services. 1989. *Human Health Services News*. Rockville, Md.: U.S. Department of Health and Human Services, February 28.

Wilson, James Q. In this volume. "Drugs and Crime."

Wish, Eric D., and Bernard A. Gropper. In this volume. "Drug Testing by the Criminal Justice System: Methods, Research, and Applications."

*Bruce D. Johnson, Terry Williams, Kojo A. Dei,
and Harry Sanabria*

Drug Abuse in the Inner City: Impact on Hard-Drug Users and the Community

ABSTRACT

Illicit drug use in the inner city expanded rapidly in the 1960s and has
continued unabated into the 1990s. While the number of heroin users has
remained relatively stable, the use and sale of cocaine have grown
tremendously since the mid-1970s. The popularity of freebase cocaine, or
"crack," exploded in 1986 and 1987; crack now dominates the illicit drug
markets in many inner cities. The structure of drug-dealing organizations
is complex and contains many roles with approximate equivalents in the
legal economy. Cocaine and crack selling by inner-city youths has had
major effects on low-income communities by offering substantial
economic opportunities that undermine the willingness of such youths to
work at low-wage legal jobs. Violence in hard-drug use and selling also
increased in the 1980s. Despite increased arrests of drug sellers,
community safety in the inner city has substantially declined in recent
years. The effects of drug abuse in the inner city have significantly
contributed to a decline in the economic well-being of most users and
sellers, an environment of poor health and risk of death at an early age,
and a weakening of family relationships.

Although many factors have contributed to the relative decline of
American inner cities, or "ghettos," this essay advances the thesis that
the expansion of use of hard drugs, and particularly the sale and distribution of heroin and cocaine, is both a symptom and an important
factor in the continued relative decline of inner-city communities and
persons who reside in those communities.

Bruce D. Johnson, Terry Williams, Kojo A. Dei, and Harry Sanabria are researchers
at Narcotic and Drug Research, Inc., New York. Support for this project was provided
by the National Institute on Drug Abuse, the National Institute of Justice, the New York
State Division of Substance Abuse Services, and Narcotic and Drug Research, Inc.

Massive amounts of evidence now document the deterioration of the inner city. During the period 1960–80, the number of persons living in communities (or census tracts) primarily occupied by low-income (including welfare and unemployed) blacks and Hispanics approximately doubled (Murray 1984; Hughes 1988; Ricketts and Sawhill 1988). Between 1968 and 1980, employment rates declined substantially (from 78 to 55 percent) for nonwhites—mainly blacks (Freeman and Wise 1982; Freeman and Holzer 1986; Larson 1988; Jaynes and Williams 1989). Minorities, especially in inner-city schools, remain educationally deprived, are less likely than whites to complete advanced courses, and are more likely to be placed in vocational tracks or to drop out (Ogbu 1978; Glasgow 1981; Reed 1988). Between 1970 and 1985, the proportion of black children living in mother-only families increased from 30 to 51 percent (Glick 1988), primarily because large proportions of black mothers never married (up from 6 to 25 percent). The chance that a black child will experience poverty is almost 90 percent if he or she lives in a family headed by a single woman under age thirty (Gibbs 1988, p. 25). The availability of affordable housing for low-income families declined dramatically in the 1980s; many persons became homeless (Johnson et al. 1988; Ropers 1988).

Living in inner-city communities with severe social and economic conditions, however, does not "select" which persons will become most impoverished and experience multiple social problems. As we argue in this essay, involvement with drugs and the criminal underclass is a major factor in creating persons who will experience such multiple social problems, with wide-ranging negative impacts on their families and neighborhoods.

The *criminal underclass subculture* refers to the values, conduct norms, lifestyles, and performance of roles in the criminal underclass (see Wolfgang and Ferracuti 1967; Johnson 1973, 1980). The criminal underclass subculture appears to have several major conduct norms:[1] illegal means are better than legal means to earn money; other people are to be manipulated and their goods or money taken for the offender's

---

[1] This concept emerges from two major and controversial intellectual traditions. The "Subculture of Violence" (Wolfgang and Ferracuti 1967; Johnson 1973, 1980) provides definitions of criminal norms and examples that are important for the arguments that follow. The recent analyses of an economic underclass in the inner city by Gibbs (1988) and Wilson (1988) are very similar to our understanding and use of the term, except that the emphasis here is on the role of drug use or sale by members of the underclass who also engage in crime.

benefit; violence and its threat should be used to gain criminal returns and maintain reputation; expenditures of illicit money should support "fast living," even at the cost of necessary items. Thus, illegal income is to be spent for luxury items (gold, fancy clothes), illicit drugs, and entertainment of friends, rather than on basic necessities (food, shelter, family obligations, and lifetime savings); participants should attempt to remain unknown to official institutions, especially police, taxing authorities, and other officials.

This essay provides an overview of the shifting patterns of drug use and sales, particularly heroin and cocaine—with a special emphasis on crack, in order to document various impacts on inner-city residents and communities. Since a full attempt to provide complete documentation is well beyond the scope of this essay, we limit our coverage in several ways. First, our review is directed mainly toward low-income, inner-city communities in which nonwhite minority residents are typically a majority of all residents. Second, we wish to make it absolutely clear that the vast majority of blacks and Hispanics in inner-city communities are not cocaine-heroin abusers or criminals. We focus primarily on the proportionately few (although numerically many) inner-city residents who commit nondrug crimes and who become frequent users of heroin, cocaine, or crack at some time during their lives.

Illustrative materials are drawn primarily from research in New York City since there exists solid documentation about the drug problem in that city and it has the nation's largest number of heroin and cocaine abusers. The general organizational structure of drug markets, patterns, and consequences of hard-drug use and sales and their impact on New York City residents and inner communities appears similar in other metropolitan areas of the country.

Section I traces the rise of heroin use and addiction in the inner cities, particularly in New York, and the expansion of use of cocaine in various forms. This section also discusses the expansion and social organization of heroin and cocaine distribution in the inner city at retail and street levels. Section II describes the rise of the cocaine/crack economy and the associated subcultural patterns that are emerging in relation to its use and distribution. Section III explores the effects of drug selling on levels of violence and neighborhood safety in inner-city areas. Section IV identifies and discusses a number of the consequences of hard-drug use and sales for individuals and families in the inner city. Section V, the conclusion, summarizes the preceding analyses and comments on promising directions for future research.

I. Heroin and Cocaine Use

The rise and spread of heroin and cocaine, and recently "crack" among inner-city communities, are primarily postwar phenomena. In this section, we briefly trace the shifts and institutionalization of subcultures of hard-drug use and dealing among the inner-city criminal underclass during the postwar period.

A. *The Institutionalization of Inner-City Heroin-Use Subcultures*

Prior to World War II, heroin was primarily confined to a few large cities, especially New York, and the prevailing stereotype of a narcotic addict was that of a white or an Asian. Prior to 1940, about 20 percent of those arrested for narcotic law violations were black, a figure that increased to over 50 percent by the mid-1950s (Courtwright 1986; Courtwright, Joseph, and Des Jarlais 1989). The war apparently disrupted illicit supplies of heroin, and white and Asian heroin users became less common (Courtwright 1986).

World War II also brought thousands of southern blacks and Puerto Ricans to New York to fill wartime industrial jobs. Due to housing discrimination, most settled in inner-city white ethnic neighborhoods. From 1945 to 1960, millions more black migrants moved from the South to the inner-city neighborhoods of New York, Chicago, Philadelphia, Detroit, Los Angeles, and, in smaller numbers, to many other metropolitan areas (e.g., Cleveland, Boston, Newark). Large numbers of Puerto Ricans also moved to the New York metropolitan area, and many Mexicans migrated to Los Angeles and other southwestern cities.

During 1945–60, these first-generation migrants to the large urban centers obtained employment in blue-collar occupations and gained housing (although located in inner-city areas) which was superior to that in their home communities. Many whites left adequate inner-city housing to move into the new suburbs. Most first-generation migrants (including those in the 1980s) avoided the drug and heroin abuse that affected their children (Lukoff and Brook 1974; Frank et al. 1988*a*, 1988*b*).

In the mid-1950s, sizable numbers of white and minority inner-city youths in New York and Los Angeles initiated heroin use and became addicted to it. Heroin became heavily adulterated and most near-daily heroin users progressed from "snorting" (nasal inhalation), to "skin-popping" (injection under the skin), to "mainlining" (injection into the vein). By 1960, a heroin injection subculture had become institutionalized in New York (Hunt and Odoroff 1962; Chein et al 1965; Feldman 1968; Preble and Casey 1969), Chicago (McFarland and Hall 1953; Finestone 1957; Hughes, Sanders, and Schaps 1972), and Los Angeles (Bullington 1977), but was rare in other major metropolitan areas (Robins and Murphy 1967). Relative to the 1970s, however, the absolute numbers of heroin users were small in these cities.

By the early 1960s, drug subcultures and most heroin users were located primarily in a few inner-city areas of the largest metropolitan areas. But this changed dramatically as the baby-boom generation reached adolescence. Different drugs became available in local areas; use became increasingly regular among core cohorts of users and became institutionalized. "New" drugs were typically added to substances already in regular use.

B. The Drug Revolution, 1960–75

Four major historical events occurring during the years 1960–75 dramatically altered the extent and pervasiveness of drug use and abuse. First, the civil rights movement greatly increased expectations and the political importance of the entire black population (and most minorities). Second, growth in the size and isolation of minority communities within major metropolitan areas led to explosive rioting in the early 1960s that badly damaged the infrastructure of most major inner-city communities (National Advisory Commission on Civil Disorders 1968). Third, America's participation in the Vietnam War bitterly divided the nation, especially alienating youths of draft age. Fourth, many in the baby-boom generation reached adolescence and young adulthood, the ages of greatest risk for drug use and delinquency. These events provided the setting for a great expansion of drug use and abuse.

Marijuana use exploded after 1965 across the United States. Surveys among high school seniors and other segments of the baby-boom generation showed that, by 1965, 5 percent of high school seniors had used marijuana in the preceding twelve months; this figure rose to 30 percent by 1970 (National Commission on Marihuana and Drug Abuse 1973), 40 percent by 1975, and 49 percent by 1980, with a slow decline afterward, to 38 percent in 1985 (Johnston, Bachman, and O'Malley 1988).

A sizable proportion of white marijuana users also progressed to irregular use of LSD and psychedelic drugs, amphetamines, barbiturates, and tranquilizers (Johnston, Bachman, and O'Malley 1988). These drugs, however, generally did not gain similar popularity among inner-city black and Hispanic marijuana users who found heroin and cocaine more attractive as secondary drugs (Langrod 1970; Johnson 1973). Unlike the situation in the pre-1965 era, illicit drug use was no longer only a big-city or inner-city problem.

C. The Heroin Generation in the Inner City, 1965–73

Heroin use and addiction, particularly among minorities in inner-city neighborhoods, exploded during the period 1965–73 (Hughes and Crawford 1972; Hughes 1976; Hunt and Chambers 1976; O'Donnell et al. 1976; Rittenhouse 1977; Brunswick and Boyle 1979; Boyle and Brunswick 1980; Clayton and Voss 1981). Most users initiated heroin use between ages fifteen and twenty-one. About half of the users became addicted within two years of initiation, but less than half of the addicted remained addicted for several years (Johnson 1978; Clayton and Voss 1981).

The most striking findings, however, concern the percentages of various age cohorts who initiated use and became addicted to heroin in adolescence. In a retrospective study of young men in Manhattan, the annual prevalence of heroin use increased from 3 percent in 1963 to 20 percent by 1970 and declined to 13 percent by 1974 (Clayton and Voss 1981, p. 42; see also Boyle and Brunswick [1980] for similar findings on Harlem youths). Since 1973, much lower proportions of blacks have been initiating heroin use and, if users, becoming addicted—even among inner-city populations.

The "heroin generation" of youths who became addicted in 1965–73 is evident in the black community in virtually every city with a population over 100,000 (Hunt 1973; Hunt and Chambers 1976) and among inner-city Puerto Ricans (in the New York City metropolitan area) and Chicanos in Los Angeles and the Southwest (Hunt and Chambers 1976; Bullington 1977; Moore 1978; Anglin and Speckart 1988).

The exact number of persons in this heroin generation cannot be accurately estimated; a low estimate would be 800,000, while a high estimate would be over four million (O'Donnell 1977). Probably half or more who were addicted to heroin at some time during the 1965–73 period have desisted from heroin use without any involvement in treatment (Johnson 1978; Brunswick 1979; Clayton and Voss 1981).

Many of the heroin generation entered detoxification, drug-free, or methadone treatment programs established during this era (Brecher 1972; Brunswick and Messeri 1986). This heroin generation remains the major population being treated for opiate addiction and has continued to be quite stable throughout the 1970s and 1980s; in the 1980s, very few new heroin addicts were from younger age cohorts. Thus, the average age of opiate addicts in treatment (Division of Substance Abuse Services 1985) and opiate-positive arrestees (Wish, Brady, and Cuadrado 1984, 1986) was in the mid-thirties at the end of the 1980s.

Heroin users from this generation are primarily multiple drug abusers who use a variety of drugs (especially alcohol, marijuana, tobacco, and cocaine) on a daily basis or several times a week. Many of these people prefer to heat heroin and cocaine together and inject the mixture as a "speedball" (Langrod 1970; Hanson et al. 1985; Johnson et al. 1985; Johnson and Wish 1986; Sanchez and Johnson 1987).

D. The Rise of Cocaine Use in the Inner City, 1975–84

As the heroin epidemic began to ease in the mid-1970s, cocaine snorting (nasal inhalation) became increasingly popular among nonheroin drug users in the inner city. Also, during 1975–83, cocaine gained the reputation of a "status drug" that was relatively innocuous; its use spread rapidly among marijuana-using segments of the baby-boom generation (Grinspoon and Bakalar 1976; Kandel, Murphy, and Karus 1985; Johnston, Bachman, and O'Malley 1988). Like middle-class drug users, large numbers of inner-city drug users were snorting cocaine when they could afford it. In New York, "afterhours clubs" were gathering places for cocaine users and dealers (Williams 1978). By 1984, 43 percent of all Manhattan arrestees tested positive in urinalyses for cocaine, while only 22 percent were positive for heroin; over half of the latter were also positive for cocaine (Wish, Brady, and Cuadrado 1984).

In the Los Angeles area, a new technique for purifying adulterated cocaine called "freebasing" emerged (Seigel 1982). Freebasing is a chemical process for converting cocaine hydrochloride powder into alkaloidal cocaine, or "freebase." Cocaine freebase is not water soluble and cannot be snorted or injected. When it is heated at low temperatures and the fumes are inhaled, the freebase user becomes euphoric within seconds. The high from freebase lasts less than 20 minutes and is followed by rapid dysphoria in which the user feels worse than usual. Consequently, episodes of use often occur in rapid succession (Van Dyke and Byck 1983).

Freebasing became an increasingly popular form of cocaine use in the Los Angeles area during 1976–83. In the New York area, freebasing became common during 1980–84; many afterhours clubs became "base houses" where cocaine could be purchased and someone would "cook up" (base) it (Williams 1978–89, field notes from 1983; Hamid 1988a, 1988b). Although some base houses were in transitional areas, most were located in minority low-income neighborhoods and run by minority owners (Williams 1978–89, field notes from 1983).

E. The Crack Generation, 1985 to the Present

In 1984, Los Angeles authorities began to encounter cocaine "rock," and, in 1985, New York officials began to uncover vials containing what users called "crack" (Brody 1985; Street Studies Unit 1985). Crack and rock are the same product: cocaine freebase packaged in retail form. In New York, crack is typically sold in a small plastic vial with a watertight cap; the asking price in 1989 was $10 for a standard vial containing about three to five chunks of freebase, but it usually sells for considerably less (frequently $5). Smaller vials with two to three chunks sell for $3 to $5 and are marketed to the poor and to youths. Thus, the cost of a dosage unit is very low, but users typically buy several vials at a time or return for more within an hour or two. Multiple purchases and use episodes occur during a typical-use day; the major limitation facing users is money to purchase crack (Williams 1989).

Crack use exploded during 1986–87 in New York, Miami, Detroit, Washington, D.C., and elsewhere; it now dominates illicit drug markets in most inner-city neighborhoods (*Newsweek* 1986a, 1986b, 1986c, 1988; *New York Times* 1986a, 1986b, 1988a). Urine testing in several major cities documents the widespread nature of recent (past forty-eight hours) cocaine use among arrestees. The Drug Use Forecasting System (National Institute of Justice 1988a, 1988b) shows that 83 percent of arrestees tested positive for cocaine at arrest in Manhattan, about 65 percent in Los Angeles and Washington, D.C., and over 50 percent in Chicago, Dallas, Houston, New Orleans, and Birmingham. The low figures were 33 percent in Phoenix and 15 percent in Indianapolis.

Although the full dimensions of this "crack generation" are not currently known, several features were clear in mid-1989. The number of cocaine users has not increased substantially due to crack. Rather, the relatively few regular cocaine users appear to have increased the frequency of their consumption (Frank et al. 1988a). While crack selling is preponderantly based in inner-city neighborhoods and among minorities, crack use and its problems have spread to virtually all neighborhoods in the New York City region (Belenko and Fagan 1987).

Thousands of persons are seeking treatment for crack addiction (Division of Substance Abuse Services 1988), thousands more are being convicted of crack sales and sent to jail or prison (Belenko and Fagan 1987; Ross and Cohen 1988), and many more users are at liberty on the streets at any given time. No treatment regime for cocaine or crack use has been demonstrated to be effective in preventing relapse to cocaine for large proportions of dependent users (*Science* 1988). No long-acting cocaine derivative (like methadone for heroin) has been developed to prevent the rapid swings between euphoria and depression, although some new drugs and acupuncture may help alleviate symptoms (*Science* 1988; Smith 1988).

It is unclear how long this crack epidemic will last. Will this "crack generation" continue to recruit newcomers and low-income youths for many years (as was the case with marijuana use)? Will crack users begin to consume cocaine freebase mixed with heroin freebase (referred to as "crank" in New York) and become dependent on both (*New York Times* 1989a)? Or will new cohorts of inner-city adolescents in the 1990s not initiate crack use as their counterparts of 1973–78 chose not to initiate heroin use?

II. Drug Selling and Drug Business in the Inner City

The rise, institutionalization, and organizational improvements of the illicit distribution of heroin and cocaine have become serious problems confronting inner-city communities. Unfortunately, very little systematic scientific research has been conducted on the organization of the drug business. The scant available evidence about cocaine selling has generally come from research conducted outside inner-city communities (Adler 1985; Inciardi 1986; Mills 1986; Waldorf and Murphy 1987; Carpenter et al. 1988).

A. Heroin and Cocaine Selling in the Inner City

While Jewish bootleggers probably began systematic importation and sale of heroin in New York City, Italians became important prior to World War II. But they relied on black associates to conduct retail sales in Harlem both before and after the war (Courtwright, Joseph, and Des Jarlais 1989).

While Italian mobsters controlled heroin importation and upper-level distribution in New York during 1940–70 (Maas 1968), the fact that most of the market was in black communities led to the rise of black distributors. During the 1960s, blacks such as Nicky Barnes developed important distribution networks based on the work of minority heroin user-dealers.

The Italians generally imported kilograms and sold them to black (and sometimes Puerto Rican) wholesalers on a regular basis. At the lower levels of the heroin distribution system, heroin user-dealers would generally be advanced several "bags" of heroin to sell; they would use some and sell enough to pay their supplier in order to "re-up"—gain the next "bundle" of heroin to sell (Johnson et al. 1985). So many different suppliers were cutting, adulterating, bagging, and supplying user-dealers in New York that suppliers began advertising their wares by marking their heroin bags (Goldstein et al. 1984).

Cocaine selling, as well as its supply, was less common than heroin prior to 1970. Most cocaine sellers were also heroin sellers. But when supplies and profits of cocaine began to increase dramatically in the late 1970s and 1980s, many sellers of heroin began to sell cocaine. By 1976, Preble (1977) estimated that there were two cocaine sellers for every heroin seller in East and Central Harlem. But the organizational structure at the street level of cocaine sales was very similar and parallel to that of heroin, as the following structural analysis suggests.

B. The Social Structure of the Inner-City Drug Business

The structure of dealing organizations is complex and filled with different roles performed in various ways by many individuals. Moreover, the terminology and drug argot vary greatly across geographical jurisdictions. The following discussion provides a paradigm of several major roles and relations among dealers identified in the literature. Table 1 identifies various roles, suggests their approximate role equivalents in the legal economy, and briefly describes activities occurring at each level (Johnson et al. 1987).

Inner-city residents typically have access to and routinely perform the lower-level roles as dealers, sellers, and low-level distributors. Preble and Casey (1969) and Moore (1978) differentiated about six levels of inner-city heroin distributors, of which the kilo dealers, house connections, street sellers, and "jugglers" are the most important. Kilo dealers

TABLE 1

Roles and Functions at Various Levels of the Drug Distribution Business

Approximate Role Equivalents in Legal Markets	Roles by Common Names at Various Stages of the Drug Distribution Business	Major Functions Accomplished at This Level
Grower/ producer	Coca farmer, opium farmer, marijuana grower	Grow coca, opium, marijuana; the raw materials
Manufac- turer	Collector, transporter, elaborator, chemist, drug lord	All stages for preparation of heroin, cocaine, marijuana as commonly sold
	Traffickers	
Importer	Multikilo importer, mule, air- plane pilot, smuggler, trafficker, money launderer	Smuggling of large quantities of substances into the United States
Wholesale distributor	Major distributor, investor, "kilo connection"	Transportation and redistribu- tion of multikilograms and single kilograms
	Dealers	
Regional dis- tributor	"Pound and ounce men," "weight dealers"	Adulteration and sale of moder- ately expensive products
Retail store owner	House connections, suppliers, crack-house supplier	Adulteration and production of retail level dosage units ("bags," "vials," "grams") in very large numbers
Assistant manager, security chief, or accountant	"Lieutenant," "muscle men," transporter, crew boss, crack- house manager/proprietor	Supervises three or more sellers, enforces informal con- tracts, collects money, dis- tributes multiple dosage units to actual sellers
	Sellers	
Store clerk, salesmen (door-to- door and phone)	Street drug seller, "runner," juggler, private seller	Makes actual direct sales to con- sumer; responsible for both money and drugs
	Low-Level Distributors	
Advertiser, security guards, leaflet dis- tributor	Steerer, tout, cop man, look- out, holder, runner, help friend, guard, go-between	Assists in making sales, adver- tises, protects seller from police and criminals, solicits customers; handles drugs or money—but not both
Servant, temporary employee	Run shooting gallery, injector (of drugs), freebaser, taster, apartment cleaner, drug bag- ger, fence, launder money	Provides short-term services to drug users or sellers for money or drugs; not responsi- ble for money or drugs

buy heroin or cocaine in large amounts (usually pounds and kilos) from importing organizations and typically supply several house connections with ounces of adulterated drugs. The house connection and his associates typically generate hundreds or thousands of retail dosage units (bags of heroin or powder cocaine or vials of crack).

Street sellers receive several retail units ("bundles" of ten to twenty-five bags or vials) on consignment to sell on the streets or elsewhere; they are expected to return about 60 percent of the value to their suppliers. Street sellers might be assisted by "steerers" who refer customers, "touts" who are employed to find customers, "middle men" or "cop men" who transport money and drugs between buyers and sellers who do not meet, and "jugglers" who buy several bags and further adulterate their contents and resell them (Hanson et al. 1985; Johnson et al. 1985).

Through the 1960s and 1970s in New York City, the primary business relationship among occupants of these various roles may be described as free-lance or loose cooperation. A house connection might supply drugs to several street sellers, but each worked day-by-day, with neither party committed to the following days or weeks. Thus, a house connection might supply very different street sellers thirty days apart. A street seller may also switch to several different suppliers and choose his own time and locations for "work" (Hanson et al. 1985; Johnson et al. 1985, 1987; Williams and Kornblum 1985; Johnson, Kaplan, and Schmeidler 1990). Studies of traffickers and dealers (Adler 1985; Waldorf and Murphy 1987) and adolescent marijuana suppliers (Carpenter et al. 1988; Chaiken and Johnson 1988) suggest this same free-lance organization structure.

C. The Rise of Vertically Controlled Selling Organizations

Although free-lance selling was the standard economic relationship among dealers, sellers, and low-level distributors, Nicky Barnes in New York, the Young Boys in Detroit (Ianni 1974; Mieczkowski 1986), and CRIPS and Bloods in Los Angeles (Drug Enforcement Administration 1988) had developed semivertical organizations prior to 1985. Such exceptional organizations, however, rarely gained a near monopoly over heroin sales in certain areas.

The explosion of crack use appears to be fundamentally altering the social structure of dealing networks from primarily a confederation of free-lance sellers and dealers to vertically organized dealing groups or organizations. A dealer who can buy a kilogram of cocaine a week is pressured by police, competitors, and supply-demand considerations to build and carefully control a vertically organized crack-selling group.

The vertical organization structure makes it difficult for police to arrest "sellers" with standard buy-and-bust techniques because a variety of roles are performed by several persons: "holders" conceal bulk crack supplies on the street, "counters" or "money men" check and receive buyers' money, "hand-off men" provide the drug to buyers, "lookouts" warn of police or competitors, "muscle men" serve as guards and intimidate passersby and competitors, "lieutenants" or "crew bosses" supervise the whole street operation and collect money at regular intervals, "storekeepers" commingle drug money with legal store income, "runners" take cocaine to different buyers, "transporters" transfer larger amounts across state lines and "baby-sit" in prearranged locations. The lead "supplier" maintains separate apartments for "stashes" of drugs and money, as well as several locations for "packaging" and "selling."

In such vertically organized selling groups, sellers and support staff are frequently assigned to particular locales, work for a specific time, hand over all money to the lieutenant or money collector, and are paid at the end of the day in either drugs or money. Recent reports suggest that some crack-dealing groups recruit juveniles as lookouts and train them in a variety of other dealing roles (*Newsweek* 1986*b*; Hopkins 1988; Street Studies Unit 1988; *Time* 1988; Williams 1989).

As police have become increasingly sophisticated and effective at breaking up large congregations of crack sellers in a particular locale (Kleiman and Smith, in this volume; also see police tactics below), crack-dealing groups have become very mobile in New York, Los Angeles, Detroit, and other cities (*Newsweek* 1986*b*, 1988; *New York Times* 1988*b*). They immediately cease sales if any unknown outsider or a police unit enters the block, move indoors until the danger passes, and then resume regular sales activity. Crack may be made and sold from several different apartments during the week (Williams 1989).

While free-lance relationships among dealers and sellers are common in Los Angeles, two loosely organized black gangs, the CRIPS and the Bloods, have become heavily involved in selling heroin, cocaine, and crack ("rock" in Los Angeles) (Drug Enforcement Administration 1988), although Klein, Maxson, and Cunningham (1988) found only a loose overlap among gang members and drug sellers. The Drug

Enforcement Administration (1988) believes that these two Los Angeles gangs control and distribute crack throughout most West Coast cities and even in the South.

D. Minority-controlled Dealing Organizations

A major shift in drug dealing occurred during the late 1980s. Crack-dealing groups in the inner city are owned, organized, run, and controlled by members of minority groups. The Drug Enforcement Administration (1988) reports that four major groups control crack trafficking: Jamaicans on the East Coast and in midwestern states; Haitians in Florida and within 200 miles of Washington, D.C.; Dominicans in New York and Massachusetts; and black street gangs in Los Angeles for most West Coast and western states.

Whites are seldom encountered at the upper or lower levels of crack-selling groups. In New York, persons from two or three ethnic backgrounds appear to be disproportionately important at upper levels. Colombians appear to control very large proportions of cocaine sold in the New York metropolitan area.

The Colombians also appear to have developed transshipment arrangements and good working relationships with New York–based Jamaicans and Dominicans who head localized crack-selling groups. Williams (1989) reports on the origins and innovations of one such local selling group, most of whose members were youths from the Dominican Republic. During four years of fieldwork studying crack users, base houses, and dealing groups, Williams has also met approximately fifty persons (mostly Dominicans) who were upper-level suppliers in Harlem and Washington Heights and has encountered Jamaicans leading dealing groups in Brooklyn and Queens. Hamid (1988a, 1988b) has documented the shift from marijuana to crack selling among West Indian migrants in Brooklyn.

Newspaper reports (*New York Times* 1988b, 1988c, 1988d) and New York City police suggest that American blacks direct several local crack-selling groups in Brooklyn, Queens, and other boroughs. American blacks appear to have developed crack-selling groups in Detroit, Washington, D.C., Chicago, and Los Angeles. While the ethnic composition of upper-level crack suppliers will probably never be well documented, youths and young adults from American black, Puerto Rican, other Hispanic (Cuba, El Salvador, Panama) backgrounds and, occasionally, white backgrounds are employed in street-level roles.

Other than police reports and newspaper or newsmagazine articles (generally based on police sources), very little is known about crack-dealing groups. How many people are employed at one time? How much crack is sold? What are the drug-use and career histories of such sellers and employees? How many are successful in maintaining a middle-class lifestyle or better? How many become crack dependent? How many become impoverished by crack use? How do the groups relate to inner-city residents who do not use crack or other drugs? To such questions, few answers exist.

E. The Cocaine Economy near the Street Level

The President's Commission on Organized Crime (1986) reported that the total value of illicit drugs was over $100 billion annually, and about half of this was cocaine. This estimate was based on cocaine powder sales before the advent of crack; the value is probably even higher now (Mills 1986). While this gross estimate includes cocaine sales among middle- and upper-class users from all areas of the country, and although these sales are conducted by a variety of sellers, we focus below on some economic and subcultural aspects of cocaine and crack selling by inner-city youths whose activities appear to have had major effects on low-income communities.

In this section, we draw extensively from a major ethnographic study conducted in 1984–88 in the Washington Heights section of New York City, when that area became a major center for cocaine and crack dealing in New York and the eastern seaboard (Williams 1989). This case study illustrates how the "crack" market operates in one major city.

Max (age eighteen in 1985) was the organizer and leader of the crew. Chillie was the crew chief who directed house and street sellers. Splib supplied cocaine to others and was a "con artist." Kitty worked for a "dial-a-gram" service that sold cocaine mainly to middle-class buyers. Charlie preferred direct sales to customers from the street corners.

1. *The Economics of a Cocaine Crew.* Max's supplier "loaned" him three to five kilos a week of pure cocaine (street value between $180,000 and $360,000 in 1985) to be distributed. Max was responsible for returning about $100,000 a week to his Colombian connection, Ramon. The amount of cocaine advanced varied according to the amount sold in the previous week, how much Max had on hand, and the amount he had committed himself to deliver both to his crew and to others.

When the crew was first formed and began cocaine sales in 1983, Max would supply each member with the amount of cocaine they needed. The crew members were then responsible for selling their shares to customers, frequently with assistance from others. After a designated time, either money or unsold cocaine was returned to Max. Max then paid the connection or returned the cocaine (the latter practice was frowned on).

In the cocaine economy, suppliers like Max provide retail cocaine sellers with a variety of different units of cocaine and expect them to return at a specified time with about 60–75 percent of the potential gross sales in cash before "re-upping." Among the "cocaine kids," Max provided Chillie with the largest amounts of cocaine ("weight") at one time. For an adulterated "eighth" of a kilo valued at $3,000 (1983 prices), Chillie was to return $4,000 in cash from sales in one week. The profit for Max was $1,000 less expenses.

Chillie adulterated the cocaine further, however, by mixing one part adulterant to one part cocaine, creating a potential of approximately 250 "grams" for sale at $80 each, which Kitty would sell to middle-class buyers. Or Chillie could create about 1,200 retail "bags" (for retail at $10 each) of cocaine powder (averaging 200 milligrams). Thus, the potential retail value for an adulterated "eighth" of a kilo ranged from $12,000 to $20,000. But many of these bags may be consumed by crew members, other street sellers, or steerers, touts, and copmen who work for Chillie, and buyers may insist on discounts ("shorts"). Expenses to feed and entertain the crew during the week may be high (see Johnson et al. 1985). Chillie would be fortunate to gain a gross cash income of $6,000–$10,000 from all sales from a given "eighth." After paying Max $4,000, Chillie would realize a profit of between $2,000 and $6,000. On an annual basis, Max and Chillie (and others dealing above the street level) could easily make a tax-free income of $100,000 or more after expenses. This potential income is a very attractive incentive for young men and women in the inner city who most likely would be otherwise unemployed.

2. *Economic Importance of Middle-Income Buyers for Inner-City Crews.* Although such crews of inner-city youths are primarily from low-income minority backgrounds, their buyers are not limited to low-income minority drug abusers. A sizable proportion of cash income came from cocaine purchasers who were middle- and working-class persons from all ethnic backgrounds. The dial-a-gram service primarily served a middle- and upper-class clientele. Kitty and other women delivered grams of cocaine to middle-class men who frequently paid high prices for cocaine ($80–$100/gram) and tipped them well (and offered additional money for sex).

Max had several white buyers from New Jersey, suburban New York, and elsewhere on the eastern seaboard. Many of these were sellers and dealers in their home communities and would pay high prices for "eighths," "quarters," and even kilos. Thus, Max was a major "connection" for middle-class cocaine dealers in the entire region. Even street dealers like Charlie made a sizable but unknown proportion of their sales to middle- and working-class buyers who never left their cars or who came by subway to buy.

For all practical purposes, inner-city minority youths working in the illicit cocaine economy are selling their labor, sales skills, and willingness to risk very substantial prison penalties. The willingness to take such risks is the only service that middle-class persons value and pay for. Most middle-class buyers did not socialize with Max's crew and would avoid them entirely otherwise. Only by selling the highest quality cocaine at the lowest prices in the region were Max and his crew able to interact with middle-income persons and participate in American prosperity.

Given the important structural factors leading to the deprivation that residents of inner-city communities face, some members of cocaine and crack-selling crews have made an apparently reasonable economic decision. With few or no economic opportunities for an honest living, they have chosen the opportunities of making "crazy money" by working in the cocaine economy and using their communities as a locale for such illegal behavior.

3. *Benefits for a Few.* While the overall impact of cocaine use and dealing is primarily negative, several persons may benefit from the cocaine economy. While Max's crew was operating at its maximum (1984–86), he was earning "crazy money." Although not strongly pressed about how much he made, Max routinely made large cash gifts to his extended family back in Santo Domingo. About weekly, a trusted relative would fly to the island with $5,000 in cash, converting it at a very favorable exchange rate to the national currency. In this impoverished country, Max's otherwise destitute relatives now have comfortable homes that approach middle-class standards in the United States. Max even exported a Cadillac to the island for his uncle, but a general's son seized it and told Max that he would turn him over to U.S. authorities as a drug dealer (Williams 1978–89, field notes from 1988). Moreover, several of Max's relatives arrived destitute in New York but were soon proprietors of bodegas (grocery stores) and other cash businesses.

Several inner-city residents other than Max's relatives also appeared to be benefiting. By 1988, Max's crew reached their early twenties. Their cocaine selling ended, but not because of arrest or homicide (although Chillie was shot). Max was last reported living comfortably in Florida at the request of his wife. Kitty was married and living in a New York City suburb. Only Charlie was still selling cocaine. Although most are too young to "retire," most of Max's crew are much more prosperous than virtually all their counterparts of similar age.

Of course, there is no way of knowing exactly how many cocaine dealers do become prosperous or wealthy from their participation in the cocaine economy. Many more probably aspire to such success than succeed.

F. Impact of Drug Use and Sale on Conduct Norms in the Criminal Underclass Subculture

Drug use and selling is also transforming the conduct norms of the criminal underclass subculture. Earlier, we defined five major conduct norms of the criminal underclass. Crack has dramatically expanded the prosperity of the criminal underclass economy as well as incorporated and strengthened new elements into the criminal underclass subculture.

1. *Rejection of Conventionality and Manipulation of Others.*   Even prior to the 1960s, the criminal underclass subculture placed low value on conventional behaviors. As the economic situation of inner-city males declined and as hard-drug use and sales became important components of the criminal underclass, the disdain for conventional jobs appears to have continued. Working-class jobs and food-industry employment are viewed as providing wages that are only "chump change" (Williams 1978–89, field notes from 1989). Persons working at honest jobs and supporting their families are disparagingly referred to as "squares," "geeks," and worse.

Nevertheless, persons who made a living from crime were admired for their hustling ability. "Hustling" and "getting over" (Goldstein 1981) also refers to the ability to "con" or manipulate others to gain what is wanted. This includes not only true crimes (three-card monte, confidence games for money) but also a wide variety of manipulations of others that are not illegal.

Virtually all persons in the social environment are to be manipulated. Women are viewed as "hos" (whores or holes) and valued only for their sexual favors. Mothers, siblings, and the extended family are expected to provide basic necessities (shelter, food, clothes), while able-bodied males make few contributions to the family or its well-being Family members who try to change such values are seen as "nags" and disregarded.

2. Violence and Its Threat.   Hard-drug sales have dramatically strengthened the subculture of violence (Wolfgang and Ferracuti 1967). Old patterns of using violence and its threat to obtain money via crime, and to defend masculinity, have been further transformed. Protection of economic interests and drug markets are now important considerations. In addition to evading police, sellers and suppliers must now defend their "businesses" against robbers, competitors, and ordinary citizens who will call police. The entire population of the inner city (and elsewhere) may contain potential enemies against whom the threat of violence and actual violence may need to be used.

> Max told me about the shooting on 155th Street. "Three kids were shot dead," he murmured in Spanish to Jake and turning to me, repeated his words in English. "Those kids don't know what they're doing. They're not professional. They are only so smart. They take three ounces of material and think they don't have to pay for it. So, they get killed." Jake takes pinches from a dollar bill hidden underneath the counter edge, while Chillie chimes in (between sniffs of cocaine). "It's good," Chillie says matter-of-factly, "because it teaches the others not to do what only professionals should do." [Williams 1978–89, field notes from 1988]

3. The New Meaning of Fast Living.   Hard-drug-use patterns and the thriving cocaine economy have dramatically transformed the meaning of "fast living." While criminals continue to respect criminal underclass members who can afford middle-class lifestyles, housing, clothes, parties, and cars, drug-dealing organizations have greatly expanded the type and magnitude of wealth necessary to support fast living. Particularly important is the belief that successful and "respectable" dealers can use as much cocaine or other drugs as they want and still afford other luxury items. "Parties" given by dealers are expected to be lavish affairs with lots of "free" drugs, alcohol, and women.

> At a more mundane level, dealers reward impoverished youths who function in street selling and support roles with expensive sneakers, clothes, gold rings, and "ropes" (expensive gold chains) that weigh a lot. Chillie, Jake, Kitty, Splib, Charlie, and Masterrap are not on the same level as Max but they do generate

enough cash to keep them in the street, their families fed and clothed, with enough hope to carry on another day. Of course, they had several changes of designer clothes and shoes. They also had rings and several gold chains that they wore at parties, but usually not when dealing. [Williams 1978–89, field notes from 1989]

4. *Incubators of Criminal Underclass Subculture.* For the most part, new standards have emerged from two sets of institutions: drug-selling groups and social-recreational groups of drug users. The leaders of drug-selling groups had to be very innovative in order to gain and maintain routine sales. Such innovations emerged mainly from personal experience, not from advanced education (where the basic principles of good team management are taught).

Dealing groups now rent several apartments within the same building or neighborhood and a couple outside that area where large quantities of drugs, money, or both are stored. They switch dealing activities from one apartment to another, depending on neighbors and police. When police began systematic raids of apartments where crack was sold to arrest dealers, Max was one of the first to develop "piggybacking." He and his crew would effectively take over an abandoned building or three to four apartments in a low-income building. They would deal crack from one apartment for a while. When it was raided and closed, selling would begin shortly after the police left, but from another ("piggyback") apartment in the same building. Of course, the police subsequently changed their tactics to close all crack apartments in a building (Williams 1978–89, field notes from 1986).

In New York City, a variety of supportive social and recreational institutions have evolved in response to the changing demands of clientele and police or community pressure. These institutions have various names and informally approved activities: shooting galleries (where heroin users can rent equipment and inject drugs), after-hours clubs (where alcohol is sold after closing time and cocaine is snorted or sold), social clubs (for dancing, where illicit alcohol and drugs are frequently sold), base houses (where someone freebases cocaine, and the base is consumed), and crack houses (where crack is used or sold).

In the early 1970s, after-hours clubs in inner-city black neighborhoods were transformed from places where alcohol was illegally available after liquor stores closed into locales for cocaine snorting and use (Williams 1978, 1989; Williams and Kornblum 1985). At first a few persons would bring cocaine and snort it while drinking. Early on cocaine sellers became regular and high-spending patrons; they effectively converted after-hours clubs into their social institution. Users and sellers developed effective social rituals and norms that emphasized moderation in cocaine snorting, social controls for "overindulgers," and social status symbols (gold or platinum coke spoons, hundred dollar bills, etc.) (Williams 1978).

The rise of freebasing in the early 1980s dramatically altered after-hours clubs. Cocaine users now wanted someone to "base" their cocaine for them. The resulting freebase was quickly "smoked up," and the resulting cocaine-induced paranoia and depression set in quickly. The ratio of controlled cocaine users to overindulgers declined (Williams 1978–89, field notes from 1983; Hamid 1988a, 1988b). Freebasing dramatically affected cocaine dealers. Their clients were demanding purer cocaine for purposes of basing. They wanted to purchase the base and smoke it on the premises. Cocaine snorters did not want to continue associating with basers, so some after-hours clubs became "base houses." While they made a lot of money, base houses were very hard to run because of the distrust and paranoia of basers.

While the crack user has become very disreputable, crack dealers and dealing have become the center of subcultural values. Persons who can organize and systematically control crack-selling groups (as described above) are highly respected in the criminal underclass and become very rich quickly. Crack suppliers from inner-city backgrounds can rapidly attain great wealth, especially when they do not use crack themselves and devote full-time effort to supervising their "employees."

Although many cannot sustain such networks for several years, during their period of active dealing the leaders of crack-selling groups can and do define the rules for work and promote a lifestyle that many others attempt to emulate. In order for their organization to survive (evade police and resist competition), such leaders must be constantly innovative and entrepreneurial in their businesses. For every tactic used by police or their competitors, new selling strategies must be copied (from competition) or developed to avoid detection and disruption by police.

The need for such innovations means that organizational patterns of crack selling continue to evolve. Because of the attraction of high cash income and unavailability of legal jobs for inner-city youths, crack-selling groups increasingly prefer to hire noncrack users or irregular users for selling roles.

When crack users are hired, they are warned not to smoke while working. In short, crack-selling groups are moving toward an organizational structure very similar to legal businesses. The reward system is also being altered by suppliers. While user-sellers are still given a choice of money or drug supplies (or both) as payments, many of the noncrack sellers are also rewarded with gold chains, luxury clothing, and automobiles. The norms of this cocaine subculture stress high expenditures at parties and fast living that absorb most of the funds earned.

Thus, many of these same youths remain unable to obtain good legal housing and improved economic well-being for themselves and their families. Moreover, most low-income dealers know little about the legal banking and credit system, have no legal "job" to earn credit, and wish to avoid asset seizure in the event of arrest.

As of 1989 in New York (and many other cities), sales of heroin, cocaine, and crack have been incorporated as vital activities of the criminal underclass economy and subculture. Returns from drug-dealing activities probably earn much larger amounts than all other forms of nondrug crime combined. Likewise, many values and norms have been developed regarding the use and sale of heroin, cocaine, and crack that now influence and are central to the criminal underclass subculture.

Hence, the cocaine/crack economy and subculture provide norms, values, and money that are very attractive to large numbers of inner-city youths who have no or few other options. Such norms and values are taught to youths by adult suppliers who gain most of the cash returns from their labor and the risks such youths assume. Such crack-selling groups also hire many otherwise unemployable inner-city youths to perform risky jobs paying much higher wage rates than they could earn at legal jobs, if legal jobs were available.

In short, the criminal underclass economy now offers real and substantial economic opportunities that can effectively employ the talents and labors of inner-city minority youths; this economy now competes directly with and frequently undermines the willingness of such youths to work at low-wage legal jobs.

III. Increasing Violence and Declining Safety in the Inner City

Perhaps no other effect of hard-drug use and selling becomes more visible or arouses greater public concern than the increasing levels of violence associated with drug selling and the perception (and perhaps reality) of declining safety in inner-city neighborhoods. In this section, we describe a combination of factors that may help efforts to understand the role of violence in the late 1980s.

A. *Changing Patterns of Drug-Law Enforcement*

New York City has always had the nation's largest number of addicts and drug abusers. Moreover, the high population densities and lack of cars among low-income communities in the city have meant that much social and illegal activity takes place in streets and public locales (parks, bars, social clubs). As the heroin epidemic and heroin selling expanded in the 1950s and 1960s, corruption of local police officers by heroin sellers became a reality in New York City. The investigation and trials instigated by police officer Serpico led to police policies that were implemented in the following years (Zimmer 1987). To prevent future police corruption, precinct police officers were discouraged and prevented from making drug sale/possession arrests; sergeants and officers in the narcotics bureau squads were routinely transferred; the narcotics bureau concentrated on investigations involving higher-level distributors.

A major unstated and unintended result of these policies was that few major police resources were devoted to arresting or controlling low-level street sellers. During the 1970s, thousands of free-lance user-sellers found that they could sell drugs with little fear of arrest or, if arrested, with only slight possibility of serious penalties. By 1978, many streets and most parks in Manhattan had become "drug-copping" communities (Hughes 1976), locations where sellers and steerers routinely conducted business (Kornblum, Williams, and Boggs 1978). In some locations, over 100 persons at a time could be observed buying or selling in what had become "drug supermarkets" (Zimmer 1987). Some streets in Harlem and the Lower East Side had become locales where all passersby were assumed to be buyers and offered drugs or intimidated to buy them. Particularly in the Lower East Side, thousands of buyers and sellers controlled the streets; shooting galleries and dealing organizations operated in the numerous abandoned buildings (Street Studies Unit 1988). Mayor Koch and the police commissioner agreed that law enforcement had lost control and that something drastic had to be done (Zimmer 1987).

The city's first black police commissioner, Benjamin Ward, instituted Operation Pressure Point with the avowed intention of eliminating drug supermarkets and making the streets safe for ordinary citizens. In 1983–84, Operation Pressure Point moved thousands of police into the Lower East Side where they made thousands of arrests of sellers, steerers, and buyers; meanwhile, bulldozers leveled abandoned buildings, and storefronts rented to dealers were padlocked (Zimmer 1987). In the subsequent years, Operation Pressure Point and its descendants have spread to all other areas of the city (Toledo 1988). Similar police operations in Los Angeles have been directed against "rock houses" and rock sellers (Klein, Maxson, and Cunningham 1988).

Since 1984, new public and police policy gives very high priority to preventing large congregations of street sellers in a given area, but this requires very large expenditures of police manpower. From the end of 1984 to the present time, Operation Pressure Point and related police "crackdowns" have essentially cleared many former drug supermarkets in the Lower East Side (Zimmer 1987), Harlem, and other areas of the city. Where previously 10–100 user-sellers loitered and sold drugs all day prior to 1983, the streets now appear much clearer, and uniformed officers were frequently observed in the summer of 1989 (Williams 1978–89, field notes from 1985, 1988, and 1989).

Such intense police pressure, however, did not eliminate drug-selling activity or make major reductions in the number of sellers. Rather, heroin and cocaine sellers developed new strategies for marketing their products. Suppliers now prevented loitering and kept potential purchasers moving; they frequently made buyers pool their money and purchase bundles (twenty-five bags) that were subsequently divided (Hopkins 1988; Toledo 1988). Nevertheless, police actions made it harder for sellers to locate large numbers of buyers and decreased the number of sellers from whom buyers could select the best price. In short, police action probably increased somewhat the time between sales for sellers and the "search" time by buyers (Kleiman 1986; Kleiman and Smith, in this volume).

New York City was fortunate that such drug supermarkets had been essentially eliminated by 1985 because the emergence of crack and crack-selling groups would have made a bad situation even worse. When crack selling exploded in the city in 1986, the number of drug sellers increased (and possibly doubled). Police made thousands of crack-related arrests, even in the many areas of the city where few sellers had been arrested in previous years (Belenko and Fagan 1987; Nickerson and Dynia 1988). Crack and drug sellers had to shift their selling strategies to cope with police pressure and competition from other sellers.

B. The Growing Cohesiveness of Drug-Selling Groups

Throughout the 1970s and into the 1980s, most user-sellers worked on a consignment basis and took their returns as drugs consumed while selling (Johnson et al. 1985; Johnson and Williams 1987). They essentially bartered their labor for drugs and obtained relatively modest cash incomes on active days (Johnson, Kaplan, and Schmeidler 1990). Their "employment" was intermittent because it depended on finding a supplier who would provide drugs to sell.

Such free-lance selling worked best in "supermarkets" where a large number of buyers could select from a large number of sellers. The search time for buyers and sales time for sellers were reduced to about the same time it took to buy a quart of milk (Kleiman 1986). But Operation Pressure Point and subsequent police enforcement essentially ended such favorable conditions for free-lance sellers. While free-lance selling of heroin and cocaine powder, and even crack, remains very common for most user-sellers of these drugs, crack selling is becoming much better organized. Many crack users who would prefer free-lance arrangements find that only support roles in crack-selling groups are available.

1. *Declining Cocaine Prices Increase Monetary Profits for Inner-City Sellers.* Another factor greatly influenced the organization of crack selling in the last half of the 1980s. An oversupply of cocaine in the producing countries (Peru, Bolivia, and Chile) forced foreign suppliers to cut their kilogram prices. The price of a kilogram of pure cocaine declined dramatically in New York City from $100,000 in 1980 to $40,000 in 1986 to $16,000 in 1988 (Drug Enforcement Administration 1988). The possibilities for making large monetary profits, due to low wholesale prices, became a striking reality to many persons in the criminal underclass. An effective but relatively small-time seller could be advanced or could purchase an ounce or two of cocaine, freebase it, and make several hundred vials of crack which street sellers could sell within a day or two. Such suppliers could quickly double or triple their investments and monetary incomes, instead of working primarily for the drugs they consumed (Williams 1978–89, field notes from 1988; Williams 1989). This affected the noncash (barter of labor for drugs) market. As kilogram prices dropped so dramatically, low-level dealers began to receive and retain more cash than ever. And there was much more cash available to everyone.

2. *Most Crack Abusers Cannot Be Reliable Sellers.* Persons who had been effective street user-sellers but became multiple daily users of

crack (a sizable proportion) quickly smoked up the drugs to be sold; they were "always late, always short, and always with a story" (Williams 1978–89, field notes from 1987; Williams 1989). If not assaulted for nonpayment, most crack abusers were "cut off" from consignments by their former suppliers but offered other roles. Sellers who avoided crack use, but snorted cocaine in moderation or were irregular or nonusers of drugs, could be "trusted" by suppliers and earned good money (Williams 1989).

In order to make "crazy money," however, the supplier needed to prevent his or her user-sellers from consuming the product while selling and to ensure (like legal businesses) that virtually all dollars received (gross sales) be returned to the supplier. This led to several major changes in the social organization of crack selling, which was still evolving in 1989.

3. *Centralized Management Controls Crack Abusers and Counters Police Tactics.* Crack-dealing groups now generally have one primary boss ("supplier") who has established connections and can routinely obtain an eighth to a full kilogram of cocaine from a higher level of traffickers, usually on consignment. Depending on the size of the operation, the supplier may have four to fifty persons "working" for him in various roles. The identity and location of the supplier is usually concealed from all but a few trusted workers.

One or more trusted "lieutenants" or "crew bosses" oversee street- and house-dealing operations. Street-selling operations divide illegal sales into several roles (lookouts, guards or muscle men, steerers, touts, holders, money counters, drug dispensers, money handlers, etc.). Such role separation provides work and drugs to crack users (but they are not responsible for *both* money and drugs). Likewise, role separation is designed to counteract police buy-and-bust and street-sweep tactics, making it very difficult for police to trace either the drugs or money back to its "owner," even if some lower-level sellers can be "turned."

Running such a street-selling operation necessitates "managers" having high levels of performance and coordination that are rare among free-lance sellers. Such organizations assure that most buyers pay the "asking price," that the gross cash income is returned to the supplier, and that workers are paid on an hourly or daily basis. A smooth-functioning operation can generate gross sales of $5,000 or more a day, equivalent to a small supermarket. Individual employees may earn $100–$400 a day or more but are frequently offered drugs or goods (gold jewelry, women, cars, etc.). In short, such crack-selling groups are now managed and function more like legal businesses than previously (except that they do not keep detailed financial records or pay taxes).

But such "crazy money" can be gained only under optimum conditions: no problem employees, no police, no complaining citizens, and no competition in the area. Violence and its threat, however, are almost always necessary even to approach these conditions.

C. Systemic Violence to Control "Employees" and Free-Lancers

Because sales of heroin, cocaine, and crack are illegal and serious felony crimes, persons and groups selling these drugs cannot seek protection from law enforcement agencies and constantly oppose them. Thus, the use of violence and, even more important, threats of physical violence become essential elements in controlling the many persons who do not comply with the selling group's conditions for optimum functioning.

1. *Self-Selection and Social Selection of Violent Persons.* Drug-selling organizations frequently recruit persons who have previous histories of violence and who are physically menacing and verbally aggressive (Chaiken and Chaiken 1982; Johnson et al. 1985). Such persons also seek out drug-selling groups. Persons who have no fear of violence and enjoy violence are particularly valuable in roles of lieutenant or crew boss and as muscle men or guards, although the violence-prone members also perform other roles.

2. *Weapons Intimidate Workers and Competitors.* Crack-selling groups now spend money to buy the latest weapons and guns (semiautomatics and small handguns), which guards may deploy in public view. Guards and lieutenants routinely show such weapons and threaten violence to those who work for their selling group. Street sellers know that if they run off with drugs or money, or fail to repay debts, or act as informers to police, they are likely to be physically assaulted or killed (Goldstein 1985; Johnson et al. 1985). In addition, free-lance sellers depart rapidly from good selling locations when threatened by weapon-carrying guards. Such threats, in addition to payments for work performed, are the "glue" that keeps drug-selling groups functioning effectively and prevents persons "laid off" from complaining to police and others about their mistreatment.

3. *Intimidation of Neighborhood Citizenry.* With the mobile and rapid deployment of narcotics bureau squads, which target both street sellers

and house or apartment selling operations, crack-selling groups have also developed highly mobile tactics. Because police and narcotics squad activity are frequently based on calls from community leaders and citizen complaints identifying specific locations, crack-selling groups undertake efforts to control ordinary or "straight" citizens and prevent them from calling police. Two major tactics are routinely employed.

One method consists of using money to overcome resistance to the drug trade. Crack-selling groups attempt to "buy" the cooperation or silence of citizens. Such groups make very attractive offers to landlords or low-income citizens to vacate their apartments or permit them to be used as a location for selling or packaging. They often employ young children, mothers with baby carriages, grandmothers, or other inno-cent-appearing persons as lookouts or drug "holders." They also pro-vide their selling "staff" with badly needed money to give to mothers, parents, or spouses to suppress their opposition to selling crack. (When crack sales are the only "job" to be found in inner-city neighborhoods, high cash payments are frequently accepted by "straights.") In short, crack-selling groups may make concerted efforts to buy the cooperation of ordinary citizens who would be present to observe their illegal activi-ties and might call police.

Of equal or greater importance to crack-selling groups, however, is a second tactic that calls for the use of violence in order to intimidate most citizens in their selling territory. Such citizen intimidation ranges from loud, aggressive talk among sellers to shootouts with rival groups. A common form of intimidation consists of implicit verbal threats ("you better not cause trouble") to persons who refuse generous "offers" of money for the use of their apartments or who refuse to "work" for the organization.

After gaining and using an apartment in a building for selling, crack-selling groups and crack users may also destroy plumbing or vandalize the building, thus threatening the marginally decent living accommo-dations of inner-city residents. Several crack users and sellers may make loud, verbal threats to each other and to passersby. Guards in crack organizations may display weapons (semiautomatic guns are especially effective). Sellers and lookouts may attend "anticrack" rallies to see who is opposing them. Some persons, especially leaders in low-income neighborhoods, may be physically assaulted; some have even been killed.

The end result of many hours and days of crack selling and related dealing activity is that most members of the inner-city community are bought off or sufficiently intimidated; police are rarely contacted or neighborhood organizations cannot generate sufficient support to demand improved police protection.

Police ability to eliminate crack sellers for long periods of time without large manpower resources is spotty. From June 1986 to August 1988, Manhattan's prosperous West Side was a favorite sales location for many crack sellers, including Max's crew, because many middle-class buyers would come to the neighborhood. By October 1988 most crack dealers were gone:

> But for many [repeat crack dealers] the door is slamming shut; not only arrests, but convictions are up, the result of a highly focused effort by diverse groups of government agencies who've joined forces with the community to combat drugs. Amsterdam Avenue, plagued in recent years by thickets of drug dealers, appears to be clearing up, according to a task force team who've been targeting Amsterdam and intersecting streets for the past five months. During that time 450 drug-related arrests were made. The District Attorney's office had been responsible for the conviction of and sentence of 158 persons . . . and had obtained particularly stiff penalties. The Westside Crime Prevention Program involved top commanders of two precincts, housing police, the D.A., and local politicians. The reclamation of Amsterdam Avenue seems now a work-in-progress. [*Westsider* 1988]

Similar results have yet to be accomplished in Harlem and Washington Heights, partially due to the magnitude of the problem and a citizenry that is less effective in demanding action from city government than are the middle-class elites of the West Side. Neighborhood intimidation and effective control by crack-selling groups is particularly evident in many inner-city public housing projects, especially in Chicago, Detroit, and St. Louis (*Newsweek* 1988).

4. *Violence among Crack-Selling Groups.* Crack-selling organizations ("gangs," "crews," and "posses") face several fundamental problems. They are all trying to sell the same undifferentiated product to a relatively small number of crack abusers who use it frequently and always try to bargain the price down. Price reductions by and competition from free-lancers and other crack-selling groups are probably the major

constraint limiting profits. Competition among selling groups is probably more important than police tactics (which usually result in arrests of lower-level sellers rather than upper-level management).

Emerging crack-selling groups have, for the most part, been effective in controlling free-lance sellers by moving them out of their "turf" or by providing employment in their groups. The major problems arise over which organization is going to sell crack within a specific area. Well-managed crack-selling groups typically gain and maintain control of most crack sales within a building or perhaps several blocks. The presence of armed guards and other muscle men is designed to frighten off other crack sellers and crack-selling groups (although citizen intimidation is also an important factor).

Other crack-selling groups, however, will frequently challenge and try to establish their sellers in particularly good locations. Such efforts to break into a local near monopoly of sales frequently generate the most serious street violence. Armed guards and employees may engage in executions or gunfire with guards and employees of another crack-selling group. Such shoot-outs by persons with no firearm training sometimes occur in busy neighborhoods and may wound or kill innocent persons. The shootings are almost always reported on television and in the local press. The publicized incidents provide a most effective form of citizen intimidation.

5. *Cumulative Impact of Crack-Selling Groups.* Crack-selling groups have expanded dramatically since 1985. Many have a vertical, business-like, organizational structure, control the actions of several employees, have well-armed guards, and are willing to use violence and its threat on a daily basis to maintain optimal selling conditions. Well-armed and well-financed organizations now exist in New York, Los Angeles, Detroit, Chicago, and Washington, D.C., and can be found in the inner sections of most cities of over a million and in many smaller urban areas. They maintain effective paramilitary control much of the time in many inner-city streets and neighborhoods, although they generally cede control to police when they pass through.

From 1986 to the present, the police in most communities with crack have devoted major resources to arresting crack sellers. For example, the monthly number of crack arrests in New York City increased from 3,000 in the fall of 1986 to 6,000 in the fall of 1988 (New York City Police Department 1989). Moreover, in comparison with cocaine arrestees in 1983–84 (primarily Operation Pressure Point arrestees), crack arrestees in 1986 were more likely to be held at every stage of criminal-justice processing and to be sentenced to more severe penalties (Belenko and Fagan 1987; Nickerson and Dynia 1988; Ross and Cohen 1988).

The end result is that persons convicted of drug sales, especially of crack, have surpassed robbery convictions and now constitute the largest proportion of all inmates entering jails and prisons in New York (Ross and Cohen 1988). The results are similar nationally; jails and prisons bulge with inner-city crack user-dealers arrested and convicted on a variety of charges, but especially for sales.

Few officials believe that inner-city neighborhoods are much safer because so many crack user-dealers have been incarcerated. Moreover, the core members of crack-selling organizations are rarely arrested and convicted, so that arrested street-level sellers are rapidly replaced (Chaiken and Chaiken 1984, 1985; Chaiken and Johnson 1988; Williams 1989). General agreement exists that community safety in the inner city and other neighborhoods declined substantially during the latter half of the 1980s (Newsday 1988; Newsweek 1988; New York Times 1988a, 1988e).

IV. Consequences of Drug Use and Dealing for the Inner City

The vast majority of inner-city users and dealers of cocaine, heroin, and crack come from backgrounds that generally exhibit two or more of the following interrelated social problems: broken or disturbed families, illegitimacy, abuse or neglect by parents, parental alcoholism or drug abuse, parental deviance or criminality, poor housing, below-average school performance, failure to finish school, part-time work or unemployment (or no legal employment), welfare dependency, and long-term economic impoverishment. Such multiple problems are common in the social backgrounds of many, if not most, inner-city residents. Even in the worst communities, however, most inner-city residents deal in their own ways with poverty, poor housing, low education, welfare, family dissolution, and other problems. Despite their severely disadvantaged backgrounds, the vast majority of inner-city residents do not become regular users or dealers of heroin, cocaine, or crack, although regular use of marijuana and alcohol may be common (Clayton and Voss 1981; Frank et al. 1988a, 1988b).

Despite their own lack of personal involvement with heroin, cocaine, or crack, however, most inner-city residents in the 1980s routinely confront hard-drug use and dealing in their neighborhoods and among their families, relatives, and friends. Moreover, with the advent of crack dealing and use, these impacts have apparently worsened significantly in the last half of the 1980s.

A. The Rise and Economic Importance of Drug Dealing for the Criminal Underclass

In 1960, probably less than 5 percent of the total population, and probably less than a quarter of the criminal underclass, had ever used any type of illicit drug. While drug possession and selling were classified as felony crimes in 1960, relatively few persons sold drugs because the demand was not large and supplies were very limited. With the dramatic rise in marijuana consumption after 1965, the heroin epidemic (1965–73), the cocaine epidemic (1975–84), and the crack epidemic (1985–present), the number of persons involved and the frequency of felony crimes of sale and possession of illicit drugs expanded dramatically.

For all practical purposes, drug sales were like a "new crime" after 1960. Like alcohol during prohibition, illicit drugs were commodities that many persons valued and for which they willingly paid a high price. Drug sales were a "victimless" crime (Schur 1962; Scher 1967) in which the buyer would generally not cooperate with—much less complain to—police. The actual economic costs of producing marijuana, heroin, and cocaine were low for suppliers. The major costs were the risks of arrest, apprehension, and imprisonment for violation of drug laws (Moore 1977).

Drug selling and related dealing roles rapidly became a favorite crime for many inner-city youths participating in the criminal underclass. For poorly educated, unemployable, impoverished youths, drug selling had few skill or training requirements; all skills could be learned "on the job" from other suppliers and sellers. Several hours of selling would consistently net greater dollar returns than the commission of almost every other form of crime (e.g., robbery, burglary, and theft) and had a lower probability of arrest and incarceration because the "victims" sought out the seller (Johnson et al. 1985; Johnson, Kaplan, and Schmeidler 1990).

Somewhat like legal businesses, the real economic rewards from drug dealing came from employing and supervising others to conduct the routine sales work and to assume the risks of arrest and incarceration. Criminals who could organize and supervise three to five street dealers to make over 200 transactions or about 400 sales units (bags, vials, etc.) a day would make "crazy money" (Williams 1989).

The labor of the drug-abuser "junkie" became valuable. While the junkie might not be trusted to sell his drug of addiction, he would work much of the day to assist sellers by performing other key roles (lookout, tout, holder, etc.) and take payments in drugs rather than cash (Johnson et al. 1985; Johnson and Williams 1987). As a victimless crime that had eager buyers paying large cash amounts for illegal drugs, drug selling rapidly became the most frequently committed crime, even among criminals who otherwise seldom used drugs (Chaiken and Chaiken 1982, 1985). Especially among daily users of marijuana, heroin, cocaine, and crack, virtually all engage in direct sales and related roles. They engage in hundreds or thousands of drug transactions annually (Inciardi 1979; Ball et al. 1982; Chaiken and Chaiken 1982; Chaiken and Johnson 1988).

B. The Hard Drugs/Crime Connection

An extensive research literature now documents the linkages between heroin and criminality and, increasingly, between cocaine and crime (Ball et al. 1981; Johnson et al. 1985; Nurco et al. 1985; Johnson, Lipton, and Wish 1986; Wish and Johnson 1986; Chaiken and Johnson 1988; Wexler, Lipton, and Johnson 1988; also see Hunt, in this volume).

There are several ways in which hard-drug use or sales have increased criminality. First, among youths who initiate criminality at an early age (thirteen or under), sizable proportions also initiate drug use and hard-drug use at early ages. In short, those predisposed toward criminality are at high risk for also becoming hard-drug users, although the majority may not become lifelong hard-drug users (Robins and Wish 1978; Brunswick 1979, 1988; Elliott and Huizinga 1984).

Second, even among persons not predisposed to criminality and those from stable working-class or middle-class origins, a small proportion (but with sizable absolute numbers) become regular users of heroin, cocaine, or crack, commit several felony crimes, and become participants in the criminal underclass subculture (sometimes while also holding steady employment). Thus, drug abusers from outside the poverty class may also be recruited to the criminal underclass.

Third, heroin and cocaine, and recently crack, are drugs that rapidly lead to dependence. They produce euphoria (highs) that many users find extremely rewarding, but after several administrations users experience dysphoria or depression or withdrawal symptoms that the next administration of the drug quickly, but temporarily, relieves. Even after several days or weeks without such drugs, users experience strong cravings for use; relapse is the usual, predictable outcome (Des Jarlais et al. 1983; Gold 1984; Anglin and Speckart 1988; Anglin and Hser, in this volume). Such cycles of repeated administration, euphoria, and dysphoria, occasionally punctuated by days or months of abstinence (followed by relapse), create pressure on the user to commit crimes to obtain the drugs or funds with which to purchase hard drugs.

Fourth, since heroin, cocaine, and crack are expensive illicit drugs, many users, especially from inner-city poverty origins, quickly exhaust their legal resources and engage in cash-generating crimes (primarily thefts, burglary, robbery, and female prostitution) or drug-dealing crimes on a regular basis, from several times a week to two to ten times a day (Ball et al. 1981, 1982; Johnson and Wish 1987; Anglin and Speckart 1988; Johnson, Anderson, and Wish 1988; Johnson, Kaplan, and Schmeidler 1990; Chaiken and Chaiken, in this volume).

Fifth, although the majority of heroin and cocaine users have initiated criminality prior to their use of these drugs, their crime rates increase from relatively few felony crimes (under fifty annually) prior to addiction to many crimes (about 200 nondrug crimes and over 300 drug sales annually) during periods of daily and multiple daily use. If such hard-drug users temporarily abstain or reduce consumption to less than weekly use, their crime rates decline to approximately their preaddiction levels but increase when they relapse to daily use (Ball et al. 1981, 1982; Ball, Shaffer, and Nurco 1983; Nurco et al. 1985, 1988; Anglin and Speckart 1988).

Sixth, the most serious crimes (robbery and assaults) are committed primarily during periods of heaviest (daily, multiple daily) use of heroin and cocaine; such offenders rarely commit these crimes during periods of less-than-weekly use of these drugs (Hunt, Lipton, and Spunt 1984). Criminal income from robbery is rapidly expended, primarily on heroin and cocaine among speedballers in New York (Johnson and Wish 1987; Johnson, Anderson, and Wish 1988).

Seventh, persons who engage in hard-drug sales must systematically protect themselves against arrest and incarceration and have no access to law enforcement to protect their property. Sellers at all levels must be prepared to resort to violence or its threat to control their associates.

Eighth, the economic returns to dealing organizations from drug sales are so substantial that many expensive goods and services can be afforded to maintain control. Particularly important is the ability to purchase weapons, especially guns and automatic weapons.

Hence, hard-drug use and sales have probably increased the number of participants in the criminal underclass substantially since the 1960s. The participants appear more likely to commit serious crimes and to commit all felony crimes at higher frequencies than prior to 1960 and in comparison with criminals who do not use hard drugs. The dramatic expansion of drug selling and related roles since 1960 and the economic values of illicit drugs have provided the criminal underclass with very real and substantial economic power and criminal means to prevent law enforcement from imposing sanctions on the majority of offenders.

The central conclusion is that the criminal underclass in the inner city has experienced substantial growth since 1960. Drug use and sales have been incorporated, and have surpassed all other criminal offenses, in the criminal underclass economy. The monetary returns from drug sales have so dramatically expanded the economic value and importance of the criminal underclass economy that it may rival or surpass the licit economy in inner-city neighborhoods (although hard data on this point are impossible to obtain). The consequences of such growth in the criminal underclass economy and its subculture for individuals are discussed in the following sections.

C. Declines in Economic Well-Being of Drug Abusers in the Inner City

While a few upper-level suppliers like Max make "crazy money" from cocaine and crack sales, the vast majority of inner-city youths who enter the cocaine-heroin world and the criminal underclass rarely improve their economic positions in American society. Instead, the regular use of heroin, cocaine, and crack frequently brings about rapid impoverishment (Williams and Kornblum 1985). The following paradigm of "declining economic well-being" among drug abusers is designed to help organize and understand diverse findings about family disintegration (Hoefferth 1985; Deren 1986; Gibbs 1988; Glick 1988; McAdoo 1988), homelessness (Johnson et al. 1988; Ropers 1988), unemployment and underemployment (Glasgow 1981; Freeman and Wise 1982; Williams and Kornblum 1985; Freeman and Holzer 1986; Larson 1988), and the economic underclass (Shannon 1986; Hughes 1988; Ricketts and Sawhill 1988; Wilson 1988).

"Economic well-being" may be defined as the ability to gain and maintain housing and food, to accumulate tangible assets, and—in the illicit markets—to acquire drugs for consumption. It also refers to intangible assets such as good relationships with other persons to gain assistance in hard times. Economic well-being can be measured by the dollar amounts expended on housing and food plus the dollar value of tangible assets acquired (value of house, furniture, cars, etc.) plus cash savings and investments, plus the dollar value of legal and illegal drugs consumed. At very low levels, economic well-being may also be conceptualized as including the dollar value of "avoided expenditures" (Johnson et al. 1985) for housing, food, or drugs that may be given by the "good will" of others who provide such subsistence.

The majority of near-daily users of heroin and cocaine experience severe declines in, and have very low, economic well-being because most of their resources are expended for drugs—regardless of how much they earn from legal work, illegal activities, and drug dealing. The majority of cocaine or heroin abusers and even dealers experience absolute declines in economic well-being within both the licit economy and the drug-dealing economy.

1. *The Downward Cycle in the Licit Economy.*   The lifestyle of drug abusers during typical cycles of daily or multiple daily use of heroin or cocaine, or of crack, needs to be placed within its context. Most inner-city adults have welfare support or a legal job providing modest legal income that supports expenditures for a home or apartment, sufficient food, and some household furniture. They are also likely to have friends and extended family willing to "help during hard times" (McAdoo 1988, pp. 160–66). While several adults may use heroin or cocaine recreationally (once or twice a week or less often), among persons who become daily users of heroin or cocaine, the following scenario—drawn mainly from Hanson et al. (1985), Johnson et al. (1985), and Williams (1989)—is common.

Users enjoy drug-induced euphoria so much, and they feel so sick or depressed shortly afterward, that they *must* have their drug of choice again, and again, and again. If available, cash savings are spent, the entire paycheck or welfare check is spent in a couple of days, and credit is borrowed up to the limit. Their food consumption and expenditures drop (heroin and cocaine suppress appetite). Phone service is disconnected, and the rent is not paid. In about six months (unless a spouse or family member or police or treatment intervenes), all tangible assets have been sold or traded for drugs, and a permanent residence is lost. Frequently, a legal job has been lost as well. Legal economic well-being has declined below federal poverty levels, if not to near zero. The frequency of criminality increases.

Next comes the "couch person" or "garage person" phase. Drug abusers avoid expenditures by sleeping on a couch or floor (or garage) of a relative or friend who will provide them with a meal or two. After the theft of some goods or several days' stay, however, this hospitality typically ends, and the drug abuser must find another friend who will provide shelter and some food. Depending on the extent of the kinship and friendship network, most drug abusers become homeless shortly afterward.

The "homeless" phase occurs when the drug abuser has exhausted virtually his entire economic well-being, owning only the clothes he wears. He eats at soup kitchens or spends a few dollars on snacks and sleeps outdoors, in abandoned buildings, or, in cold weather, in public shelters. Arrest or jail or residential treatment entry provides a few limited opportunities to eat and sleep reasonably well.

2. *The Downward Cycle in the Drug-Dealing Economy.* During the process of losing legal economic well-being, however, heroin abusers report earning substantial cash incomes—about $8,000 annually in 1982 in New York (Johnson et al. 1985)—from nondrug crimes such as burglary and shoplifting for males, or theft and prostitution for females. Most of the returns from each crime episode are spent within a day on drugs, and very little will be spent for food (Johnson, Anderson, and Wish 1988).

Prior to becoming "homeless," most heroin and cocaine abusers also engage in drug dealing. Suppliers may advance them "bundles" of ten to twenty-five dosage units (bags or vials) to sell. Average sellers can easily make gross sales of $200 to over $1,000 a day, of which about 60 percent must be returned to the supplier in order to "re-up." Such gross sales should generate $80–$400 a day in cash income, but this is rarely the case. User-sellers frequently consume some of the drug consignment as their "returns" in drugs. In addition, the user-sellers must frequently give drugs to others who steer or find customers or who protect them (Johnson et al. 1985; Williams 1989).

Recently, as crack-selling groups have become vertically organized with crack users (and nonusers) being hired to sell at assigned street locations for a wage, persons who do not make enough sales during the week are not rehired. Moreover, as users of heroin or crack begin to use several times daily, their reliability as sellers declines. They consume so much of their drug consignment that they cannot return the expected cash amount to their supplier, or they use as much as they sell (Williams 1989). Soon their reputations spread, and suppliers will no longer advance them drugs to sell. Nevertheless, a variety of roles in assisting sellers remain available; users can tout drugs, steer buyers, look out for police or competitors, hold money or drugs, and so on. The key feature of these roles is that the person is responsible for either money or drugs, but not both, and for some roles he has access to neither.

If their crack-induced paranoia or excessive consumption of heroin or cocaine bothers suppliers or impedes performance in these roles, however, user-sellers will be discharged. Thus, they can no longer obtain supplies to sell; nor will others hire them to assist in selling drugs. They have exhausted their economic well-being and reputation even within the dealing economy. They can no longer earn drugs easily. Especially when they can no longer share their occasional supplies of drugs, they may not be welcome to stay at apartments of other drug abusers or, more specifically, crack abusers.

At the end of the downward spiral, economic well-being in both the legal economy and the drug-dealing economy has reached near zero. Abusers become unemployed, homeless, without tangible assets, can get neither meals nor shelter from friends and relatives, and have lost their earning powers and reputations in the drug-dealing economy. Despite such near-zero economic well-being, a relatively large number of drug abusers persists in living at that level. Only nondrug crimes (and prostitution for females) will raise the money needed to purchase their valued drugs and minimal food. Many become mendicants, depending primarily on panhandling, the least reputable hustle in the criminal underclass subculture.

> I was waiting at a small restaurant to meet Headache. When I saw him, we walked about halfway down the block. He was approached by a scrawny young girl named T-bird who apparently knew him. She asked him for some money. He said no and wanted to know would I lend her anything. I gave her a dollar and she left immediately for the local groceria. We were standing on the corner talking a few minutes later when she walked by. She held several party cakes in one hand, a Coca-Cola in the other and a bag of potato chips between her teeth. Over the course of the summer I saw her begging many times. Headache said she only begged for money to buy food because she could get crack from a friend named Rock at the crack spot because he (Rock) liked to have her oral sex talents. T-bird was not an isolated case. Begging has become so prevalent among the female (and male) crack users to the point where it was routine behavior that bor-

dered the con game. Many wanted money for drugs while others obviously needed food or transportation. [Williams 1978–89, field notes from 1988]

Arrest and incarceration or admission to inpatient drug detoxification (if they have Medicaid) are two primary routes that provide a break in this bleak lifestyle. Occasionally, some enter methadone treatment or residential drug programs and begin a process of rehabilitation. But usually after several months of abstention or low to intermittent use, most relapse to daily use, and the cycle is likely to repeat itself.

Remarkable though it may seem, many heroin and crack abusers subsist at a very low level of economic well-being, even though their illicit incomes may greatly exceed federal poverty levels and sometimes would provide a comfortable middle-class existence, if they were not all expended for drugs.

3. *Homelessness and Shelters.* Declining economic well-being has added many hard-drug abusers to the growing numbers of homeless and "couch people." While the number of homeless cannot be estimated with precision, the large numbers of drug abusers are clearly evident among the two major institutions for the homeless: public shelters and low-income hotels. In New York City, the Human Resources Administration (Crystal and Goldstein 1984; Human Resources Administration 1987) estimates that approximately 10,000 persons live in "welfare hotels" and "single-room occupancy hotels" or other "low-income hotels"; this number is half of the figure in 1970. In addition, a stable population of 7,000 resides in public shelters; however, that figure swells to nearly 10,000 on the coldest winter nights. Moreover, several thousand homeless sleep in bus, train, and subway stations. Many others sleep in parks, on the street, and in abandoned buildings or drug-taking locations. Los Angeles has approximately 3,500 homeless living in private emergency shelters, but probably 35,000 more sleep in garages and outdoors (Ropers 1988).

Studies of New York City shelter residents (Division of Substance Abuse Services 1988; Joseph 1988; Street Studies Unit 1988; Struening and Kolmar 1988) found that approximately a quarter of "transient" respondents admitted to the use of heroin, cocaine, or crack, and two-fifths admitted to recent marijuana use (Johnson et al. 1988). Such figures must be considered as minimal estimates due to underreporting. Moreover, among "couch persons" and homeless hard-drug abusers, public shelters are frequently the last resort; bus and train stations and the streets (in mild weather) are generally preferred (Joseph 1988). Hard-drug abusers will likely continue to provide a sizable and probably increasing share of the nation's homeless in the near future as well. This may be partially due to extraordinary difficulties in rehabilitating drug abusers.

4. *The Difficulty of Rehabilitation.* The drug-abuser lifestyle is very difficult to alter for long periods of time, especially for abusers from poor inner-city backgrounds. A large and complex literature on treatment of heroin abuse documents these difficulties (DeLeon 1985; Johnson, Lipton, and Wish 1986; Wexler, Lipton, and Johnson 1988; Anglin and Hser, in this volume). While probably over half of heroin abusers seek treatment during their careers, the long-term rehabilitative prognosis is least favorable for detoxification, which addicts prefer (Lipton and Maranda 1982).

Methadone maintenance and therapeutic communities keep addicts in treatment longer; their drug abuse and criminality are substantially reduced while enrolled. On departure from such treatment, however, relapse occurs within a year for about two-thirds of the addicts. Additional cycles of treatment, relapse, and treatment are associated with slow improvements toward rehabilitation (Simpson 1984; Tims and Ludford 1984). Two groups of heroin addicts have particularly poor prognoses: those who are criminally active and the homeless from inner-city backgrounds. Both groups are particularly likely to depart from treatment against medical advice and relapse rapidly to heroin, cocaine, and crack.

Rehabilitation difficulties have increased dramatically with crack. The only "treatment" that consistently rehabilitates crack users is total abstinence from all drugs, but those who abstain are a distinct minority (Washton 1989). Even programs designed for middle-class and employed working-class crack users have dismal outcomes. Over 80 percent relapse to crack and other drug use within a year, most within 30 days of treatment exit. While a variety of experimental treatments are underway, the current prognosis for finding a treatment that can keep the one-year relapse statistic under 50 percent appears distant (Barnes 1988; Gawin and Ellinwood 1988; O'Brian 1988).

In the late 1980s and into the early 1990s, the demand for treatment greatly exceeded available slots—and the vast majority of heroin, cocaine, and crack abusers are not seeking treatment. Most of those who enter will rapidly depart and relapse. Those who remain in treatment for nine to twelve months have the best prognosis toward rehabilitation in future years, but even a majority of these will relapse. With the dramatic rise in crack abuse and the lack of cocaine-specific treatments for the many inner-city drug abusers, very large numbers appear likely to continue their addiction cycles, depleting their economic well-being, have few opportunities for rehabilitation to legitimate activities, and continue to overwhelm the criminal justice, correctional, drug-treatment, and health-care systems.

D. Morbidity and Mortality in the Inner City

The abuse of heroin, cocaine, and crack is also associated with difficulties in achieving gains in inner-city public health. While public-health indicators are generally improving for the United States as a whole, virtually all studies (Centers for Disease Control 1985, 1986; Brunswick and Messeri 1986) show inner-city communities to have the worst measures on virtually all indices of public health. The data are suggestive, but not conclusive, that cocaine and heroin abusers are at highest risk for almost all health measures and that they contribute a very disproportionate share of all persons who are "ill," regardless of the specific sickness.

1. *Accumulation of Years of Poor Health Practices.* The basic reasons for the poor health of heroin, cocaine, and crack users are easily understood. First, regular nutrition, sleep, and preventive health practices are typically neglected. These drugs are appetite suppressants, so the user does not eat as often or as much as normal. Users frequently spend "food" money for drugs, and eat "sweets" (sodas and candy) rather than a variety of foods. Normal sleep and rest are not routine. During runs of cocaine or crack use, users may be awake for several days.

Second, these drugs are effective at suppressing a variety of physiological symptoms, so that warning signs of illness and chronic poor health are masked by these effective painkillers or ignored by users. Users typically seek medical attention only for acute and life-threatening episodes.

Third, cocaine and heroin abusers frequently engage in many practices dangerous to their health and are prone to the development of chronic diseases such as lung and heart diseases (due to multiple daily smoking of tobacco or marijuana), cirrhosis of the liver (due to high alcohol intake), sexually transmitted diseases (due to sexual practices with several sex partners), hepatitis B, and AIDS (due to injection and needle sharing).

Particularly during their teens and twenties, and after onset to near-daily use of heroin, cocaine, or crack, such abusers typically accumulate several years of poor nutrition and sleep, consistently high rates of tobacco and alcohol consumption, and intravenous injections. Sometimes earlier, but usually when in their thirties and forties, many, if not most, cocaine and heroin abusers experience chronic ill health from several diseases, have several hospital episodes, or even die.

Although public-health indicators are not specifically focused on the inner city, the following subsections summarize a few major studies that have examined the relation of indicators of morbidity, mortality, and AIDS among hard-drug users.

2. *Morbidity Indicators: Drug Abusers Often Have a Variety of Serious Illnesses.* Goldstein et al.'s (1987) review of several studies of public-health indicators point out that these may be related to heroin and cocaine abuse. While many studies demonstrate that most measures of poor health are highest in inner-city communities (Gibbs 1988) and that many drug abusers in inner-city health facilities (hospitals and clinics) have these diseases, very few studies directly show what proportion of persons with a specific disease are heroin abusers. The studies strongly suggest that heroin abusers constitute a substantial proportion of all reported cases of the following conditions: hepatitis B, endocarditis, pneumonia, and trauma from assault.

Goldman and Sixsmith (1982) investigated direct linkages between heroin use and medical disease at seven public hospitals in New York City; they examined the patient's entire medical record (including urinalysis, blood tests, and self-reported drug use—including alcohol use) for evidence of addictive status, regardless of the admitting or presenting problem or disease. A sizable proportion of patients, about 20 percent, had evidence of substance abuse, frequently for several substances such as alcohol, heroin, cocaine, and methadone. In cases where some drug use was present, approximately two-thirds of the medical diagnoses were clearly caused by drug use, and only a quarter were clearly not caused by drug use. Drug abusers entered via emergency care and stayed hospitalized longer for their illnesses than other patients. About 20 percent left against medical advice prior to completing the prescribed treatment. About a quarter of the drug abusers had three or more previous hospitalizations compared with 18 percent of other cases. They absorbed a disproportionate share of medical and economic resources at these hospitals.

3. *Mortality Indicators: Drug Abusers are at High Risk for Death at an Early Age.* The evidence is much clearer regarding the association of

heroin abuse and premature death. Even before the AIDS epidemic, heroin abusers had much higher early death rates than their non-drug-using counterparts, and evidence for cocaine and crack abuse suggests similar findings (Sells and Simpson 1976; Dole and Joseph 1978; Simpson and Sells 1982; DeLeon 1985; Joseph and Appel 1985; Des Jarlais and Friedman 1987; Des Jarlais et al. 1989).

During periods when drug abusers remained in treatment, their annual death rate was about five per 1,000 person-years. But when they relapsed to daily heroin use, the annual death rate increased to about fifteen per 1,000 person-years. The three leading causes of death were narcotics overdose, alcoholism (cirrhosis of liver, etc.), and homicide. Other causes of death (traffic or other accidents, heart or lung diseases, natural causes) were much less frequent.

Another grim set of statistics documents the increasingly close connection between drug abuse and homicide. In New York City, estimates of the proportion of homicides which were "drug related" have increased from about 24 percent in 1984 to about 56 percent in 1988 (*New York Newsday* 1988—part of this increase may be due to improved definitions and recording practices).

Goldstein (1985; Goldstein and Brownstein 1987) proposed and measured three ways in which homicides in New York State in 1984 may be "drug related." Because New York City cases could not be back coded, only figures for homicides outside New York City were available. Although widely feared by the public, the "economic-compulsive" variety (homicides committed during robbery of ordinary citizens) was relatively uncommon (less than 2 percent of all homicides). The "psychopharmacological" variety (homicides committed while very heavily intoxicated with alcohol or heroin or while paranoid after heavy use of cocaine) occurred in about 25 percent of the homicides. The "systemic" variety (murders committed among persons involved in drug-dealing networks) accounted for about 10 percent. Approximately 40 percent were clearly not drug related (wife kills husband, fight between friends where drugs are not involved, etc.), and in 20 percent of the homicides the circumstances were unknown.

A recent review of the "new mortality" among young black males by Jewell Taylor Gibbs (1988) revealed that homicide was a leading cause of death, as well as suicide, accidents, and other life-threatening behavior (such as alcoholism and lung cancer). She summarizes her book-length review with this strong statement: "The evidence is overwhelming that young black males are truly endangered—not only indirectly from society's neglect and abuse, but quite directly by their own actions and activities. . . . [They] are continuing to kill, maim, or narcotize themselves faster than they could be annihilated through wars or natural disasters. They not only destroy themselves, but also jeopardize their families and friends, restrict family formation for young black women, threaten the stability of the black community, and endanger the health and welfare of the entire society" (Gibbs 1988, pp. 281–82).

In the early 1980s, medical examiner reports of deaths among those with narcotic drugs in their systems began to grow in number, a harbinger of a new cause of inner-city mortality: AIDS.

4. *AIDS as the Grim Reaper of the Heroin Generation.* Acquired Immunodeficiency Syndrome (AIDS) was first diagnosed in 1981 as a distinct disease, and a test for exposure to the Human Immunodeficiency Virus (HIV) was developed in 1984. Data from the 1970s show that exposure began among New York City heroin injectors in 1976 (Des Jarlais et al. 1989).

Intravenous drug abusers, primarily blacks and Hispanics from inner-city neighborhoods, now constitute a majority of detected AIDS cases in New York City (Stoneburner et al. 1988). Over 90 percent of female AIDS cases have occurred among intravenous drug abusers or spouses of such abusers; they also have virtually all the prenatal transmissions or AIDS babies (Des Jarlais and Friedman 1988; New York City Department of Health 1988).

In 1988, approximately 50–60 percent of intravenous drug abusers in New York City tested positive for HIV. Needle sharing and frequent rental of "works" at "shooting galleries" are primary causes for the high levels of exposure to HIV in New York (Des Jarlais and Friedman 1987; Marmor et al. 1987; Des Jarlais et al. 1988, 1989).

In Los Angeles and many other major urban centers, shooting galleries and needle sharing among heroin abusers do not appear as commonly as in New York City. Less than 5 percent of heroin abusers test HIV positive. Addicts are getting the messages about AIDS and are increasingly reluctant to share needles (Friedman and Des Jarlais 1987).

Probably 250,000 or more New Yorkers have injected heroin or other drugs during the past decade (1978–88) (Des Jarlais, Friedman, and Stoneburner 1988; New York State Department of Health 1988, 1989); this is a conservative estimate. Persons who have injected drugs since 1976 and become HIV infected are at very high risk of death, although no accurate estimate can be made that predicts how many will die of AIDS or HIV related diseases. Tens of thousands will die before the year 2000 (assuming no medical breakthroughs).

AIDS has killed and will continue to kill thousands of heroin injectors nationally before they reach their fiftieth birthday (New York State Department of Health 1988, 1989). Although many addicts do not know it (and avoid tests), many are already HIV positive. The Grim Reaper is working steadily to remove them from society before the end of the twentieth century.

E. Family and Kinship Ties

Recent reviews (Gibbs 1988; McAdoo 1988; Wilson 1988) of family research provide extensive evidence of deterioration in the status of minority males and their families since 1965 (Nobles 1975). Despite mountains of fine research into the causes and consequences of the declining well-being of black (and Hispanic) families, the roles of drug use and abuse and drug dealing are routinely ignored. We suggest that patterns of hard-drug abuse (since 1965) among parents continue to undermine and weaken inner-city families and reduce the support provided by kinship networks among inner-city families.

1. *The Rationale.*   Alcohol abuse affects more families than drug use, but most families can adapt to the alcoholic parent. In families in which a spouse (or even an adult-aged child) becomes an alcoholic or a marijuana abuser, a limited share, probably under 10 percent, of family economic resources (income and savings) goes to the purchase of alcohol or marijuana. The major impacts of alcohol abuse primarily involve affective relationships within the family. Nonalcoholic family members and children may develop elaborate defenses to deny a problem, protect outsiders from knowing, and cover up for the alcoholic family member (Hendin et al. 1987).

The economic impact is far more important when family members become regular or near-daily heroin or crack abusers. If such abusers obtain legal income (via jobs or welfare) for the family, they soon spend most of such money for drugs and cease monetary contributions to the family. When their legal incomes are insufficient to buy drugs, they frequently will turn to stealing family possessions (televisions, appliances, etc.), which they sell to buy drugs (Hanson et al. 1985; Johnson et al. 1985).

In order to protect the family's economic well-being, non-drug-abusing family members must take steps to remove the abuser from imposing further hardships on the family. This usually means denying him or her access to the house, denying food and shelter, and literally being "put out" on the street. In short, family breakup due to drug abuse becomes the responsible solution to preserve the rest of the family (Rosenbaum 1981).

Hard-drug abuse may badly damage or end relationships among family members. Companionship and sexual pleasure between adults decline due to drug consumption. Time spent with children frequently ends; the abuser's erratic and unreliable behavior undermines parent and child relationships. Once out of the household, the male drug abuser rarely has contact with his children, although female addicts may try to maintain contact (Deren 1986). In short, cocaine-heroin abuse (unlike alcoholism and daily marijuana use) severely and rapidly undermines, if not destroys, the family as an economic and affective unit; frequently such dissolution represents responsible action on the part of the family member who remains (*New York Times* 1989*b;* Williams 1989).

2. *The Children of Alcoholics and Substance Abusers.*   One of the best-documented findings in the alcohol literature is that the children of alcoholics are at high risk of becoming alcoholics themselves. Especially during the 1960s, 1970s, and 1980s, children growing up in inner-city families with an alcoholic member were also at high risk of becoming abusers of drugs as well as alcohol. Members of the heroin generation have had several children (two to three on the average), although parents were infrequently married and rarely living with their families. In short, these children of substance abusers in inner cities may not know who their fathers are. If they know their fathers' identity, contacts with them may be very rare, as have been the fathers' economic contributions to the family (Deren 1986).

> The effects of drug abuse on the abusers' children may begin during the prenatal phase, extend to neonatal withdrawal symptoms, and continue as the child is raised in a drug-abusing environment . . . it has been estimated that more than 234,000 children in the U.S. have heroin-addicted mothers. Addicted mothers usually receive little or no prenatal care . . . and suffer complications during pregnancy. Newborns of addicted mothers are more likely to be born prematurely, and about 50 percent are low birth-weight infants. Up to 90 percent of infants born to heroin-addicted mothers experience withdrawal symptoms. . . . In New York City, between 1979 and 1981, (such) infants had a

mortality rate almost three times that of the general population. Substance abuse in parents has been associated with higher rates of substance abuse in children. [Goldstein et al. 1987, pp. 96–97]

If mothers are hard-drug abusers, the children are frequently raised by grandparents, kin, or the foster-care system. And these children of heroin abusers, as well as many children of the inner city, are now at high risk for becoming crack abusers.

Female crack abusers are very active sexually and engage in prostitution as a common source of support. Although many claim to use condoms, they frequently do not employ effective birth control or follow accepted patterns of prenatal care when pregnant; most also smoke tobacco and marijuana and drink alcohol heavily. Over 10 percent of babies born in New York City (*New York Times* 1988e) test positive for cocaine. A sizable proportion of them are abandoned by their mothers before leaving the hospital and are never reclaimed.

Society appears to have a growing number of children with a "no parent" family (Moynihan 1988). That is, no natural parent of the child is responsible enough to raise the offspring; few or no members of the child's kin network are willing to assume this responsibility. Finding relatives or foster homes willing to accept high-risk babies (born to heroin or cocaine abusers or mothers who are HIV positive) who are abandoned in hospitals has challenged the welfare, foster-care, and adoptive systems and will continue to do so for years to come.

V. Concluding Comments

This essay has provided an overview of the major impacts of hard-drug use and sale on the lives and quality of life of inner-city communities and residents. In this section, we comment on the largely negative "progress" that has occurred in the inner city by reflecting on the past to provide a window into the future. We compare the situation in 1965 to 1988 to suggest some general prognoses about the year 2000.

Prior to 1965, the civil rights movement had ignited expectations of improved conditions for blacks and minorities all across America. Yet the inner cities exploded in riots or near-riots in Watts (Los Angeles), Detroit, Newark, and many other cities. New York was largely spared because Mayor Lindsay met often with black leaders and visited the streets (National Advisory Commission on Civil Disorders 1968). Despite the civil disorders, however, black males were only somewhat less likely than white males to be employed, although primarily in low-wage unskilled jobs. Most inner-city minority residents had homes, stable legal income (jobs or welfare), low education, and a variety of other supports (see several essays in Gibbs [1988]). While heroin addicts were present in several inner cities, they were few in number. Cocaine and hallucinogens were not well known. Illicit sales of drugs were relatively uncommon and typically occurred in private places among the few users. Drug use and drug sales were relatively unimportant in the economy and had little visible impact on inner-city communities.

By 1988, the situation had changed dramatically for the worse. We may briefly summarize the major points of this essay as follows:

1. The drug revolution has brought American society epidemics of drugs: marijuana and LSD (1960–75), heroin (1955–73), cocaine powder (1975–84), and crack (1985–present).

2. Drug selling and business have expanded dramatically in economic importance, and the cocaine economy has become a major factor in the inner city and is a major employer of otherwise unemployable youths.

3. Drug use and selling have had substantial impact on the economy and subculture of the criminal underclass.

4. The economic importance of the drug trade has increased the systematic use of violence by dealers; drug-selling organizations can be found in most inner-city neighborhoods.

5. As drug sales have become particularly prominent in the inner city, criminality by users and dealers has increased, becoming more frequent and severe.

6. Most hard-drug abusers experience important declines in their economic well-being and typically live well below poverty levels—regardless of their cash earnings.

7. Drug abuse appears to be associated with a variety of morbidity and mortality indicators. Sharing needles is a primary cause of AIDS among heroin abusers.

8. Family formation, child rearing, and responsible parenting are very difficult if not impossible during daily use of hard drugs. Children of substance abusers are at high risk for similar outcomes as they grow up.

The analyses above have implications for social policy toward drugs in spite of President Bush's declaration that "this scourge will end." The most critical implication is that the already adverse conditions in the inner city have been further harmed and continue to be aggravated by the growth and violence of drug distribution groups. The cocaine and crack economy has become a major factor in expanding the criminal underclass in the inner city, enriching a few upper-level distributors, but impoverishing thousands of compulsive users. Moreover, the expansion in the number of sellers and low-level distributors plus the flexible organizational structure of crack distribution groups in the inner city give every indication that the crack economy will expand well into the 1990s.

Researchers must continue to provide vital information designed to improve public understanding about the impact of drug use and abuse and related public policies on inner-city residents and communities. Three major lines of research are badly needed but are not now occurring. First, much more interdisciplinary and systematic research is needed about the structure, functions, and economics of the drug distribution industry and about the impact of current policies that support police crackdowns on street dealers and imprisonment of thousands of sellers. Second, researchers need to provide improved understanding of how drug use, abuse, and distribution affect family formation, structure, and functioning in the inner-city communities. Third, innovations and demonstration programs designed to increase the effectiveness of treatment for crack abuse are essential.

An optimistic forecast for the inner city in the 1990s is that the drug problem will not get worse. But a more likely scenario for the 1990s is that thousands of inner-city youths will be attracted by the rewards of drug distribution groups, or bullied into working for them, in part because few other legitimate jobs or economic activities will be available in their communities.

We conclude this essay by asking a question. Will policymakers in the year 2000 consider the drug use and sale problem of the inner cities in the late 1980s to be as benign as today we consider the inner-city drug problem to have been in the early 1960s? The whole history of drug abuse in the inner city in the past thirty years suggests that the answer may be "yes."

REFERENCES

Adler, Patricia A. 1985. *Wheeling and Dealing: An Ethnography of Upper-Level Drug Dealing and Smuggling Communities.* New York: Columbia University Press.

Anglin, M. Douglas, and Yih-Ing Hser. In this volume. "Treatment of Drug Abuse."

Anglin, M. Douglas, and George Speckart. 1988. "Narcotics Use and Crime: A Multisample, Multimethod Analysis." *Criminology* 26(2):197–231.

Ball, John C., Lawrence Rosen, John A. Flueck, and David N. Nurco. 1981. "The Criminality of Heroin Addicts When Addicted and When Off Opiates." In *The Drugs-Crime Connection*, edited by James Inciardi. Beverly Hills, Calif.: Sage.

———. 1982. "Lifetime Criminality of Heroin Addicts in the United States." *Journal of Drug Issues* 12:225–39.

Ball, John C., John W. Shaffer, and David N. Nurco. 1983. "The Day-to-Day Criminality of Heroin Addicts in Baltimore: A Study in the Continuity of Offense Rates." *Drug and Alcohol Dependence* 12(1):119–42.

Barnes, Deborah M. 1988. "Breaking the Cycle of Addiction." *Science* 241:1029–30.

Belenko, Steven, and Jeffrey Fagan. 1987. *Crack and the Criminal Justice System.* New York: New York City Criminal Justice Agency.

Boyle, John, and A. F. Brunswick. 1980. "What Happened in Harlem? Analysis of a Decline in Heroin Use among a Generation Unit of Urban Black Youth." *Journal of Drug Issues* 10(1):109–30.

Brecher, Edward M. 1972. *Licit and Illicit Drugs.* Boston: Little, Brown.

Brody, Jane. 1985. "Crack: A New Form of Cocaine." *New York Times* (November 29).

Brunswick, Ann F. 1979. "Black Youths and Drug-Use Behavior." In *Youth and Drug Use: Problems, Issues and Treatment*, edited by G. Beschner and A. Friedman. Lexington, Mass.: Lexington.

———. 1988. "Young Black Males and Substance Use." In *Young, Black, and Male in America: An Endangered Species*, edited by Jewell Taylor Gibbs. Dover, Mass.: Auburn House.

Brunswick, Ann F., and John Boyle. 1979. "Patterns of Drug Involvement: Developmental and Secular Influences on Age at Initiation." *Youth and Society* 11(2):139–62.

Brunswick, Ann F., and P. Messeri. 1986. "Drugs, Life Style and Health." *American Journal of Public Health* 70:52–57.

Bullington, Bruce. 1977. *Heroin Use in the Barrio.* Lexington, Mass.: Lexington.

Carpenter, Cheryl, Barry Glassner, Bruce D. Johnson, and Julia Loughlin. 1988. *Kids, Drugs, Alcohol, and Crime.* Lexington, Mass.: Lexington.

Centers for Disease Control. 1985. "Homicide among Young Black Males—United States, 1970–82." *Morbidity and Mortality Weekly Report* 34:629–33.

———. 1986. "Premature Mortality due to Suicide and Homicide—United States, 1983." *Morbidity and Mortality Weekly Report* 35:357–67.

Chaiken, Jan M., and Marcia Chaiken. 1982. *Varieties of Criminal Behavior.* Santa Monica, Calif.: Rand.

Chaiken, Marcia, and Jan M. Chaiken. 1984. "Offender Types and Public Policy." *Crime and Delinquency* 30(2):195–226.

———. 1985. "Who Gets Caught Doing Crime?" Discussion paper. Bureau of Justice Statistics, Washington, D.C.

———. In this volume. "Drugs and Predatory Crime."

Chaiken, Marcia R., and Bruce D. Johnson. 1988. "Characteristics of Different Types of Drug-involved Offenders." *Issues and Practices*. Washington, D.C.: National Institute of Justice.

Chein, Isidor, Donald L. Gerard, Robert S. Lee, and Eva Rosenfeld. 1965. *The Road to H*. New York: Basic.

Clayton, Richard R., and Harwin L. Voss. 1981. *Young Men and Drugs in Manhattan: A Causal Analysis*. Rockville, Md.: National Institute on Drug Abuse.

Courtwright, David. 1986. *Dark Paradise*. Cambridge, Mass.: Harvard University Press.

Courtwright, David, Herman Joseph, and Don Des Jarlais. 1989. *Addicts Who Survived: An Oral History of Narcotics Use in America, 1923–1965*. Knoxville: University of Tennessee Press.

Crystal, Stephen, and R. Goldstein. 1984. *Shelter Residents in New York City*. New York: Human Resources Administration.

DeLeon, George. 1985. *The Therapeutic Community: Study of Effectiveness*. Rockville, Md.: National Institute on Drug Abuse.

Deren, Sherry. 1986. "Children of Substance Abusers: A Review of the Literature." *Journal of Substance Abuse Treatment* 3:77–94.

Des Jarlais, D. C., and S. R. Friedman. 1987. "HIV Infection among Intravenous Drug Users: Epidemiology and Risk Reduction." *AIDS* 1:67–76.

———. 1988. "Gender Differences in Response to HIV Infection." In *Psychology, Neuropsychiatry and Substance Abuse Aspects of AIDS*, edited by T. P. Bridge, A. F. Mirsky, and F. K. Goodwin. New York: Raven Press.

Des Jarlais, D. C., S. R. Friedman, D. Novick, J. L. Sotheran, S. R. Yancovitz, D. Mildvan, J. Weber, M. J. Kreek, R. Maslansky, T. Spira, P. Thomas, and M. Marmor. 1989. "HIV-1 Infection among Intravenous Drug Users Entering Treatment in Manhattan, New York City, 1978–87." *Journal of the American Medical Association* 261:1008–12.

Des Jarlais, D. C., S. R. Friedman, J. L. Sotheran, and R. Stoneburner. 1988. "The Sharing of Drug Injection Equipment and the AIDS Epidemic in New York City." In *Needle Sharing among Intravenous Drug Abusers: National and International Perspectives*, edited by R. J. Battjes and R. W. Pickens. Research Monograph no. 80. Rockville, Md.: National Institute on Drug Abuse.

Des Jarlais, D. C., S. R. Friedman, and R. L. Stoneburner. 1988. "HIV Infection and Intravenous Drug Use: Critical Issues in Transmission Dynamics, Infection Outcomes, and Prevention." *Reviews of Infectious Diseases* 10(1):151–58.

Des Jarlais, Don C., Herman Joseph, Vincent P. Dole, and James Schmeidler. 1983. "Predicting Post-treatment Narcotic Use among Patients Terminating from Methadone Maintenance." *Advances in Alcohol and Substance Abuse* 2(1):57–68.

Division of Substance Abuse Services. 1985. "Five Year Plan: 1984–85 through 1988–89." Albany, N.Y.: Division of Substance Abuse Services.

———. 1988. "Five Year Plan: 1984–85 through 1988–89." Fourth annual update. Albany, N.Y.: Division of Substance Abuse Services.

Dole, Vincent, and Herman Joseph. 1978. "Long-Term Outcome of Patients with Methadone Maintenance." *Annals of the New York Academy of Sciences* 311:181–89.

Drug Enforcement Administration. 1988. "Crack Cocaine Availability and Trafficking in the United States." Washington, D.C.: U.S. Department of Justice, Drug Enforcement Administration, Cocaine Investigations.

Elliott, Delbert S., and David Huizinga. 1984. *The Relationship between Delinquent Behavior and ADM Problems*. Boulder, Colo.: Behavioral Research Institute.

Feldman, Harvey W. 1968. "Ideological Supports to Becoming and Remaining a Heroin Addict." *Journal of Health and Social Behavior* 9(2):131–39.

Finestone, Harold. 1957. "Cats, Kicks and Color." *Social Problems* 5(1):3–13.

Frank, Blanche, Rosanne Morel, James Schmeidler, and Michael Maranda. 1988*a*. *Cocaine and Crack Use in New York State*. Albany, N.Y.: Division of Substance Abuse Services.

———. 1988*b*. *Illicit Substance Use among Hispanics in New York State*. Albany, N.Y.: Division of Substance Abuse Services.

Freeman, R. B., and H. Holzer. 1986. *The Black Youth Employment Crisis*. Chicago: University of Chicago Press.

Freeman, R. B., and D. A. Wise. 1982. *The Youth Labor Market Problem: Its Nature, Causes and Consequences*. Chicago: University of Chicago Press.

Friedman, Samuel, and Don C. Des Jarlais. 1987. "Knowledge of AIDS, Behavioral Change, and Organization among Intravenous Drug Users." In *Proceedings of the Fifteenth International Institute on the Prevention and Treatment of Drug Dependence*. Rotterdam: Institute for Preventive and Social Psychiatry.

Gawin, Frank H., and E. H. Ellinwood. 1988. "Cocaine and Other Stimulants: Actions, Abuse, and Treatment." *New England Journal of Medicine* 18:1173.

Gibbs, Jewell Taylor, ed. 1988. *Young, Black, and Male in America: An Endangered Species*. Dover, Mass.: Auburn House.

Glasgow, D. 1981. *The Black Underclass*. New York: Vintage.

Glick, Paul C. 1988. "Demographic Pictures of Black Families." In *Black Families*, edited by Harriet McAdoo. Beverly Hills, Calif.: Sage.

Gold, Mark S. 1984. *1-800-COCAINE*. New York: Bantam.

Goldman, Fred, and Diana Sixsmith. 1982. "Medical Care Costs of Drug Abuse." Final report to the National Institute on Drug Abuse. Columbia University, New York.

Goldstein, Paul J. 1981. "Getting Over: Economic Alternatives to Predatory Crime among Street Drug Users." In *The Drugs-Crime Connection*, edited by James Inciardi. Beverly Hills, Calif.: Sage.

———. 1985. "The Drugs/Violence Nexus." *Journal of Drug Issues* 15(4):493–506.

Goldstein, Paul J., and Henry H. Brownstein. 1987. "Drug Related Crime Analysis—Homicide." Paper presented at the annual meeting of Drugs-Crime Grantees, National Institute of Justice, Salem, Mass.

Goldstein, Paul J., Dana Hunt, Don C. Des Jarlais, and Sherry Deren. 1987.

"Drug Dependence and Abuse." In *Closing the Gap: The Burden of Unnecessary Illness*, edited by Robert W. Amler and H. Bruce Dull. New York: Oxford University Press.

Goldstein, Paul J., Douglas Lipton, Edward Preble, Ira Sobel, Tom Miller, William Abbott, William Paige, and Franklin Soto. 1984. "The Marketing of Street Heroin in New York City." *Journal of Drug Issues* 14(3):553–66.

Grinspoon, Lester, and T. B. Bakalar. 1976. *Cocaine: A Drug and Its Social Evolution*. New York: Basic.

Hamid, Ansley. 1988*a*. "From Ganja to Crack: Caribbean Participation in the Underground Economy in Brooklyn, 1976–86." In *Drugs and Drug Abuse: A Reader*, edited by Ansley Hamid. Littleton, Mass.: Copley.

————. 1988*b*. "From Ganja to Crack: Establishment of the Cocaine (and Crack) Economy." In *Drugs and Drug Abuse: A Reader*, edited by Ansley Hamid. Littleton, Mass.: Copley.

Hanson, Bill, George Beschner, James M. Walters, and Elliot Bovelle. 1985. *Life with Heroin: Voices from the Inner City*. Lexington, Mass.: Lexington.

Hendin, Herbert, Ann Pollinger Haas, Paul Singer, Melvin Ellner, and Richard Ulman. 1987. *Living High: Daily Marijuana Use among Adults*. New York: Human Sciences Press.

Hoefferth, S. L. 1985. "Updating Children's Life Course." *Journal of Marriage and the Family* 47:93–116.

Hopkins, William. 1988. "The Changing Street Drug Scene." Plenary address to the statewide drug abuse conference, Rochester, N.Y., June.

Hughes, Mark Alan. 1988. "Concentrated Deviance or Isolated Deprivation?: The 'Underclass' Idea Reconsidered." Report prepared for the Rockefeller Foundation. Princeton, N.J.: Princeton University, Princeton Urban and Regional Research Center.

Hughes, Patrick H. 1976. *Behind the Walls of Respect: Community Experiments in Heroin Addiction Control*. Chicago: University of Chicago Press.

Hughes, Patrick H., and Gail A. Crawford. 1972. "A Contagious Disease Model for Researching and Interviewing in Heroin Epidemics." *Archives of General Psychiatry* 27(2):149–55.

Hughes, Patrick H., Clinton R. Sanders, and Eric Schaps. 1972. "The Impact of Medical Intervention in Three Heroin Copping Areas." Paper presented at the fourth national conference on methadone, San Francisco, Calif., January.

Human Resources Administration. 1987. *New York City Shelter Plans*. New York: Human Resources Administration.

Hunt, Dana. In this volume. "Drugs and Consensual Crime: Drug Dealing and Prostitution."

Hunt, Dana, Douglas S. Lipton, and Barry Spunt. 1984. "Patterns of Criminality among Methadone Clients and Current Narcotics Users Not in Treatment." *Journal of Drug Issues* 14(4):687–702.

Hunt, G. Halsey, and Maurice E. Odoroff. 1962. "Followup Study of Narcotic Drug Addicts after Hospitalization." *Public Health Reports* 77(1):41–54.

Hunt, Leon G. 1973. *Heroin Epidemics: A Quantitative Study of Current Empirical Data*. Washington, D.C.: Drug Abuse Council.

Hunt, Leon G., and Carl D. Chambers. 1976. *The Heroin Epidemics: A Study of Heroin Use in the U.S., 1965–75 (Part 2)*. Holliswood, N.Y.: Spectrum.

Ianni, Francis A. J. 1974. *Black Mafia: Ethnic Succession in Organized Crime*. New York: Simon & Schuster.

Inciardi, James A. 1979. "Heroin Use and Street Crime." *Crime and Delinquency* 25:335–46.

———. 1986. *The War on Drugs: Heroin, Cocaine, Crime and Public Policy*. Palo Alto, Calif.: Mayfield.

Jaynes, Gerald D., and Robin M. Williams, eds. 1989. *A Common Destiny: Black and American Society*. Washington, D.C.: National Academy Press.

Johnson, Bruce D. 1973. *Marijuana Users and Drug Subcultures*. New York: Wiley-Interscience.

———. 1978. "Once an Addict, Seldom an Addict." *Contemporary Drug Problems* 7(1):35–53.

———. 1980. "Towards a Theory of Drug Subcultures." In *Theories on Drug Abuse: Selected Contemporary Perspectives*, edited by Dan Lettieri, Mollie Sayers, and Helen W. Pearson. Rockville, Md.: National Institute on Drug Abuse.

Johnson, Bruce D., Kevin Anderson, and Eric D. Wish. 1988. "A Day in the Life of 105 Drug Addicts and Abusers: Crimes Committed and How the Money Was Spent." *Sociology and Social Research* 72(3):185–91.

Johnson, Bruce D., Blanche Frank, Rosanne Morel, James Schmeidler, Michael Maranda, and Cherni Gillman. 1988. *Illicit Drug Use among Transient Adults in New York State*. Albany, N.Y.: Division of Substance Abuse Services.

Johnson, Bruce D., Paul Goldstein, Edward Preble, James Schmeidler, Douglas S. Lipton, Barry Spunt, and Thomas Miller. 1985. *Taking Care of Business: The Economics of Crime by Heroin Abusers*. Lexington, Mass.: Lexington.

Johnson, Bruce D., Ansley Hamid, Edmundo Morales, and Harry Sanabria. 1987. "Critical Dimensions of Crack Distribution." Paper presented at the thirty-ninth annual meeting of the American Society of Criminology, Montreal, November.

Johnson, Bruce D., Mitchell A. Kaplan, and James Schmeidler. 1990. "Days with Drug Distribution: Which Drugs? How Many Transactions? With What Returns?" In *Drugs, Crime, and the Criminal Justice System*, edited by Ralph A. Weisheit. Cincinnati, Ohio: Anderson.

Johnson, Bruce D., Douglas S. Lipton, and Eric D. Wish. 1986. "An Overview for Policymakers: Facts about Cocaine and Heroin Abusers and Some New Alternatives to Incarceration." Report to the National Institute of Justice. Narcotic and Drug Research, Inc., New York.

Johnson, Bruce D., and Terry Williams. 1987. "Economics of Dealing in a Nonmonetary Labor Market." In *Proceedings of the Fifteenth International Institute on the Prevention and Treatment of Drug Dependence*. Rotterdam: Institute for Preventive and Social Psychiatry.

Johnson, Bruce D., and Eric D. Wish. 1986. "Crime Rates among Drug-abusing Offenders." Final report to the National Institute of Justice. Narcotic and Drug Research, Inc., New York.

————. 1987. "Criminal Events among Seriously Criminal Drug Abusers." Final report to the National Institute of Justice. Narcotic and Drug Research, Inc., New York.

Johnston, Lloyd D., Jerald G. Bachman, and Patrick M. O'Malley. 1988. *Use of Licit and Illicit Drugs by America's High School Students, 1984–1986.* Rockville, Md.: National Institute on Drug Abuse.

Joseph, Herman. 1988. "Homeless Drug Abusers and AIDS." In *Community Research and AIDS*, edited by Carl Leukefeld. Rockville, Md.: National Institute on Drug Abuse.

Joseph, Herman, and Phil Appel. 1985. "Alcoholism and Methadone Treatment: Consequences for the Patient and Program." *American Journal of Drug and Alcohol Abuse* 11:37–53.

Kandel, Denise B., Debra Murphy, and Daniel Karus. 1985. "Cocaine Use in Young Adulthood: Patterns of Use and Psychosocial Correlates." In *Cocaine Use in America: Epidemiologic and Clinical Perspectives*, edited by Nicholas J. Kozel and Edgar H. Adams. Rockville, Md.: National Institute on Drug Abuse.

Kleiman, Mark A. R. 1986. "Bringing Back Street-Level Heroin Enforcement." Working paper. Cambridge, Mass.: Harvard University, Program in Criminal Justice Policy and Management.

Kleiman, Mark A. R., and Kerry D. Smith. In this volume. "State and Local Drug Enforcement: In Search of a Strategy."

Klein, Malcolm W., Cheryl L. Maxson, and Lea C. Cunningham. 1988. "Gang Involvement in Cocaine 'Rock' Trafficking." Final report to the National Institute of Justice. University of Southern California, Los Angeles.

Kornblum, William, Terry Williams, and Vernon Boggs. 1978. *West 42nd Street: The Bright Light Zone.* New York: Ford Foundation.

Langrod, John. 1970. "Secondary Drug Use among Heroin Users." *International Journal of the Addictions* 5(4):611–35.

Larson, Tom E. 1988. "Employment and Unemployment of Young Black Males." In *Young, Black and Male in America: An Endangered Species*, edited by Jewell Taylor Gibbs. Dover, Mass.: Auburn House.

Lipton, Douglas S., and Michael J. Maranda. 1982. "Detoxification from Heroin Dependency: An Overview of Method and Effectiveness." *Advances in Alcohol and Substance Abuse* 2(1):31–55.

Lukoff, Irving F., and Judith S. Brook. 1974. "A Sociocultural Exploration of Reported Heroin Use." In *Sociological Aspects of Drug Dependence*, edited by Charles Winick. Cleveland: CRC Press.

Maas, Peter. 1968. *The Valachi Papers.* New York: Putnam.

McAdoo, Harriet Pipes, ed. 1988. *Black Families.* Beverly Hills, Calif.: Sage.

McFarland, Robert L., and William Hall. 1953. "A Survey of One Hundred Suspected Drug Addicts." *Journal of Criminal Law, Criminology, and Police Science* 44(3):308–19.

Marmor, M., D. C. Des Jarlais, H. Cohen, S. Friedman, S. T. Beatrice, N. Dugan, W. El-Sadr, D. Mildvan, S. Yacovitz, U. Mather, and R. Holzman. 1987. "Risk Factors for Infection with Human Immunodeficiency Virus among Intravenous Drug Abusers in New York City." *AIDS* 1:39–44.

64   Bruce D. Johnson et al.

Mieczkowski, Thomas. 1986. "Geeking Up and Throwing Down: Heroin Street Life in Detroit." *Criminology* 24(4):645–66.
Mills, James. 1986. *The Underground Empire*. New York: Bantam.
Moore, Joan. 1978. *Homeboys*. Philadelphia: Temple University Press.
Moore, Mark. 1977. *Buy and Bust*. Lexington, Mass.: Lexington.
Moynihan, Daniel P. 1988. "Epidemics." Newsletter to constituents, New York, July 1.
Murray, C. 1984. *Losing Ground: American Social Policy, 1950–80*. New York: Basic.
National Advisory Commission on Civil Disorders. 1968. *U.S. Riot Commission Report*. New York: Bantam.
National Commission on Marihuana and Drug Abuse. 1973. *Drug Abuse in America: Problem in Perspective*. Washington, D.C.: U.S. Government Printing Office.
National Institute of Justice. 1988a. *Drug Use Forecasting*. Washington, D.C.: U.S. Department of Justice, National Institute of Justice (February).
———. 1988b. *Drug Use Forecasting*. Washington, D.C.: U.S. Department of Justice, National Institute of Justice (September).
Newsday. 1988. "The City Is Losing" (May 20).
Newsweek. 1986a. "Kids and Cocaine: An Epidemic Strikes Middle America" (March 17).
———. 1986b. "Crack and Crime" (June 16).
———. 1986c. "Can You Pass the Job Test?" (May 5).
———. 1988. "Losing the War?" (March 14).
New York City Department of Health. 1988. *AIDS in New York City*. New York: New York City Department of Health.
New York City Police Department. 1989. Monthly statistical reports on arrest activity. New York.
New York Newsday. 1988. "Homicide, Drug Link Increasing" (October 3), pp. 3, 22.
New York State Department of Health. 1988. *AIDS in New York State through 1988*. Albany: New York State Department of Health.
———. 1989. *AIDS: New York's Response*. Albany: New York State Department of Health.
New York Times. 1986a. "Cuomo Says State Is Widening Effort to Combat Crack" (June 16).
———. 1986b. "Laws Alone Won't Stop Crack" and "Public Found Ready to Sacrifice in Drug Fight" (September 2).
———. 1988a. "Devastating Effect of Drugs on City" (September 16).
———. 1988b. "Irregulars in the Drug War" (June 9).
———. 1988c. "Crack Addicts at a Young Age, and No Place to Get Aid" (May 2).
———. 1988d. "Police Broaden Queens Drug Crackdown" (May 5).
———. 1988e. "More Infants Showing Signs of Narcotics" (April 1).
———. 1989a. "Cocaine and Heroin Smoking Now Common" (July 12).
———. 1989b. "In Cities, Poor Families are Dying of Crack" (August 11).
Nickerson, Gary W., and Paul A. Dynia. 1988. *From Arrest to Jail: Arraignment*

Processing and the Detention Population, New York: New York City Criminal Justice Agency.

Nobles, W. W. 1975. *A Formulative and Empirical Study of Black Families*. San Francisco, Calif.: Westside Community Mental Health Center.

Nurco, David N., John C. Ball, John W. Shaffer, and Thomas E. Hanlon. 1985. "The Criminality of Narcotic Addicts." *Journal of Nervous and Mental Disease* 173(2):94–102.

Nurco, David N., Thomas E. Hanlon, Timothy W. Kinlock, and Karen R. Duszynski. 1988. "Differential Criminal Patterns of Narcotic Addicts over an Addiction Career." *Criminology* 26(3):407–23.

O'Brian, Charles P. 1988. "Pharmacological and Behavioral Treatments of Cocaine Dependence: Controlled Studies." *Journal of Clinical Pharmacology* 49:17.

O'Donnell, John A. 1977. "Comments on Hunt's Estimation Procedures." In *Epidemiology of Heroin and Other Narcotics*, edited by Joan D. Rittenhouse. Rockville, Md.: National Institute on Drug Abuse.

O'Donnell, John A., Harwin L. Voss, Richard R. Clayton, Gerald T. Slatin, and Robin G. W. Room. 1976. *Young Men and Drugs: A Nationwide Survey*. Rockville, Md.: National Institute on Drug Abuse.

Ogbu, John U. 1978. *Minority Education and Caste*. New York: Academic Press.

Preble, Edward J. 1977. Personal communication with author, Narcotic and Drug Research, Inc., July.

Preble, Edward J., and John J. Casey. 1969. "Taking Care of Business: The Heroin User's Life on the Street." *International Journal of the Addictions* 4(1):1–24.

President's Commission on Organized Crime. 1986. *The Impact: Organized Crime Today*. Washington, D.C.: U.S. Government Printing Office.

Reed, Rodney J. 1988. "Education and Achievement of Young Black Males." In *Young, Black and Male in America: An Endangered Species*, edited by Jewell Taylor Gibbs. Dover, Mass.: Auburn House.

Ricketts, E., and I. Sawhill. 1988. "Defining and Measuring the Underclass." *Journal of Policy Analysis and Management* 7:316–25.

Rittenhouse, J. D., ed. 1977. *The Epidemiology of Heroin and Other Narcotics*. Rockville, Md.: National Institute on Drug Abuse.

Robins, Lee N., and George Murphy. 1967. "Drug Use in a Normal Population of Young Negro Men." *American Journal of Public Health* 57(9):1580–96.

Robins, Lee N., and Eric D. Wish. 1978. "Childhood Deviance as a Developmental Process: A Study of 223 Urban Black Men from Birth to 18." *Social Forces* 56:448–73.

Ropers, Richard H. 1988. *The Invisible Homeless: A New Urban Ecology*. New York: Insight.

Rosenbaum, Marsha. 1981. *Women on Heroin*. New Brunswick, N.J.: Rutgers University Press.

Ross, Richard A., and Marjorie Cohen. 1988. *New York State Trends in Felony Drug Processing, 1983–87*. Albany: New York State Division of Criminal Justice Services.

Sanchez, Jose E., and Bruce D. Johnson. 1987. "Women and the Drugs-Crime

Connection: Crime Rates among Drug Abusing Women at Rikers Island." *Journal of Psychoactive Drugs* 19(2):205–16.

Scher, Jordan. 1967. "Patterns and Profiles of Addiction and Drug Abuse." *International Journal of the Addictions* 2(2):171–90.

Schur, Edwin M. 1962. *Narcotic Addiction in Britain and America.* London: Social Science.

Science. 1988. "Breaking the Cycle of Addiction." 241:1029–30.

Sells, Saul B., and D. Dwayne Simpson. 1976. *Effectiveness of Drug Treatment*, vols. 3–5. Cambridge, Mass.: Ballinger.

Shannon, Lyle W. 1986. "Ecological Evidence of the Hardening of the Inner City." In *Metropolitan Crime Patterns*, edited by Robert M. Figlio, Simon Hakkim, and George F. Rengert. Monsey, N.Y.: Criminal Justice Press.

Siegel, Ronald K. 1982. "Cocaine Smoking." *Journal of Psychoactive Drugs* 14(4):277–359.

Simpson, D. Dwayne. 1984. "National Treatment System Evaluation Based on the Drug Abuse Reporting Program (DARP) Followup Research." In *Drug Abuse Treatment Evaluation: Strategies, Progress, and Prospects*, edited by Frank M. Tims and Jacqueline P. Ludford. Rockville, Md.: National Institute on Drug Abuse.

Simpson, D. Dwayne, and Saul B. Sells. 1982. "Effectiveness of Treatment for Drug Abuse: An Overview of the DARP Research Program." *Advances in Alcohol and Substance Abuse* 2(1):7–29.

Smith, David. 1988. Personal communication with author, Haight-Ashbury Free Clinic, August.

Stoneburner, Rand, Don Des Jarlais, Diane Benezra, Leo Gorelkin, Jo L. Sotheran, Samuel R. Friedman, Stephen Schultz, Michael Marmor, Donna Mildvan, and Robert Maslansky. 1988. "A Larger Spectrum of Severe HIV-1 Related Disease in Intravenous Drug Users in New York City." *Science* 242:916–19.

Street Studies Unit. 1985. Staff reports. New York Division of Substance Abuse Services, New York.

————. 1988. Staff reports. New York Division of Substance Abuse Services, New York.

Struening, Elmer L., and Mary E. Kolmar. 1988. "Characteristics of New York City Shelter Residents: Drug Utilization Summer 1987." Unpublished manuscript, New York State Psychiatric Institute.

Time. 1988. "Kids Who Sell Crack" (May 9).

Tims, Frank M., and Jacqueline P. Ludford, eds. 1984. *Drug Abuse Treatment Evaluation: Strategies, Progress, and Prospects.* Rockville, Md.: National Institute on Drug Abuse.

Toledo, Raymond J. 1988. *A Study of Drug Activity in South Jamaica Queens Area following Special Police Efforts to Reduce Drug Dealing.* New York: Division of Substance Abuse Services, Bureau of Research and Evaluation.

Van Dyke, Craig, and Robert Byck. 1983. "Cocaine." *Scientific American* 246(3):128–41.

Waldorf, Dan, and Shiegla Murphy. 1987. "Business Practices and Social

Organization of Cocaine Sellers." Paper presented at the thirty-ninth annual meeting of the American Society of Criminology, Montreal, November.

Washton, Arnold. 1989. *Cocaine Addiction: Treatment, Recovery, and Relapse Prevention.* New York: Norton.

Westsider. 1988. "The Door Slams Shut" (October 13).

Wexler, Harry K., Douglas Lipton, and Bruce D. Johnson. 1988. "A Criminal Justice Strategy for Treating Drug Offenders in Custody." *Issues and Practices.* Washington, D.C.: National Institute of Justice.

Williams, Terry. 1978. "The Cocaine Culture in After Hours Clubs." Ph.D. dissertation, City University of New York.

———. 1978–89. Field notes from ethnographic observations of cocaine dealers in New York City. Narcotic and Drug Research, Inc., New York.

———. 1989. *The Cocaine Kids.* New York: Addison-Wesley.

Williams, Terry M., and W. Kornblum. 1985. *Growing Up Poor.* Lexington, Mass.: Lexington.

Wilson, William J. 1988. *The Truly Disadvantaged.* Chicago: University of Chicago Press.

Wish, Eric D., Elizabeth Brady, and Mary Cuadrado. 1984. "Drug Use and Crime of Arrestees in Manhattan." Paper presented at the forty-seventh annual meeting of the Committee on Problems of Drug Dependence, St. Louis, June.

———. 1986. *Urine Testing of Arrestees: Findings from Manhattan.* New York: Narcotic and Drug Research, Inc.

Wish, Eric D., and Bruce D. Johnson. 1986. "The Impact of Substance Abuse on Criminal Careers." In *Criminal Careers and "Career Criminals,"* vol. 2, edited by Alfred Blumstein, Jacqueline Cohen, Jeffrey A. Roth, and Christy A. Visher. Washington, D.C.: National Academy Press.

Wolfgang, Marvin E., and Franco Ferracuti. 1967. *The Subculture of Violence: Toward an Integrated Theory in Criminology.* London: Tavistock.

Zimmer, Lynn. 1987. "Operation Pressure Point: The Disruption of Street-Level Trade on New York's Lower East Side." Occasional papers from the Center for Research in Crime and Justice, New York University School of Law.

Mark A. R. Kleiman and Kerry D. Smith

State and Local
Drug Enforcement:
In Search of a Strategy

ABSTRACT

Increasing public concern about drug dealing, particularly the spread of
the market for cocaine in smokable form ("crack"), has dramatically
increased the volume of drug-enforcement activity by state and local
police. Drug enforcement serves multifarious and sometimes competing
goals: reducing drug abuse, controlling predatory crime, preventing the
growth of large criminal enterprise, and protecting neighborhoods from
the ill effects of drug dealing on community life. Theory and evidence
agree that it is extremely difficult to put enough pressure on mid- and
high-level dealers to reduce markedly the volume of drugs consumed.
Retail-level enforcement has some clear theoretical advantages but risks
swamping the courts and jails. Focusing retail enforcement on specific
neighborhoods is attractive in concept and has succeeded in some places
but not in others.

The explosive growth of the market for cocaine in smokable form
(known variously as "crack" or "rock") and the associated violence
among dealers have created public demand for more vigorous enforcement of the drug laws. As a result, drug enforcement is commanding a
growing share of local police, prosecution, and corrections resources.
In Washington, D.C., felony drug-law prosecutions rose 503 percent

Mark A. R. Kleiman is lecturer in public policy and research fellow in the Program in
Criminal Justice at the John F. Kennedy School of Government, Harvard University.
Kerry D. Smith is a Ph.D. candidate in history and East Asian languages, Harvard
University. This study was supported by the Smith-Richardson Foundation. James Q.
Wilson, Mark H. Moore, and Saul N. Weingart provided helpful comments and other
assistance. Rebecca M. Young provided invaluable editorial assistance.

between 1983 and 1987. More than half of the district's prosecution activity is directed toward drug enforcement (Office of Criminal Justice Plans and Analysis 1988); the same is true in Baltimore (Coyle 1988). The backlog of cases in New York's criminal court was around 34,000 in 1987 (Press 1987); former New York mayor Edward Koch sought to increase the narcotics division of the police department by 50 percent, 775 new officers, in a city where felony drug arrests rose 70 percent between 1985 and 1987 (Kerr 1988*b;* Wines 1988). In Detroit, police have pursued a series of raids on crack houses; warrants served and arrests made rose 300 percent from 1987 to early 1988 (Calkins 1988). This response is natural and perhaps inevitable: an increase in the level of illegal activity calls forth an increase in the enforcement response. The public demand to "do something about drugs" is certainly very powerful.

Indeed, the public fury about drug dealing and the public frustration about the inability of police to control it have become so great that extralegal measures against drug dealers—extending even to mayhem and arson—have been both practiced and condoned (Davidson 1988). A jury in Detroit, for example, acquitted two men who admitted setting fire to a crack house (Wilkerson 1988*a*). Police have found it necessary to protect drug-dealing suspects being arrested from assailants with pipes, rocks, and baseball bats.

But while "the drug problem" and responses to it seem simple enough from the distance of a politician's podium, a preacher's pulpit, or an editorialist's desk, from close up they reveal an almost disorienting complexity of goals, techniques, and targets. How best to use limited, and largely uncoordinated, enforcement, adjudication, and punishment resources to address the multifaceted drug problem is anything but obvious.

As drug enforcement grows, decision makers must at least implicitly make a complicated series of choices. How much effort should be put into drug enforcement? Which drugs should receive the most attention? How should enforcement effort be divided among high-level dealers, retailers, and drug users? Should enforcement be concentrated or spread throughout a city? What is the role of police and corrections agencies in the prevention and treatment of drug abuse?

The relationship between the level of enforcement activity and the suppression of undesirable behavior is not nearly as direct or as clearcut for drug enforcement as it is for, say, arresting armed robbers. In the armed robbery case, more arrests, convictions, and sentences are likely, in relatively straightforward ways, to reduce the unincarcerated population's average propensity to commit robbery, both through deterrent effects—by changing the perceived costs of robbery—and through incapacitative effects—by placing temporarily out of action some persons with particularly high propensities to rob.

The benefits of arresting more cocaine dealers are less obvious because drugs are bought and sold in markets. The imprisonment or retirement of a drug dealer opens a niche for a new dealer far more directly than the imprisonment or retirement of a robber opens a niche for a new robber.[1] Enforcement has to be thought of as changing the conditions confronting buyers and sellers of illicit drugs, and its effects have to be traced through the drug markets before any conclusion can be drawn about whether those effects are, on balance, beneficial. At least one veteran of the war on drugs is pessimistic about the role of enforcement. Francis C. Hall, recently retired commander of the New York Police Department's narcotics division, notes that "there comes a point when you have to say, what is the optimum number of people we should have directly involved in narcotics enforcement? We may have reached it. If we continue to pour in resources, it may not make things much better" (Pitt 1989).

A mayor, police chief, or district attorney wanting to allocate drug-enforcement resources to achieve socially valuable results would confront four distinct, and sometimes competing, sets of goals: first, limiting the number of persons who use various illicit drugs and the physical, psychological, behavioral, and moral damage they suffer as a result; second, reducing the violence connected with drug dealing and the property and violent crimes committed by users, whether to obtain money for drugs or as a result of intoxication; third, preventing the growth of stable, wealthy, powerful criminal organizations; and fourth, protecting the civility of neighborhoods, and thus their attractiveness as places to live, work, shop, and raise children, from the disorder caused by open drug dealing.[2] As shorthand, these goals might be thought of, respectively, as drug-abuse control, crime control, organized-crime control, and neighborhood protection.

---

[1] But see Cook (1986) for the complexities surrounding the suppression of even "predatory" crime.

[2] Wilson and Kelling (1982) have argued that reducing disorder reduces both the fear of crime (since residents take disorder as a danger signal) and the actual rate of serious crime (because potential offenders take disorder as a signal that deviant behavior is tolerated).

Given the enormous contribution of heroin addiction to the AIDS epidemic (Des Jarlais, Friedman, and Hopkins 1985), as it had contributed earlier to the epidemic of hepatitis-B and the evidence of the rapid spread of syphilis in drugs-for-sex transactions at crack houses (Kerr 1988a), one might add the control of communicable disease as a fifth objective of drug enforcement. If greater weight were given to AIDS control, police might devote more effort to retail heroin enforcement vis-à-vis other drugs and take more aggressive measures to shut down the "shooting galleries" where heroin users go to inject themselves. At the same time, they might refrain from confiscating users' own injection equipment. But few law-enforcement officials consider public health to be central to their mandate, and consequently, local drug policies have not been consciously redesigned to meet the AIDS challenge (Kleiman and Mockler 1988).

Drug-law enforcement sometimes helps one goal at the expense of another.[3] For example, drug-abuse control can compete both with crime control and with organized-crime control (see Moore, in this volume).

If drug enforcement raises the price of illicit drugs, the result will be decreased consumption and thus decreased abuse. But the effect of a price rise on income-producing crime will depend on how sharply drug buyers cut back on their consumption. A 10 percent heroin price increase that leads to only a 5 percent quantity decrease (the situation economists call "relatively inelastic demand") will generate a 4.5 percent increase in the total dollars going to pay for heroin and thus, presumably, an increase in income-producing crime by heroin users. By contrast, if demand is relatively elastic and a 10 percent price increase generates a 20 percent drop in quantity, then total dollars spent will fall by 12 percent, and income-producing crime will presumably fall as well.

One careful econometric study of the issue suggests that, in one market almost two decades ago, rising heroin prices in fact led to rising crime rates. Brown and Silverman (1974) generated price series for heroin in nine major United States cities using monthly reports submitted by agents of the Bureau of Narcotics and Dangerous Drugs. Based on data from the Uniform Crime Reports (reported Part I offenses), and focusing especially on New York City (where the price

---

[3] For a discussion of some trade-offs, see Reuter et al. (1988). See also Moore (1979).

series were most reliable and the addict population the largest), the authors demonstrated the existence of a positive relationship between heroin prices and crime. While it would be imprudent to regard that result as conclusive, it does suggest that the possibility of a tradeoff, at least in the short run, between reducing drug consumption and reducing crime is not merely hypothetical (see also Johnson et al. 1985).

A different line of reasoning suggests the potential tension between drug-abuse control and organized-crime control (Kleiman 1987). Thomas C. Schelling (1971) was the first to point out that an organized-crime monopoly would tend, like all monopolies, to lead to higher prices and lower quantities of, in his example, bookmakers' services. In markets for illicit goods and services, this monopoly effect is desirable; the Mafia helps the police reduce the volume of gambling. Breaking up such illicit cartels helps the struggle against organized crime but expands the availability of illicit goods and services.

Substitute the Medellin cartel or the local drug kingpin for the Mafia and cocaine for the horse bets, and this argument applies to the drug markets. More recently, Frederick Martens (1988) has made the converse point: enforcement can create conditions favorable to transforming drug markets into a cartel. Martens argues that overcoming this tendency requires a redirection of drug-enforcement attention away from drug transactions and toward specific organizations identified on the basis of their violent and corrupting tendencies rather than their mere size. This sort of targeting is far more characteristic of organized-crime and gang enforcement than it is of most narcotics operations (Kleiman 1989).

The problem facing local drug-policy decision makers is further complicated by the wide array of enforcement tactics available to them; the difficulty of balancing the various parts of the criminal justice process managed by independent agencies (e.g., finding enough judges or prison cells to handle the results of a surge in arrests); and the diversity of the drugs themselves and their user populations.

This last point alone ought to be enough to keep a responsible official awake nights. Crack, powder cocaine, heroin, PCP, "pills"—each drug type has a different volume, different user demographics, a different relationship to dealer and user crime. To an outsider, deciding how to divide enforcement attention among them would seem both difficult and important. In fact, except for a widespread belief that marijuana is less important than other illicit drugs, the distinctions among drugs occupy little of police managers' thoughts. They want "good," that is, valid and prosecutable, felony arrests. Chief Hall (1988, p. 1) seems to speak for most of his peers when he writes, "Arrests by this Division are the result of complaints from the public. If cocaine/crack is the drug of choice for abusers, then it follows that more arrests will be made for its possession and sale."

Given these conditions, a prudent elected official may be pardoned for deciding to "handle" the problem by proposing the execution of drug dealers, the legalization of cocaine, military action against Colombia, or other measures so clearly outside a local official's jurisdiction that voters are unlikely to demand any very precise accounting.[4]

The lack of current measurements of the level of activity in drug markets only adds to the confusion about how best to go about enforcement. It might make sense, given the wide range of goals, tactics, drugs, and resources confronting policymakers, and the variations in conditions from place to place, to try something to see if it works. But even this simplest of policy approaches is frustrated by lack of current city-by-city (or, better yet, neighborhood-by-neighborhood) data. The number of crack smokers in New York City is far harder to measure than the reading level of its tenth graders. Thus drug-enforcement effectiveness is even less easy to measure than educational effectiveness.[5] To this lack of data there corresponds a lack of theory. A conscientious local official, eager to create as much public value as possible from the resources at hand, would find only limited help in the published research on the topic. A comprehensive and persuasive answer to the question, How should local officials discharge their drug-enforcement responsibilities? has yet to be offered.

If policymakers are unclear about what they should be doing in their own cities, they are even less clear about what others are doing in theirs. There exists no regular forum for the discussion of strengths and weaknesses of alternative drug strategies. Even the simplest facts from which comparisons might be drawn are hard to come by. Criminal justice data vary around a rather low average in quality, coverage, and specificity: the Federal Bureau of Investigation's Uniform Crime Re-

[4] Mayor Edward Koch of New York City has proposed the death penalty for "drug kingpins" (*New York Times* 1988); Baltimore Mayor Kurt Schmoke has proposed a national debate on the decriminalization of drugs (Coyle 1988); and Isaac Fulwood, Jr., assistant chief of police for field operations in Washington, D.C., has called for U.S. military intervention in drug-producing countries (Fulwood 1989).

[5] For an extended discussion of the data needs of drug-enforcement planning and the inadequacy of current collection efforts, see Kleiman 1986b; Reuter 1984.

ports, for example, lump heroin and cocaine together. Information about the incidence of drug abuse derived from national surveys is not available on a metropolitan-area basis; information about some of its consequences (overdose deaths and emergency room visits) is available through the Drug Abuse Warning Network (DAWN) system. Journalistic accounts often provide useful insights but tend not to develop the quantitative evidence necessary for a full assessment. The scholarly literature is scant and often focused on something other than enforcement policies. A recent Rand study (Reuter et al. 1988) analyzed enforcement, market conditions, and treatment in the Washington, D.C., area; no similar study exists for any other major metropolitan area. In order to get a clearer picture of what major departments are doing and why, the authors met with police officers, prosecutors, federal agents, treatment personnel, and others in New York, Los Angeles, and Detroit.

Section I reviews the relations between drugs and crime, models of the drug market, and likely limits on the ability of the criminal justice system to cope with an increasing volume of drug-related cases. Section II presents six "bundles" of drug-enforcement tactics, each designed to address a particular facet of drug-market activity and reach a well-defined goal. In Section III, we discuss drug enforcement as practiced in New York, Los Angeles, and Detroit. The final section presents some conclusions and policy suggestions.

I. Prior Research

Decisions on drug enforcement are made every day. Resources are allocated, targets chosen, and goals defined, largely without reference to the scholarly literature on the subject, which, to be sure, is not overwhelmingly helpful. Still, the theoretical and empirical studies that do exist can provide some guidance for local officials in their efforts to stem the tide of drug abuse and associated violence.

A. The Drug-Crime Link

Two sets of studies document the link between drug use (heroin addiction) and crime by users (see Chaiken and Chaiken, in this volume, for a review of this literature). This research demonstrates that interventions directed at decreasing the drug use of drug-involved offenders can effectively reduce their offense rates.

Since 1967, Douglas Anglin and his colleagues have collected longitudinal data on the criminal activity of a large number of heroin users during periods of addiction and of abstinence (e.g., Anglin and Mc-Glothlin 1984; Anglin and Speckart 1988). Decreases in drug use, especially those that come with periods of drug treatment, correlate with periods of decreased criminal activity. Treatment, even involuntary treatment, reduces criminal activity, and this effect remains after the treatment regimen ends. A natural experiment that accidentally assigned one group to mandatory treatment, while leaving another virtually identical group untouched, shows that more is at work than self-selection. The importance of Anglin's work lies in its demonstration of the causal relationship between heroin use and crime, and of the effectiveness of policy interventions in manipulating that relationship. The relationship is best demonstrated for heroin, though preliminary results suggest it will prove true for crack as well (Anglin 1988).

David Nurco and his associates (1985) studied the self-reported criminal activity of a set of heroin users and found it extremely high. They conclude that a very large portion of crime in some cities is committed by heroin users. However, the selection of the sample population reduces the force of this result. Nurco's sample is drawn exclusively from addicts known to the Baltimore Police Department, and thus may overstate the criminal activity of heroin users as a class, given that heroin users not known to the police might reasonably be expected to engage in less criminal activity than those who are known to police. His estimates are so high that, combined with the national estimate of the number of heroin users and the national victimization rates, they suggest that heroin users commit more crimes than, in fact, occur. (For earlier estimates, see Singer [1971].) However, even substantial modifications of Nurco's estimates would leave unchanged his conclusion that heroin addicts on average commit enormous numbers of crimes. This conclusion is reinforced by Jan and Marcia Chaiken's survey of male prison and jail inmates in California, Michigan, and Texas. Both early heroin abuse and polydrug abuse turned out to be strong predictors of high-rate offending (Chaiken and Chaiken 1982).

A third set of studies often cited to support the proposition that drug use is linked to crime uses the National Institute of Justice's Drug Use Forecasting (DUF) system. The DUF system collects data from many cities on new arrestees whose urine tests positive for any of ten illicit drugs. In those cities, between 39 and 80 percent of arrestees participating in the study in the first quarter of 1988 tested positive for one or more illicit drugs (excluding marijuana) (National Institute of Justice 1988). It does not, of course, follow from these figures that 39–80 percent of the crime problem is caused by drug use among offenders. Without an otherwise-matched sample of nonusers of illicit drugs or of nonoffenders, the DUF results are effectively silent about the causal link between drug use and crime. In the absence of such a control group, DUF may simply be detecting a high rate of drug use in the populations from which urban arrestees are drawn: young, poor males.

The Drug Use Forecasting system was developed to look at drug-use trends among arrestees and at variations in those trends between cities. It was not designed to indicate drug-use trends among the general population. The lack of localized measures of drug-use prevalence makes it impossible to calibrate the DUF arrestee findings to the general population.

Tom Mieczkowski has expanded the DUF program in Detroit to include a series of additional questions for those subjects who indicate crack use. His work has elicited a wide range of information on production and distribution methods within crack markets (Mieczkowski 1989a, 1989b, 1989c). The success of the methodology employed in Detroit suggests that the DUF system could be a useful and timely source of information, one that would lend itself well to comparisons between cities.

Perhaps the greatest usefulness of the DUF results is their ability to identify very large city-to-city variances in use of particular drugs. In Washington, D.C., 33 percent of arrestees tested positive for PCP, which is almost nonexistent in other DUF cities. Similarly, San Diego stands out for its high rate of amphetamine use. Marijuana, by contrast, holds at between 40 and 50 percent virtually everywhere (except in New York, where it is markedly lower). Unfortunately, the current DUF system makes it hard to measure differences in the use of such widely consumed drugs as cocaine, because some jurisdictions (Chicago, for instance) are core cities only, while others (such as Indianapolis) include large suburban areas as well.

On an individual and social level, some drug use by some users causes some predatory crime. To that extent, drug-abuse control can contribute to crime control. But some drug users commit little or no crime; others commit much but would commit no less were they drug free. With current knowledge, no claim of the form, "Drugs cause 40 percent of the burglaries in Cleveland," can be emphatically demonstrated or refuted. (See Anglin and Speckart [1988] on the difficult methodological issues in testing such a statement.) Attempts to understand that relationship lead to a series of even more difficult questions for enforcement officials. What effects can enforcement efforts have on drug sellers and purchasers, and what steps will lead to the most beneficial results? One way to address these issues is to develop explicit models of drug sales and purchases.

B. Theories of the Drug Markets

Drugs are traded in markets. Economists understand markets in terms of prices and quantities. Thinking of drug distribution in this way yields some powerful insights, but it is not without its pitfalls as well. Illicit markets are not as different from ordinary ones as many enforcement professionals believe, but neither are they quite as similar as economists are likely to assume.

Some of the differences are straightforward. Illicit markets face higher costs because participants cannot advertise, enter into contracts the courts will enforce, sue to recover for injuries, or even effectively call the police if they are shot, beaten, or robbed. Information travels slowly. A peculiar kind of reputation turns out to be a key resource (see the general discussion of illicit markets in Reuter [1982], [1983]).

Other differences are more obscure and harder to accommodate within standard economic models. Perhaps the most important of these was first identified by Mark Moore (1973, 1976): drug buyers, particularly at retail, are discouraged from buying by many factors other than cash expense. They must spend time finding a willing seller; they must undergo the risk of arrest, the risk of being robbed, the risk of being defrauded, the risk of being poisoned by adulterated drugs; and they are sometimes unable to complete a transaction at all. Lumping these nonmoney disincentives together as "search time," Moore pointed out that search time has the essential characteristic of a price: as it goes up, the quantity demanded goes down. This nonmoney price may be as substantial a factor in the drug-purchase decision as the money price. It is likely to be higher for new drug users than for experienced users, and both the average search time and the differential are likely to grow with enforcement pressure.

Search time and money price give enforcement policymakers two distinct conditions to manipulate in their attempt to minimize the total social costs imposed by the illicit drug industry. The money price of heroin depends largely on the risks faced by high-level drug dealers. If enforcement can increase those risks, the price will rise and some users will refuse to pay it. The nonmoney price of heroin depends on how many street dealers there are, who they are, where they are, and how aggressively they look for new customers. If street-level enforcement can shrink their numbers, restrict their location, and make them more cautious, it can influence drug consumption even if the money price of heroin remains unchanged.

Reuter and Kleiman (1986) attempt to explain the impact of enforcement on prices and quantities in drug markets. Their "risks and prices" model treats enforcement as imposing costs on illicit markets, similar in effect to excise taxation. Increased costs will result in increased prices for goods; higher prices lead to lower levels of consumption. How much enforcement increases price depends on the extent of the costs imposed (e.g., asset seizures, drug seizures, and prison time) and on the size of the underlying market. How much an increase in price decreases consumption levels depends on the behavior of consumers.

The "risks and prices" analysis leads to pessimistic conclusions about the ability of local enforcement changes to create substantial impacts on very large drug markets because the enforcement burden on the market depends on the ratio of enforcement activity to illicit activity. In New York, for example, if authorities were to seize an additional 500 kilograms of cocaine annually or imprison an additional 200 cocaine dealers annually for one year each, the result would be only a 1 percent increase in the price of cocaine.[6]

Reuter and Kleiman (1986) point out that, at very high ratios of enforcement pressure to market activity, the "risks and prices" model and the markets will tend to break down. If, as enforcement activity rises, the market shrinks in response, and if effective enforcement pressure depends on the ratio of the two, then at some point the shrinkage of the market may become self-sustaining. (For a general discussion of such situations, see Schelling 1978.) In the case of retail-level enforcement, the possibility of inducing market collapse is reinforced by the importance of nonmoney transactions costs in the calculations of buy-

---

[6] The "risks and prices" model is applied to federal marijuana enforcement in Kleiman (1989), and to the question of capital punishment for drug dealing in Kleiman (1988*b*). Both Reuter and Kleiman have subsequently questioned one of its crucial assumptions: zero long-run "pure" profits in the drug industry, which implies that all enforcement costs will essentially be passed on to consumers. See Cave and Reuter (1988) and Kleiman (1989, chap. 4).

ers and sellers alike. This suggests that concentrated retail enforcement may have exceptional advantages not shared by higher-level enforcement activity.

The "risks and prices" model is attractive in that it allows quantitative predictions of the effects of new enforcement policies. At least one jurisdiction, Santa Cruz County, has attempted to plan its drug-enforcement programs on the basis of a "risks and prices" analysis, which identified some of the county's problems as beyond the likely reach of any enforcement program the county could afford though others seemed within reach of control if efforts were directed at them (Kleiman, Lawrence, and Saiger 1987). Officials responsible for the resulting program report what they regard as successful outcomes, though no formal evaluation has been conducted.

Kleiman (1986a, 1988a) gives two examples of the "risks and prices" model's apparent success (Lynn, Mass., and Operation Pressure Point in New York City) as well as one example of apparent failure (Lawrence, Mass.). Over the first year of the Lynn Drug Task Force's operation, reported robberies were down 18.5 percent compared with the previous year while reported burglaries were down 37.5 percent, and reported crimes against the person were down 66 percent (Kleiman, Holland, and Hayes 1984). Crime rates seem to have remained at their new, lower levels for several years. However, data for the year following the study period suggest that rates began to rise, perhaps because enforcement attention was shifted away from the neighborhood (Barnett 1989).

Operation Pressure Point I targeted the Alphabet City area for enforcement attention (Zimmer 1987). The New York Police Department saturated the area with large numbers of both plainclothes and uniformed police officers; at $12 million a year for its first two years of operations, Operation Pressure Point I was roughly 25 times as costly as the Lynn Task Force. However, the effort disrupted the drug market, improved the quality of life (perhaps too much, judging by the charges of "gentrification" now heard in the area), and reduced crime in the Alphabet City neighborhood. Between 1983 and 1984, robberies fell 47 percent, burglaries, 37 percent, and homicides, 62 percent (13 as against 34) (Kleiman 1988a). Crime rates in surrounding areas either fell or remained stable.

The apparent failure was in Lawrence, Massachusetts. While heroin was described as somewhat harder to find in Lawrence, and drug-dealing neighborhoods clearly felt the benefits of a reduction in open trafficking, the existence of a vigorous heroin market in nearby Lowell kept supplies readily available. Crime rates actually increased slightly, although not significantly so. The fact that the market in Lawrence was more dispersed, that police resources were increasingly diverted to attempt to control the growing cocaine market, and that nearby drug markets not under comparable pressure were accessible help account for the relatively poor showing of operations in Lawrence (Kleiman et al. 1988). As against this discouraging account, the local prosecutor responsible for the Lawrence effort points to substantial neighborhood-protection benefits (Burke 1989).

Both the theory and the evidence from the Lynn, Lawrence, and Operation Pressure Point I experiences single out the concentration of enforcement resources on the market for one drug in one neighborhood as an important contributor to success. In each case, the drug is heroin, raising questions about the applicability of this approach to much larger markets for crack. In addition to the complexities introduced by the wide variety of drugs, enforcement officials must also contend with the limits imposed by other elements of the criminal justice system.

C. Criminal Justice System Constraints

Aric Press (1987) discusses what happened to the criminal justice system in New York when police stepped up pressure on that city's burgeoning crack market. Felony drug arrests in New York increased 159 percent between July 1985 and July 1987. The problem was that the courts could not handle the increased caseload. In 1986, the backlog of cases in the criminal court was 27,694; in 1987, it leveled off at about 34,000. Already-crowded prisons, and particularly jails, were forced to accommodate the influx of new prisoners generated by the anticrack operations. The combination of crowded court dockets and crowded jails created pressure on prosecutors to let drug cases "plead out" cheaply.

Press (1987) compares the New York City criminal justice system to a person with bulimia, gorging itself on masses of arrests only to vomit them back up in plea negotiation. Press makes it clear both that the police can easily swamp the courts with drug cases, and that the courts will respond to control their own workloads in ways that may largely neutralize the value of mass-arrest programs.

Research and experience have led scholars to reach tentative conclusions about the link between drugs and crime, the nature of retail drug markets, and the capacity of criminal justice systems. Law-enforcement officials have a wide range of tactics available to enforce drug laws. Policymakers are now faced with the task of incorporating research results and the tools of police work into a coherent drug-enforcement strategy. This has proven to be a difficult task.

II. Tactics and Strategies

The list of tactics available to drug enforcement officials is long (see the Appendix). The problem is to assemble a coherent strategy from this plethora of things that might be done. Should the next fifty officer-years of effort be put into bringing down the largest crack dealership in the area, or into making 1,500 additional felony arrests for retail dealing? Is another Spanish-speaking undercover agent needed more or less than a wiretap expert? Should drug enforcement efforts be concentrated in one or a few neighborhoods (either those where the problem is most serious or those where the chances of turning the area around are best) or spread around the city? Should explicit priorities among drugs be set, or should the narcotics squad make as many good cases as it can, regardless of drug?

One way to organize thought on this subject is to create a set of stylized "strategic bundles," each aimed at a particular intermediate goal. (See Moore 1989 for a similar account with a different set of "bundles.")

A. Getting Mr. Big: High-Level Enforcement

"High-level" drug enforcement attacks the operators of large-scale distribution systems. The idea is that identifying and convicting ("immobilizing" in the parlance of federal narcotics enforcement) the top layer of one of the major drug distribution groups will shut down at least one drug conduit into a city. Drugs will be harder to find, prices will rise, and consumption will decrease. Moreover, justice will be served by punishing a kingpin rather than the usual miscellaneous collection of low-level operatives.

Getting Mr. Big relies on tactics similar to those employed by the Drug Enforcement Administration and the Federal Bureau of Investigation in their drug-enforcement work: long-term, high-level undercover operations; developing informants, often by making cases against low-level dealers that can then be bargained away in return for their help against their suppliers ("working up the chain"); searching through police files, financial records, telephone logs, and the like to demonstrate connections; and, most powerful but most expensive, electronic surveillance (wiretaps and, less frequently, bugs). In addition to convictions and prison terms, agents pursuing Mr. Big try to take financial and material assets as well: bank accounts, real estate, and vehicles.

That getting Mr. Big will, if successful, serve the ends of justice is hard to deny. That it serves the ends of drug-abuse control, crime control, neighborhood protection, or even organized-crime control is less clear.

It might be true—and enforcement professionals often talk after a successful case as if it will be true—that eliminating a major dealing organization will reduce the supply of illicit drugs and thus increase their prices. For example, the assertion that the Chambers Brothers group (an organization founded by four siblings from Marianna, Arkansas, known for its business-like approach to drug dealing, and dismantled early in 1988 after a joint federal-local operation) supplied half of the Detroit area's cocaine (Wilkerson 1988a) would seem to suggest that the arrest of the brothers could halve Detroit's cocaine problem. But there are two problems with such an optimistic belief.

First, it assumes that no new management group will develop to continue the affairs of the organization. But there may be almost as many potential kingpins as there are second- and third-level dealers. Newspaper accounts of the careers of major convicted dealers often feature astonishingly rapid ascents from low-level dealing to the top of the trade; this suggests that no long apprenticeship is required. Nor is it evident that the basic financial and personnel-management skills required of a drug kingpin are in short supply compared to the number of job openings that enforcement can plausibly be expected to create.

Second, it assumes both that existing organizations cannot grow to meet the unfilled demand created by the demise of their competitor and that new organizations cannot quickly come into existence. But with the ample cash flows that characterize the narcotics trade, the ready supplies of raw materials in the form of bulk drugs and of labor in the form of youngsters to whom $100 a day seems a generous wage, and the already-developed and now unserved customer base left by the dismantled organization, it is hard to see what will inhibit the rapid growth of existing and new organizations alike.

If a successful Mr. Big attack transformed a tightly cartelized drug market into a fragmented one, the result might well be reduced drug prices and wider availability as the result of replacing a monopoly with open competition. Alternatively, a succession of successful attacks might narrow down the field of major organizations to the one or two toughest and most enforcement resistant. By picking off the weak, enforcement can toughen the breed of drug dealers, as wolves toughen the breed of deer.

Even if the result of a successful attack on Mr. Big were an increase in the price of illicit drugs—not by creating a shortage but by increasing the costs of doing business as major suppliers reacted to an increasingly risky enforcement environment—raising drug prices is a two-edged sword. Depressing consumption is all to the good. However, as argued above, if consumption declines less (proportionately) than the price rises, both dealers' revenues and users' income-producing criminal activity may rise. Moreover, users who spend more money on drugs will have less money left to spend on food, clothing, and shelter, and this effect tends to offset the health benefits of reduced drug abuse.

The best conceivable result of the Mr. Big strategy would be a reduction in drug consumption mediated not by an increase in price but by increased difficulty of purchase (what Moore calls "increased search time" and drug agents usually call "decreased availability"). This would reduce drug abuse, user crime, and illicit revenues all at once and would not impoverish the remaining users.

But no one has offered a plausible account of why successful attacks on kingpins should reduce the numbers or increase the caution of drug retailers, the two factors that might cause search times to rise. What is to keep a retail drug pusher with an established client base from finding a new wholesale supplier if his current connection is put out of action by enforcement? To put the same question another way, what essential service does Mr. Big provide to the retail dealer that someone else will not supply just as well if he is made to disappear?

If there were even a single documented instance in which one or a succession of high-level drug cases coincided with substantial reductions in drug consumption in a city, the above reflections would need to be taken with considerable skepticism; complicated markets can easily overwhelm the explanatory reach of simple models. As the engineers say, "Just because it works in practice doesn't mean you can do it in theory." But no such success has been reported. Given the paucity of data, such negative evidence is far from conclusive. Still, a strategy whose advocates can show neither theory nor evidence in its support ought to be regarded as speculative rather than self-evidently valuable.

If the retail conditions of availability matter more to us than price, and if those conditions are determined at the retail or street level, then the Mr. Big strategy—no matter how professionally rewarding and morally satisfying—only diverts resources from the real business at hand.

B. Sweeping the Streets: Retail-Level Enforcement

If the business end of drug enforcement is to be aimed at the final retail transaction, its key tactics will be those that make those transactions riskier and less convenient. Some retail transactions go on discreetly, in indoor locations primarily used for nondrug activity: bars, hotel and office elevators, customers' living rooms. Others are indiscreet, taking place either out in the open or in locations such as "rock houses" (locations dedicated to the sale of illicit drugs).

Indiscreet drug dealing is both more noxious and more susceptible to control than discreet dealing: more noxious because it is more available to new users and more obtrusive on the sensibilities of others, more susceptible to control because open dealing can be observed, and dedicated locations provide ready targets for police search. Thus a second strategic bundle aims to push indiscreet retail drug dealing underground, reducing the availability of drugs rather than increasing their price.

Though the targets here are retail, the tactics are wholesale. While getting Mr. Big pays attention to this year's major case, sweeping the streets involves making today's seventy-fifth bust. Tactically, this involves arrests based on police observations of actual sales (often by patrol forces rather than specialized detectives), low-level and short-term undercover activity, massive uniformed presence in drug-dealing hot spots, enforcement of ancillary laws (traffic, parking, disorderly conduct, code violations), and changes in physical conditions such as lighting to make things more difficult for drug buyers and sellers.

Chiefs of narcotics bureaus, exposed to the influence and example of the federal Drug Enforcement Administration, tend to hold street sweeping in some contempt because it fails to make "quality" busts. They also worry that the necessary involvement of uniformed patrol officers in drug enforcement will lead to corruption. This worry seems ironic in light of the fact that all of the department-shattering drug corruption cases, typified by the "Prince of the City" case in New York (in which almost every member of the city's elite Special Investigations Unit preyed on the drug-selling community in a lengthy run of extortion and theft), have centered on narcotics detectives rather than patrol officers (Daley 1978). To this result of experience one might add a theoretical result: the more complete the "protection" from enforcement attention any one police unit can provide to a criminal organization, the greater the feasibility of establishing and maintaining corrupt relationships. That thought suggests that concentrating all narcotics enforcement in a single narcotics or vice bureau is unlikely to minimize the corruption problem. Even if it did, keeping uniformed patrol officers away from drug cases has two significant costs: it frustrates them, and it convinces citizens that police must be on the take, for otherwise why do they not go out and arrest the dope dealers everybody sees?

The characteristic problem of street sweeping is not financial corruption but abuses of authority: harassment of citizens going about their lawful business, illegal searches (and false reports to conceal their illegality), even the planting of evidence. These problems are illustrated by Philadelphia's ill-fated and short-lived "Operation Cold Turkey," in which precinct-level street-corner sweeps resulted in the arrest of significant numbers of otherwise law-abiding residents who happened to be in the wrong place at the wrong time (Pothier 1987). Avoiding these problems may demand a higher-than-average ratio of supervisors to patrol officers.

Street sweeping, if it works, serves all four goals of drug enforcement. It reduces drug abuse by reducing availability; it reduces user crime by reducing consumption without raising price; by the same token, it weakens major drug-dealing organizations by reducing the dollar value of the market; and it protects neighborhoods by reducing the flagrancy of illicit drug activity.

But can it work? Even a huge street-sweeping effort may be inadequate to suppress a growing retail drug trade. As a result of an increased interest in street-level enforcement, felony drug convictions in Washington, D.C., from 1981 to 1986 grew by more than a factor of ten (from 273 to 3,309), and aggregate drug sentences by almost a factor of twenty (from 470 years to 9,200 years) without noticeably interfering with the growth of drug abuse (Reuter et al. 1988).

One obvious problem is that drug dealers and police officers do not work the same hours. The received wisdom among the police we talked with is that drug dealing is at its peak during the late night and early morning hours, particularly on weekends. But those tend to be times when big-city police forces are struggling just to respond to emergency calls for service. When one of us scheduled weekend visits to New York and Los Angeles to "ride along" on police narcotics operations, he had great difficulty finding any operations to ride along with. In New York, over the long Labor Day weekend, it appeared that there was not a single retail-level narcotics operation in the entire city.

Even if the number and timing of arrests were adequate, the quality of subsequent processing might not be. Street sweeping yields far more arrests per officer-year than does high-level enforcement. This sounds efficient until it is considered that more arrests mean more postarrest processing, with consequent strains on prosecutors, courts, and corrections facilities.

Not only does a flood of arrests take resources away from other law-enforcement efforts against drug dealing and predatory crime alike but prosecutors, judges, and corrections officials are also likely to adapt to a sudden burst of not-very-exciting retail drug cases with cheap plea bargains, time-served sentences, and early-release policies. (Press's [1987] essay on crack enforcement in New York makes this point powerfully, while Peter Reuter and his colleagues at the Rand Corporation [1988] note that the judicial system in the Washington, D.C., area responded well to the increase in drug-related cases there.) In consequence, as the number of retail drug arrests rises, the significance of each one is likely to fall. As a result, the drug markets may be able to absorb enormous numbers of arrests without substantially shrinking or changing their conduct.

This response on the part of prosecutors, judges, and corrections officials may be a serious mistake from a long-term social viewpoint. It might be far better to accept a period of a year or two when drug enforcement strangles the rest of the system in return for what could be a substantial and lasting shrinkage in drug activity since the same level of enforcement pressure can be maintained on a smaller market with a smaller allocation of enforcement energy. Whatever the truth of the matter, a mayor or a police chief contemplating a street sweeping strategy needs to anticipate the reactions of other officials with independent authority and their own agendas.

Street sweeping is probably the most powerful and valuable drug-enforcement approach where indiscreet markets exist on a small enough scale so that attacking them will not cause the rest of the system to come to a grinding halt. Any city without a massive street drug-dealing problem should go to enormous lengths to avoid developing one. But in the cities with the biggest drug problems, effective street sweeping may not be among the practicable options. Ineffective street sweeping— doing half the amount that would be required to shrink substantially the volume of transactions—is a little like plugging half the holes in the dike.

C. Concentrating on One Market: Focused Crackdowns

If retail-level enforcement is more valuable than getting Mr. Big, but a city-wide sweep of the streets would yield more arrests than can be adequately prosecuted and punished, one alternative is to sweep only some of the streets. Focused crackdowns use virtually the same tactics as more dispersed retail enforcement efforts, except that bigger investments can be made in acquiring tactical intelligence and other forms of cooperation from neighborhood residents. Devices for doing so include "hot-line" telephone numbers connected directly with the crackdown's command center rather than through the 911 response system. Los Angeles, New York, and Detroit all have hot lines in operation. Commander Warren Harris reports that Detroit's 224-DOPE went into operation in February of 1988 and averaged roughly 200 calls a day from concerned citizens over the first few months. The hope is that concentrated enforcement will produce dramatic results in some places with greater total benefits than might accrue from producing slight improvements everywhere.

In particular, concentrated street-level enforcement can hope to take advantage of a form of positive feedback peculiar to illicit markets. From the viewpoint of drug buyers and sellers, big, active markets have two advantages over smaller, slower markets. First, it is easier for a buyer to find a seller, or vice versa, where there are many of both kinds; this effect is common to all markets. Second, any given number of officers pose a smaller threat to any one transaction if there are many other transactions going on in the same area; in effect, illicit-market participants unwillingly compete for unwanted enforcement attention. As a few buyers and sellers leave, the rest face increased enforcement risks as well as increased search times. Under these circumstances, a market that can easily absorb a small or temporary increase in enforcement activity without greatly changing or shrinking may be profoundly altered by a large, persistent increase. (For a general discussion of such multiple-equilibria or "tipping" phenomena with a wealth of examples, see Schelling 1978.)

There are other arguments for focus and against dispersion. A dramatic police effort may call forth increased neighborhood efforts at self-protection against drug-dealing activity; given limited police resources, such self-defense may be essential to long-run control of drug dealing.

The same police activity, dispersed across an entire city, may be below citizens' thresholds of perception. By the same token, even if the total decline in dealing activity were the same in a focused crackdown as it would be in a citywide sweep of the streets, the benefits might be greater in terms of drug consumption and neighborhood amenity.

Virtually eliminating drug dealing in one drug-infested neighborhood—thus creating an area where residents feel safe and parents can let their children roam free—may be more valuable than reducing drug activity by 10 percent in each of ten drug-infested neighborhoods, just as picking up all the litter in one filthy park creates a clean park, while picking up 10 percent of the litter in each of ten filthy parks leaves ten slightly less filthy parks, none of them attractive as places to play or relax. The same logic applies to search time: removing 10 percent of the sellers may leave search time virtually unchanged, while removing 90 percent of them raises it to prohibitive levels.

The ideal focused crackdown strategy in a big city would move slowly from neighborhood to neighborhood, leaving behind vigilant citizens and residual markets small enough to be controlled with residual enforcement efforts. That ideal awaits its first instance.

The Lynn and Lower East Side (Operation Pressure Point I) experiences, discussed above, illustrate the promise of focused crackdowns in reducing drug abuse and crime and improving the quality of neighborhood life. The Lawrence experience demonstrates that the promise will not always be kept.

The obvious problem with focused enforcement activity is the displacement of illicit transactions from one neighborhood to another. It is sometimes asserted that this displacement is automatic and complete: as if dope deals, like mass and energy, were subject to a conservation law and incapable of being increased or decreased in total (Bouza 1989). There is no evidence for such a sweeping generalization, and many reasons to believe that it does not hold (see Barr and Pease 1990).

Some neighborhoods are more convenient than others as places for drug buyers and sellers to meet, owing to convenient transportation, relative safety from street crime (always a worry for those who must carry valuable drugs and cash), and the presence of natural or man-made cover in the form of parks, courtyards, and abandoned buildings. Even if all neighborhoods were equally attractive, disrupting an established market confronts participants with a complicated coordination problem in finding a new place to meet; one of the consequences of product illegality is that information moves more slowly and with greater cost than is true when retailers can advertise. Finally, it may matter, particularly to novice users and ex-users trying to remain drug free, whether drugs are easily available in their own neighborhoods. If this is true, reducing the number of active drug-dealing areas by one will, net, reduce the size of the market.

Still, even if displacement is likely to be neither instantaneous nor total, it is likely to take place. Some users and some dealers will look for new places to buy and sell. Residents of some areas outside the crackdown are likely to suffer. This, and the evident benefits of the crackdown where it happens, will generate citizen demand for expansion of the crackdown area or the creation of new task forces for other neighborhoods. This demand is unlikely to be matched by any willingness of the residents in the original target area to see "their" officers moved away. A successful focused crackdown, whatever its operational benefits, is likely to leave some substantial management problems in its wake.

D. Suppressing Gang Activity

Aside from the emergence of crack as a mass-market drug of abuse, the most frightening drug-market phenomenon of the past decade has surely been the emergence of youth gangs as prominent drug-dealing organizations. The most famous of them are the congeries of factions, ranged under the rival labels "CRIPS" and "Bloods," who are shooting each other and innocent bystanders at the rate of about one a day in Los Angeles (Nazario 1988; see also Spergel 1990) and spreading to cities as far away as Kansas City and Anchorage.

These groups originated as youth gangs of the "West Side Story" variety, which were based on the need of adolescents for physical protection and something to join and which engaged in partying, hell raising, combat with rival gangs, and low-grade extortion and theft. How it was that growth of the crack market in Los Angeles allowed substantial illicit enterprises to be built on these collections of hooligans—why crack, why Los Angeles, why these two black organizations rather than their Latino and Anglo counterparts—remains obscure. What is clear is that the social structure of the gangs proved valuable in the drug-distribution business, and that the wealth available from the drug business fueled both a recruiting boom and an armaments race among the various "sets." An encounter that is no more than a "rumble" when conducted with rocks, chains, and knives becomes a massacre when the weapons are fully automatic rifles that fit under a windbreaker.

To some of the cities now being "colonized" by the Los Angeles gangs, their arrival may represent a substantial increase in the availability of crack and thus a threat on the drug-abuse front. The case is different in Los Angeles itself; no one believes that crack availability would change noticeably, one way or the other, if the CRIPS and Bloods disappeared entirely. Los Angeles is worried, not about the contribution of the gangs to the drug problem, but about the contribution of drugs to the gang problem.

Equal opportunity, transaction-oriented drug enforcement, whether street level or high level, has little to offer in the way of help for this problem. Gang members' unwillingness to inform on each other may give them competitive advantages in the face of routine drug enforcement. To place them at a competitive disadvantage instead, enforcement officials and prosecutors would have to single out gang-related drug activity for special attention; they would have to acknowledge that a crack dealer wearing Blood red or CRIP blue is a target of a distinct and more important type than a crack dealer dressed otherwise, just as the federal Organized Crime Strike Forces treat Mafia labor racketeering or loansharking as a species of activity distinct from other labor racketeering or loansharking.

Treating youth gangs as organized crime means a heavy investment in intelligence gathering and analysis, with special emphasis on membership lists, aggressive use of field interrogation both to gather information and to establish police presence, and vigorous investigation and prosecution of even relatively minor crimes if connected with gang activity. In general, it will require the creation of a police unit organizationally separate from the narcotics squad in order to maintain both distinct routines and a distinct scoring system. The Los Angeles Community Resources against Street Hoodlums (CRASH) program is such a unit.

The Los Angeles district attorney's office has proposed the next logical step in treating youth gangs as a species of organized crime: a new law, based loosely on the Federal Racketeer Influenced and Corrupt Organizations Act, 18 USC 1961–65, creating felony criminal liability for what otherwise would be misdemeanor activity if committed in connection with the operation of a gang. It is conceivable that such a law, if vigorously enforced, could make the CRIPS and Bloods high-cost producers in the drug-distribution business, as the federal organized-crime effort has made the "families" of the Mafia largely unable to compete in the national narcotics distribution markets. Successful organized-crime enforcement makes the criminal reputation, which is a major asset of durable criminal enterprises, carry a cost (Reuter 1982, 1983).

Another—not necessarily competing—approach would be to attack youth gangs by making recruitment more difficult. Boys' clubs and police athletic leagues attempt to do so by replacing some of the gangs' social functions, "keeping the kids off the streets and out of trouble." But gangs also serve (and help create) the need among youngsters in tough neighborhoods for simple physical protection. In some Los Angeles neighborhoods, being a Blood is safer than not being a Blood because it offers protection both from the Bloods themselves and from random bullying and theft.

Police could attempt to compete with gangs in supplying this want. After all, providing protection against assault and theft by threatening assailants and thieves with arrest and punishment is what the police are all about. However, activities which among adults would qualify as robbery, extortion, and aggravated assault tend to be classified as "boys will be boys" if the predators and victims are adolescent males. This may be a serious mistake in social policy, though the mechanics and the implications of changing it have yet to be worked out (Jencks 1987).

E. Controlling User Crime

One way to reduce user crime is to reduce the availability of drugs and thus the need for income to buy drugs and the number of crimes committed while intoxicated. (This latter effect is far more important with respect to cocaine than with respect to heroin, which is not pharmacologically crime inducing.) But, as we have seen, reducing the availability of drugs is hard sledding.

One alternative would be to identify drug-involved offenders (not very difficult, since many of them are arrested frequently) and attempt to reduce their drug use as a way of reducing their criminal activity. Mandatory drug treatment as an alternative to incarceration, as exemplified by the Treatment Alternatives to Street Crime programs now in widespread operation and by the earlier California civil commitment program (see, e.g., Anglin and McGlothlin 1984) or voluntary drug treatment during incarceration (Wexler and Williams 1986; Wexler, Lipton, and Johnson 1988), is among the more conventional direct attacks on the problem of drug-involved offenders. Even very expensive drug-treatment programs begin to look cheap when they make substantial cuts in drug users' often-astronomical personal crime rates.

Instead of mandating or offering treatment, authorities could mandate abstinence instead and leave the problem of choosing and finding programs up to the user or offender (Carver 1986). Abstinence could be verified by urine testing at frequent but random intervals, with the frequency increasing if a test comes back positive or a test appointment is missed, and decreasing after a long series of negative results. Repeated missed tests or "dirty" samples would result in jail or prison time, for longer or shorter periods, depending on the frequency of misbehavior. Such a program could be instituted for persons awaiting trial (though not without facing constitutional challenge), as an alternative to incarceration (formally, as a condition of a suspended or probation sentence) or after incarceration (formally, as a condition of "split-sentence" probation or parole) (Kaplan 1988).

This approach might reduce crime in two ways. It would deter some drug-involved offenders from continued drug use (and thus, in part, from continued income-producing crime), and it would lead to the speedy identification and incarceration of those who insist on continuing careers of drug use and crime. The result need not, on balance, be increased prison populations; judges could incarcerate a smaller fraction of the drug-involved convicts before them if letting an offender "walk" did not mean letting him go back to addiction and crime.

The most intractable problem in mounting such a program is the unwillingness of judges to be consistently tough in imposing sanctions for missed or positive tests. With jails and prisons full to bursting, the logic of incarcerating someone "only" for using drugs is difficult to make clear. This problem is visible between the lines of published reports of the District of Columbia's pretrial urine-monitoring program (Toborg and Kirby 1984) and is made explicit in accounts of the Lawrence, Massachusetts, experience (Kleiman et al. 1988).

Several programs of intensive supervision probation (ISP) have been started within the last few years. One of the most promising attempts to evaluate the effectiveness of drug testing in controlling criminal activity is the Rand Corporation's ongoing study of eleven ISP programs throughout the United States. The demonstration programs assign parolees or probationers to either an ISP or non-ISP (control) group. Subjects in the ISP group undergo frequent drug testing and experience additional constraints. Subjects in the non-ISP group receive "normal" supervision. Some of the programs have had substantial difficulty in delivering their planned levels of supervision. In particular, urine tests are far less frequent in practice than was planned (Petersilia 1990). At least one such program, however, in Santa Cruz County, California, is reportedly working well (Frank 1989).

Monitoring the behavior of ex-offenders in the community was a traditional function of the police. Big-city departments abandoned that function about the same time they began to treat rapid response to calls for service as their most important goal. It may be time to reconsider that abandonment, particularly in the case of drug-involved offenders. Police could help enforce abstinence orders (and orders to stay away from specified drug-dealing locations) if they were prepared to treat a probation, parole, or bail revocation as equivalent to a good felony bust.

F. Protecting the Youth

Drug abuse by adolescents (and, now, even preadolescents) is worse than drug abuse by adults. Adolescents are more helpless because they are less able to grasp the risks they run. They are perhaps even more subject to fashion, suggesting that drug use by one child will tend to increase drug use by his or her peers. They may be more profoundly affected by drug experiences than they would be if they were older; in particular, their educational performance is likely to suffer. They have most of their lives—and virtually all of their prime potential crime-committing years—still ahead of them. More than that, they have parents who worry about them and react with intense rage to the fact that drug dealers are out there offering temptation to the (relatively) innocent.

One response to this special concern is the development of enforcement efforts aimed particularly at dealing to minors. Consequently, various state and federal statutes impose specific penalties based on the age of the user or the proximity of a school. Alas, most final sales to adolescents are made by other adolescents young enough to qualify for juvenile treatment. Moving middle-level suppliers 1,000 yards from the nearest school is unlikely to substantially decrease the accessibility of drugs to schoolchildren.

Dealing on the school grounds or inside school buildings may be a more attractive target. Attacking it calls for joint efforts by school authorities and police. Even in the most violence-ridden schools, principals are traditionally nervous about having guns and uniforms around. Moreover, there is a problem of control; a principal enthusiastic about having a chronic troublemaker arrested for selling crack may still want to avoid having his valedictorian busted for possession of a small amount of marijuana. Police departments vary in their willingness to provide a presence on demand while ceding control to the schools.

The other approach to reducing drug abuse by young people is education. This might properly seem the province of teachers rather than police, but in some drug-infested areas the teachers know less about practical psychopharmacology than do some of the students. A drug-education program that gives the most drug-involved student in the class an opportunity to show up the teacher's ignorance is unlikely to do its job.

In this context, police have several advantages. They are knowledgeable. They give the appearance of being less willing to take verbal abuse. They also command substantially higher salaries and more respect from television scriptwriters and presidential candidates alike; some of this surely communicates itself to students. They talk, dress, and act differently from the teachers whom students are used to seeing in the classroom; this gives police at least some novelty value. In addition, school systems are delighted to have what amounts to a financial contribution from police budgets.

For many, the idea of a police presence in schools is a bitter pill to swallow. The potential for the abuse of state power looms large, and it remains difficult to weigh the benefits of having police in schools against the harm they might do there. In any case, it makes sense to examine carefully the long-term implications of such a policy. For whatever reason, school systems around the country have welcomed uniformed officers as drug educators. The most widely publicized and emulated program is DARE (Drug Abuse Resistance Education) which has spread out from Los Angeles (Gates 1987).

Drug Abuse Resistance Education officers work full time on drug education. They spend an hour a week with each class. The current curriculum runs thirteen weeks in the seventh grade and another thirteen in the eighth grade, with more material under development. The substance of the program is not particularly drug focused; a decade ago it would have been called "values clarification." It stresses thinking about reasons for and against courses of action, resisting peer pressure and emotional arguments, and saying "no" gracefully. This last point is reinforced by a series of role-playing exercises.

A careful evaluation of DARE's pilot year in Los Angeles found that students exposed to DARE were significantly, though not vastly, less likely to use illicit substances than a control group. Troublingly, DARE students were also reading and doing math at slightly lower levels (Evaluation and Training Institute 1988). This pilot evaluation has not been repeated now that DARE is systemwide in Los Angeles. For a thorough discussion of the effectiveness of earlier nonpolice "drug education" programs, see Polich et al. (1984).

Frustration with the apparent inability of enforcement to get the big-city drug problem under anything resembling control makes DARE-style programs attractive. The size of their contribution to long-term drug-abuse control remains to be established.

The actual approach of any jurisdiction will involve elements of several of the "bundles" outlined above. The mix will depend on local conditions, history, bureaucratic habits and interests, and deliberate choice. The experiences of New York, Los Angeles, and Detroit illustrate just how diverse those responses can be.

III. Drug Enforcement in Three Cities

New York, Los Angeles, and Detroit are all big cities with big drug problems. The enforcement response in each city has been subject to more or less media attention, but none has had a comprehensive evaluation of its drug-enforcement activities. In August and September 1988 we traveled to each city, and there met with members of the law-enforcement community.[7] The discussion below is based on the results

---

[7] In Detroit, Wayne County Prosecutor John O'Hair and his associates, Andrea L. Solak, George Best, and Richard Padzieski, were extremely helpful. Commander Warren Harris of the Detroit Police Department offered several useful insights, as did many other members of the law-enforcement community who asked that their names not be disclosed. Dennis Nordmoe and Don Davis of the Bureau of Substance Abuse gave freely of their time; Dr. Theda Bishop explained the workings of the Treatment Alternatives to Street Crime (TASC) program in careful detail. Tom Mieczkowski of Wayne State University shared not only the results of his work but also suggested useful avenues for further research. In Los Angeles, Captain Michael Bagdonis of the Narcotics Division and Chief Glenn Levant of the Special Operations Division of the Los Angeles Police Department were generous with their time. In New York, we benefited from the advice of Robert Stuttman of the Drug Enforcement Administration and Inspector Al James of the Narcotics Division of the New York Police Department. Michael Scott of the New York City Police Commissioner's Office gave much of his own time and was helpful in setting up meetings with other members of the department.

of those meetings, firsthand observations, and data provided by enforcement agencies. Our accounts of drug enforcement in these cities are, of course, highly impressionistic and rely heavily on information provided by individual police officers with whom we spoke. Some of what we were told may represent police aspirations rather than police operations. Some of what we saw may be unrepresentative. Some of what we describe may, for those reasons, be inaccurate, incomplete, or insufficiently appreciative of important contextual information. Nonetheless, big city police departments do differ substantially in their approaches and attitudes toward drug law enforcement, and we believe the following capsule descriptions reasonably depict differences between New York, Los Angeles, and Detroit.

A. New York

The illicit drugs that flow into the New York area's three airports and its busy seaport are consumed in vast quantities by the city's residents; by one estimate, the New York metropolitan area is home to one-third of the nation's heroin users. Drugs are also sold in bulk in New York for final distribution elsewhere.

The narcotics division is the largest component of the New York Police Department's Organized Crime Control Bureau. With more than 2,000 sworn personnel assigned, it is about two-thirds the size of the federal Drug Enforcement Administration. New York narcotics detectives work closely with the New York Drug Enforcement Administration office—the nation's largest—in pursuit of some of the most important drug dealers in the country.

The leadership of the narcotics division is committed to the value of getting Mr. Big. Like the rest of New York's police leadership, it is also deeply committed to avoiding another major corruption scandal. This commitment makes narcotics division commanders worry about any street-level enforcement program that involves the uniformed patrol force.

Nevertheless, New York is the home of the largest and longest-continued focused drug crackdown, Operation Pressure Point I, which substantially reduced drug dealing in "Alphabet City" on the Lower East Side of Manhattan. Operation Pressure Point has been in operation continuously since January 1984. It is a joint operation of the narcotics unit and Patrol Borough Manhattan South, and relies on a massive uniformed presence in addition to a substantial commitment of detectives.

The New York City Police Department, and particularly Commissioner Benjamin Ward, who boasts of his personal role in launching Operation Pressure Point I, is proud of its success. But the experiment has not been repeated. Neighborhood pressure has made it impossible to wind the operation down even after drug dealing had substantially diminished, leaving an excessive concentration of increasingly bored officers in a relatively small area of the city. Accordingly, the department wonders how many comparable successes it can afford.

Instead, the narcotics division has developed its own version of street-level enforcement under the label TNT (Tactical Narcotics Team). The Tactical Narcotics Team, strictly a narcotics squad operation, rigidly excludes precinct police, who thoroughly resent the exclusion and the implied slur on their integrity.

By some measures, TNT is effective. In the first TNT target area in southeast Queens, dealing was reduced so substantially that even long-term drug users reported difficulty in obtaining drug supplies, according to an evaluation by the New York State Division of Substance Abuse Services (Toledo 1988). However, the results show little tendency to outlast the operations themselves; the southeast Queens area was again home to a thriving narcotics bazaar within a few weeks of the withdrawal of the TNT unit.

Under pressure from city hall, TNT has grown by leaps and bounds; late in 1988 the mayor imposed citywide budget cuts specifically to fund 700 new narcotics officers. City hall's enthusiasm for TNT was not fully matched within the police department; the commissioner even took the extraordinary step of telling newspaper reporters, on the record, that expanded TNT operations should not be expected to dramatically reduce the level of drug dealing citywide (*New York Newsday*, 1988).

Narcotics commanders are at least equally skeptical; their recurrent metaphor is the war in Vietnam; as one of them put it, "the country has to learn that another division, and another division, doesn't win the war." "Can I guarantee you another 21,000 quality felony narcotics busts? Yes. Can I tell you that will do anything about drug dealing? No," says one senior official of the narcotics division. Chief Hall is equally frank: "People expect us to eliminate drugs. Some of them use expressions like drug-free zones, drug-free communities. Unrealistic! Totally unrealistic. It's certainly not going to happen in my lifetime" (Pitt 1989).

D. Los Angeles

The Los Angeles Police Department (LAPD) and the Los Angeles County Sheriff's Department share responsibility with a number of smaller city police departments for drug enforcement in sprawling Los Angeles County. Their combined strength is substantially lower per capita, and enormously lower per square mile, than is the case in New York. Though Los Angeles has its share of major drug dealing, the LAPD makes no real effort to compete with federal authorities in pursuing major drug cases. Barely a hundred of its officers work on anything that could be described as high-level drug enforcement.

Even less in Los Angeles than in New York is drug-enforcement policy driven by a belief that arresting drug dealers can make a substantial contribution to reducing drug abuse. While New York police are likely to describe their apparent inability to stop the flood of drugs with something approaching desperation, Los Angeles police report the same situation with calm acceptance, perhaps reflecting the more sanguine mood of the department generally. Again and again, a visitor hears the matter-of-fact assertion that "the current generation of drug users is lost."

In the short run, reducing drug abuse takes a back seat to controlling gang violence. A local initiative called Community Resources against Street Hoodlums (CRASH) has given its name to a citywide gang-control unit. Officers of CRASH combine traditional "gang work" tactics (arranging truces among rival factions, establishing personal relationships with gang leaders, developing credible contingent threats if bounds are overstepped) with intelligence gathering that more closely resembles the routines of Federal Bureau of Investigation organized-crime squads. The striking difference between gang organized-crime enforcement and Mafia organized-crime enforcement is that the "members and associates" lists involve not hundreds, but literally tens of thousands, of individuals.

Whether CRASH's attempts to combine West Side Story's Officer Krupke with television's Elliot Ness are operationally successful remains to be seen; gang homicides have yet to be brought under control (Nazario 1988). But CRASH officers obviously believe deeply that they are doing an important job and that they understand how to go about it; even at a routine roll call the air of determination and elite-unit pride is obvious.

The rest of the LAPD's retail drug-enforcement effort is not targeted directly at gang activity per se. The nightly round of retail undercover buys are made from gang members and independent operators with a fine impartiality. The immediate goals are to rack up some good felony busts, to make the dealers keep their heads down, and to give some respite to threatened neighborhoods. The high-level enforcement effort, while it pays considerable attention to postadolescent ex-gang members now acting as middlemen between drug importers and gang-affiliated retailers, hardly reaches the gangs themselves.

Los Angeles police are unanimous in describing their enforcement efforts as a mixed and balanced strategy. To an outsider, they look more like three independent programs without a central theme.

But even if this account were accepted, it would bother the LAPD relatively little because its officers and leaders have come to regard drug enforcement as merely a "holding action" designed to keep the city from falling apart while waiting for the effects of demand-reduction programs to make themselves felt. Unlike the belief that the problem can be solved in Colombia, this belief does not serve as a device for distancing police from responsibility. The Los Angeles Police Department backs its belief in demand reduction with a commitment of ninety full-time officers to the DARE program, about equivalent to the department's entire high-level drug-enforcement effort. These officers, carefully selected and trained, wear uniforms but make no arrests. All they do is classroom teaching, and they and their superiors believe that they represent the long-term hope for controlling drug abuse in Los Angeles.

C. Detroit

Detroit has a major crack problem and a major murder problem. Though Detroit's homicide rate fell 8 percent from 1987 to 1988, while other crack-hit cities (Miami, Baltimore, Washington, D.C., and Boston) experienced double-digit increases, that rate is still the highest in the nation. The city's unenviable reputation as a "murder capital" predates the introduction of crack, but the strong link between homicide and drugs remains an article of faith.

The Detroit Police Department assigned "more than 200" of its sworn strength of 4,800 officers to narcotics work.[8] Most, if not all, of that personnel energy has been committed to street-level enforcement. The Narcotics Enforcement Units (NEUs), the operational elements of

---

[8] The actual number is not a matter of public record.

the division, function at the precinct level. The most recent undertaking of the division has been Operation Maximum Effort, which began in December 1987.

Maximum Effort is street sweeping in its purest form. Using surveillance, informants, and undercover purchases against both indoor and outdoor markets throughout the city, Maximum Effort targets "rock houses" and street-corner markets. Citizen complaints are often the starting point for investigations and generate quick, reactive operations; enforcement crews may be expected to conduct at least one raid a day, and sometimes two. As a result, arrest, raid, and seizure figures were all up 300 percent through mid-1988 from the same period the previous year. Police cite the 75 percent reduction in calls to their twenty-four-hour 224-DOPE hotline as evidence that the drug problem is being brought under control.

Privately, however, skepticism about these claims and about the goals of drug enforcement in the city runs deep among police officers and the public alike. One problem is that the focus on street-level enforcement has come at the expense of high-level investigations; the "Mr. Bigs" of the city have been left to the federal agencies. Organizations are not explicit targets, nor are the groups or individuals that supply the "rock houses." Police officers are unhappy about what they see as pointless activity on their part and about the need to generate "numbers" for their bosses. Morale is low; officers feel as if they are accomplishing nothing. Some attribute the lack of high-level enforcement activity to high-level corruption. Recent events have added to public anxiety. In May 1988, it was disclosed by federal authorities that a list of the home and office numbers of Detroit police officers and an original set of secret police narcotics reports were recovered in a raid on the home of Cathy Volsan-Curry, the wife of convicted drug dealer Johnny Curry, and niece of Mayor Coleman Young (Wark 1989).

Nor has public reaction to police efforts been entirely positive. Narcotics officers move from house to house, and thus often from neighborhood to neighborhood, with each complaint. Thus, while the number of arrests, raids, and warrants has increased overall, it has been difficult for residents of neighborhoods with large drug markets to notice any long-term improvement.

In addition, the City of Detroit is now also facing a series of legal challenges related to its drug enforcement strategy. Some of the search warrants used in Operation Maximum Effort have been challenged in court, and some of the people whose homes were searched have gone to the press with horror stories about thefts and threats by the police. The cost to the city in lawsuits may well outweigh the social benefit of "kicking in doors" on a regular basis.

IV. Conclusions

In principle, the right way to choose a drug policy for a city would be to describe the problem, invent some alternative approaches to addressing that problem, predict the costs and the likely results of each approach, and choose the least painful. Then, after a while, one could measure the results and compare them with the predictions. Unexpected results or new situations would call for changes in policy.

In practice, no city has anything resembling a quantitatively accurate description of its own drug problem. Nor is there a well worked-out body of theory or experience to allow predictions of the likely results of alternative approaches.

Theory and experience agree that neither high-level enforcement nor unfocused retail-level enforcement is likely to contribute much to solving the problem under current big-city conditions. Yet local drug enforcement consists primarily of a mix of those two strategies. A growing share of local law-enforcement budgets is thus being committed to programs that are both unproven and implausible.

Law-enforcement agencies, like boxers, need to learn to fight their weight. In a city that has a small crack market, for instance, investing early and heavily may succeed in keeping the market small or driving it out. Where a large crack market already exists, consideration should be given to whether even maximal efforts are likely to have much effect. There will come a point of diminishing returns, when throwing more police resources into the pot will no longer produce significant social benefits. Refining the techniques for making those calculations poses a substantial intellectual and practical challenge.

Crackdowns focused on particular neighborhoods have some theoretical advantages and a little experience to suggest they can work. But the extent to which they simply push the problem around is undetermined. For neighborhood crackdowns to be a viable citywide strategy, it must be possible after a time to move enforcement resources to a new area and repeat the process. That, in turn, requires both the development in the crackdown area of indigenous capacity to resist the return of drug dealing and a willingness on the part of residents to see the focus of police attention shift once the problem has subsided. How local governments can create that capacity and that willingness remains an open problem.

Drug markets dominated by warring youth gangs will leave more corpses behind them than drug markets not so dominated. Routine drug enforcement may have little to contribute to gang control; police need to learn how to make life particularly miserable for gang-related drug dealers (and for gang members committing other crimes).

There is some evidence—not yet much—that putting police in the classroom as "drug-education" teachers can reduce the rate at which adolescents are initiated into illicit drug use. Whether such programs are an efficient use of police work-years depends in part on the value of alternative uses of the same work-years. If current drug activities are already overloading the capacity of prosecutors, courts, and jails, the arrests sacrificed by putting some police in classrooms may not matter much.

Considering how much of the public concern about drugs centers on the link between drugs and crime, it is surprising how ill designed current policies are to discourage the long drug and crime careers characteristic of heroin users (and almost certainly of some crack users). Mandatory drug abstinence for drug-involved offenders, verified by testing and backed with the threat of reincarceration, ought to be a centerpiece of any serious "career-criminal" or "dangerous-offender" program.

Research, which has contributed relatively little to the current decision-making process, seems ill positioned to contribute much more. The most obvious need is for a set of plausible, computable models of local drug sales activity as a function of local enforcement activity. This would be likely to involve some combination of microeconomics and operations research.

But better models will be of limited practical use unless someone collects the data to feed them. Number of users, number of sellers, number of transactions, total revenue; all of these data are needed, and needed right down to the neighborhood level. This requires some very expensive data collection: surveys, street ethnography, and the development of user, ex-user, and potential-user panels. No police chief will ever know as much about the cocaine market in his or her city as the local manager for R. J. Reynolds knows about the cigarette market, but we can be, and need to be, much closer to that position than we are now.

One way to start would be to collect more information about drug enforcement. Local, state, and national data collection systems often fail to make essential distinctions or to record data in comparable categories; the Uniform Crime Reports, for example, lump heroin and cocaine together. Questions of the form, "How many crack sellers were arrested in Chicago last year, and how many aggregate years of confinement were they sentenced to?" need to be routinely answerable before any serious study can be made of the results of alternative strategies.

Beginning to collect at least that minimal level of information would suggest a new level of seriousness about developing responses to the drug problem that produce publicly valuable results. Until then, state and local drug enforcement will remain a collection of activities in search of a strategy.

APPENDIX
Drug Enforcement Tactics

1. Observation arrests
2. Undercover operations:
    Short-term/long-term
    Buy-and-bust/sell-and-bust
3. Exploitation of physical evidence:
    Laboratory analysis of drug samples
    Finding and using fingerprints
4. Historical conspiracy investigation:
    Searching the files
    Questioning convicted dealers
    Finding paper trails
    Informant development
5. Electronic surveillance
6. Ancillary attacks:
    Changes in publicly owned spaces:
        Locking exterior doors of housing projects
        Lighting and landscape changes to deny cover to dealers
    Parking and traffic enforcement in market areas
    Code violation on dealing premises
7. Community-based intelligence gathering:
    Hotlines
    Beat cops
    Work with citizens' groups
8. Going after assets:
    Civil forfeiture
    Criminal forfeiture
9. User control programs:
    Treatment Alternatives to Street Crime (TASC)
    Mandatory treatment
    Mandatory abstinence and urine monitoring
10. Drug education by police officers (DARE, etc.)

REFERENCES

Anglin, M. Douglas. 1988. Personal communication with authors, September.
Anglin, M. Douglas, and W. H. McGlothin. 1984. "Outcome of Narcotic Addict Treatment in California." In *Drug Abuse Treatment Evaluation: Strategies, Progress, and Prospects*, edited by Frank M. Tims and Jacqueline P. Ludford. Research Monograph Series 51. Rockville, Md.: National Institute on Drug Abuse.
Anglin, M. Douglas, and George Speckart. 1988. "Narcotics Use and Crime: A Multi-sample, Multi-method Analysis." *Criminology* 26:197–233.
Barnett, Arnold. 1989. "Drug Crackdowns and Crime Rates: A Comment on the Kleiman Paper." In *Street Level Drug Enforcement: Examining the Issues*, edited by Marcia Chaiken. Issues and Practices in Criminal Justice. Washington, D.C.: National Institute of Justice.
Barr, Robert, and Ken Pease. 1990. "Crime Placement, Displacement, and Deflection." In *Crime and Justice: A Review of Research*, vol. 12, edited by Michael Tonry and Norval Morris. Chicago: University of Chicago Press.
Bouza, Anthony V. 1989. "Evaluating Street Drug Enforcement." In *Street Level Drug Enforcement: Examining the Issues*, edited by Marcia Chaiken. Issues and Practices in Criminal Justice. Washington, D.C.: National Institute of Justice.
Brown, George F., and Lester P. Silverman. 1974. "The Retail Price of Heroin: Estimation and Applications." *Journal of the American Statistical Association* 347(69):595–606.
Burke, Kevin M. 1989. "Comments on Street-Level Drug Enforcement." In *Street Level Drug Enforcement: Examining the Issues*, edited by Marcia Chaiken. Issues and Practices in Criminal Justice. Washington, D.C.: National Institute of Justice.
Calkins, Richard F. 1988. "Drug Abuse Trend Update, Detroit/Wayne County, Michigan." Community Epidemiology Work Group Report. Rockville, Md.: National Institute on Drug Abuse.
Carver, John A. 1986. "Drugs and Crime: Controlling Use and Reducing Risk through Testing." *Research in Action*. Washington, D.C.: National Institute of Justice.
Cave, Jonathan, and Peter Reuter. 1988. *The Interdictor's Lot: A Dynamic Model of the Market for Drug Smuggling Services*. Report no. N-2832-USDP. Santa Monica, Calif.: Rand.
Chaiken, Jan, and Marcia Chaiken. 1982. *Varieties of Criminal Behavior*. Santa Monica, Calif.: Rand.
———. In this volume. "Drugs and Predatory Crime."
Cook, Philip J. 1986. "The Supply and Demand of Criminal Opportunities." In *Crime and Justice: An Annual Review of Research*, vol. 7, edited by Michael Tonry and Norval Morris. Chicago: University of Chicago Press.
Coyle, Marcia. 1988. "Prosecutors Admit: No Victory in Sight." *National Law Journal* 10(48):S2–S3.
Daley, Robert. 1978. *Prince of the City*. Boston: Houghton Mifflin.
Davidson, Joe. 1988. "Street Sweepers: Some Citizen Patrols Bully Drug Traffickers until They Flee Area." *Wall Street Journal* (September 26).
Des Jarlais, Don C., Samuel R. Friedman, and William Hopkins. 1985. "Risk

Reduction for the Acquired Immunodeficiency Syndrome among Intravenous Drug Users." *Annals of Internal Medicine* 103:755–59.

Evaluation and Training Institute. 1988. *DARE Longitudinal Evaluation Annual Report, 1987–88.* Los Angeles: Evaluation and Training Institute.

Frank, Merle. 1989. Personal communication with authors, April 14.

Fulwood, Isaac, Jr. 1989. "Washington's Year of Shame." *Washington Post* (January 1).

Gates, Daryl F. 1987. "Project DARE—a Challenge to Arm Our Youth." *Police Chief* 54(10):100–101.

Hall, Francis C. 1988. Personal communication with authors, November 28.

Jencks, Christopher. 1987. "Genes and Crime." *New York Review of Books* 2(34):33–41.

Johnson, Bruce D., Paul Goldstein, Edward Preble, James Schmeidler, Douglas S. Lipton, Barry Spunt, and Thomas Miller. 1985. *Taking Care of Business: The Economics of Crime by Heroin Abusers.* Lexington, Mass.: Lexington.

Kaplan, John. 1988. "Taking Drugs Seriously." *Public Interest* 92(Summer):32–50.

Kerr, Peter. 1988a. "Syphilis Surge with Crack Use Raises Fears on Spread of AIDS." *New York Times* (June 29, eastern ed.).

———. 1988b. "Koch Seeking 775 More Police Officers for an Anti-Drug Blitz." *New York Times* (August 10, eastern ed.).

Kleiman, Mark A. R. 1986a. "Bringing Back Street-Level Heroin Enforcement." Working Paper no. 86–01–08. Program in Criminal Justice Policy and Management. Cambridge, Mass.: Harvard University, John F. Kennedy School of Government.

———. 1986b. "Data and Analysis Requirements for Policy toward Drug Enforcement and Organized Crime Control." In *America's Habit: Drug Abuse, Drug Trafficking, and Organized Crime*, edited by the President's Commission on Organized Crime. Washington, D.C.: U.S. Government Printing Office.

———. 1987. "Organized Crime and Drug Abuse Control." In *Major Issues in Organized Crime Control*, edited by Herbert Edelhurtz. Bellevue, Wash.: Northwest Policy Studies Center.

———. 1988a. "Crackdowns: The Effects of Intensive Enforcement on Retail Heroin Dealing." In *Street Level Drug Enforcement: Examining the Issues*, edited by Marcia Chaiken. Issues and Practices in Criminal Justice. Washington, D.C.: National Institute of Justice.

———. 1988b. "Dead Wrong." *New Republic* (September 26), pp. 15–16.

———. 1989. *Marijuana: Costs of Abuse, Costs of Control.* New York: Greenwood/Praeger.

Kleiman, Mark A. R., William Holland, and Christopher Hayes. 1984. "Report to the District Attorney of Essex County: Evaluation of the Lynn Drug Task Force." *Papers in Progress* series. Program in Criminal Justice Policy and Management. Cambridge, Mass.: Harvard University, John F. Kennedy School of Government.

Kleiman, Mark A. R., Mary Ellen Lawrence, and Aaron Saiger. 1987. *A Drug Enforcement Program for Santa Cruz County.* Cambridge, Mass.: BOTEC Analysis.

Kleiman, Mark A. R., and Richard Mockler. 1988. *Heroin and AIDS: Strategies for Control.* Washington, D.C.: Urban Institute.

Kleiman, Mark A. R., Christopher E. Putala, Rebecca M. Young, and David P. Cavanagh. 1988. *Heroin Crackdowns in Two Massachusetts Cities.* Prepared for the office of the district attorney for the eastern district, Commonwealth of Massachusetts, the Honorable Kevin M. Burke, under National Institute of Justice Grant no. 85-JJ-CX-0027.

Martens, Frederick T. 1988. "Narcotics Enforcement: What Are the Goals and Do They Conflict?" Paper prepared for the Organized Crime Narcotics Enforcement Symposium, Villanova University, May.

Mieczkowski, Tom. 1989*a*. "Crack Distribution in Detroit." *Journal of Drug Issues* (forthcoming).

————. 1989*b*. "The Damage Done: Cocaine Methods in Detroit." *International Journal of Comparative and Applied Criminal Justice* (forthcoming).

————. 1989*c*. *Studying Crack Use in Detroit: An Application of the Drug Use Forecasting System.* Washington, D.C.: National Institute of Justice.

Moore, Mark H. 1973. "Achieving Discrimination on the Effective Price of Heroin." *American Economic Review* 63(2):270–77.

————. 1976. *Buy and Bust: The Effective Regulation of an Illicit Market in Heroin.* Lexington, Mass.: Heath.

————. 1979. "Limiting the Supplies of Drugs to Illicit Markets in the United States." *Journal of Drug Issues* 9:291–308.

————. 1989. "The Police and Drugs." *Perspectives on Policing.* Washington, D.C.: U.S. Department of Justice, National Institute of Justice.

————. In this volume. "Supply Reduction and Drug Law Enforcement."

National Institute of Justice. 1988. *Drug Use Forecasting.* Washington, D.C.: U.S. Department of Justice, National Institute of Justice.

Nazario, Sonia L. 1988. "Turf Wars: How a Deputy Stresses Brains over Brawn in Battling Gangs." *Wall Street Journal* (December 29).

New York Newsday. 1988. Untitled article (September), p. 42.

New York Times. 1988. "Adding Warriors to the Drug War" (editorial) (May 22).

Nurco, David N., John C. Ball, John W. Shaffer, and Thomas E. Hanlon. 1985. "The Criminality of Narcotic Addicts." *Journal of Nervous and Mental Disease* 173(2):94–102.

Office of Criminal Justice Plans and Analysis. 1988. *1987 Crime and Justice Report for the District of Columbia.* Washington, D.C.: Office of Criminal Justice Plans and Analysis.

Petersilia, Joan. 1990. "Implementing Randomized Experiments: Lessons from BJA's Intensive Supervision Project." *Evaluation Review* (forthcoming).

Pitt, David E. 1989. "Report from the Field on an Endless War." *New York Times* (March 12, eastern ed.).

Polich, J. Michael, Phyllis L. Ellickson, Peter Reuter, and James P. Kahan. 1984. *Strategies for Controlling Adolescent Drug Abuse.* Santa Monica, Calif.: Rand.

Pothier, Dick. 1987. "Department's 'Reputation Grew Uglier' over the Years." *Philadelphia Inquirer* (March 11).

Press, Aric. 1987. *Piecing Together New York's Criminal Justice System: The Response to Crack.* New York: New York Bar Association.

Reuter, Peter. 1982. *The Value of a Bad Reputation: Cartels, Criminals, and Barriers to Entry*. Report no. P-6835. Santa Monica, Calif.: Rand.

———. 1983. *Disorganized Crime: The Economics of the Visible Hand*. Cambridge, Mass.: MIT Press.

———. 1984. "The (Continuing) Vitality of Mythical Numbers." *Public Interest* 75(Spring):135–47.

Reuter, Peter, John Haaga, Patrick Murphy, and Amy Praskac. 1988. *Drug Use and Drug Programs in the Washington Metropolitan Area*. Report no. R-3655-GWRC. Santa Monica, Calif.: Rand.

Reuter, Peter, and Mark A. R. Kleiman. 1986. "Risks and Prices." In *Crime and Justice: An Annual Review of Research*, vol. 7, edited by Michael Tonry and Norval Morris. Chicago: University of Chicago Press.

Schelling, Thomas C. 1971. "What Is the Business of Organized Crime?" *Journal of Public Law* 20:71–84.

———. 1978. *Micromotives and Macrobehavior*. New York: Norton.

Singer, Max. 1971. "The Vitality of Mythical Numbers." *Public Interest* 23(Spring):3–9.

Spergel, Irving A. 1990. "Youth Gangs: Continuity and Change." In *Crime and Justice: A Review of Research*, vol. 12, edited by Michael Tonry and Norval Morris. Chicago: University of Chicago Press.

Toborg, Mary A., and Michael P. Kirby. 1984. "Drug Use and Pretrial Crime in the District of Columbia." *Research in Brief*. Washington, D.C.: U.S. Department of Justice, National Institute of Justice.

Toledo, Raymond J. 1988. *A Study of Drug Activity in a South Jamaica Queens Area Following Special Police Efforts to Reduce Drug Dealing*. New York: Bureau of Research and Evaluation, Division of Substance Abuse Services.

Wark, John T. 1989. "Drugs Scourge Hasn't Bypassed Detroit Police." *Detroit News* (February 21).

Wexler, Harry K., Douglas S. Lipton, and Bruce D. Johnson. 1988. "A Criminal Justice System Strategy for Treating Cocaine-Heroin Abusing Offenders in Custody." *Issues and Practices in Criminal Justice*. Washington, D.C.: U.S. Department of Justice, National Institute of Justice.

Wexler, Harry K., and Ronald Williams. 1986. "The 'Stay'n Out' Therapeutic Community: Prison Treatment for Substance Abusers." *Journal of Psychoactive Drugs* 18(3):221–30.

Wilkerson, Isabel. 1988*a*. "Detroit Drug Empire Showed All the Traits of Big Business." *New York Times* (December 18, eastern ed.).

———. 1988*b*. "'Crack House' Fire: Justice or Vigilantism?" *New York Times* (October 22, eastern ed.).

Wilson, James Q., and George Kelling. 1982. "Broken Windows: The Police and Neighborhood Safety." *Atlantic Monthly* (March), pp. 29–36.

Wines, Michael. 1988. "Against Drug Tide, Police Holding Action." *New York Times* (June 24, eastern ed.).

Zimmer, L. 1987. "Operation Pressure Point: The Disruption of Street-Level Drug Trade on New York's Lower East Side." Occasional paper. New York: New York University School of Law, Center for Research in Crime and Justice.

Mark H. Moore

Supply Reduction and Drug Law Enforcement

ABSTRACT

Efforts to control the supply of drugs to illicit markets in the United States through law-enforcement measures must be evaluated from three different perspectives: their efficacy in reducing the availability of drugs in illicit markets; their impact on the wealth and power of ongoing criminal organizations; and their impact on foreign-policy objectives of the U.S. government. Available evidence suggests that supply-reduction efforts have been successful in dealing with heroin and, perhaps, with marijuana, but not yet with cocaine. Government efforts to attack the supply system include an international program to eradicate crops, interdiction of shipments crossing U.S. borders, investigations and prosecutions of high-level drug trafficking networks, and state and local enforcement efforts directed at street-level drug dealing. A portfolio of programs is stronger than any single program alone. The primary thrust of the effort must be to frustrate illicit transactions at every level and to immobilize those groups that seem to have solved the problem of executing reliable transactions.

Within the United States, and throughout the world, psychoactive drugs are legally controlled.[1] Those with no legitimate uses are generally entirely prohibited. Those with recognized medical uses are more or less tightly regulated depending on their potential for abuse. In the United States, for example, heroin, marijuana, and hallucinogens are,

Mark H. Moore is Daniel and Florence V. Guggenheim Professor of Criminal Justice Policy and Management at the John F. Kennedy School of Government, Harvard University, Cambridge, Mass.

[1] For an enlightening discussion of the origins of the international system of drug controls, see Bruun, Pan, and Rexed (1975).

for all practical purposes, prohibited. Cocaine, which has limited medical uses, is very tightly controlled. Tranquilizers, which have more widely recognized medical uses, are more loosely regulated.

The aim of such regulation, of course, is to minimize drug abuse. It does so partly by affecting demand. By marking the boundaries of socially sanctioned drug use, the government teaches the proper uses of these drugs. To the extent that citizens accede to the government's judgments, or are deterred by the prospect of criminal sanctions, the statutes limit the demand for drugs.

The more important effect of these statutes, however, is probably to suppress supply. These laws guarantee that, at any given price, the quantity of drugs available to users will be less than would be true if the drugs were less tightly controlled.

This effect is, to some degree, produced directly by the statutes without any further governmental efforts. By outlawing drug distribution, the statutes remove drug traffickers from the protection of the law. As a result, they must operate without the police to guard them against robbery, and without the protection of courts to enforce contracts (Schelling 1980). In that underworld, dealers' fears of other criminals make them less efficient, higher-cost suppliers than they would be otherwise.

The supply-reduction effect is strengthened, however, by explicit government efforts to disrupt the supply of drugs to illicit markets. These efforts include the following: *international efforts* (including crop eradication, crop substitution, the negotiation of mutual legal-assistance treaties, and cooperative international enforcement efforts); *interdiction* (including border inspections and patrols conducted by the U.S. Customs Service and the U.S. Immigration and Naturalization Service, the interdiction of ships and planes suspected of carrying contraband by the U.S. Coast Guard, and, increasingly, the U.S. Armed Forces); *investigation* (including efforts by the U.S. Drug Enforcement Administration, the Federal Bureau of Investigation, and the U.S. attorneys to investigate and prosecute drug trafficking organizations); *state and local drug enforcement* (including the enforcement activities of the nation's 40,000 municipal police departments directed at traffickers and users). These efforts now absorb about $6 billion a year in government spending (Bodshaw, Koppel, and Pancoast 1987, pp. 1, 10).

Elsewhere in this volume, Kleiman and Smith address the issue of state and local drug enforcement. My task is to report what can be said about the efficacy of federal supply-reduction efforts—specifically, whether these efforts are worth their costs, and which approaches seem more promising than others. Although the evidence about these matters is not particularly strong, my principal conclusions are these:

1. While the value of supply-reduction efforts must be reckoned primarily in terms of their impact on the price and availability of drugs to illicit markets in the United States (and the impact that higher effective prices have on levels of drug use and their adverse consequences), it is also important that we consider the impact of supply-reduction efforts on the organized crime problem and the foreign policy objectives of the United States.

2. Supply-reduction efforts have raised the cost and (probably) reduced the consumption of heroin. They may also have succeeded to some degree with marijuana. So far, they have failed to produce these results with cocaine.

3. To improve supply-reduction efforts in terms of drug-policy objectives, we must identify the key factors of production and distribution that are in long-run short supply, and then attack those factors. Otherwise, our efforts will be absorbed by the illicit drug markets with little effect.

4. The factor that currently seems to be in long-run short supply is not land, personnel, raw materials, or technology but reliable "connections." By connections, I mean the continuing capacity among illegal traffickers to execute transactions in which huge financial sums and evidence that could condemn the parties to life imprisonment are on the table.

5. Connections and transactions can usefully be attacked by law enforcement at many different levels of distribution—including at the street level. Moreover, unselective enforcement efforts in foreign drug bazaars, along the borders, and on the streets of the nation's cities not only produce important supply-reduction benefits in their own right but also provide important intelligence about new, unsuspected trafficking networks. Thus, it is a mistake to think of "supply reduction" as chiefly involving crop eradication, transport interdiction, or arresting "Mr. Big."

6. Because we are uncertain about the effectiveness of any given instrument, because the world is dynamic and adaptive, and because there are important synergistic effects among the various instruments of the supply-reduction strategy, it is wise to rely on a portfolio of

supply-reduction programs—not on any single device. Wisdom in managing that portfolio requires adjustments in the balance of efforts in accord with policy objectives and information about which programs seem to be working.

Here is how this essay is organized. Section I sets out frameworks within which supply-reduction strategies can be evaluated. Section II examines how these strategies affect illicit drug pricing and availability and the organizational activities surrounding crop control and interdiction. Existing and alternative theories to guide supply-reduction efforts are discussed in Section III. The strengths and limitations of supply-reduction programs, from international efforts to local enforcement, are assessed in Section IV. Section V offers guidelines for supply-reduction efforts.

I. Supply Reduction: Three Evaluative Perspectives

In the past, supply-reduction strategies could be evaluated wholly in terms of the objectives of drug-abuse policy. The emergence of cocaine traffickers, powerful enough to intimidate national governments, has changed that. Now, prudent policymakers must evaluate supply-reduction efforts in terms of their impact on the wealth and power of organized criminal enterprises and their implications for the broader foreign-policy objectives of the United States.

Such aspects of supply-reduction policies have always been present, of course. In the late sixties, the zealous attack on the "French Connection" was animated at least partly by a desire to attack the Mafia, as well as to disrupt the flow of heroin to the East Coast (Select Committee on Crime 1970, pp. 45–70, 142–64; 1971, pp. 61–76). In Southeast Asia, efforts to reduce the export of opium and heroin were complicated by our interests in using Laotian tribesmen (who were notorious opium growers and traffickers) to help fight the Vietnam War (McCoy 1973, pp. 150–52; Bureau of International Narcotics Matters 1988, p. iv). The point, however, is that these concerns can no longer be treated as mere side effects; they have become sufficiently important to be reckoned alongside drug-policy objectives.

A. The Drug-Policy Perspective

From the perspective of drug-abuse policy, the objectives of supply-reduction efforts are to minimize the supply, increase the price, and reduce the availability of drugs to illicit markets.[7] Such objectives are valuable to drug policy insofar as they lead to reduced drug consumption and reduced adverse consequences of drug use.

Many analysts argue that the demand for drugs is "inelastic" and that supply-reduction efforts will therefore fail to reduce drug consumption. Or they argue that supply-reduction efforts alter the conditions of availability in ways that worsen the consequences of drug consumption—for example, by leading to sales of impure, unpredictable doses that threaten users' lives and health or by drawing users into an illicit underworld that tempts them to commit crimes to finance their drug use (e.g., Nadelmann 1988a).

This is not the place to examine the reasoning and evidence on the effects of drug prohibition on the *consequences* of illicit drug use. James Q. Wilson discusses these matters briefly in his essay in this volume. The issue of whether supply-reduction efforts can reduce drug consumption, however, is sufficiently germane to judging the value of supply-reduction strategies that it is worth pausing for a moment to consider the question.

Those who believe that the demand for drugs is "inelastic" rely on two different arguments. One is that drug users are addicted and, therefore, will do anything to maintain their consumption. A second is that there are certain kinds of people who want to use drugs, and they cannot be dissuaded by laws, social disapprobation, price, or inconvenience.

In evaluating these arguments, one must keep two quite different claims in mind. One is that drug consumption will not decrease *at all* in the face of price increases. That claim requires the demand for drugs to be "perfectly inelastic." A less restrictive claim is that the percentage reduction in consumption caused by an increase in the price will be less than the percentage change in price. That more modest claim is what it means for the demand for drugs to be "inelastic" but not "perfectly inelastic."

The difference between an "inelastic" demand for drugs and a "perfectly inelastic" demand is enormous. Unless the demand for drugs is "perfectly inelastic," drug consumption will decrease to some degree as a result of price increases. How much depends on how inelastic the

[2] I am following a line of argument developed previously and more extensively in Moore (1979, pp. 291–308).

demand. In all but those cases in which the demand for drugs is perfectly inelastic, then, there might be a justification for supply-reduction efforts if the amount that consumption can be reduced is large enough, and the cost of producing the price increases small enough.

There are many reasons to believe that the demand for illicit drugs is far from perfectly inelastic. For one thing, no good ever analyzed has ever been perfectly inelastic—not gasoline, not alcohol, not tobacco. Indeed, even those who are most dependent on these commodities, such as salesmen, alcoholics, and chain-smokers, seem to adjust their consumption as prices change (Nicholson 1985, pp. 184–87). Everything seems to respond to price.

For another, the equation of physiological dependence with a perfectly inelastic demand reveals a fundamental misunderstanding of addiction and dependence. The physiological mechanisms of addiction and dependence are nowhere near as compelling as this simple equation suggests. The physiological consequences of withdrawal are often overdramatized (Nyswander 1956, pp. 121–24). Drug users often stop using drugs with or without the aid of treatment (Vaillant 1969). Anthropological studies of users on the street reveal that they vary their drug consumption depending on how much money they have been able to obtain through fair or foul means (Johnson et al. 1985). So, addiction and dependence do not necessarily imply that users are entirely unresponsive to price or inconvenience.

Even if it were true that the physiological mechanisms of addiction and dependence were powerful in determining the consumption of committed drug users, they would not be relevant to those experimental users of drugs who were not yet addicted (Moore 1973). Indeed, one would expect inexperienced users to be among those most influenced by changes in price and availability since their knowledge and commitment to drug use are the weakest. To the extent that their demand was relatively elastic, they would make the aggregate demand for drugs at least somewhat elastic.

As to the claim that there are certain people who are destined to use drugs, one cannot help but be impressed by the enormous changes in the demographic patterns of drug use over the last few decades. Heroin use seems to have increased in the late sixties and early seventies, and then held steady (Kozel 1985). Marijuana use seems to have increased dramatically in the late sixties and early seventies, and recently declined (National Institute on Drug Abuse 1988). Starting in the middle classes in the late seventies, cocaine seems to have spread rapidly through all segments of American society during the eighties (Kozel and Adams 1985). The fluidity of these patterns over time and across demographic groups seems inconsistent with the hypothesis that there are some people who by virtue of their biology, upbringing, or character are simply destined to use drugs. Those patterns seem much more consistent with the hypothesis that patterns of drug use, like the patterns of consumption for many other things, are vulnerable to changes in tastes, prices, and availability.

It seems unlikely, then, that the demand for drugs is perfectly inelastic. Therefore, increases in the price of drugs will produce reductions in consumption. Exactly how much consumption can be reduced through price increases depends on exactly how inelastic the demand is. One can get a sense for the range of possibilities from the following estimates: the best estimate of the elasticity of the demand for marijuana is -1.50 (Misket and Vakil 1972); for alcohol, -0.8 (Cook 1988); for tobacco, -0.4 (Harris 1987). All these estimates, except for marijuana, indicate an inelastic demand. They also imply, however, that a doubling in the price of the good would result in reductions in consumption from 80 percent to 40 percent.

Whether this is important for policy depends on how easy it is to affect the price of the drugs, and how valuable the reductions in consumption are. It is significant, then, that the prices of heroin and marijuana have about doubled—even in constant dollars—over the last fifteen years (Flanagan and Jamieson 1988). It is apparently not so difficult to increase prices to levels that produce significant results. While a 40 percent reduction in drug consumption is not as good as a 100 percent reduction, it is nothing to sneeze at.

From the perspective of drug-abuse policy, then, the basic goals of supply reduction and drug law enforcement are to minimize the supply of drugs to illicit markets and to increase the price and inconvenience of acquiring drugs. Obviously, society would also like to pay the smallest possible cost in achieving these objectives. The costs are reckoned not only in terms of money but also in terms of reliance on our most intrusive investigative methods such as informants, electronic surveillance, and undercover operations for producing these effects, and in terms of increasing the vulnerability of criminal justice institutions to corruption.[3]

---

[3] For an explanation of why such methods are necessary, see Moore (1983). For a discussion of the costs of such activities, see Marx (1988).

B. Organized Crime Policy

From the perspective of organized-crime policy, supply-reduction objectives are slightly different. Here the principal concern is that illegal drug production and distribution provide an economic base that nourishes existing organized criminal enterprises or gives rise to new ones.

Drug traffickers behave in all the ways that make organized crime offensive to the society (Moore 1986). They frustrate the aims of drug policy by continuing to supply drugs to illicit markets. They produce a great deal of violence.[4] They corrupt, and sometimes intimidate, enforcement agencies. They grow rich in the process of violating the laws and taunt society with their financial success. The aims of organized-crime policy are to reduce these bad aspects of organized crime by weakening the organizations and bringing those who participate in the enterprises to justice.

To a degree, these objectives are congruent with the objectives of drug policy. To the extent that organized-crime policy attacks existing drug traffickers, reduces their capacity to supply drugs to illicit markets, and weakens them as ongoing criminal enterprises, the objectives of both drug policy and organized-crime policy are served.

There are, however, two ways in which the objectives of drug-abuse policy and organized-crime policy conflict. Suppose for a moment that society viewed the organized-crime aspects of drug trafficking as the worst part of the problem, and drug use itself as less urgent. In that case, a new option for controlling the organized-crime elements would become available, namely, legalizing the supply of drugs. If drug distribution were legalized, the organized criminal groups that now dominate the industry would have no particular competitive advantage. Their current capacity for violence and corruption, so essential in operating an illicit enterprise, would suddenly become nothing more than costly overhead. The corrupting, violent organized-crime groups would be outcompeted by legitimate firms that specialize in low prices, convenient access, and reliable quality, and who could mobilize the police to protect their operations from direct threats or indirect competition from organized-crime groups.

---

[4] For an analytic account of why violence is valuable to drug dealers, see Moore (1976, pp. 41–45). For more descriptive accounts of the activities of drug dealers, see Siegel (1978), Mills (1986), and Shenon (1988).

Legalization would not, of course, necessarily shrink the overall supply of drugs. Indeed, the supply would almost certainly increase as the licensed dealers took their place alongside the illegal dealers and developed their own markets. Nor would legalization entirely eliminate the black market. All plausible legalization schemes include restrictions on who can legally buy drugs. Minors, for example, are generally excluded. Any such restriction creates an incentive for a black market to emerge.

The point is simply that legalization would change the size and character of the illicit supply system that remained after legalization. The residual black market for heroin, cocaine, or marijuana would probably resemble the current black market for amphetamines and tranquilizers: a large number of small, transient firms supplied by diversion from the legitimate market. That sort of black market presents fewer organized-crime problems than does the current system.

That drug prohibition creates fertile soil in which organized-crime groups can grow is one way in which the objectives of drug policy are not quite aligned with the objectives of organized-crime policy. The second way is even more frustrating and paradoxical. Effective law-enforcement attacks on drug traffickers eliminate those drug dealers who are least resistant to law-enforcement efforts and leave in place those drug traffickers who are most resistant, thereby exacerbating the organized-crime aspects of the drug problem (Kleiman 1985, chap. 7). Criminal enterprises that are most successful in resisting effective enforcement are likely to be the ones that are large, violent, and corrupting.

Perhaps the easiest way to understand the relationship between organized-crime policy and drug-abuse policy is this: having decided to pay a price in terms of organized-crime control by prohibiting drug distribution in the interests of discouraging drug consumption, and having acknowledged that successful enforcement directed at drug traffickers can reduce the supply of drugs but only at the expense of making the remaining drug traffickers tougher and more powerful, it is still valuable to strike at the remaining drug traffickers to achieve additional results in both organized-crime and drug-policy terms.

C. The Foreign-Policy Perspective

Most of the drugs that reach illicit markets in the United States are produced, processed, and exported by foreign countries. In the past, the impact of drug trafficking on relations with foreign governments and the objectives of U.S. foreign policy was considered sufficiently small as to be insignificant—something that could be handled at technical, bureaucratic levels rather than in meetings of heads of state (Nadelmann 1987a). No longer is this true.

What so dignifies drug use as an issue of foreign policy is the concatenation of two facts. First, the commerce in illegal drugs has become large enough to figure prominently in the international financial positions and the national political economies of some countries, principally in Latin America. As Richard Craig (1987, p. 4) reports, "Cocaine was perhaps the only Latin American commodity in the late 1970's and early 1980's whose price showed any real increase. Illicit narcotics have in fact kept several Latin American economies afloat in a sea of regional depression. It is even more ironic that the principal means by which peasants in many source countries manage to earn above starvation wages are both illegal drug cultivation and clandestine emigration."

Second, the countries for which the illegal drug trade has become economically important have recently assumed particular importance in the overall foreign policy of the United States. It was one thing to have the drug problem associated with Turkey, Afghanistan, and Southeast Asian countries at a time when U.S. foreign-policy interests in these areas were waning; it is quite another to have the drug industry be important in Colombia, Bolivia, Peru, Panama, and Mexico at a time when the U.S. government sees "stemming the tide of communism" in Central and South America as a dominant foreign-policy objective. That supply-reduction efforts have now become entangled in important foreign-policy issues complicates both the calculation of U.S. interests and the successful implementation of supply-reduction efforts.

In some cases, of course, the entanglement of drug trafficking and foreign policy is helpful: each gives impetus to the other. This occurs when a powerful regime, allied with the United States, sees drug trafficking as a threat to its internal security. It could make this judgment because the trafficking in the country is creating a domestic drug-abuse problem, or embarrassing the country in international diplomatic arenas, or fueling guerrilla movements, or distorting the national economy, or threatening to corrupt the regime. Whatever the reasons, if a friendly regime is opposed, the United States and its ally can join arm in arm to attack the traffickers.

In many other situations, however, foreign-policy interests diverge from supply-reduction objectives. Consider, first, the situation in which the United States is dealing with a friendly regime. No significant external or internal political threat to the regime seems to exist. The only problem is that the regime seems to be founded at least partly on the control of narcotics trafficking. The profits to high officials are important to them—so important that if they are threatened, the leaders would move farther away from their current alignment with the United States. The enterprise as a whole is important enough to the overall economy that many ordinary citizens would support this move as well. In this situation, the United States is faced with a choice between advancing its foreign-policy interests or its supply-reduction efforts. While the analysis is far too simplified, this seems to have been the recent situation with Panama and might have been part of our problem in Vietnam (McCoy 1973, chap. 5; Bureau of International Narcotics Matters 1988, pp. 146–49).

Consider, now, a second situation in which the United States is dealing with a friendly but somewhat shaky regime. There is no substantial internal threat to the regime yet, but the economic and social situation is deteriorating. There is some question about the regime's capacity to solve economic and social problems and to enforce law and order throughout the country. Within the country, illicit drugs are becoming economically, and therefore politically, important.

The country is opposed to narcotics trafficking and is not thoroughly corrupted but is a little anxious about attacking the illegal drugs zealously lest these attacks create powerful political opposition. The political opposition could appear as legitimate political challenges from candidates and parties financed by drug traffickers, or it could take the form of more popular support for existing guerrilla movements.

An aggressive attack on drug trafficking would require tough action from the police and the military. Two things could happen if such an attack were launched: the police and military might destroy the drug trade and, in the process, create powerful political opposition, or they might become corrupted and undermine the government from within. In this case, the friendly government would like to avoid the issue for a while and not take zealous action against the drug traffickers.

Again, there is a trade-off between our interests in shoring up a friendly regime and in attacking the illegal drug industry. If we press the regime to take vigorous action against drugs, we may weaken it to the disadvantage of foreign-policy objectives. If we are tolerant of less vigor, we will take a loss in terms of drug-control objectives in the short run, and perhaps allow the drug traffickers to become too powerful over the long run. Again, while far too simplified, this could be a sketch of the current situation in Mexico and Peru.[5]

Now consider a third situation in which the United States confronts an unfriendly regime in a politically important area. In that country, a guerrilla movement exists favorable to U.S. interests. The guerrillas are in need of both international financing to buy weapons and political support from the local peasantry. While the United States would like to support the guerrilla movement, it cannot do so overtly. The local peasantry is now growing marijuana, cocaine, or opium poppies. These crops, far from U.S. markets, have little value. Once connected to U.S. markets, however, the value of the crops soars. Consequently, there is an opportunity for the guerrilla movement to solve its financial and local support problem by becoming an international drug trafficker.

In this situation, the United States must choose between assisting the guerrilla movement by ignoring or facilitating their drug trafficking, or weakening the guerrilla movement by restraining it from the lucrative and locally attractive narcotics business. While much oversimplified, this seems to have been the situation the United States faced in Southeast Asia during the Vietnam War, recently faced in Nicaragua, and is facing now in Afghanistan (McCoy 1973, chap. 5; Bureau of International Narcotics Matters 1988, pp. iv, 144–45, 174–79).

These scenarios illustrate the point that a foreign-policy perspective requires one to view supply-reduction efforts in terms of their impact on the power and stability of friendly regimes. If supply-reduction efforts will strengthen the hands of our friends, then the policy is clear. If supply-reduction efforts force previously supportive regimes to move away from support for the United States, or if they weaken regimes with which the United States has strong and valuable relations, then an issue arises as to which concerns should predominate. Often it will be the right judgment for the United States to advance foreign-policy objectives at the cost of reduced achievement of drug-policy objectives.

These complex interactions among legitimate public policy concerns relating to drug control, organized crime, and foreign policy are not new. They need to be highlighted, however, because they dictate that

[5] These comments are based in part on personal conversations with Mexican officials. See also Nadelmann (1987*b*, pp. 35–36); Bureau of International Narcotics Matters (1988, pp. iii, 131–43, 104–10).

efforts at drug control will inevitably sometimes be weaker and less single-minded than if drug-control policies were the only legitimate considerations shaping governmental policy.

II. Assessing Effectiveness

To base supply-reduction policies on firm knowledge, it would be necessary to know the impact of current (or proposed) supply-reduction strategies on drug policy, organized-crime policy, and foreign-policy objectives. Unfortunately, we have only recently begun to think systematically about the impact of our efforts on organized-crime and foreign-policy objectives. And, with respect to the more familiar and limited interests in the impact on drug-policy objectives, we are handicapped by the slowness with which experience accumulates and by the difficulty of capturing that experience with accurate data.

The sad fact is that, in gauging the potential efficacy of supply-reduction efforts, there is little a priori reasoning or knowledge from laboratory experiments that can give us the answer. We must rely instead on our cumulative, historical experience as it is reflected in our statistical systems. These systems are currently impossible to use in judging effectiveness in terms of organized-crime and foreign-policy objectives. They are only of limited value in judging effectiveness in drug-policy terms (e.g., Kleiman 1986a).

A. Price and Availability

The single most important bit of empirical evidence on the effectiveness of supply-reduction efforts is data on the price and availability of drugs in illicit markets in the United States. Such data provide direct measures of an important objective of supply-reduction policies. They are relatively easy to measure and record. And we have recorded these data long enough to observe trends. However, several complications arise in using these measures for assessing effectiveness.

First, the implicit sampling procedures for estimating retail price are quite weak. Basically, price data come from records of narcotics buys by agents or their informants. For any geographic area at any given time, very few transactions are recorded. Consequently, all price estimates implicitly have high variances.

An even greater sampling problem comes from worries about the consistency and representativeness of the transactions that make up the sample. Narcotics agents buy at different levels of the market—

sometimes at wholesale, sometimes at retail. Naturally, prices differ by level. Similarly, narcotics agents may not be typical customers. Less familiar to dealers, less knowledgeable about local conditions, and more eager to make purchases, drug agents might well pay systematically higher prices than other purchasers. These need not be problems if the biases introduced remain constant over time, and if analysts restrict their attention to trends in prices rather than absolute estimates. But if these assumptions are not true, the errors introduced by failing to take account of the level of the buy and the agents' unique status will be crippling.

Second, the purchase price may be the wrong measure of supply-reduction impact. It may be much more important to record how difficult, time consuming, and dangerous it was for consumers to obtain the drug. These elements of the street-level drug transaction are arguably more important than mere dollar price in discouraging new use and persuading older users to seek treatment. More important, these dimensions might be differentially affected by different supply-reduction instruments. Street-level drug enforcement, for example, affects convenience more than price, while crop eradication produces the opposite effect (Reuter and Kleiman 1986, pp. 328–29).

These observations have led some to the conclusion that the appropriate measure of price and availability is not the dollar price but the effective price of drugs—a measure that incorporates dollar cost, the time and effort required to "score," and the risks of being arrested or "ripped off" in the course of the purchase (Moore 1973). This concept adds precision to the measure, but at the price of necessitating additional data collection and introducing a difficult scaling problem in representing the "effective price" as a single index number. Moreover, to the extent that these other measures are highly correlated with money price, little new information is provided about the impact of supply-reduction efforts. So far, the collection and recording problems have proved so crippling, and the assumption that the effective price is highly correlated with the money price so convenient, that the dollar price of drugs remains the standard measure.

Third, there is a problem in separating the effects of supply-reduction efforts on the price of drugs from the many other factors that affect the price of drugs in illicit markets. The overall level of demand affects prices. Consequently, if supply remains constant but demand increases, prices will increase even if the supply-reduction efforts are no more successful than in the past. Conversely, if the demand for drugs falls, the price of drugs may also fall even if supply-reduction efforts dramatically improve. On the supply side, many things that are beyond the control of supply-reduction efforts can also affect prices. Supplies can be reduced by bad weather, local labor shortages, and military hostilities.[6] All this makes the interpretation of the impact of supply-reduction efforts on drug prices a treacherous enterprise.

These problems can be dealt with, of course. Separate estimates of movements in the demand for drugs can be obtained by means of annual surveys of the population, or counts of people showing up in emergency rooms with drug problems, or overdose deaths (e.g., Kleiman 1986a). Estimates of growing conditions for illicit drugs can be obtained through satellite surveillance. Such observations might make it possible to tease out the independent effects of supply-reduction efforts. Alternatively, an arbitrary approach can be taken by setting the goal of supply reduction and drug law enforcement as increasing the effective price of drugs no matter what else is going on, and using that as a benchmark for evaluating performance regardless of its imprecision. In reality, however, these difficulties of interpretation weaken the usefulness of this measure as an indicator of supply-reduction effectiveness.

Despite these difficulties, the price of drugs in illicit markets remains one of the principal empirical measures available for assessing the effectiveness of supply-reduction efforts. That the problems described above exist, however, means that the data on prices reveal much less than might be imagined.

Table 1 compares the current retail prices of the primary drugs of abuse with their estimated prices in a regulated but legal market. In all cases, the drugs are significantly more expensive than legal substitutes. These data make it clear that prohibition and supply-reduction efforts can increase the price of psychoactive drugs well above levels that would obtain in a legal market. In an important sense, this difference constitutes the most significant result of supply-reduction efforts.

Note, however, that not all of the observed differential can be attrib-

[6] In Afghanistan, the 1985 and 1986 opium poppy harvests yielded considerably more opium than the abnormally small 1984 crop, which was reduced by unfavorable weather conditions and the disruptions caused by the war (National Narcotics Intelligence Consumers Committee 1987, p. 74).

TABLE 1

Illegal versus Legal Drug Prices

Drug	Current Retail Price ($)	Estimated Legal Price ($)	Ratio
Heroin (pure gram)	2,280	30–35	70:1
Cocaine (pure gram)	143	15–20	8:1
Marijuana (cigarette, in ¢)	95	6–7	15:1

SOURCES.—Retail prices from Flanagan and Jamieson (1988), table 3-76. Legal heroin price is estimated from prevailing legal prices for morphine and methadone. Legal cocaine price is estimated from prevailing prices for cocaine. See *Drug Topics Redbook* (1988). Legal marijuana price is estimated from prevailing prices of tobacco cigarettes.

uted to explicit supply-reduction efforts. Some portion must be attributed directly to the legal regime prohibiting drugs—leaving aside any specific effects of other concrete efforts to enforce these laws such as crop eradication, interdictions, or successful enforcement operations.

Figure 1 presents the available data on trends in the retail price of the principal drugs of abuse. The data indicate that the retail price of heroin steadily increased through the decade of the seventies and has since held constant or slightly declined. The price of marijuana has increased dramatically since the late seventies. The price of cocaine has declined since the late seventies. If we ignore the effects of everything else that might be influencing these observed prices, such as changing levels of demand or changes in growing conditions in foreign source countries, and impute all of the observed changes in price to supply-reduction efforts, the implications for the effectiveness of supply-reduction strategies are mixed. We seem to be able to control heroin, but not cocaine. We might be able to control marijuana. That conclusion is particularly discouraging because much of our recent effort has gone into the control of cocaine (U.S. Department of Justice 1986).

An improved estimate of supply-reduction effectiveness could be made if we could remove the effect of demand on the observed price. That could be done if we had good independent measures of the underlying demand for drugs, but we do not. All we have are imperfect measures of attitudes toward drugs and levels of consumption developed from surveys (Kleiman 1986a, p. 12) and changes in levels of adverse consequences of drug use such as overdose deaths, emergency room visits, and arrests of drug users (Kleiman 1986a, pp. 25–26).

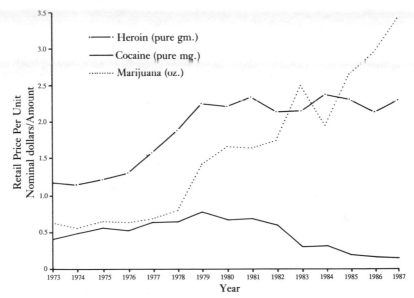

FIG. 1.—Retail price per unit of drug: heroin, cocaine, and marijuana. Sources.—
Flanagan, van Alstyne, and Gottfredson (1982), p. 329; and Flanagan and Jamieson
(1988), p. 289.

Still, there is a crude approach to this problem that is robust and
yields some interesting results (Boyum 1989). By comparing the data
on *prices* with the direct measures and indications of *consumption*, we can
identify historical periods in which observed trends in prices and observed trends in consumption were moving in opposite directions. In
some cases, prices were increasing while consumption seemed to be
declining. Such situations indicate an *unambiguous downward* shift in the
supply curve: at any given price, fewer drugs were being supplied in
that period than previously. In other cases, prices were decreasing
while consumption was increasing. These situations represent an *unambiguous upward* shift in the supply curve: at any given price, more drugs
were being supplied than in the previous periods. Although shifts in
supply curves can be clearly identified in new situations, a shift in the
supply curve cannot be taken as clear evidence of successes and failures
in supply-reduction efforts, however, for there are factors other than
explicit supply-reduction efforts that are influencing the supply curves.
Still, with this evidence, we are closer to observing real supply-
reduction effects with these methods than with those previously relied
upon.

Figures 2, 3, and 4 present the relevant data for heroin, cocaine, and

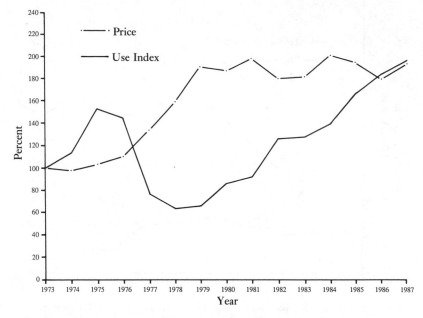

Fig. 2.—Relation between price and use index for heroin, 1973–87. Sources.—National Institute on Drug Abuse (1983, 1987); and see fig. 1 and n. 7.

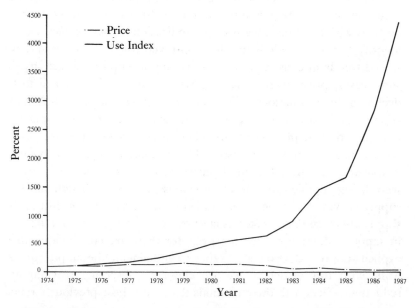

Fig. 3.—Relation between price and use index for cocaine, 1974–87. Sources.—National Institute on Drug Abuse (1983, 1987); and see fig. 1 and n. 7.

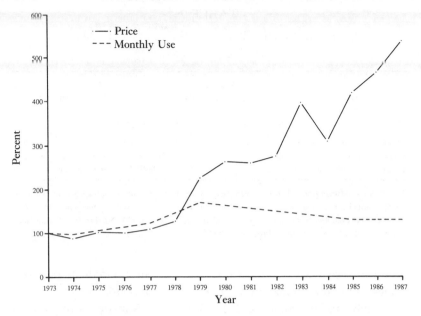

FIG. 4.—Relation between price and use index for marijuana, 1973–87. Sources.—National Institute on Drug Abuse (1983, 1987); and see fig. 1 and n. 7.

marijuana, respectively.[7] Table 2 describes these periods of apparent success and failure in supply-reduction efforts. Apparently, we were successful in controlling heroin in the later seventies. We may also have succeeded recently in reducing the supply of marijuana. We have failed dismally to deal with the cocaine problem in the eighties.

---

[7] Data collected by the Drug Abuse Warning Network (DAWN) were used to compose both the heroin and cocaine use indexes. There is no single source that presents all of the DAWN data, nor is there a single publication series for the entire period of DAWN data. Consequently, the DAWN data were pieced together from a variety of sources, doing a lot of arithmetic along the way. Most of the DAWN data are presented as gross figures. But these estimates are potentially biased over time since inconsistent reporting is widespread (hospitals drop in and out of the program or report infrequently). The National Institute on Drug Abuse occasionally publishes DAWN "consistent panel estimates" that only include data from particular hospitals that have reported consistently over a certain period of time. Since the consistent panel estimates offer more accurate figures—more accurate in terms of representing change—they were used wherever possible. Two problems arise, however. First, consistent panel estimates were not available for the early years. Second, the consistent panel is not always the same; it is merely "consistent" over a certain period of time. Since indexes were constructed, only data that accurately represented percentage changes—precisely what the "consistent panel" data does—were needed. Basically, gross figures were used for the first few years of the indexes, and then consistent panel estimates were used to determine the subsequent percentage changes in those indexes. Averages were made where conflicting information existed.

TABLE 2

Periods of Supply-Reduction Successes and Failures
(Values in Percent)

	Heroin (1976–79)		Marijuana (1979–Present)		Cocaine (1979–Present)	
Retail price:	+73	Retail price:	+139	Retail price:		−82
Emergency room mentions:	−45	Monthly use:	−20	Annual use:		+20
Medical examiner mentions:	−65			Emergency room mentions:		+1,527
Treatment admissions:	−33			Medical examiner mentions:		+2,226

SOURCES.—Retail prices: Flanagan, van Alstyne, and Gottfredson (1982); Flanagan and Jamieson (1988). Annual use: Household Survey, National Institute on Drug Abuse. Emergency room mentions, medical examiner mentions: Drug Abuse Warning Network (DAWN). Treatment admissions: Client Oriented Data Acquisition Process (CODAP).

A third clue about the effectiveness of supply-reduction efforts comes from an examination of price differentials at different stages of production and distribution. Table 3 presents estimates of the price of drugs at four different stages in the process of production and distribution and the ratios of those prices (Reuter and Kleiman 1986).

One way to think about the observed differences in these prices is in terms of the value added at each stage of production and distribution. To a degree, the price differentials reflect added value associated with incurring real underlying costs of production and distribution—the costs of materials, personnel, supplies, and transportation.

The observed price differential could also reflect market power. The large ratio between the farm prices and the prices at the border, for example, may reflect the existence of a powerful monopoly or cartel at the export level that can claim a larger portion of the total value to be created by setting prices above the level that simply compensates them for their costs and risks.

From the perspective of those interested in analyzing supply-reduction efforts, however, the most interesting interpretations view the price differentials as indicators of where the greatest risks to dealers lie. Indeed, to the extent that the greatest cost associated with the illicit business is the risk of being caught, the value that is created in moving drugs along this pipeline is that some risks have been avoided. Similarly, to the extent that enforcement pressures tend to concentrate the market by eliminating inefficient firms, market power will be associated with high levels of enforcement pressure. Thus, the large price differ-

TABLE 3

Structure of Drug Prices, 1980 (per Pure Kilogram)

Drug and Stage of Production/ Distribution	Price ($)	Transfer Activity	Markup (×)
Heroin:			
Farm-gate	350–1,000	} Cultivation and processing	11.9
Processed	6,000–10,000	} Overseas packaging	11.9
Export	95,000	} Smuggling	2.4
Import	220,000–240,000	} Domestic distribution	8.3
Retail	1.6–2.2 million		
		Total markup	2,815
Cocaine:			
Farm-gate	1,300–10,000	} Cultivation and processing	1.2
Processed	3,000–20,000	} Overseas packaging	2.1
Export	7,000–20,000	} Smuggling	3.7
Import	50,000	} Domestic distribution	13.0
Retail	650,000		
		Total markup	115
Marijuana:			
Farm-gate	7–18	} Cultivation and processing	4.4
Processed	55	} Overseas packaging	2.5
Export	90–180	} Smuggling	4.0
Import	365–720	} Domestic distribution	3.1
Retail	1,250–2,090		
		Total markup	134

SOURCE.—Reuter and Kleiman (1986), p. 293.

entials observed between stages of production may indicate differences in the threats to dealers posed by supply-reduction efforts.

If this interpretation were correct, one could plausibly draw the following conclusions. First, the greatest pressure seems to be on heroin. That is the implication of the overall markup from farm-gate prices.

Second, the location of the maximum pressures differs among drugs. For heroin, the principal difficulties seem to lie in processing, exporting, and distributing the drug in the United States, rather than in getting it across the border. For cocaine, the greatest difficulty lies in distributing it in the United States; getting it processed and smuggling it into the country appear much less difficult. For marijuana, the great-

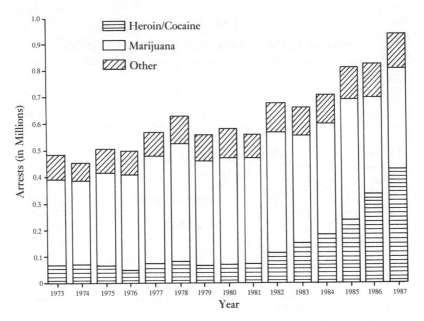

FIG. 5.—Arrests for drugs by type, 1973–87. Sources.—Federal Bureau of Investigation (1973–87).

est difficulties are in collecting and processing the plants and in smuggling it across the border.

B. Measures of Organizational Production

The other empirical measures of supply-reduction effectiveness are measures of organizational activity rather than the achievement of social objectives. With respect to the international crop-control programs, there are the counts of acreage destroyed. With respect to interdiction and domestic enforcement, there are measures of arrests made, drugs seized, and, more recently, assets seized in association with drug investigations.[8] Figure 5 presents the available data on drug arrests by type of drug. Table 4 presents the data on drug seizures (represented in terms of dosage units) by type of drug.

Two points seem worth making about these data. First, the trends in these data are up sharply since 1980, reflecting both the onslaught of cocaine and the former and current administrations' emphases on drug

[8] The National Narcotics Intelligence Consumers Committee (e.g., 1987) and the President's Commission on Organized Crime publish these figures. Reuter and Kleiman (1986) point to the limited value of these figures as a measure of the effectiveness of supply-reduction efforts.

TABLE 4

Drug Seizures by U.S. Customs Service, U.S. Coast Guard, and Other Agencies with Coast Guard Participation
(in Thousands of Dosage Units)

Type of Drug Seized	1975	1976	1977	1978	1979	1980	1981	1982	1983	1984	1985	1986
Heroin	5,221	16,694	12,608	8,562	5,562	12,199	10,655	13,161	26,949	30,159	35,621	31,417
Cocaine	18,912	28,427	24,699	36,804	37,307	123,300	100,582	310,963	535,643	767,046	1,502,054	1,666,644
Marijuana	897,901	1,771,094	4,583,872	13,223,596	10,592,146	8,216,836	12,698,921	12,285,950	8,438,244	9,673,519	7,647,063	6,249,090

SOURCES.—Flanagan, van Alstyne, and Gottfredson (1982); Flanagan and Jamieson (1988).

control, particularly supply-reduction efforts. Second, the focus of the effort seems to be shifting from marijuana to cocaine.

These measures are much maligned by academics, policy analysts, and program evaluators who are interested in measuring the ultimate effectiveness of supply-reduction efforts. To a great degree, their disdain is justified, for it is true that these measures of enforcement efforts alone cannot justify supply-reduction efforts. Still, there are some important contributions that these measures make to our understanding and control of supply-reduction efforts. The contributions are of two kinds.

First, they help us evaluate programs by providing direct evidence on the extent to which a given policy is being implemented. The alternative measures of governmental effort such as the passage of a law or the expenditure of money intended for a given purpose do not really measure the implementation of a policy and therefore leave us uncertain about whether a finding that a policy has had little impact should be attributed to a faulty program design or a faulty process of implementation.[9]

Second, these measures are managerially useful. When paired with cost data, they allow public managers and those who oversee their operations to determine how much it costs to produce outputs that are thought to be related to the overall objectives of supply reduction and to see whether productivity is increasing or decreasing. As such, they provide information useful to policymakers and incentives for managers to improve their performance (Brace et al. 1980).

The more important weakness of these measures is not that they fail to describe the ultimate, socially valuable impact of supply-reduction efforts but that they are essentially unaudited. Given that they are under the control of operating agencies and are routinely used for performance measurement, it is always possible that they will be distorted to make the agency look better. These fears are reasonable, for the occasional audits that have been done have revealed substantial double counting (e.g., General Accounting Office 1983, pp. 35–39). The only way to make these measures credible is by routine outside auditing.

In addition, these output measures ignore quality differences. A crop destroyed after the yield has been harvested is worth less in supply

---

[9] That implementation of policies cannot be taken for granted is now well established in the political science literature (see, e.g., Mazmanian and Sabatier 1983; Wildavsky and Pressman 1984).

reduction than the same crop destroyed before the crop has been harvested. This distinction is not reliably made (nor audited) in crop-
eradication programs. Similarly, the arrest of a major trafficker or the
immobilization of a whole network is probably worth more than a large
number of arrests of low-level traffickers in terms of interrupting the
supply of drugs, but that difference is only imperfectly reflected (and
unaudited) in the existing arrest data.[10] Arrests that lead to convictions
are also more valuable than those that do not. Without such distinctions, it is hard to know what exactly is being produced.

III. Theories Guiding Supply-Reduction Efforts

Given the weakness of the empirical evidence, we are thrown back on
common sense and theory to guide judgments about supply-reduction
effectiveness. The concepts that now shape policy debates about supply-reduction efforts are what might be called "theories in use."[11] They
are broad concepts that appeal to common sense and serve political
mobilization purposes but have not been clearly set out, reasoned
through, or empirically tested.

A. Theories in Use

The conventional theory of supply reduction is that the best place to
strike is "at the source."[12] That assertion appeals to the common intuition that permanent solutions to problems can be found by striking at
root causes.

The difficulty is that it is not clear what "the source" is. Does this
refer to the crops in the field, the traffickers who organize the collection, refinement and export, the laboratories and processing facilities,
or the users whose willingness to purchase the drugs seems to generate
such powerful economic forces that agricultural patterns and cultures
are transformed throughout the world?

Moreover, the logic is incomplete. What if the source cannot be
reached because the sovereignty of another country intervenes, or the
operational capacities to implement the desired program do not now

---

[10] This statement is strictly applicable to the hundreds of thousands of arrests made by
state and local governments. For a while, the Drug Enforcement Administration sought
to grade arrests through the G-DEP system. For a description, see Wilson (1978, pp.
113–22). This system does not seem to be used in the Federal Bureau of Investigation's
drug enforcement work.

[11] See Argyris and Schon (1978), in which the theory of action perspective is applied
to the problem of organizational capacity for learning.

[12] I am, again, following a line of analysis that is presented in more detail in Moore
(1979).

exist and cannot easily be created? Is it still desirable to strike at the source?

Another conventional theory much in use is that it is best to stop drugs at the border.[13] There may be some merit to this claim insofar as there are special legal powers at the border that facilitate searches and insofar as these searches lead to the seizure of particular shipments headed for the nation's streets. But stopping drugs at the border is no easy task given the thousands of miles of U.S. borders that must be patrolled, the huge volumes of cargo and people who daily cross these borders, and the relative ease with which shipments and smugglers can be replaced by others waiting to take their places.[14]

A third conventional theory is that supply-reduction efforts will be effective if only the major traffickers are arrested and successfully prosecuted (Moore 1979, pp. 300–301; 1986, pp. 70–71). Again, there may be merit in this view insofar as the major traffickers provide much of the capital and managerial impetus behind drug trafficking. But if it proves impossible to arrest high-level traffickers, or if there are many traffickers positioned to take the places of those arrested, or if those arrested can continue to operate from behind prison walls, then this argument is called into doubt.

Examination of these theories in use reveals them for what they are: pieces of organizational ideology buttressing the bureaucratic claims of the principal operating agencies involved in supply-reduction efforts. The question is whether there is anything better. Or, in the absence of any better current theory, we need to know which of these theories has the soundest reasoning behind it.

B. An Alternative Theory: The Economics of Supply

The principal competitive theory to those now in use is an economic theory of drug supply that seeks to identify the effects of attacking the industry through crop-eradication efforts, legal prohibitions, and enforcement.[15] This reasoning typically proceeds through an analysis of

[13] New York Mayor Ed Koch, Florida Congressman Larry Smith, and Harlem Congressman Charles Rangel, who recognize government's inability to deal with the drug problem in the cities, are among the most vocal supporters of stepping up interdiction efforts (see Nadelmann 1988a, p. 6).

[14] For a detailed account of the problems with stopping drugs at the border, see Reuter (1988, pp. 51–65).

[15] See, e.g., Wisotsky (1983). Economic theories and graphs are used throughout the article to illustrate and analyze the effects of various forms of enforcement on the illegal industry. Also see Reuter and Kleiman (1986).

"comparative statics"—a time-honored methodology in economics. The idea is to compare the structure, conduct, and performance of the drug industry in a legal, competitive market with its performance in a highly taxed or regulated market or in an illegal market. More precisely, the likely directions of change in the performance of the industry are analyzed as a function of changing the legal regime or altering the levels of taxation and enforcement.[16]

This method leads to some important predictions and conclusions. For example, compared with a legal market in drugs, an illegal market will supply less drugs for any given price, charge higher prices for any given quantity supplied, and will be more concentrated in its structure. It will also engage in violence and corruption. To the extent that the screws are tightened with more aggressive enforcement, these effects will be exaggerated. Moreover, money profits (but not necessarily gains in the overall welfare of the dealers) will increase because the suppliers will be dealing with increased likelihoods of arrest and successful prosecution, and will demand compensation for these risks.[17]

Similarly, economic theory tells us that there will always be some offsetting reactions to any control measures.[18] If crops are successfully eradicated in one area, new areas, previously underused because of undertrained labor or poor soil conditions, might suddenly attract development. Similarly, if enforcement gets much tougher at the ports of entry along the border, drug traffickers might reduce the size of their shipments, or elaborate the hiding places in which the drugs are stored. Or, if enforcement becomes more effective through reliance on infor-

[16] For a discussion of this methodology, see Samuelson (1983). For an application to supply-reduction efforts, see Wisotsky (1983), which discusses the characteristics of the industry under a variety of assumptions, and Nadelmann (1988b, p. 105).

[17] This is best understood in terms of "economic welfare," which is often expressed through a person's "utility." For example, given a set of occupational characteristics (e.g., income, hours, risks, boredom, flexibility), a person will have a certain level of "utility" for the job (which translates into happiness or satisfaction with the job). Assuming that the person dislikes risks, many increases in the riskiness associated with the occupation (e.g., a higher rate of lung cancer) will lower his "utility" for the job, everything else constant. Now, assume that the person likes money and prefers more to less so that any increase in the income of the job will also raise his "utility" for the job, everything else constant. Thus, it is conceivable that a combination of increased risks and increased pay might leave him at the same level of "utility" as before. In this case, his overall welfare will not change. The effect of greater enforcement on the overall welfare of the drug dealers can be assessed under the same analysis. Their monetary rewards rise, but since the risk of going to prison also rises, their overall welfare will not necessarily rise.

[18] Economic adjustments and adaptations are bound to occur. For examples of how the market has adapted to drug enforcement efforts in the past, see Reuter (1988, pp. 54–56).

mants, drug traffickers may shrink the number of new people with whom they deal, or deal more harshly with those they suspect of informing. Such adaptations often mean that control efforts will have less impact on original objectives than anticipated or that unintended consequences of the policy will occur.

These insights are extremely valuable. Indeed, the power of economic theory to give reasonably good predictions with very little data about the responses to changes in controls is crucial to our current beliefs and understandings about supply-reduction efforts. What this sort of economic theory cannot do, however, is tell us much about how much difference marginal changes in the current control regime will make over the next few years.

A concrete example may make the point. In 1973–74, due to a confluence of luck and skill, the U.S. government was able to produce a significant interruption in the flow of heroin from Turkey and France to the United States. This was achieved by new restrictions on and more effective control of opium poppies in Turkey, by effective enforcement by the French and Italians, and by effective enforcement by the United States. The result was a shortage of heroin use on the East Coast that seemed to last for about two years (Bartels 1975). Eventually, supplies from Mexico and Southeast Asia expanded and reduced the net effect of the successful control of Turkish heroin (Nadelmann 1987*b*, p. 40).

From one perspective, interruption could be seen as unimportant, or even counterproductive. The shortage soon disappeared, and the attack on Turkey resulted in a more diversified supply system that made control more difficult for the future. Alternatively, one could say that the effort was valuable because a cohort of American teenagers passed through a period of vulnerability under relatively safer conditions, and because it led to a lower level of heroin use than would have existed if the Turkish ban had not succeeded.

The point of the example is not to prove that the Turkish effort was successful. It is simply to illustrate the difference between viewing things in terms of "comparative statics" versus the "dynamics of adjustment." The mere fact that there are offsetting reactions to a policy intervention does not mean that it was useless. The crucial questions involve the detailed, quantitative characteristics of the dynamics that result in a shift from one position to another and the new position that is achieved.

Economic analysts are now beginning to develop dynamic theories describing the adjustments and adaptations that the illegal drug industry makes to different kinds of supply-reduction efforts (e.g., Crawford et al. 1988). These analyses demand more data and produce less deterministic results than the simpler comparative statics models.

C. An Alternative Theory: The Organization of Production and Distribution

A different way to analyze the likely effects of supply reduction is to identify the particular factor of production or distribution for illicit drugs that is in long-run short supply (Moore 1979). As a matter of logic, some such factor must exist. It will be the factor that is exercising the most important constraint on the overall performance of the system. The difficulty is that we do not know what it is. Moreover, it may not remain constant over time. A certain amount of informed speculation is possible.

To supply drugs to illicit markets in the United States, certain factors of production and distribution must be combined. There must be sufficient capital to see farmers through growing periods, to buy chemicals and equipment to process and package the drugs, and to purchase land for airfields and warehouses. There must be technical knowledge about growing and processing the drugs and about smuggling them past interdiction efforts. There must be entrepreneurs willing to risk arrest or criminal attack by their colleagues, and laborers willing to engage in illegal activity for wages rather than equity. There must be enough structure and governing capacity in the illegal enterprise to insure that those who engage in the activity will be able to conduct their business without constant violence and theft and to hold onto their returns. And there must be some prospect that the dealers will be able to spend their profits.

If one considers which of these factors of production and distribution are expensive and in short supply, certain things become obvious. First, raw materials and suitable growing areas are far from limited. The total U.S. demand for illicit drugs accounts for a tiny fraction of the overall world production and can be supplied by crops grown on a very small amount of acreage. Moreover, it now seems that there are many parts of the world in which opium poppies, coca shrubs, and marijuana plants can be grown (Reuter and Kleiman 1986, pp. 306–15).

Second, there is no scarcity of human capital prepared to enter the business. Entrepreneurs have arisen in many different parts of the world. They have come from many different ethnic and class backgrounds. The supply is not limited to those with prior criminal records or with a taste for violence and corruption. Laborers and specialists are easily recruited. All that seems to matter in constructing trafficking networks is some degree of personal connection with one's associates and a desire for money (Reuter and Haaga 1987).

Third, technical knowledge and equipment are not tightly constraining. Not much technical knowledge is required for crop production or drug processing, and that which is required is relatively easy to learn. Although the chemical precursors required to process some drugs are in somewhat short supply owing to governmental restrictions, most of the necessary materials and equipment are readily available because they have legitimate as well as illicit uses. A cocaine "laboratory" is often nothing more than a set of barrels, water tubs, and hoses.

As analysts have considered which factor of production or distribution is in short supply, they have tended to come to the conclusion that what is consistently difficult about drug trafficking is the process of reliably executing large financial transactions in a crooked world with no police or courts to enforce the contracts. The importance of this problem is signaled by the importance of a "connection" in the parlance and operations of the trade. Dealers at all levels of the system constantly talk in terms of "making connections." When they have a "connection," things go well. When they do not, they are essentially out of business.

Making a connection is a difficult, somewhat haphazard process of finding others who are involved in drug dealing and persuading them that one can be trusted. The problem of making connections exists on both sides. Looking up, one must find someone with regular access to drugs. Looking down, one must find customers who buy drugs regularly and can be trusted to pay cash and not to inform. As Reuter and Haaga (1987) describe it, most of the business is the process of "brokerage."

The reason this is true, of course, is that transactions are vulnerable in a world of prohibition and active law enforcement. They are vulnerable to theft and violence by greedy business associates and to the enforcement efforts of informants, undercover operations, and electronic and physical surveillance. Protecting transactions from these vulnerabilities absorbs resources and time. That, in turn, increases the price of any given supply of drugs or reduces the volume supplied at any given price. It also gives a competitive advantage to any illegal enterprise that learns how to solve the problem of making the transactions secure by building confidence through repeated deals, or by developing a sufficient reputation for violence that it can do its own contract enforcement.

If it is correct that what is scarce in the illicit drug industry is the ability to execute transactions, then it follows that the most important supply-reduction instruments will be those that continue to exacerbate these problems (assuming that they are as easy to deploy as other instruments). Other instruments that attack other factors of production may occasionally be valuable if they can produce a large gain all of a sudden. But over the long run, the instruments that will be doing the most work in reducing the supply of drugs will be those that keep making it difficult to establish "connections" in the drug business.

IV. Assessing Strengths and Limitations of Programs

With neither empirical evidence nor proven theory to guide us, we find ourselves in what could best be called a clinical world. Government efforts are now under way to reduce the supply of drugs. These efforts are undoubtedly producing effects. We are just not sure what they are or how they could be improved. Given an understanding of the organizational vulnerabilities of drug production and distribution systems, it is nonetheless possible to advance some hypotheses about the features of current policies that are more or less effective and about what could be done to improve our overall performance.

A. The International Program

The international program has two major limitations. First, it is inevitably hostage to the interests and capabilities of source country governments. Second, it now tends to be focused primarily on crop-control strategies such as eradication and crop-substitution programs.

Of course, there are things the United States can do to increase the motivation and capacities of source country governments to control drugs. It can point to the obligations a country has under international treaties, or appeal to the country's self-interest by documenting the extent of the country's domestic drug problem, or indicate the importance the United States attaches to drug control by its willingness to sacrifice other interests. To strengthen capabilities, the United States can contribute money, equipment, technical assistance, or training. In the end, though, these efforts run up against limitations such as the inefficiency and corruption of government agencies, or the limited control of central governments over outlying areas of a country, or the reluctance of the U.S. government to elevate its drug-control objectives over other foreign-policy concerns.[19]

Moreover, even if the United States could be successful in persuading or equipping foreign countries to control crops, it would run up against the limitations of controlling crops as a supply-reduction strategy. There is no particular reason to believe that the raw materials for heroin, cocaine, or marijuana are in long-run short supply. Indeed, as noted above, all our experience and intelligence suggest that potential growing areas for these drugs are widespread and that the elimination of fields in one place will soon be replaced by cultivation elsewhere (Reuter 1985, pp. 13–16).

These limitations are sufficiently forbidding that it would probably be a mistake to rely on the international program as the primary instrument of an overall supply-reduction strategy. It simply cannot do enough work to affect prices reliably enough to merit that position. Having said this, however, there are two important contributions that the international program *can* make.

First, occasions will arise when the focus on crop controls suddenly *does* become effective in constraining the supply of drugs. This occurs when an important source country suddenly becomes highly motivated to control drugs. Then, support from the United States can produce a significant shortage. Typically, the shortage lasts no longer than a year or two as the illicit industry adjusts to the new conditions. But even so, that temporary shortage is often worth producing.

Indeed, as noted above, this is what happened in the early part of the seventies when Turkey suddenly shut down its legitimate production of opium and helped to produce a two- to three-year shortage in the supply of heroin. It seems to have occurred again in the latter part of the seventies when Mexico introduced an effective program of aerial spraying of poppy fields (Kozel 1985). The results of these successes were increased effective prices for heroin in the United States and reduced incidence and prevalence of heroin use. Keeping open such opportunities and being in a position to exploit them when they come along is an important contribution of the international drug program.

Second, the international program can contribute to supply-reduction efforts by shifting its focus from crop-control efforts to inter-

---

[19] For a powerful critique, see Nadelmann (1987*a*).

national criminal enforcement. Concretely, this means that the international program should negotiate extradition treaties with countries that now harbor traffickers and improve operational coordination between foreign and U.S. police agencies to take advantage of both extradition and of investigations and prosecutions within the host country.[20]

Such a thrust has potential for two reasons. First, an enforcement program is narrowly focused. It has none of the logistical and bureaucratic difficulties of massive crop-control programs. Second, it is targeted against a factor of production and distribution that is likely to be in long-run short supply, namely, individuals with a sufficiently well-established reputation for both reliability in successful transactions and viciousness in betrayals that they become major connections.

B. Interdiction

In recent years, the interdiction program has grown faster than any other component of the supply-reduction effort. The growth has come primarily as a result of engaging the U.S. Coast Guard and other military agencies in the pursuit of smugglers on the ocean and in the air. As table 4 indicates, this has produced large increases in the volume of seized drugs. Indeed, the best current estimate is that we are now seizing a quarter to a third of all the marijuana shipped to U.S. markets (Kleiman 1985, chap. 3). The results of this effort can be seen generally in the dramatic difference in the price of drugs that land in the United States as compared with prices offshore or in source countries, and in the recent increases in the retail price of marijuana (Reuter and Kleiman 1986).

Two main limitations hamper the ultimate effectiveness of the interdiction program. First, it is limited by its dominant focus on finished inventories of drugs rather than trafficking networks. Of course, there is much to be said for the value of drug seizures. There is undeniable, concrete satisfaction in capturing drugs that would otherwise reach illicit markets. It is also true that the seized drugs have economic value. If these drugs are eliminated, drug traffickers are deprived of valuable working capital (e.g., Stellwagen 1985).

As in the case of crop eradication, however, one must wonder

[20] For a detailed country-by-country account of the problems associated with drug supply-reduction efforts within the host country (i.e., hindered investigations and prosecutions, slow negotiations of extradition treaties), see Lupsha (1988).

whether seizing inventories has a substantial long-run impact on drug supplies. After all, we do not think of inventories of finished goods as particularly important for the future of legitimate businesses. For example, when Tylenol had to be taken off the market in response to the poisoning of the capsules, no one expected the company to go out of business, even though a month's worth of production had to be written off. It seemed far more likely that the company would continue to produce and market Tylenol, for there were still people who wanted the product and the organization still had the capacity to produce it. It is hard to understand, then, why we think it is so important when finished inventories of drugs are seized.

Moreover, the financial impact of the seizure is important only if the seized shipment represents a large fraction of the entrepreneur's total assets. But there is no particular reason to believe this. Indeed, smugglers often divide shipments precisely to hedge against the loss of their total shipment. Thus, seizures usually represent only a minor inconvenience to continued operations.

The second limitation of the interdiction program is that it is primarily focused on marijuana. A review of table 4 clearly indicates the extent to which the interdiction effort is absorbed by the flow of marijuana. It also seems clear from table 3 that interdiction efforts are relatively more important in affecting the price of marijuana than the other drugs.

The reason for the emphasis on marijuana is not that anyone intends that result. It is simply that the current interdiction efforts seem most effective against bulk shipments in noncommercial vessels. Marijuana is the drug whose sheer volume makes shipment in noncommercial vessels the most attractive option. Smugglers of heroin and cocaine have many more options—including general aviation and shipments through commercial ships and planes.[21]

The implicit focus on marijuana is shifting a little as cocaine interdiction efforts gather momentum and as the flow of cocaine has increased. But it seems unlikely that cocaine will ever replace marijuana as the drug most often seized. To the extent that marijuana is currently believed to be a high-priority drug to control, this may be counted a benefit rather than a problem. To the extent that other drugs warrant

---

[21] For an estimate of interdiction seizures by drug, see Reuter and Kleiman (1986, p. 316). The amount of marijuana seized far exceeds that of cocaine.

higher priority, however, or to the extent that one wanted flexible supply-reduction instruments that could be used for controlling several different drugs, the current interdiction program has significant disadvantages.

C. Federal Investigation

The standard criticism of the federal investigative program is that it is too far from the source of drugs to allow effective control. By this reckoning, both the international program and the interdiction program are preferred instruments because they attack the chain of production and distribution at an earlier stage than federal investigation. Moreover, the quantity of drugs seized in federal investigations seems too small for it to produce much supply reduction.

The difficulty with these criticisms is that they rely on assumptions about the best way to control the supply of drugs that have little evidence or reasoning to back them up. They emphasize physical relationships over economic relationships. A priori there is no particular reason to assume that resources are better spent nearer the source. True, if drugs are stopped earlier rather than later, they need not be worried about in the later stages. And, true, the drugs may be at their maximum concentration with respect to volume at the point where they are processed into finished products.

But neither of these points indicates that the source is the most important target to attack. As we have seen, it may be quite difficult to mount an attack at that point. Moreover, both these arguments make too much of the drugs and not enough of the entrepreneurs and firms whose continued determination and adaptability keep the drugs coming even if production runs are spoiled and inventories seized.

If the principal risks facing dealers are risks posed by enforcement agents and other criminals, then the crucial factors of production and distribution are not raw materials, technology, or warehouses but the capacity to complete transactions in this risky environment. It is with respect to transactions that the federal investigative program has distinct advantages.

The principal tactics include informants, undercover agents, and wiretap investigations. The first two attack the ability to make transactions by forcing dealers to be wary of associates, employees, and customers since any of these might become an informant or might be an undercover agent. The third makes it difficult for traffickers to communicate efficiently with associates, employees, and customers. Thus, domestic enforcement presses hard on the factors of production and distribution that seem in long-run short supply.

It is worth noting that forcing dealers to be cautious and therefore slowing transactions has value in reducing supply at all stages of production and distribution. Even at the lowest levels of distribution, such efforts have value, for they slow the recruitment of new customers and the flow of drugs to regular customers. At intermediate or high levels, each slowed transaction reduces the overall capacity of the system to supply drugs, and each trafficking network that is taken out results not only in the loss of current inventories but also of the future capacity to supply.

Moreover, it is possible that the same techniques of attacking transactions and immobilizing those networks that have developed a continuing capacity to execute transactions in a risky environment would have enormous value in the international program as well as in the domestic program. Indeed, while it cannot be assumed that foreign countries have laws and enforcement agencies that allow them to attack criminal trafficking organizations, it is primarily convention that makes us think of the international program as focused on raw materials and the domestic program as focused on trafficking networks. In principle, a criminal enforcement program could move across national boundaries. And that might hold the best chance not only for minimizing the supply of drugs to illicit markets but also for advancing the objectives of organized-crime policy as well.

D. State and Local Enforcement

The impact of the state and local enforcement program on drug-related crime is the subject of a detailed analysis by Kleiman (1986b). What is important to consider here is the impact that state and local enforcement efforts might have on broad supply-reduction objectives.

Many people believe that state and local efforts, particularly those directed at street-level dealing, are not important in reducing supplies. In their view, there are so many locations in which street-level drug dealing can occur and so many people willing to enter the business at this level that any effects of local enforcement pressure soon disappear. Even worse, this sort of activity tempts local and state police into corruption and abuses of state power and therefore should be resisted.

Recently, this thinking has been challenged by a revisionist view that sees far more value in attacks directed at street-level drug dealing—

even if one restricts one's attention to the impact that these efforts will have on supply-reduction objectives (Kleiman 1986*b*). Three points from that analysis are worth making in the context of assessing the contribution to supply-reduction objectives.

First, if it is true that the important objective of the supply-reduction strategy is to increase the effective price of drugs rather than simply the money price, then street-level enforcement is important because that program has the greatest impact of any supply-reduction instrument on the openness of drug dealing and the amount of time it will take drug users to score. The impact of international crop control, interdiction efforts, and high-level drug enforcement is generally reflected in wholesale prices of drugs and the difficulty of making wholesale transactions. They do not necessarily produce much of an impact on the ease of availability at the street level.

Street-level drug enforcement, on the other hand, forces dealers at the street level to operate more covertly. They must hide their transactions in alleyways and hallways. They must change the location of their business often. And they must screen their customers for informants and undercover agents. All this reduces the openness and accessibility of drugs on the street. To the extent that "time to score" is an important component of the effective price of drugs, street-level drug enforcement is uniquely able to increase the effective price at retail levels.

Second, street-level drug enforcement plays an important role in facilitating higher-level enforcement activities. A key to the success of high-level investigative efforts is an informant who can guide investigative efforts, interpret what the investigators are observing, introduce undercover agents, or help directly gather evidence of crimes by wearing a wire or purchasing drugs. Such informants are hard to come by. Some are recruited with monetary rewards. Some do the job for vengeance. But most do it to work off a charge that is pending against them (Wilson 1978, pp. 65–68). An important source of informants is the users and dealers who are picked up in street-level investigations.

This pool of potential informants is not necessarily a rich one. The street-level people may not know much about higher-level traffickers, or they may be terrified of revealing what they do know. But even if there is a low probability of any particular arrest producing a valuable informant, if there are enough arrests, state and local enforcement can be an important source of informants for high-level investigations. The crucial issue is not how many local arrestees turn out to be valuable informants, but rather how many informants who turn out to be valuable were initially encountered in state and local enforcement operations. Currently, we do not know the answer to this question, but it would be worth finding out.

Third, state and local enforcement may help to target higher-level investigations by alerting them to the existence of previously unknown trafficking networks. The strength of investigative agencies is their capacity to establish links among known facts and figure out how to penetrate known trafficking organizations. Their weakness is that they become narrowly targeted on the particular trafficking organizations that are their current targets. They tend to discount, even discard, information that comes their way but cannot be related to their main investigative targets. That is not a problem if the investigative agencies do, in fact, have the major trafficking organizations in their sights. But it is a problem if there are newly emerging trafficking organizations that they do not know.

In attacking something as mysterious and dynamic as the illicit drug industry, this tendency to become narrow is potentially very dangerous. There is always the chance that attention is concentrated on only a small piece of the overall supply system, and that there is a newer or better-shielded trafficking organization that has so far escaped notice. If this is true, the only way that enforcement agencies could discover this is to look in areas that are not now being closely investigated. That is an important contribution that broad, untargeted low-level enforcement agencies make to the overall supply-reduction strategy. Like pickets and patrols sent out by a main military force to maintain contact with a mysterious enemy force, police on the street help the main investigative forces stay in touch with the emergence and development of new trafficking capabilities (Moore 1987). Indeed, it was precisely through such efforts that the "pizza connection" was discovered in New York City.

V. Toward an Effective Supply-Reduction Strategy

Given the complex objectives and instruments of supply-reduction efforts, the lack of evidence or well-developed theory to guide calculations of effectiveness, and the limitations of any particular approach, it is impossible to reach a simple, definitive conclusion about the most efficient overall supply-reduction strategy. Instead, wisdom in guiding supply-reduction efforts consists of the following key recommendations.

1. *Instead of choosing one particular program as essential to supply-reduction efforts, it is better to think in terms of managing a portfolio of programs.*

The concept of a portfolio seems useful for at least three reasons

(Moore 1979). First, when not enough is known, a useful strategy is to hedge. One can and should emphasize the programs that seem most likely to be effective in reducing the supply of drugs, disrupting orga- nized-crime groups, and strengthening the political economies of our foreign allies. But because we cannot be certain that our judgment is correct about the efficacy of the other approaches, it is worth also pursuing them. It might be that a successful eradication program is right around the corner. It might be that the military could effectively seal the border. It might be that local law enforcement could produce the informants that would allow enforcement agencies to penetrate previously unknown and significant trafficking groups. Without being able to eliminate these possibilities, it is wise to keep the programs in place that create the opportunities to exploit them.

Second, investing in the portfolio of programs is probably more effective than investing the whole lot of resources in a single approach. This is true even if we hold costs of the overall effort constant and ignore the benefits that are associated with hedging against our current uncertainty. The reason is that there do seem to be some synergistic effects among the programs. The most important is that operations in source-country fields, at the border, and on city streets all help to expose drug trafficking entrepreneurs who would otherwise not be noted by investigative agencies. It also seems significant that street- level operations can have an important impact on the effective price of drugs by forcing street-level dealers to be cautious. This is an effect that cannot be produced by crop eradication, interdiction, and high- level enforcement. Synergistic effects such as these make the overall strategy more effective than the sum of its parts.

Third, the world keeps changing. The supply system changes as new drugs are created, new methods of growing and processing the drugs are invented, new routes for smuggling the drugs and laundering the profits are devised, and new entrepreneurs become involved in the business. The supply-reduction efforts change as foreign governments change, new laws are passed that facilitate or frustrate criminal investi- gations, new technologies become available to support supply- reduction efforts, and new investigative and patrol tactics emerge. Since we cannot know how the supply system will adapt in the future, or where valuable innovations will occur in the supply-reduction effort, it is probably wise for the effort to be distributed across a variety of approaches rather than concentrated in a single all-or-nothing effort that risks becoming obsolete.

Uncertainty, potential synergies, and change make it wise for society to diversify its supply-reduction effort. But to say that diversification is valuable is not quite the same thing as saying that the resources should be evenly distributed across all the programs or distributed as they now are. To determine the focus and concentration of the portfolio as well as its range, one must decide where the society should place its biggest bets.

2. *The main thrust of the diversified supply-reduction strategy should be to make it hard for drug traffickers to make connections. More specifically, the objective should be to frustrate transactions at all levels of the system and to immobilize those particular trafficking networks that develop enough experience with one another to complete transactions easily and efficiently.*

This conclusion is based on a judgment—not yet firmly established by evidence and reasoning—that the difficulty of executing transactions in the illicit industry is the principal factor constraining the supply of drugs (for any given price) over the long run, and is therefore the most valuable target for the supply-reduction strategy to attack.

If this judgment is accepted, it changes fundamentally the way that we should view and evaluate supply-reduction efforts. First, it alerts us to the fact that legal prohibition in itself, independent of any concrete enforcement efforts, contributes to supply-reduction efforts by making transactions vulnerable to theft and betrayal by other criminals.

Second, the focus on transactions shifts judgments about the relative importance of the different programs. The international efforts to control crops retain their special but occasional value. The arguments about the value of keeping pressure on street-level drug dealing also remain strong. But if the principal operational objectives of the supply-reduction strategy are to frustrate transactions and disrupt successful trafficking networks, then the investigative program moves to the position of central importance. It is drug investigations that put pressure on transactions and make it possible to disrupt and immobilize trafficking networks that become expert in completing the transactions.

Third, the focus on transactions indicates how the other programs might be improved. The international program's focus on crop control looks less important than strengthening foreign governments' capacities to pressure drug transactions and immobilize trafficking networks. Interdiction programs and state and local enforcement programs contribute less by removing drugs or disrupting open markets than by producing intelligence on heretofore unknown trafficking networks.

3. *Success in frustrating transactions and immobilizing trafficking networks depends on the development of more successful enforcement capabilities than now*

exist. That, then, requires us to strengthen current capabilities in the areas of investigation, intelligence, and patrolling, and to insure that these diverse func tions are effectively coordinated.

If the task is to frustrate transactions at all levels of the system, then it is clear that drug investigations are the key function in the supply-reduction strategy. It is the prospect that transactions will be physically observed by agents, recorded through electronic equipment, or infiltrated by informants or undercover agents that is the government's contribution to the difficulty of making transactions.

If the objective is also to immobilize those trafficking networks that have become particularly effective in executing transactions, then the general increase in investigative activity must also be able to disrupt the trafficking networks that have become most effective. That means that the investigators must be able to determine who the traffickers are and develop evidence against them. To do this effectively requires much greater investigative capabilities than now exist and much greater coordination among the investigators, the intelligence analysts, and those involved in broader, less focused enforcement activities along the border, on city streets, and in foreign drug-growing areas.

With respect to the investigative function, two new capabilities must be developed. First, the international program has to raise the priority now given to strengthening international investigative efforts. Second, it is important that investigative agencies be prepared to undertake the sophisticated investigations that expose trafficking networks to criminal liabilities associated with conspiracy laws, violations of banking and tax laws, and anti-organized-crime statutes such as the Racketeering Influenced and Corrupt Organizations (RICO) laws. Such approaches are proving to be quite effective in prosecuting individuals and crippling networks (Lynch 1987; U.S. Senate Permanent Sub-committee on Investigations 1988). But they demand a great deal from investigative agencies and prosecutors.

The challenges are partly technical. Electronic surveillance is often essential and requires a high degree of technical sophistication. Financial investigations are also extremely valuable not only to identify silent partners but also to expose traffickers to additional penalties through the use of forfeiture statutes that will take from convicted traffickers money, vehicles, and other property used to carry out their illegal enterprise (Fried 1988). These, too, require special training.

Another part of the challenge, however, is not so much technique as style and attitude. These elaborate investigations require patience, a patience that extends to allowing dealers to continue to operate even though enough evidence has already been gathered to make the arrests. They also require agents to pass over good arrests that could be made now for uncertain but more important cases later. The hope that other defendants might become visible and indictable if one continues the investigation is not always realized. The targets of the investigation may discover the investigation and flee before they can be arrested.

Finally, these cases depend on elaborate accounts of ongoing activities and relationships revealed through patterns of events rather than single events. Even though such accounts constitute a more accurate description of what has been done that is both problematic to the society and illegal, it requires a real knack for analysis and inference to make such stories plausible. It is much easier to plunk a bag of powder down on the evidence table, testify that it was in the possession of the defendants, and leave it at that. Patience, a willingness to take current risks for uncertain future gain, and careful thought are required of investigators and prosecutors. These qualities are not always in plentiful supply in action-oriented enforcement agencies (Wilson 1978).

To support these investigative efforts, it is also important that the operational intelligence capabilities of investigative agencies be developed. By operational intelligence, I mean the capacity of international, national, state, and local enforcement agencies to use their past investigative efforts and their current access to informants to identify trafficking networks that are emerging as unusually efficient suppliers of drugs. For the most part, improvements in this area do not require more intelligence *collection*. The agents and their informants, if induced to divulge what they know and think about it, have a great deal of information. In essence, it is the intelligence *analysis* function that must be improved. If improved, it will help to support the sophisticated investigations described above.

There is one further reason to be interested in improving the quality of the intelligence function at all levels of the enforcement system. It has to do with being able to keep informants productive. One of the sad ironies of drug law enforcement is that the agencies must often rely on drug dealers to help them make cases against other drug dealers. That makes sense if the drug dealers who are acting as informants are less active and less dangerous than those on whom they are informing. But there is no guarantee that this is true. Moreover, there are some reasons, other than corruption, for enforcement agencies to want to avoid looking too closely at this problem. After all, if an informant is helping an agent make cases, that makes the agent and his agency look good.

The fact that the informant might be systematically misleading the agency and focusing their attention on relatively unimportant traffickers is unwelcome. The only way to guard against such problems is to have as accurate information as one can get on both the informant and the investigative targets and to have someone other than the case agent monitoring the situation. That function is something that good intelligence analysis, carried out by a separate organizational unit, could supply.

To wring the maximum advantage from investigative efforts, coordination between the investigative capabilities and the broader "patrol functions" carried out by the interdiction program, the local enforcement effort, and the source country enforcement efforts must be improved. I describe these efforts as "patrol" efforts precisely because they are not focused on particular trafficking networks. Instead, they attack drugs when they become visible in foreign drug markets, along the borders, and on the streets. They attack what is visible in these locations. This relatively unfocused enforcement effort is a crucially important complement to the investigative and intelligence functions for two reasons.

First, the patrol function produces a general deterrent effect on drug trafficking. Its persistent vigilance forces caution at all levels of drug distribution. Its more or less random quality means that no transaction, shipment, or trafficking organization is ever entirely secure. Slight mistakes can be discovered and exploited by a large, observant patrol function.

Second, the patrol function, if properly executed and integrated into the investigative effort, can insure that the investigative function is properly targeted on the most important drug trafficking networks. As noted above, the strength of the investigative function is its ability to focus on known trafficking networks. If the supply system is dynamic in that new groups are always arising, then the strength of the investigative function becomes its weakness. Its tendency to narrow its focus and concentrate on known traffickers prevents it from noticing the emergence of new trafficking groups. The best way to counteract that tendency is to have some portion of the supply-reduction strategy remain in intimate contact with the markets for the drugs where they come into the open. That typically occurs overseas as drugs are being grown and collected for processing, along the border as special attention becomes focused on movements of people and goods, and on the streets as dealers search for customers. It is in those places that the police can find the threads that lead back to new, unsuspected trafficking networks, and correct the focus of investigative efforts.

Note that a key feature of the scanning function is that it not be too specifically targeted. If it is narrowly focused to increase the chance of arrests, its efficiency in making cases and removing drugs might be enhanced, but its crucial role in providing a general deterrent and a check on investigative efforts would be lost. The supply-reduction strategy as a whole would be weakened by becoming too narrowly targeted on trafficking networks that were assumed but not definitively known to be the most important.

4. *Since the current strategy is based on bets and gambles, it is vital that capacities be improved for measuring not only the impact of the supply-reduction effort but also its own operations. Without such measurements that provide evidence about what works and what does not, there is no prospect for improving either our knowledge or our performance.*

The key to improving measurement is to spend more money to take the measurements. It is absurd to spend $750 million on federal supply-reduction efforts and begrudge $10 million to measure the effective prices of drugs in illicit markets in the United States, to analyze growing conditions in host countries, and to produce responsible estimates of supplies reaching the United States. But it is also essential that the measurements be audited by people who have no stake in the success of the strategy to insure that they are accurate numbers. And, it is important that there be some mechanism for resolving interagency disputes about the numbers and their implications.

A useful model might be the establishment of the National Defense Intelligence Board after the Second World War that assumed the responsibility for reconciling conflicting estimates of Soviet intentions and capabilities. Over time, this agency, with its complement of academic outsiders, dramatically improved both the quality of the estimates made and the underlying data. So far, informal arrangements among the drug-law-enforcement agencies have failed to produce even a coherent language and concept, much less an analysis, of supply-reduction efforts based on solidly established measurement systems.

These observations and judgments lead to some obvious implications for the important academic research that must be conducted in this area. Probably the most important study would be one that attempted to draw together a variety of sources and give as accurate a report as possible about the dynamics of the illicit supply system over the last twenty-five to thirty years. A great deal of experience has accumulated over that period. There are also some good historical sources. If the agencies could be induced to open their files for a historical study, we would learn a great deal more than we now know about the structure of the illicit supply systems and how they react to supply-reduction efforts.

It would also be extremely valuable to do more detailed analytic and modeling work than has so far been attempted. A great deal more can be done to describe and analyze the industrial organization of the illicit drug industry. And simulation models might tell us a great deal about the likely efficacy of supply-side interventions.

Finally, it would be important to see whether any relation can be established between the effective prices of various drugs and the incidence and prevalence of use. The few pieces of evidence now available on this subject are remarkably thin, given the importance of this assumed relationship as a justification for supply-reduction efforts. Obviously, this study cannot be done until we develop improved measures of price and consumption and allow them to be recorded long enough to develop variation for us to analyze.

The more one thinks about and analyzes supply-reduction efforts, the more one realizes that our efforts in this domain are guided by hopes and intuitions rather than by facts and analysis. It is essential that our society invest in an analysis that can underwrite and guide a federal effort, the annual costs of which now exceed $1 billion. What is now available is simply not enough to satisfy any reasonably demanding investor such as a U.S. citizen.

REFERENCES

Argyris, Chris, and Donald A. Schon. 1978. *Organizational Learning: A Theory of Action Perspective.* Reading, Mass.: Addison-Wesley.

Bartels, John. 1975. "Testimony before Select Committee on Narcotics, Washington, D.C." Mimeographed, in author's possession.

Bodshaw, Gerald, Ross Koppel, and Russell Pancoast. 1987. *Anti-Drug Law Enforcement Efforts and Their Impact.* Balla Cynwyd, Penn.: Wharton Econometrics.

Boyum, David. 1989. "A Second Look at Drug Supply Reduction Effectiveness: New Methods and Applications." Working paper. Program in Criminal Justice Policy and Management. Cambridge, Mass.: Harvard University, John F. Kennedy School of Government.

Brace, Paul K., Robert Elkin, Daniel Robinson, and Harold I. Steinberg. 1980. *Reporting of Service Efforts and Accomplishments*. Stamford, Conn.: Peat, Marwick, Mitchell & Co.

Bruun, Kettil, Lynn Pan, and Ingemar Rexed. 1975. *The Gentlemen's Club: International Control of Drugs and Alcohol*. Chicago: University of Chicago Press.

Bureau of International Narcotics Matters. 1988. *International Narcotics Control Strategy Report*. Washington, D.C.: U.S. Department of State.

Cook, Philip J. 1988. Personal correspondence with author, December 6.

Craig, Richard. 1987. "Illicit Drug Traffic: Implications for South American Source Countries." Paper presented at the Conference on International Drugs: Threat and Response, Defense Intelligence College, Washington, D.C., June.

Crawford, Gordon B., Peter Reuter, Karen Isaacson, and Patrick Murphy. 1988. *Simulation of Adaptive Response*. Santa Monica, Calif.: Rand.

Drug Topics Redbook. 1988. Oradell, N.J.: Medical Economics Co.

Federal Bureau of Investigation. 1973–87. *Uniform Crime Reports for the United States*. U.S. Department of Justice. Washington, D.C.: U.S. Government Printing Office.

Flanagan, Timothy J., David J. van Alstyne, and Michael R. Gottfredson, eds. 1982. *Sourcebook of Criminal Justice Statistics—1981*. U.S. Department of Justice, Bureau of Justice Statistics. Washington, D.C.: U.S. Government Printing Office.

Flanagan, Timothy J., and Katherine M. Jamieson, eds. 1988. *Sourcebook of Criminal Justice Statistics—1987*. U.S. Department of Justice, Bureau of Justice Statistics. Washington, D.C.: U.S. Government Printing Office.

Fried, David J. 1988. "Rationalizing Criminal Forfeiture." *Journal of Criminal Law and Criminology* 72:328–436.

General Accounting Office. 1983. *Federal Drug Interdiction Efforts Need Strong Control Oversight*. Washington, D.C.: General Accounting Office.

Harris, Jeffrey E. 1987. "The 1983 Increase in the Federal Cigarette Excise Tax." In *Tax Policy and the Economy*, edited by L. H. Summers. Cambridge, Mass.: MIT Press.

Johnson, Bruce D., Paul Goldstein, Edward Preble, James Schmeidler, Douglas Lipton, Barry Spunt, and Thomas Miller. 1985. *Taking Care of Business: The Economics of Crime by Heroin Abusers*. Lexington, Mass.: Heath.

Kleiman, Mark A. R. 1985. "Allocating Federal Drug Enforcement Resources: The Case of Marijuana." Ph.D. dissertation, Harvard University.

———. 1986a. "Data and Analysis Requirements for Policy toward Drug Enforcement and Organized Crime." In *America's Habit: Drug Abuse, Drug Trafficking, and Organized Crime Control*, edited by the President's Commission on Organized Crime. Washington, D.C.: U.S. Government Printing Office.

———. 1986b. "Bringing Back Street-Level Heroin Enforcement." Working Paper no. 86-01-08. Program in Criminal Justice Policy and Management.

Cambridge, Mass.. Harvard University, John F. Kennedy School of Government.

Kleiman, Mark A. R., and K. D. Smith. In this volume. "State and Local Drug Enforcement: In Search of a Strategy."

Kozel, Nicholas J. 1985. *Epidemiology of Heroin: 1964–84.* Rockville, Md.: U.S. Department of Health and Human Services, National Institute on Drug Abuse.

Kozel, Nicholas J., and Edgar H. Adams, eds. 1985. *Cocaine Use in America: Epidemiologic and Clinical Perspectives.* Rockville, Md.: U.S. Department of Health and Human Services, National Institute on Drug Abuse.

Lupsha, Peter A. 1988. "Drug Trafficking Policy and Politics: The United States and Latin America." Albuquerque: University of New Mexico, Department of Political Science.

Lynch, Gerald E. 1987. "The Crime of Being a Criminal." *Columbia Law Review* 87(4):661–764; (5):920–84.

McCoy, Alfred W. 1973. *The Politics of Heroin in Southeast Asia.* New York: Harper & Row.

Marx, Gary. 1988. *Undercover Policing.* Berkeley and Los Angeles: University of California Press.

Mazmanian, Daniel, and Paul Sabatier. 1983. *Implementation and Public Policy.* Glenview, Ill.: Scott, Foresman.

Mills, James. 1986. *Underground Empire.* New York: Doubleday.

Misket, T. C., and F. Vakil. 1972. "Some Estimates of Price and Expenditure Elasticities among UCLA Students." *Review of Economics and Statistics* 54:474–75.

Moore, Mark H. 1973. "Achieving Discrimination on the Effective Price of Heroin." *American Economic Review* 63(2):270–77.

———. 1976. *Buy and Bust: The Effective Regulation of an Illicit Market in Heroin.* Lexington, Mass.: Heath.

———. 1979. "Limiting Supplies of Drugs to Illicit Markets in the United States." *Journal of Drug Issues* 9:291–308.

———. 1983. "Invisible Offenses." In *Abscam Ethics,* edited by Gerald Caplan. Washington, D.C.: Police Foundation.

———. 1986. "Drug Policy and Organized Crime." In *America's Habit: Drug Abuse, Drug Trafficking, and Organized Crime,* edited by the President's Commission on Organized Crime. Washington, D.C.: U.S. Government Printing Office.

———. 1987. "International Narcotics and the U.S. Supply Reduction Strategy." Paper presented at the Conference on International Drugs: Threat and Response, Defense Intelligence College, Washington, D.C., June.

Nadelmann, Ethan A. 1987a. "Cops across Borders: Transnational Crime and International Law Enforcement." Ph.D. dissertation, Harvard University, Department of Government.

———. 1987b. "International Narcotics Control Strategy Report." Working Paper no. 87-01-10. Program in Criminal Justice Policy and Management. Cambridge, Mass.: Harvard University, John F. Kennedy School of Government.

———. 1988a. "The Case for Legalization." *Public Interest* 92(Summer):32–50.

———. 1988*b*. "U.S. Drug Policy: A Bad Export." *Foreign Policy* 70:89–105.

National Institute on Drug Abuse. 1983. *National Household Survey on Drug Abuse: Summary of Selected Findings 1982*. U.S. Department of Health and Human Services. Washington, D.C.: U.S. Government Printing Office.

———. 1987. *National Household Survey on Drug Abuse: Population Estimates 1985*. U.S. Department of Health and Human Services. Washington, D.C.: U.S. Government Printing Office.

———. 1988. *National Household Survey on Drug Abuse: Main Findings 1985*. U.S. Department of Health and Human Services. Washington, D.C.: U.S. Government Printing Office.

National Narcotics Intelligence Consumers Committee. 1987. *The NNICC Report, 1985–86: The Supply of Illicit Drugs to the United States from Foreign and Domestic Sources in 1985 and 1986*. Washington, D.C.: National Narcotics Intelligence Consumers Committee.

Nicholson, Walter. 1985. *Microeconomic Theory*. 3d ed. Chicago: Dryden.

Nyswander, Marie. 1956. *The Drug Addict as Patient*. New York: Grune & Stratton.

Reuter, Peter. 1985. "Eternal Hope: America's International Narcotics Efforts." *Public Interest* 79(Spring):13–94.

———. 1988. "Can the Borders Be Sealed?" *Public Interest* 92(Summer):51–65.

Reuter, Peter, and John Haaga. 1987. *The Organization of High Level Drug Markets: An Exploratory Study*. Santa Monica, Calif.: Rand.

Reuter, Peter, and Mark A. R. Kleiman. 1986. "Risks and Prices." In *Crime and Justice: An Annual Review of Research*, vol. 7, edited by Michael Tonry and Norval Morris. Chicago: University of Chicago Press.

Samuelson, Paul A. 1983. *Foundations of Economic Analysis*. Cambridge, Mass.: Harvard University Press.

Schelling, Thomas C. 1980. "Economics and Criminal Enterprise." In *The Economics of Crime*, edited by Ralph Andreano and John J. Siegfried. Cambridge, Mass.: Schenckman.

Select Committee on Crime, U.S. House of Representatives. 1970. "Crime in America—Heroin Importation, Distribution, Packaging and Paraphernalia." Hearings before the Select Committee on Crime, U.S. House of Representatives, 91st Congress, New York, June 25, 26, 27, 29, and 30.

———. 1971. "Narcotics Research, Rehabilitation and Treatment." Hearings before the Select Committee on Crime, U.S. House of Representatives, 92d Congress, Washington, D.C., April 26, 27, and 28.

Shenon, Philip. 1988. "Enemy Within: Drug Money Is Corrupting the Enforcers." *New York Times* (April 11, eastern ed.).

Siegel, Max H. 1978. "U.S. Indictments Tell of Swimmers and Ships and Murder for Cocaine." *New York Times* (March 21, eastern ed.).

Stellwagen, Lindsey D. 1985. "Use of Forfeiture Sanctions in Drug Cases. *Research in Brief*. Washington, D.C.: U.S. Department of Justice, National Institute of Justice.

U.S. Department of Justice. 1986. *Report of the Drug Policy Review Board*. Washington, D.C.: U.S. Department of Justice.

U.S. Senate Permanent Sub-committee on Investigations. 1988. *Organized*

Crime 25 Years after Valachi. Washington, D.C.: U.S. Government Printing Office.

Vaillant, George E. 1969. "The Natural History of Urban Narcotic Drug Addiction." In *The Scientific Basis of Drug Dependence,* edited by Hannah Steinberg. New York: Grune & Stratton.

Wildavsky, Aaron, and Jeffrey Pressman. 1984. *Implementation.* Berkeley and Los Angeles: University of California Press.

Wilson, James Q. 1978. *The Investigators.* New York: Basic.

————. In this volume. "Drugs and Crime."

Wisotsky, Steven. 1983. "Exposing the War on Cocaine: The Futility and Destructiveness of Prohibition." *University of Wisconsin Law Review,* pp. 1305–1426.

Dana E. Hunt

Drugs and Consensual Crimes: Drug Dealing and Prostitution

ABSTRACT

Ethnographic field research has provided important qualitative data on the relation between drugs and consensual crimes, such as drug dealing and prostitution. Dealers often share background characteristics with their clients. Drug use varies from none to daily among dealers, but the proportion of dealers who use the drugs they sell is difficult to assess. Drug-dealing organization varies greatly in its structural complexity; acceptance into dealing groups often depends on situational factors, familiarity, and financial resources. Research findings indicate that more than half of street prostitutes are drug users. Prostitutes who are heavy drug users often engage in crime to help support their habit.

The relations between drugs and crime have been a consistent theme in both the research and popular literatures of this country for almost a century. Several findings have emerged. Persons who abuse drugs, particularly expensive drugs such as heroin and cocaine, are more likely than nonusers to be involved in a lifestyle that includes a great variety of illegal activities, from property offenses to confidence games and prostitution. However, the majority of drug users in this country—an estimated 25 million people each month (National Institute on Drug Abuse 1987)—are not involved in these crimes. In most cases, drug use does not cause the user to become involved in crime. Drug use and consensual crimes are complexly intertwined, but there is no invariant sequence of which precedes which.

In this essay, I deal with a subset of the user population, the criminally involved substance abuser, the person who frequently uses illicit

Dana E. Hunt is senior analyst with Abt Associates, Inc., Cambridge, Massachusetts.

substances and is concurrently involved in other illicit activities. They are the same persons addressed in Chaiken and Chaiken (in this volume). Both essays examine the tangled relation between drug use and crime in the population that is involved in both.

I concentrate on drug dealing and prostitution, *consensual crimes* in which the victim is a willing participant in the offense. A variety of data sources are considered—surveys, Drug Enforcement Administration (DEA) and police reports, and ethnographic studies of the drug world. In general, these are studies of "accessible populations," which are unlikely to be representative of all addicts and offenders. Both drug users and offenders are hidden populations; portions of both are inaccessible to research, and truly random samples are beyond the reach of most studies. Moreover, the few doors of ready access often lead to skewed populations. Access is possible to incarcerated populations, for example, but this sampling approach omits both users not involved in crime and the more successful addict offenders who have not yet been caught. Drug-treatment programs or hospitals provide handy "patient" populations, but samples from them overlook the broad range of addicts and addict offenders not currently seeking treatment. Finally, samples of drug users are reached through field studies that enter the milieu of the drug world where researchers study small specialized groups of users through observation and interview.

Because of the hidden nature of drug dealing and prostitution, and the low ratio of apprehension to commission, combinations of data sources often provide the most accurate picture of the nature and extent of the crimes. Qualitative or ethnographic data, for example, provide detail on the structure of the crime not readily apparent from statistical analysis alone. In this essay, I draw more heavily on qualitative sources than on the quantitative analyses discussed in the Chaiken and Chaiken essay (in this volume) so that together the essays draw a more complete picture of the relation between drug use and these crimes than does either alone.

Information collected by ethnographic research provides an important data source for this essay. Ethnographic methods and an overview of the relevant ethnographic studies are presented in Section I. Sections II and III look at the extent of drug dealing, the characteristics of dealers, and the relation of drug use to dealing. Section IV discusses the social organization of street dealing. Section V provides a discussion of the extent of drug-related prostitution and the role that drugs may play in that crime. The last section provides a summary and suggests future research needs.

I. Methods. Use of Ethnographic Data

The criminology literature is rich in ethnographic data on the crimes of drug users, including observations of prostitution in the first part of this century (see Woolston 1921; Dai 1970), characterizations of the drug trade in the 1950s and 1960s (Preble and Casey 1969), studies of the professional thief and the stolen merchandise trade in the 1970s (Chambliss 1972; Klockars 1974), and studies of crack dealing in the 1980s (Johnson, Hamid, and Morales 1987; Mieczkowski 1989). The term "qualitative methods" incorporates an enormous range of techniques and is part of a long-standing research tradition in sociology and anthropology. In the 1930s, sociologists at the University of Chicago employed them to study a variety of inner-city problems—the hobo, the delinquent, and the gang (Thrasher 1926; Shaw and McKay 1942; Shaw 1966). In the 1950s, anthropologist Erving Goffman used ground-breaking qualitative methods to analyze the structure of institutions (Goffman 1961), and sociologists soon extended the approach to a variety of criminal activities (Finestone 1958; Becker 1963; Petersen and Truzzi 1972).

More recently the term "ethnography" has been used to describe the analysis of behaviors of individuals or groups using the definitions or "worldview" of these groups rather than any external cultural definition; that is, the analysis is done within the framework of the "knowledge and beliefs that generate and interpret those behaviors" (Walters 1980, p. 17). To summarize briefly, ethnographic studies use methods of intensive field observation and interviews to gather data in the natural setting of the behaviors under study from what is generally a nonrandomly selected, purposive or snowball sample (Biernacki and Waldorf 1981). These methods can generate many different kinds of data within a single investigation: case studies, structured interview data, systematic field observations (i.e., drug deals within a time/space frame), film or photographic records, archival or historical data, and testimonials. Diverse sources are then combined with demographic, socioeconomic, and even individual psychological or medical data (Walters 1980) to produce the analysis, which in the best studies can also include a rigorous quantitative component.

The ethnographic approach is particularly useful in the investigation of new phenomena of which little is known or when appropriate measurements are unspecified, in the detection and analysis of changing phenomena, and in the examination of hidden or officially unrecorded behaviors or events. However, it also has major limitations as a research tool. First, both by virtue of the design and size, the samples are not generalizable to the population of interest. Second, because the studies occur in natural settings, the control that is desirable for rigorous hypothesis testing is also often not possible. Therefore, these methods are not to be used to make causal inferences from the street scene, but rather to detect "patterns; that is, meaningful correlations in real life social contexts" (Walters 1980, p. 19).

Throughout this essay, there is a heavy reliance on ethnographic data. Because consensual crimes involve the active participation (if not enthusiasm) of both the offender (the seller of drugs or sex) and the "victim" (the buyer), the offense is seldom reported. Street dealers are busted, illegal laboratories are discovered, and smugglers are caught at the border. Prostitutes are picked up in sweeps to clean up the streets. However, the ratio of these occurrences to the actual volume of the crimes committed is small; consequently, as with much of our current information about interactions between drug use and criminality, what we know about the world of drug dealing or prostitution often comes from unusual sources.

Examples of ethnographic research methods and combinations of qualitative and quantitative methods are found throughout this essay. In order to explain their methods more clearly and to eliminate repetition of research descriptions throughout the essay, in the next few pages I briefly describe some of the most frequently cited research projects. All of these studies combine the variety of tools used in ethnographic work—interview, detailed field reporting, and observation.

Narcotic and Drug Research, Inc. (NDRI), a research group operating in conjunction with the New York State Division of Substance Abuse Services, has a long tradition of ethnographic research beginning with the works of the late anthropologist Edward Preble (Preble and Casey 1969). For over fifteen years NDRI has operated a series of store fronts in sections of New York City from which indigenous workers (generally ex-addicts) identify and recruit drug users for various studies. The research operations are known on the street as trustworthy sources of conversation, coffee, money, and sometimes shelter. In a study of economic behavior of street addicts (Johnson et al. 1985) cited throughout this article, two store fronts in East and Central Harlem, an area heavily populated with drug users and sellers, were maintained and staffed with ex-addicts and professional staff to study the day-to-day economic activities of heroin addicts. Addicts were obtained through snowball sampling (using information provided by one interviewee to locate others) and street surveys of the area. The interviewees reported on a regularly scheduled basis to the store front for an initial life history interview, which was updated weekly with their activities, sources of income, and drug use. These interviews were supplemented by observations in the neighboring areas, and by informal interviews and discussions with other persons in the neighborhood. Interview data were analyzed in a format that allowed examination of days per month in which the individual was actively using drugs, actively committing crimes, or both. Observational data, and transcribed data from field notes and informal conversations, provided important contextual information for the analysis of each respondent's daily activities. A total sample of 201 heroin users provided 11,417 person-days of data over a three-year period.

Other work by members of this group at NDRI (Wish and Johnson 1986; Johnson, Hamid, and Morales 1987) is also discussed. Wish and colleagues, operating out of the NDRI store front, conducted a series of studies on the time period around the commission of a crime and drug use. Through street outreach, they identified persons who had committed a crime within forty-eight hours prior to being interviewed about the circumstances of the crime and their drug use. Field data were used to substantiate stories and details of the crime given, and urine screens were conducted to verify reported drug use.

The research group of the Division of Substance Abuse Services, working in close association with NDRI, has operated a street research unit in New York City for almost ten years. The street unit is a full-time team of male and female ex-addicts who daily observe the drug scene in the city. They report daily on changes in drug price, purity, and availability and carry out a wide variety of special state research projects related to substance abuse. For example, the unit has reported on the growth and development of the crack trade, systematically observed cocaine dealers and runners on Wall Street, and detailed the use of video parlors in drug distribution. Their results are published in regular reports to the state (Street Studies Unit 1986, 1987) as well as in professional journals (Des Jarlais, Friedman, and Hopkins 1985).

Inciardi (1986, pp. 115–74) and colleagues conducted a series of interview studies with heroin and cocaine users in Dade County,

Florida, from 1977 to 1985, which are also extensively cited here. For comparison, additional samples of informants were interviewed during this time in three other cities, bringing the total number of face-to-face interviews to over 3,000. The subjects consisted of persons contacted through detention centers and outpatient drug-treatment programs, during a period when two-thirds of them were actively using drugs and committing crimes in their communities. They were located through snowball sampling from one user to others in communities in which the field interviewers were known and trusted. Field data from observations in the area and conversations with other informants provided additional sources of information.

My colleagues and I (Hunt, Lipton, and Spunt 1984; Hunt et al. 1985; Hunt, Spunt, and Lipton 1985) conducted a study of methadone clients and addicts not in treatment in four cities in New York, New Jersey, and Connecticut from 1980–83 (TRISEP). These data are cited throughout this essay. Project data were derived from several sources: two structured interviews with a sample of 368 methadone clients drawn randomly from program rosters and 142 narcotics addicts not in treatment developed from snowball sampling and indigenous worker contacts, informal interviews and taped conversations with drug users in the area, formal interviews with treatment-program staff, many months of structured and unstructured field observation at each site recorded weekly and transcribed for analysis, state drug-abuse data, and journals or logs kept by both professional staff and indigenous workers. Each city area was mapped for drug-dealing areas, hangouts, and similar features, and observations concentrated on those areas where drug users congregated and did business. All data (with the exception of workers' journals) were computerized for analysis. A simple coding scheme allowed thousands of pages of transcribed material to be easily retrieved by topic. Transcribed material from this project is referred to in its coded, unpublished form throughout this essay (Hunt et al. 1985).

Adler's (1985) work on mid- to upper-level drug dealers in Southern California took a different approach. After preliminary work as a graduate student on drug dealing in the San Diego area, Adler became friendly with a group of marijuana and cocaine dealers operating there and in the Los Angeles area in the early 1980s. Identifying herself as a researcher and gradually gaining their confidence, she was able to live among and interview a sample of dealers, observing first-hand their operations, parties, and daily lives. Her study consists of intensive taped interviews with a sample of twenty-four dealers, and observations of sixty-five others in the dealing network. An aggressive research strategy of active participant observation over a period of six years in which the researcher became friends and even a helper (e.g., she posted bail) to respondents produced case-study-level data on a small sample of persons that resulted in a detailed picture of their dealing activities and connections over a period of years.

Finally, Rosenbaum's (1981) work on prostitution is reported in Section V. Rosenbaum's sample consisted of 100 active women addicts identified by posting notices in treatment facilities, in "copping" (buying) areas, and in detention centers. A series of intensive (two to three hours) interviews were conducted with these women in their homes, in project offices, and on the street, focusing on their drug-using careers. In addition, fieldwork in high-drug-use areas, shooting galleries, and community treatment facilities provide contextual detail.

The studies described are only a few of the many research projects in the drug literature on drugs and crime that combine qualitative and quantitative techniques. While often limited in their ability to generalize insights, they provide invaluable information about the world of the substance abuser.

II. The Extent of Dealing and Characteristics of Dealers

The extent of drug dealing is very difficult to measure with existing data. However, some estimates using official data are reported here. Depending on their position in the distribution scheme, dealers may be drug users or ex–drug addicts, and their characteristics also vary considerably from area to area.

A. The Extent of Drug Dealing

The quality is good because I know down 163rd St. by the old court house you get coke two bags for $15. Usually, coke was $10 a bag, but now you can get it for $9. When people hears it's two for $15, they go down to get what they need. You figure you can get four for $30 so you can get eight for $60. You go uptown, you can make ten or twenty bucks for yourself.

Most people have been sitting across the street because there is trees there and the shade. It's shady there and there is a dice game once in a while. . . . I have been going down with Jake just to see what's goin' on and it's business as usual. [Hunt et al. 1985]

These two separate quotes, from studies of drug users in four north-eastern cities (Hunt, Lipton, and Spunt 1984; Hunt et al. 1986), reveal two important aspects of the street-drug trade. Buying and selling drugs, or "taking care of business" (Preble and Casey 1969), is both a hustling, money-making enterprise and an intrinsic part of the social life of some drug abusers. Most frequent drug abusers have at some point dealt, sold, or distributed drugs; far fewer support themselves through dealing. The street-level, highly visible "drug pusher" is often this user, selling relatively small amounts from a capital outlay or on consignment for a larger-scale operator. He or she may, as in the first case, seize the opportunity of low prices to get his or her own supply and "make ten or twenty bucks" at the same time. Dealing a little, talking with others, playing dice or cards also constitute "business as usual" in drug-dealing areas, areas that can vary from burned-out apartments in the South Bronx from which cocaine is dealt, to the relaxed New Jersey park described above in the second quote, and even to high-rise office buildings. Methods and organization change depending on the drug dealt, the area of the country, and the characteristics of the users. The "dealer," however, is an enduring part of the drug world, the "day laborer" (Preble and Casey 1969) in a business that has very few heavy users at the top and an ever-changing agglomeration of amateurs and professionals at the bottom. It is also violent "business," because violence is used on the street level to maintain reputation or control and on the upper levels of drug distribution to maintain markets or organization.

Drug dealing is perhaps the most pervasive and enduring crime in the drug world. It is the behavior least responsive to changing levels of use and the economic behavior with the most lasting value for both current and ex–drug abusers (Anglin and Speckart 1986). At some time in their drug careers, persons at almost all levels of drug use distribute drugs; that is, sell or share them. Occasional drug users may distribute small amounts as a part of sharing drugs or obtaining them for their own use and often do not classify their activities as dealing or selling. Among serious drug abusers, "becoming an occasional dealer is almost an inevitable consequence of becoming a competent regular user" (Faupel and Klockars 1987, p. 60). Dealing, for a variety of reasons, may in fact be *the* preferred method of making money among serious drug users (Goldman 1981; Goldstein 1981).

While we know drug dealing is widespread, the true extent is difficult to estimate. Two sources can be used for extrapolation: official records of drug arrests and self-report data from active drug dealers. Both sources have limitations. Official records such as Uniform Crime Report (UCR) arrest data represent only those dealers who are caught rather than the number of persons committing the crimes (Federal Bureau of Investigation 1987). Some addicts report that they commit hundreds, even thousands, of drug transactions each year with few resultant arrests (Ball, Shaffer, and Nurco 1983; Johnson et al. 1985; Inciardi 1986). Official arrest data is also biased toward both the visible street-level dealer and, to some degree, the less successful or less careful offender, for example, one who is intoxicated and more easily apprehended. Finally, jurisdictions also vary as to the rigor with which they pursue dealers of particular drugs, resulting in additional time- and area-specific biases in these data.

Self-report data of active users also introduce bias in estimating the extent of dealing. Generally, these studies are examining the most active users and dealers, often persons in treatment or incarceration. This population provides a look at the high-frequency end of the dealing trade but does not represent the occasional user or dealer whose drugs and crime involvement has not put him or her in touch with these agencies.

Given these caveats, I cautiously offer some numbers on drug dealing. Uniform Crime Report (UCR) data and Bureau of Justice Statistics data[1] show that drug-abuse arrests constituted about 7 percent of the total crimes reported to UCR in 1986 (Federal Bureau of Investigation 1987), a 30 percent increase over the 1982 levels (table 1). Recent data from the Drug Use Forecasting (DUF) system indicate that an even more substantial portion of all arrests are for drug law violations (National Institute of Justice 1988). Drug Use Forecasting is a program established by the National Institute of Justice in 1987 to track drug-use trends in arrestees and is now operating in twenty-one cities. Samples of male and female arrestees are tested for the presence of drugs in their urine and interviewed while in lockup. Drug Use Forecasting

---

[1] Even though federal, state, and local agencies are responsible for the enforcement of drug laws, most enforcement is done at the state and local level. Federal drug offenses reported in the Chaiken and McDonald (1988) report for the Bureau of Justice Statistics consist primarily of manufacture and international or interstate trafficking. Arrests for drug law violations reported to the UCR are defined as violations of state and federal drug laws, i.e., possession of controlled substances or drug paraphernalia (where this constitutes a violation), manufacture or distribution of controlled substances, and smuggling. Many jurisdictions allow possession of small amounts of drugs without incurring a felony charge, although possession of large quantities of drugs is, by definition, generally seen as intent to distribute.

TABLE 1
Drug Abuse Violation Arrests and Prostitution Arrests, Total and by Sex, 1982 and 1986

	Male			Female			Total		
	1982	1986	Change (Percent)	1982	1986	Change (Percent)	1982	1986	Change (Percent)
Drug abuse violations*	424,253	546,293	+28.8	67,243	92,664	+37.8	491,496	638,957	+30.0
Total (percent)	6	7	...	5	6	...	6	7	...
Prostitution and commercialized vice†	26,392	31,883	+20.8	67,243	60,364	−10.2	93,635	92,247	−1.5
Total (percent)	...‡	...‡	...	5	4	...	1	1	...
Total all crimes	7,244,900	7,623,244	+5.2	1,414,064	1,604,298	+13.5	8,658,964	9,227,542	+6.6

SOURCE.—Federal Bureau of Investigation (1987).

* State and local offenses related to the unlawful possession, sale, use, growing, and manufacturing of illicit drugs.

† Sex offenses of a commercialized nature, such as prostitution, keeping and procuring or transporting women for immoral purposes.

‡ Less than 1 percent.

TABLE 2

Percentage Distribution of Arrests for Drug Sale/Possession and Prostitution, Each Site, at Cities Tested during April–June 1988

	Males		Females	
	Drug Sales	Sex Offense	Drug Sales	Sex Offense
Los Angeles	30	2	22	14
San Diego	35	2	46	7
Portland	13	2	9	18
Phoenix	10	3	6	9
Dallas	7	5	14	14
Houston	31	2	*	*
New Orleans	11	3	10	15
Chicago	26	2	36	8
Indianapolis	1	14	*	*
Detroit	28	10	*	*
New York	17	2	21	25

SOURCE.—National Institute of Justice (1989).
* Data not available.

interviewers intentionally undersample persons arrested for drug violations because their large numbers would overload the interviewers (Wish, O'Neil, and Baldau 1988). Even with this undersampling among arrestees, 13 percent of males and 17 percent of females were arrested for dealing or possession. In some cities, such as San Diego, the percentage is as high as 35 percent (table 2).

Data from the Bureau of Justice Statistics (Chaiken and McDonald 1988) show increasing numbers of drug offenders in the federal system. Twenty-one percent of all federal offenses reported to U.S. attorneys from October 1985 to September 1986 were drug offenses; 87 percent of these involved distribution or manufacture; 9 percent involved smuggling; and 4 percent involved possession with intent to distribute. It should be noted that these Bureau of Justice Statistics sources are biased toward the importer or smuggler, because they are primary targets of federal drug law enforcement efforts, rather than the street hustler, and toward drugs (primarily heroin and cocaine) that are imported. By contrast, DUF data are probably overrepresentative of the visible street-level hustler and/or drug user buying drugs in public areas.

It is obvious from official data that there are large numbers of arrests

TABLE 3

1985 NIDA Household Survey Responses to Any Illicit
Drug Use Ever, in Past Year, and Past Month

Age/Sex	Ever Used (Percent)	Used in Past Year (Percent)	Used in Past Month (Percent)
12–17:			
Male	31.3	23.9	16.6
Female	27.7	23.3	13.4
18–25:			
Male	66.5	47.3	30.0
Female	63.1	36.7	21.0
26–34:			
Male	69.8	38.1	26.2
Female	54.6	25.1	15.4
35 and older:			
Male	25.3	9.1	5.1
Female	16.1	4.5	2.9
All ages:			
Male	42.0	23.3	15.0
Female	32.2	15.6	9.3

SOURCE.—National Institute on Drug Abuse (1987).

for drug offenses. The absolute numbers of drug-dealing activities, particularly among drug users who deal, are often startling and place the official data in better perspective. Inciardi (1979, 1986) states that drug dealers in his Miami sample report committing 1,000 drug deals for every two for which they were apprehended. Ball (1986) found only seven arrests for every 1,000 drug deals committed during high-criminal-activity periods of heroin users. Other researchers (Chaiken and Chaiken 1982; Johnson et al. 1985; Johnson and Wish 1986) also report that the most active dealers commit an average of 1,000 drug-dealing crimes in each year that they are at liberty.

Numbers of drug users can also provide some insight into the extent of dealing. Twelve percent of the total U.S. population (table 3) reported the use of some illicit substance in the thirty days prior to interview in the 1985 household survey (National Institute on Drug Abuse 1987); 42 percent of those eighteen to twenty-five years old reported some illicit use in the past year. For cocaine, a drug whose popularity has been increasing in the past decade, 6 percent of the population had used it in the past year (table 4). If even *1 percent* of the almost twenty-three million illicit substance users were to sell or share

TABLE 4

1985 NIDA Household Survey Response to Cocaine Use

Age/Sex	Ever Used (Percent)	Used In Past Year (Percent)	Used In Past Month (Percent)
12–17:			
Male	6.1	5.1	2.0
Female	4.2	3.3	1.4
18–25:			
Male	28.9	20.2	9.0
Female	21.4	12.4	6.2
26–34:			
Male	30.0	17.1	8.6
Female	18.4	8.3	3.8
35 and older:			
Male	7.2	1.5	.7
Female	1.6	.8	*
All ages:			
Male	15.4	8.4	3.9
Female	8.3	4.4	2.0

SOURCE.—National Institute on Drug Abuse (1987).
* Less than 1 percent.

drugs occasionally, the number of dealers and deals unaccounted for by official records would be staggering. Fagan, Piper, and Moore's (1986) study of self-reported delinquency indicated that of all 863 juveniles studied from court records and field interviews, 16 percent had used illicit drugs (not counting alcohol) and 12 percent had sold them; among those classified as violent delinquents, 36 percent had used illicit drugs and 25 percent had sold them.

Reuter and Kleiman (1986) offer an interesting estimate of the total number of dealers of marijuana, heroin, and cocaine operating in the country based on an estimate of the user-to-dealer ratio. They estimate that there are 500,000 marijuana dealers, 180,000 cocaine dealers, and 45,000 heroin dealers, not including small-scale street-addict dealers. They estimate these numbers by dividing the number of users from the National Institute on Drug Abuse Household Survey (National Institute on Drug Abuse 1987) by an estimate of the number of customers a retailer might handle. The denominator is affected by the riskiness of the dealing operation in terms of penalties. They estimate forty marijuana users per dealer, twenty-five cocaine users per dealer, and ten heroin users per dealer. They suggest, however, that these are conservative estimates of the number of drug dealers and deals undetected by official sources.

B. Who Deals Drugs?

Typically, persons arrested for drug law violations as reported in the UCR are white males and under thirty years old, though minorities are disproportionately represented among these offenders (Federal Bureau of Investigation 1987). About 26 percent of the drug violators are under twenty-one years old, though the greatest increases recently have been among older offenders. This may be due to the "aging" of the large cohort of still-active narcotics addicts from the 1960s and 1970s, or a recently noted return to drug use and the drug lifestyle of ex-addicts, which has occurred with the new availability of cocaine (Siegel 1982; Strug et al. 1985).

There has been a 38 percent increase in the number of female arrestees for drug offenses since 1985 (Federal Bureau of Investigation 1987), a trend also reported in ethnographic research. Traditionally, it has been thought that female dealers of narcotics or cocaine have been rare, with women generally acting as "holders" (Goldstein 1979) or peripheral members of a male-dominated dealing group. Hunt and colleagues (Hunt, Lipton, and Spunt 1984) found almost one-third of all dealers in their sample were women, many of whom were among the most active dealers. Mauge (1981) reported that 37 percent of 256 women readmitted to treatment for heroin use were involved with drug dealing. And Inciardi's (1986) interviews with drug-using females show that 72 percent had been involved in drug dealing at some time, 69 percent before the onset of heroin use.

Dealer characteristics also vary considerably with the area of the country, though there is a fairly logical rule of thumb. Dealers with direct contact with their customers ("street level") are likely to look like the customers, and in fact be customers at other points in time. Therefore, the cocaine seller in a Wall Street building is likely to be a white male in his twenties (Hopkins 1989); a cocaine dealer working Southern California beach towns looks like, and often is, a surfer (Adler 1985); and the inner-city Washington, D.C., cocaine dealer is likely to be a young black or Hispanic man (Hanson et al. 1985).

Distribution of a particular drug may follow ethnic lines in some areas though, overall, ethnic associations with particular drugs are not consistent and more often represent media stereotyping. Because Colombians or other South Americans are often involved as the source and in the manufacture and import of cocaine (Inciardi 1986; Rinfret 1988), local cocaine distributors at the top-to-middle level in some areas may be disproportionately Hispanic, though dealer characteristics at the retail level still tend to resemble characteristics of the user population in that area. Adler (1985) found that southwestern U.S. dealers and smugglers who handled marijuana and cocaine in the early 1970s became exclusive cocaine traffickers when its popularity soared in the late 1970s. These importers were primarily white U.S. citizens but dealt with South American cocaine brokers at the import level. The same importer-level dealers in New York City in the early days of cocaine's rise to popularity were likely to be black or Hispanic.

What is known about distributors of crack cocaine indicates that users and distributors are young, members of minority groups, and residents of the urban areas where the crack is sold. Street dealers in New York City reflect the ethnicity of their neighborhoods and clientele (Johnson, Hamid, and Morales 1987). In cities like Washington, D.C., and in some areas of New York City, it is believed that Jamaicans are "controlling" the crack trade (Johnson, Hamid, and Morales 1987). However, in New York City this seems to be linked to neighborhood distribution rather than to citywide control. Though still fairly confined to large urban areas, crack has increasingly been appearing in urban areas throughout the country (Community Epidemiology Work Group 1988); and since it is a drug easily manufactured from a relatively small supply of cocaine hydrochloride (Hunt 1987), it has been an easy market for young distributors to enter. Consequently, unlike other drug-distribution networks, crack "organizations" are often headed by young entrepreneurs operating with relatively little capital.

Distributors may "specialize" in a particular drug, that is, handle only one type of drug. Johnson, Hamid, and Morales (1987) report that the distributors of heroin in New York City are not the major distributors of other drugs like crack, powdered cocaine, marijuana, or illicit prescription drugs; they "specialize" in heroin or carry heroin and a few related narcotics like methadone, Demerol, or Dilaudid. Conversely, studies of cocaine hydrochloride distributors (that is, dealers of the powdered form) indicate that most deal primarily in cocaine powder and avoid heroin (Waldorf 1977; Williams 1978; Adler 1985). Retail crack dealers in New York City are not likely to deal heroin or even cocaine hydrochloride but concentrate their efforts on crack cocaine (Johnson, Hamid, and Morales 1987). One reason for some specialization is the smaller costs of crack manufacture and the lack of "connections" to other drug sources. Young dealers need only local connections for obtaining cocaine hydrochloride. One exception to the trend toward specialization is the dealer of "pills," who often handles a range of tranquilizers, sedatives, amphetamines, and marijuana.

Certain areas of a city are often known for particular drugs. Morganthau and Miller (1989) have described crack "bazaars" in the southeast section of Washington, D.C., from which the majority of the city's crack cocaine is distributed. Interesting geographic variations in street-level Harlem dealers were explained to the author by a current cocaine user who had previously dealt the drug: "Between 125th St. and 123rd Street on Lexington there are approximately six (regular) cocaine dealers, all Hispanic. The black guys in the area they deal only with heroin, maybe methadone and various pills . . . on the West Side, like around 109th and Columbus, you find a lot of Cubans . . . and then on the East Side around 110th, a lot of Puerto Ricans deal cocaine" (Hunt et al. 1985).

The ethnicity of dealers is likely to be different in different cities, but the homogeneity cited above is often apparent within a dealing group in a specific area due primarily to the social network on which the dealing group is based. Friends deal with friends and recruit friends into the business. The differences between dealing groups are also less attributable to drug preference than to neighborhood characteristics or friendship networks within the drug world from which the groups spring.

III. The Relation between Dealing and Drug Use

Are most drug dealers also drug users? This question generates two conflicting answers. At the upper levels of drug distribution and import, the answer is most often negative. Bureau of Justice Statistics (1984) data on persons arrested for violation of federal drug laws indicate that 80 percent of those arrested are not regular users. Upper-level dealers[2] (importers, smugglers, and wholesale dealers), whom federal arrest data are especially likely to include, may be binge users or recreational users of the drugs dealt, but are not often seriously impaired by or addicted to the substances. If they become so, they are not likely to remain successful dealers. Adler (1985) reports that the smugglers and top-level dealers she studied used marijuana recreationally and were sometimes binge consumers of cocaine. The easy access to large quan-

---

[2] Violators picked up at the federal level are often upper-level dealers, in that their crimes are likely to involve international or interstate transport or distribution.

tities that dealing offers allowed dealers to consume thousands of dollars worth of cocaine in weekend partying, but this practice often "broke" or ruined the dealer. More typically, the dealers in upper-level management were more moderate users not seriously involved with the substance dealt, particularly in the case of heroin. These dealers were businessmen and women motivated by a quick return on their investment; their use was not related to the crime or its profit motive.

However, dealers at the middle and lower portions of the trade often *are* users. Table 2 indicates the percentages of persons in the DUF research who were arrested for drug dealing or sex offenses; for many urinalysis tests were positive for the presence of illicit substances at the time of arrest (National Institute of Justice 1988). Across all cities the percentage of offenders arrested for dealing or possession who were currently using drugs is uniformly and consistently high. These data support earlier findings that half the persons arrested for drug-dealing crimes report that they were under the influence of drugs, alcohol, or both at the time of the crime (U.S. Department of Justice 1984). We cannot, of course, infer causality between presence of drugs in system at arrest and a "drug-related" crime, or take the presence of drugs in the system to imply abusive levels of use. These data do confirm, however, that, of persons picked up for dealing, a large percentage have also recently used drugs. While these data undoubtedly do not represent the drug involvement of the universe of dealers, it may be representative of the street dealer, the most visible part of the trade. As many other researchers have noted, the "loser" or least successful predatory offender is especially likely to be caught and to have some concurrent drug involvement (Chaiken and Johnson 1988). The same is true for street-level dealing; the visible street dealer is the most likely to be arrested *and* to have some concurrent drug use. In any event, it seems that lower- and middle-level dealers typically are themselves abusive users of drugs.

Are most drug users also dealers? Of the many millions of drug users in the country, most are not drug dealers in any conventional sense. However, many, if not most, *serious* or high-frequency drug abusers, particularly heavy heroin and cocaine users, at some point distribute drugs or drug services in exchange for drugs, money, or both. Studies of narcotic addict populations show drug dealing as an almost universal activity at some point in the drug-use career. Ball and his associates interviewed 2,394 methadone clients in seven treatment programs in 1985–86 in three states (Ball et al. 1987) and found that during clients' last periods of addiction, 85 percent had been involved in drug dealing or falsifying prescriptions to obtain drugs. Hunt, Lipton, and Spunt (1984) found that 30 percent of the methadone client sample and 56 percent of their sample of addicts not in drug treatment reported that they had sold drugs or drug services in the week prior to interview. A variety of drugs were reportedly dealt by these groups. Addicts not in treatment were more likely to deal heroin (33 percent dealt heroin in the prior week) than were methadone clients, though both groups were active in the cocaine and marijuana trade. The prior arrest records of both of these groups also showed that drug-dealing crimes featured prominently in their arrest histories as the most common offense committed.

Throughout the literature drug dealing appears endemic to settings of serious drug abuse. In 1969, Preble and Casey conducted a series of interviews and observations with heroin addicts contacted through addict-friendship networks in New York City in an attempt to characterize the structure of the street heroin trade. All addicts they interviewed had some involvement in the drug trade. In the 1970s, Waldorf (1977), in an ethnographic study of cocaine users dealing in the San Francisco area, reported high levels of involvement of cocaine users. In an ethnographic study of the organization of a heroin-dealing area (Hughes et al. 1971), one-third of the addicts interviewed claimed to support themselves solely through dealing. Ball, Shaffer, and Nurco (1983) studied 243 heroin addicts through extensive life-history interviews in the late 1970s and early 1980s. In these interviews, they found addicts committing drug-dealing crimes on 27 percent of the days they were criminally active. Inciardi (1986), in his Miami research, reported that 38 percent of the total crimes committed in a twelve-month period by his sample of 573 narcotics users were drug-dealing crimes.

Drug dealing also may be the crime least responsive to change in addiction status of serious drug users (Anglin and Speckart 1986). Anglin and colleagues (Brecht, Anglin, and Woodward 1987) at the University of California at Los Angeles have followed a sample of 581 narcotics addicts admitted to the California civil commitment program during 1962–64. Eighty-four percent of the subjects have been reinterviewed (161 were deceased) at two points since that time, establishing a twenty-five year picture of addiction careers. Their data provide compelling information on the enduring nature of drug-dealing activities even during periods of limited use or abstention. It is a behavior readily resorted to during relapse periods and is often sustained during "off" periods, when the individual is off drugs himself. These authors also find that a history of drug dealing is predictive of decreased likelihood of "maturing out" or voluntarily leaving addiction. In a real sense, it is the hustling activity most closely tied to "the life" in that it places the person daily in the middle of the user subculture, regardless of whether he or she is a current user.

These most active drug dealers are most likely to be daily or near daily users of narcotics or cocaine, even within treatment settings (Chaiken and Chaiken 1982; Johnson et al. 1985; Anglin and Speckart 1986; Ball et al. 1987). While less than 17 percent of a sample of methadone clients (Hunt, Lipton, and Spunt 1984) reported heroin use in the week prior to being interviewed, of those who *were* using heroin, 37 percent committed some type of drug-dealing crime—significantly more than the nonheroin users. The relation is also significant for cocaine use and drug dealing; not surprisingly, the most active client dealers are those using heroin, cocaine, or both at the highest frequency. Seventeen percent of all methadone clients reported use of cocaine three or more times in the week prior to the interview; of that group, 31 percent report committing five or more property crimes and 41 percent report committing five or more drug-dealing crimes in the prior two-week period. Heavy users of illicit prescription drugs also deal the drugs they use. However, in this study as well as in Inciardi (1986), even high-frequency nonopiate, noncocaine users are involved in dealing at lower levels than are the daily narcotics users.

Overall, there has been an increase in the use of cocaine among persons who are arrested (National Institute of Justice 1989). In the twelve cities tested in the DUF program during April-June 1988, half the male arrestees and 42 percent of the females tested positive for cocaine (National Institute of Justice 1989). Mieczkowski (1989) also reports that, of the sample of 241 arrestees in Detroit tested in a DUF data-collection cycle in 1987, 64 percent tested positive for cocaine, of whom 43 percent used crack cocaine.

It should be understood that the highest-frequency dealers are not confined to dealing as their sole criminal activity. Only a third of all sales can be attributed to "specialists" (dealing activity only). Among career criminals who report drug sales activity, about half are responsible for 99 percent of all sales reported (Johnson and Wish 1986), but they are also responsible for considerable amounts of nondealing crime. In a population of user/dealers not in treatment from the TRISEP study (Hunt, Lipton, and Spunt 1984), high-frequency dealers (more than five times/deals per week) were concurrently involved in numerous other crimes: 11 percent were also shoplifting, 15 percent were involved in burglary, 8 percent in robbery, 15 percent in con games, and 29 percent in dealing stolen merchandise. Inciardi's (1986) Miami sample of 573 drug users reported committing 82,000 drug sales, 6,000 robberies and assaults, 6,700 burglaries, 900 vehicle thefts, 25,000 instances of shoplifting, and 46,000 other larceny or fraud events in a one-year period prior to interview. Among female addicts, the battery of crimes included dealing, prostitution, shoplifting, burglary, and larceny (Inciardi 1986; Anglin and Hser 1987).

In summary, the proportion of dealers who use the drugs they sell is difficult to assess. Drug Use Forecasting data indicate that a substantial portion of persons arrested for dealing have a variety of illegal drugs present in their bodies at arrest. This population is, however, overrepresentative of street-level, visible dealers who are most likely to be users, so these data do not adequately answer the question. There is no evidence that the majority of *all* dealers are users; and both ethnographic (Mieczkowski 1986) and survey data (Bureau of Justice Statistics 1984) indicate that there are a substantial number of nondrug-using dealers. Mieczkowski (1986), through observation and interviews conducted in 1985, studied crews of young men who sold heroin and cocaine in Detroit. These young men distributed both drugs without using them. Bureau of Justice Statistics (1984) data, based on self-reports of arrested offenders, also show large proportions of nonusers among those convicted of federal drug offenses. Both of these sources are limited for making an accurate assessment of the number of nonuser dealers. The percentage of serious drug users who deal is easier to estimate. Anywhere from a third to more than half of serious drug users, particularly the users of heroin and cocaine, have at some time dealt drugs.

Why is occasional dealing so pervasive among drug users and endemic among heavy users of narcotics and cocaine? Faupel and Klockars (1987) argue that any competent user will at some point stumble on an opportunity to deal or distribute an amount of drugs for profit. Even as a "break even" enterprise, distribution is a natural outgrowth of obtaining the drugs they use for themselves or for friends. It is also an easy money-making activity that can be incorporated into activities in the daily round of other hustling or simply socializing with other users. Thus, the more frequently the user is consuming or buying drugs, particularly expensive drugs, the more likely he is to have the opportunity and inclination to deal. These are the user/dealers who become what Preble and Casey (1969) called the "day laborers" in the drug trade—operating at the street level of the business hierarchy.

IV. The World of Drug Dealing

In the studies of the drug trade (the narcotics or opiates trade in particular) which have been done in the last twenty years, there is a remarkable consistency in descriptions of the structure of dealing groups. While researchers have called the players different names, the characteristics and functions of roles at each point in the structure are similar. Perhaps it is this consistency and the natural fascination with this world that have made this structure appear far more organized and formal than it is.

There are two images of the drug-dealing world, neither of which seems adequately to describe the real thing. Although the picture of highly organized crime families controlling distribution almost to the street level is an anachronism perhaps not appropriate since the 1950s (Reuter and Kleiman 1986), a view of all levels of dealing as unconnected, entrepreneurial operations is also incomplete. The truth is somewhere in between. The international connections needed to purchase, manufacture, process, and import many drugs mandate dealing operations or syndicates that function as organized big businesses or at a minimum as very "disciplined criminal entrepreneurs" (Inciardi 1986, p. 52) with large individual organizations. A Drug Enforcement Administration (DEA) official recently estimated that, in the case of narcotics, fewer than ten major international operations control manufacture and import to next-level U.S. distributors (Rinfret 1988). These individuals and their organizations are obviously not visible to most research and may only surface as part of other criminal investigations. The DEA also estimates that there are but a handful of U.S. manufacturers of LSD, a substance whose raw materials are available domestically, and that they are located primarily in Northern California and the Pacific Northwest. These manufacturers then distribute through a changing network to more local distributors (Rinfret 1988). By contrast, the number of crack manufacturers is impossible to count. Crack can be manufactured locally in kitchens with kitchen supplies; the step from crack manufacturer to crack user is a short one.

Different drugs show greater or lesser degrees of centralization in distribution. The resurgent interest in injectable methamphetamines has given rise to new laboratory operations in Southern California and the mid-Atlantic area, though the nature of these operations appears entrepreneurial and locally based (Rinfret 1987). Areas where methamphetamine or PCP labs flourish are also areas where use of those drugs concentrates, indicating that the drugs are not shipped out to distant points in any global distribution scheme. By contrast, accounts of heroin traffickers such as reported by Inciardi (1986) often reveal complex worldwide connections. "In early 1983, a Miami heroin trafficker indicated that, as the result of an arrest in Turkey, an assassination in Kuwait and a plane crash in Corsica, one shipment of drugs had to be diverted through at least eight countries before it reached its final destination" (Inciardi 1986, p. 57). The ability to divert the shipment through eight countries when the system is disrupted speaks to the organizational structure needed to manufacture and import drugs not produced domestically. While this organization is necessary, it is not necessarily of long duration. Cocaine importers may operate for one to two transactions (Adler 1985) or for years. The organization does not appear, however, to be the stable crime structure of the heroin trade in past decades. It is also not until these international links are broken that they are visible. What *is* visible to researchers are the small entrepreneurial groups and individuals with little formal structure beyond behavioral roles members play in dealing. These are the players in the system on which I concentrate here. (See Moore, in this volume, for a discussion of law enforcement strategies for dealing with international aspects of drug manufacture, collection, and importation.)

Descriptions of the world of drug dealing that I use in this section are drawn primarily from ethnographic research conducted in different cities. In selecting research on the structure or organization of dealing, it is always tempting to include the numerous journalistic accounts of crack operations, preteen dealers with beepers, or drug gangs moving into farm communities. All of these news items may, in fact, be true. However, the ethnographic work on which I rely uses the multiple methods discussed in the introduction. Work that does not meet adequate research criteria has not been included.

Prior research has described the distribution network for heroin and cocaine as a hierarchy of roles with increasing financial responsibility and decreasing visibility as one moves from street distributor to importer and manufacturer (Preble and Casey 1969; Moore 1977; Goldstein 1979; Adler 1985; Johnson, Hamid, and Morales 1987). These reports describe a social organization that varies somewhat over time, by the drug dealt, and by area of the country. The structure can include as many as five or six levels, as with heroin or cocaine hydrochloride, from importer to user, or as few as two or three, as with marijuana (Reuter and Kleiman 1986). Levels in the structure may be linked to the adjoining players (i.e., source and next-level customer) but have no link to any other part of the structure. Structures may also vary widely from one geographic area to another. For example, Adler (1985) reports a looser structure, more personal drug use among dealers, and a more highly visible lifestyle among the upper-level dealers and smugglers of cocaine and marijuana in Southern California than has traditionally been found among dealers in the Northeast. The use of small children as drug runners or "holders" in areas of New York City is also not commonly found in other areas. In addition, the heroin trade is currently a more "stable" market than the cocaine market (particularly the crack cocaine market), having established lines of distribution in this country for a longer period of time. Roles in the heroin distribution network are better defined and have been more completely researched. Therefore, the hierarchy of roles described here should be viewed as somewhat generic rather than representing details specific to all dealing networks. For example, the street dealing of illegal prescription drugs (or drugs requiring no preparation or import) generally has a very simple distribution system: the person steals the product from a pharmaceutical house or obtains an illegal prescription through forgery or fraud and sells directly to the user.

There are some commonalities, however, found in dealing structures that cross geographic areas and drugs dealt: first, the structure of distribution is better characterized as groups of dealers and individual entrepreneurs throughout, rather than as a single, highly organized and centralized criminal operation; and second, entrance and acceptance into the dealing groups are based on familiarity, friendship ties, situational factors ("the right place at the right time"), and available capital.

A. The Structure of Distribution

Over twenty years ago Preble and Casey (1969) outlined a structure of distribution of narcotics found in New York City. Much of their description still holds true today, though terms used for persons at each level have changed or vary by geographic area. At the top of the dealing world are the "importers" or "traffickers" (Johnson, Hamid, and Morales 1987). These persons may never see the imported product but simply provide the capital, equipment, or organization to others to make the connections with the overseas growers, processors, or manufacturers. While some traffickers or importers may have ties to or be part of traditional organized-crime structures, there are numerous individual entrepreneurs in the drug trade of the 1980s. Many of Adler's (1985) cocaine smugglers fall into these top positions, dealing directly with international sources and investing large sums of money for planes and boats for transport of quantities of cocaine. Inciardi (1986) describes the incongruity of the sleepy river towns in the jungles of South America filled with hundreds of fast, expensive air and water vehicles belonging to an odd array of South American and U.S. buyers of coca paste, some well established with local growers, others new to the business. At this level, traffickers buy either unprocessed paste or (more often) already processed cocaine hydrochloride and arrange its transport into the United States to be distributed to the next-level dealer. They may be large-volume importers with a history of trafficking or short-term entrepreneurs trying to make a big return on an investment.

The next-level dealer may have some structural or organization connection to the distributor or, more commonly, be one of a group of different buyers who trade with the distributor. Preble's (Preble and Casey 1969) second-level "captains" or "kilo connections" are analogous to Adler's (1985) next-level dealers and those described as "top dealers" by Chaiken and Johnson (1988). These individuals buy large quantities of drugs from importers, and divide and cut them into smaller units to sell to other dealers, in what Adler (1985) terms "straight dealing." These substances are cut with a variety of adulterants to decrease purity and increase bulk for distribution at the next level. Over the last few years there has been little variation in heroin prices at this level, but there have been dramatic decreases in the price of cocaine (Street Studies Unit 1987), due primarily to increased availability and greater numbers of dealers entering this market (Inciardi 1986).

The next level of distributor sells somewhat smaller amounts. These are the "ounce men," or "dealers in weight" and the first dealers who may be regular users of the drugs themselves. These individuals may be known to users by sight and have the reputation of "big dealers" (Preble and Casey 1969) on the street because of the investment they make and the quantity they handle, even though they are actually quite removed from the drug's source. The "big dealer" may also operate as a "house connection" selling to users and street dealers out of apartments or houses. They may also operate a lower-tier distribution structure of street dealers and other functionaries responsible to them directly. The suppliers of Mieczkowski's (1906) young men's dealing syndicates described in Detroit are these "big dealers."

The following conversation with a cocaine user who previously dealt cocaine hydrochloride describes this level of the hierarchy and a "house connection." He goes on to talk about "N.B.", a kilo-level dealer, who had recently been arrested on tax fraud charges.

Q. Is it easy to get cocaine? How do you approach a dealer?
. . . is no big mystery. You are going to get cocaine, he knows what you want and you [know] that he has it. He takes you to his apartment, shows you his product. He might let you snort a little . . . taste first and see what it is.

Q. What level dealer would he be?
Below middle, because you have guys who deal to him. He is only dealing grams. You have guys dealing ounces, pounds and kilos. They [the bigger dealers] live in the same area, but you would not find them outside. I mean these are the guys they [the "big dealers"] go to.

Q. What level dealer would N.B. be?
Ultra high. N.B. was dealing some cocaine, though mostly heroin. He would be buying direct from overseas. . . . He got to the point where he was dealing direct with Turkey and France.

Q. Now, people on the street used to see him, didn't they?
Yeah, but they know he didn't have anything [drugs] on him. . . . The only place he would go near is the garage and that's because that was one of his businesses [a legitimate business]. [Hunt et al. 1985]

"Big dealers" may also employ "lieutenants" or "crew bosses" as middlemen between themselves and street-level sellers (Johnson et al. 1985; Mieczkowski 1986).

A user/dealer describes his activities as a lieutenant for a middle level dealer: "You would never see him [on the street]. I was his lieutenant. He lived way up in the Bronx. He would cut it and parcel it . . . and bring it to my house and I would take it to the other people" (Hunt et al. 1985).

The final level, the street-level dealer, falls into the category of "dope hustler" (Hanson et al. 1985) or "juggler" (Preble and Casey 1969; Johnson et al. 1985): an individual who buys small quantities of drugs, who may or may not repackage, cut or "stop on" it further, and who sells directly to other users. Levels of capital investment vary widely within this group. Some street dealers may invest fairly substantial amounts of money, others may hustle only five or ten bags ($50–$100 worth) of heroin, as little as one or a few ounces of marijuana or even "loose joints" (single marijuana cigarettes). Street dealers often take drugs "on consignment" with no initial investment and divide subsequent profits with the source. For example, a street dealer may be given three $10 bags of heroin (or $30) for every $100 sold (Goldstein et al. 1984). Street dealers may also work for a higher-level dealer in a number of dealing-related roles.

These street-level dealers are the most visible and are arrested most often both because of the frequency with which they ply their trade and the degree of openness necessary for high-volume business. The likelihood that these "day laborers" (Preble and Casey 1969) would be connected to upper-level dealers in an organized sense is essentially nil. They may move up in the profits with bigger individual "scores," but they typically lack either the funds or connections to become a "big dealer." While most are users themselves, there are distributors at this level who are not users (Mieczkowski 1986) and who are simply in it for the money. The commitment to dealing at this level also tends to be transitory or intermittent (Johnson et al. 1985). A street dealer may deal drugs on one or two days a week, run con games on another day, and burglarize property on another. For example, one regular dealer of illegal prescription drugs in my earlier work routinely dealt Valium from his car, was involved in commercial burglary, and fenced stolen merchandise in the two-year period that his activities were regularly reported to the project (Hunt, Lipton, and Spunt 1984).

The street-level dealer is often an individual entrepreneur, working his or her own area in connection with the source, but clearly as a "private business." The decision to cut the product again, even give it a brand name, usually falls with this level of dealer. The volume he or she wishes to deal also depends on personal circumstances: "connections," capital, individual enterprise, and his or her own consumption patterns. A methadone client with a history of dealing explained the street dealer network in Harlem:

> talking about 127th Street and 123rd Street, there are about seven people dealing [regularly] and they all get it from the same person, but they cut and dip . . . they are all getting it from one thing [source] but you might cut it again because you want to double your money. But me, I'm selling mine as the man gave it to me

and that means mine would be better than yours; but we both got
it from the same person. But you might try to be greedy. . . . He
[the source] already got his money so if you want to cut it twenty
times that's your business. [Hunt et al. 1985]

The volume of drugs dealt is an obvious status differential in the
dealing hierarchy. The high-status "big dealer" is the one who has
made "the big score" and handles large quantities of drugs. Within this
hierarchy, prestige is also based on reputation, business savvy, and
what is often called "carrying yourself well." "Carrying yourself well"
implies control of a wheeling and dealing lifestyle and includes avoidance of arrest, appearing well-dressed and affluent, and exhibiting control of personal drug use and visible generosity with drugs and money.
Southwestern cocaine dealers (Adler 1985) prided themselves on their
clothes, their often elaborate homes, and the free-flowing availability of
drugs. These were seen as tangible markers of success and the foundation of a good reputation in the business.

Other more service-oriented roles played at the street level of dealing
are "steering," "touting," "copping" for others, and providing drug-use
resources (selling or renting injection equipment, injecting another user
for a fee, or running a shooting gallery). "Steering" involves directing
users to a dealer in exchange for money or drugs; "touting" is acting as a
"barker" or advertiser for a dealer. "Copping" for others is simply
buying drugs for someone else in exchange for money or, more often, a
portion of the drugs. Playing these roles may provide entree into a
dealing group. Additional roles and functionaries include lookouts,
guards, collectors of money, and "strong arms."

The distribution networks for crack cocaine appear unique, though
little systematic information about them is available. Though the processing of crack cocaine relies on a supply of cocaine hydrochloride,
only small quantities are needed for a large return and can be purchased
by entrepreneurial manufacturers from local rather than international
sources (Johnson, Hamid, and Morales 1987). Crack's popularity may
have some impact on the overall amount of cocaine hydrochloride imported into the United States. Yet, manufacture of crack itself still
appears to be carried out by mid- to lower-level dealers, using apartments or makeshift crack labs and local cocaine supplies. "Crack
houses" can refer to apartments or buildings where crack is made, sold,
or both. They may spring up overnight and disappear just as quickly.

Johnson, Hamid, and Morales (1987) suggest that a "freelance model" of distribution—in which all parties work without clear status distinctions on an as-needed or temporary basis—was most applicable to the street-level trade in cocaine powder. The crack trade, however, they describe as more "vertically organized" (Johnson, Hamid, and Morales 1987, p. 5); that is, it is a market of numerous entrepreneurial sellers who need to employ role-specific employees to consolidate their business—enforcers, collectors, guards, hawkers, supervisors of street sellers' own use—all of whom may be assigned to a particular location. Therefore, several members of a gang or team of dealers work together with defined functions and a status hierarchy. While highly organized at first glance, these crews or gangs of crack dealers may be more fluid than they first appear, with a small core of central players and many "temps" or transitory members (Hopkins 1989). The heavy competition among young entrepreneurs over crack distribution in the same urban areas is one important source of the well-publicized violence among them.

Distribution of illegal sedatives or tranquilizers and methadone occurs almost exclusively at the dealer/user level. A distributor will "bust a script"; that is, obtain a legal prescription through fraud or pass a forged prescription as a legitimate one. In the course of prior research by me and others, several local physicians were cited by pill dealers as particularly lenient or cooperative in prescribing sedatives. Obtained in this fashion or through script forgery, quantities of pills make their way onto the drug market.

One dealer of tranquilizers, sedatives, and amphetamines who was part of this earlier study had enough inventory to sell daily from a van in the Bronx, operating with remarkable regularity from one location between 1 P.M. and 3 P.M. each day. One such user/dealer explains a particularly lucrative source of "legal" pills: "You walk into the place (doctor's office) and the 250 lb. nurse with the 38 under his sleeve would say 'Sit down.' You fill out a 7 page questionnaire on why I want to lose weight, why I'm not a drug addict and, yes, I cannot sleep because of my problems. . . . So what they would do is give you a script at the end" (Hunt et al. 1985). The user/dealer rode into New York City to visit this source and returned to Connecticut with his merchandise. Hustling a variety of such doctors could produce enough inventory to make a small income and provide his own drug supply.

Distribution of illicit methadone is also a street-level operation (Spunt et al. 1986). Methadone dealers are primarily clients in methadone treatment who sell a portion of their daily dosage. Little methadone is diverted by staff or during transport. A portion of clients will sell take-home dosages or "spitbacks" (medication held in the mouth and spit into a container after leaving the program). Sporadic selling is fairly widespread, though regular selling is confined to a smaller number, generally clients who are not working or who continue to abuse heroin or cocaine while in methadone treatment (Spunt et al. 1986). Considering the source, it is not surprising that the heaviest distribution of methadone occurs in the immediate neighborhood of treatment programs, though some dealers, particularly those also selling other illicit substances, may sell methadone in traditional dealing areas. Similarly, because the "owner" of the bottle sells directly to the user, there is no hierarchy in most methadone dealing.

Cocaine and heroin are marketed at the street level in packets, envelopes, or glassine bags containing variable purity levels and price variation depending on the dealer and the market. On the street, marijuana is sold in loose cigarettes, bags of rolled joints, and in bags or bricks of larger amounts. The quality of marijuana is also variable depending on availability, the tetrahydrocannabinol (THC) level of the crop (its strength), and whether an exotic blend or sinsemilla. Much of the marketing of marijuana and other drugs, however, is done under the caveat emptor philosophy—what you are told you are getting is rarely the actual quality. Crack is packaged in small vials or plastic bags containing one to four "rocks" or chunks or as sets of vials or bags bound together (Street Studies Unit 1987). Sedatives, tranquilizers, and capsule amphetamines are sold in large lots (100 or even 1,000 pills per bottle) or, more often, a few at a time.

The "seals" are the bag markings or names heroin dealers place on their products to distinguish one distributor from another and such "brand names" abound in areas where heroin is plentiful (Hanson et al. 1985; Inciardi 1986; Goldstein et al. 1987). For instance, as a former New York dealer explains: "I have a good bag this way I'll name it 'devil wish.' So I go to the store, buy a stamp, and stamp it on the bag. There are all kinds of names like 'Cadillac,' 'Eldorado' " (Hunt et al. 1985). Bag marking for cocaine packaged in small amounts is reported in New York City (Goldstein et al. 1984) but does not seem to be as common in other areas. While some names are simple ("Blue Tape," "Penny Stamp"), promises of "Sudden Death" potency or "Lamb" smoothness are not uncommon.

Street-level dealing does not offer much career stability and so is most often an intermittent activity for the dealer. Even many mid- to upper-level cocaine dealers such as those studied by Adler (1985) remain in the trade for relatively short periods. Similarly, studies of street-level heroin dealers (Johnson et al. 1985; Mieczkowski 1986) and many adolescent marijuana sellers (Carpenter et al. 1988) show that this is sporadic work or work alternating with other legal and illegal income activities.

B. Entrance or Recruitment into Dealing Groups

Entrance or recruitment into dealing can result from a decision to "make a score" or simply as an outgrowth of one's own use. In all cases, familiarity with other users and suppliers is essential. Even though the open dealing that is often seen in some urban areas implies a haphazard or very risky selling operation, this is rarely true. The phrase, "You gotta know somebody," has real meaning in this context.

Two persons recently involved in dealing in New York City and northern New Jersey explain two different methods of entering the business:

> Now, if I want to get a job dealing for the people, right? The first thing I would find out [is] who is the man that has the dope. Then I say to the man, 'Let me tout for you.' Tout—that means that I will get the people to him and he will give me a cut for getting the people for him. Now, if I'm getting enough people and the people know me, he is making that money, so eventually he will give me a job.

> If you want to deal, you have to get yourself a couple hundred, one hundred at least. By yourself, go to the man. . . . When you bring your package out you say to him I have so much money, what can you do for that? . . . Then you put it in your little bags and you put your seals on it. Then, you just pass the word, 'I got.' [Hunt et al. 1985]

Familiarity is an essential element in entrance into and maintenance of the world of drug dealing, as both parties are agreeing to engage in an illegal activity and each is a potential threat to the other: they could be police, they could sell inferior or tainted goods, they could refuse to pay or produce the goods. In general, the dealer tries to "know" the buyer by sight, by referral, or by association. As a New York cocaine user explains the mutual consent: "Most of the time you know them [dealers] by name, or you have seen them before. And the dealers on the corners are the ones that are there every day . . . They don't know you by name—it's a face thing. It's a contract you have between dealer and buyer" (Hunt et al. 1985).

Familiarity between dealers and buyers is found in the distribution of most drugs at both the upper levels and the street level. Adler (1985) reports that the network of Southwest cocaine dealers she studied was made up of "connections"—intimate partnerships, suppliers, customers, and acquaintances—all persons known to the dealer by sight if not by name. Marijuana dealing on college campuses runs similarly: students buy from one another in a network of acquaintanceships. While the term "friends" is hardly appropriate for many distributor-dealer relationships, the necessity of being a member of an in-group of users or dealers, for example, not straights or police, is essential. Mieczkowski's (1986) adolescent dealers follow the same familiarity principle in acquiring new customers through established contacts, preferring to keep their trade within a group of known customers.

Persons may be recruited into the business because of special skills they bring to the operation, or they may be trained on the job. Adler's (1985) cocaine dealers and importers had developed necessary skills (e.g., pilot, sales manager) prior to entering the business rather than learning these skills on the job. Some were recruited for their specific skills, such as the ability to fly an airplane. Mieczkowski's (1986) adolescent dealers, however, entered the selling of narcotics, marijuana, and illicit prescription drugs as relatively unskilled amateurs, with acquaintances recruiting each other into informal "clubs" or crews of sellers. Newcomers learned business and marketing strategies from the more seasoned "runners," as well as more covert techniques for stretching their profit. One risky skimming technique used to produce extra bags of heroin is called "pinching." Small amounts skimmed from many bags yield an extra bag to be sold as pure profit for the runner. Pinching was frowned on by upper management and these clever entrepreneurs, if discovered, were severely dealt with by crew bosses and other superiors in the trade.

Research in New York City (Johnson, Hamid, and Morales 1987; Street Studies Unit 1987) reports that recruitment into dealing crack comes from both persons previously involved with street sales of other drugs and persons with no prior dealing experience. The novices are young crack users who begin selling shortly after initiation to defray costs of their own use. Ethnographic data from the Street Studies Unit group conducting daily systematic monitoring of drug use and prices in

New York City (Street Studies Unit 1987) indicate that novice crack distributors appear to be of three types: youths (under eighteen) whose first serious drug involvement is with crack; female users of soft drugs and cocaine hydrochloride who now use crack; and adults with a history of marijuana and irregular cocaine snorting who now use crack. Each of these types deals crack primarily in return for supplies for his or her own use. The "manufacturer" or even crew boss in this operation may be an occasional user, but is not the heavy user his or her staff represent.

Recruitment into upper levels of cocaine traffickers (Adler 1985) has some of the same elements as becoming a street-level dealer—peripheral involvement with the drug world, increasing familiarity, sponsorship, and acceptance. In contrast, however, Adler found that middle-level dealers, particularly those who became major dealers, often jumped right into large quantity purchases, even if they had no substantial trafficking experience. (One is reminded of the alleged foray by John DeLorean into the business.) Unlike the transitory or sporadic commitment of the street hustler, these dealers may sometimes stay in the business through several "scores" or larger transactions. Presumably, the establishment of international ties, payoffs to officials, and expensive equipment make it more likely that the top-level dealer or importer will remain in the business longer.

How do patterns of drug dealing differ between persons who use and deal regularly and those who deal drugs but do not use them? I have been describing the first case in the description of the lower-echelon dealer and the street hustler. For them, dealing is one element in a repertoire of hustling activities and sources of legal income: it is done for money, as part of social activity, as a way of obtaining a supply of their own drugs. The second case, the nonusing street dealer, falls generally into three types: the upper-level distributor or trafficker mentioned earlier, the former user returning to or continuing dealing to make money, and the adolescent dealer.

The former user who deals has been identified by many other researchers (Ball, Shaffer, and Nurco 1983; Collins, Hubbard, and Rachal 1985; Anglin and Speckart 1986). During periods of abstinence the drug user may reduce overall criminal activity but may continue to deal as a source of income. In my study of methadone clients (Hunt, Lipton, and Spunt 1984), 5 percent of clients used no opiates, cocaine, or illegal prescription drugs, but *were* currently involved in drug dealing as an income-generating activity. Of that number, 16 percent were dealing opiates and 11 percent were dealing cocaine.

The abstinent adolescent dealer has been less frequently studied. Mieczkowski (1986) describes small networks of young heroin dealers in Detroit who do not use nor have ever used heroin themselves. These dealers operated in a far more organized manner than the drug-using street dealer. They were organized into "crews" with "crew bosses" and a runner system similar to the consignment system used by more opportunistic user/dealers. The greater organization may be possible due to the greater sobriety of participants (use of *any* drug while working was strongly disapproved, even though some crew members used marijuana and/or cocaine recreationally) and due to the focus on making money rather than a focus on *both* making money *and* obtaining one's own drugs found among user/dealers. Mieczkowski's young men are more typical of the occasional or recreational user/dealers found among upper levels of dealing and may represent a retail version of that entrepreneur.

C. Dealing and Violence

A great deal of attention has been paid by the media to the violence associated with the drug trade, a type of violence termed "systemic violence" by Goldstein et al. (1987) to distinguish it from violence resulting from the psychopharmacological properties of the drugs themselves or violence committed by a drug user in the course of other crimes such as robbery. It is mentioned only briefly here since violence and drugs are covered in this volume by Chaiken and Chaiken. Estimates of the extent of this type of drug-related violence are impossible to make. Inciardi (1986) described a marked increase in homicide in south Florida occurring in conjunction with the rapidly expanding cocaine trade, as well as a rise in related crimes such as piracy, firearms violations, and assassinations. A 1981 New York City police study (New York City Police Department 1983) estimated that 24 percent of known homicides were drug related. In approximately 40 percent of those cases, the victim was a known drug dealer. In the first six months of 1988, 80 percent of New York City homicides were judged to be drug related (Morganthau et al. 1989). Both the nature of the business and the state of the customer—often nervous, perhaps feeling deprivation effects—make violence a frequent outcome in the drug trade. Goldstein et al. (1987) describe types of "systemic" violence: "Wars over territory between rival drug dealers, assaults and homicides committed within dealing hierarchies as a means of enforcing normative codes, robberies of drug dealers and the usually violent retaliation by the dealer or his bosses, elimination of informers and punishment for selling adulterated or phony drugs or failing to pay one's debts" (Goldstein et al. 1987, p. 95).

There are, of course, no legal channels for the types of management problems dealers face. Mieczkowski (1986) describes the disciplinary measures, including homicide, used by crew bosses to keep adolescent distributors in line. The crew bosses often use violence against a runner to serve as an example or warning to other members. My initiation into ethnographic research included witnessing a homicide in Philadelphia in the mid-1970s of a heroin dealer/user who had repeatedly "burned" other users and was finally killed by one disgruntled customer in the street. While the dramatic violence of gangs warring for territory is often what is covered in the press, the day-to-day violence, such as the incident described above, is far more commonplace. A former Harlem narcotics dealer summarized the hazards of local competition: "When you are running, if you have a good bag, you have no problem. Now, you might have to risk somebody taking you off anyway, because the man over there he have a mediocre bag and he's been doin' all right. And now you come saying you will take all his business. Now he might be the jealous type. . . . It's quick money, but it's dangerous" (Hunt et al. 1985).

The current crack market can be compared to the early market structures for other drugs, such as heroin or cocaine hydrochloride. New distributors or distributors of other substances are "shaking down" the market, eliminating competition, and establishing distribution territories. Since this settling of the market is occurring among young and extraordinarily well-armed dealers, the level of violence is often numbing.

V. Prostitution

Prostitution is a profession that attracts a wide variety of men and women. Some persons develop careers in prostitution spanning several years while others work intermittently or part time (Bryan 1965). Status differences also exist within prostitution based on the cost of the sexual encounter or where the contact or encounter takes place—the street, a car, a hotel, the sex worker's apartment. Like drug dealing, its true extent is almost impossible to estimate. It is a crime well hidden, with sporadic enforcement and few victim complaints; the ratio of commissions to arrests is extremely high. In Inciardi's (1986) sample of 573 narcotic users in Miami, there were 16,045 prostitution offenses reported resulting in only 89 arrests. Among his sample of 429 nonnarcotic drug users (of alcohol, sedatives, marijuana, and cocaine), 24,966 prostitution offenses were reported resulting in only 49 arrests. In Goldstein et al.'s (1988) interviews with 133 female offenders conducted in 1986 and 1987 on the Lower East Side of New York City, 39 percent reported engaging in prostitution activities in the eight-week period being monitored. Of the women reporting regular use of drugs, 79 percent reported engaging in prostitution in the prior two-week period.

These data indicate that figures on prostitution from state and local law enforcement records reflected in the UCR seriously underestimate the actual commission rate of this crime (see table 1). Uniform Crime Report data show that prostitution routinely accounts for about 5 percent of the total female arrests. Drug Use Forecasting data show a higher proportion of prostitution arrests (22 percent) in the urban areas in which DUF operates. In both cases, the numbers represent a small portion of the total prostitution committed and are weighted heavily toward the more visible streetwalker prostitutes.

Like the apprehended drug dealer, the apprehended prostitute is often a heavy drug user but may be unrepresentative of call girls and less conspicuous prostitutes. A survey of street prostitutes in New York City (Des Jarlais and Friedman 1987) revealed a large proportion of serious drug users. One-half reported having injected drugs at some point, and one-third reported doing so within the prior two-year period. Darrow (1988), drawing on a study of prostitutes by the Centers for Disease Control, reports that 50 percent of the 1,456 prostitutes interviewed in eight cities were intravenous drug users of heroin or cocaine. In a National Institute on Drug Abuse study currently under way, preliminary data indicate that 72 percent of the one hundred prostitutes interviewed in a Connecticut site reported frequent use of crack; many were former intravenous drug users. As with research on drug dealers, however, the prostitute samples available to researchers and represented in these studies are of street level or lower status, often minority prostitutes who are more likely to be drug users than the more costly call girls (Bryan 1965; Carmen and Moody 1985; Delacost and Alexander 1987; Shedlin 1987). In short, it is very difficult to estimate the extent of drug use among prostitutes, but the data do suggest that suggest that among IV drug users, prostitution is common. It should also be stressed that the serious drug user engaging in prostitution rarely confines illegal activities to that single source of income. Inciardi, Pottieger, and Faupel (1982) report that of the sixty-three black female heroin users interviewed, 64 percent engaged in prostitution in the prior twelve-month period, but prostitution accounted for only one-fourth of all offenses they committed during this period. Prostitution was only one of a number of ways these addicted women supported themselves.

The large number of drug users who engage in prostitution prompts the notion of compulsion or "enslavement." Indeed, an "enslavement theory" (Inciardi 1986, p. 156) of prostitution and drugs has been a popular one in American culture for over fifty years. Assuming that only women forced by physiological need and dire economic straits would choose prostitution, the media and some researchers have argued that drug enslavement drives the crime. Consequently, statements such as the following have not been uncommon in the research literature: "That the pimp in his attempt to entice a girl to his service not seldom 'dopes' her and makes her an addict so that she will depend on him for her drug and thereby becomes his woman is a matter of common knowledge" (Dai 1970; reprinted in Inciardi 1986, p. 156).

Many investigators have found a quite different pattern. The sequence of serious drug use and criminal activity, including prostitution, is in most instances reversed. Among the female addicts studied by Inciardi in Miami (1986), the median age of first use of heroin was 17.3 years old, of regular heroin use was 18.6 years, and of prostitution was 19.2 years. However, while only 17.4 percent were involved in prostitution prior to heroin use, among opiate-using prostitutes their other criminal activities began a full year prior to narcotics use. Inciardi concludes: "As such, the opiate using prostitutes were meshed within their criminal careers well before the beginning of heavy narcotics use. This would suggest that rather than a simple cause and effect connection between narcotics and prostitution, individuals prone to heavy drug use on a regular basis are also prone to criminal activity on a regular basis" (Inciardi 1986, p. 160).

Prostitutes in Inciardi's sample were also likely to be engaged in drug dealing prior to prostitution and often switched to prostitution when the drug market or supply was low or when it appeared that prostitution was either easier or more profitable.

The female drug user will therefore often report prostitution as an income-generating activity. Her activities, however, may also include an array of other offenses, such as dealing and property crimes, and she is likely to have little career commitment to prostitution. It is the non-drug-using prostitute who is more likely to sustain a career in prostitution (Bryan 1965). Rosenbaum's (1981) in-depth interviews with 100 women report similar findings. Women drug users were involved with criminal activity, including prostitution, prior to addictive use of narcotics. In Goldstein's (1979) sample, most regular drug use took place concurrently with prostitution among those who were drug users. (This study provides no detailed information about the occurrence or sequencing of other criminal activities.)

Anglin and Hser (1987) report on a sample of female drug abusers that a variety of criminal activities, including but not dominated by prostitution, may precede addiction, but that there are significant increases during periods of heavy drug use. While the costs of drugs were not the likely reason for entering into prostitution or other offenses, there is an escalation of these offenses during periods of heavy drug use. They found that among non-Hispanic white women, 14 percent engaged in prostitution during periods of daily narcotics use, compared with 5 percent during periods of less-than-daily use, and averaged five times as much prostitution income during daily use periods. As one woman eloquently explained in the Rosenbaum study: "The first time I turned a trick, I wasn't using at the time. The guy I was with knew some girls—some working girls that had a book—$100 tricks. That sounded a lot better to me than making $10 a day working in a restaurant. That's how I got into it. I needed the money" (Rosenbaum 1981, p. 72). When the respondent began using narcotics, she used her prostitution proceeds to buy them.

The relation between drug use and prostitution is then one of engaging in a crime to help support a drug habit among heavy drug users. Among heavy drug users, particularly those who have limited means of support, prostitution is a common alternative at some point in the drug-use career. Because of both the expense of the drugs and because of the lifestyle of those users, the heavy users of heroin and cocaine are particularly likely to be involved in prostitution. This may involve an exchange of sex for money or sex for drugs, and may be of limited duration or span several years. However, the serious substance abuser who is engaged in prostitution is also likely to be involved in a host of other illegal activities such as dealing, shoplifting, burglary, and con games. She is likely to have limited social resources and employment skills, is more likely to be a minority group member, and is more likely to live in areas of high poverty and crime than the middle- or upper-income substance abuser not involved in prostitution or other criminal activity. In this regard, prostitution is different from drug dealing. Many if not most heavy drug users at some point may involve themselves in obtaining their supply or in selling or sharing a supply with friends. This is not true with prostitution. While many serious drug users report prostitution, it is generally an activity confined to those drug users already involved in other criminal activities. Unlike dealing, prostitution does not necessarily place a person in day-to-day contact with illicit substances.

VI. Summary and Research Priorities

Consensual crimes, such as dealing and prostitution, are activities in which participants purposely engage, making instances of offending almost impossible to enumerate. The numbers and characteristics of persons arrested for drug law violations or prostitution reflect only a portion of these trades. Seizure information gives us another source of information about what is being sold or imported, and DUF data provide another source on what drugs are currently being used by the people handling drugs or engaged in prostitution, both generally at the street level.

The data tell us that only a portion of all dealers and prostitutes use drugs heavily. There are occasional users who regularly deal, for example, for the profits involved and upper-level dealers who are not involved in drug use but are involved in dealing purely as a business. Particularly with expensive drugs not domestically grown or produced, the dealing business involves large capital outlays but returns enormous profits and is of interest to persons looking for quick returns rather than simply personal drug supplies. There are working girls turning tricks for extra income or as full-time jobs because they see it as a better or more profitable alternative to the low-paying jobs available to them.

Among drug abusers, however, particularly the frequent users of heroin and cocaine, dealing or prostitution may be a common part of their regular activities. Dealing is done as part of sharing or obtaining drugs with friends, part of regular social activities, or is done as a money-making enterprise that fits easily into their regular round of drug-seeking activities. A portion of these user/dealers, the lower-

income, daily narcotics or cocaine users, are the most active dealers
and the most criminally active drug users in general. They do not
specialize in dealing but add it to a battery of other illegal activities.

While drug use may not be the precipitating agent in the crimes
discussed in this essay, it is a driving force in continued involvement in
those activities. Continued drug use is the single best predictor of a
career in crime for drug-using offenders, and disruption of that drug
use dramatically affects the criminal patterns of heavy abusers (see
Anglin and Hser, in this volume). Disruption of use removes the added
financial burdens the drug use often represents to the user and, impor-
tantly, helps remove him or her from the drug lifestyle.

Reporting the role that drugs play in criminal activity is always
frustrating. While the topic of drugs and crime is both timely and
compelling, data available to help draw an accurate picture of even the
extent of drug-related crimes are poor and rely on highly specialized
segments of drug-using populations. We have rich descriptions of
street-level hustlers and prostitutes, but these tell us little about their
less-visible and perhaps more successful counterparts, involved both in
drug use and "straight" lifestyles. Consequently, a stereotype of heroin
users or cocaine users emerges that may or may not represent the norm
for that group.

In examining drug dealing, the data are always incomplete, relying
on seizure information, arrest data, interviews with street dealers, or
autobiographical accounts of reformed or incarcerated drug "kingpins."
What is needed is systematic and continuous data collection on drug
markets, prices, availability, fads, and distribution patterns. This could
be a much expanded version of the National Institute on Drug Abuse
Community Epidemiology Work Group (CEWG), coupled with local
versions of the New York State Street Studies Unit described above.
Drug dealing varies by geographic area, by drug, and over time. We
have no systematic mechanism to capture any of these data. For example, the emergence of new drugs such as crack can occur, and dealing networks become established before criminal justice practitioners
are knowledgeable or able to respond. Early warning systems combining existing data sources, such as DUF, street studies, or the CEWG,
can be vital in this regard.

The understanding of the relation between drugs and crime remains
fraught with problems, caveats, and special circumstances. The heroin
addict is likely to be involved in crime prior to heroin use. He or she is
also likely to be a member of a minority group, to have poor resources

and skills, and to come from disruptive social settings. Early drug use predicts later trouble of all sorts, as it places the user in a life track quite different from the nonuser in terms of friends, interests, activities, and values. Lifestyle feeds drug use and crime, and each has a direct impact on the other. In short, only large longitudinal studies of samples of users and nonusers, coupled with detailed street-level and market data about prices, availability, and even fads in use, will allow us to draw a full picture of the roles drugs play in the lives of offenders and in the crimes they commit.

REFERENCES

Adler, Patricia A. 1985. *Wheeling and Dealing*. New York: Columbia University Press.

Anglin, M. Douglas, and Yih-Ing Hser. 1987. "Addicted Women and Crime." *Criminology* 25:359–97.

————. In this volume. "Treatment of Drug Abuse."

Anglin, M. Douglas, and George Speckart. 1986. "Narcotics Use, Property Crime and Dealing: Structural Dynamics across the Addiction Career." *Journal of Quantitative Criminology* 2(4):355–75.

Ball, John C. 1986. "The Hyper-criminal Opiate Addict." In *Crime Rates among Drug Abusing Offenders*, edited by Bruce Johnson and Eric Wish. Final report to the National Institute of Justice, U.S. Department of Justice, Washington, D.C.

Ball, John C., Eric Corty, S. Paul Petroski, Henrietta Bond, Anthony Tommasello, and Teri Baker. 1987. *Patient Characteristics, Services Provided and Treatment Outcomes in Methadone Maintenance Programs in Three Cities, 1985 and 1986*. Baltimore: University of Maryland School of Medicine.

Ball, John C., John W. Shaffer, and David N. Nurco. 1983. "The Day-to-Day Criminality of Heroin Addicts in Baltimore: A Study in the Continuity of Offense Rates." *Drug and Alcohol Dependence* 12:119–42.

Becker, Howard. 1963. *Outsiders: Studies in the Sociology of Deviance*. New York: Free Press.

Biernacki, Patrick, and Dan Waldorf. 1981. "Snowball Sampling: Problems and Techniques of Chain Referral Sampling." *Sociological Methods and Research* 10:131–63.

Brecht, M., M. D. Anglin, and J. Woodward. 1987. "Conditional Factors of Maturing Out: Personal Resources and Pre-addiction Sociopathy." *International Journal of the Addictions* 22:55–69.

Bryan, James. 1965. "Apprenticeships in Prostitution." *Social Problems* 12:287–97.

Bureau of Justice Statistics. 1984. *Federal Drug Law Violations*. Washington,
    D.C.: U.S. Department of Justice, Bureau of Justice Statistics.
Carmen, A., and H. Moody. 1985. *Working Women: The Subterranean World of
    Street Prostitution.* New York: Harper & Row.
Carpenter, Cheryl, Barry Glassner, Bruce Johnson, and Joyce Loughlin. 1988.
    Kids, Drugs, and Crime. Lexington, Mass.: Lexington.
Chaiken, Jan, and Marcia Chaiken. 1982. *Varieties of Criminal Behavior.* Santa
    Monica, Calif.: Rand.
———. In this volume. "Drugs and Predatory Crime."
Chaiken, Jan, and Douglas McDonald. 1988. "Federal Offenses and Offenders:
    Drug Law Enforcement 1980–86." Report to the Bureau of Justice Statis-
    tics, U.S. Department of Justice, Washington, D.C.
Chaiken, Marcia R., and Bruce D. Johnson. 1988. "Characteristics of Different
    Types of Drug Involved Offenders." *Issues and Practices.* Washington, D.C.:
    U.S. Department of Justice, National Institute of Justice.
Chambliss, William. 1972. *The Box Man.* New York: Harper & Row.
Collins, James, Robert Hubbard, and Valley Rachal. 1985. "Expensive Drug
    Use and Illegal Income: A Test of Explanatory Hypotheses." *Criminology*
    23:743–64.
Community Epidemiology Work Group. 1988. *Epidemic Trends in Drug Abuse.*
    Proceedings, U.S. Department of Health and Human Services, National
    Institute on Drug Abuse, Washington, D.C., December.
Dai, Brigham. 1970. *Opiate Addiction in Chicago.* New Jersey: Patterson Smith.
Darrow, William. 1988. "The Potential Spread of HIV Infection in Female
    Prostitutes." Paper presented at the annual meeting of the American Psycho-
    logical Association, August.
Des Jarlais, Don, and Samuel Friedman. 1987. "HIV Infection among Intrave-
    nous Drug Users: Epidemiology and Risk Reduction." *AIDS* 1:67–76.
Des Jarlais, Don, Samuel Friedman, and William Hopkins. 1985. "Risk Reduc-
    tion for the Acquired Immunodeficiency Syndrome among Intravenous
    Drug Users." *Annals of Internal Medicine* 103(5):755–59.
Delacoste, F., and P. Alexander, eds. 1987. *Sex Work: Writings by Women in the
    Sex Industry.* Pittsburgh, Penn.: Cleis Press.
Fagan, J., E. Piper, and M. Moore. 1986. "Violent Delinquents and Urban
    Youths." *Criminology* 24:439–64.
Faupel, Charles E., and Carl B. Klockars. 1987. "Drugs-Crime Connections:
    Elaborations from the Life Histories of Hard Core Heroin Addicts." *Social
    Problems* 34:54–68.
Federal Bureau of Investigation. 1987. *Crime in the United States, 1986.* Wash-
    ington, D.C.: U.S. Government Printing Office.
Finestone, Harold. 1958. "Cats, Kicks, and Color." *Social Problems* 5:39–45.
Goffman, Erving. 1961. *Asylums.* New York: Free Press.
Goldman, Fred. 1981. "Drug Abuse, Crime Economics: The Dismal Limits of
    Social Choice." In *The Drugs-Crime Connection*, edited by James Inciardi.
    Beverly Hills, Calif.: Sage.
Goldstein, Paul J. 1979. *Prostitution and Drugs.* Lexington, Mass.: Lexington.
———. 1981. "Getting Over: Economic Alternatives to Predatory Crime

among Street Drug Users." In *The Drugs-Crime Connection*, edited by James Inciardi. Beverly Hills, Calif.: Sage.

Goldstein, Paul J., Patricia Belluci, Barry Spunt, and Thomas Miller. 1988. "Frequency of Cocaine Use and Violence: A Comparison between Men and Women." National Institute on Drug Abuse Technical Review, Rockville, Md., May 4.

Goldstein, Paul J., Dana E. Hunt, Don Des Jarlais, and Sherry Deren. 1987. "Drug Abuse and Dependence." In *Closing the Gap: The Burden of Unnecessary Illness*, edited by Robert Amler and H. Bruce Dull. New York: Oxford University Press.

Goldstein, Paul J., Douglas Lipton, Edward Preble, Ira Sobel, Tom Miller, William Abbott, William Paige, and Franklin Soto. 1984. "The Marketing of Street Heroin in New York City." *Journal of Drug Issues* 14:553–56.

Hanson, William, George Beschner, James M. Walters, and Elliott Bovelle. 1985. *Life with Heroin*. Lexington, Mass.: Lexington.

Hopkins, William. 1989. Personal communication with author. New York: Division of Substance Abuse Services, New York State Street Research Unit.

Hughes, Patrick H., Gail Crawford, N. W. Barker, S. Schumann, and Jerome Jaffe. 1971. "The Social Structure of a Heroin Copping Community." *American Journal of Psychiatry* 125(5):551–58.

Hunt, Dana E. 1987. *Crack*. Los Angeles, Calif.: Drug Abuse Series, Drug Abuse Information and Monitoring Project.

Hunt, Dana E., Douglas Lipton, Douglas Goldsmith, Barry Spunt, and David Strug. 1985. Transcription of In-State Ethnographic Project (TRISEP). Unpublished data. Narcotic and Drug Research, Inc., New York.

Hunt, Dana E., Douglas Lipton, Douglas Goldsmith, David Strug, and Barry Spunt. 1986. "It Takes Your Heart: The Image of Methadone Maintenance in the Addict World and Its Effect on Recruitment into Treatment." *International Journal of the Addictions* 20(11,12):1751–71.

Hunt, Dana E., Douglas S. Lipton, and Barry Spunt. 1984. "Patterns of Criminal Activity among Methadone Clients and Current Narcotics Users Not in Treatment." *Journal of Drug Issues* 14:687–702.

Hunt, Dana E., Barry Spunt, and Douglas S. Lipton. 1985. "The Costly Bonus: Cocaine Related Crime among Methadone Clients." *Advances in Alcohol and Substance Abuse* 15(3):54–62.

Inciardi, James A. 1979. "Heroin Use and Street Crime." *Crime and Delinquency* 26:335–46.

———. 1986. *The War on Drugs*. Palo Alto, Calif.: Mayfield.

Inciardi, James, Anne Pottieger, and Charles Faupel. 1982. "Black Women, Heroin and Crime: Some Empirical Notes." *Journal of Drug Issues* 12:241–50.

Johnson, Bruce D., Paul J. Goldstein, Edward Preble, James Schmeidler, Douglas Lipton, Barry Spunt, and Thomas Miller. 1985. *Taking Care of Business: The Economics of Crime by Heroin Abusers*. Lexington, Mass.: Lexington.

Johnson, Bruce D., Ansley Hamid, and Edmundo Morales. 1987. "Critical

Dimensions of Crack Distribution." Paper presented at the annual meeting of the American Society of Criminology, Montreal, November.

Johnson, Bruce D., and Eric Wish. 1986. "Highlights of Research on Drug and Alcohol Abusing Criminals." Report prepared for the National Institute of Justice, U.S. Department of Justice, Washington, D.C.

Klockars, Carl B. 1974. *The Professional Fence.* New York: Free Press.

Mauge, Conrad. 1981. "Criminality and Heroin Use among Urban Minority Women." *Journal of Addictions and Health* 2:84–96.

Mieczkowski, Thomas. 1986. "Geeking Up and Throwing Down: Heroin Street Life in Detroit." *Criminology* 24:645–65.

———. 1989. "The Damage Done: Cocaine Methods in Detroit." *International Journal of Comparative and Applied Criminal Justice* (forthcoming).

Moore, Mark. 1977. *Buy and Bust.* Lexington, Mass.: Lexington.

Morganthau, Tom, and Mark Miller. 1989. "The Drug Warrior." *Newsweek* (April 10), pp. 19–22.

Morganthau, Tom, Mark Miller, Richard Sandza, and Pat Wingret. 1989. "Murder Wave in the Capital." *Newsweek* (March 13):16–20.

National Institute on Drug Abuse. 1987. *National Household Survey on Drug Abuse, 1985 Population Estimate.* Washington, D.C.: U.S. Department of Health and Human Services, National Institute on Drug Abuse.

National Institute of Justice. 1988. *Drug Use Forecasting (DUF).* Washington, D.C.: U.S. Department of Justice, National Institute of Justice.

———. 1989. *Drug Use Forecasting (DUF).* Washington, D.C.: U.S. Department of Justice, National Institute of Justice.

New York City Police Department. 1983. *Homicide Analysis 1981.* New York: New York City Police Department.

Petersen, D. M., and M. Truzzi. 1972. *Criminal Life: Views from the Inside.* Englewood Cliffs, N.J.: Prentice Hall.

Preble, Edward, and John H. Casey. 1969. "Taking Care of Business— the Heroin User's Life on the Street." *International Journal of the Addictions* 4:1–24.

Reuter, Peter, and Mark Kleiman. 1986. "Risks and Prices: An Economic Analysis of Drug Enforcement." In *Crime and Justice: An Annual Review of Research*, vol. 7, edited by Michael Tonry and Norval Morris. Chicago: University of Chicago Press.

Rinfret, Maurice. 1987. "Cocaine Price, Purity and Traffic Trends." Unpublished. Drug Enforcement Administration, Washington, D.C.

———. 1988. Personal communication with author. Washington, D.C.: Office of Intelligence, Drug Enforcement Administration.

Rosenbaum, Marsha. 1981. *Women on Heroin.* New Brunswick, N.J.: Rutgers University Press.

Shaw, Clifford R. 1966. *The Jack Roller.* 2d ed. Chicago: University of Chicago Press.

Shaw, Clifford R., and H. D. McKay. 1942. *Juvenile Delinquency and Urban Areas.* Chicago: University of Chicago Press.

Shedlin, Michelle. 1987. "If You Wanna Kiss, Go Home to Your Wife: Sexual

Meanings for the Prostitute." Presented at the annual meeting of the American Anthropological Association, November.

Siegel, Ronald K. 1982. "Cocaine Smoking." *Journal of Psychoactive Drugs* 14(4):271–343.

Spunt, Barry, Dana E. Hunt, Douglas S. Lipton, and Douglas Goldsmith. 1986. "Methadone Diversion: A New Look." *Journal of Drug Issues* 16:569–83.

Street Studies Unit. 1986. Staff reports. New York Division of Drug Abuse Services, New York.

———. 1987. Staff reports. New York Division of Drug Abuse Services, New York.

Strug, David, Dana E. Hunt, Douglas Goldsmith, Douglas S. Lipton, and Barry Spunt. 1985. "Patterns of Cocaine Use among Methadone Clients." *International Journal of the Addictions* 20(8):1163–75.

Thrasher, Frederick. 1926. *The Gang*. Chicago: University of Chicago Press.

U.S. Department of Justice. 1984. *Report to the Nation on Crime and Justice*. Washington, D.C.: U.S. Department of Justice, Bureau of Justice Statistics.

Waldorf, Dan. 1977. *Doing Coke: An Ethnography of Cocaine Users and Sellers*. Washington, D.C.: Drug Abuse Council.

Walters, James. 1980. "What Is Ethnography?" In *Ethnography: A Research Tool for Policymakers in the Drug and Alcohol Fields*, edited by C. Akins and G. Beschner. Rockville, Md.: National Institute on Drug Abuse.

Williams, Terry. 1978. "The Cocaine Culture in After-Hours Clubs." Ph.D. dissertation, City University of New York, Department of Sociology.

Wish, Eric, and Bruce Johnson. 1986. "The Impact of Substance Abuse on Criminal Careers." In *Criminal Careers and "Career Criminals,"* vol. 2, edited by Alfred Blumstein, Jacqueline Cohen, Jeffrey Roth, and Christy Visher. Washington, D.C.: National Academy Press.

Wish, Eric, Jacqueline O'Neil, and Virginia Baldau. 1988. "Lost Opportunity to Combat AIDS: Drug Abusers in the Criminal Justice System." Presented to the Drug Abuse Technical Review, National Institute on Drug Abuse, Washington, D.C., July.

Woolston, H. B. 1921. *Prostitution in the United States*. New York: Century.

Jan M. Chaiken and Marcia R. Chaiken

Drugs and Predatory Crime

ABSTRACT

Drug abuse and predatory criminality are behavior patterns that coexist in certain social groups. In other groups, drug abuse often occurs without predatory criminality. Among populations involved in drug abuse and predatory crime, a temporal sequence from drug abuse to predatory criminality is not typical; on the contrary, predatory criminality more commonly occurs before drug abuse. Drug-abusing offenders who display increasingly deviant behavior over time may eventually cross over a threshold to heroin addiction or frequent polydrug abuse. The intensity of their criminal behavior typically escalates substantially. If these high-rate offenders subsequently decrease the amount of drugs they use, they typically also lessen their rate of criminal activity. Among offenders who use multiple types of drugs, individual predatory crime commission frequencies are typically two or three times higher among offenders when they use multiple types of drugs than they are for the same offenders when they are in drug treatment or abstain from drug abuse.

A strong association has long been surmised between illicit drug use and predatory crime. Almost twenty years ago, Sutherland and Cressey (1970, p. 164) pointed out that in the United States "felons are overrepresented in the addict population, [and] crime rates are increased considerably by drug addiction." But, although they proposed

Jan M. Chaiken is deputy manager of the law and justice area at Abt Associates, Inc., Cambridge, Massachusetts. Marcia R. Chaiken is director of research, LINC, Lincoln, Massachusetts. The authors thank Alfred Blumstein, Albert J. Reiss, Jr., Bernard Gropper, the authors of other essays in this volume, and the volume's editors for their many constructive suggestions. They also would like to acknowledge support from the National Institute of Justice and the Bureau of Justice Statistics in carrying out research projects that provided a basis for this essay.

several hypotheses to explain the relationship, they summarized the state of knowledge at the time by saying that "a precise definition of the process by which narcotic drugs are related to criminal behavior has not been made" (p. 167).

Ten years later, numerous studies of incarcerated or addicted populations had increased knowledge of the drug/crime nexus; but the information was still complex and incomplete. Only in regard to heroin addiction did a coherent viewpoint prevail, but it was not universally accepted. The prevailing view, summarized by Gandossy et al. (1980), was that drug use propelled income-producing crime primarily because addicts required money to buy drugs. This view was supported by the following findings: many serious offenders were drug users and had started using drugs as juveniles; not all drug users became addicts, but continued drug use frequently led to heroin addiction; minority group members were proportionately more likely than nonminority group members to be drug users and to be arrested for crimes; many (although not all) drug users became addicted before they were involved in criminal pursuits or arrest; among arrestees and prisoners, drug users were more likely than nondrug users to have been arrested for income-generating crimes rather than crimes of violence; drug users in treatment were more likely to have been arrested for property crimes than for violent crimes; and the drug users who were most likely to commit numerous crimes were heroin addicts.

At the time, some researchers and many policymakers were convinced from this evidence that a fairly simple causal relation existed between drug use and criminality, especially for minority group members who were disproportionately likely to become involved in drug use: first came some form of drug use as juveniles, then drug use progressed to heroin addiction, and, as heroin addicts, these users committed many nonviolent income-producing crimes to support their habits. But many countervailing facts were already known, such as that a substantial number of casual users of heroin (nonaddicts) existed and were not heavily involved in crime (e.g., Robins, Davis, and Wish 1980).

The picture available from today's research indicates that, while the progression to heroin addiction and income-producing crimes may apply to some drug users, other behavioral sequences also occur often (even *more* often), for example, patterns involving drugs other than heroin, or predatory crime before drug addiction, or violent rather than nonviolent criminality. Some patterns are applicable only in particular subgroups of the population.

In short, no single sequential or causal relationship is now believed to relate drug use to predatory crime. When the behaviors of large groups of people are studied in the aggregate, no coherent general patterns emerge associating drug use per se with participation in predatory crime, age at onset of participation in crime, or persistence in committing crime. Rather, different patterns appear to apply to different types of drug users (Chaiken and Johnson 1988). But research does show that certain types of drug abuse are strongly related to offenders' committing crimes at high *frequencies*—violent crimes as well as other, income-producing crimes. The observed relationship applies to various population subgroups, including groups defined by age, race, or sex.

This essay summarizes the known research information—with emphasis on quantitative research—about the association between drug use and *predatory crime*. The association between drug dealing and predatory crime is also discussed, because it is often more pertinent or stronger than the association between drug use and crime.

In discussing predatory crime, we have in mind instrumental offenses committed for material gain. We do not include aggressive crimes such as marital violence, homicide, or assault unrelated to robbery or burglary; public disorder crimes; driving under the influence of alcohol or drugs; or consensual crimes such as prostitution. However, in reviewing the results of published works, some nonpredatory crimes may be included with predatory crimes if they were studied together or summarized together by the original authors.

In summarizing and commenting on the literature on drug use and predatory crime, we use a specialized vocabulary that has been developed in the study of criminal careers (Blumstein et al. 1986). The terms *onset*, *participation*, *frequency*, *desistance*, and *persistence* are drawn from the concept of a criminal career as a sequence of crimes committed by an individual offender (Blumstein et al. 1986). A person's criminal career has its *onset* when he or she commits a crime for the first time, at which time the offender is said to be *participating* in crime. A *participation rate* is the proportion of a group of people who engage in crimes during a specified period. The *frequency* or *rate* of crime commission is the number of crimes committed per year when the offender is free to commit crime (that is, unincarcerated). *Desistance* is the end of the criminal career, and *persistence* refers to a career that lasts a long time between onset and desistance. (Details are in Section III.)

Since this essay focuses on predatory crime and not on assaultive or other destructive behavior resulting from physiological effects of drugs, we do not distinguish among pharmacological classes of drugs such as amphetamines, barbiturates, or hallucinogens. However, as shown in the sections that follow, the types of drugs used by offenders and the frequency with which they use them are important in understanding the connections between drug abuse and predatory crime. Most drug users abuse at least two types of substances; therefore many research studies summarized in this essay categorize types of *drug abuse* rather than types of *drugs* abused. Commonly employed categories of drug abuse, in order of increasing seriousness, are: marijuana and alcohol abuse; use of other nonopiate illicit drugs (possibly in addition to marijuana and alcohol); and opiate or cocaine use, including various derivative forms of those substances.

People are generally considered to be involved in a specific category of drug abuse if they have a sustained pattern of involvement. For example, most researchers would not classify as a drug abuser a person who has used marijuana two or three times. Similarly, a person who frequently drinks and also smokes marijuana would be classified by most researchers as involved in marijuana use; this would be the case even if he or she is also known to have used cocaine on one occasion. However, people who have a sustained pattern of relatively serious drug abuse would be classified as involved in that form of drug abuse even though they were more likely to indulge in less serious forms of abuse. For example, people who use heroin every week would be classified as heroin users even if they drank alcohol and smoked marijuana every day.

Almost all the studies discussed in this essay were based on self-reports of drug use and crime. Self-reports are less likely than criminal justice system records or other forms of agency records to underestimate study subjects' involvement in crime, delinquency, or drug use. However, the validity of self-report information about drug abuse and criminality is questionable because respondents may have had difficulty recalling past behavior, may not have understood the questions they were asked, or may either have concealed or exaggerated their illegal activities. Researchers who conduct these studies are aware of these validity issues and use methods that minimize the possible distorting effects on their findings.

The studies most likely to avoid problems of recall are those in which subjects are interviewed at set intervals over a period of time. These studies provide valuable information on the relationships between predatory crime and drug use over the life course. However, many other studies learn about respondents' past behavior retrospectively.

When findings from prospective and retrospective studies are similar, they reinforce each other.

The methods used for collecting data about drug use and criminality range from relatively large national surveys to in-depth interviews and observations of small groups. The study subjects include random samples of the nation's youth, groups of school children, addicts in treatment centers, inmates in prisons and jails, defendants whose cases had been just concluded, samples of inner-city youth, probationers, and adult street populations. Aside from studies of addicts in treatment, important data sources drawn on in this essay are the National Youth Survey, a Rand Corporation inmate survey, and interview data from street addicts in New York City. Brief descriptions of these data sources are given here.

1. *National Youth Survey*. The National Youth Survey is a prospective longitudinal study of delinquent behavior, alcohol and drug use, problem-related substance abuse, and mental health problems in a representative sample of American youth (Elliott, Huizinga, and Menard 1989). To date, seven waves of data have been collected on a panel of youths covering the period from 1976 to 1986. (However, published analyses cover only six waves, representing the seven-year period from 1976 to 1983.) The random sample was drawn in 1976 and contained 2,360 eligible youths aged eleven to seventeen at the time of the initial interview. Of these, 1,735 agreed to participate; by age, sex, and race they were representative of the total eleven- through seventeen-year-old youth population of the United States in 1976. Respondent loss over the six waves of the survey has been 13 percent. Comparisons of participants across the first six waves indicated that loss by age, sex, ethnicity, class, place of residence, and self-reported delinquency did not substantially influence the underlying distributions on these variables.

Annual involvement in delinquent behavior, use of alcohol and drugs, and mental health problems were self-reported in personal face-to-face interviews, usually in the respondents' homes. Confidentiality was guaranteed, and no information about individuals collected in the National Youth Survey can be released to any person or agency without the respondent's written consent. Delinquent behavior was conceptualized as a parallel measure to official arrest, so that offenses self-reported in the survey can be categorized as Uniform Crime Report (UCR) Index offenses (which are murder and nonnegligent manslaughter, forcible rape, robbery, aggravated assault, burglary, larceny-theft, motor vehicle theft, and arson; murder is not included in the National

Youth Survey), UCR Part II offenses (all other criminal offenses), and juvenile status offenses. For each offense, the response set involves an open-ended frequency estimate; respondents who reported ten or more occurrences of a particular offense during the year were also offered a set of categorical responses ranging from "mostly" to "two to three times a day."

Although the delinquency offenses include some drug-related offenses (e.g., selling marijuana), the National Youth Survey includes separate questions about first use, quantity, reasons for using, and sources of alcohol (beer, wine, and hard liquor), marijuana, hallucinogens, amphetamines, heroin, cocaine, and barbiturates. Questions related to mental health capture dimensions of social isolation, depression, and use of mental health services.

The results of the National Youth Survey are extensively reported in papers by the primary data collectors, and the data are also archived and available for secondary data analysis.

2. *Rand Inmate Survey*.[1] In 1978, the Rand Corporation carried out a survey of convicted male offenders housed in prisons and jails in California, Michigan, and Texas. (An earlier anonymous Rand survey of California prisoners obtained only nonspecific information about respondents' drug use and is not cited in this essay.) Self-report data on criminal activity, personal characteristics, and criminal record were obtained from 2,316 inmates by means of a group-administered written questionnaire. In addition, official record data were collected for the prison inmates (and obtained for 1,214 of the 1,380 prison inmates surveyed).

The survey provided detailed information about crimes that respondents had committed during a one- to two-year measurement period immediately prior to their arrest for their current sentenced crime. Inmates reported the date of their arrest and then followed questionnaire instructions to identify the beginning of the measurement period, which was January 1 of the year preceding this arrest. They then answered questions about their activities during the measurement period related to commissions of burglary, robbery, assault, automobile theft, other theft, fraud, drug trafficking, and forgery, check, or credit card offenses. Inmates indicated whether or not they had committed each of these offenses and either the number of commissions (if less

---

[1] This description relies heavily on Peterson et al. (1982).

than ten) or the number of months during which they committed each crime and their rate of commission in those months. They also answered questions for the same measurement period concerning heavy drinking and use of drugs other than marijuana (subdivided into three categories: heroin/methadone, barbiturates/"reds"/downers, and amphetamines/uppers/"whites"). To obtain data on a retrospective longitudinal basis, the questionnaire also asked briefly about crime commissions and drug use during two two-year reference periods preceding the main measurement period.

The Rand inmate survey was administered at twelve prisons and fourteen county jails. The institutions were selected to yield a broad sample of offenders active in both urban areas and smaller cities within each of the three study states. The prisons included all custody levels within each prison system. The sample was drawn randomly using selection probabilities that resulted in approximating the characteristics of inmates coming into prison or jail during a limited period of time—an "incoming cohort."

The results of the survey and the quality of the self-report data are extensively documented in procedural, methodological, and analytical reports. Also, the data have been archived and are available for secondary analysis.

3. *Street Addicts in New York City*.[2] During 1980–82 the New York State Division of Substance Abuse Services and Narcotic and Drug Research, Inc., collected information from heroin or methadone addicts who lived on the streets in East and Central Harlem and were engaged in some form of criminality. The field workers were exaddict, exoffender staff, who were sent into the streets to locate subjects. They sometimes approached persons on the street who were unknown to them. More often they found an acquaintance who informally introduced them to potential respondents. The field workers attempted to recruit about one female for every two or three males.

Individuals who were willing to participate in the study were taken by field workers to a research storefront. After obtaining the subjects' informed consent, research workers asked them to report the following information about the previous day: types of crimes committed, criminal income, drugs used, purchased, sold, or distributed, cash income from all sources, cash expenditures, involvement in drug treatment,

---

[2] This description relies heavily on Johnson et al. (1985); see their book for further discussion.

and drugs received at no cost ("in-kind"). Respondents were initially interviewed for five consecutive days and then asked to return once a week for the next four weeks. A longitudinal research design was approximated with the East Harlem subjects, by conducting additional cycles of data collection at three- to six-month intervals.

In general, when broad populations are surveyed, as in the National Youth Survey, the results are representative of "typical" behavior. But broad samples often include only small numbers of people who are serious drug abusers or predatory criminals. Studies that focus on populations of drug abusers, like the New York City street addict studies, or on offender groups, such as the Rand inmate survey, are more valuable for amassing detailed data about seriously deviant behavior. Through a combination of findings from these and other sources described in the remainder of this essay, we can piece together the rich complex of relationships between drug use and predatory crime.

Here is how this essay is organized. Section I summarizes research that indicates the absence of a simple or unified association between drug use and participation in crime. It also discusses the limitations of research based on information about arrested or incarcerated offenders, who are atypical of offenders in general in regard to their drug use. Section II presents evidence showing there is no coherent, general association between drug use and onset or persistence of criminality. Section III reviews the quantitative measures that are used to describe levels of offending activity by discussing and comparing the wide variety of such statistics that appear in the drug literature. Section IV describes the relationships between an offender's drug use and his contemporaneous amount of criminal activity, based partly on a reanalysis of drug abusers' offending frequencies that have been presented in a number of studies. Section V discusses the implications of the observed relationships between drug abuse and predatory crime.

I. Summary of Findings from Recent Research

People who commit predatory crimes over long periods tend also to commit other crimes and to have begun their criminal careers at young ages. Similarly, people who use illicit drugs often or in large quantities tend to use a variety of drugs and to have begun using drugs during adolescence. These seemingly similar groups of persistent offenders and persistent drug users are not necessarily the same people. There appears to be no simple general relation between high rates of drug use and high rates of crime.

A. Patterns of Criminal Behavior and Drug Use

Research on criminal behavior over the past decade has demonstrated strong interrelationships among age at onset of a criminal career, persistence of criminal activity, rates of committing offenses, and types of offenses committed. In any population of offenders, most commit non-violent offenses and at low rates. Even adult offenders who were incarcerated for violent crimes such as robbery or assault typically committed only one or two of these offenses in the year preceding their incarceration (Chaiken and Chaiken 1982; Visher 1986; Mande and English 1988; Chaiken and Chaiken 1989). However, a relatively small group of offenders commits crimes at very high rates—hundreds of crimes per year when they are free to do so (Chaiken and Chaiken 1982; Ball, Shaffer, and Nurco 1983; Johnson et al. 1985; Ball 1986; Mande and English 1988; Chaiken and Chaiken 1989). Those who frequently commit violent crimes also are very likely to commit other crimes, such as burglary and theft, and to commit one or more of these types of crimes at high rates (Chaiken and Chaiken 1982; Chaiken and Chaiken 1985; Johnson et al. 1985). Moreover, this small group of adult offenders is likely to have started committing crimes as young adolescents (Chaiken and Chaiken 1982; Hanson et al. 1985; Johnson et al. 1985).

Studies of patterns of drug use have produced parallel findings. Most people who use illicit drugs confine their use to sporadic use of marijuana, while relatively few use other illicit drugs such as barbiturates, amphetamines, cocaine, or heroin (Miller et al. 1983; Johnston, O'Malley, and Bachman 1985, 1986). An even smaller number of people use these drugs frequently (e.g., daily or more often); and those who use any drug in high quantities or at high frequencies are likely to be using also several other types of illicit drugs frequently, often in combination with alcohol (Elliott and Huizinga 1985; Wish and Johnson 1986; Elliott, Huizinga, and Menard 1989). The high-frequency users are also more likely than other users to have started using drugs as adolescents (Newcomb and Bentler 1988).

While these parallel patterns of criminal behavior and drug abuse are strongly interrelated, research does not support the view that they are basically overlapping descriptions of the same people. There are a few severely addicted people who commit no crimes aside from illegal possession of drugs (Collins et al. 1982); and there are criminals who commit numerous serious crimes but are not involved in drug use (Chaiken and Chaiken 1985; Innes 1988). Moreover, for most people, changes over time in individuals' use or nonuse of drugs are not systematically related to changes in their participation or nonparticipation in criminal activity (Kandel, Simcha-Fagan, and Davies 1986; Newcomb and Bentler 1988). One exception, discussed in Section IV, is a repeated finding that, among heroin-using high-rate offenders, intensity of offending appears to vary directly with intensity of drug use (e.g., Anglin and Speckart 1986; Nurco et al. 1988).

Research does not support the view that drug abuse necessarily precedes onset of criminal activity, nor does it demonstrate a causal ordering between drug use and criminality. A more coherent interpretation is that drug abuse and participation in crime coexist in some social groups. Rather than having a cause-and-effect relationship, the onset of drug use, the onset of predatory crime, or both, can occur in early puberty as products of similar external factors. Fagan and others have found that both or either of these behaviors can be explained by intervening variables such as destructive factors in the environment (e.g., physical abuse or criminal siblings) or the absence of traditional social controls (e.g., lack of parental attention or participation in rewarding school activities) (White, Pandina, and LaGrange 1987; Fagan and Weis 1990). The more deviant the environment, the more likely an adolescent is to perform poorly in school, to use multiple forms of illicit drugs frequently, and to participate frequently in predatory crime (Williams and Kornblum 1985; Simcha-Fagan and Schwartz 1986).

From analysis of self-report surveys of male prison and jail inmates in three states in the late 1970s, we concluded that predatory criminals may be involved in drug use as a part of their nontraditional lifestyle, which in most instances is also evidenced by other factors such as irregular employment and absence of marital ties (Chaiken and Chaiken 1982). However, many long-term offenders in these inmate surveys had never used drugs; in fact, nearly half (47 percent) of inmates who had never used drugs were persistent offenders (they had committed crimes for more than five years prior to their arrest). Generally, older criminals are less likely than younger offenders to use illicit drugs (Wish and Johnson 1986); but even among young delinquents who committed crimes such as robbery, burglary, or serious assaults in inner-city areas, most have been found not to use drugs (Fagan and Weis 1990).

Where, then, lies the strong relationship between drug use and criminality? A large body of research, discussed in the remainder of this essay, shows that, among predatory offenders, the ones who are *high-frequency* drug users are also very likely to be *high-rate* predators and to commit many different types of crimes, including violent crimes, and to use many different types of drugs. This finding has been confirmed for adolescents and adults, across states, independent of race, and in many countries. It also is the same for both males and females with one notable exception: females who use drugs frequently are less likely than males to commit violent crimes (but women drug users are more likely to resort to prostitution, shoplifting, and similar covert, nonviolent crimes at high rates [Sanchez and Johnson 1987]).

The relationship between high-frequency drug use and high-frequency criminality is intensified by long durations of involvement in drug use and predatory crime (Nurco et al. 1988). Adult offenders who commit robbery and burglary at the highest rates typically have been persistent offenders and drug users since they were juveniles, for example, using heroin as juveniles and starting to commit predatory crimes before they were sixteen years old (Chaiken and Chaiken 1982). The earlier the age of onset of cocaine or heroin use, the more likely persistent offenders are to be serious predatory offenders as adults (Chaiken and Chaiken 1985; Collins and Bailey 1987).

B. Drug Sellers

In all studies that have examined the issue, the relationship between drug use and criminality has been found to be substantially weaker than the relationship between drug *sales* and other forms of criminality (Chaiken and Chaiken 1982; Johnson et al. 1985; Chaiken 1986). Most people who sell drugs do so occasionally and privately and are not likely to be involved in predatory crimes. But those who sell drugs publicly, for example in parks, streets, or back alleys, are likely to commit predatory crimes and to commit them at higher rates than people who commit the same type of offenses but do not sell drugs (Johnson et al. 1985; Williams and Kornblum 1985).

Based on surveys of inmates and interviews with other offenders, adult robbers who sell drugs on average report committing many more robberies than robbers who do not sell drugs; these *robbers* also report committing more *burglaries* than many other burglars, especially burglars who do not distribute drugs (Johnson et al. 1985; Chaiken 1986). Among urban youth, drug sales were also found to have a strong association with committing numerous serious crimes, including armed robbery (Fagan and Weis 1990).

While many public drug dealers are themselves frequent users of various types of drugs, others are careful not to mix business with pleasure; they only sporadically use their own illicit merchandise. Yet these nonuser drug dealers still commit predatory crimes, including numerous robberies and burglaries (Chaiken and Chaiken 1982; Williams and Kornblum 1985; Mieczkowski 1986).

Some of the robberies and other assaultive crimes committed by offenders who also sell drugs are systemic aspects of the drug trade (Johnson et al. 1985). Given the highly competitive nature of drug distribution (Kleiman and Smith, in this volume; Moore, in this volume) and the obvious lack of official regulation, violence and robbery are sometimes used to drive competitors out of business or to protect a dealer's money, supplies, and connections (Adler 1985; Johnson et al. 1985). Other assaults and predatory crimes committed by drug dealers arise from their need for money for drugs and are opportunistically focused on the first available target (Williams and Kornblum 1985)—although many addicts are able to sustain their use by committing less serious crimes (Goldstein 1985; Hunt, in this volume). However, many predatory crimes are committed by dealers who find vulnerable victims with cash, follow them to a secluded area, threaten or actually injure them, and take their money (Chaiken and Chaiken 1985; Hanson et al. 1985).

C. Arrestees Are Not Typical Offenders

Researchers' difficulties in sorting out details of the drug/crime nexus can in part be traced to the misleading and unrepresentative nature of information and statistics derived for readily accessible study populations such as arrestees and prisoners. High-rate criminals who do not use drugs, or use them only sporadically, are far less likely to be arrested than are their counterparts who use drugs frequently (Chaiken and Chaiken 1985). Most offenders who are arrested for predatory crimes commit few crimes but do exhibit at least low levels of drug use (National Institute of Justice 1988). Among offenders who commit crimes at high rates but are arrested infrequently (so-called "high-rate winners"), many started using illicit drugs as juveniles and continued to use illicit drugs other than marijuana as adults, but only a quarter of them are high-frequency drug users, such as daily users of heroin. Among incarcerated offenders, the ones who are arrested frequently are actually a mix of offenders including two very distinct types of chronic offenders: inept, emotionally disturbed people (as described by Elliott and Huizinga 1985) who do not commit many predatory offenses but are arrested nearly every time they commit a crime (Chaiken and Chaiken 1985); and frequent users of multiple drugs who commit predatory crimes at high rates and are frequently caught because they are opportunistic and do not plan their criminal activities to avoid detection. Over one third of these high crime rate, high arrest rate of fenders reported onset of heroin use as juveniles and daily heroin use during the period before their last arrest (Chaiken and Chaiken 1985), but they are not characteristic of all offenders who are arrested frequently.

Obviously, a typical group of arrestees or prisoners includes disproportionate numbers of offenders who are arrested frequently and much smaller proportions of offenders who are arrested infrequently. Thus researchers and policymakers alike must be careful not to draw overly broad conclusions about the drug-use patterns of *offenders in general* by examining information about the drug-use patterns of arrestees or prisoners.

II. Chronology of Participation in Use of Illegal Drugs and Predatory Crime

The criminal careers model provides a useful framework for organizing the discussion of research on the relationship between drug use and predatory crime. Similarities and differences between the onset and persistence of these two types of behaviors are discussed in this section. Particular emphasis is given to research on the interrelatedness of the onset and persistence of drug use and predatory crime.

A. Onset of Criminal Behavior

Research does not support the hypothesis that use of illicit drugs ultimately results in the user's involvement in predatory crime, or even that this is a predominant pattern. Studies of youths' drug use and crime that refute this hypothesis have included repeated interviews with over 1,500 youngsters selected as a representative sample for a National Youth Survey (Elliott and Huizinga 1985); in-depth interviews with 100 youngsters in a medium-size upstate city in New York (Carpenter et al. 1988); surveys of over 800 inner-city youth including almost 200 school dropouts (Fagan and Weis 1990); repeated surveys from age fifteen to age twenty-five with a sample of over 1,000 youths selected to be representative of students enrolled in New York State secondary schools (Kandel, Simcha-Fagan, and Davies 1986); and repeated interviews over a period of eight years with a sample of 1,000 youths who originally attended Los Angeles County schools (Newcomb and Bentler 1988).

Virtually all these studies have found that many more youngsters use illicit drugs than are involved in predatory crime. As youthful users of illicit substances approach adulthood, they are likely to continue to use drugs, but they are less likely—not more likely—to commit predatory crimes (Kandel, Simcha-Fagan, and Davies 1986). Moreover, youths who commit serious predatory crimes are more likely to use illicit drugs frequently than are youthful users of illicit drugs to engage in predatory crime (Fagan and Weis 1990).

Research evidence provides little support for the popular conception that most drug-involved offenders begin committing predatory crimes because they want money to buy drugs. In fact, many of them were involved in juvenile delinquency, including minor forms of predatory crime, before they were involved in illicit drug use. The data are more consistent with the commonsensical notion that minor predatory crime is a precursor to serious predatory crime. Prospective longitudinal self-report data from the National Youth Survey (Elliott and Huizinga 1985) and studies based on a sample of New York youngsters (Kandel, Simcha-Fagan, and Davies 1986) demonstrate that, among youngsters who both use drugs and commit nondrug offenses, delinquency is about as likely to begin before as after initial use of illicit drugs.

For example, table 1, which summarizes data from the National Youth Survey, shows that 16.3 percent of this sample were involved in both drug use and delinquency. Of these, half (8.1 percent) reported initial drug use after delinquency involvement, and the other half reported drug use in the same year as delinquency involvement (3.7 percent) or earlier (4.5 percent). Ethnographic studies, in which researchers spend long periods of time observing and talking to youngsters, have also found that among youths who use drugs and commit predatory crimes, the connection appears to be due more to a style of everyday life than to simply committing predatory crimes to get money for drugs (Williams and Kornblum 1985; Mieczkowski 1986). For example, although youngsters involved in the street drug trade in Detroit used drugs occasionally, they were not addicted and had contempt for the addicts to whom they distributed heroin; as part of being involved in the drug trade they were also involved in more predatory activities involving weapons (Mieczkowski 1986).

These observations, derived from prospective and ethnographic studies of juveniles, find confirmation in retrospective studies of adult

TABLE 1

Self-Report of Drug Use and Delinquency, National Youth Survey

Behavior	Percent of Subpopulation	Percent of Total Population
No drug use and no delinquency		46.0
Drug use and no delinquency:		26.5
Alcohol	18.6	
Alcohol and marijuana	7.1	
Alcohol, marijuana, and other drugs	.6	
No drug use but delinquent		8.9
Initial drug use a year or more *before* delinquency involvement:		4.5
Alcohol	3.9	
Alcohol and marijuana	.5	
Alcohol, marijuana, and other drugs	.1	
Initial drug use a year or more *after* delinquency involvement:		8.1
Alcohol	4.7	
Alcohol and marijuana	2.1	
Alcohol, marijuana, and other drugs	1.3	
Initial drug use and delinquency involvement occurred in same year:		3.7
Alcohol	1.6	
Alcohol and marijuana	2.0	
Alcohol, marijuana, and other drugs	.1	
Other or not classifiable		4.3

SOURCE.—Elliott and Huizinga (1984), table 9.

NOTE.—Drugs mentioned refer to those used during the period specified. *Delinquency* is self-reported commission of an Index crime during the reference period (12 months). Percentages do not add to subtotals due to rounding.

offenders. The Rand inmate survey (Chaiken and Chaiken 1982) in three states showed that 12 percent reported committing predatory crimes as adults after using drugs for two or more years; but 15 percent started committing predatory crimes as adults and two or more years later began to use illicit substances (see table 2). When the surveyed inmates were asked about their main reasons for first becoming involved in crime, only 26 percent of those who used illicit drugs cited their drug involvement as a primary motive, and only 20 percent of them cited their drug involvement as their sole reason for getting into crime.

Anglin and Speckart (1987) and Anglin and Hser (1987) have applied sophisticated statistical methods to examine the temporal ordering between addicts' criminality and drug use, using data describing the ad-

TABLE 2

Relationship between Drug Use and First Involvement in Crime:
Survey of Prison and Jail Inmates in Three States

Response	Subtotals	Percent of Respondents with Usable Data
No drug use during the five- to six-year reference period:		42
Began crime during last two calendar years	6	
Began crime during middle two-year period	12	
Began crime during first two-year period	5	
Began crime prior to the entire reference period	19	
Began both crime and drug use prior to entire reference period		26
Began onset of drug use and crime simultaneously during any one of the two-year reporting periods		5
Began crime prior to drug use, during reference period		15
Began drug use prior to crime, during reference period		12

SOURCE.—Chaiken and Chaiken (1982), table 5.10.
NOTE.—Respondents in 1978–79 provided self-reports on drug use and crime during a thirteen- to twenty-four-month-long measurement period that ended with their arrest on the charge for which they were incarcerated and began on January 1 of the preceding year. This is called the "last two calendar years." Respondents also provided self-reports for the two-year period prior to the measurement period (called the "middle two years") and the two-year period before that (the "first two years"). Missing or unusable data accounted for 12.5 percent of the sample and were excluded from the analysis.

dicts' behavior in the periods prior to and during their addiction. They find that involvement in property crime activities generally tends to precede the onset of addiction. In particular, approximately half of all first burglaries and more than half of all first thefts precede addiction. (These studies also illuminate the relationship between addiction and crime *frequency*, the topic of Section IV below.)

In sum, use of illicit drugs may be a primary cause for initial participation in predatory crime for some offenders; however, for the vast majority of offenders who commit predatory crimes, use of illicit substances appears to be neither a necessary nor a sufficient cause of onset of predatory criminal behavior. Even onset of *narcotic addiction* often does not appear to be causally related to onset of involvement in property crime. Rather, the onset of heroin addiction is often a key point in accelerating an existing criminal career.

B. Persistence of Drug Use and Predatory Crime

Studies that have followed the behavior of youngsters over the span of early adolescence to young adulthood indicate that drug use is more likely to persist over this life span than is involvement in predatory crime (Kandel, Simcha-Fagan, and Davies 1986; Newcomb and Bentler 1988). Further, continued criminality is more predictive of future drug use than is drug use predictive of criminality. Although over two-thirds of youthful users of drugs are likely to continue use as adults, as they approach their late teens and early twenties, half of the juveniles who commit crimes stop (Elliott and Huizinga 1985; Kandel, Simcha-Fagan, and Davies 1986). As they grow older, delinquents are likely to use more addictive drugs—starting with marijuana, progressing to hallucinogens, sedatives and analgesics, and then to cocaine and heroin (Inciardi 1987b). Delinquents most likely to engage in drug use are those who have been sexually abused as children (Dembo et al. 1987). Moreover, almost all persistent serious delinquents are likely eventually to use drugs. Only 18 percent of chronic, serious offenders in the National Youth Survey remained drug free as they aged (Elliott and Huizinga 1985).

A review of cohort studies covering nearly 12,000 boys in Philadelphia, London, Racine (Wisconsin), and Marion County (Oregon) suggests that youngsters are most likely to continue committing serious crimes as adults if they behave badly in school, come from poor families, have other criminals in their immediate family, have a low IQ, and receive inadequate parental attention (Blumstein, Farrington, and Moitra 1985). Retrospective studies of the careers of predatory adult offenders suggest that essentially the same factors are characteristic of persistent offenders who commit the most serious predatory crimes (robbery and burglary) at high rates (Chaiken and Chaiken 1985). While drug abuse may often be concomitant with these predictive factors, it generally has not been shown to have independent value as a predictor of persistent offending.

Although sustained drug use cannot, in general, be considered a cause of predation, involvement in predatory crime increases the probability of serious forms of drug use which in turn enhance continuation and seriousness of a "predatory career." This self-reinforcing relationship has been demonstrated by interviews conducted with patients in methadone treatment about their "addiction careers"; in these studies, Anglin and Speckart (1986) found that theft precedes addiction more frequently than it follows addiction; however, burglary and robbery are more likely to follow than precede addiction; and there is positive covariation between the levels of narcotics use and the numbers and seriousness of crimes committed.

Ethnographic studies of street addicts suggest that these relationships may be explained by involvement in a lifestyle of "taking care of business" in which "the hustle" is any legitimate or illegal activity that can generate income (Hanson et al. 1985). Theft and other minor predatory crimes become a "normal" activity for relatively many elementary school–aged boys raised on inner-city streets. As they approach adolescence, boys in many major cities have the opportunity to participate in the drug trade (Mieczkowski 1986; Hunt, in this volume). Part of the street drug trade often involves keeping a small amount of drugs for personal use and robbing street drug distributors or other community residents of drugs or cash (Johnson et al. 1985). As adults, heroin use may continue as part of this lifestyle, but even regular users of heroin may abstain for relatively long periods in the absence of a safe and lucrative hustle (Hanson et al. 1985). Among hustlers, robbery is not generally considered a safe means of obtaining money; however, a relatively small proportion of adult hustlers like to do "stick-ups" (robberies) because they consider the activity adventuresome and exciting (Hanson et al. 1985).

Little is known about the end of hustling lifestyles or the termination of predatory careers among drug-involved persistent offenders. Recent research suggests that addicted adult offenders often continue to use drugs and commit crimes for twelve or more years in the absence of effective treatment and supervision (Anglin, Piper, and Speckart 1987). There is some evidence that mortality rates are relatively high for this population and that almost half of the deaths are due to drug use (Joe and Simpson 1987). There is also evidence, based on in-depth interviews with over 100 ex-addicts, that the end of a hustling lifestyle can be self-initiated because of a personally negative incident endemic to hustling, such as a threat of bodily harm from another dealer, and can take place in the absence of formal treatment (Biernacki 1986).

Future research is urgently needed on the causes and reasons for desisting from a life of drug use, crime, or both. Most pertinent for policy purposes will be improved information on the manner and extent to which drug addiction extends an addict's criminal career.

III. Measuring and Describing the Intensity of Criminal Activity

Moving on from issues related to individuals' *onset* and *termination* of criminal careers, this section and Section IV focus on the *participation rate* in specified types of crimes at various times during the criminal career, and *offending frequencies* (number of crimes per year for individuals who commit a specified type of crime) (Blumstein et al. 1986, pp. 17–20). Information about participation rates and offending frequency has appeared in many guises in the literature on the relationship between drug abuse and criminality, making comparisons across studies quite difficult.

Commonly, and quite consistently, *prevalence* percentages are used in this literature to describe the participation rate of a specified population in some type of criminal activity. But the *offending frequency* lambda (λ), as defined by the National Academy of Sciences Panel on Research on Criminal Careers (Blumstein et al. 1986)—namely the annual rate of committing crimes among those who commit a particular type of crime—is not commonly tabulated or analyzed in the drug-related literature. In our review, we found statistics concerning the values of λ among groups that differ according to their levels and types of drug use only in the appendix of Johnson et al. (1985, table B-13, "Mean Lambdas").

In nearly all cases where an *incidence*, or crime commission, rate is reported in the drug-related literature, it is the aggregate crime rate per capita, which by definition is the offending frequency multiplied by the participation rate *d*. Whereas the offending frequency λ applies to people who *are* committing the type of crime in question, aggregate crime commission rates apply also to offenders in the group who do not commit the crime (counted as having a zero crime rate) along with those who do commit the crime.

For this reason, aggregate crime rates per capita may differ among study populations, even if the offenders in the populations have similar criminal behavior. For example, if a population of arrestees is divided into subgroups of, say, cocaine users and nonusers, both subgroups can be expected to have higher aggregate robbery rates than the corresponding cocaine users and nonusers in a random sample of the general population. This is because the general population would naturally have a smaller overall participation rate d in robbery, and thus a smaller λd. So it is not possible to learn anything useful about robbers' behavior when using or not using cocaine from these aggregate figures. But comparing the values of the offending frequency (λ) for cocaine users and nonusers in two populations is meaningful and interesting, since λ (for robbery) refers to those members of the study population who do commit robbery. Thus, aggregate crime rates, as the name implies, are useful for studying characteristics of groups, while offending frequencies λ are useful for studying criminal behavior of individuals.

Any research that reports the participation rate d along with the incidence rate allows quantitative comparisons of offending frequencies to be made with other studies since λ can be calculated by dividing λd by d. For example, in a subgroup 35 percent of whose members commit robbery and whose one-year incidence rate for robbery for the total larger group is 2.3, the mean annual offending frequency λ for those who commit robbery is 6.6 robberies per year (2.3 divided by .35). Researchers (and journal editors) ought to be aware of this benefit of publishing participation rates along with aggregate crime rates, even if one or the other is not particularly pertinent to the analysis in question.

Many different formats have been used for presenting and analyzing aggregate crime-rate information per capita, but these definitional differences have little substantive importance when comparing high-rate with low-rate offenders. This section gives some examples of statistics commonly used for presenting crime-rate information, and the relationships among them. A description of the numerical values of these various statistics, and the conclusions that can be drawn from them, appears in Section IV below.

A. Group Crime Rates per Unincarcerated Year

Average crime rates per year of street time are rarely calculated for subgroups of offenders defined by their extent of drug use. Chaiken (1986) presents crime rates for subgroups defined by extent of heroin use; these are estimates of the average aggregate number of crimes committed per year of unincarcerated time per person in each subgroup.

B. Annual Incidence Rates

Annual incidence rates are more common in the literature (e.g., Elliott and Huizinga 1985). These are aggregate crime rates per calendar year (not unincarcerated year). They are also group rates, but they

confound the influences of criminal justice system behavior with indi
viduals' crime commission behavior. Individuals who happened to be
incarcerated for part or all of the study year could possibly contribute
fewer crimes to the average than they would have contributed if they
were free, or "on the street." The *annualized crime rates* reported by
Johnson et al. (1985, table 7–2) are definitionally identical to annual
incidence rates.

If the incarcerating behavior of the criminal justice system is not
pertinent to a study nor expected to change, incidence rates unadjusted
for street time are entirely satisfactory for comparing behavior of individuals. However, data concerning crime rates per year of street time
are valuable for estimating the specific effects of incarceration on crime
rates, especially if one posits possible changes in sentencing policies, or
for comparing offending behavior across jurisdictions with different
incarceration patterns.

The appropriate crime-rate statistic for any purpose depends on the
policy context or research issue under consideration. For example,
Marsden, Collins, and Hubbard (1986) point out that publishing average crime rates per unincarcerated year can have a discriminatory policy impact on minority groups whose members are less likely than
others to spend an entire year unincarcerated—their crime rates per
unincarcerated year can be substantially higher than their annual incidence rates.

A related concern is that offending frequencies that are measured
immediately prior to some salient event, such as an arrest or entry into
incarceration or drug treatment, are necessarily on average overestimates of "true" offending rates since in some instances the offender's
behavior must have contributed to the occurrence of the event in question. Rolph and Chaiken (1987) have shown how to adjust each individual's data about offending frequency so as to estimate a "steady state
offending frequency"—that is, the individual's offending rate at a time
somewhat remote from the special triggering event. Generally this adjustment was found to be much smaller than a 25 percent reduction
(Rolph and Chaiken 1987, app. A).

Some incidence rates are presented for *periods other than a year*, normally the period covered by the data collected in the study. For example, in their study of 175 women in a New York City jail who, in
1983, volunteered to answer questions about their previous drug use
and criminal behavior, Sanchez and Johnson (1987) presented six-
month incidence rates.

C. Crime-Day Measures

Crime-day measures were first presented by Ball et al. (1982) in their analyses of data obtained in retrospective interviews about past crimes committed by 243 male opiate addicts. These subjects were randomly selected from a population of addicts identified by Baltimore police between 1952 and 1971. These researchers defined a crime-day as "a 24-hour period during which one or more crimes is committed by a given individual. Each day of the year, then, is either a crime-day or a non-crime day" (p. 228). Crime-days are actually incidence rates which have been capped at a level of no more than one offense per day. Their primary advantage, as compared to crime-rate data, is their reliability when self-reports are obtained about frequently occurring crimes— respondents can more reliably report that they committed drug sales on a given day than they can report they committed seventeen drug sales. A disadvantage of crime-day measures is their lack of additivity across types of crimes: two robbery crime-days plus three burglary crime-days may equal three, four, or five total crime days, depending on whether the burglaries were committed on the same days as the robberies or not.

Since most offenders commit most types of predatory crimes at low rates, the differences between a group's average number of crime-days per year and average crime commission rate for predatory crimes are likely to be unimportant for policy purposes. For example, in an analysis for this essay of self-report data from Rand's 1978–79 inmate survey in three states (Chaiken and Chaiken 1982), we found average annual robbery rates to be 1.0 to 1.2 times higher than the number of robbery days per year among various subgroups of the population (that is, average annual crime rates for these groups are at most 20 percent higher than average crime-days per year). We also calculated these ratios from data from Johnson et al. (1985), resulting in exactly the same range for robbery and a range of 1.4–1.8 for theft. By contrast, our calculation for nonpredatory crime showed that drug-sale rates for Rand inmate survey respondents ranged from 3.1 to 5.1 times the number of drug-sale-days per year. (All these ratios reflect the average number of offenses committed per day when the offense is committed.)

Variations among researchers in handling respondents' unclear answers to survey questions contribute a larger uncertainty to estimated annual robbery commission rates than a factor of 1.2, so crime-days per year can be compared with annual crime rates within a smaller degree of error than exists within the crime-rate measure itself. (See Visher

[1906] for a discussion of estimating in the face of respondent ambiguity.)

The statistics reported by Ball, Shaffer, and Nurco (1983) and many others who present crime-day measures are *crime-days as a percent of total days*; thus, if subjects report committing crimes on ten of thirty interview days, the crime-day rate is 33 percent. Such figures can be multiplied by 365 to obtain crime-days per year.

Other variations on crime-day measures include *crime-days per month* (e.g., Anglin and Speckart 1986) and *crime-days per unincarcerated year* (Anglin and Speckart 1987), which are directly comparable with aggregate crime rates per capita for low-rate types of crimes.

D. Pseudo-Crime-Day Measures

To facilitate comparisons among studies, some approximations of crime-day measures have been published. These are produced by capping individuals' self-reported crime commissions at thirty crimes per month or 365 crimes per year and averaging the resulting capped rates. (In other words, the day-by-day information is not available to the researcher but is approximated.) For example, Chaiken and Chaiken (1982, p. 161) report capped aggregate crime commission rates for California jail and prison inmates who reported different levels of heroin use. Pseudo-crime-day figures are useful because averages of offense rates are highly sensitive to outliers (e.g., respondents who report thousands of robberies per year). To develop realistic averages, most investigators must cap their data in some way, for example, at the ninetieth percentile, and a cap at 365 crimes per year is as sensible and easy to understand as any other.

Although the literature on criminal behavior of drug users is characterized by a nearly dizzying array of disparate measures of crime frequency, they can be quite easily compared after standardizing them on an annual basis. We do so in the next section.

IV. Magnitudes of Differences in Crime Rates at Different Levels of Drug Use

Despite differences among publications in their study populations, types of crimes examined in the study, and definitions of levels of drug use, general consistency emerges in the quantitative picture of the magnitude of crime-rate spread between high-drug-use and low-drug-use populations. This pattern is illustrated in this section by reference to offending frequencies calculated in nine different studies.

Although the source literature does not separate out a category of crime called "predatory crime," many studies that mention particular types of crimes do list statistics for robbery, theft, and burglary, which we include as predatory crime; so, to the extent possible, our summary tabulations here list these crimes separately. Most of the available data showing quantitative levels of offending frequencies are cross-sectional in nature, comparing high-drug-use and low-drug-use offenders during the same period of time, even when the study design is longitudinal (following the same subjects over time).

For example, the figures in table 3, calculated from Elliott and Huizinga's (1984) nationally representative longitudinal sample of youth, demonstrate many of the primary patterns in the relationship between drug abuse and offending frequencies. Contemporaneous drug abuse is very strongly associated with offending frequency. With one exception, the value of λ for multiple drug users is higher than for nonusers. In general, the values of the aggregate crime rate λd for multiple, illicit drug users are ten to twenty times as high as for nonusers (even larger ratios apply for theft). The offending frequency λ is essentially characteristic of groups of offenders categorized by their drug-use levels, while reported participation rates in most types of crimes (especially theft) decline with age. For example, the average individual robbery λ was six for the multiple illicit drug users aged eleven to seventeen and also six for multiple illicit drug users aged fifteen to twenty-one. But the value of the group robbery rate λd for the multiple illicit drug users declined from 1.2 to 0.4, a drop of nearly 70 percent which is explained by the older group's lower reported participation rate d in robbery. (This decline may be a genuine aging effect, or it could be that older respondents who are offenders drop out of the survey.)

In table 3, the subgroups of subjects are not the same people followed longitudinally over the two time periods (except of course for the "total" category); rather, the subgroups are subjects displaying the same form of drug-use behavior in the two time periods. The sample sizes show that the older youths are substantially more likely to be involved in some form of drug abuse than are the younger subjects (over three times as likely to be involved in multiple illicit drug abuse), but the participation rates in criminal activity are lower for the older subjects. Only the individual frequencies (crime commission rates for those who commit the type of crime in question) have been remaining fairly stable among subgroups over time. These observations may be taken as dem-

TABLE 3

Crime-Commission Rates per Year among Drug Users and Nonusers Ages Eleven to Seventeen in 1976 and Fifteen to Twenty-one in 1980

| | | Average Crime Rates | | | | | |
| | | Robbery | | Felony Theft | | Total Delinquency* | |
Drug Use	N	Indi-vidual	Group	Indi-vidual	Group	Indi-vidual	Group
Multiple illicit drug use:							
1976	58	6	1.2	16	8.7	92	84.0[†]
1980	187	6	.4	9	2.4	84	71.7[‡]
Nonuse (or use of a drug three or fewer times):							
1976	1,244	3	.1	2	.1	16	8.7[†]
1980	483	13	.1	2	.0	11	3.0[‡]
Total sample:[§]							
1976	1,719	6	.3	6	.7	25	16.1
1980	1,494	6	.1	5	.4	30	14.5

SOURCE.—National Youth Survey, reported in Elliott and Huizinga (1984), tables 1 and 2.

NOTE.—"Individual" refers to crimes per calendar year, for those who commit that type of crime. "Group" refers to crimes per calendar year, for all subjects in the category, including those who don't commit the crime. The multiple illicit drug use category includes use of alcohol, marijuana, and other drugs (amphetamines, barbiturates, hallucinogens, cocaine, or heroin) four or more times each.

* The delinquency scale used in this table is the National Youth Survey scale SRD-C. It includes the following offenses: stole motor vehicle, went joy riding, stole something less than $5, stole something $5–$50, stole something greater than $50, bought stolen goods, broke into building/vehicle, carried hidden weapon, aggravated assault, gang fight, hit teacher, hit parent, hit student, prostitution, sold marijuana, sold hard drugs, disorderly conduct, sexual assault, strongarmed students, strongarmed teachers, strongarmed others, panhandled. Robbery includes strongarmed students, strongarmed teachers, strongarmed others. Felony theft includes stole motor vehicle, stole something greater than $50, bought stolen goods, broke into building/vehicle.

† The ratio for 1976 of the aggregate crime rate for multiple illicit drug users to the aggregate crime rate for nonusers is 9.7:1.

‡ The ratio of the 1980 aggregate crime rates is 23.9:1.

§ The total sample includes two intermediate categories of drug use, not shown separately in the table. These omitted categories are alcohol use (use of alcohol four times or more but no use of any other drug) and alcohol and marijuana use (use of alcohol four times or more and use of marijuana four times or more but no use of other drugs).

onstrating that as drug abuse becomes more widespread among a population, it becomes less indicative of deviance in general and hence of participation in criminal activity.

Among known offender populations, the picture is even clearer. The ratios of crime commission rates between drug users and nonusers in offender populations are comparable to the ratios in general populations, but the rates themselves are substantially higher for offender populations. Chaiken and Chaiken (1982) and Chaiken (1986) present information about preincarceration predatory crime rates derived from the Rand inmate survey's self-reports. Selected figures from these studies, with summaries calculated for this essay, appear in tables 4 and 5.

TABLE 4

Pseudo-Crime-Days per Year:*
Jail and Prison Inmates Surveyed in Three States

				Pseudo-Crime-Days per Year		
Drug Use	N	Robbery	Burglary	Theft other than Auto Theft	All Study Crimes Except Drug Dealing	All Study Crimes[†]
Heroin addiction	357	24.4	51.3	68.7	186.7[‡]	224.4[§]
Heroin use, not addicted	224	9.7	32.2	34.6	100.7	156.2
No drug use	939	4.7	6.8	9.2	35.7[‡]	40.1[§]

SOURCES.—Chaiken and Chaiken (1982), p. 161, for California. Chaiken (1986) for Texas and Michigan. Summary statistics calculated by the authors. Subjects are adult male prison and jail inmates (prison inmates only in Texas).

NOTE.—A fourth drug-use category (use of barbiturates, amphetamines or any drug other than marijuana or prescribed drugs, but no use of heroin) is not shown in this table. Survey respondents are omitted from the tables if their crime-commission rate could not be calculated or their level of heroin use could not be determined from their responses.

* Average crime-commission rates per unincarcerated year, including (with zero crime-days) offenders who do not commit the listed crime, each person's crime rate truncated at 365 per year. The calendar reference period for reporting criminal activity was twelve to twenty-four months long, beginning January of the year before the respondent's arrest. The survey was conducted in 1978 and 1979.

[†] The study crimes are robbery, burglary, auto theft, other theft, forgery and credit card crimes, fraud, assault, and drug dealing.

[‡] The ratio in this column of crime-days for heroin addicts to crime-days for nonusers is 5.2:1.

[§] The ratio in this column of crime-days for heroin addicts to crime-days for nonusers is 5.6:1.

TABLE 5

Pseudo-Crime-Days per Year:
Jail and Prison Inmates Surveyed and Listed by State

Drug Use	N	Robbery	Burglary	Theft other than Auto Theft	All Study Crimes Except Drug Dealing	All Study Crimes
California:						
Heroin addiction	204	33.6	67.6	65.8	214.7*	239.2†
Heroin use	94	13.1	31.4	40.2	100.8	156.0
No drug use	225	2.3	3.4	6.2	23.8*	33.1†
Michigan:						
Heroin addiction	94	16.6	26.3	50.4	120.5	189.9
Heroin use	82	9.2	34.9	23.7	103.1	167.8
No drug use	394	8.3	9.0	12.1	50.6	54.4
Texas prisoner:						
Heroin addiction	59	4.9	34.9	107.7	195.6	228.4
Heroin use	48	3.9	29.2	42.3	96.6	137.0
No drug use	320	2.0	6.6	7.7	25.7	27.6

SOURCES.—Chaiken and Chaiken (1982), p. 161, for California. Chaiken (1986) for Texas and Michigan. Summary statistics calculated by the authors. Subjects are adult male prison and jail inmates (prison inmates only, in Texas).

NOTE.—See table 4 for explanation of the crime-rate measure, drug-use categories, and study crimes.

* The ratio in this column of crime-days for heroin addicts to crime-days for nonusers is 9:1 for California. The similar ratio for Michigan is 2.4:1 and for Texas, 7.6:1.

† The ratio in this column of crime-days for heroin addicts to crime-days for nonusers is 7.2:1 for California. The similar ratio for Michigan is 3.5:1, and for Texas, 8.3:1.

The prodigious criminal activity levels of offenders who are heavily involved in drug use have been often mentioned but are nonetheless striking when one looks at these tabulated statistics. Table 5 indicates that the *average* heroin addict offender spends more days per year (239 in California, 228 in Texas) working at his chosen (criminal) trade than does the typical factory worker. Since many heroin addicts must commit crimes more frequently than average, they obviously are hard at work on weekends and vacation days as well as weekdays.

Heroin addicts have typically somewhere between five and ten times as many crime-days per year as do offenders in this sample who do not take illicit drugs. (The exception in table 5, for Michigan, is explained by the high levels of auto theft for all incarcerated offenders in Michigan. Auto theft is not shown in the table but is included in the category All Study Crimes.) Considering the generally poor predictability of offenders' crime commission rates that can be obtained by examining their personal characteristics and criminal history (see, e.g., Monahan 1981; Chaiken and Chaiken 1982; Gottfredson and Gottfredson 1986; Farrington 1987; Rolph and Chaiken 1987; Chaiken and Chaiken 1989), ratios as high as 5:1 to 10:1 represent striking distinctions among offender groups.

Comparable figures for an entirely different incarcerated population examined at a later time period, Sanchez and Johnsons's study (1987) of 175 women in jail in New York City, are presented in table 6. Here again, the crime commission rates for property crimes amount to hundreds of offenses per year, and the ratios in crime commission rates between the frequent drug users and the infrequent or nonusers are similar to those presented above for male prison inmates.

The studies discussed in the remainder of this section describe crime frequencies among drug-user populations. The primary observations that we draw from these studies are, first, that it is not drug abuse per

TABLE 6

Crime-Commission Rates:
175 Female Jail Inmates—Riker's Island, New York

Drug Use	N	Property Crimes*		All Study Crimes[†]	
		Individual	Group	Individual	Group
Daily heroin and cocaine use	119	309	226	448	471
No use in past sixty days	25	184	74	186	128

SOURCE.—Sanchez and Johnson (1987), table IX.
NOTE.—"Individual" refers to the offending frequency, that is, crimes per calendar year for those who commit that type of crime. "Group" refers to crimes per calendar year, for all subjects in the category, including those who don't commit the crime. Two categories of drug use are omitted from the table: one to twenty times use of heroin or cocaine in the past sixty days, and twenty-one to fifty-nine times use of heroin or cocaine in past sixty days.
* "Property crimes" include burglary, shoplifting, motor vehicle theft, theft from a motor vehicle, picking pockets, criminal possession of stolen property, and other thefts.
[†] "All study crimes" include property crime, drug sales to dealers and users, violent offenses (robbery, aggravated assault, homicide, attempted homicide), fraud offenses (check and credit card forgeries, con games, loan sharking), and prostitution.

se, but the amount or frequency of drug use, that is strongly related to crime commission rates, and, second, that as drug abusers go through some periods of heavy use and other periods of nonuse or lesser drug use, their crime-committing behavior varies over time with their amount of drug use.

Table 7 presents statistics for a street drug-user population. Approximately 200 heroin (or methadone) users provided information about drugs they were using and crimes they had committed in periods between recurrent interviews with researchers; the interviews were conducted in neighborhood storefronts (Johnson et al. 1985). In contrast with tables 3 and 4, which compared daily heroin or cocaine users with nonusers, table 7 compares daily heroin users with irregular heroin users.

The comparisons in table 7 are cross-sectional; that is, the study subjects were classified once as daily, regular, or irregular heroin users and did not shift among categories. Thus, the irregular users include some people who use heroin frequently on occasion. The table illustrates that even within drug-using populations, the ratio in crime commissions for some types of crime range as high as 5:1 between addicts and irregular users and average 2.4:1 to 2.8:1 for all types of crimes. The offending frequencies in table 7 illustrate that the distinctions in offending behavior between daily heroin users and irregular users are not simply in participation rate. Heroin addicts who commit robbery have an offending frequency of twenty-seven robberies per year, while irregular users who commit robbery have an offending frequency of twelve robberies per year, a ratio of 2.3:1.

Inciardi's (1987a) data for drug-abusing populations in Miami show similar ratios, for example $\lambda = 24$ robberies per year for narcotics users and fourteen robberies per year for other drug users. Ball et al. (1986, table 631) provide data confirming the same general level of individual crime commission frequencies among addicts in New York, Baltimore, and Philadelphia (121 theft crime-days per year for addicts who commit theft in their last addiction period, eighty-nine burglary crime-days per year for those who commit burglary).

Studies of drug addicts who have entered treatment programs give the clearest picture of the extent to which drug abuse is contemporaneously related to crime commission behavior (as opposed to being a persistent characteristic of the particular person). Periods of addiction, or daily drug use, are accompanied by much higher crime commission rates than periods of lesser drug use for the same individual. An illus-

TABLE 7

Crime Commission Rates per Year: Street Drug Users in New York City

Drug Use	N	Robbery			Burglary			Theft			All Nondrug Crimes*			All Study Crimes†	
		Indi-vidual	Group	Crime-Days	Indi-vidual	Group	Crime-Days	Indi-vidual	Group	Crime-Days	Indi-vidual	Group	Crime-Days	Indi-vidual	Group
Heroin use all days	62	27	12	10	60	34	29	131	65	92	216	209	122‡	1,447	1,447§
Irregular use	61	12	2	2	14	4	4	69	41	23	133	116	50‡	515	515§
Total sample (including regular users)	201	29	21	6	44	41	18	103	67	43	176	163	88	1,074	1,073

SOURCE.—Johnson et al. (1985), tables 7-2, 8-6, 8-13.

NOTE.—"Individual" is the offending frequency, that is, crimes per calendar year for those who commit that type of crime. "Group" is aggregate crimes per calendar year for all subjects in the category, including those who don't commit the crime. "Crime-days" is crime-days per calendar year. The category of regular users is not separately shown in the table but is included in the total.

* Nondrug crimes include robbery, burglary, theft (larceny plus shoplifting for resale only), forgery, con games, prostitution, pimping.
† Total study crimes include nondrug crimes plus drug sales, steering, copping, touting, drug thefts, shoplifting for own use, and fare evasion.
‡ The ratio in this column of crime-days for daily heroin users to crime-days for irregular users is 2.4:1.
§ The ratio in this column of crime-days for daily heroin users to crime-days for irregular users is 2.8:1.

TABLE 6

Crime-Days per Year: Male Methadone Maintenance Patients

	N	Robbery	Burglary	Theft	All Property Crimes
Year following first daily use:					
Anglos	362	1	31	46	83*
Chicanos	284	2	38	52	94[†]
Year following last daily use:					
Anglos	318	0	3	7	10*
Chicanos	233	0	5	8	15[†]

SOURCE.—Anglin and Speckart (1987), tables 6 and 7.

NOTE.—"All property crimes" include robbery, burglary, theft, and forgery. Anglin and Speckart do not include drug crimes in the study. The figures given here do not entirely agree with published monthly crime commission rates for the same subjects (Anglin and Speckart 1986); however, Anglin (1987) indicates the figures tabulated here are internally consistent, using the definitions in Anglin and Speckart (1987).

* The ratio of crime-days for Anglos between first daily use and following last daily use is 8.3:1.

[†] The ratio for Chicanos is 6.3:1.

tration is given in table 8, which shows ratios of 6:1 to 8:1 between crime rates in high and low periods of drug use. Anglin and Speckart (1987), commenting on these subjects, indicate that the choice of *initial* drug addiction in this table is particularly pertinent:

> Although most studies examining the narcotics use and crime connection begin with a statement that this is a controversial area of research and that absolute conclusions cannot be drawn, the present authors disagree. Both current and earlier works, . . . we believe, present strong evidence that there is a strong causal relationship, at least in the United States, between addiction to narcotics and to property crime levels. . . . To a lesser extent nonaddicted narcotics use may also contribute significantly to levels of property crime activities. The largest increase of property crime activities during the addiction career, however, occurs at that point at which daily narcotics use is initiated. It is also clear that the reduction of individual level of addiction, while moderating criminality significantly for most and essentially terminating it for some, does not resolve the problem of property crime behaviors for all. [Anglin and Speckart 1987, p. 33]

Similar, but not quite as strong, changes in criminal behavior over time have been reported for other treatment populations. For example, Ball, Shaffer, and Nurco (1983) show aggregate theft rates for male heroin addicts in Baltimore of 125 per year at the start of addiction and thirty-four per year during the first "off" period (under treatment). Marsden, Collins, and Hubbard (1986) show aggregate predatory crime rates for addicts in ten cities entering treatment. Before treatment, clients' crime rates were 12.2 per year, and after treatment, they were 5.4 per year. These represent ratios of two- or three-to-one between crime commission rates before and after treatment, but they do not focus on precisely the same time periods that Anglin and Speckart (1987) found revealed the strongest differences (the period following first addiction versus the period after last addiction).

Another study with parallel findings involved approximately 200 male heroin addicts who were enrolled in methadone maintenance programs in New York and Baltimore, half of whom reported committing no predatory crime before heroin addiction (Nurco et al. 1988). This half differed little from those who committed predatory crime prior to addiction in terms of the types of illicit drugs they used prior to addiction. But the predatory criminals were significantly more likely to have used illicit drugs *frequently* than were the nonpredators during the pre-addiction period.

These respondents, as with other groups of addicts studied, cycled in and out of addictive use of heroin. During periods of nonaddiction, both groups of respondents committed predatory crimes at lower rates than they did during periods of addiction. But the former nonpredators once again committed crimes at lower rates than those who had been predators before addiction (Nurco et al. 1988).

V. Conclusions and Implications for the Justice System

Use of illicit drugs does not appear to be strongly related to onset and participation in predatory crime; rather, drug use and crime participation are weakly related as contemporaneous products of factors generally antithetical to traditional United States lifestyles. Most of the underlying causative factors, such as irregular employment or weak attachment to school or parents, are not amenable to intervention by the justice system. Moreover, general prevalence figures for drug use do not give much hope that even major reductions in the numbers of people who use illicit drugs could significantly reduce the numbers of incidents of predatory crime.

More specifically, among adolescents and adults who use illicit drugs, most do not commit predatory crimes. Reducing the number of adolescents who are sporadic users of illicit drugs, especially marijuana, may possibly affect the incidence and prevalence of some types of crime, such as disorderly conduct and driving under the influence of controlled substances, but not predatory crime. In addition, most adults who sporadically use drugs such as hallucinogens, tranquilizers, or cocaine do not commit predatory crimes. Therefore, reducing the number of *adults* who are sporadic users of these types of drugs may also affect the incidence and prevalence of some types of crime, but is unlikely to affect the incidence of predatory crime.

About 50 percent of delinquent youngsters are delinquent before they start using drugs; about 50 percent start concurrently or after. Reducing the number of adolescents who sporadically use illicit drugs may potentially reduce the incidence and prevalence of minor predatory crime; but these types of crime are more likely to be reduced through comprehensive delinquency prevention measures which do not focus exclusively or particularly on drug abuse.

Persistent use of drugs other than heroin (and perhaps also excluding cocaine) appears to be unrelated to persistence in committing predatory crimes. Among youngsters who use drugs and commit theft or other predatory crimes, most continue to use drugs as adults but stop committing crimes at the end of adolescence. Moreover, almost half of convicted offenders who are persistent offenders never used drugs. Therefore preventing persistent use of drugs other than heroin and cocaine is not likely to reduce the numbers of persistent predatory offenders.

However, there is strong evidence that predatory offenders who persistently and frequently use large amounts of multiple types of drugs commit crimes at significantly higher rates over longer periods than do less drug-involved offenders, and predatory offenders commit fewer crimes during periods in which they use no heroin.

These findings suggest that criminal justice programs that focus resources on high-rate predatory offenders should include among their selection criteria evidence of persistent, frequent use of multiple types of illicit drugs. In addition, criminal justice system programs that effectively prevent addicted predatory offenders from using heroin appear promising when measured against the goal of reducing the incidence of predatory crime.

REFERENCES

Adler, Patricia A. 1985. *Wheeling and Dealing: An Ethnography of Upper-Level Drug Dealing and Smuggling Communities.* New York: Columbia University Press.

Anglin, M. Douglas. 1987. Personal communication with authors, November 30.

Anglin, M. Douglas, and Yih-Ing Hser. 1987. "Addicted Women and Crime." *Criminology* 25:359–97.

Anglin, M. Douglas, Elizabeth S. Piper, and George Speckart. 1987. "The Effect of Legal Supervision on Addiction and Criminal Behavior." Paper presented at the thirty-ninth annual meeting of the American Society of Criminology, Montreal, November.

Anglin, M. Douglas, and George Speckart. 1986. "Narcotics Use, Property Crime, and Dealing: Structural Dynamics across the Addiction Career." *Journal of Quantitative Criminology* 2:355–75.

———. 1987. "Narcotics Use and Crime: A Multisample, Multimethod Analysis." University of California, Los Angeles, Department of Psychology. Mimeographed.

Ball, John C. 1986. "The Hyper-Criminal Opiate Addict." In *Crime Rates among Drug Abusing Offenders,* edited by Bruce D. Johnson and Eric Wish. Final report to the National Institute of Justice. New York: Narcotic and Drug Research, Inc.

Ball, John C., Eric Corty, S. Paul Petroski, Henrietta Bond, Anthony Tommasello, and Teri Baker. 1986. "Characteristics of 633 Patients in Methadone Maintenance Treatment in Three United States Cities." University of Maryland School of Medicine, Department of Epidemiology and Preventive Medicine, Baltimore. Mimeographed.

Ball, John C., Lawrence Rosen, John A. Flueck, and David N. Nurco. 1982. "Lifetime Criminality of Heroin Addicts in the United States." *Journal of Drug Issues* 3:225–39.

Ball, John C., John W. Shaffer, and David N. Nurco. 1983. "The Day-to-Day Criminality of Heroin Addicts in Baltimore: A Study in the Continuity of Offense Rates." *Drug and Alcohol Dependence* 12(1):119–42.

Biernacki, Patrick. 1986. *Pathways from Addiction: Recovery without Treatment.* Philadelphia: Temple University Press.

Blumstein, Alfred, David P. Farrington, and Soumyo Moitra. 1985. "Delinquency Careers: Innocents, Desisters, and Persisters." In *Crime and Justice: An Annual Review of Research,* vol. 6, edited by Michael Tonry and Norval Morris. Chicago: University of Chicago Press.

Blumstein, Alfred, Jacqueline Cohen, Jeffrey A. Roth, and Christy A. Visher, eds. 1986. *Criminal Careers and "Career Criminals."* Washington, D.C.: National Academy Press.

Carpenter, Cheryl, Barry Glassner, Bruce D. Johnson, and Julia Loughlin. 1988. *Kids, Drugs, Alcohol, and Crime.* Lexington, Mass.: Lexington Books.

Chaiken, Jan M., and Marcia R. Chaiken. 1982. *Varieties of Criminal Behavior.* Santa Monica, Calif.: Rand.

Chaiken, Marcia R. 1986. "Crime Rates and Substance Abuse among Types of Offenders." In *Crime Rates among Drug-abusing Offenders*, edited by Bruce D. Johnson and Eric Wish. Final report to the National Institute of Justice. New York: Narcotic and Drug Research, Inc.

Chaiken, Marcia R., and Jan M. Chaiken. 1985. "Who Gets Caught Doing Crime?" Discussion paper. Washington, D.C.: Bureau of Justice Statistics.

———. 1989. *Redefining the Career Criminal: Priority Prosecution of High-Rate Dangerous Offenders*. Washington, D.C.: National Institute of Justice.

Chaiken, Marcia R., and Bruce D. Johnson. 1988. *Characteristics of Different Types of Drug-involved Offenders*. Washington, D.C.: National Institute of Justice.

Collins, James J., and Susan L. Bailey. 1987. *Early Drug Use and Criminal Careers*. Research Triangle Park, N.C.: Research Triangle Institute. Mimeographed.

Collins, James J., J. Valley Rachal, Robert L. Hubbard, Elizabeth R. Cavanaugh, S. Gail Craddock, and Patricia L. Kristiansen. 1982. *Criminality in a Drug Treatment Sample: Measurement Issues and Initial Findings*. Research Triangle Park, N.C.: Research Triangle Institute.

Dembo, Richard, Mark Washburn, Eric D. Wish, Horatio Yeung, Alan Getreu, Estrellita Berry, and William R. Blount. 1987. "Heavy Marijuana Use and Crime among Youths Entering a Juvenile Detention Center." *Journal of Psychoactive Drugs* 19:47–56.

Elliott, Delbert S., and David Huizinga. 1984. "The Relationship between Delinquent Behavior and ADM Problems." Prepared for the Alcohol, Drug Abuse, and Mental Health Administration/Office of Juvenile Justice and Deliquency Prevention State-of-the-Art Conference on Juvenile Offenders with Serious Drug, Alcohol, and Mental Health Problems, April.

———. 1985. "The Relationship between Delinquent Behavior and ADM Problems." Proceedings of the Alcohol, Drug Abuse, and Mental Health Administration/Office of Juvenile Justice and Delinquency Prevention Research Conference on Juvenile Offenders with Serious Drug, Alcohol, and Mental Health Problems, Washington, D.C.

Elliott, Delbert S., David Huizinga, and Scott Menard. 1989. *Multiple Problem Youth: Delinquency, Drugs, and Mental Health Problems*. New York: Springer-Verlag.

Fagan, Jeffrey, and Joseph G. Weis. 1990. *Drug Use and Delinquency among Inner City Youth*. New York: Springer-Verlag (forthcoming).

Farrington, David P. 1987. "Predicting Individual Crime Rates." In *Prediction and Classification: Criminal Justice Decision Making*, edited by Don M. Gottfredson and Michael Tonry. Vol. 9 of *Crime and Justice: A Review of Research*, edited by Michael Tonry and Norval Morris. Chicago: University of Chicago Press.

Gandossy, Robert P., Jay R. Williams, Jo Cohen, and Hendrick J. Harwood. 1980. *Drugs and Crime: A Survey and Analysis of the Literature*. Washington, D.C.: U.S. Department of Justice, National Institute of Justice.

Goldstein, Paul J. 1985. "Drugs and Violent Behavior." *Journal of Drug Issues* (Fall), pp. 493–506.

Gottfredson, Stephen D., and Don M. Gottfredson. 1986. "Accuracy of Prediction Models." In *Criminal Careers and "Career Criminals,"* vol. 2, edited by Alfred Blumstein, Jacqueline Cohen, Jeffrey A. Roth, and Christy A. Visher. Washington, D.C.: National Academy Press.

Hanson, Bill, George Beschner, James M. Walters, and Elliott Bovelle. 1985. *Life with Heroin: Voices from the Inner City.* Lexington, Mass.: Lexington Books.

Hunt, Dana. In this volume. "Drugs and Consensual Crimes: Drug Dealing and Prostitution."

Inciardi, James A. 1987a. "Exploring the Drugs/Crime Connection." Newark: University of Delaware, Division of Criminal Justice. Mimeographed.

———. 1987b. "Beyond Cocaine: Basuco, Crack, and Other Coca Products." Paper presented at the annual meeting of the Criminal Justice Sciences Association, St. Louis, March.

Innes, Christopher A. 1988. *Profile of State Prison Inmates, 1986.* Special report. Washington, D.C.: Bureau of Justice Statistics.

Joe, George W., and D. Dwayne Simpson. 1987. "Mortality Rates among Opioid Addicts in a Longitudinal Study." *American Journal of Public Health* 77:347–48.

Johnson, Bruce D., Paul Goldstein, Edward Preble, James Schmeidler, Douglas S. Lipton, Barry Spunt, and Thomas Miller. 1985. *Taking Care of Business: The Economics of Crime by Heroin Abusers.* Lexington, Mass.: Lexington Books.

Johnston, Lloyd D., Patrick M. O'Malley, and Jerald G. Bachman. 1985. *Use of Licit and Illicit Drugs by America's High School Students, 1975–84.* Rockville, Md.: National Institute on Drug Abuse.

———. 1986. *Drug Use among American High School Students, College Students, and Other Young Adults, National Trends through 1985.* Rockville, Md.: National Institute on Drug Abuse.

Kandel, Denise B., Ora Simcha-Fagan, and Mark Davies. 1986. "Risk Factors for Delinquency and Illicit Drug Use from Adolescence to Young Adulthood." *Journal of Drug Issues* 16:67–90.

Kleiman, Mark A. R., and Kerry D. Smith. In this volume. "State and Local Drug Enforcement: In Search of a Strategy."

Mande, Mary J., and Kim English. 1988. *Individual Crime Rates of Colorado Prisoners.* Denver: Colorado Department of Public Safety, Division of Criminal Justice.

Marsden, Mary Ellen, James J. Collins, and Robert L. Hubbard. 1986. *Effects of Adjusting Individual Offense Rates for Time at Risk.* Research Triangle Park, N.C.: Research Triangle Institute.

Mieczkowski, Thomas. 1986. "Geeking Up and Throwing Down: Heroin Street Life in Detroit." *Criminology* 24:645–66.

Miller, Judith D., Ira Cisin, Hilary Gardner-Keaton, Adele Harrell, Philip W. Wirtz, Herbert Abelson, and Patricia Fishburne. 1983. *National Survey on Drug Abuse: Main Findings 1982.* Report no. (ADM)83-1263. Rockville, Md.: National Institute on Drug Abuse.

Monahan, John. 1981. *Predicting Violent Behavior; An Assessment of Clinical Techniques.* Beverly Hills, Calif.: Sage.

Moore, Mark. In this volume. "Supply Reduction and Drug Law Enforcement."

National Institute of Justice. 1988. *Drug Use Forecasting (DUF).* Washington, D.C.: National Institute of Justice.

Newcomb, Michael D., and Peter M. Bentler. 1988. *Consequences of Adolescent Drug Use Impact on the Lives of Young Adults.* Beverly Hills, Calif.: Sage.

Nurco, David N., Thomas E. Hanlon, Timothy W. Kinlock, and Karen R. Duszynski. 1988. "Differential Criminal Patterns of Narcotic Addicts over an Addiction Career." *Criminology* 26:407–23.

Peterson, Mark, Jan Chaiken, Patricia Ebener, and Paul Honig. 1982. *Survey of Prison and Jail Inmates: Background and Method.* Santa Monica, Calif.: Rand.

Robins, Lee N., Darlene H. Davis, and Eric Wish. 1980. "Vietnam Veterans Three Years after Vietnam: How Our Study Changed Our View of Heroin." In *Yearbook of Substance Abuse,* edited by L. Brill and C. Winick. New York: Human Sciences Press.

Rolph, John E., and Jan M. Chaiken. 1987. *Identifying High-Rate Serious Criminals from Official Records.* Santa Monica, Calif.: Rand.

Sanchez, Jose E., and Bruce D. Johnson. 1987. "Women and the Drugs-Crime Connection: Crime Rates among Drug-abusing Women at Rikers Island." *Journal of Psychoactive Drugs* 19(2):205–16.

Simcha-Fagan, Ora, and Joseph E. Schwartz. 1986. "Neighborhood and Delinquency: An Assessment of Contextual Effects." *Criminology* 24:667–95.

Sutherland, Edwin H., and Donald Cressey. 1970. *Criminology.* Philadelphia: Lippincott.

Visher, Christy. 1986. "The Rand Second Inmate Survey: A Reanalysis." In *Criminal Careers and "Career Criminals,"* vol. 2, edited by Alfred Blumstein, Jacqueline Cohen, Jeffrey A. Roth, and Christy A. Visher. Washington, D.C.: National Academy Press.

White, Helene Raskin, Robert J. Pandina, and Randy LaGrange. 1987. "Longitudinal Predictors of Serious Substance Use and Delinquency." *Criminology* 25:715–40.

Williams, Terry M., and William Kornblum. 1985. *Growing Up Poor.* Lexington, Mass.: Lexington Books.

Wish, Eric D., and Bruce D. Johnson. 1986. "The Impact of Substance Abuse on Criminal Careers." In *Criminal Careers and "Career Criminals,"* vol. 2, edited by Alfred Blumstein, Jacqueline Cohen, Jeffrey A. Roth, and Christy A. Visher. Washington, D.C.: National Academy Press.

Jeffrey Fagan

Intoxication and Aggression

ABSTRACT

Evidence of an association between use of illicit substances and aggressive behavior is pervasive. But the precise causal mechanisms by which aggression is influenced by intoxicants are still not well understood. Research on intoxication and aggression often has overlooked the nonviolent behavior of most substance users, controlled use of substances, and the evidence from other cultures of a weak or nonexistent relation between substance use and aggression. There is only limited evidence that ingestion of substances is a direct, pharmacological cause of aggression. The temporal order of substance use and aggression does not indicate a causal role for intoxicants. Research on the nexus between substance use and aggression consistently has found a complex relation, mediated by the type of substance and its psychoactive effects, personality factors and the expected effects of substances, situational factors in the immediate settings where substances are used, and sociocultural factors that channel the arousal effects of substances into behaviors that may include aggression. Contemporary explanations of the intoxication-aggression relation offer only limited explanatory power in view of the occurrence of controlled use of substances, the mutability of cultural norms, and cross-cultural differences.

Among contemporary explanations of violence and aggression, few have been more enduring than the presumed effects of intoxication from drugs or alcohol. There is pervasive evidence of an association between substance use and aggressive behavior. For example, drug abuse has been found to be a critical factor in homicide (Wolfgang and Strohm 1956; McBride 1981; Goldstein 1989), robbery and other "predatory" crime (Petersilia 1980; Chaiken and Chaiken 1982, in this

Jeffrey Fagan is associate professor in the School of Criminal Justice, Rutgers.

volume; Johnson et al. 1985), school violence (Gold and Moles 1978), and violence among adolescents (Tinklenberg et al. 1981; Hartstone and Hansen 1984; Elliott, Huizinga, and Ageton 1985; Fagan, Piper, and Moore 1986; Johnson et al. 1986a; White, Pandina, and LaGrange 1987; Fagan 1989). Goldstein (1985) found that drug use and drug trafficking were etiological factors in violence, while McBride (1981) and Goldstein et al. (1989) found that systemic factors in drug dealing were causal factors in homicides.

Adolescent drug abuse has been cited as a predictor of violent adult crime and criminal careers (Monahan 1981; Greenwood 1982; Wish and Johnson 1986). Among both the general youth population (Elliott, Huizinga, and Ageton 1985; Johnson et al. 1986a) and adult criminal groups (Gandossy et al. 1980; Chaiken 1986; Wish and Johnson 1986; Wish 1987), both official and self-reported crime rates are highest for heroin or cocaine users. There is a general and long-standing consensus that criminality among heroin addicts is quite high (McGlothlin, Anglin, and Wilson 1978; Nurco et al. 1984; Johnson et al. 1985; Anglin and Speckart 1988), particularly during periods of addiction (Ball et al. 1982). There also is evidence that rates of violence are associated with more frequent and abusive drug use; as drug and alcohol use becomes more frequent and abusive, the strength of the association increases. For example, Johnson et al. (1986b) found that adolescent violence may be a consequence of drug use—more frequent and intensive highs are associated with serious and frequent delinquency.

Alcohol intoxication also is often cited as contributing to violence and aggression. Alcohol use has been associated with assaultive and sex-related crimes (Rada 1975; Ladouceur and Temple 1985; Prentky, Knight, and Rosenberg 1988), serious youth crime (Akers et al. 1979; Elliott, Huizinga, and Ageton 1985; White, Pandina, and LaBouvie 1985; Fagan, Weis, and Cheng 1990), family violence toward both spouses (Coleman and Straus 1983; Hotaling and Sugarman 1986) and children (McGaghy 1968; Mayer and Black 1981), being both a homicide victim (Wolfgang 1958; Haberman and Baden 1974) and perpetrator (Wolfgang 1958; Tanay 1969), and persistent aggression as an adult (Collins 1981, 1989; McCord 1983). Alcohol "problems" occur disproportionately among both juveniles (White, Pandina, and LaBouvie 1985) and adults (Collins 1986) who report violent behaviors.

Accordingly, drugs, alcohol, and aggression have become major public health problems as well as a focal point in crime control policies

(Epstein 1977; Inciardi 1981; Musto 1981).[1] The World Health Organization (1979) concluded that alcohol was implicated worldwide in 13–50 percent of rapes, 24–72 percent of assaults, and 28–86 percent of homicides. In a sample of 1,000 consecutive decedents in New York City over eighteen years of age, Haberman and Baden (1974) found blood or brain alcohol concentrations in excess of 10 percent in 30 percent of accident victims, 26 percent of suicide victims, and 43 percent of homicide victims. Similarly, Goldstein et al. (1989) found that drugs were involved in 54 percent of New York City homicides. Studies with prison populations cite the predictive efficacy of juvenile drug use (especially opiates) in combination with early onset of delinquency and drug dealing, to explain chronic adult predatory crime (Greenwood 1982). Petersilia (1980) found that among prison inmates, the most serious offenders were involved with *both* alcohol and drug abuse, although those who used only alcohol committed fewer and less serious crimes.

Yet the link between intoxication and aggression is less certain than is implied by the scientific literature and popular opinion. Despite overwhelming evidence that drug and alcohol use and aggression are related, this essay shows that intoxication does not consistently lead to aggressive behavior. How aggressive behavior is influenced by the ingestion of various substances is not well understood. There are fundamental differences between substances in their association with aggression; various intoxicants affect both mind and body differently. Research on the nexus of aggression and substance use has consistently found a complex relation, mediated by personality and expectancy factors, situational factors, and sociocultural factors that channel the arousal effects of substances into behavior types which may or may not involve interpersonal aggression. The effects of intoxicants also differ according to the amounts consumed per unit of body weight, tolerances, and genetic or biological predispositions.

Accordingly, there is only limited evidence that consumption of alcohol, cocaine, heroin, or other substances is a direct, pharmacologically based cause of crime. Although intoxication is widely found to be

---

[1] It is not surprising that this concern has translated into policy. New calls have gone out for stiffer sentences for dealers, increased testing for arrestees in detention and during pretrial periods (irrespective of offense or prior record), and greater emphasis on drug-use patterns in detention and sentencing decisions (e.g., selective incapacitation, preventive detention of arrestees who test positive).

associated with aggressive conduct, the association is far from consistent and the reasons are diverse and poorly understood. Research has not identified specific drug-produced motivations for violence by adolescents that did not exist prior to using drugs (Akers 1984), and there have been few studies that found that aggression did not precede substance use.

The research traditions that have guided inquiries into the relation between substance use and aggression reflect the competing explanations that today characterize empirical knowledge on how substance use modifies behavior. Despite the partition of research among the natural, social, and medical sciences, the relative contributions of the separate disciplines offer an impressive array of information about the relation between aggression, alcohol, and drug use. For example, Boyatzis (1983, p. 314) concludes that we know "who should drink what, when, and where if we are looking for a fight."

Yet the specialization of research within disciplines also hinders the accumulation of knowledge and the development of theory. The dominant research models do not lend themselves easily to synthesis or integration. For example, the results of controlled experiments in the "competitive reaction" paradigm, in which subjects can set the shock level an opponent receives in a reaction time test (e.g., Taylor, Gammon, and Capasso 1976), are not generalized easily to knowledge from cross-cultural studies. While ethnographic studies attend to the roles of setting and expectations, they cannot achieve the controlled conditions of experimental psychologists who can vary the intensity of intoxication and degree of provocation of stimuli of aggression. Each discipline also reflects separate traditions of empirical research by type of substance, in part reflecting separate problem definitions by substance and the attendant separation of research support and policy in governmental agencies.

Scientific advances within disciplines are also hindered by their own methodological concerns and procedures. Despite advances in cross-disciplinary integration of theory and methods in the study of addictions, researchers in each discipline have difficulty reaching consensus on definitions and measurement issues concerning aggression, intoxication, and addiction. Ethical and human subject issues are a further source of complexity and limitation.[2] Accordingly, the current knowl-

[2] One should think twice before administering alcohol or drugs to addicted subjects, crossing threshold levels of aversive stimuli, or allowing unlimited severity of aggression in either experimental or natural designs.

edge base is extremely complex, reflecting not just different assumptions across disciplines about the linkages between aggression and intoxication but also important epistemological differences that separate the disciplines.

The diversity of research traditions naturally leads to controversy in defining aggression and intoxication. An example illustrates the complexity in defining aggression. Predatory behavior, learned aggression, and fear-induced aggression are included in broad, encompassing definitions of aggression, yet the biological, psychological, and social influences that determine them seem to differ. Also, corporal discipline or punishment rarely is included in definitions of aggression, nor is it defined as a crime in most states. Apparently, the social and legal meanings of aggression and violence differ, depending on the victim-offender relationship and the presence or absence of physical injury (Fagan and Wexler 1985).

Research paradigms also influence definitions. Aggression may be operationally defined and measured by (1) the intensity and duration of shocks administered in experimental studies; (2) bites, noises, and postures in ethological studies; (3) physical assaults or other antisocial behaviors in sociological research; and (4) a variety of culture-specific behaviors in comparative studies. Pihl (1983) suggests that aggression is a multidimensional concept where the intent of the aggressor and the legitimation of the aggressive act must be part of the definition. This suggests that aggression can be defined as any behavior whose intent is to deliver harmful stimulation; research on aggression, in turn, requires quantifiable dimensions of the behavior that vary in intensity.

A brief review of the definitions in contemporary studies offers common ground for reconciling the diverse research traditions. Bandura (1973) defined aggression as behavior that results in personal injury or property destruction. We cannot exclude property destruction, however, since it may also include the intention to harm the owner of the property. Bandura's definition is consistent with the definition of violence offered by Gelles and Straus (1979) as "an act carried out with the intention of, or perceived intention of, physically hurting another person." Gelles and Straus (1988) distinguish violence from aggression, which includes *any* malevolent act, regardless of whether physical harm is involved.

If we define aggression to include the important dimension of *intent* to harm, then symbolic and verbal aggression, as well as nonverbal aggression (e.g., bodily gestures or postures), also are types of aggression (Boyatzis 1975). Vogel (1983, p. 245) adds the element of *unjust* harm to his definition of aggression but does not include what he defines as normative assertiveness which is "absolutely necessary for men and women to live and survive, find their places in society, and advance to the fullest extent of their potentials." Moyer (1968) found different neural and hormonal determinants for each of the following types of aggression: predatory aggression, intermale aggression, fear-induced aggression, irritable aggression, maternal aggression, sex-related aggression, and instrumental aggression. Miczek and Thompson (1983) further distinguish between offensive and defensive aggression.

Obviously, aggression is not a unitary phenomenon, and the number of different kinds of aggressive behavior suggests that they cannot be reconciled within a single theoretical model. In this essay, aggression is defined as behaviors that reflect either the intent to harm, by inflicting physical pain or noxious emotional or psychic conditions, or the intent to create a noxious condition for the target. Collins (1983, 1988), focusing exclusively on violent behaviors defined as an actual or attempted physical attack, terms this "expressive interpersonal violence." Research on aggression within families, gangs, or other social settings shares these definitional components with research on aggression among animals, and also in experimental studies with human subjects and animals, that measured threats, postures, and declarations of hostility or rage. Such a broad *conceptual* definition requires careful attention to the *operational* definitions and attendant measures in the studies reviewed.

Similar problems arise in the definitions of substance use and intoxication. The interactions of physical tolerance or habituation, physiological predispositions such as metabolic rates, and the effects of substances also should be considered in definitions of intoxication. For example, blood-alcohol counts produce varying states of intoxication for individuals with different tolerances, metabolic rates, and body weights. Although most studies strive to generalize from alcohol or drug use to the effects of intoxication, few operationalize and measure intoxication or addiction or the factors that mediate them with enough care to distinguish between these states. These problems confound the distinctions between alcoholism and alcohol use, or drug addiction and drug use. For example, Gottheil et al. (1983) question whether it is practical or theoretically significant to label alcoholics on the basis of their genetic predisposition or their behavior, especially if such predispositions exist among individuals who do not drink.

Attention to these definitional and measurement distinctions will permit estimates of the extent to which empirical research on the intoxication-aggression relation reflects measurement and design artifacts or "true" effects.

This essay addresses the fundamental question of how aggressive behavior, given any particular model and research paradigm, is influenced by the ingestion of various substances. There are also additional questions of central importance, such as whether aggressive individuals differ from others in their patterns of substance use and also whether substance use has differential effects in instigating aggressive behavior among different individuals and in different settings. When the interactions of substance, individual factors, setting, and culture are considered, to what extent is there a pharmacological and biological basis for the assumption of an aggression-intoxication linkage? How much of the explained variance in the intoxication-aggression relation is attributable to biological, psychological, social, or cultural sources of influence? Does the ingestion of substances "cause" specific individuals to become violent or aggressive, while for others intoxication becomes a suppressor of violence? In the end, the essay asks whether the linkage between intoxication and aggression is evident independent of socially learned cues and the determining influences of culture and expectancy.

There has been an abundance of research to contribute empirical and theoretical knowledge to answer these questions. The studies range in discipline and method from controlled experiments on psychological disinhibition to cross-cultural research to biochemical and neurological examinations of both humans and other mammals. Within each of these paradigms, the effects of alcohol, tetrahydrocannabinol (cannabis, or, more commonly, marijuana), amphetamines, phencyclidine (PCP, or "angel dust"), cocaine, and opiates have been examined. Until recently, these inquiries have proceeded in parallel paths, with few efforts to synthesize knowledge across either substances or disciplines. Current research has recognized the importance of interactions between the disciplines.

In Section I, the essay reviews the empirical knowledge within each discipline, contrasting findings for different substances. Research within psychological, biological, pharmacological, and sociocultural disciplines is discussed. The strategy is to report critical findings from specific studies, chosen from the hundreds of citations that make up that empirical literature, that are representative of the dominant views in that discipline for that substance. Section II critically examines the dominant explanations and theories of the relations between substances and aggression. Section III analyzes promising areas for theoretical integration and model development and concludes with a research agenda and recommendations for integrative research.

I. Theory and Research on the Relations between Substance Use and Aggression

The robust association between substance use and aggression has been observed in a wide variety of sampling and measurement conditions. Although the frequency and intensity of aggression that follows intoxication varies extensively, there can be little doubt that, for many people in diverse settings and cultures, substance use may be causally related to aggression. However, the relation between substance use and aggression also may be accidental or facilitative. These relations leave unanswered the precise mechanisms by which these two factors are related.

Efforts to explain the relation generally fall into one of four disciplines. Biology and physiology seek to identify unique physiological, endocrinological, or neural factors that are activated by substances to induce aggressive responses. Psychopharmacological research focuses on the psychoactive properties of specific substances that are likely to cause aggression. Psychological and psychiatric study relies on personality theory and dynamics to identify the behavioral manifestations of intoxication. More important, these disciplines view intoxication as simply a sideshow in the service of a more significant dynamic of internal conflict or emotional pathology (Jessor and Jessor 1977; Mayfield 1983). Sociological and cultural research is concerned with setting, expectancy, social interactions, cultural norms and sanctions, and other processes that differentiate the aggregate behaviors of individuals following intoxication.

A. Biological and Physiological Perspectives

Contributions from the medical and biological sciences to explanations of the intoxication-aggression relation encompass several specific subdisciplines, including neural mechanisms, endocrine and other glandular responses to substances, and comparative ethological processes. Accordingly, mediators such as brain response (electroencephalogram), testosterone levels (glandular responses), and catecholamine measures such as norepinephrine levels have been examined. However, Mayfield (1983) doubts whether these theories can be tested or advanced within the controlled laboratory setting for two reasons. First,

there is little understanding of how alcohol intoxication causes drunkenness, despite the significant advances in explaining the actions of
opiates, anticonvulsants, and neuroleptic drugs. There is little knowledge of what specific brain regions are affected by high blood-alcohol
levels. Second, most research with human subjects in this paradigm has
been done at the "minimum end of the spectrum where normal subjects
are drawn primarily from university populations and studied under
conditions of mild intoxication and simulated stress" (Mayfield 1983, p.
146). Despite the experimental rigor that characterizes these studies,
they often produce small changes in behavior.

Accordingly, theoretical interpretations are likely to be constrained
by the restricted range of behavioral responses (Taylor and Gammon
1976). It is uncertain whether the dynamics produced under subtle
laboratory conditions would be valid under extreme conditions of intoxication or aggressive behavior. Nevertheless, there is sufficient empirical evidence to evaluate the contention that basic brain and glandular functions are altered following the ingestion of a wide range of
substances.

1. *Psychophysiological Effects.* Research on the psychophysiological
bases for aggression typically examines the effects of electrical and
chemical stimulation of brain pathways, as well as lesion studies, in the
production of aggressive behaviors. Research in this area has sought to
identify specific pathways and stimulus thresholds that provoke aggression (Moyer 1976). Moyer states that the basic premise of this model is
"that there are in the brains of animals and humans neural systems that
when fired in the presence of a relevant target result in aggressive or
destructive behavior towards that target. In the case of humans, the
actual aggressive behavior may be controlled, but the individual will
have the appropriate feelings of hostility. There is now abundant evidence to support that premise" (1983, p. 191).

The "abundant evidence" includes studies of brain stimulation in
humans, brain tumors and aggression, aggression during epileptic seizures, weakened suppressor systems and hereditary influences, and
blood chemistry changes in aggressive subjects. For example,
Robinson, Alexander, and Bowne (1969) illustrated innate aggression
in monkeys based on electrical stimulation of the anterior hy-
pothalamus. However, though Moyer (1983) cautions against broad
generalizations from one species to another, he reports similar behavioral changes following brain stimulation of human subjects with low
base rates of aggression.

Sano (1962) reported on 1,800 cases of tumors in regions of the brain that produce irritability and aggression: the septal region, temporal lobe, and the frontal lobe. Similar findings have been reported for epilepsy; the probability of aggression increases with the occurrence of temporal-lobe epilepsy. For example, Schwab et al. (1965) reported destructive behavior and bursts of anger among about half the psychomotor epileptic patients. Studies of blood chemistry influences on aggression range from analysis of testosterone levels in sex offenders (Bradford 1988) and animals (Beeman 1947) to violence that occurs during the premenstrual week. Hypoglycemia, a condition marked by a sudden drop in blood sugar levels, also has been associated with aggression (Bolton 1973, cited by Moyer 1983).

Though this literature pinpoints specific neural systems where aggression results from stimuli of neurotransmitter, endocrine, and pharmacological manipulations, there has been little experimental evidence that employs alcohol or psychoactive drugs as stimuli. Accordingly, there is little evidence that intoxicants either decrease or increase aggression by their actions as stimuli of the different neural systems and brain pathways of aggressive behavior. Moreover, how intoxicants actually stimulate these systems remains little understood. Advances in this area await such research.

2. *Comparative Research among Species.*   Ethological analyses of the influence of substance use on aggression provide comparisons of the effects of intoxication on behavior of different species. In a survey of research on controlled laboratory experiments with animals, Miczek and Thompson (1983) reported that amphetamines, PCP, and ethanol increase attack and threat behaviors in specific species, with each substance producing behaviorally distinct effects. They also reported that THC (a cannabis-based substance) and opioids appear to have selective antiaggressive effects. Their survey included several paradigms often used in animal research on aggression, with variation in the dimension of aggression (e.g., defensive or attack behaviors), the stimulus (resident-intruder, shock-induced aggression, brain stimulation, predatory aggression), and measurement of behavior (e.g., bites, gestures, vocalizations).

Phencyclidine has received little attention in controlled experiments with animals; the few studies offer conflicting evidence between species. In one experiment involving monkeys, PCP led to apparently inappropriate social behavior, producing aggression by nondrugged members against drugged animals in the setting (Miller, Levine, and

Mirsky 1973). Alcohol's effects on aggression have been studied widely on different animal species and in varying experimental circumstances. For example, high doses of alcohol decreased defensive biting and postures in mice and monkeys, while low doses seemed to enhance aggression in other circumstances (Miczek and Thompson 1983). Also, low alcohol doses increased aggressive postures and other acts characteristic of rat aggression among dominant rats confronting subordinate opponents, but higher doses had the opposite effect.

Miczek and Thompson cite several studies that illustrate that the introduction and continued administration of opiates suppress aggressive behaviors among various species and in several settings. However, when morphine is given regularly and then withdrawn, several animal species exhibit nonspecific aggressive acts such as posturing and biting random targets (e.g., Gellert and Sparber 1979). These effects seem to be further mediated by the contributions of endogenous opioids such as naloxone or maltrexone, substances that affect the opiate receptors in the brain.

The pharmacological effects of substances also seem to affect social behaviors among animals that also are associated with aggression. For example, substances that induce changes in an opponent's behavior may result in increased aggression by a drug-free attacker. Thus, defensive-aggressive behavior in reaction to attack may be suppressed by specific drug treatment of the defender. In other words, intoxication may lead to the alteration of a victim's behavior, and, in turn, may increase its risk of attack. This was found for several substances in intruder-resident paradigms, including PCP, methamphetamine, and THC (Miczek and Thompson 1983), and often stands in sharp contrast to the effects of the same drugs administered to resident attackers.

The pharmacological effects of drug administration on aggressive behavior in these experiments suggest specific causal linkages among various species. However, the causal linkage implied by aggression among nondrugged animals toward animals whose behaviors are altered by specific intoxicants suggests the possibility of a social etiology of aggression. The social origins of such aggression suggest a fertile area for new investigation.

3. *Endocrinological Research.*   Cicero (1983) reviewed the literature on alcohol-induced disturbances on the hypothalamic-pituitary-gonadal system among males and its contributions to aggression and sexual activity and found an overall decline in reproductive endocrinology in both male humans and animals. However, Cicero is critical of the

popular acceptance of the influence of alcohol on aggression and sexual arousal, since alcohol's effects on endocrine secretions are paralleled by alcohol's effects on other glandular, metabolic, and physiological functions that influence behavior. Moreover, Cicero found that the failure objectively to measure aggression or sexual arousal in most studies involving endocrinological mediators, and the inability in experimental studies to disentangle psychosocial factors,[3] makes it impossible to conclude that alcohol-induced changes in endocrine states (including testosterone levels) can increase sexual behavior or aggression. Cicero found no evidence that alcohol or hormonal activity dictates the display of aggressive behavior or sexual arousal in a direct fashion.

Langevin et al. (1988) failed to detect significant differences in testosterone levels among aggressive sex offenders who abused alcohol or drugs, despite a correlation between amounts of alcohol consumed and the degree of force used in the sexually aggressive acts. Mayfield (1983) concludes that the contributions of intoxication to the testosterone-aggression relation are inconclusive since the relation is quite broad, while the alcohol-testosterone relation is mediated by dose-response factors.

There has been little research on endocrinological changes that result from intoxication from substances other than alcohol. Recently, Schuckitt (1988) examined the effects of anabolic steroids on social behaviors. Steroids are not intoxicants but have been reported widely to have behavioral effects following prolonged use. Steroids appear to reduce testosterone production and, in turn, produce hormones more closely resembling the female hormone, estrogen. According to Schuckitt's interviews with weight lifters, 10 percent of the sample reported feelings of aggressiveness and irritability following prolonged use.

Hormonal changes from opiate addiction were examined by Mendelson et al. (1975), who found short-term dose-related effects of both heroin and methadone in the suppression of testosterone levels. Testosterone levels returned to normal after two months or longer of methadone treatment, indicating tolerance develops following initial changes in endocrinological functions. Woody et al. (1983) examined hostility and anxiety among opiate addicts, based on changes in endocrinological factors that are associated with anxiety. They found higher anxiety and hostility among addicts during drug-free periods, and reduced levels during methadone maintenance. Testosterone levels were

[3] Specifically, expectancies, drinking contexts, and social controls.

suppressed during periods of addiction (or maintenance), and their increase following detoxification also was associated with increases in hostility and anxiety. Accordingly, Woody et al. (1983) conclude that opiates may alter levels of other endocrinological activity which, in turn, affect hostility or anxiety.[4]

Finally, Mayfield (1983) examined the relations between alcohol consumption, increases in noradrenergic activity (e.g., adrenalin release), and aggression. Noradrenergic activity is associated with readiness for a fight or flight. Despite ample evidence that alcohol ingestion increases norepinephrine levels, there are no data to link such events to increased aggression.

4. *Genetic Predispositions.*   Despite numerous suggestions of a genetic predisposition to pathological alcohol intoxication or similar sensitivity to opiate addiction (based on recent studies of deficits in natural opioids and hypersensitivity in opioid receptors), there is no evidence of a genetic predisposition to an intoxication-aggression relation. Maccoby and Jacklin (1974) found evidence of genetic predispositions to aggression among males. The consistent evidence in cross-cultural and subspecies studies shows that males are more aggressive than females. Their review also showed that male aggression is evident early in life and, among nonhuman primates, aggression is related to the concentration of testosterone. Eron, Walder, and Lefkowitz (1971) suggest that violent parents produce violent children (Widom 1989). However, there has not been systematic research to disentangle genetic predispositions to *drug-* or *alcohol-induced* aggression. Moreover, empirical tests of such a relation might be beyond the limits of social or laboratory experimentation.

B. *Psychopharmacological Perspectives*

Historically, intoxication and aggression have been associated in both popular images and behavioral science. Early formulations of the relation between substance use and aggression focused on the changes in behavior that resulted from ingestion of intoxicants. There have been numerous reviews of the empirical evidence of relations between aggression and alcohol, PCP, opiates, barbiturates, and cocaine (Tinklenberg 1973; Pernanen 1976, 1981; Gandossy et al. 1980; Collins 1981;

---

[4] Not only may this be related to aggression but it also may provide an internal stimulus for a return to opiate use (or use of other substances to reduce anxiety) following detoxification or cessation. This has clear implications for understanding the biological bases of relapse among opiate addicts.

Watters, Reinarman, and Fagan 1985). Each concluded that there is a remarkably strong association but no conclusive evidence to establish either a causal direction[5] or mediating linkages. Psychopharmacological theories provide a convenient framework for explaining this widespread association.

Psychopharmacological theories differ from pharmacological perspectives. Pharmacological theories suggest that intoxicants have direct psychoactive effects on behavior independent of intervening psychological processes. Behavioral change following intoxication results from changes in physiological response, intensified primary drives such as sex, food, or aggression, or activation of specific brain functions or dysfunctions. These theories view the intoxication-aggression relation as exclusively biological. Psychopharmacological perspectives also differ from psychological perspectives, which regard intoxication as activating the psychic processes that are casually linked to aggression: personality factors, psychological predisposition to aggression, or pathologies. They presume that individuals' psychological predispositions precede intoxication, and intoxication is viewed as either a manifestation of these predispositions or as servicing a more significant personality dynamic (Mayfield 1983).

Psychopharmacological perspectives marry these two views of the interaction of psyche and substance and also attend to the inherent weaknesses in the separate explanations. Specifically, this perspective rejects explanations of aggression based on the psychoactive properties of substances. Rather, this perspective suggests that following ingestion of intoxicants, individuals may exhibit aggressive behaviors that result from effects of intoxicants on personality and affective states.

For example, Wikler (1952) found that alcohol had a weak and inconsistent pharmacological effect, although behaviors would emerge during alcohol intoxication that did not appear under any other circumstances. Yet aggression was rarely associated with alcohol intoxication. Wikler concluded there was no basis for a purely pharmacological explanation of the alcohol-aggression association. When Wikler compared alcohol and opiates, he found that opiates had a stronger pharmacological "signature" than alcohol. Yet there was equivocal evidence of an

---

[5] There is conflicting evidence to suggest that substance use may cause violence, violence may cause substance use, that a reciprocal relation exists between the two phenomena, that shared "third" factors cause the two behaviors (i.e., that they are spuriously related), or that they are simply correlated without any significant shared causal linkages (Watters, Reinarman, and Fagan 1985).

association between opiate use and aggression, usually based on behavior evidenced during withdrawal. Once again, Wikler concluded that
other factors were necessary to explain the association between intoxication and aggression.

For alcohol, the dose-related association with aggression suggests
that the relation might be strongest at the extreme manifestations of
alcohol use. This generally acknowledges that the association is not
idiosyncratic but is associated with a pattern of alcohol use. Under such
circumstances, the paradigm of pathological intoxication suggests that
long-term ingestion of high doses of substances may induce psychological pathologies that are activated by alcohol. However, this association
also suggests possible interactions between dosage and habituation in
relation to effects on aggression.

The general paradigm for studying this association is dose-control
experiments comparing subjects with different violence histories. For
example, Maletsky (1976) reported significantly higher violence rates
among alcohol-intoxicated subjects with prior violence, compared to
rates for nonviolent subjects, but only at higher doses. Maletsky concluded that alcohol activated psychological pathologies that were not
manifested during periods of sobriety.[6]

Illicit and licit substances other than alcohol are also associated with
aggression, though some have no association. Marijuana and opiate
ingestion suppress hostility and aggression, though withdrawal from
long-term opiate use is consistently associated with irritability, hostility, and other affective symptoms. Barbiturate use appears to have the
strongest relation to aggression. Collins (1982) found that aggravated
assaults and robberies among treatment clients in the year preceding
admission were highest among barbiturate users. Tinklenberg (1973)
identified barbiturates as the drug most likely to enhance assaultiveness
among incarcerated juvenile offenders. Lion, Azarte, and Koepke
(1975) induced a "paradoxical rage" reaction in experimental studies
with patients in psychiatric facilities. The "paradox" involved the man-

---

[6] This paradigm also addresses a major weakness in experimental studies focusing on
the alcohol-pathology-aggression association: the use of subjects (primarily university
students) drawn from the minimal range of a behavior whose distribution is highly
skewed. Moreover, the dose levels in these studies produce only mild conditions of
intoxication, again not approaching what Mayfield (1983) and, earlier, Wikler (1952)
termed the conditions of pathological intoxication. Mayfield goes on to describe the
conundrum of researchers who require appropriate subjects for research within this
paradigm, yet in settings where the risks to subjects and experimenters are far greater
than the traditionally milder settings and behaviors of the traditional experimental setting.

ifestation of rage following ingestion but in the absence of other signs of intoxication.

Amphetamine use also has been associated with aggressive behaviors. Ellinwood (1971) and Asnis and Smith (1978) reported high rates of amphetamine abuse in incidents of assault and homicide. However, there appears to be little evidence to establish a psychopharmacological link between amphetamine use and aggression. Mayfield (1983) reports that amphetamine use stimulates noradrenergic activity and increases general levels of arousal and that long-term use may produce paranoid psychosis with some regularity. However, there is little experimental evidence of aggression resulting from either short- or long-term amphetamine abuse. Among delinquent boys, Simonds and Kashani (1980) reported that amphetamine use had a weaker correlation with crimes against persons than did several other substances.

Phencyclidine has also been associated with aggression, particularly assaultive behavior (Simonds and Kashani 1979, 1980). However, its effects are highly idiosyncratic and unpredictable. Feldman, Agar, and Beschner (1979) examined PCP use in six cities comparing ethnographic data from local researchers. They found that behaviors under PCP were mediated not only by sociocultural factors but also by geographic region.

Frequent and high levels of cocaine use similarly have been associated with a variety of personality disorders. Washton, Gold, and Pottash (1984) reported findings from a study of seventy upper-income users[7] who had contacted the 1-800-COCAINE hotline. Nearly two in three callers (65 percent) reported paranoid feelings, and 87 percent reported depression. However, these high levels of adverse reactions are likely to be attributable to the self-selected sample of help-seekers who had sought advice for their drug problems. Small clinical samples (e.g., Spotts and Shontz 1980) also found that paranoid ideation was a common problem. Again, though, those seeking treatment differ significantly in their patterns of use and reactions to cocaine and cannot be generalized to the broader population of cocaine users (Chitwood and Morningstar 1985; Erickson et al. 1987). For example, low-dose cocaine users report being high as a "mellow" and positive experience (Goldstein et al. 1987). However, this depends in part on route of ingestion (smoking, intravenous injection, or nasal inhalation) (Siegel 1980, 1982a).

[7] Incomes over $50,000 annually in 1982–84.

Erickson et al. (1987) surveyed 145 adults in Ontario about the frequency of their cocaine use and reactions. Overall, about one in six (17 percent) reported becoming violent or aggressive after using cocaine. About one in three frequent users reported feelings of aggression, compared to 20 percent of intermediate users and 10 percent of infrequent users. Factor analyses indicated that aggression and paranoia reactions formed a single dimension of cocaine reactions, though the differences by frequency of cocaine use for the factor score were not significant. However, the differences were positively related to the combined use of alcohol and cocaine, and inversely related to social class. Goldstein et al. (1988), relying on drug users' self reports, found that the frequency of cocaine use is associated with a greater likelihood of involvement *as a perpetrator* in violent behaviors.

Recent indications of frequent pharmacologically induced violence associated with use of "crack" cocaine, a smokable cocaine derivative that produces a nearly instantaneous and intense high, are based on reports from treatment populations and anecdotes conveyed in the mass media. To date, there has been no systematic research linking crack cocaine use with increased violence. However, there is evidence of a sudden and precipitous depression following crack use, leading to anxiety and depression (Washton and Gold 1987). While aggression has been reported among crack users following intoxication and withdrawal (Bourgois 1989), it appears to conform with an economic-compulsive model of drug-related violence (Goldstein 1985), rather than a pharmacological response.

Accordingly, there is empirical evidence of a psychopharmacological basis for aggression following intoxication only for alcohol and cocaine. Only in the alcohol studies and in very few studies with cocaine were there experimental investigations of psychodynamic processes or pathologies that were posited as causal mechanisms. Despite empirical evidence that other substances may produce such behaviors, none of the studies with illicit or prescription drugs were experimental. They relied on cross-sectional designs and a general analytic model comparing users and nonusers or the coincidence of psychological pathology and aggression and often were confounded by expectancies and social context. Moreover, they neither explicitly hypothesized nor examined specific causal links between substance use and aggression.

However, research on the pharmacological treatment of psychiatric disorders where aggressive behavior also is manifested suggests a psychopharmacological basis for the intoxication-aggression relation.

Kramer (1983) reviews evidence from clinical treatment that shows that the pharmacological treatment of aggression may be accomplished by the treatment of more general psychiatric disorders, of which aggression may be a manifestation. These include mania, major depression, schizophrenia, organic mental disorders that produce episodic dyscontrol, and seizure disorders. However, it is not certain whether the pharmacological agents are suppressing the behaviors or acting on the psychiatric disorders. For example, Bell (1972) reports that the chlorpromazine treatment of amphetamine intoxication can reduce not just paranoid ideation but also cardiovascular effects following intoxication. But in these tests, the researchers do not distinguish the competing effects of the physiological and psychiatric manifestations of the substances and their reduction in curbing aggression. Nor do these studies always measure aggression or violence, more often either excluding or confounding these two behaviors. Instead, the studies cited by Kramer *assume* that the psychiatric state includes an aggressive behavioral manifestation, and, in turn, that the treatment of the disorder also will suppress aggression. Though Kramer identifies an important paradigm for explaining the intoxication-aggression relation, experimental evidence is needed to sort out the physiological and psychopharmacological effects of the treatment drugs.

C. Psychological and Psychiatric Perspectives

The psychopharmacological perspective on the intoxication-aggression relation posits direct effects of substance use on behavior. In contrast, psychological perspectives link intoxication to changes in personality or psychopathological factors that may be associated with aggression. Since alcohol or drug use does not lead inevitably to aggression, psychologists have turned to individual and conditional relations (between personality and social context) to explain aggression among a relatively small proportion of substance users. Various theories of personality and cognition suggest contradictory perspectives on the effects of substance use on the emotional and personality dynamics associated with aggressive behavior.

For example, there is evidence that alcohol or other psychoactive drugs may either dampen or intensify emotions such as hate, rage, or contempt that often accompany aggressive behavior. There also is evidence that substance use may either suppress or deny certain emotions that may precede aggressive behavior, for example, shame or guilt. Rather than a stimulation of aggressive behaviors, alcohol or drug use may also be a "defense" to excuse or justify behavior, or to deny responsibility for aggression. Still other perspectives suggest that the effects of substances on personality factors are not psychoactive but are social in origin. That is, certain emotional correlates of aggression—shame, guilt, rage—which are stimulated by substance use may result from the social processes of substance abuse. Substance use also may be spuriously related to psychological processes that underlie aggression. For example, both aggressive behaviors and substance use (particularly alcohol abuse) arise from severe family pathology (McCord 1988). This brief overview suggests several competing and conflicting hypotheses on the complex relations among substance use, personality or psychopathology, and aggression.

Research strategies also vary within this set of explanations. The general theoretical model for studying the substance use-aggression relation suggests that intoxication conditionally affects either personality variables or psychodynamic processes which, in turn, are associated with aggression. At the extremes of aggressive behavior, the clinical study of psychopathology relies on small clinical samples and often idiographic approaches to assign theoretical meaning to observations with individuals or small groups. Cross-sectional studies with general populations or populations "at risk" provide opportunities to test the hypothesized associations between personality variables, substance use, and behaviors. Longitudinal studies have been used to examine the causal order of substance use and aggression and attendant hypotheses regarding psychological processes. Experimental studies also have been used both to standardize measurement and to control interactions between victims and aggressors—that is, to provide direct controls on stimulus while covarying personality variables through sampling. The majority of experimental and clinical studies of psychological variables have examined the effects of alcohol. The discussion in this section reflects this imbalance in empirical research.

1. *Personality Development and Emotions.*   Studies of patients in intensive and lengthy psychotherapy suggest psychodynamic processes that link aggression and substance use. Pihl (1983) and Wurmser and Lebling (1983) suggest several types of relations among personality factors, substance use, and aggression. They are illustrated in the Appendix. Most (93 percent) of the studies tested personality concepts with clinical (treatment) samples, and fewer than half (47.4 percent) had control groups (Pihl and Spiers 1978). The results have contributed to the tendency to assign a causal role to personality disorder in a hypothetical

causal sequence leading to aggression. But evidence from clinical samples tells us more about individuals who reach treatment programs and how they are labeled than about aspects of intoxication or aggression. Typically, these studies use measures that rarely are linked theoretically to aggression.

Research on psychoanalytic theories of aggression and substance use has involved three theoretical frameworks. One class of theories suggests that personalities predisposed to substance use also suffer from severe conflicts that produce aggressive behavior. Substance use either dampens or strengthens these conflicts. Accordingly, this formulation states that substance use intervenes in the relation between personality and behavior. A second class of theories suggests that personality factors that are associated with aggression are also related etiologically to substance use. That is, substance use and psychopathology are related spuriously. For example, the antecedents of family dysfunction may produce both aggression and compulsive or pathological intoxication. A third perspective suggests that the personality traits of aggression are antecedents of substance abuse behaviors and that substance abuse "serves" the interests of aggression for these individuals.

a) Intoxication Strengthens or Dampens Emotional States Associated with Aggression. In this framework, intoxication affects the motivation for or restraints against aggressive feelings. This hypothesis is the basis for the widely discredited "disinhibition" hypothesis (Room and Collins 1983; Reinarman and Critchlow-Leigh 1987; Collins 1988, 1989).[8] Both psychoanalytic experience and experimental evidence underlie this proposition. Alcohol, stimulants, and psychedelics may neutralize moral or emotional restraints that, in a sober state, effectively control aggression. Wurmser and Lebling (1983) cite case studies in which cocaine and methedrine enhanced patients' feelings of power and control and, in turn, diminished feelings of helplessness and dependence. However, when feelings of loss of power or control were evident, depression and fear set in. Aggression in these circumstances was either external (sexual aggression, intimidation, or interpersonal violence) or internal (sado-masochism, suicidal ideation, or attempts at self-harm).[9]

Alternately, Wurmser and Lebling (1983) cite reports from other patients that intoxication numbed aggressive feelings associated with

---

[8] The debate over this hypothesis is analyzed in detail in a later section which reviews several contemporary views and explanations.

[9] One patient reported that alcohol actually increased the threshold of physical pain she could endure, allowing aggressive behaviors to become more salient and endurable.

personality disturbance. Typically, barbiturates and opiates were reported as anesthetics against feelings of rage, despair, or loneliness. Stimulants, psychedelics, and alcohol were used to offset feelings of depression, guilt, shame and weakness, or vulnerability. There appear to be characteristic correlations between the drug chosen, emotional state, and the type of affect sought. Rage, shame, and loneliness seem to be characteristic of patients who are narcotic users and may be associated with aggression when users are not intoxicated. Stimulants and alcohol, conversely, seem to be used by patients seeking to enhance emotional states which serve aggressive purposes. Accordingly, the psychopharmacological effects of specific drugs appear to be consciously monitored in the selection of substances to intervene in the dynamics of the personality-aggression relation.

In psychoanalytic terms, intoxication defends the ego against the superego's efforts to resist the neutralization of values, authority, temporal perceptions, and control or delay of gratification. This is one hypothesis for the effectiveness of treatments that provide substitute conscience figures such as Alcoholics Anonymous and its derivatives (e.g., Narcotics Anonymous). Transference in psychotherapy serves a similar purpose. These external authorities either temporarily suppress or outweigh the emotional or ego states that are evident in the intoxication-aggression dynamics (Kubie 1963, cited in Wurmser and Lebling 1983).

b) Substance Use and Aggression Share Common Antecedents. Research on causes of both aggression and pathological intoxication or addiction has identified shared antecedents, especially family pathology and early childhood victimization experiences. Wurmser and Lebling (1983) emphasize the essential role of violence and sexual overstimulation in the family background in more than half the substance abusers in psychotherapy. Early childhood victimization by one's parents is thought to generate acute feelings of powerlessness that result in later loneliness and alienation, precursors to self-victimization as an adult. The specific sequence leading to aggression and addiction begins with anxiety and conflict from the suppression of rage (against the victimizer) and guilt (from evoking parental anger and disapproval). The developmental deficit fuels the twin reactions of addiction and aggression.

Other views on personality suggest a developmental perspective, where gaps in cognitive and emotional skills may lead to "problem behaviors." Jessor and Jessor (1977) identified deficits in personality development leading to both aggression and substance use during the transition from adolescence to adulthood. They cite "problem behaviors" by young males in this period as evidence of a strain resulting from a discrepancy between social role expectations and personality development. "Problem behaviors" include both substance abuse and aggression, especially their joint occurrence. Fagan et al. (1987) suggest that these behaviors reflect weak development of social judgmental skills for analyzing ambiguous moral situations or managing emotional responses to complex social cues. This developmental period also has been cited as a period of vulnerability to compulsive masculinity that contributes to aggression and drinking (McClelland and Davis 1972). Kohlberg (1973) cites weak moral development as an antecedent of both aggression and substance use.

   c) *Does Aggression Precede Substance Use, or Does Substance Use Precede Aggression?*   Longitudinal research provides empirical evidence to disentangle the effects and antecedents of compulsive substance use. For example, Robins (1979, 1984) has made important contributions to the study of the natural histories of addiction and adolescent substance use. McCord (1983, 1988) followed subjects in the Cambridge-Somerville Youth Study (Powers and Witmer 1951), begun in 1936, for four decades and examined antisocial behaviors including alcohol use and criminal activity. Subjects were classified during childhood as aggressive or nonaggressive based on teacher evaluations at seven to eight years of age, well before their initiation into substance use. At followup, subjects were classified as alcoholic ($N = 107$) or nonalcoholic ($N = 283$), and information was collected about their criminal activity from official records. About half the alcoholics (47 percent) had been aggressive youngsters, compared to 40 percent of the nonalcoholics. Accordingly, there was no conclusive evidence that aggression preceded alcoholism.

   The results showed that aggressiveness in childhood predisposed subjects to adult criminal behavior, and that alcoholic subjects were convicted of more crimes regardless of their early childhood aggressiveness. Moreover, alcoholism and early childhood aggression were associated with different forms of adult aggression. Alcoholic subjects who were aggressive during childhood more often were convicted of interpersonal crimes as adults than nonalcoholic subjects. In other words, early childhood aggressiveness and alcoholism as an adult were found to interact and predict the highest levels of interpersonal violence.

The McCord study makes a singular contribution in its multidecade span. However, it relies more on the classification of early childhood behaviors than assessment of personality variables that might influence aggression as a child and thereby overlooks alternate views of the development of aggression in childhood. This is typical of longitudinal studies that seek to disentangle the sequence of behaviors between intoxication and aggression. Unfortunately, few other studies have examined the temporal order of aggression and substance use, much less other etiological factors, and accordingly the causal mechanisms remain tangled. There are a few exceptions, however. Greenberg (1977) reviewed empirical research on amphetamine abuse and violence. She found consistent evidence that delinquency preceded amphetamine abuse. Collins, Hubbard, and Rachal (1985) suggested that criminal violence preceded certain types of substance use among adults. Unfortunately, problems of accurate recall of temporal order or specific experiences in most retrospective studies pose threats to the validity of their results.

d) *Substance Use and Aggression Are Spuriously Associated.*   Numerous researchers have suggested that the intoxication-aggression relation is spurious rather than causal, especially among adolescents (see the literature reviews in Elliott and Ageton 1976; Gandossy et al. 1980; Collins 1981; Inciardi 1981; and Watters, Reinarman, and Fagan 1985). In this view, a "third factor" or common cause underlies both crime and drug use. Longitudinal studies have been unable to establish conclusively a causal ordering and may interpret as causal what may actually be reciprocal relations. Several longitudinal studies (Johnston, O'Malley, and Eveland 1978; Elliott, Huizinga, and Ageton 1985; Kandel, Simcha-Fagan, and Davies 1986; White, Pandina, and LaGrange 1987) found little evidence that drug use either precedes or follows crime, only that they tend to co-occur and are associated in frequency and severity.

There also seems to be considerable variation in the strength of the drug-violence association, with simple correlations ranging from 0.4 to 0.6 (Clayton 1981). Thus, over 60 percent of the variance in drug use and criminality is not shared by a common set of etiological factors. White, Johnson, and Garrison (1985) analyzed longitudinal data from a probability sample of New Jersey adolescents through eighteen years of age. They report even lower correlations (0.2 to 0.4) when controlling for severity of use, with gender and age differences between middle (fifteen years of age) and later (eighteen years) adolescence. And crime variables added less to predictions of substance use than substance use did to predictions of crime, suggesting that the relation may be asymmetrical: there may be more drug users who avoid crime than delinquents who avoid substance use.

Accordingly, there is little doubt that adolescents who drink or use drugs are more likely to commit violent acts than are those who avoid substance use. Among delinquents, the probability of more frequent and severe[10] drug use increases with the severity and frequency of violent delinquency (Johnson et al. 1986b). Yet consensus on the intoxication-aggression relation among adolescents seems to end there.

2. *Experimental Studies.*   Direct, systematic experimental studies of the effects of intoxication on aggression provide further evidence of the complexity of the association. These studies generally occur within a laboratory setting where the experimenter monitors aggressive behavior that may occur following controlled (and manipulated) interactions between an aggressor and a potential victim. Measurement of aggression requires a valid index of aggressive behaviors. Intoxicants are given in varying doses to the potential aggressor, often in a double-blind condition. The amounts are almost always less than the threshold for sensory impairment (drunkenness). Subjects are nearly always male college students.

Taylor (1983) summarized the results of research using two major experimental models: the teacher-learner paradigm and the competition paradigm. Conclusions about the strength and nature of the relation varied by experimental model used and several design characteristics. In the teacher-learner paradigm, the subject, or teacher, helps the learner, who is engaged in a memory task, by administering electric shocks of varying intensities when the learner makes a mistake. The competition paradigm allows a subject to commit aggressive acts against an opponent during competition in a reaction time test.[11] Taylor described this method succinctly:

---

[10] Use of drugs other than alcohol or marijuana, specifically hallucinogens, opiates, cocaine, barbiturates, amphetamines, or PCP.

[11] One might rightfully wonder about the human subjects procedures in these experiments. Subjects are informed about the procedures involved, including the potential for receiving electric shocks. The discomfort is compared to pain encountered in daily routines, such as a pinprick or a mild burn from a hot kitchen surface. Subjects are told they may terminate their services at any time, without penalty. They are asked to sign a statement acknowledging that they have had some previous experience with alcohol, or the substance to be investigated. They also authorize their medical records to be examined to rule out participation where medical conditions so indicate. To consume alcohol, subjects place a small amount of crushed ice in their mouths and consume two drinks, fifteen minutes apart. Each drink consists of the alcohol (100 proof), a quantity of ginger ale that is 1.5 times the amount of the alcohol, and peppermint oil to mask the taste.

Prior to each competitive trial, the subject, and presumably his opponent, is signaled to select the intensity of the shock he wishes to administer to his competitor. The subject and his opponent then compete on a reaction time trial. The person with the slower reaction time receives the shock that had presumably been selected by his competitor. The person with the faster reaction time does not receive a shock; however, he is informed, by means of feedback lights, of the intensity of the shock his opponent had set for him. Thus, the subject realizes that either he or his opponent will receive a shock, depending on the outcome of the competitive trial, and that each can select the intensity of the shock the other will receive. In actuality, the opponent is simulated. [Taylor 1983, p. 281]

Several studies using the competition paradigm suggest that intoxicated subjects behave more aggressively than nonintoxicated subjects. Shuntich and Taylor (1972) reported that intoxicated subjects behaved more aggressively than did subjects who either consumed a placebo or had no beverage at all.[12] Taylor and Gammon (1975) replicated this experiment, varying the quantity of alcohol consumed. Their results indicated there is a positive and linear association between aggression and the quantity of alcohol consumed. Accordingly, Taylor (1983) suggests that there initially appears to be a relation between alcohol and aggression.

Other studies sought to determine whether similar associations were evident for the effects of marijuana (considered to have hallucinogenic effects) or diazepam, a minor tranquilizer, generally classified as a central nervous system suppressant. Taylor et al. (1976) found that high doses of delta-9-tetrahydrocannabinol (THC) did not produce aggressive responses. The high-dose THC condition tended to suppress aggression. Myerscough (1980) replicated the Taylor et al. study, but with a higher maximum dose of THC and a highly provocative (simulated) opponent.[13] Only subjects in the low-dose condition showed aggressive behavior over the two control conditions and were

---

Thirty minutes after the last drink, the subject is taken to the area where the experiment proceeds.

[12] The no-beverage controls and the placebo groups did not differ in their shock settings.

[13] The simulated opponent set intense shocks and, on two occasions, attempted to deliver a shock that was twice as strong as the pain threshold.

also the only ones to retaliate against the provocative opponent. Pagano (1981) compared the effects of high and low doses of diazepam to both a placebo and a nonintoxicating condition. Diazepam, a central nervous system depressant, increased subjects' aggression, but only at high dosage.

Research using the teacher-learner paradigm produced quite different results, suggesting that the intoxication-aggression relation is mediated by social and environmental factors. This is the basis for rejection of the simple disinhibition hypothesis, a form of psychopharmacological determinism that, until recently, was uncritically accepted to explain the intoxication-aggression relation. Factors such as threat, learned social responses, and expectancy have been shown empirically to mediate the intoxication-aggression relation.

Bennett, Buss, and Carpenter (1969) found no relation between alcohol consumption and aggression, contradicting the Shuntich and Taylor (1972) results obtained using the competition paradigm. Analyzing the differences between these studies, Taylor, Gammon, and Capasso (1976) suggested that differences between the paradigms explained the discrepancy. They argued that the teacher-learner paradigm is inherently nonthreatening since the learner cannot retaliate. But in the competition paradigm, opponents not only can retaliate but also initiate physical attacks.

Taylor and colleagues tested this hypothesis by having subjects compete with a silent or active opponent. The silent opponent was considered to be nonthreatening, and even went so far as to audibly say to the experimenter, within earshot of the subject, "I have strong convictions about hurting people and I'd feel more comfortable about this thing if I just set the 'one' button all the time" (Taylor 1983, p. 285). Intoxicated subjects behaved more aggressively than the sober subjects but only under the threatening conditions. Taylor, Gammon, and Capasso concluded that aggression is not simply a pharmacological effect of ingestion of alcohol but instead results from the interaction of consumption and threatening environmental cues.

In later experiments, Sears (1977) and Taylor et al. (1979) each modified this experimental framework. Results were consistent with the earlier studies: intoxicated subjects still behaved more aggressively. Taylor et al. (1979) allowed subjects actually to see an opponent attempt to harm him, making the threat real rather than potential. Sears used social cues conveyed verbally by peers, instead of potential threat, to instigate aggression. Finally, Taylor and Gammon (1975) found that intoxicated subjects also were receptive to social pressure to reduce shock, even when opponents administered intense shocks.

Accordingly, both threat and other instigative cues interacted with intoxication to produce aggressive responses in a competition paradigm. The absence of aggression in the noninstigative conditions provides strong evidence to dismiss disinhibition models based on either physiological or psychopharmacological processes. However, not all theories of disinhibition are based on psychoactive or physiological responses. The learned disinhibition model suggests that the effects of alcohol are learned rather than physiologically determined, and that subjects who consume alcohol simply behave consistently with their expectancy that intoxication will instigate aggression. That is, belief that one is intoxicated is itself a cue for specific aggressive behaviors. (Also, see Briddell et al. 1978, regarding sexual arousal).

In experimental conditions, learned disinhibition suggests that those who consume a placebo which they believe to be alcohol should become more aggressive than those individuals who do not believe they have consumed alcohol, independent of dose. Moreover, since the belief that one has consumed alcohol is the critical condition, aggression should be constant for those who believe they have not received alcohol, regardless of whether, in fact, they receive placebos or varying doses of alcohol. Taylor (1983) reports several studies that contradict the learned disinhibition hypothesis (Shuntich and Taylor 1972; Taylor and Gammon 1975; Zeichner and Pihl 1979, 1980). Taylor (1983, p. 228) concludes that the evidence "provides strong support for a model that assumes that neither the pharmacological effects of alcohol, nor cues in the drinking situation, can independently account for the aggression expressed by intoxicated persons. In the absence of instigation, alcohol consumption has not been shown to increase aggressive responding. However, in the presence of instigative cues, alcohol has been reported to facilitate intense aggression. While these instigations were only minimally effective in producing aggression among sober subjects, they were very effective among intoxicated subjects."

Instead, it appears more likely that alcohol influences the perception or attribution of threat (Taylor, Gammon, and Capasso 1976; Schmutte, Leonard, and Taylor 1979). Boyatzis (1977) cites evidence that alcohol affects the same physiological processes stimulated during an aggressive encounter, an endocrinological effect. Both Moyer (1983) and Vogel (1983) suggest that this process decreases the threshold of provocation or stimulation for aggression.

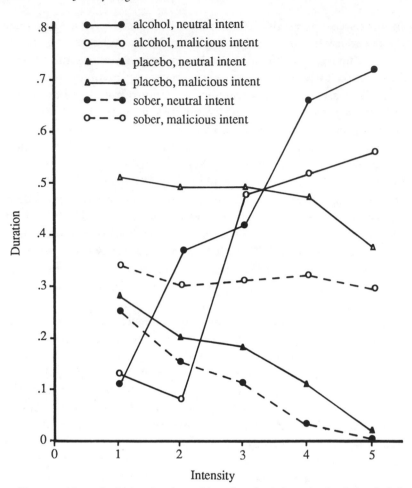

FIG. 1.—Mean shock duration (seconds) at five shock intensity levels in alcohol, placebo, and nondrinking ("sober") groups. Source.—Zeichner (1980), cited in Pihl (1983), p. 297.

Zeichner and Pihl (1979, 1980) reported evidence confirming a corollary hypothesis: intoxication reduces the ability to perceive the negative consequences of an aggressive act or at least interferes with individuals' abilities to process information about behavioral contingencies. Again using a competition paradigm, they found that intoxicated subjects more often failed to consider the possible consequences of their behavior, and responded aggressively to provocations regardless of the level of retaliatory threat. Figure 1 illustrates the significant effect of alcohol (compared to a placebo) on shock administration and also the interaction of provocation (malicious or neutral), expectancy, and substance. Russell and Mherabian (1974) found that increased risk taking occurs during intoxication, indicating that judgments about contingencies and consequences alter rather than simply impair.

Accordingly, these studies suggest that intoxication either intensifies or diminishes perceptions of the social contexts of drinking situations. That is, they suggest the presence of mediating cognitive and emotional mechanisms that qualify the intoxication-aggression relation. Specifically, the effects of anticipation or expectation on aggressive responses to intoxicants have important implications for understanding the occurrence of violence following substance use. Unfortunately, the preponderance of experimental research has examined the effects of alcohol as an intoxicant; empirical evidence from experiments with other substances is simply not available or lacking in rigor.

3. *Summary.* The results of both psychoanalytic and experimental studies suggest that intoxication is associated with aggression but that cognitive and emotional states mediate the intoxication-aggression relation. Moreover, the association is substance specific, with evidence available that some substances suppress aggression while others intensify either the behavior or its emotional or cognitive antecedents. The preponderance of empirical studies have examined the effects of alcohol, most often with subjects drawn from college student pools, and they suffer from marked intrasubject variability. The paradigms employed may be artifactual and fail to simulate credible social contexts. Nevertheless, there is evidence of the antecedent effects of alcohol on aggression, and that expectancy also plays a significant role in the intoxication-aggression relation.

There is some evidence that alcohol in particular may increase one's preparedness to aggress, akin to a "fight or flight" reaction, or, alternatively, reduce the threshold for aggression by altering perceptions of its consequences. Aggression also is more likely to occur in response to provocation or perception of threat in specific social contexts. There appears to be little support for a neurochemical model of disinhibition, despite the evidence that aggression increases at higher doses of alcohol, or for alcohol in comparison to beer (Pihl 1983). But Pihl (1983) suggests that prior associations with alcohol may significantly influence expectancy. The expectancy relation is further modified by the social contexts in which alcohol is consumed and the beliefs of behavioral expectations in specific circumstances (Wilson and Lawson 1976; Boyatzis 1983). It is plausible that the alcohol's antecedent effects simply reflect social cues or other social-psychological factors that are spuriously related to aggression. These factors are analyzed in the next section.

D. Social and Cultural Explanations

Empirical evidence of subcultural variation in the intoxication-aggression relation challenges theories based on chemical disinhibition. Despite evidence that intoxication may alter social judgment and arousal states, the many observations of subcultural, cross-cultural, and socially mediated variation contradict theories of intoxication-caused aggression based on biological, psychopharmacological, cognitive, or personality factors. Goldstein's (1985) important work, and subsequent empirical validation (Goldstein et al. 1988), suggests that even when there exists an intoxication-aggression relation, there are several meanings and explanations to observed patterns of substance use and aggression. Social and cultural explanations of the intoxication-aggression relation do not deny the contributions of individual factors; however, biological or psychological factors simply cannot explain the cross-cultural or subcultural variation that dominates the empirical literature on intoxication and aggression.

The evidence of social influences encompasses three broad areas: cross-cultural and subcultural studies of societies where there is conflicting evidence of aggression during intoxication; social structural patterns in the intoxication-aggression relation by race, region, age, and social class; and evidence from specific varieties of intoxication-related aggression which demonstrate the sociocultural patterns that shape these behaviors.

1. *Cross-cultural Variation.* In 1969, MacAndrew and Edgerton demonstrated that alcohol use does not lead to aggressive behavior in all cultures, but that aggressive behavior accompanies alcohol use in some cultures but not others, and that individuals may be aggressive in some situations but not others. Their study, *Drunken Comportment*, essentially dismissed the notion that the physiological effects of ethanol are the major or sole cause of aggressive behavior when intoxicated. Other cross-cultural studies have confirmed the MacAndrew and Edgerton (1969) finding. For example, Schaefer (1973) examined ethnographic reports from a probability sample of sixty small-scale and folk societies and concluded that men frequently get drunk in most (forty-six) of them but are involved in drunken brawls in fewer than one-half (twenty-four). A decade earlier, Lemert (1962) noted that drinking may

be interpreted either as a cultural pattern, a symbol of cultural stress, a symbolic protest, or a form of collective behavior. Accordingly, regardless of how substances are used, cultural meanings and practices will contribute to some degree in determining the circumstances of how people use intoxicants and how they behave afterward. Levinson (1983*b*) suggests three explanations of cultural influences that may mediate the intoxication-aggression relation: cultural norms or patterns, cultural "defense," and ethnic and subcultural determinants.

a) Cultural Patterns. The cultural pattern model rests on two broad assumptions: first, that aggressive behavior is learned and transmitted by social and cultural processes and, second, that different forms of aggression tend to co-occur (e.g., assaults, homicide, warfare). Accordingly, Wolfgang and Ferracuti (1967) sought to explain the existence of violence within subcultural groups as intrinsic to those groups, culturally legitimated in a wide range of social situations, and reproduced or passed on intergenerationally. With respect to intoxication, the cultural pattern model suggests that the intoxication-aggression relation will be strongest in subcultures or societies where aggression is normative.

Many cultures have no association between intoxication and aggression. Heath (1983) cites the Camba tribe of Bolivia, who get drunk on 178 proof rum twice a month, but who experience no verbal, physical, or sexual aggression during those periods or between them. Instead, drinking for the Camba is a welcome and necessary "time out" from the difficult routines facing these subsistence farmers. For the Camba, aggression is virtually nonexistent and hence does not occur during their predictable periods of intoxication. In contrast, the Lapps of Finland also drink in periodic binges. But fighting is commonplace and homicide is a frequent result of knife fights during their drinking episodes (Ahlstrom 1981, cited in Heath 1983). However, there is no evidence that the Lapps are particularly violent when sober. Levinson (1983*b*) links the generally higher levels of homicide and aggression in the American South to its high rates of alcohol-related aggression. Citing national surveys of drinking patterns, Levinson states that both alcohol use and violence are higher in the southern United States, calling it a pattern of "belligerent drinking."

In an earlier study, Heath (1964) cited other sociocultural factors that illustrate the culturally unique patterns of aggression while intoxicated. Heath showed the importance of individual relationships within the kinship structure of the Navajo that determine who will fight when drunk. For example, the Navajo fight exclusively within their kinship structures (e.g., between uncles and nephews), rather than indiscriminately between members of different families within the tribe. Even within cultures, the norms and expectation of "drunken comportment" may change over time—Hill (1974) cites changes in expected behaviors while intoxicated of young Plains Indians, from "hell raiser" as a youth to a sober and gentle "family man" as an adult who avoids violence when intoxicated. Common experience tells us that, in American culture, there is less physical aggression among businesspersons than "blue-collar" workers despite the higher alcohol dose in businesspersons' martinis than there is in the beers consumed by working-class men in neighborhood taverns.

There also is ample evidence of cross-cultural variation in the intoxication-aggression relation for other substances. Morales (1989) studied coca farmers in Peru who chewed coca leaves to increase their energy and productivity. The term "drug abuse" itself originally reflected prejudice by American southerners against black cocaine users rather than any attribution of its dangerous effects (Musto 1973; Helmer 1975). The term later was extended to opium smoking by Chinese Americans, another expression of fear against a minority who were despised at the time (Zinberg 1984). Clausen (1968) pointed out that a particular drug (in his writing, marijuana) may be accepted as part of a religious ritual in one society, an enhancement to routine social interactions in another society, and a dangerous substance in a third society. The work of Carlos Castaneda illustrates the importance of hallucinogens in spiritual observance and as religious sacraments (Castaneda 1967).

Evidently, cultural and ecological factors influence the intoxication-aggression relation. However, research has provided few valid explanations of why and how cultural factors influence the intoxication-aggression relation. Achte et al. (1969) and Room (1970) adopt a drive-discharge model to explain the Finnish aggression and American belligerent drinking in the South, respectively.[14] However, comparing drive discharge and cultural pattern models, several studies have found little support for drive-discharge explanations of intoxication-related aggression (Berkowitz 1962; Straus 1974; Levinson and Malone 1980).

[14] The drive-discharge model of human aggression suggests that all groups have basic aggressive instincts that must be discharged periodically (Levinson 1983a). The processes of a drive-discharge model generally include five components: ambivalence about aggressive feelings, guilt feelings about the behavior once it is initiated, authoritarian control that suppresses the expression of basic instincts or behaviors, tension or difficulty in expressing the guilt or ambivalence produced by the behavior, and expression of the frustration and rage from the pent-up aggressive feelings.

Moreover, individual variation within cultures suggests that cultural pattern models suffer from ecological fallacy limitations. Heath (1983) suggests that situational factors are necessary to explain individual variation within a culture, although the situational factors themselves are created by unique cultural processes. Heath suggests that cultural patterns of "drunken comportment" are perhaps best explained as communicating the shared values and norms of a culture or social group.[15] Accordingly, aggression while intoxicated may be a social, interactive ritual with specific meaning in specific social contexts that links the participants in terms of their social roles and connections.

b) Cultural Defense. Many studies have shown how intoxication is used as an excuse for behavior that is socially disapproved or controlled in most contexts. MacAndrew and Edgerton (1969) use the notion of "time out" to explain how people are not held accountable for behaviors that occur while intoxicated. These cultural practices help reduce tensions and hostilities within cultures or social groups by creating situations in which it is permissible to express such conflicts. Marshall (1983) suggests three reasons why drunken aggressiveness is an efficient cultural defense. First, aggressiveness while intoxicated is widespread, both between strangers and in domestic situations. Its common occurrence suggests that it plays some useful social purpose within cultural systems. Second, feigned drunkenness often accompanies aggressive behavior. Apparently, drunken behavior is associated with a social context that is important in facilitating aggressiveness. Third, aggressiveness while intoxicated involves a highly ritualized set of learned behaviors and specific social rules that dictate the conditions for becoming intoxicated and the participants in episodes of aggression.

The ritualization of cultural defense provides participants a set of rules governing the boundaries of aggression: locations, participants, and severity. Levinson (1983*b*) suggests that ritualization of aggression during intoxication reduces ambiguity in social cues in drinking contexts and, accordingly, may help reduce random, uncontrolled violence. Thus, provocation from a *known* drunken aggressor can be interpreted appropriately and met with tactics that deflect the aggression, while *arbitrary* aggression that occurs outside accepted boundaries more often will result in violence (Pernanen 1976).

---

[15] As an anthropologist, Heath regards behaviors while intoxicated as expressions of other social or psychological processes, what sociologists often term symbolic interactions (Blumer 1971).

Brisset (1978) cites cross-cultural evidence that individuals in various cultures around the world admit to planning asocial or antisocial acts and then drinking as an "excuse" for the behaviors that follow. A corollary of cultural defense is the concept of drinking to embolden behavior. Levinson (1983*b*) and Roizen (1983) each cite evidence that drinkers intended to alter their mood by consuming alcohol, but they did not anticipate specific behaviors that might accompany their changed mood. Vigil (1988) described how Mexican American youth gangs in East Los Angeles used PCP and alcohol to achieve a state of *locura*, where a variety of antisocial and aggressive acts could occur. Feldman, Mandel, and Fields (1985) found similar processes among Latino youths in San Francisco. However, they discovered quite opposite effects among black youths in the same city, who preferred substances that enhanced their ability to maintain reserve or *cool*, their culturally valued mood and behavior. Thus, both the *defense* (excuse) and *embolden* hypotheses view intoxicants as enablers or facilitators of certain culturally specific emotional or behavioral states while intoxicated.

c) Ethnic and Subcultural Determinants. There is an extensive literature on ethnic and subcultural differences in alcohol studies (Wechsler et al. 1980), and there are some studies on other substances (see Feldman, Agar, and Beschner [1979], for PCP use; and Feldman, Mandel, and Fields [1985], regarding alcohol, marijuana, and PCP). These studies focus mainly on the behaviors and problems of males while intoxicated. Levinson (1983*a*) explains ethnic differences in consumption and problem behavior patterns in terms of the extent to which cultural processes incorporate intoxication into subcultural social systems. Accordingly, where intoxication is well integrated into the rituals of a subculture, problems related to intoxication are rare. Where there exists cultural dissonance about alcohol or drug use (i.e., where it is poorly integrated), or where intoxication results from the social or economic isolation of an ethnic group, problems such as aggression and violence will be evident. The evidence of differences between Latino and black youths in San Francisco in Feldman, Mandel, and Fields (1985) also illustrates ethnic and subcultural differences.

Anomie theory (Merton 1957) suggests that deviant behavior (such as aggression while intoxicated) is more likely to occur in a situation in which individuals lack access to legitimate means to achieve their economic goals. The resulting means-ends disjunction may produce individual and social pressures to engage in alternative behaviors. Levinson

(1983*b*) suggests that excessive drinking and drunken brawling may be two common expressions, citing three studies to support this interpretation. First, Robbins (1979) found that aggressive drinkers among Naskapi men in northern Canada were men who were unsuccessful as iron miners in a mining community. Nonaggressive drinkers included those who were successful economically, and accordingly had greater access to status-conferring social ceremonies or to important goods that could be other indicators of their social status. Second, Gordon (1978) found that Dominican immigrants to the United States had greater economic opportunities after migration. The social meaning of drinking changed for Dominican immigrants when their cultural role changed in response to their new economic condition, and aggression while drinking changed in turn. They placed a greater value on discipline, sacrifice, and family. In turn, their drinking locale changed from male-only bars to their homes, often in the company of wives and relatives, and aggression decreased as their embedment in the male culture lessened.

Finally, Gordon (1982) discovered the opposite pattern among Guatemalan immigrants to the United States and attributed the differences to the absence of women in their immigrant communities compared to the Dominicans. Guatemalan immigration was confined largely to males, but Dominican *families* migrated to the United States. Thus, while Dominican men spent more time at home, Guatemalan men continued to drink in bars with other men, maintaining the social immersion in male cultures that prevailed in Guatemala, and that have been associated with violent behavioral norms among males (Bowker 1986*a*, 1986*b*).

Burns (1980) provided an ethnographic account of typical drinking behavior of male adolescents in Boston by charting the events of an evening of drinking and socializing with four young males from Charlestown, a homogeneous working-class section of the city. The displays of aggression were integral to the social bonds between the young men and included seventeen distinct aggressive acts.[16] Their behaviors varied widely by type of setting. They were quiet and deferential in the local tavern with elder members of the Charlestown neighborhood. However, they were most aggressive in the "adult entertainment"

---

[16] Loud conversation, good-natured wrestling, piling into a car, speeding, verbal boasting, verbal threatening, raucous comments, verbal disparagement, being rowdy, yelling, screaming, arguing, putting a fist through a store window, fighting, bottle crashing, threatening with a gun, and sexual aggressiveness.

neighborhoods of the downtown areas. Burns concluded that drinking served aggression and allowed them to express their masculinity, but the boys shifted their setting to a milieu where aggression was more acceptable, or where social controls were less salient. Moreover, Burns's account suggested that aggression was associated with the amount of alcohol consumed. In other studies cited by Levinson (1983b), the correlations between the amount consumed and aggression ranged from .28 to .42, suggesting that at least 50–70 percent of the variance in aggression while drinking is explained by other factors than the amount consumed. Yet the causal direction is uncertain—the boys in the Burns study drank beer to become aggressive, and the more they drank, the more aggressive they became.

Missing from these studies are efforts to examine interactions between cultural and economic variables. It is conceivable that cultural meanings associated with intoxication may mediate the relation between economic attainment and aggression while intoxicated. These anthropological studies generally use the occurrence of alcohol- or drug-related aggression to illuminate aspects of their subjects' social lives and their relation to the dominant cultures in which they exist. It is also likely that there is an interaction between cultural or ethnic groups and social controls regarding intoxication, factors that both impart meaning to intoxication and proscribe impermissible behaviors (Morgan 1983).

Accordingly, the cultures where aggression often accompanies intoxication are likely to vary in the cohesion or looseness of their social and economic structures (Levinson 1983a). Factors such as kinship structures, collective property ownership, or divisions of labor are dimensions of cultural cohesion. In cohesive cultures, not only is there economic integration of its members, but also intoxication rituals are integrated into their social rituals, and cultural and social controls are present to proscribe behavior while intoxicated. In these cohesive societies, Levinson (1983b) hypothesizes that few differences in behaviors exist whether members are intoxicated or sober. Thus, the extent of integration of the factors that operate in different realms and levels (social, economic, cultural) influences the occurrence of aggression during intoxication.

2. *Social Structural Patterns and Social Correlates.* Much of the research on the social sources of substance use and aggression has examined the joint occurrence of substance use and criminality. Over fifty years of research on the relation between substance use and violence

has yielded contradictory and ambiguous findings (Austin and Lettieri 1976; Elliott and Ageton 1976; Gandossy et al. 1980; Inciardi 1981; Clayton and Tuchfield 1982; Watters, Reinarman, and Fagan 1985; Collins 1906, Johnson et al. 1906b). Although there is little doubt that individuals who drink or use drugs are more likely to commit crimes than those who avoid substance use, there is conflicting evidence on the strength or direction of the association. Recent evidence suggests that there may be "common causes" or a "third factor" that explains the joint behaviors or suggests whether the same factors may be equally efficient at explaining them independently (Elliott, Huizinga, and Ageton 1985; White, Pandina, and LaGrange 1987). Among delinquents, the probability of more frequent and severe[17] drug use increases with the severity and frequency of delinquent involvement (see Chaiken and Chaiken, in this volume, and Hunt, in this volume, for reviews of research on drug-crime relationships).

The age and gender distribution of criminal violence seems also to describe the intoxication-aggression relation. Violence while intoxicated is the province of young males (Gandossy et al. 1980). Analysis of national survey data (Cahalan and Cisin 1976; Blane and Hewitt 1977) shows that drinking patterns of younger males tend to be characterized by binge drinking, often associated with aggressive behavior. These studies found the highest rates of violence and verbal aggression following drinking among twenty-one to twenty-four-year-old respondents. Wechsler (1979) surveyed college undergraduates in the New England states and found nearly ten times the rate of aggression while drinking for males. Among adolescents, Jessor and Jessor (1973, 1977) found more deviant behavior (especially assaultive behavior) among students who drink than among nondrinkers. However, Jessor and Jessor report also that youths who are aggressive while drinking also are aggressive while sober, suggesting a spurious relation between alcohol use and aggression among adolescents.

In inner-city areas, where the social correlates of both substance use and crime are concentrated, violent youths were more likely to be involved in frequent alcohol and drug use, though the majority of alcohol and drug users were involved infrequently in violent behaviors (Fagan et al. 1987). White, Pandina, and LaGrange (1987) analyzed longitudinal data from a representative sample of New Jersey adoles-

---

[17] Use of drugs other than alcohol or marijuana, specifically hallucinogens, opiates, cocaine, barbiturates, amphetamines, or PCP.

cents and found that few respondents reported concurrent involvement in "serious" alcohol use, drug use, or delinquency.[18] Elliott, Huizinga, and Ageton (1985) analyzed a national probability sample of adolescents and also found that alcohol and substance abuse were highest for "multiple index offenders," but the explanatory variables of substance use overlapped with those for delinquency.

Chaiken and Chaiken (in this volume) summarize empirical research on substance use and "predatory" crimes and find that predatory offenders commit violent crimes at a high rate and are also likely to be frequent users of several drug types and alcohol. They are also likely to have irregular employment and weak family (marital) ties. However, the Chaikens are quick to point out that addiction or pathological intoxication often are not associated with violence. Moreover, changes over time in individuals' substance-use patterns are not a function of their participation in criminal activity. However, Ball et al. (1982) and Speckart and Anglin (1986) show that heroin addicts commit far more crimes during periods of addiction than during periods of abstinence or withdrawal.

Some of these empirical trends may result from the design artifacts of the studies that characterize this literature. There seems to be more empirical evidence available about adolescents in general population samples, often in longitudinal studies. In contrast, few cross-sectional or longitudinal studies are available about the substance use and illegal behaviors of adults. Rather, empirical evidence on adults is based often on either clinical samples (substance users or offenders in treatment) or on criminal justice populations. There are few efforts, other than national surveys on alcohol and (rarely) on drug use, that include responses from general adult populations. Accordingly, both epidemiological knowledge and assessments of risk factors and etiological variables are concentrated on adolescent behaviors.

Despite controversy over the direction and strength of the drug-crime relation, the consistent association between them suggests that there are correlates of the joint behaviors as well as potential discriminators of the individual or joint behaviors. In general, the correlates of criminality generally mirror the correlates of substance use. Both literatures agree on age, sex, and ethnic relations, as well as on a variety of social factors including family relations and peer groups. For both race and class relations, the relation to delinquency and drug use is

[18] Their definition of "serious" use was three or more occasions in the past year of each behavior.

ambiguous other than for the more serious delinquent activities (Weiner and Wolfgang 1985) or persistent drug use behaviors (Johnston, O'Malley, and Bachman 1985). The incidence of delinquency and the drug-delinquency correlation are higher among males than females, especially for harder drugs (Johnson et al. 1986b), and among minority youths (Elliott and Huizinga 1983; Newcomb and Bentler 1988).

Numerous studies have identified common social correlates of delinquency and drug use, including family structure and process, school performance and experience, religious ties and commitments, and a variety of psychological, interpersonal, and attitudinal variables (see Huba and Bentler 1984; Kaplan, Martin, and Johnson 1986; and Newcomb and Bentler 1988, for thorough analyses of these literatures). Other studies have examined risk factors across time periods. For example, Kandel et al. (1986) analyzed risk factors for both delinquency and drug use in the transitional years from adolescence to young adulthood. They found that transitions into conventional roles of adulthood, such as continuous employment and marriage, in the period *subsequent* to adolescence predicted future drug use but not delinquent involvement.

However, peer associations have been the most consistent and strongest correlates of both delinquency and drug use. Specifically, the behavior of close friends appears to be most strongly associated with both avoidance and participation in deviant behaviors, including initiation, development of approving attitudes, social reinforcement, and progression from experimental or occasional use to more serious and sustained behaviors (Jessor and Jessor 1977; Kandel, Kessler, and Margulies 1978; Akers et al. 1979; Kandel 1980, 1985, 1986; Elliott, Huizinga, and Ageton 1985; Giordano, Cernkovich, and Pugh 1985; Kaplan, Smith, and Robins 1986; Fagan et al. 1987; White, Pandina, and LaGrange 1987). Jessor and Jessor (1977) suggest that qualitatively different behaviors may serve similar purposes (e.g., expressions of independence from parental control). Schwendinger and Schwendinger (1985) suggest that peer networks form according to similar processes and exert similar social influences on their members with respect to delinquency but remain separate and distinct. There indeed may be synchronous group processes in separate networks but with similar influences, which would explain the parallel contributions to dissimilar behaviors within deviance-specific groupings.

Thus, it is not clear if there is one deviant subculture or many. If there were one generally deviant subculture, it would be hard to conceptualize why a group or individual chose a particular behavior to the exclusion of the others. For crossover or joint behaviors, the network may simply be one that supports both behaviors, with similar processes (and correlates) in delinquent networks that eschew drug use but whose behavioral norms develop independently. But if there are separate (but perhaps parallel) subcultures, the similarities and differences between these groups are as yet little understood. Yet they are critically important in explaining variation among similar groups within cultures.

3. *Violence and Substance Use in Specific Social Contexts.* Research on social processes and causes of the intoxication-aggression relation has focused on specific social contexts. Studies of barroom brawls typify this approach (Gottlieb 1957). In contrast, the Burns (1980) and Zinberg (1984) studies illustrate the interaction between social set and setting that determines when intoxication can contribute to aggression, and when context mitigates violence while intoxicated. Youth gangs and family violence, two well-studied areas, are discussed below; these are realms in which the intoxication-aggression relation is well established but where violence also occurs often in the absence of intoxication. These perspectives illustrate the theories of cultural defense and social determinism that explain a significant portion of the intoxication-aggression relation.

a) Youth Gangs. In this decade, gang violence increasingly has been linked to drug use and drug dealing (Klein 1985; Mieczkowski 1986; Fagan 1989). The relation between drug use and serious youth crime is consistently strong under a variety of sampling and measurement conditions. However, gangs are diverse, complex, and shifting organizations whose members participate variably in crime and drug use (Stumphauzer, Veloz, and Aiken 1981; Hagedorn 1988; Klein and Maxson 1989; Spergel 1990). Accordingly, the social organization of substance use and its influence on aggression is likely to vary.

Recent evidence suggests that gang members may also have greater involvement in drug distribution than do other adolescent youths, increasingly for "hard" drugs, leading to what Goldstein (1989) terms "systemic violence" involving drugs. Analyses of gang and nongang homicides (Maxson, Gordon, and Klein 1985), and gang involvement in rock cocaine trafficking (Klein, Maxson, and Cunningham 1988), suggest that Los Angeles gangs increasingly are involved in drug selling. Mieczkowski (1986) reported on adolescent heroin sellers in Detroit, while Cooper (1987) described Detroit youth gangs organized around crack cocaine distribution. Each study reported that gang members used violence both to maintain organizational discipline and for market regulation and control. In several Chicago neighborhoods, gangs control drug sales to juveniles (Rechtenwald and Sheppard 1984; Spergel 1984). Dolan and Finney (1984), among many, clearly show the economic lure of drug sales for gang members, relative to other economic opportunities. Klein (1985) suggests that the sudden emergence of "rock" or "crack" cocaine provided unique economic opportunities which Los Angeles gangs quickly took advantage of.

Drug use among gang members has been noted consistently in gang research. However, until recently, there has been little distinction made regarding patterns of drug use among gangs and the relation between drug use, gang cohesion, and gang activities. Stumphauzer, Veloz, and Aiken (1981) noted that patterns of drug use varied within and among Los Angeles gangs. Campbell (1984) and Dolan and Finney (1984) illustrated the commonplace role of drug use in gang life among both males and females. Vigil (1985, 1988) described a variety of meanings and roles of drug use among Chicano gang members in East Los Angeles, from social "lubricant" during times of collective relaxation to facilitator for observance of ritual behaviors such as *locura* acts of aggression or violence. In these contexts, drug use provided a means of social status and acceptance as well as mutual reinforcement, and was a natural social process of gang life.[19]

Feldman, Mandel, and Fields (1985) observed three distinct "styles" among Latino gangs and street-corner groups in San Francisco that in part were determined by the role and meaning of drug use in their social processes. The "fighting" style included males in gangs who were antagonistic toward males in other gangs. They aggressively responded to any perceived move into their turf by other groups or by any outsider. Drug use and selling were evident but were only situationally related to their violence through territoriality. Violence occurred in many contexts unrelated to drug use or selling and was an important part of the social process of gang or group affiliation. The "entrepreneurial" style consisted of youths who were concerned with attaining social status by means of money and the things money can buy. They were very often active in small-scale illegal sales of marijuana, pill amphetamines, and PCP. While fighting and violence were part of this

[19] Vigil notes that these patterns are confined to substances that enhance gang social processes—alcohol, marijuana, PCP, and crack cocaine. There is a sanction against heroin use among Chicano gangs. Heroin involvement is seen as a betrayal of the gang and the barrio: one cannot be loyal to his addiction and the addict ("tecato") culture while maintaining loyalty to the gang.

style, it was again situationally motivated by concerns over money or drugs. The last style was evident in gangs whose activities were social and recreational, with little or no evidence of fighting or violence.

Drug use also is disallowed in some youth gangs, regardless of the gang's involvement in drug selling. Chin (1986) found that drug use was rejected entirely by Chinese gangs in New York City, despite their involvement in heroin distribution. They used violence to protect their business territories from encroachment by other gangs and to coerce their victims to participate in the gang's ventures. These gangs were hierarchically organized with strict codes and violent consequences for rule violations by members. Cooper (1987) described organizations of adolescent crack sellers in Detroit who prohibited drug use among their members. Leaders in these groups were wary of threats to efficiency and security if street-level sellers were high and to the potential for co-optation of its business goals if one of its members became involved with consumption of their goods. The gangs were organized around income and saw drug use as detracting from the selling skills and productivity of its members. Expulsion from the gang resulted from breaking this rule, but other violent reprisals also were possible.

Mieczkowski (1986) studied adolescent heroin runners (street dealers) in heroin-dealing organizations, also in Detroit, and found a rejection of heroin use by members of the runner organization. However, these gangs accepted recreational use of other drugs by members, primarily marijuana and cocaine, in social situations not involved with dealing. They particularly found danger in being high on any drug while on the job, and superiors in the gang enforced the prohibition against heroin use while working by denying runners their consignment and, accordingly, shutting off their source of income. Violence was occasionally used by superiors (crew bosses) to enforce discipline. Gang members looked down on their heroin-using customers, despite having tried it at some point in their lives, which in part explains the general ideology of disapproval of heroin use.

The discovery of diverse patterns of criminality and drug involvement among gang members and gangs suggests that there are factors in the social organization of gangs and processes of affiliation and cohesion that either encourage or discourage these patterns (Fagan 1989; Spergel 1990). Such diversity also exists among general adolescent populations (Schwendinger and Schwendinger 1985; Fagan, Weis, and Cheng 1990) and suggests that gangs reflect patterns of affiliation and collective behavior similar to other adolescent subcultures. Accordingly, violence and drug involvement, which historically have been taken as defining features of gangs, may be more accurately conceptualized as contingent behaviors that vary by factors that have not been given adequate theoretical or empirical attention.

b) Family Violence. There is widespread belief that intoxication, particularly drunkenness, is a major cause of wife beating and child abuse. Historical analyses by Pleck (1987) trace these beliefs in American society to the colonial era. A Gallup poll, cited by Coleman and Straus (1983), found that almost one in four respondents believed alcohol to be the cause of family violence. Winick (1983) described how popular culture portrayed the effects of drinking on wife beating: in Tennessee Williams's *A Streetcar Named Desire*, a drunken Stanley Kowalski strikes his pregnant wife Stella, and later on strikes his sister-in-law Blanche DuBois (herself a former alcoholic) on the night that Stella delivers their first baby. Similar episodes occurred in Edward Albee's *Who's Afraid of Virginia Woolf*, when George and Martha drink through the night and become increasingly abusive to each other, though only verbally.[20] In *The Brothers Karamazov*, Dostoevski hints (but does not directly assert) that alcohol may have led Dmitri to kill his father. In the 1980s, the musical satirist Kinky Friedman penned the darkly humorous song, "I'd Kill My Mother for Another Line of Cocaine." Kantor and Straus (1987) point out that these images not only link drug use and aggression, but also directly attribute stranger and family violence to intoxication and portray it as an underclass phenomenon.

The empirical evidence on the contribution of intoxication to aggression in families is equivocal. Wolfgang (1958) coined the phrase "victim-precipitated homicides" based on the incidence of intoxication of homicide victims, including victims of domestic homicides. Bard and Zacker (1974), studying a broader range of domestic violence cases, found only a weak association between alcohol and family violence. Kantor and Straus (1987) reviewed fifteen empirical studies on alcohol and spouse assault and found a wide range of reports of the presence of alcohol—from 6 to 85 percent. Fagan, Hansen, and Stewart (1983) reported that the severity of spouse abuse was positively associated with alcohol use by the assailant, but there was a weak, negative association with use of other substances. Coleman and Straus (1983) suggest

---

[20] Martha then went on to have sexual relations with their young male dinner guest, illustrating the image of alcohol as a disinhibitor of sexual behaviors as well as of aggression.

that although reports of alcohol use are high among spouse abusers, the rates are no higher than among the general population. Bard and Zacker (1974) conclude that the relation between spouse abuse and alcohol use was spurious. Establishing a precise relation is made difficult by variation in measures of spouse assault, alcohol or drug use (frequency, severity of intoxication, and impairment), and the variety of sampling and research designs. Thus, for example, Kantor and Straus (1987) reviewed clinical samples of spouse abuse victims (in shelters) or abusers (in batterer treatment) and found higher incidences of alcohol use among spouse abusers than in general population studies or police samples.

Mayer and Black (1981) reviewed the limited evidence on intoxication in cases of child abuse and found a similar broad range of reports of the presence of alcohol problems—from 32 to 65 percent—in families where a child had been abused. However, Steele and Pollack (1968) found no incidence of alcoholism among sixty families where child abuse had occurred. Such discrepancies may result from design and measurement problems that are typical of empirical research on child and spouse abuse.

Hotaling and Sugarman (1986) used a different research strategy to address the question of the intoxication-aggression relation for husband-to-wife violence. They analyzed case-control studies of spouse and child abuse, concentrating on the strength of effects of variables across studies that met minimal design criteria. Alcohol was one of the variables that met their criteria of a positive, significant association in two-thirds of the studies in their analysis which established it as a risk factor for husband-to-wife violence. Abuse of other substances was not found to be a significant risk factor that was positively correlated with spouse assault. Rather, they found an equal number of studies that indicated either positive or negative associations of spouse abuse with other substances. Accordingly, alcohol appears to be a significant correlate of wife abuse, but not child abuse, while drug use is associated with neither form of intrafamily violence.

Two studies examined the incidence of alcohol use in a nationally representative population of families. Coleman and Straus (1983) analyzed data from a 1975 nationwide survey of a representative sample of 2,143 American couples (married and cohabiting) who were interviewed on the frequency of violence between partners in the relationship and the frequency of intoxication from alcohol. The results showed a positive association between the frequency of alcohol consumption and violence between cohabitants. Rates of violence were nearly fifteen times greater for husbands who were drunk "often" compared to "never" during the past year.[21]

In the second study, Kantor and Straus (1987) analyzed data from telephone interviews conducted in 1983 with a nationally representative sample of 5,159 households.[22] Unlike the Coleman and Straus (1983) study, this study asked if there was drinking at the time of a violent incident. In 76 percent of the households where violence occurred, alcohol was *not* used immediately prior to the incident. However, controlling for respondents' *usual* drinking patterns, there was a positive association between the percent who were violent and who were drinking immediately prior to the violent incident. Among "binge" drinkers, nearly half (48.4 percent) were drinking prior to a violent episode, compared to fewer than one in five (19.4 percent) for "infrequent" drinkers. The authors caution that over 80 percent of all respondents in the highest frequency drinking categories did not assault their female partners *at all* in the past year, and nearly two-thirds of blue-collar workers were nonviolent during the study year.

Star (1980) characterized persons violent toward family members as needing power and control and likened violent spouses to alcohol users in such characteristics as extreme jealousy, external blame, sexual dysfunction, and bizarre mood shifts. Speiker (1983) found that both spouse abusers and their victims tended to blame alcohol for the violence, and that men used it as an excuse for their violence. Coleman and Straus (1983) draw on deviance disavowal theories to explain behaviors among people who do not view themselves (or their behaviors) as deviant but need some excuse (such as alcohol) for their unacceptable behavior. By "explaining" violence toward spouses as the result of intoxication, their social standing and self-image are preserved. The behavior is deviant, but not the individual. Intoxication provides a "time out" for such deviance to occur.

Similar to processes described by MacAndrew and Edgerton (1969)

---

[21] However, for men who were the most frequent alcohol users (i.e., those who were "almost always" drunk), violence rates were half those of the "often" drunk respondents. The survey did not inquire about the co-occurrence of intoxication and spouse abuse—whether violence occurred while either of the partners was intoxicated. The authors conclude that the heaviest drinkers are "anesthetized," both emotionally and physiologically.

[22] Eligible households included an adult female (over eighteen years of age) who was either married, recently divorced or separated (within the past two years), not married but cohabiting with a male as a "couple," or a single parent with a minor (less than eighteen years of age) child in the household.

in their cross-cultural studies, the norms for conventional and appropriate behavior were set aside temporarily. However, the process of redefinition uses some external factor (e.g., intoxicants), rather than a conscious decision to behave outside acceptable boundaries. Coleman and Straus (1983) suggest that these processes actually could promote the behavior by offering an advance excuse for their acts. This is similar to the behaviors of gang members and others whose use of substances is designed to create the circumstances when violence can occur.

Both the Kantor and Straus (1987) and Coleman and Straus (1983) studies also suggest that expectancy develops via social learning processes. They conclude that persons learn reactions to alcohol and behaviors while intoxicated through observations in the family context. Other theories also would apply, if we accept the claims of Star (1980) and Speiker (1983) that violence in the family is an expression of power and control. Power-motivation theory (McClelland and Davis 1972; McClelland 1975) suggests that drinking and violence may be a means of asserting power and control in the family. However, other studies of family violence (Dobash and Dobash 1979; Bowker 1983) conclude that the maintenance of masculine power and control is a motivation for domestic violence, independent of external factors.

The findings regarding alcohol and the Bowker (1983) and Dobash and Dobash (1979) studies agree that socioeconomic status also is important and interacts with intoxication to increase the severity of violence.[23] Bowker (1983) found that the men most violent toward spouses were working-class men who were most deeply embedded in "male subcultures," as measured by time spent in bars with male comrades. However, the intoxication-family aggression relation is present even when there is disapproval of violence, for example, among middle-class men. Accordingly, it is likely that, for middle-class men, processes of deviance disavowal and "time out" may permit the assault of spouses. For working-class men, expectancy of behaviors during intoxication, reinforced by both social learning experiences and societal approval for the use of force within families to assert and maintain supremacy, contributes to violence during intoxication. Kantor and Straus (1987) suggest that both processes operate among working-class men.

---

[23] This does not deny the distribution of family violence across social classes. See Straus, Gelles, and Steinmetz (1980), and Straus and Gelles (1986).

Thus the interaction of personality, social network, situation or setting, and cultural norms provides a powerful influence on individual behaviors in the family while intoxicated (and among strangers, as illustrated by Darns's study of the Charlestown youths). Though most violence occurs in the absence of alcohol or other intoxication, there appear to be parallel etiological processes leading to the onset of family violence, and substance abuse contributes to the continuation of aggression over a "battering career."

II. Explanatory Models of Intoxication and Aggression

The association between intoxication and aggression has been noted by researchers for centuries. However, despite a vast literature spanning several disciplines, there is little empirical evidence within or across disciplines to support the separate explanations of the precise causal mechanisms by which the measurable effects of intoxication may lead to specific aggressive behaviors. There is no empirical evidence for attribution of a *causal* relation of intoxication to aggressive behavior—regardless of the type of substance—on the basis of strong correlations. The most influential evidence shows that one's belief that he or she is intoxicated (especially from drinking) affects behavior in much the same way as the actual consumption of a substance. Although experiments offer reliable evidence that aggression increases during intoxication, that evidence cannot account for the results of cross-cultural studies, the high base rates of intoxication without aggressive behaviors, and the mediating effects of social setting and expectancy. Moreover, the empirical literature also contains far more information about alcohol than other substances, and there have been extremely few studies that compare the effects of different substances within controlled settings or similar experimental frameworks. Watters, Reinarman, and Fagan (1985) examined the literature on both alcohol and other intoxicants and concluded that situational and conditional factors still make causal connections difficult to demonstrate. Wolfgang's (1981) conclusions, though referring to alcohol, apply equally to the broader knowledge base on all intoxicants: "The presence of alcohol may be a *contributing* factor, may be positively *correlated*, may be a determinant, but our scholars are unwilling to assert *cause*. And rightly so, for the best available evidence is sometimes contradictory and never fully compelling and convincing. Alcohol may arouse aggression or may augment aggressive behavior which may, in turn, result in criminal assault. But many other things also promote aggression, and even aggression aroused need not lead to criminal behavior" (Wolfgang 1981, p. ix, emphasis in original).

The influence of intoxication on aggression is a complex phenomenon, and explanations that draw narrowly from within disciplines are likely to have weak explanatory power. For example, theories that might explain the interaction of substance and expectancy should incorporate pharmacological, physiological, social-psychological, cultural, and emotional (or cognitive) factors. Understanding the intoxication-aggression relation may require several explanatory frameworks.[24] However, few theorists have developed explanations or models that integrate factors from several disciplines into a unified theoretical framework that specifies causal mechanisms and mediating processes.

This section reviews three theoretical frameworks that integrate explanations and empirical evidence from different disciplines and sources of effects. Collins (1983) and Reinarman and Critchlow-Leigh (1987) fault previous theories for failing to specify the precise mechanisms that explain how intoxication can cause aggression under certain conditions. The frameworks reviewed in this section meet this criterion in that they attempt to integrate empirical evidence and theoretical perspectives from several disciplines.

A. Power-Motivation and Developmental Explanations

Young adult males are involved disproportionately in violent behavior resulting from problem drinking (Cahalan and Room 1974; Jessor and Jessor 1977; Collins 1983; Levinson 1983*b*) or drug use (Elliott and Huizinga 1984; Wish and Johnson 1986; Fagan et al. 1987). There also is a general association of young males with violent behavior (Weiner and Wolfgang 1985). Collins (1981) concludes that the social-

---

[24] Writing specifically about alcohol, but again with broader implications for the intoxication-aggression relation, Pernanen (1976, 1981) suggests that several frameworks may be necessary to explain the empirical correlations between consumption of intoxicants and interpersonal aggression. Fagan et al. (1987), writing specifically about adolescent violence and drug use, also suggest that different explanatory models are necessary given the diversity of observed patterns. Pernanen suggests a typology of causal models, similar to the typologies discussed in earlier sections of this essay. First, the *common* cause theory assumes that the factors that cause aggression and violence are similar to the factors that cause extreme forms of intoxication, especially alcoholism or addiction. Second, he posits a *conditional* relation, where the intoxication-aggression relation is mediated by the social context in which substances are used, the nature of an individual's personality, or socialization that determines one's expectations for behaviors while intoxicated. Third, a *spurious* model suggests that there simply is a correlation without theoretical meaning.

psychological dynamics of the transition from adolescence to adulthood are particularly important to understanding the intoxication-aggression relation. He suggests that theories that account for the social status of youths, as well as their transitional developmental stages, are necessary to explain the frequent joint occurrence of aggression and substance use.

Power-motivation theories were developed by McClelland and colleagues (McClelland and Davis 1972; McClelland et al. 1972; McClelland 1975) to explain motivations for drinking. His theory that people drink in response to a desire for personal dominance offers a potential link to the relation between alcohol use and violence. The basic premise is that drinking enhances personal power, particularly the power to gain victories in confrontations with personal adversaries. The theory is specific to males and has been applied by Kantor and Straus (1987) to examine the alcohol-family violence relation. The perspective suggests that violence can occur during drinking episodes when an intoxicated male may resort to violence to win in a conflict situation.

Transitional developmental periods also are periods when problem behaviors are evident (Jessor and Jessor 1977; Kandel, Simcha-Fagan, and Davies 1986). Kandel, Simcha-Fagan, and Davies (1986) found that the drug use-crime relation was strongest for twenty-four-year-old males when they encountered problems entering the "traditional" roles of worker and marital partner during their transitions from adolescence. Jessor and Jessor (1977) also suggest that problems in life cycle transitions are accompanied by problem behaviors, resulting from changes in expected social roles and behaviors. Fagan et al. (1987) found that among adolescents, the presence of such problems had strong explanatory power in distinguishing controlled drug use from problem drug use and drug use that occurred jointly with violent crimes. These periods also seem to be marked by what Collins (1983) refers to as "hypermasculinity."

There seems to be a close relation between male sex role socialization and aggressive behaviors while intoxicated during the uncertain periods of transition from adolescence to adulthood (McClelland and Davis 1972). Kantor and Straus (1987) suggest an interaction between power-control theories, male sex role socialization, and the co-occurrence of drunkenness and family violence. Young men are at particularly high risk for domestic violence (Hotaling and Sugarman 1986). Violence in the home often manifests a compulsive need to maintain power and control (Bowker 1983, 1986b; Walker 1984), especially against the threat of loss of dominance or control (Dobash and Dobash 1979). Bowker (1983) suggests that the deeper males are embedded in social systems that reinforce their domination and control in the home, the more likely they are to use force to maintain control. Not coincidentally, bars are locales where such socialization often occurs, according to Bowker, as well as to Shields, Hannecke, and McCall (1989).[25]

Thus for family violence there may be several cognitive connections to alcohol: social cue, socialization process, and behavioral expectancy for violence. Similar interpretations may be applied to the use of substances within youth gangs, where intoxication provides both the social "glue" that causes the gang to cohere as well as the "fuel" for the inevitable intergang conflicts that maintain gang boundaries and social relations (Vigil 1988). Burns (1980) also demonstrated the motivation of power-control drives in *specific settings* during the socially complex night of drinking of the Charlestown youths.

The convergence of factors related to the intoxication-aggression association for young males in several settings suggests that young adulthood is a period when there is an exaggerated dependence on socially expected behaviors, in which the social context of substance use conveys several meanings—the enhancement of personal power that is not yet available through "traditional" social roles and the maintenance of power through force. Also, the limited social and personality development of young males in early adulthood may create dependency on external norms for determining expected and appropriate behaviors. Accordingly, the integration of power-motivation theories with perspectives on moral (e.g., Kohlberg 1973) and social (e.g., Jessor and Jessor 1977) development, as well as explanations of violence toward intimates, provides potentially fertile ground for understanding the causal role of intoxication in aggression.

B. Pathology, Cognitive Functioning, and Disinhibition

Physiological and pharmacological explanations of the intoxication-aggression relation share the perspective that ingestion of drugs or

---

[25] The socialization that may occur in that setting can set expectations among males for control over their spouses or female cohabitants, and also legitimate the use of force to maintain it, in a milieu that links violent behaviors to the social cues of drinking. Such contexts provide the frames of reference and cues with which drinkers may make sense of the social interactions. Reinarman and Critchlow-Leigh (1987) refer to alcohol in this context as communicating specific social meanings within a culture. This is similar to what Heath (1983) discusses as the importance of *semiotics* to interpret the meanings of words and actions.

alcohol leads to changes in physiological or psychological functioning that, in a sober state, restrain behavior. The pathological framework states that a pathological condition in the individual can lead to aggression following substance use, either alone or in combination with other factors. Intoxication also may result in cognitive impairment that alters the processing of information or interpretation of social cues, leading to contingencies that produce aggressive responses. A third class of explanations attributes a direct pharmacological or psychoactive effect to substances, though failing to specify neurological or other linkages between substance, brain function, and behavior. This is the classic disinhibition hypothesis.

1. *Pathology and Psychological Impairment.* One simple explanation of the aggression-intoxication relation is the underlying pathology of the individual who uses substances excessively. The American Psychiatric Association acknowledges a disorder characterized by a "marked behavioral change—usually to aggression—that is due to the recent ingestion of an amount of alcohol that is insufficient to produce intoxication in most people" (American Psychiatric Association 1987, p. 128). Other conceptualizations suggest that underlying pathologies are activated by the ingestion of substances (Kramer 1983; Mayfield 1983), leading to states of anxiety, hostility, or paranoia. These conceptualizations leave open the etiological roots of the pathology, though none suggests that substances directly cause personality disorder. At least one study (Ylikahri et al. 1978) claims that alcohol may stimulate the production of cortisol, an arousal or stress hormone that has been linked to aggression. An alternate view is that prolonged substance abuse can itself produce pathologies or emotional states that may lead to aggression (Wilson and Abrams 1977).

2. *Cognitive Impairment.* There is substantial evidence that various substances may impair cognitive functioning (see Pernanen 1976 and 1981, regarding alcohol; and Woody et al. 1983, regarding several types of drugs). Pernanen (1981) developed a model in which intoxication has a disorganizing effect on cognitive functions, especially the ability to process the cues of communication, and causes a general narrowing of the perceptual field. In turn, this may lead to a random determination of behavior, rather than to the contingent behaviors that result from accurate perceptions of social cues. Accordingly, an interpretation of another person's behavior as arbitrary can lead to aggressive behavior. Also, intoxication may reduce an individual's ability to use various coping devices in situations seen as arbitrary or threatening (Collins

1983). However, the effects of intoxication on behavior are not uniform and tend to vary by individual personality factors and emotional or affective states (Holcomb and Adams 1985). These emotional states are also subject to interpretations that are filtered through cultural beliefs, circumstances, and personality, factors that are not easily explained at the individual level (Room 1983).

3. *The Disinhibition Hypothesis.*   Until recently, the disinhibition hypothesis has been prominent in explanations of behavioral changes during intoxication. Its basic underlying premise is that intoxication alters central nervous system or psychological functions that are thought to control or inhibit aggression. Once intoxicated, individuals were free of moral or cognitive restraints on behavior. Competing explanations within this framework suggested that substances either accelerated processes that contributed to behavior, or loosened the moral or learned restraints against behavior. It has been most prominently applied in explanations of the alcohol-violence relation (see Collins 1983, for a critical review) and sexual behaviors (see Reinarman and Critchlow-Leigh 1987, for a critical review) and sexual aggression (Langevin et al. 1988).

However, the inadequacy of these three perspectives is readily demonstrated. For example, pathological intoxication is characterized by nonaggressive states more often than violent behavior. In common lore, the "maudlin," "amorous," and "gregarious" drunks all typify behaviors that were not manifest before but that emerge following alcohol intoxication (Mayfield 1983). The "giggles" and "munchies" are states often produced by marijuana intoxication (Zinberg and Jacobson 1976). But there is virtually no evidence of aggression resulting from the pharmacological effects of marijuana.

The phenomenon of controlled drug use also contradicts the concept of an inevitable relation between drug abuse and aggression, even during periods of frequent opiate use (cf. Ball et al. 1982; Johnson et al. 1985). Waldorf (1973) described the controlled heroin use of the majority of addicts, while Waldorf (1983) and Biernacki (1986) reported on desistance from opiate use by long-term addicts without treatment. Waldorf, Reinarman, and Murphy (1990) studied over 200 high-rate cocaine users (over two grams per week for at least six months) who reported acute changes in their personalities but avoided interpersonal aggression. Woods and Mansfield (1983) reviewed physiological research on disinhibition and concluded that there are no explanations for the effects of substances that span the course from ingestion of ethanol to neuron transmission to central nervous system functions. Simply, there is too much unknown about the processes that might link *behavior* and *substance* to conclude that there exists such a process as "disinhibition." Research on expectancy, summarized earlier in this essay, further disputes the notion of pharmacologically-induced changes in affective states. The effects of expectancy on interpretation of social cues in competition paradigms further mitigates explanations regarding the specific physiological effects of intoxicants on cognitive or emotional states that do mediate aggression.[26]

Research on intoxication and aggression often has overlooked the distinction between acute and chronic intoxication and their differential effects on affective or personality states. Collins (1988) specifically analyzes this distinction for alcohol: acute effects include short-term physiological, cognitive, and mood alterations following ingestion of a substance. Chronic effects, including personality deterioration and physical disabilities, take place over longer periods of prolonged use. He suggests that acute drinking effects may be more important to the occurrence of aggression. Analyses of similar phenomena for heroin use (Zinberg 1984), cocaine inhalation (Erickson et al. 1987; Waldorf, Reinarman, and Murphy 1990), cocaine smoking (Siegel 1982a, 1982b), and marijuana use (Zinberg and Jacobson 1976) do make this distinction but fail to find differences in effects on the intoxication-aggression relation.

Collins (1989) cites several studies that link problem drinking to a multiple-disorder configuration in which individuals with alcohol disorders frequently have other personality disorders such as crippling anxiety or sudden changes in affective states (Harwood et al. 1985; Stinson and Williams 1986). Accordingly, the etiology of compulsive intoxication also may be etiologically relevant to other types of personality or psychiatric disorders that, in turn, mediate aggression. Whether aggression follows intoxication depends in part on the psychological processes that either precede substance use or are intensified following ingestion.

C. Culture and Context: Situational and Sociocultural Factors

There is a growing consensus that the effects of culture, setting, and expectancy shape behavioral responses to intoxication. The ethnographic work of MacAndrew and Edgerton (1969), discussed earlier,

---

[26] Only Steele and Southwick (1985) have found a measurable "alcohol effect" apart from cognitive expectancy, in the relation between alcohol and aggression. However, the preponderance of evidence continues to suggest that expectancy, socially learned, is the strongest argument to dispute disinhibition effects.

found that attitudes toward drinking and rules that govern behavior after drinking are variable across cultures, within the same culture at different times, and even within subcultural networks of the same culture. Comparative analyses of ethnographic research on drug use among adolescents revealed similar diversity in the behaviors that accompanied its use (Feldman, Agar, and Beschner 1979; Feldman, Mandel, and Fields 1985). Accordingly, understanding the origins of expectancy and social controls regarding drinking requires an examination of the factors within cultures that shape beliefs about the effects of substances, the history of social meanings assigned to intoxication from various substances, the social controls that permit or sanction behaviors while intoxicated, and the communication of those rules across diverse circumstances.

1. *Situational Factors.* Substance use and behavioral norms vary both by culture and the specific social setting within the culture. For example, there is a cultural tendency to ascribe blame to alcohol for most of the negative behaviors that occur following its consumption. This "malevolence assumption" (Hamilton and Collins 1981) suggests a moral status of alcohol. The same has developed over time regarding most illicit drugs (Musto 1981), despite empirical evidence that their ill effects are not felt by the majority of users. There can be little doubt that these attributes of most substances influence their cultural phenomenology and, in turn, expectancies of their effects on behaviors. However, analyses of expectancy (e.g., Critchlow-Leigh 1986) suggest that beliefs about expected behavioral effects of substances vary according to the social situations where intoxication occurs.

Social situational factors are attributes of an immediate setting that directly or indirectly influence the behavior of intoxicated people in that setting. Both Burns (1980) and Levinson (1983a) cite three situational factors that influence the social processes of a setting: the number of people present, the nature of their relationships (intimate, familial, adversarial), and the permissiveness of the situation. Interpersonal violence seems to occur in some situations more than others and even in different venues of the same type of setting. For example, there is more violence in some bars than others, though there also is more violence in bars than in other social contexts where alcohol is used. Aggression occurs in some sports stadiums and more often during some types of sporting events than others. The absence of informal social controls, external restraints, or perceptions of societal approval may contribute to interpersonal aggression between intimates following intoxication (Straus 1978).

Permissiveness describes the social controls of the setting that sanction or accept behaviors. The origins of these norms or permitted behaviors is uncertain, but some research suggests how controls against aggression during drug or alcohol use are maintained. For example, the peer processes within the groups described by Reinarman (1979) for cocaine and Zinberg (1984) for heroin suggest a strict social setting that does not tolerate behaviors not approved by the group's norms. And among adolescents, the use of certain intoxicants (e.g., PCP or alcohol) that produce exaggerated, boisterous behaviors can result in ostracism from a cohesive social group (Feldman, Mandel, and Fields 1985).

Roman (1981) defined a "situational ecology" that either constrains or permits specific behaviors. An ecology of aggression might include the nature of the relationships among those in the setting and the type of environment (private home, tavern, open space, public event). Steadman (1982) suggests that we study "violence prone situations," defined as the interaction between specific types of people and situations.[27] Levinson (1983a), Roman (1981), and Steadman (1982) include in this ecology factors that exist at different levels and may interact to produce aggression: social setting at the small group or situational level and cultural processes at the societal or subcultural level. In this ecology, aggression during intoxication may convey several meanings or purposes: interpersonal or intergroup conflict, ritual or social adjunct, or expression of power and control. Understanding the dimensions of an ecology of behavior during intoxication may contribute to explanations of the social sources of aggression during drug or alcohol use.

2. *Deviance Disavowal.* Beliefs about the effects of specific substances have fostered the "excuse function" of substances and "relaxed standards of accountability" under the influence of substances (Collins 1988). Similar patterns are noted within subcultures regarding other substances—although within the United States, the meanings and norms of substance use differ widely across adolescent subcultures (Beschner and Friedman 1986). Heath (1978) suggests that there are special beliefs in nearly all cultures regarding alcohol, but the rules for drunken comportment are contradictory across cultures. It is likely, then, that the "excuse" function of intoxicants also has largely cultural determinants.

---

[27] Steadman found that violence in interpersonal disputes was greatest when the dispute was outside the home, late at night, when alcohol or drugs were used by either party involved, in the presence of third parties, where strangers were involved, and where one party was physically dominant over the other.

This notion of the disavowal of deviance essentially relocates blame for behavior from the individual to the substance. Reinarman and Critchlow-Leigh (1987) suggest that this not only serves to excuse misbehavior while intoxicated but it also reassures others that the behaviors themselves do not challenge the legitimacy of the violated norms. Thus wife beaters do not challenge the sanctity of marriage or the societal laws against assault. The use of rationalization or externalization of blame has been used to explain other forms of deviance and criminality. Sykes and Matza (1957) suggested that the denial of responsibility was one of several "techniques of neutralization" that individuals use to justify criminal behavior. Disavowal also permits behaviors that violate nonlegal social taboos, especially sexual behaviors or revelry (MacAndrew and Edgerton 1969; Reinarman and Critchlow-Leigh 1987).

The plausibility of the disavowal framework depends on the acceptance of these accounts of behavior by society. Such accounts help avoid the assignment of an identity to an individual consistent with their deviant behavior (e.g., Scott and Lyman 1968).[28] Collins (1983) suggests that there is a synergistic relation between cultural acceptance of such accounts and the relocation of blame to substances that are widely thought to "cause" or at least excuse such behaviors. When cultural evaluations accept the view that substances cause aggressive or illegal behavior, then these accounts are more often honored by society, and the use of such excuses also is greater. However, acceptance of "excuses" is mutable and is vulnerable to historical and cultural shifts in societal attitudes about substances (see Silver 1979, regarding marijuana; Reinarman 1979, regarding cocaine; Musto 1981, regarding opiates; and Reinarman 1988, regarding Mothers against Drunk Driving and the modern temperance movements).

3. *Interactions between Culture and Behavior.* Collins (1989) suggests that expectancy also has cultural roots—beliefs and expectations about the psychopharmacological effects of a substance that help shape the rules governing its use and the behavioral effects anticipated after ingestion. Understanding controlled drug use tells us much about the cultural and social factors that shape expectancy toward aggressive or nonaggressive behaviors. In turn, these may influence changes in cognitive, affective, or emotional states following intoxication.

---

[28] Legitimate accounts, for example, are those that rely on widely shared underlying assumptions, and that are understood by the situationally relevant group as applying to it.

Zinberg (1984) analyzed interviews with 153 controlled opiate users.[29] He identified four controlling rituals and social sanctions that promote controlled use within subcultures of drug users: (1) rules and boundaries that defined moderate and compulsive use; (2) norms that limited use to physical and social settings that were conducive to positive or "safe" drug experiences; (3) explicit recognition of potentially harmful or unpleasant drug effects; and (4) rituals that supported users' non-drug-related relationships and obligations (e.g., family, work, money). These rituals developed within social networks of drug users and were communicated primarily through peer group processes (Zinberg 1984). Others have noted similar, parallel group processes within independent networks of drug users (Reinarman 1979; Schwendinger and Schwendinger 1985; White, Pandina, and LaGrange 1987). The social learning basis for these peer group processes is evident in the description by Zinberg (1984, p. 18): "Without doubt the most important source of precepts and practices for control is the peer using group. Virtually all of our subjects had been assisted by other non-compulsive users in constructing appropriate rituals and sanctions out of the folklore of and practices circulating in their drug-using subculture. The peer group provided instruction in and reinforced proper use; and despite the popular image of peer pressure as a corrupting force pushing weak individuals toward drug misuse, our interviews showed that many segments of the drug subculture have taken a firm stand against drug abuse."

The cultural phenomenology of different substances apparently has varying interpretations not only in different cultures (Heath 1983) but also for specific social groups within cultures. Explanations of the effects of intoxication on aggression must account for the development, maintenance, and expression of such normative processes within social groups regarding the uses of substances and the permitted behaviors following their use.

Such cultural processes themselves are mutable. Hamid (1989) studied the evolution of illicit substance use and trafficking over a ten-year period in several New York City neighborhoods with high concen-

---

[29] Controlled use was defined as consistent drug use without experiencing the potential harms of each substance. Multiple and daily use were excluded as frequency categories. The initial frequency criterion for subject selection was one use per week or less for at least one year prior to interview. Subjects had first used an opiate at least two years ago and in the past two years had had as many days of abstention as use. Moreover, they were required to have not used any substance in an uncontrolled way, using the same criterion of abstention days.

trations of Caribbean immigrants. In these neighborhoods, substance users and dealers are primarily types of laboring populations with a specific social organization that is closely tied to the economic functions of their community and are responsive to their social and economic developmental processes. As neighborhoods change in their commercial and social makeup, so, too, do patterns of substance use and the social controls on aggression that define behaviors (following drug use) that are permitted.

As new drugs entered the study neighborhoods (from marijuana in the 1960s and 1970s, to opiates in the 1970s, and then to cocaine and crack in the 1980s), profound changes occurred in the intoxication-aggression patterns among the residents. Hamid's ethnographic research found that the forms of social organization and social rituals of drug use were established, then dismantled and reconstituted in novel ways when use of one substance was succeeded by use of another. As new networks of distribution developed, so, too, did new forms of social control. Specifically, marijuana dealers recycled funds in their areas, leaving intact the major forms of informal and formal social control. But cocaine and crack dealers removed money and goods from circulation, changing the social organization of drug use and weakening the formal and informal social controls. Accordingly, the intoxication-violence relation strengthened in this decade in the areas studied by Hamid (1989). He concludes that a political-economic analysis is necessary to understand the social controls on substance use and violence, apart from systemic violence associated with dealing. Not only do the cultural phenomenology of a substance and the immediate social network of the user influence expectancy but also the norms within these networks may develop and change in response to social and economic influences on the users' social milieux.

III. An Integrated Perspective on Aggression following Intoxication

The deficiencies of these separate perspectives result not from the individual weaknesses of each explanation but from dependence on any one framework as a unicausal theory to explain the variation in the intoxication-aggression relation. Each has some validity but offers only a partial explanation for the empirical knowledge on aggressive behavior following intoxication. No single framework can be expected to explain what obviously is an extremely complex relation between substance use and aggression. Nor can any framework explain the variation in why people use substances. It is more likely that the separate frameworks offer complementary explanations, and each perspective adds a unique contribution to the development of more complex models of the effects of substances on behavior.

A. An Integrated Model of Substance Use and Aggression

The evidence from several disciplines suggests that individual attributes, both psychological and physiological, combine with cognitive and emotional factors that are interpreted through social-psychological contexts and situational factors to explain the interaction between substance and individual, set, culture, and behavior. There is little explanatory power to the intoxication-aggression association when the partial correlations of culture and social interaction are removed. Moreover, these processes vary by type of substance. Social networks and their subcultural *milieux* determine the social construction of substance-use patterns and shape the cognitive and emotional processes that transform the effects of substances from physiological response to aggressive behavior.

Evidence from the studies of alcohol on both sexuality (Wilson and Lawson 1976; Reinarman and Critchlow-Leigh 1987) and interpersonal aggression (Steadman 1982; Collins 1983, 1988), as well as on drug use and interpersonal behaviors (Steadman 1982; Zinberg 1984; Feldman, Mandel, and Fields 1985), converges in one critical area: intoxication affects cognitive processes that shape and interpret perceptions of both one's own physiology (i.e., expectancy) and the associated behavioral response. The cognitive processes themselves are influenced by cultural and situational factors that determine the norms, beliefs, and sanctions regarding behaviors following intoxication.

In developing a general model of the influence of alcohol on aggression, Collins (1983) suggests two major independent variables that increase the probability of violence during social interactions following alcohol use: psychological proclivity toward the exercise of personal power in an overt manner and beliefs that alcohol causes aggression. Each of these factors in turn influences cognitive processes that interpret both the situation and the appropriate behavioral response. One effect of alcohol on cognitive processes is a reduction in behavioral repertoire, and the use of violence results either from personal proclivity or cultural beliefs, forces that further proscribe responses to social interactions during drinking situations.

The sources of aggression in this stochastic model operate mainly at the individual level. Propensity toward aggression reflects explanations regarding the use of personal power to resolve perceived conflicts. This concept resembles Megargee's (1983) concept of "habit strength" in his "algebra of aggression," but it also includes basic intrinsic motivations for violence. It also is similar to the "set" in Zinberg's (1984) theory of behavior as the result of interactions between set (personality), setting, and substance. Cultural beliefs are expressed through the individual who believes, as does the society, that intoxication (especially drunkenness) induces aggression. Culture, therefore, has both direct effects (through expectancy) and indirect effects through its influence on mediating cognitive processes. Moreover, cultural beliefs are likely to produce "accounts" that allow him or her to shift blame to alcohol and therefore perceive fewer social rules against aggressive behaviors.

The empirical evidence with respect to both drugs and alcohol suggests that individual behaviors vary by set and setting; that is, the same individual consuming the same substance will behave differently in different situations. For example, gang members use alcohol in two distinctly different contexts: to embolden members for aggression in one setting and to make the group socially cohesive in another (Moore 1978; Vigil 1988). Beliefs about behaviors that are permissible, and the effects of specific substances, accordingly are determined by processes that are social and vary by situation. Drug- or alcohol-use behaviors themselves vary by social setting and are shaped by the norms and rituals of the setting. These may include social norms that either promote or impede aggression. Also, cognition interacts with social cues to produce an interpretation of the setting where drinking or drug use takes place, while personality variables also affect the cues (and their interpretation) that trigger cognitive reactions. This suggests three processes that are needed to explain aggression following intoxication: first, the probability of exposure to a situation that is associated with aggression; second, the probability that an individual will react aggressively when exposed to the same contextual stimuli; and third, the probability that the factors favoring an aggressive response outweigh the restraints or sanctions against it.

In sum, rather than being a linear process, aggression following intoxication is more likely to be a reciprocal process in which expectancies and physiological factors, social norms, events in specific situations where substances are used, and cultural factors have multiple and recursive interactions leading to aggressive or nonaggressive behaviors when intoxicated. That is, situational variables and group processes

(conveyed through social learning processes) are likely to affect variations in the behaviors that follow intoxication; these relations then will
alter the individual's selection of contexts and his or her social construction or cognitive interpretation of these contexts and will affect the
probability of aggressive behaviors in subsequent encounters. The influence of larger political, economic, and social organizational influences on culture and social controls on drug use and aggression also
must be acknowledged.

Emerging from this perspective is an integrated model presented in
figure 2. The psychoactive properties of various substances, their availability, and individual physiological and psychological factors are exog-
enous factors that influence other social-psychological processes. An
example of an individual personality factor is the propensity to use
violence to resolve interpersonal conflicts or the habit strength of violence that has been socially reinforced through past experiences during
stages of social and personality development. Cultural factors include
beliefs about permitted behaviors for each substance and the meaning
of substances in various cultural processes and subcultural groups (ceremonies, spiritual or religious uses, social interaction). These factors in
part determine the settings where substances are used and influence
individual choices about when and where to use them. The settings and
social contexts also influence the choice of substance, convey the rules
and norms proscribing behaviors, the cognitive interpretation of the
situation, and, accordingly, the probability of aggression in that situation.

The interaction between personality and social context to produce
controlled or uncontrolled substance use and manage aggression is critical to this model. Individuals form perceptions of their environments
and internalize the expected responses to social situations through the
development of personality. Social-learning processes affect these internal perceptions and the capacity to activate internal controls. Experiences with intoxicants, both psychoactive and social experiences,
socialize users not only to the effects of the substance but also to the
expected social behaviors that accompany that state. Zinberg (1984)
suggests that people select explanatory constructs from a range of cognitive and emotional perceptions available to them, and their responses
would follow the available explanations of their situation. The boundaries of those responses are determined by three factors: perceptions of
the expected environment, personality variables such as relative ego
autonomy, and responses to the substance itself. These three processes

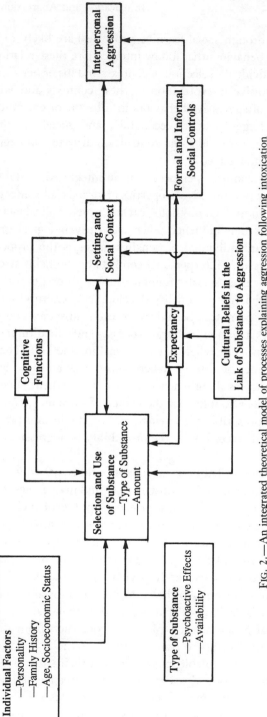

FIG. 2.—An integrated theoretical model of processes explaining aggression following intoxication

are influenced strongly by social-learning processes. Social-learning processes teach users about the expected behaviors in various social settings, determine perceptions of the psychoactive effects of the substance itself,[30] and also influence personality factors by raising apprehensions about danger or moral ambiguity. The delicate interplay of these factors responds to the social cues of the setting where substances are used and reciprocally may determine the selection of setting where people go to use substances. From these cues, aggression may follow logically from the controls that are internally activated and the social controls present in the setting.

However, unlike a linear model, these relations also have "backward" effects on the same social processes. For example, an individual who is apt to exhibit aggressive behaviors in bars is unlikely to select bars where aggression is negatively sanctioned. Or an individual may choose to use substances he or she can manage effectively to remain in a social context that has some utilitarian value or emotional attachment. At the social and cultural levels, weak social organization may permit or promote certain specific forms of intoxicated behaviors at the group or neighborhood level. Thus patterns of aggression following intoxication develop over time through socialization within specific social contexts and the shaping of behaviors through social-learning processes. Individuals may initially have diverse experiences with settings and substances but ultimately are likely to gravitate toward social contexts that offer a match between personal proclivities (base rates of aggression, beliefs in the legitimacy of violence, use of accounts based on cultural interpretations of intoxication) and the social rituals of that scene. However, such personal proclivities also may include a desire for acceptance in nonviolent social worlds, and, accordingly, selective processes of affiliation may ensue depending on the type of social gratification sought.

B. Implications for Research and Policy

This model is a first step in articulating reciprocal processes that operate at multiple levels to explain sociocultural-cultural processes underlying the intoxication-aggression relation. Similar models have been developed to explain the etiology of delinquent conduct, combining individual and socialization processes (Thornberry 1987). Such

---

[30] See Becker (1967) for a description of how social-learning processes were influential in determining responses to LSD.

models require extensive development to describe and define their constructs in a way that permits study in diverse settings. One task for future research is to learn the forms of these interactions and the processes by which factors at one level of influence are linked to processes at another level. Thus the origins of controlled use and the social processes that support that use are as critical to understand as are the methods by which groups enforce and communicate those norms. These questions will be answered through multimethod and multilevel analyses involving experiments in different social contexts with different substances, surveys in different cultures and social groups, aggregate data analysis of consumption and behavioral patterns, and ethnographic reports to unravel multilevel causal sequences and reciprocal effects.

APPENDIX

Psychoanalytic Theory of Addiction (From Pihl [1983], p. 307)

Addiction Is
  Substitute for sexual pleasure
  A fixation at the oral stage
  And/or the anal stage
  And/or the phallic stage
Irrespective of Stage, Addicted Individuals Show
  A polymorphous-perverse need for love
  Repressed but sometimes blatant homosexuality
  Mild neuroticism hiding anger and low self-esteem
  A counterphobic tendency
  Expression of unmet dependency needs
  Ambivalent feelings toward parents
  Self-destructive drives
  Hysteria
  Obsessive-compulsive neuroses
  Sexual disorder
  Suicide
  Psychoses

REFERENCES

Achte, K., S. Kalevi, L. Ginman, and N. Colliander. 1969. *Alcohol Psychoses in Finland.* Helsinki: Finnish Foundation for Alcohol Studies. Cited in D. Levinson. 1983. "Social Setting, Cultural Factors and Alcohol-related Aggression." In *Alcohol, Drug Abuse and Aggression*, edited by E. Gottheil, K. A. Druley, T. E. Skoloda, and H. M. Waxman. Springfield, Ill.: Thomas.

Ahlstrom, S. 1981. *Finnish Drinking Habits: A Review of Research and Trends in Acute Effects of Heavy Drinking*. Report no. 150 from the Social Research Institute of Alcohol Studies, Helsinki. Cited in *Alcohol, Drug Abuse and Aggression*, edited by E. Gottheil, K. A. Druley, T. E. Skoloda, and H. M. Waxman. Springfield, Ill.: Thomas.

Akers, R. L. 1984. "Delinquent Behavior, Drugs and Alcohol: What Is the Relationship?" *Today's Delinquent* 3:19–48.

Akers, R. L., M. D. Krohn, L. Lanza-Kaduce, and M. Radosevich. 1979. "Social Learning and Deviant Behavior: A Specific Test of a General Theory." *American Sociological Review* 44:636–55.

American Psychiatric Association. 1987. *Diagnostic and Statistical Manual*. Washington, D.C.: American Psychiatric Association.

Anglin, M. Douglas, and George Speckart. 1988. "Narcotics Use, Property Crime, and Dealing: Structural Dynamics across the Addiction Career." *Criminology* 26:197–233.

Asnis, S. F., and R. C. Smith. 1978. "Amphetamine Abuse and Violence." *Journal of Psychedelic Drugs* 10:317–77.

Austin, G. A., and D. J. Lettieri. 1976. "Drugs and Crime: The Relationship of Drug Use and Concomitant Criminal Behavior." In *Research Issues*, edited by G. A. Austin and D. J. Lettieri. National Institute on Drug Abuse. Washington, D.C.: U.S. Government Printing Office.

Ball, J. C., L. Rosen, J. A. Flueck, and D. N. Nurco. 1982. "Lifetime Criminality of Heroin Addicts in the United States." *Journal of Drug Issues* 12:225–39.

Bandura, A. 1973. *Aggression: A Social Learning Approach*. Englewood Cliffs, N.J.: Prentice-Hall.

Bard, M., and J. Zacker. 1974. "Assaultiveness and Alcohol Use in Family Disputes: Police Perspectives." *Criminology* 12:281–92.

Becker, Howard S. 1967. "History, Culture, and Subjective Experiences: An Exploration of the Social Bases of Drug Induced Psychoses." *Journal of Health and Social Behavior* 8:163–76.

Beeman, E. A. 1947. "The Effect of Male Hormone on Aggressive Behavior in Mice." *Physiological Zoology* 20:373–405.

Bell, C. S. 1972. "The Experimental Reproduction of Amphetamine Psychosis." *Archives of General Psychiatry* 29:35–40.

Bennett, R. M., A. H. Buss, and J. A. Carpenter. 1969. "Alcohol and Human Physical Aggression." *Quarterly Journal of Studies on Alcohol* 30:870–76.

Berkowitz, L. 1962. *Aggression: A Social Psychological Analysis*. New York: McGraw-Hill.

Beschner, G. M., and A. Friedman. 1986. *Teen Drug Use*. Lexington, Mass.: Heath.

Biernacki, P. 1986. *Pathways from Heroin Addiction: Recovery without Treatment*. Philadelphia: Temple University Press.

Blane, H. T., and L. E. Hewitt. 1977. "Alcohol and Youth: An Analysis of the Literature, 1960–75." Final report prepared for the National Institute on

Alcohol Abuse and Alcoholism, contract no. ADM 281-75-0026. Rockville, Md.: U.S. Public Health Service.

Blumer, H. 1971. "Social Problems and Collective Behavior." *Social Problems* 18:298–306.

Bolton, R. 1973. "Aggression and Hypoglycemia among the Quolla: A Study in Psychobiological Anthropology." *Ethnology* 12:227–57.

Bourgois, Phillipe. 1989. "In Search of Horatio Alger: Culture and Ideology in the Crack Economy." *Contemporary Drug Problems* (forthcoming).

Bowker, L. 1983. *Beating Wife-beating*. Lexington, Mass.: Heath.

———. 1986*a*. "The Meaning of Wife Beating." *Currents* 2:39–43.

———. 1986*b*. "Empowering Women: The Only Way to End Domestic Violence." Paper presented at the third national conference of the National Coalition against Domestic Violence, St. Louis, July.

Boyatzis, R. E. 1975. "The Predisposition toward Alcohol-related Interpersonal Aggression in Men." *Journal of Studies on Alcohol* 36:1196–1207.

———. 1977. "Alcohol and Interpersonal Aggression." In *Alcohol Intoxication and Withdrawal*, vol. 3B, edited by M. M. Gross. New York: Plenum.

———. 1983. "Who Should Drink What, When, and Where If Looking for a Fight." In *Alcohol, Drug Abuse and Aggression*, edited by E. Gottheil, K. A. Druley, T. E. Skoloda, and H. M. Waxman. Springfield, Ill.: Thomas.

Bradford, J. M. W. 1988. "Organic Treatment for the Male Sexual Offender." *Annals of the New York Academy of Sciences* 528:193–222.

Briddell, D. W., D. C. Rimm, G. R. Caddy, G. Dorawitz, D. Sholis, and R. J. Wunderlin. 1978. "Effects of Alcohol and Cognitive Set on Sexual Arousal to Deviant Stimuli." *Journal of Abnormal Psychology* 87:418–30.

Brissett, D. 1978. "Toward an Interactionist Understanding of Heavy Drinking." *Pacific Sociological Review* 21:3–20.

Burns, T. F. 1980. "Getting Rowdy with the Boys." *Journal of Drug Issues* 10:273–86.

Cahalan, D., and I. Cisin. 1976. "Drinking Behavior and Drinking Problems in the United States." In *The Biology of Alcoholism*, vol. 4, edited by B. Kissin and H. Begleiter. New York: Plenum.

Cahalan, D., and R. Room. 1974. *Problem Drinking among American Men*. New Brunswick, N.J.: Rutgers Center of Alcohol Studies.

Campbell, A. 1984. *The Girls in the Gang*. New Brunswick, N.J.: Rutgers University Press.

Castaneda, Carlos. 1967. *The Teachings of Don Juan*. New York: Simon & Schuster.

Chaiken, Jan M., and Marcia Chaiken. 1982. *Varieties of Criminal Behavior*. Santa Monica, Calif.: Rand.

———. In this volume. "Drugs and Predatory Crime."

Chaiken, Marcia. 1986. "Crime Rates and Substance Abuse among Offenders." Unpublished manuscript. New York: Narcotic and Drug Research, Inc.

Chin, Ko-Lin. 1986. "Chinese Triad Societies, Tongs, Organized Crime, and Street Gangs in Asia and the United States." Ph.D. dissertation, University of Pennsylvania, Department of Sociology.

Chitwood, D. D., and P. J. Morningstar. 1985. "Factors Which Differentiate Cocaine Users in Treatment and Non-treatment Users." *International Journal of the Addictions* 20:449–60.

Cicero, T. J. 1983. "Behavioral Significance of Drug-induced Alterations of Reproductive Endocrinology in the Male." In *Alcohol, Drug Abuse and Aggression*, edited by E. Gottheil, K. A. Druley, T. E. Skoloda, and H. M. Waxman. Springfield, Ill.: Thomas.

Clausen, J. A. 1968. "Drug Addiction: Social Aspects." In *International Encyclopedia of the Social Sciences*, vol 4., edited by D. L. Sills. New York: Macmillan.

Clayton, R. R. 1981. "The Delinquency and Drug Use Relationship among Adolescents." In *Drug Abuse and the American Adolescent*, edited by D. J. Lettieri and J. P. Ludford. Rockville, Md.: National Institute on Drug Abuse.

Clayton, R. R., and B. S. Tuchfield. 1982. "The Drug-Crime Debate: Obstacles to Understanding the Relationship." *Journal of Drug Issues* 12:153–66.

Coleman, D. H., and M. A. Straus. 1983. "Alcohol Abuse and Family Violence." In *Alcohol, Drug Abuse and Aggression*, edited by E. Gottheil, K. A. Druley, T. E. Skoloda, and H. M. Waxman. Springfield, Ill.: Thomas.

Collins, J. J., Jr. 1981. "Alcohol Use and Criminal Behavior: An Empirical, Theoretical and Methodological Overview." In *Drinking and Crime: Perspectives on the Relationship between Alcohol Consumption and Criminal Behavior*, edited by J. J. Collins, Jr. New York: Guilford.

———. 1982. "Drugs and Violence: The Relationship of Selective Psychoactive Substance Use to Assault and Robbery." Paper presented at the thirty-fourth annual meeting of the American Society of Criminology, Toronto, November.

———. 1983. "Alcohol Use and Expressive Interpersonal Violence: A Proposed Explanatory Model." In *Alcohol, Drug Abuse and Aggression*, edited by E. Gottheil, K. A. Druley, T. E. Skoloda, and H. M. Waxman. Springfield, Ill.: Thomas.

———. 1986. "The Relationship of Problem Drinking to Individual Offending Sequences." In *Criminal Careers and "Career Criminals,"* vol. 2, edited by A. Blumstein, J. Cohen, J. A. Roth, and C. A. Visher. Washington, D.C.: National Academy Press.

———. 1988. "Suggested Explanatory Frameworks to Clarify the Alcohol Use/Violence Relationship." *Contemporary Drug Problems* 15:107–21.

———. 1989. "Alcohol and Interpersonal Violence: Less than Meets the Eye." In *Pathways to Criminal Violence*, edited by N. A. Weiner and M. E. Wolfgang. Newbury Park, Calif.: Sage.

Collins, J. J., Jr., R. L. Hubbard, and J. V. Rachal. 1985. "Expensive Drug Use and Illegal Income: A Test of Explanatory Hypotheses." *Criminology* 23:743–64.

Cooper, Barry M. 1987. "Motor City Breakdown." *Village Voice* (December 1), pp. 23–35.

Critchlow-Leigh, B. 1986. "The Powers of John Barleycorn: Beliefs about the Effects of Alcohol on Social Behavior." *American Psychologist* 41:751–64. (Original publication as Critchlow, B.)

Curry, G. D., and I. A. Spergel. 1988. "Gang Homicide, Delinquency and Community." *Criminology* 26:381–407.

Dobash, R. E., and R. Dobash. 1979. *Violence against Wives: A Case against the Patriarchy*. New York: Free Press.

Dolan, E. F., and S. Finney. 1984. *Youth Gangs*. New York: Simon & Schuster.

Ellinwood, E. H. 1971. "Assault and Homicide Associated with Amphetamine Abuse." *American Journal of Psychiatry* 127:1170–75.

Elliott, D. S., and A. R. Ageton. 1976. "Subcultural Delinquency and Drug Use." In *Drug Use and Crime: Report of the Panel on Drug Use and Criminal Behavior*, Research Triangle Institute. Springfield, Va.: National Technical Information Service.

Elliott, D. S., and D. Huizinga. 1983. "Social Class and Delinquent Behavior in a National Youth Panel." *Criminology* 21:149–77.

———. 1984. "The Relationship between Delinquent Behavior and ADM Problems." National Youth Survey Report no. 26. Boulder, Colo.: Behavioral Research Institute.

Elliott, D. S., D. Huizinga, and S. Ageton. 1985. *Explaining Delinquency and Drug Abuse*. Beverly Hills, Calif.: Sage.

Epstein, E. J. 1977. *Agency of Fear: Opiates and Political Power in America*. New York: Putnam.

Erickson, P. G., E. M. Adlaf, G. F. Murray, and R. G. Smart. 1987. *The Steel Drug: Cocaine in Perspective*. Lexington, Mass.: Heath.

Eron, L. D., L. O. Walder, and M. M. Lefkowitz. 1971. *Learning of Aggression in Children*. Boston: Little, Brown.

Fagan, J. 1989. "The Social Organization of Drug Use and Drug Dealing among Urban Gangs." *Criminology* 27:633–69.

Fagan, J., K. V. Hansen, and D. K. Stewart. 1983. "Violent Men or Violent Husbands? Background Factors and Situational Correlates of Violence toward Intimates and Strangers." In *The Dark Side of Families: Current Family Violence Research*, edited by D. Finkelhor, R. J. Gelles, G. T. Hotaling, and M. A. Straus. Beverly Hills, Calif.: Sage.

Fagan, J., E. S. Piper, and M. Moore. 1986. "Violent Delinquents and Urban Youth." *Criminology* 23:439–66.

Fagan, J., J. G. Weis, and Y. T. Cheng. 1990. "Drug Use and Delinquency among Inner City Students." *Journal of Drug Issues* (forthcoming).

Fagan, J., J. G. Weis, Y. T. Cheng, and J. K. Watters. 1987. "Drug Use, Violent Delinquency and Social Bonding: Implications for Theory and Intervention." Final report. Grant no. 85-IJ-CX-0056, National Institute of Justice. Washington, D.C.: National Institute of Justice.

Fagan, J., and S. Wexler. 1985. "Complex Behaviors and Simple Measures: Understanding Violence and Aggression in Families." Paper presented at the thirty-seventh annual meeting of the American Society of Criminology, San Diego, Calif., November.

Feldman, H. W., M. Agar, and G. M. Beschner. 1979. *Angel Dust: An Ethnographic Study of PCP Users*. Lexington, Mass.: Lexington.

Feldman, H. W., J. Mandel, and A. Fields. 1985. "In the Neighborhood: A

Strategy for Delivering Early Intervention Services to Young Drug Users in Their Natural Environments." In *Treatment Services for Adolescent Substance Abusers*, edited by A. S. Friedman and G. M. Beschner. Rockville, Md.: National Institute on Drug Abuse.

Gandossy, R. P., J. Williams, J. Cohen, and H. Hardwood. 1980. *Drugs and Crime: A Survey and Analysis of the Literature*. Washington, D.C.: National Institute of Justice.

Gellert, V. F., and S. B. Sparber. 1979. "Effects of Morphine Withdrawal on Food Competition Hierarchies and Fighting Behavior in Rats." *Psychopharmacology* 60:165–72.

Gelles, R. J., and M. A. Straus. 1979. "Determinants of Violence in the Family: Toward a Theoretical Integration." In *Contemporary Theories about the Family*, edited by W. Burr, R. Hill, F. I. Nye, and I. L. Reiss. New York: Free Press.

———. 1988. *Intimate Violence*. New York: Touchstone.

Giordano, P. C., S. Cernkovich, and M. D. Pugh. 1985. "Friendships and Delinquency." *American Journal of Sociology* 91:1170–1202.

Gold, M., and O. C. Moles. 1978. "Delinquency and Violence in Schools and the Community." In *Violent Crime*, edited by J. A. Inciardi and A. E. Pottieger. Beverly Hills, Calif.: Sage.

Goldstein, P. J. 1985. "The Drugs-Violence Nexus: A Tri-partite Conceptual Framework." *Journal of Drug Issues* 15:493–506.

———. 1989. "Drugs and Violent Crime." In *Pathways to Criminal Violence*, edited by N. A. Weiner and M. E. Wolfgang. Newbury Park, Calif.: Sage.

Goldstein, P. J., P. A. Belluci, B. J. Spunt, and T. Miller. 1988. "Frequency of Cocaine Use and Violence: A Comparison between Men and Women." Unpublished manuscript. New York: Narcotic and Drug Research, Inc.

Goldstein, P. J., H. H. Brownstein, P. J. Ryan, and P. A. Belluci. 1989. "Crack and Homicide in New York City, 1988: A Conceptually-based Event Analysis." *Contemporary Drug Problems* (forthcoming).

Goldstein, P. J., D. S. Lipton, B. J. Spunt, P. A. Belluci, T. Miller, N. Cortez, M. Khan, and A. Kale. 1987. "Drug Related Involvement in Violent Episodes." Final report. Grants DA-03182 and DA-04017, National Institute on Drug Abuse. New York: Narcotic and Drug Research, Inc.

Gordon, A. J. 1978. "Hispanic Drinking after Migration: The Case of Dominicans." *Medical Anthropology* 2:61–84.

———. 1982. "The Cultural Context of Drinking and Indigenous Therapy for Alcohol Problems in Three Migrant Hispanic Cultures." *Journal of Studies on Alcohol* 42:217–40.

Gottheil, E., K. A. Druley, T. E. Skoloda, and H. M. Waxman. 1983. "Aggression and Addiction: Summary and Overview." In *Alcohol, Drug Abuse and Aggression*, edited by E. Gottheil, K. A. Druley, T. E. Skoloda, and H. M. Waxman. Springfield, Ill.: Thomas.

Gottlieb, D. 1957. "The Neighborhood Tavern and the Cocktail Lounge: A Study in Class Differences." *American Journal of Sociology* 62:550–62.

Greenberg, S. W. 1977. "The Relationship between Crime and Amphetamine

Abuse: An Empirical Review of the Literature." *Contemporary Drug Problems* 5:101–30.

Greenwood, P. W. (with A. Abrahamse). 1982. *Selective Incapacitation*. Santa Monica, Calif.: Rand.

Haberman, H. E., and M. M. Baden. 1974. "Alcoholism and Violent Death." *Quarterly Journal of Studies on Alcohol* 35:221–31.

Hagedorn, J. 1988. *People and Folk: Gangs, Crime and the Underclass in a Rustbelt City*. Chicago: Lake View Press.

Hamid, A. 1989. "The Political Economy of Crack-related Violence." *Contemporary Drug Problems* (forthcoming).

Hamilton, C. J., and J. J. Collins, Jr. 1981. "The Role of Alcohol in Wife Beating and Child Abuse: A Review of the Literature." In *Drinking and Crime: Perspectives on the Relationship between Alcohol Consumption and Criminal Behavior*, edited by J. J. Collins, Jr. New York: Guilford.

Hartstone, E. C., and K. V. Hansen. 1984. "The Violent Juvenile Offender: An Empirical Portrait." In *Violent Juvenile Offenders: An Anthology*, edited by R. A. Mathias, P. DeMuro, and R. A. Allinson. San Francisco, Calif.: National Council on Crime and Delinquency.

Harwood, H. J., D. Napolitano, P. Kristiansen, and J. J. Collins, Jr. 1985. "Length of Stay in Treatment for Alcohol Abuse and Alcoholism: National Estimates for Short-term Hospitals, 1983." Technical report no. RTI-2979-01DR. Research Triangle Park, N.C.: Research Triangle Institute.

Heath, D. B. 1964. "Prohibition and Post-repeal Drinking Patterns among the Navajo." *Quarterly Journal of Studies on Alcohol* 25:119–35.

———. 1978. "The Sociocultural Model of Alcohol Use: Problems and Prospects." *Journal of Operational Psychiatry* 9:55–66.

———. 1983. "Alcohol and Aggression: A 'Missing Link' in Worldwide Perspective." In *Alcohol, Drug Abuse and Aggression*, edited by E. Gottheil, K. A. Druley, T. E. Skoloda, and H. M. Waxman. Springfield, Ill.: Thomas.

Helmer, J. 1975. *Drugs and Minority Oppression*. New York: Seabury.

Hill, T. W. 1974. "From Hell-Raiser to Family Man." In *Conformity and Conflict: Readings in Cultural Anthropology*, edited by J. Spradley and D. McCurdy. Boston: Little, Brown.

Holcomb, W. R., and N. A. Adams. 1985. "Personality Mechanisms of Alcohol-related Violence." *Journal of Clinical Psychology* 41:714–22.

Hotaling, G. T., and D. B. Sugarman. 1986. "An Analysis of Risk Markers in Husband to Wife Violence: The Current State of Knowledge." *Violence and Victims* 1:101–24.

Huba, G. J., and P. M. Bentler. 1984. "Causal Models of Personality, Peer Culture Characteristics, Drug Use, and Criminal Behaviors over a Five-Year Span." In *Longitudinal Research in Alcoholism*, edited by D. W. Goodwin, K. van Dusen, and S. Mednick. Boston: Kluwer-Nijhof.

Hunt, D. E. In this volume. "Drugs and Consensual Crime."

Inciardi, J. A. 1981. "Introduction." In *The Drugs-Crime Connection*, edited by J. A. Inciardi. Beverly Hills, Calif.: Sage.

Jessor, R., and S. L. Jessor. 1973. "Problem Drinking in Youth: Personality,

Social and Behavioral Antecedents and Correlates." Publication no. 144.
Boulder: University of Colorado, Institute of Behavioral Sciences.

———. 1977. *Problem Behavior and Psychosocial Development: A Longitudinal Study of Youth.* New York: Academic Press.

Johnson, B. D., P. J. Goldstein, E. Preble, J. Schmeidler, D. Lipton, B. Spunt, and T. Miller. 1985. *Taking Care of Business: The Economics of Crime by Heroin Abusers.* Lexington, Mass.: Heath.

Johnson, B. D., J. Schmeidler, E. Wish, and D. Huizinga. 1986a. "Drug- and Alcohol-preceded Delinquencies: Substance Abuse near the Time of the Crime." Unpublished manuscript. New York: Narcotic and Drug Research, Inc.

———. 1986b. "The Concentration of Delinquent Offending: The Contribution of Serious Drug Involvement to High Delinquency Rates." Unpublished manuscript. New York: Narcotic and Drug Research, Inc.

Johnston, L. D., P. M. O'Malley, and J. G. Bachman. 1985. "Use of Licit and Illicit Drugs by America's High School Students: 1975–84." Rockville, Md.: National Institute on Drug Abuse.

Johnston, L. D., P. M. O'Malley, and L. K. Eveland. 1978. "Drugs and Delinquency: A Search for Causal Connections." In *Longitudinal Research on Drug Use*, edited by Denise Kandel. New York: Wiley.

Kandel, Denise. 1980. "Drug and Drinking Behavior among Youth." In *Annual Review of Sociology*, vol. 6, edited by A. Inkeles, N. J. Smelser, and R. H. Turner. Palo Alto, Calif.: Annual Reviews.

———. 1985. "On Processes of Peer Influences in Adolescent Drug Use: A Developmental Perspective." *Advances in Alcohol and Substance Use* 4:139–63.

———. 1986. "Processes of Peer Influences in Adolescence." In *Development as Action in Context: Problem Behavior and Normal Youth Development*, edited by R. K. Silberstein, K. Eyferth, and G. Rudinger. Berlin: Springer-Verlag.

Kandel, D., R. Kessler, and R. Margulies. 1978. "Adolescent Initiation into Stages of Drug Use: A Sequential Analysis." In *Longitudinal Research on Drug Use: Empirical Findings and Methodological Issues*, edited by Denise Kandel. New York: Wiley.

Kandel, D., R. Simcha-Fagan, and M. Davies. 1986. "Risk Factors for Delinquency and Illicit Drug Use from Adolescence to Young Adulthood." *Journal of Drug Issues* 16:67–90.

Kantor, G. K., and M. A. Straus. 1987. "The 'Drunken Bum' Theory of Wife Beating." *Social Problems* 34:213–31.

Kaplan, H. B., S. S. Martin, and R. J. Johnson. 1986. "Self-Rejection and the Explanation of Deviance: Specification of the Structure among Latent Constructs." *American Journal of Sociology* 92:384–411.

Kaplan, H. B., S. S. Smith, and C. Robins. 1986. "Pathways to Adolescent Drug Use: Self-Derogation, Peer Influences, Weakening of Social Controls, and Early Substance Use." *Journal of Health and Social Behavior* 25:270–89.

Klein, M. W. 1985. "Gang Involvement in Cocaine Rock Trafficking." Grant application from the University of Southern California, Social Science Research Institute, Los Angeles, to the National Institute of Justice.

Klein, M. W., and C. Maxson. 1989. "Street Gang Violence." In *Violent Crime, Violent Criminals*, edited by N. A. Weiner and M. E. Wolfgang. Newbury Park, Calif.: Sage.

Klein, M. W., C. Maxson, and L. Cunningham. 1988. "Gang Involvement in Cocaine Rock Trafficking." Final report. Grant 85-IJ-CX0057, to the National Institute of Justice. Washington, D.C.: U.S. Department of Justice.

Kohlberg, L. 1973. "Continuities in Childhood and Adult Moral Development Revisited." In *Life-Span Developmental Psychology—Personality and Socialization*, edited by Paul B. Baltes and K. W. Schaie. New York: Academic Press.

Kramer, M. S. 1983. "Pharmacotherapy for Violent Behavior." In *Alcohol, Drug Abuse and Aggression*, edited by E. Gottheil, K. A. Druley, T. E. Skoloda, and H. M. Waxman. Springfield, Ill.: Thomas.

Kubie, L. S. 1963. "The Central Affective Potential and Its Trigger Mechanisms." In *Counterpoint—Libidinal Object and Subject*, edited by H. S. Gaskill. New York: International Universities Press.

Ladouceur, P., and M. Temple. 1985. "Substance Abuse among Rapists." *Crime and Delinquency* 31:269–94.

Langevin, R., J. Bain, G. Wortzman, S. Hucker, R. Dickey, and P. Wright. 1988. "Sexual Sadism: Brain, Blood and Behavior." *Annals of the New York Academy of Sciences* 528:163–71.

Lemert, E. M. 1962. "Alcohol, Values and Social Control." In *Society, Culture and Drinking Patterns*, edited by J. Pittman and C. Snyder. New York: Wiley.

Levinson, D. 1983a. "Social Setting, Cultural Factors, and Alcohol-related Aggression." In *Alcohol, Drug Abuse and Aggression*, edited by E. Gottheil, K. A. Druley, T. E. Skoloda, and H. M. Waxman. Springfield, Ill.: Thomas.

———. 1983b. "Alcohol Use and Aggression in American Subcultures." In *Alcohol and Disinhibition: Nature and Meaning of the Link*, edited by R. Room and G. Collins. Research Monograph no. 12. National Institute on Alcohol Abuse and Alcoholism. Washington, D.C.: U.S. Department of Health and Human Services, U.S. Public Health Service.

Levinson, D., and M. J. Malone. 1980. *Toward Explaining Human Culture*. New Haven: HRAF Press.

Lion, J. R., C. L. Azarte, and H. H. Koepke. 1975. "Paradoxical Rage Reactions and Induced Hostility." *Diseases of the Nervous System* 36:537–58.

MacAndrew, C., and R. Edgerton. 1969. *Drunken Comportment: A Social Explanation*. Chicago: Aldine.

Maccoby, E. E., and C. N. Jacklin. 1974. *The Psychology of Sex Differences*. Palo Alto, Calif.: Stanford University Press.

McBride, Duane C. 1981. "Drugs and Violence." In *The Drug-Crime Connection*, edited by J. A. Inciardi. Beverly Hills, Calif.: Sage.

McClelland, D. C. 1975. *Power: The Inner Experience*. New York: Irvington.

McClelland, D. C., and W. N. Davis. 1972. "The Influence of Unrestrained Power Concerns on Drinking in Working Class Men." In *The Drinking Man*, edited by D. C. McClelland, W. N. Davis, R. Kalin, and E. Wanner. New York: Free Press.

McClelland, D. C., W. N. Davis, R. Kalin, and E. Wanner, eds. 1972. *The Drinking Man*. New York: Free Press.

McCord, Joan. 1983. "Alcohol in the Service of Aggression." In *Alcohol, Drug Abuse and Aggression*, edited by E. Gottheil, K. A. Druley, T. E. Skoloda, and H. M. Waxman. Springfield, Ill.: Thomas.

————. 1988. "Parental Aggressiveness and Physical Punishment in Long-Term Perspective." In *Family Abuse and Its Consequences: New Directions in Research*, edited by G. T. Hotaling, D. Finkelhor, J. T. Kirkpatrick, and M. A. Straus. Newbury Park, Calif.: Sage.

McGaghy, C. H. 1968. "Drinking and Deviance Disavowal: The Case of Child Molesters." *Social Problems* 16:43–49.

McGlothlin, W. H., M. D. Anglin, and B. D. Wilson. 1978. "Narcotic Addiction and Crime." *Criminology* 16:293–315.

Maletsky, B. M. 1976. "The Diagnosis of Pathological Intoxication." *Journal of Studies on Alcohol* 37:1215–28.

Marshall, M. 1983. "Four Hundred Rabbits: An Anthropological View of Ethanol as a Disinhibitor." In *Alcohol and Disinhibition: Nature and Meaning of the Link*, edited by R. Room and G. Collins. Research Monograph no. 12. National Institute on Alcohol Abuse and Alcoholism. Washington, D.C.: U.S. Department of Health and Human Services, U.S. Public Health Service.

Maxson, C. L., M. A. Gordon, and M. W. Klein. 1985. "Differences between Gang and Non-gang Homicides." *Criminology* 23(2):209–22.

Mayer, J., and R. Black. 1981. "The Relationship between Alcoholism, and Child Abuse and Neglect." In *Currents in Alcoholism*, vol. 2, edited by F. A. Sexias. New York: Grune & Stratton.

Mayfield, D. 1983. "Substance Abuse and Aggression: A Psychopharmacological Perspective." In *Alcohol, Drug Abuse and Aggression*, edited by E. Gottheil, K. A. Druley, T. E. Skoloda, and H. M. Waxman. Springfield, Ill.: Thomas.

Megargee, E. I. 1983. "Psychological Determinants and Correlates of Criminal Violence." In *Criminal Violence*, edited by M. E. Wolfgang and N. A. Weiner. Beverly Hills, Calif.: Sage.

Mendelson, J. H., R. E. Meyer, J. Ellingboe, S. Mirin, and M. McDougle. 1975. "Effects of Heroin and Methadone in Plasma Cortisol and Testosterone." *Journal of Pharmacological Experimental Therapy* 195:296–302.

Merton, R. K. 1957. *Social Theory and Social Structure*. New York: Free Press.

Miczek, K. A., and M. L. Thompson. 1983. "Drugs of Abuse and Aggression: An Ethnopharmacological Analysis." In *Alcohol, Drug Abuse and Aggression*, edited by E. Gottheil, K. A. Druley, T. E. Skoloda, and H. M. Waxman. Springfield, Ill.: Thomas.

Mieczkowski, T. 1986. "Geeking Up and Throwing Down: Heroin Street Life in Detroit." *Criminology* 24:645–66.

Miller, R. E., J. M. Levine, and I. A. Mirsky. 1973. "Effects of Psychoactive Drugs on Nonverbal Communication and Group Social Behavior of Monkeys." *Journal of Personality and Social Psychology* 28:396–405.

Monahan, J. 1981. *Predicting Violent Behavior*. Beverly Hills, Calif.: Sage.

Moore, J. W. 1978. *Homeboys*. Philadelphia: Temple University Press.

Morales, E. 1989. *Cocaine: White Gold Rush in Peru*. Tucson: University of Arizona Press.

Morgan, P. 1983. "Alcohol, Disinhibition and Domination: A Conceptual Analysis." In *Alcohol and Disinhibition: Nature and Meaning of the Link*, edited by R. Room and G. Collins. Research Monograph no. 12. National Institute on Alcohol Abuse and Alcoholism. Washington, D.C.: U.S. Department of Health and Human Services, U.S. Public Health Service.

Moyer, K. E. 1968. "Kinds of Aggression and Their Physiological Basis." *Communications in Behavioral Biology* 2:65–87.

———. 1976. *The Psychobiology of Aggression*. New York: Harper & Row.

———. 1983. "A Psychobiological Model of Aggressive Behavior: Substance Abuse Implications." In *Alcohol, Drug Abuse and Aggression*, edited by E. Gottheil, K. A. Druley, T. E. Skoloda, and H. M. Waxman. Springfield, Ill.: Thomas.

Musto, D. 1973. *An American Disease: Origins of Narcotic Control*. New Haven, Conn.: Yale University Press.

———. 1981. "Review of Narcotic Control Efforts in the United States." In *Substance Abuse: Clinical Problems and Perspectives*, edited by J. H. Lowinson and P. Ruiz. Baltimore: Williams & Wilkins.

Myerscough, R. 1980. "The Effect of Delta-9-Tetrahydrocannabinol on Human Physical Aggression." Masters thesis, Kent State University, Department of Psychology.

Newcomb, M. D., and Paul M. Bentler. 1988. *Consequences of Adolescent Drug Use*. Newbury Park, Calif.: Sage.

Nurco, D. N., J. W. Schaffer, J. C. Ball, and T. W. Kinlock. 1984. "Trends in in the Commission of Crime among Narcotic Addicts over Successive Periods of Addiction." *Journal of Drug and Alcohol Abuse* 10:481–89.

Pagano, R. 1981. "The Effects of Diazepam on Human Physical Aggression." Ph.D. dissertation, Kent State University, Department of Psychology.

Pernanen, K. 1976. "Alcohol and Crimes of Violence." In *The Biology of Alcoholism: Social Aspects of Alcoholism*, vol. 4, edited by B. Kissin and H. Begleiter. New York: Plenum.

———. 1981. "Theoretical Aspects of the Relationship between Alcohol Use and Crime." In *Drinking and Crime: Perspectives on the Relationship between Alcohol Consumption and Criminal Behavior*, edited by J. J. Collins, Jr. New York: Guilford.

Petersilia, Joan. 1980. "Career Criminal Research: A Review of Recent Evidence." In *Crime and Justice: An Annual Review of Research*, vol. 2, edited by Norval Morris and Michael Tonry. Chicago: University of Chicago Press.

Pihl, R. O. 1983. "Alcohol and Aggression." In *Alcohol, Drug Abuse and Aggression*, edited by E. Gottheil, K. A. Druley, T. E. Skoloda, and H. M. Waxman. Springfield, Ill.: Thomas.

Pihl, R. O. and P. Spiers. 1978. "Individual Characteristics in the Etiology of Drug Abuse." In *Progress in Experimental Personality Research*, vol. 8, edited by B. Maher. New York: Academic Press.

Pleck, E. 1987. *Domestic Tyranny: The Making of American Social Policy against Family Violence from Colonial Times to the Present.* New York: Oxford University Press.

Powers, E., and H. Witmer. 1951. *An Experiment in the Prevention of Delinquency: The Cambridge-Somerville Youth Study.* New York: Columbia University Press.

Prentky, R. A., R. A. Knight, and R. Rosenberg. 1988. "Validation Analyses on a Taxonomic System for Rapists: Disconfirmation and Reconceptualization." *Annals of the New York Academy of Sciences* 528:21–40.

Rada, R. T. 1975. "Alcoholism and Forcible Rape." *American Journal of Psychiatry* 132:444–56.

Rechtenwald, William, and Nathaniel Sheppard, Jr. 1984. Newspaper series on Youth Gangs in Chicago. *Chicago Tribune* (July 29–30).

Reinarman, C. 1979. "Moral Entrepreneurs and Political Economy: Historical and Ethnographic Notes on the Construction of the Cocaine Menace." *Contemporary Crises* 3:225–54.

———. 1988. "The Social Construction of an Alcohol Problem: 'Mothers Against Drunk Drivers,' Restrictive Alcohol Laws, and Social Control in the 1980s." *Theory and Society* 17:91–120.

Reinarman, C., and B. C. Critchlow-Leigh. 1987. "Culture, Cognition and Disinhibition: Notes on Sexuality and Alcohol in the Age of AIDS." *Contemporary Drug Problems* 14:435–60.

Robbins, R. H. 1979. "Alcohol and the Identity Struggle: Some Effects of Economic Changes on Interpersonal Relations." In *Beliefs, Behaviors and Alcoholic Beverages: A Cross-cultural Survey*, edited by M. Marshall. Ann Arbor: University of Michigan.

Robins, L. N. 1979. "Addict Careers." In *Handbook on Drug Abuse*, edited by R. L. DuPont, A. Goldstein, and J. O'Donnell. Washington, D.C.: U.S. Government Printing Office.

———. 1984. "The Natural History of Adolescent Drug Use." *American Journal of Public Health* 74:656–75.

Robinson, B. W., M. Alexander, and G. Bowne. 1969. "Dominance Reversal Resulting from Aggressive Responses Evoked by Brain Telestimulation." *Journal of Neurophysiology* 26:705–20.

Roizen, R. 1983. "Loosening Up: General Population Views of the Effects of Alcohol." In *Alcohol and Disinhibition: Nature and Meaning of the Link*, edited by R. Room and G. Collins. Research Monograph no. 12. National Institute on Alcohol Abuse and Alcoholism. Washington, D.C.: U.S. Department of Health and Human Services, U.S. Public Health Service.

Roman, P. A. 1981. "Situational Factors in the Relationship between Alcohol and Crime." In *Drinking and Crime: Perspectives on the Relationship between Alcohol Consumption and Criminal Behavior*, edited by J. J. Collins, Jr. New York: Guilford.

Room, R. 1970. "Drinking in the Rural South: Some Comparisons in a National Sample." Paper presented at the Symposium on Law and Drinking Behavior at the Center for Alcohol Studies, University of North Carolina, Chapel Hill.

————. 1983. "Alcohol and Crime." In *Encyclopedia of Crime and Justice*, vol. 1, edited by S. H. Kalish. New York: Macmillan.

Room, R., and G. Collins. 1983. "Introduction." In *Alcohol and Disinhibition: The Nature and Meaning of the Link*, edited by R. Room and G. Collins. Research Monograph no. 12. National Institute on Alcohol Abuse and Alcoholism. Washington, D.C.: U.S. Department of Health and Human Services, U.S. Public Health Service.

Russell, J. A., and A. Mherabian. 1974. "The Mediating Role of Emotions in Alcohol Use." *Journal of Studies on Alcohol* 36:1509–36.

Sano, K. 1962. "Sedative Neurosurgery: With Special Reference to Postremedial Hypothalamotomy." *Neurologia Medico-Chirurgica* 4:112–42.

Schaefer, J. M. 1973. "A Hologeistic Study of Family Structure and Sentiment, Supernatural Beliefs, and Drunkenness." Ph.D. dissertation, State University of New York at Buffalo, Department of Anthropology.

Schmutte, G. T., K. E. Leonard, and S. P. Taylor. 1979. "Alcohol and Expectations of Attack." *Psychological Reports* 45:163–67.

Schuckitt, M. A. 1988. "Weight Lifters Folly: The Abuse of Anabolic Steroids." *Drug Abuse and Alcoholism Newsletter* 17:8.

Schwab, R. S., W. H. Sweet, V. H. Mark, R. N. Kjellberg, and F. R. Ervin. 1965. "Treatment of Intractable Temporal Lobe Epilepsy by Stereotactic Amygdala Lesions." *Transactions of the American Neurological Association* 90:12–19.

Schwendinger, H., and J. Schwendinger. 1985. *Adolescent Subcultures and Delinquency*. New York: Praeger.

Scott, M. B., and S. M. Lyman. 1968. "Accounts." *American Sociological Review* 33:46–62.

Sears, J. 1977. "The Effects of Social Pressure on the Aggressive Behavior of Intoxicated and Non-intoxicated Subjects." Masters thesis, Kent State University, Department of Psychology.

Shields, N., C. R. Hanneke, and G. J. McCall. 1989. "Patterns of Family and Non-family Violence: Violent Husbands and Violent Men." *Violence and Victims* 3:83–98.

Shuntich, R., and S. P. Taylor. 1972. "The Effects of Alcohol on Human Physical Aggression." *Journal of Experimental Research in Personality* 6:34–38.

Siegel, R. K. 1980. "Long Term Effects of Recreational Cocaine Use: A Four Year Study." In *Cocaine 1980*, edited by F. R. Jeri. Lima, Peru: Pacific Press.

————. 1982a. "History of Cocaine Smoking." *Journal of Psychoactive Drugs* 14:277–99.

————. 1982b. "Cocaine Free Base Abuse: A New Smoking Disorder." *Journal of Psychoactive Drugs* 14:321–37.

Silver, G. 1979. *The Dope Chronicles: 1850–1950*. San Francisco, Calif.: Harper & Row.

Simonds, J. F., and J. Kashani. 1979. "Phencyclidine (PCP) Use in Males Committed to Training School." *Adolescence* 14:721–25.

————. 1980. "Specific Drug Use and Violence among Delinquent Boys." *American Journal of Drug and Alcohol Abuse* 7:305–22.

Speckart, George, and M. Douglas Anglin. 1986. "Narcotics and Crime: A Causal Modeling Approach." *Journal of Quantitative Criminology* 2:3–28.

Speiker, G. 1983. "What Is the Linkage between Alcohol Abuse and Violence?" In *Alcohol, Drug Abuse and Aggression*, edited by E. Gottheil, K. A. Druley, T. E. Skoloda, and H. M. Waxman. Springfield, Ill.: Thomas.

Spergel, I. A. 1984. "Violent Gangs in Chicago: In Search of Social Policy." *Social Service Review* 58:199–226.

———. 1990. "Youth Gangs: Continuity and Change." In *Crime and Justice: A Review of Research*, vol. 12, edited by Michael Tonry and Norval Morris. Chicago: University of Chicago Press.

Spotts, J. V., and F. C. Shontz. 1980. *Cocaine Users: A Representative Case Approach*. New York: Free Press.

Star, B. 1980. "Patterns in Family Violence." *Social Casework* 61:339–46.

Steadman, H. J. 1982. "A Situational Approach to Violence." *International Journal of Law and Psychiatry* 5:171–86.

Steele, B. F., and C. A. Pollack. 1968. "A Psychiatric Study of Parents Who Abuse Infants and Small Children." In *The Battered Child*, edited by R. Helfer and H. Kempe. Chicago: University of Chicago Press.

Steele, C., and L. Southwick. 1985. "Alcohol and Social Behavior I: The Psychology of Drunken Excess." *Journal of Personality and Social Psychology* 48:16–34.

Stinson, F. S., and G. D. Williams. 1986. "Trends in Alcohol-related Morbidity among Short-Stay Community Hospital Discharges, United States, 1977–84." National Institute on Alcohol Abuse and Alcoholism, Surveillance Report no. 4. Rockville, Md.: U.S. Public Health Service.

Straus, M. A. 1974. "Leveling, Civility, and Violence in the Family." *Journal of Marriage and the Family* 36:13–19.

———. 1978. "Wife Beating: How Common and Why?" *Victimology* 2:576–84.

Straus, M. A., and R. Gelles. 1986. "Societal Change and Change in Family Violence from 1975 to 1985 as Revealed by Two National Surveys." *Journal of Marriage and the Family* 48:465–79.

Straus, M. A., R. Gelles, and S. S. Steinmetz. 1980. *Behind Closed Doors: Violence in the American Family*. New York: Doubleday.

Stumphauzer, J. S., E. V. Veloz, and T. W. Aiken. 1981. "Violence by Street Gangs: East Side Story?" In *Violent Behavior: Social Learning Approaches to Prediction, Management, and Treatment*, edited by R. B. Stuart. New York: Brunner-Mazel.

Sykes, G. M., and D. Matza. 1957. "Techniques of Neutralization: A Theory of Delinquency." *American Sociological Review* 22:667–70.

Tanay, E. 1969. "Psychiatric Study of Homicide." *American Journal of Psychiatry* 125:1252–58.

Taylor, S. P. 1983. "Alcohol and Human Physical Aggression." In *Alcohol, Drug Abuse and Aggression*, edited by E. Gottheil, K. A. Druley, T. E. Skoloda, and H. M. Waxman. Springfield, Ill.: Thomas.

Taylor, S. P., and C. B. Gammon. 1975. "Effects of Type and Dose of Alcohol on Human Physical Aggression." *Journal of Personality and Social Psychology* 32:169–75.

———. 1976. "Aggressive Behavior of Intoxicated Subjects." *Journal of Studies on Alcohol* 37:917–30.

Taylor, S. P., C. B. Gammon, and D. R. Capasso. 1976. "Aggression as a Function of Alcohol and Threat." *Journal of Personality and Social Psychology* 34:261–67.

Taylor, S. P., G. T. Schmutte, K. E. Leonard, and J. W. Cranston. 1979. "The Effects of Alcohol and Extreme Provocation on the Use of a Highly Noxious Shock." *Motivation and Emotion* 3:73–81.

Taylor, S. P., R. M. Vardaris, A. B. Rawich, C. B. Gammon, J. W. Cranston, and A. I. Lubetkin. 1976. "The Effects of Alcohol and Delta-9-Tetrahydrocannabinol on Human Physical Aggression." *Aggressive Behavior* 2:153–61.

Thornberry, Terence P. 1987. "Toward an Interactional Theory of Delinquency." *Criminology* 25:863–92.

Tinklenberg, J. R. 1973. "Drugs and Crime." In *Drug Use in America: Problem in Perspective*. Appendix, vol. 1, *Patterns and Consequences of Drug Use*. National Commission on Marihuana and Drug Abuse. Washington, D.C.: U.S. Government Printing Office.

Tinklenberg, J. R., P. Murphy, P. L. Murphy, and A. Pfefferbaum. 1981. "Drugs and Criminal Assaults by Adolescents: A Replication Study." *Journal of Psychoactive Drugs* 13:277–87.

Vigil, J. D. 1985. "The Gang Subculture and Locura: Variations in Acts and Actors." Paper presented at the thirty-seventh annual meeting of the American Society of Criminology, San Diego, Calif., November.

———. 1988. *Barrio Gangs*. Austin: University of Texas Press.

Vogel, W. H. 1983. "Aggression-Stress-Alcoholism." In *Alcohol, Drug Abuse and Aggression*, edited by E. Gottheil, K. A. Druley, T. E. Skoloda, and H. M. Waxman. Springfield, Ill.: Thomas.

Waldorf, O. D. 1973. *Careers in Dope*. Englewood Cliffs, N.J.: Prentice-Hall.

———. 1983. "Natural Recovery from Opiate Addiction: Some Social Psychological Processes of Untreated Recovery." *Journal of Drug Issues* 13:237–80.

Waldorf, O. D., C. Reinarman, and S. Murphy. 1990. *Cocaine Charges*. Philadelphia: Temple University Press.

Walker, L. E. 1984. *The Battered Woman Syndrome*. New York: Springer.

Washton, A. M., and M. Gold. 1987. "Recent Trends in Cocaine Abuse as Seen from the 800-COCAINE Hotline." In *Cocaine: A Clinician's Handbook*, edited by A. M. Washton and M. S. Gold. New York: Guilford.

Washton, A. M., M. Gold, and A. C. Pottash. 1984. "Upper Income Cocaine Abusers." *Advances in Alcohol and Substance Abuse* 4:51–57.

Watters, J. K., C. Reinarman, and J. Fagan. 1985. "Causality, Context, and Contingency: Relationships between Drug Abuse and Delinquency." *Contemporary Drug Problems* 12:351–73.

Wechsler, H. 1979. "Patterns of Alcohol Consumption among the Young: High School, College and General Population Studies." In *Youth, Alcohol and Social Policy*, edited by H. T. Blane and M. E. Chafetz. New York: Plenum.

Wechsler, H., H. Demone, D. Thum, and E. Kasey. 1980. "Religious-Ethnic Differences in Alcohol Consumption." *Journal of Health and Social Behavior* 11:21–29.

Weiner, N. A., and M. E. Wolfgang. 1985. "The Extent and Character of Violent Crime in America, 1969 to 1982." In *American Violence and Public Policy*, edited by L. A. Curtis. New Haven, Conn.: Yale University Press.

White, H. R., V. Johnson, and C. Garrison. 1985. "The Drug-Crime Nexus among Adolescents and Their Peers." *Deviant Behavior* 6:183–204.

White, H. R., R. J. Pandina, and E. LaBouvie. 1985. "The Drug-Crime Nexus: A Longitudinal Analysis." Paper presented at the thirty-seventh annual meeting of the American Society of Criminology, San Diego, Calif., November.

White, H. R., R. J. Pandina, and R. L. LaGrange. 1987. "Longitudinal Predictors of Serious Substance Abuse and Delinquency." *Criminology* 25(3):715–40.

Widom, C. S. 1989. "The Intergenerational Transmission of Violence." In *Pathways to Criminal Violence*, edited by N. A. Weiner and M. E. Wolfgang. Newbury Park, Calif.: Sage.

Wikler, A. 1952. "Mechanisms of Action of Drugs that Modify Personality Function." *American Journal of Psychiatry* 108:590–99.

Wilson, G., and D. Abrams. 1977. "Effects of Alcohol on Social Anxiety: Cognitive versus Pharmacological Processes." *Cognitive Therapy and Research* 1:195–210.

Wilson, G., and D. Lawson. 1976. "Expectancies, Alcohol and Sexual Arousal in Male Social Drinkers." *Journal of Abnormal Psychology* 85:587–94.

Winick, C. 1983. "Drinking and Disinhibition in Popular Culture." In *Alcohol and Disinhibition: The Nature and Meaning of the Link*, edited by R. Room and G. Collins. Research Monograph no. 12. National Institute on Alcohol Abuse and Alcoholism. Washington, D.C.: U.S. Department of Health and Human Services, U.S. Public Health Service.

Wish, Eric D. 1987. "Drug Use among Arrestees in Manhattan." Unpublished manuscript. New York: Narcotic and Drug Research, Inc.

Wish, Eric D., and B. D. Johnson. 1986. "The Impact of Substance Abuse on Criminal Careers." In *Criminal Careers and "Career Criminals,"* vol. 2, edited by A. Blumstein, J. Cohen, J. A. Roth, and C. A. Visher. Washington, D.C.: National Academy Press.

Wolfgang, M. E. 1958. *Patterns in Criminal Homicide*. New York: Wiley.

———. 1981. "Foreword." In *Drinking and Crime: Perspectives on the Relationship between Alcohol Consumption and Criminal Behavior*, edited by J. J. Collins, Jr. New York: Guilford.

Wolfgang, M. E., and F. Ferracuti. 1967. *The Subculture of Violence: Toward an Integrated Theory in Criminology*. London: Tavistock.

Wolfgang, M. E., and R. Strohm. 1956. "The Relationship between Alcohol and Criminal Homicide." *Quarterly Journal of Studies on Alcohol* 17:411–25.

Woods, S. C., and J. G. Mansfield. 1983. "Ethanol and Disinhibition: Physiological and Behavioral Links." In *Alcohol and Disinhibition: The Nature and*

Meaning of the Link, edited by R. Room and G. Collins. Research Monograph no. 12. National Institute on Alcohol Abuse and Alcoholism. Washington, D.C.: U.S. Department of Health and Human Services, U.S. Public Health Service.

Woody, G. E., A. Persky, A. T. McLellan, C. P. O'Brian, and I. Arndt. 1983. "Psychoendocrine Correlates of Hostility and Anxiety in Addicts." In *Alcohol, Drug Abuse and Aggression*, edited by E. Gottheil, K. A. Druley, T. E. Skoloda, and H. M. Waxman. Springfield, Ill.: Thomas.

World Health Organization. 1979. *Health Statistics: Annual Report.* Geneva: World Health Organization.

Wurmser, L., and C. Lebling. 1983. "Substance Abuse and Aggression: A Psychoanalytic View." In *Alcohol, Drug Abuse and Aggression*, edited by E. Gottheil, K. A. Druley, T. E. Skoloda, and H. M. Waxman. Springfield, Ill.: Thomas.

Ylikahri, R. H., M. O. Huttunen, M. Harkonen, T. Leino, T. Helenius, K. Liewendahl, and S. Karonen. 1978. "Acute Effects of Alcohol on Anterior Pituitary Secretion of the Tropic Hormones." *Journal of Clinical Endocrinology and Metabolism* 46:715–20.

Zeichner, A., and R. O. Pihl. 1979. "The Interaction of Consequences and Alcohol in the Production of Human Physical Aggression." *Journal of Abnormal Psychology* 88:153–60.

———. 1980. "The Effects of Alcohol and Perceived Intent on Human Physical Aggression." *Journal of Studies on Alcohol* 41:265–76.

Zinberg, N. E. 1984. *Drug, Set, and Setting: The Social Bases of Controlled Drug Use.* New Haven, Conn.: Yale University Press.

Zinberg, N. E., and R. C. Jacobson. 1976. "The Natural History of Chipping." *American Journal of Psychiatry* 133:37–40.

Eric D. Wish and Bernard A. Gropper

Drug Testing by the Criminal Justice System: Methods, Research, and Applications

ABSTRACT

The purposes of drug testing by the criminal justice system are to screen for persons who have recently ingested a drug, to identify chronic drug users, to monitor and deter drug use, and to estimate national and local drug-use trends in criminals. Substantial work has been done on the reliability and methodology of drug-testing technologies. Most criminal justice system tests involve urinalysis. Experimental research is under way on radioimmunoassay of hair samples. Much discussion of criminal justice system drug testing focuses on pretrial drug testing, the national Drug Use Forecasting program, and the testing of juvenile detainees. Adult offenders typically began their drug use in their early teens, and drug testing of juvenile detainees may provide the most effective place for early detection and prevention of drug abuse in a high-risk population. Drug testing of persons detained or monitored by the criminal justice system raises a number of critical legal and ethical issues that differ from those raised by testing other populations.

There is a widely shared belief that national policies aimed at reducing the supply of drugs have not worked and that interdiction efforts are unlikely to prevent enough importation to influence the price of drugs on the street (e.g., Reuter 1988; Reuter, Crawford, and Cave 1988). The profits from drug dealing are enormous, and someone always seems ready to take the place of a dealer or supplier who has been forced out of business by law-enforcement actions (Nadelmann 1988).

Eric D. Wish is visiting fellow at the National Institute of Justice and research scientist at Narcotic and Drug Research, Inc. Bernard Gropper is manager of the Research Program on Drugs, Alcohol, and Crime for the National Institute of Justice. We would like to thank James K. Stewart for his strong support and Christy Visher and Joyce O'Neil who provided valuable editorial and substantive assistance.

There have been repeated calls for new policies that focus on reducing demand for drugs. A "demand-based" policy rests on the assumption that, if enough persons can be deterred from using drugs, profits will decrease and the motivation to supply drugs and to commit drug-related crimes will be diminished. One manifestation of this policy is an attitude of "zero tolerance" for persons who use illicit drugs.

To reduce demand for drugs, people must be deterred or dissuaded from initiating drug use, and persons who already use illicit drugs must be induced to cease. Drug-abuse education, prevention, and treatment programs and some law-enforcement actions are interventions intended to accomplish these goals. In the past fifteen years, with the development of cost-effective technology for measuring chemical markers of drug use in the body, a new strategy of identification through drug testing has become available for reducing demand for drugs. Knowledge that one may be tested for drugs may deter persons from initiating use, and the testing itself can identify current users for referral to treatment, to periodic urine monitoring, or to other interventions. Drug testing has been embraced more by government agencies, private corporations, the military, and drug treatment programs than by criminal justice agencies.

This essay reviews the most widely used and promising tests for identifying persons who have used drugs. The focus is on criminal justice system identification of drug-using detainees or convicted criminals. Drug testing of offenders raises legal and practical issues that are distinct from those raised when testing other populations. Throughout this essay, accordingly, we distinguish drug testing by the criminal justice system from testing by employers.

Drug-testing programs have been used with arrestees, probationers, parolees, incarcerated persons, and juvenile detainees. The White House national drug policy of 1989 asserts that "drug tests should be a part of every stage of the criminal justice process—at the time of arrest and throughout the period of probation or incarceration—because they are the most effective way of keeping offenders off drugs both in and out of detention" (White House 1989, p. 26). The applicable purposes and procedures often differ according to which population is being tested. A growing body of case law indicates that privacy and due-process rights may differ according to the stage in the criminal justice system in which a person is tested. We discuss testing programs for each of these groups and review available evidence for the usefulness of these programs.

The legal and ethical issues surrounding pretrial testing of arrestees are especially complex. The constitutionality of the nation's only fully operational pretrial testing program, in Washington, D.C., has been challenged and is under judicial review (*Berry v. District of Columbia*, 833 F.2d 1031, 1034–36 [D.C. Cir. 1987]). Much of the debate concerns whether drug-test information can legitimately be taken into account by the judge in making decisions regarding a person's pretrial release. A major question is the extent to which drug-test results at arrest are associated with a defendant's likelihood of failure to appear in court or of rearrest for another offense before trial. Because of the growing importance of pretrial testing programs and the ensuing debates, we review the evidence available regarding these questions.

We focus primarily on urine tests and the analysis of hair. Urine tests are the most commonly used method for identifying drug users, and considerable information exists regarding their accuracy, strengths, and limitations. Radioimmunoassay of hair is a promising experimental technique for detecting drug use by extracting and testing for drugs deposited in body hair (Baumgartner et al. 1979; Gropper 1987a, 1988b). Radioimmunoassay of hair is less intrusive than urinalysis, and it may enable the measurement of drug-use patterns over a longer period than is possible with urine tests. Furthermore, the risk of deception and contamination of samples may be less than with urine. To provide a comparative framework, we briefly refer to other types of tests based on measuring brain waves, speech, saliva, or blood.

We focus primarily on the common illicit drugs such as heroin, marijuana, cocaine, methamphetamine, and phencyclidine (PCP). We exclude tests for alcohol because alcohol is a licit drug that does not present as many difficulties in identification as do the illicit drugs. While alcohol use is related to the commission of violent crimes against persons (Collins 1986), unlike heroin and cocaine its use alone has not been found to be associated with elevated crime rates. With the exception of driving offenses, the criminal justice system rarely tests for alcohol use. We also exclude from consideration the expensive and technically difficult tests being developed to detect use of controlled-substance analogues, or "designer drugs" (e.g., ecstasy, china white) (Hall 1988).[1] These synthetic drugs are taken in extremely small doses that make them difficult to detect with standard laboratory tests.

---

[1] Controlled-substance analogues are synthetic drugs, often produced in clandestine laboratories. They are chemically similar to other psychoactive drugs but are often far more potent and sometimes have severe life-threatening side effects. These drugs are taken in such small doses that extremely sensitive tests are required to detect their metabolites in urine.

During 1987, the National Institute of Justice established the national Drug Use Forecasting (DUF) program, designed to monitor drug-use trends in arrestees. Anonymous voluntary urine specimens are obtained each quarter from a new sample of arrestees in the booking facilities of the largest cities in the country. Response rates are high. About 95 percent of those arrestees approached so far agreed to be interviewed. Of these, more than 80 percent provided a specimen. The DUF results have provided the first objective measure of the level of recent drug use in arrestees and have inspired city administrators to establish pretrial urine-testing programs and other programs for drug abusers. In view of the potential of the DUF program to provide a measure of drug trends in offenders, we review its methodology, strengths, and limitations.

This essay is organized into five sections. In Section I, we examine the purposes for which drug testing is used in the criminal justice system and contrast these with testing in other contexts. Section II describes and compares the testing procedures available. Section III describes criminal justice system testing programs that have been established across the country. Legal and ethical concerns are discussed in Section IV. The concluding section discusses future possibilities for drug testing and research.

I. Purposes of Drug Testing

Drug testing is used in the criminal justice system for at least four purposes: to detect persons who have recently ingested an illicit substance, to identify chronic drug users, to monitor and deter drug use among persons under the authority of criminal justice system officials, and to estimate national and local drug-use trends among criminal justice system populations.

A. *To Screen for Recent Drug Use*

The most common reason for using drug tests is to determine whether a person has used a drug in the recent past. But why is a test necessary? Why not just ask persons about their drug use? For many years social science researchers have used drug tests to assess the validity of self-report information about recent drug use (O'Malley, McGlothlin, and Ginzburg 1977). If the test results agree with what the respondent has reported, one is more confident in the accuracy of the person's interview responses. The evidence is substantial that persons will accurately report about their illicit drug use during confidential ᴵᴵ ᴵᴵ ᴵᴵᴵᴵ ᴵᴵ ᴵᴵᴵᴵᴵ ᴵᴵᴵᴵ ᴵᴵᴵ ᴵᴵᴵ ᴵᴵᴵᴵᴵ ᴵᴵ ᴵᴵᴵᴵᴵ ᴵᴵ ᴵᴵᴵ ᴵᴵ ᴵᴵᴵᴵᴵᴵᴵᴵᴵ ᴵᴵᴵᴵ ᴵᴵᴵᴵ ᴵᴵᴵ ᴵᴵ ᴵᴵᴵᴵ ᴵᴵ

sures will not produce adverse consequences (Bonito, Nurco, and Shaffer 1976; Harrell 1985).

However, the validity of self-reported drug-use information deteriorates when people are questioned within the potentially threatening criminal justice system. Thus, arrestees in Washington, D.C., and New York City have been found to underreport their recent drug use by about one-half even in confidential research interviews conducted soon after arrest (Toborg and Bellassai 1986; Dembo 1988; Wish, Toborg, and Bellassai 1988; Dembo et al. 1989). One study of intensive supervision probationers in New York City found that seventeen times more persons tested positive for cocaine than reported cocaine use in the research interview (Wish, Cuadrado, and Martorana 1986).

Each of these studies was conducted by researchers who were independent of the criminal justice system; these researchers recorded the identity of each respondent but guaranteed the confidentiality of the interview information from subpoena and use in any court proceeding. However, even when the interview information was obtained anonymously, arrestees underreported recent drug use. In those cities where arrestees are anonymously interviewed as part of the DUF program, many fewer admit to using drugs just prior to arrest than test positive by urinalysis.[2]

Certain qualifications to these findings need to be noted. While detainees are reticent to admit to recent drug use, they may be more likely to admit to lifetime use or use in the more distant past. Furthermore, the underreporting may be related to the perceived legal consequences. Juveniles are more likely to admit to recent marijuana use (perhaps perceived as less serious) than to cocaine use (Dembo 1988; Dembo et al. 1989), and adult arrestees are very likely to report alcohol use (Wish, Brady, and Cuadrado 1986) and more likely to admit to use of heroin or marijuana (National Institute of Justice 1989). While many arrestees conceal recent drug use, there is some evidence that, when they report drug abuse or dependence, the information is likely to be valid (Wish 1988b). Furthermore, self-reports are probably the most effective means to diagnose drug dependence.

---

[2] Analyses of DUF results from twenty-one cities indicate that the percentage of arrestees who tested positive and who reported using the drug twenty-four to forty-eight hours prior to arrest varies from 11 percent to about 60 percent (National Institute of Justice 1988). The amount of disclosure also varies by drug, with more persons admitting to recent marijuana or heroin use than to the use of cocaine.

If we cannot rely on persons to tell us about their drug use, can we use criminal justice records? The criminal justice system does maintain extensive files of information about offenders. However, much of the information contained in criminal justice records comes from self-reports from the offender and is therefore prone to the same kinds of reporting errors noted above. Furthermore, even when an arrest report has a place to enter information about the person's drug use, it typically is not completed. This is probably because the police officer is often unaware of the arrestee's drug use and because information not immediately relevant to the case is unlikely to be systematically recorded. In Washington, D.C., where the U.S. attorney's office has installed an automated case management information system, the arresting officers recorded as drug users only 22 percent of the persons who tested positive by urinalysis (Wish et al. 1981). Presentence investigation reports should contain more information about an offender's background. However, in the absence of urine tests, the investigator must rely solely on the defendant's admission of drug use or on information supplied by a family member or friend. In large cities, time and resources are insufficient to allow for soliciting and verifying such information.

If personal information in criminal justice records is an unreliable source of information about a person's drug use, can his record of arrests or convictions for sale or possession of a drug serve as an accurate indicator? The evidence conclusively indicates that it is not an accurate measure of drug use prevalence (Wish and Johnson 1986; Wish, Toborg, and Bellassai 1988). Only 10 percent of the 17,000 male and female arrestees who tested positive for recent drug use by urinalysis in Washington, D.C., in 1973 and 1974 were charged with a drug offense (Wish et al. 1981). Furthermore, DUF statistics from arrestees in twenty-one cities show that, while arrestees charged with a drug offense are most likely to test positive for drug use, persons charged with a variety of other offenses are only slightly less likely to test positive (National Institute of Justice 1989). In most DUF samples less than 25 percent of the arrestees are charged with a drug offense, while more than 50 percent of each sample test positive for drug use. By relying solely on a charge or conviction for a drug offense to identify the drug user, one would grossly underestimate the user population.

We conclude that the more readily available sources of information about a detainee, self-reports and criminal justice records, detect fewer drug users than do urine tests. Other advantages of urine tests for

screening criminal justice populations for drug use include their low
cost (especially when done in high volume), their accuracy, and their
ease of use. Perhaps their greatest limitation is the inability of a single
test to measure level of drug use or dependence.

B. To Identify Chronic Users

A primary justification for identifying chronic drug users is the well-
documented finding that, among offenders, persons who use illicit
drugs (especially cocaine or heroin) frequently and over long periods
tend to commit crimes at higher rates than do other offenders (Chaiken
and Chaiken, in this volume). There is evidence that many offenders
reduce their crime rates when drug use is reduced voluntarily or during
treatment (McGlothlin, Anglin, and Wilson 1977; Ball et al. 1981;
Leukefeld and Tims 1988; Anglin and Hser, in this volume). The
criminal justice system could therefore use drug-testing information in
conjunction with other information to distinguish chronic drug users
who are likely to be active criminals from less active criminals. Persons
classified as high risk could receive special conditions of release or
supervision designed to monitor or reduce their involvement with
drugs, while low-risk persons could receive less supervision (Wish,
Toborg, and Bellassai 1988).

This goal of identifying chronic drug users through testing faces
some practical problems. No single drug test can measure levels of drug
involvement. In testing a large number of persons, the group of individuals who test positive will consist of a heterogeneous collection of experimental users, occasional users, chronic users, and persons who may
not be users at all but have been erroneously labeled as such ("false
positives").

An exception may be persons who test positive for multiple drugs.
Male arrestees who tested positive for two or more drugs, usually
heroin and cocaine, in Washington, D.C., and New York City had a
greater number of subsequent arrests (Toborg and Bellassai 1986;
Wish, Brady, and Cuadrado 1986; Yezer et al. 1988a; Smith, Wish,
and Jarjoura 1989; Toborg et al. 1989) than those who tested positive
for use of a single drug. This is consistent with ethnographic research
showing that urban street criminals tend to use a variety of available
illicit drugs (Gandossy et al. 1980; Johnson et al. 1985; Inciardi 1986).

An infrequent drug user, however, may also test positive for multiple drugs, given the heavy adulteration and mixing of substances that

occurs in the uncontrolled illicit drug market. Consequently, reliance on a single test result (even if it identifies the presence of two or more drugs), without differentiating each person's level of drug use, is an insufficient basis for identification of chronic drug users.

The research literature with regard to drug abuse and crime has focused primarily on male offenders. While some epidemiological evidence shows that female arrestees in large cities are even more likely to test positive for heroin and cocaine than are male arrestees (National Institute on Drug Abuse 1979; Wish and Johnson 1986; Wish, O'Neil, and Baldau 1988), no data are available regarding the association of drug test results with the level of female criminality. Many female arrestees are charged with sex offenses; prostitutes are likely to use illicit drugs (Goldstein 1979; Wish, Brady, Cuadrado, and Alvarado 1985; Inciardi 1986) and to be repeatedly arrested. However, we do not know whether female chronic drug users commit other nondrug crimes at elevated rates. The rationales for testing female offenders rest primarily on reducing their demand for drugs and addressing the health problems resulting from their serious drug-abuse problems and their potential for transmitting the HIV virus (the virus that causes AIDS) to their babies, their sexual partners, or their needle-using companions (Wish, O'Neil, and Baldau 1988).

While a single drug test does not measure level of drug involvement, it can identify persons for further testing or assessment. If a person repeatedly tests positive, he or she is more likely to be a compulsive, uncontrolled user. Special care must be taken, however, to ensure that successive tests are spaced in time so that they do not repeatedly detect the same occasion of use. In one case, for example, a judge ruled that a person who tested positive for PCP sixteen times during pretrial release could not be considered to be in violation of his release conditions prohibiting drug use because expert witnesses could not agree on how long it took for PCP to be eliminated from the body. All of the positive tests could therefore have resulted from use before arrest, as the defendant claimed (*United States v. Phillip Roy*, Criminal no. M 12098–84, D.C. Superior Court, Order, June 26, 1985).[3]

A number of other methods exist for assessing the level of drug involvement of persons who test positive. Persons can be referred to a

---

[3] Other illicit drugs that may be found weeks after use are metabolites of marijuana. This occurs because some drugs are stored in fat tissue and released at a later time.

counselor of drug-treatment program for a diagnosis of dependence. At the end of the Vietnam War, a program of urine testing of all soldiers before return to the United States was established because of the huge problem with opiate addiction (Robins 1974; Robins et al. 1980). This public health approach to drug abuse in soldiers in Vietnam—detection by urinalysis, diagnosis, and treatment—worked so well that the initiator of the program speculated that a similar strategy might be effective for dealing with the heroin epidemic back in the United States during the 1970s (Jaffe 1973). Persons who tested positive were detained for detoxification before they were allowed to leave Vietnam. In some instances, probation officers have successfully confronted probationers with positive test results in order to encourage them to discuss their drug problems (Joseph 1970; Wish, Cuadrado, and Martorana 1986).

C. To Monitor and Deter Drug Use

A random or fixed schedule of repeated drug tests can diagnose the level of drug use. Testing can also be used to verify compliance with conditions of release and to deter use. Drug-abuse treatment programs have been relying on drug tests for some years to monitor compliance with treatment. In New York City, urinalysis testing is a requirement in programs that dispense methadone to clients (Magura et al. 1987).

Urine monitoring is sometimes ordered for suspected drug users by their parole or probation officers. The California Civil Addict Program was a civil commitment program in which incarcerated persons received treatment followed by community supervision, including urine testing. If a person relapsed to drug use, a period of reincarceration typically followed. Evaluations found that treatment with urine supervision reduced drug use and crime while persons remained in the program (McGlothlin, Anglin, and Wilson 1977; Anglin 1988).

The District of Columbia Pretrial Services Agency operates a program to monitor drug use of persons during pretrial release. Defendants who are identified at the bail-setting stage as drug users, either by urinalysis or self-reports, and who are to be released without payment of money bail to await trial, are often ordered to enter treatment or the agency's program of periodic urine testing before trial (Carver 1986; Wish, Toborg, and Bellassai 1988). If a defendant violates the pretrial release condition by continuing to use drugs, the Pretrial Services Agency reports this to the court, which may hold the defendant in contempt of court or impose sanctions for the violation. Some Treatment Alternatives to Street Crimes programs also use urine monitoring to track the drug use of persons referred to treatment from the criminal justice system (Bureau of Justice Assistance 1988a, 1988b). Treatment Alternatives to Street Crimes programs are locally funded organizations that attempt to link criminal justice agencies with drug-abuse treatment facilities.

Monitoring programs may also deter persons not being tested from using drugs. This is a primary rationale for random testing in the workplace. The largest employer in this country to use drug testing to deter drug use is the military. In the late 1970s, drug testing, prevention, health promotion, and treatment efforts were adopted by the armed forces to deal with a growing drug-abuse problem (Cohen 1986). Urine or breath testing could be requested at the direction of a commander or a physician under specified conditions. Testing was conducted either for cause or as a random screening device for entire units. All specimens are collected under direct observation to eliminate specimen substitution or adulteration (Willette 1986); any positive urine test is interpreted as evidence of abuse and constitutes evidence of unfitness for duty. One effort at rehabilitation was customarily provided to persons who tested positive.

The U.S. Navy has had the most intensive and successful testing program (Willette 1986). Almost two million specimens are tested each year. The testing is primarily random with an average rate of three tests per person per year. Because it is truly random, some persons are tested many times a year while others are not tested at all. Because an individual cannot predict how many times he will be tested, the program may be a considerable deterrent to drug use; it is rare for a person to be retained in the service following a second positive test. In 1981, 48 percent of the navy enlisted personnel under age twenty-five were estimated to be users, but all screening test results after that year showed fewer than 5 percent to test positive.

Data from four anonymous worldwide military surveys suggest that the testing program was an effective component of a strategy that reduced drug use by military personnel (Bray et al. 1988). Current drug users declined from 27 percent in 1980 to 19 percent in 1982, to 8.9 percent in 1985, and to 4.8 percent in 1988 (Bray et al. 1988). Lost productivity (measured by self-reports of lowered work performance, skipped work, intoxication at work) dropped from 14.4 percent in 1980 to 2.1 percent in 1988. Furthermore, 76 percent of the respondents in 1988 said that the urine-testing program reduced drug use in the military, and 23 percent reported that it had kept them from using drugs. Cohen (1986) claims that, although it is possible that the testing was not the major reason for successful control of drugs in the military, it is very likely that it was an important factor in the program's overall success.

Drug users in the military were at the lower pay grades and unlikely to have graduated from high school. Furthermore, persons with serious criminal records were routinely denied admission to the military, and military personnel probably differed in other ways from the typical criminal offender. For these reasons, it is not known whether the deterrent effect of drug testing with military personnel would necessarily apply to offenders.

However, in 1977, in a speech to the Federal Bar Association, Robert L. DuPont, then director of the National Institute on Drug Abuse, proposed the establishment of a new program, Operation Trip-Wire, that would use urine testing to deter drug use in probationers and parolees. He proposed that

> when placed on probation or parole—all offenders should be promptly screened for heroin use, using histories, physical examinations, and urinalysis. I propose that those probationers and parolees who have a demonstrated history of addiction [i.e., daily heroin use] be required to submit to periodic [e.g., monthly or twice monthly] urine testing. A routine, random urine testing program should also be used for all probationers and parolees; the average frequency of testing should be once or twice a year. Such random testing of the entire probation and parole population will serve both as a deterrent and as a case-finding technique. But the main thrust of Operation Trip-Wire is not the random testing; it is the systematic testing and followup of those who are known to be or have been heroin addicts. [DuPont 1977]

Operation Trip-Wire met with considerable criticism and resistance and was a factor in DuPont's being replaced as director of the National Institute on Drug Abuse. The nation was not ready in 1977 to consider wide-scale drug testing of convicted offenders. While it is conceivable that a program of random drug testing could deter convicted persons from drug use, no research is available regarding this topic.

D. To Track National and Local Drug-Use Trends

One might expect that, as an illicit drug becomes available in a community, those more deviant persons who are committing crimes might be the first to use it. The urine-test results for heroin from arrestees in the District of Columbia showed evidence of the growing heroin epidemic in Washington in the 1970s one to one-and-a-half years before other indicators such as new treatment admissions, overdose deaths, and emergency room admissions showed the increase (Forst and Wish 1983). Years later, in the early 1980s, the growing use of cocaine in Washington was clearly evident in arrestee test results (Wish and O'Neil 1990).

Drug-use trends in the United States are monitored primarily through periodic surveys of persons in households and of seniors in high school.[4] The National Household Survey is conducted every two to three years and is designed to estimate drug use in the American household population aged twelve and over. In 1988 the survey was based on 8,814 completed interviews. While the household population is estimated to include more than 98 percent of the U.S. population, it excludes persons living in group quarters or institutions such as military installations, dormitories, hotels, hospitals, and jails and transient populations such as the homeless (National Institute on Drug Abuse 1989). The annual High School Senior Survey, sponsored by the National Institute on Drug Abuse, consists of self-administered questionnaires obtained from about 16,000 students enrolled in 125–35 public and private high schools throughout the coterminous United States. The survey does not include in the target population youths who have dropped out of high school before graduation, estimated to be between 15 and 20 percent of each cohort (Johnston, O'Malley, and Bachman 1988).

Because these surveys omit both school dropouts and persons in jails and prisons, it is likely that they underestimate drug use in the total population. Extensive research has shown that persons who drop out of school are more likely than nondropouts to be using drugs (Robins and Wish 1977; Nurco 1979; Gandossy et al. 1980). Furthermore, drug

---

[4] The National Institute on Drug Abuse also sponsors the Drug Abuse Warning Network (DAWN), which collects reports of drug overdose deaths from medical examiners and of visits to hospital emergency rooms for drug-related incidents (National Institute on Drug Abuse 1988a). Both of these events represent extreme reactions to drugs and may not be sensitive indicators of changes in drug use in a community. The DAWN sample of twenty-six cities is being modified to be representative of the entire United States (National Institute on Drug Abuse 1988b).

TABLE 1

Estimates of Drug Use in the Past Month in the National Household
and Senior High School Populations in 1988

Used in Past Month	National Household Survey 1988 (Percent)	Senior High School Survey 1988 (Percent)
Marijuana	5.9	18.0
Cocaine	1.5	3.4
Heroin	. . .*	. . .*

SOURCES.—National Institute on Drug Abuse (1989); University of Michigan (1989).
* Less than 1 percent.

addicts tend to have unstable lifestyles and are likely to be homeless, in
jail, or otherwise inaccessible to a household survey (Johnson et al.
1985).

Another reason why these surveys may underestimate drug use is
their reliance on self-reports to measure drug use. Self-reports of drug
use have been repeatedly shown to be valid when obtained by researchers in a confidential, nonthreatening context. However, it is probable
that the reduced tolerance to drug use that developed in American
society during the 1980s has made respondents less willing to report
their drug use in social surveys (Kleiman 1986). In each year between
1979 and 1986, significant percentages of respondents to the Senior
High School Survey indicated that they would not have reported use of
marijuana, amphetamines, or heroin in the questionnaire if they had
ever used these drugs (e.g., 21.7 percent of black students in 1986 said
they would not have reported heroin use, and 17.2 percent, marijuana
use) (Bachman, Johnston, and O'Malley 1986, p. 206). Table 1 presents
estimates of drug use in the past month reported by respondents from
the household and senior high school surveys in 1988.

The limits of the currently available indicators of drug-use trends
and the possibility of developing a urinalysis-based measure of drug-
use trends among arrestees led the National Institute of Justice, in
cooperation with the Bureau of Justice Assistance, to establish in 1987
the DUF program. Drug Use Forecasting provides periodic urine testing of samples of arrestees in selected cities. Operational in twenty-one
of the nation's largest cities, DUF has expanded to twenty-five cities in
1989. In each DUF city, a new sample of arrestees is selected every
three months, is interviewed, and is asked to provide voluntary, anonymous urine specimens for analysis. Drug Use Forecasting findings have

shown that the rates of recent drug use among arrestees, especially of cocaine, are many times that found in surveys of the general population. While student surveys had detected a leveling off of cocaine use in 1987 (Johnston, O'Malley, and Bachman 1988), the prevalence of cocaine use among adult arrestees and juvenile detainees has continued to climb (Wish and O'Neil 1990). Furthermore, large geographical differences in drug-abuse patterns have been uncovered. The DUF findings have provided local jurisdictions with objective information on which to base planning for legislation and for programs for intervening with drug-abusing offenders.

E. Criminal Justice Testing versus Testing in Other Contexts

While some of the purposes of drug testing conducted by the criminal justice system also apply to testing in other contexts, it is important to note some differences. Some of the criticisms of criminal justice drug testing are a product of perceived abuses of drug testing in other contexts, primarily in testing of employees. The common rationale for employee testing is that drug-impaired employees have lower productivity than other employees and pose a higher risk of accidents. However, employee drug-testing programs typically make no attempt to ascertain the person's level of impairment. Instead, a single positive urine test may result in an applicant being denied employment. Employees who test positive for a drug may be fired.[5] This is because the liability to a company for retaining an employee who tested positive may be unacceptable, especially in sensitive occupations. The fear of losing one's job because of a single test result, which itself could be erroneous, and a number of highly publicized instances of laboratory errors, have engendered considerable skepticism in the public about the value of testing programs.

In the criminal justice system, a single positive test result will seldom have the drastic consequences it can have in the employment setting. The level of recent drug use in the offender population is so high (National Institute of Justice 1988; Wish, Toborg, and Bellassai 1988) that it would be counterproductive to attempt to revoke probation or parole or incarcerate all persons who tested positive. Drug testing is more likely to be used by the criminal justice system to enable more persons to be released to the community under enhanced supervision (Wish, Toborg, and Bellassai 1988) or to refer persons to treatment or

---

[5] A series of articles (Spolar 1988) documents the extreme actions sometimes taken by employers against employees who have a single positive test for marijuana.

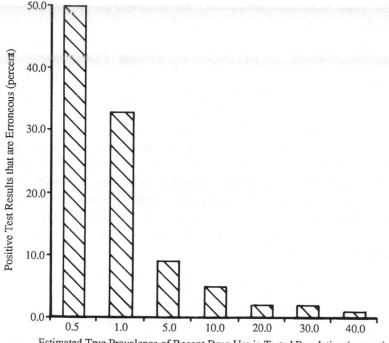

FIG. 1.—Relation between true prevalence of drug use and erroneous positive urine-test results in a population where drug use is rare. (Assume that .5 percent of all tests are positive because of test or clerical errors and that all recent users test positive.) Source.—Wish (1988*a*).

counseling. In most of these situations a single test is used to trigger more assessment, testing, or supervision and not to punish people or deprive them of their liberty.

There is another reason for differentiating drug testing of offenders from testing other populations. As figure 1 shows, the percentage of positive test results that are found to be in error is directly related to the true level of drug use in the tested population (Journal of the American Medical Association's Council on Scientific Affairs 1987). These statistics assume that a hypothetical test has a one-half of 1 percent chance of falsely labeling a person as a user because of any technical or clerical error.[6] Under these conditions, if the estimated true rate of drug use in

---

[6] This example is designed to illustrate a point. One would hope that a certified laboratory would have a false positive rate smaller than one-half of 1 percent. However, unconfirmed screening tests may have false positive error rates above 1 percent (Davis et al. 1988).

the tested population is 1 percent, 33 percent of all persons who test positive will be erroneously identified to be a drug user. While test error remains constant as the number of drug users in a population decreases, false positives increase as a percentage of all positive results. Random testing of large populations should therefore be undertaken only after estimates of the false positive rate (from all sources of error) and the level of drug use in the target population are obtained and a cost/benefit analysis completed (see Miike and Hewitt 1988; Sexton and Zilz 1988). In testing an employee population where drug use is rare, the risk of mislabeling a person a drug user and the cost of detecting a few users may be unacceptably high. This is not the case when testing offender populations, where drug use is generally found to be extensive. Section II examines the types of drug tests being used by the criminal justice system with special emphasis on urine tests and the analysis of hair.

II. Drug-Testing Methods

Evidence of drug usage may be manifested in many ways. Three categories of indicators and related tests may be defined on the basis of the body systems involved and their temporal patterns—how soon they appear and how long they remain detectable (Gropper 1987a, 1987b). *Clinical-behavioral indicators* are behavioral and central nervous system effects that tend to appear rapidly after ingestion of drugs. They are manifested by changes in speech patterns, brain waves, pupillary reaction and body coordination, and psychological orientation. Some of these effects may be measured by simple observation while others require sophisticated recording devices. *Metabolic indicators* are related to the body's metabolism, storage, and excretion of drugs. These include measures of bodily fluids such as blood, urine, saliva, and breath. *Structural indicators* measure products of the body's organic absorption of drugs in such body parts as hair or nails. Structural indicators can provide evidence of drug use long after the drug has been eliminated from other body systems and has ceased to have a psychoactive effect.

The criminal justice system has primarily used clinical-behavioral and metabolic indicators. Examples of clinical-behavioral tests are the Breathalyzer, which is typically used in drunk-driving cases, and the Los Angeles Police Department's drug detection procedure, which includes an oral interview, a physiological examination, and a battery of behavioral tests (Bureau of Justice Assistance 1989). Police officers, called drug recognition experts, are trained to detect the patterns of behavioral and physiological symptoms associated with the use of different classes of drugs and have used this technique to classify accurately the drugs used by persons arrested for driving under the influence (Anderson 1983; Compton 1986; Bureau of Justice Assistance 1989). While measures of changes in speech and brain waves produced by drugs have been developed, we know of no field tests of their use by the criminal justice system.

Urinalysis is the primary metabolic indicator of drug use. Blood tests, while accurate, involve more complex analytic procedures and require more invasive procedures to obtain a specimen (fear of transmission of the AIDS virus also makes blood tests less attractive). While drugs appear quickly in the blood, their detection is limited by the short period that they remain in circulation. Similar analytic and duration problems apply to tests of saliva, although obtaining saliva is probably the easiest and least intrusive of all biological specimens that can be obtained (Hawks and Chiang 1986).

Structural indicators of drug use have only recently been developed for possible use by the criminal justice system. The method receiving the most attention is the analysis of hair specimens by an experimental technique in which the drug is extracted from the hair and analyzed using radioimmunoassay tests (Harkey and Henderson 1988). In addition to its lesser intrusiveness, the analysis of hair has a number of other potential advantages over the metabolic tests (Gropper 1988a; Wish, Toborg, and Bellassai 1988).

A. Urinalysis

The most comprehensive general discussion of urine-testing technology and applications (irrespective of the context where testing occurs) appears in a handbook published by the National Institute on Drug Abuse (Hawks and Chiang 1986). Additional useful information about the scientific issues involved in drug testing appears in a report prepared by the Journal of the American Medical Association's Council on Scientific Affairs (1987), in an issue of a newsletter prepared by a commercial laboratory (Chang 1987), and in a review of the accuracy of urine tests (Miike and Hewitt 1988). Issues relevant to urine testing by the criminal justice system are discussed in a description of police employee drug testing (Manili et al. 1987), guidelines for Treatment Alternatives to Street Crime programs (Bureau of Justice Assistance 1988a), and in a description of research on the identification of drug-using offenders (Wish 1988*b*). The information below draws heavily from these sources.

An understanding of the different types of urine tests requires a knowledge of some basic definitions. The *sensitivity* of a test is the minimum concentration of a drug that can be reliably detected in a urine sample. Sensitivity is measured in nanograms per milliliter (ng/mL) of urine. A nanogram is one-billionth of a gram. The *cutoff* limit is the concentration limit that is used by a test to designate the specimen as positive or negative and is usually set above the minimum sensitivity limit.[7] By requiring a higher cutoff threshold, the manufacturer reduces the possibility that a specimen is erroneously designated as containing a drug. The higher cutoff, however, necessarily results in a greater likelihood that a test will fail to detect a drug that is in the urine. Thus, when manufacturers state that a test is accurate 95–97 percent of the time, most of the errors are intentionally biased toward false negative errors to protect the person (and the manufacturer) from erroneously labeling a person to be a user.[8]

The *specificity* of a urine test "refers to the ability of the assay to identify a single-chemical component in a mixture of chemicals and biological materials" (Hawks 1986). A highly specific test will accurately differentiate one drug from another. For example, the Enzyme Multiplied Immune Test (EMIT) for amphetamines will detect the presence of both amphetamines and methamphetamines. A more specific test would be required to determine which of these drugs is in the urine. Furthermore, some of the screening tests actually measure

[7] For example, the Syva Corporation markets EMIT assays for cannabinoids (marijuana) with cutoffs of 20 ng/mL, 50 ng/mL, and 100 ng/mL even though these assays are likely to be capable of detecting much smaller concentrations of the drug. The 100 ng/mL cutoff is considered more conservative because persons are unlikely to test positive at this level if they merely inhaled smoke exhaled by marijuana users (passive inhalation) or if small amounts of the drug remain in their bodies from use that occurred weeks earlier.

[8] A study by the Centers for Disease Control (CDC) has often been cited for its finding of substantial errors in the urinalysis results from the thirteen laboratories surveyed (Hansen, Caudill, and Boone 1985). In a blind experiment, the CDC sent a set of blank specimens and spiked urine specimens containing known quantities of drugs to each laboratory for analysis. A major omission in the report is that the precise urine tests used were not described. The study found that, while some laboratories failed to detect the drugs, few instances occurred where a drug was detected in the blank specimens. The average accuracy of the analyses of the blank specimens was 99 percent. False negative error rates were much higher and varied considerably by laboratory and drug. This study is often misinterpreted as indicating that laboratories frequently make false positive errors. Davis et al. (1988) also found rates of false negative errors to be substantially greater than false positive error rates.

drug degradation products (metabolites) rather than the presence of the drug itself. One must be careful in comparing test results from different methodologies because each test may measure different metabolites to detect the same drug.

An associated characteristic of urine tests is the level of potential *cross-reactivity* (Morgan 1984; Journal of the American Medical Association's Council on Scientific Affairs 1987). This refers to the ability of a substance other than the drugs in question to produce a positive result. For example, certain over-the-counter allergy and cold medicines will cause a positive test result in an EMIT amphetamine test. And in an early form of the EMIT test, an over-the-counter pain reliever, ibuprofen, caused the results to be positive. The EMIT tests were eventually redesigned to eliminate this problem (Blanke 1986). It is not practical, however, for a manufacturer to test all possible substances that might cross-react with a particular test. Cross-reactivity is especially a problem with all immunoassay tests because they measure a drug indirectly by observing the level of chemical reaction that occurs in the presence of the drug or its metabolites. Substances that are chemically similar to the drug can sometimes produce the chemical reaction measured by the test and thereby produce a false positive result (Morgan 1984).

The appropriate test to use depends on the desired combination of sensitivity, specificity, and cross-reactivity. The cheaper, more rapid urine tests available today tend to be highly sensitive, but, because of their cross-reactivity problems, it is generally recommended that they be confirmed by a second test based on a different methodology. These tests are therefore generally recommended for use for screening or monitoring large numbers of persons. The more labor-intensive and expensive urine tests tend to be both highly sensitive and highly specific. These tests are therefore most appropriate for confirming a positive screening test.

The screening test may indicate that one or more classes of drugs are present (e.g., opiates) while a confirmatory test will identify the actual drug (e.g., codeine). It is important that the confirmatory test does not rely on the same type of chemical reaction used by the screening test. In this way a false positive produced by cross-reactivity of a substance with a screening test will not "fool" the confirmatory test. For these reasons, the National Institute on Drug Abuse guidelines, some courts, and even the test manufacturers themselves recommend that an initial positive result be confirmed by a test that uses an alternative method of detection. This is particularly true in cases where decisions regarding employment and liberty are being made. Below we briefly describe the tests most commonly available for screening and confirming drug use.

1. *Screening by Thin-Layer Chromatography.*   Thin-layer chromatography, known as TLC, was one of the first analytic techniques used to screen for a broad spectrum of drugs. The test procedure can simultaneously identify the presence of a large variety of drugs. Until the development of sensitive immunoassay tests (discussed below), TLC was the method most likely to be used to screen and monitor persons in treatment programs or in criminal justice programs.

Thin-layer chromatography is labor intensive. The specimen must first be processed to extract, purify, and concentrate the drug to be detected. A measured amount of the concentrated urine specimen is then placed on a glass plate or other firm support that has been coated with a fine, sandlike material (silica gel or alumina). Special solvents are used that separate the drugs on the TLC plate. During the separation process, the solvents cause the drugs to migrate on the plate. Their locations then are determined by applying a series of color sprays. A technician compares the location and color of the spots on the plate to known drug standards on the plate. If both the location of the drug spot and the color match the standard, the drug can be identified.

One reason for TLC's popularity is that the technique is relatively inexpensive. A large number of drugs can be tested simultaneously. However, a number of disadvantages of TLC, combined with the development of immunoassay tests, have considerably reduced its use. Thin-layer chromatography is a highly subjective procedure that requires an experienced laboratory technician capable of interpreting the colors and patterns on the plate. Furthermore, there is no permanent record of the test result unless a photograph is taken; TLC plates often do not photograph accurately. Thin-layer chromatography generally is a less sensitive technique than immunoassay tests. Research has shown that compared with one such test—EMIT—TLC underdetects certain drugs (especially opiates and cocaine) by as much as two-thirds (Wish, Chedekel, Brady, and Cuadrado 1985; Magura et al. 1987). Finally, because TLC is a subjective test, requiring a decision by a technician, the technique is not very specific and should be confirmed by other methods (Journal of the American Medical Association's Council on Scientific Affairs 1987). A more sensitive variation of TLC, High Performance TLC (HPTLC), has been developed to detect drugs that appear in low concentrations in the urine. Commercial systems have also been developed (e.g., Toxi-lab) that attempt to standardize various elements of TLC, including extraction, application, and visualization. Nonetheless, the substantial disadvantages of TLC techniques make them less attractive screening tests than the newer immunoassay techniques.

2. *Screening by Immunoassays.* These tests use antibodies to detect the presence of a drug. An antibody is a protein that will react only with a specific substance, called an antigen. An antibody can be produced to react with a specific antigen, for example, a drug. During a test, a label or tag is attached to a sample of the drug to be detected. Then the tagged drug, the untagged drug (which is in the urine specimen being tested), and the antibody are combined during the test. The tagged drug and the untagged drug compete for binding with the antibody. If a high concentration of drug is present in the urine specimen, little of the tagged drug will be able to bind with the antibody. The immunoassay test measures the amount of tagged drug that was not successfully bound. The amount that was not bound is related to how much drug was in the urine. The test results generally indicate only that the presence of a drug is positive or negative (by comparison to a standard containing a known quantity of the drug), although quantitative estimates of the amount of drug present can be obtained.

The major immunoassay tests differ with regard to the "tag" that is used. Enzyme immunoassay, EIA (e.g., EMIT uses this technique), uses an enzyme to tag the drug and then measures the amount of enzyme activity occurring after the test reagents and the urine specimen have been combined. Fluorescent polarization immunoassay, FPIA (e.g., TDx), uses a substance that glows as its drug tag. Radioimmunoassay (RIA) (e.g., Abuscreen), uses an antigen tagged with a radioactive substance. Drug presence is indicated by the amount of radioactivity remaining after binding. A potential disadvantage of RIA is that it requires specially trained staff and certified laboratories to handle and dispose of radioactive materials. While the test reagents are inexpensive, the instrumentation is costly.

The most popular immunoassay test is currently EMIT. Both small portable machines and high-volume automated processors are available. While more expensive than TLC, EMIT tests are much less expensive than the more sophisticated laboratory tests discussed in the next section. One EMIT test is conducted for each drug to be identified. Depending on the laboratory, the volume of testing, and the drugs being detected, the cost may range from under $1.00 per test to over $5.00. To run EMIT tests, a minimum amount of training is required, compared to the expertise needed to run the chromatography procedures. Finally, the EMIT process is simple enough to enable some facilities to establish on-site testing programs. Like all immunoassays, EMIT tests are very sensitive. A major disadvantage is the reduced specificity and the possibility of cross-reactivity (Morgan 1984). Furthermore, immunoassay tests are subject to adulteration of the specimen which can lead to false negative results.

3. *Confirmation by Gas Chromatography.* In gas chromatography (GC), also sometimes called gas liquid chromatography, urine is extracted and a portion of the extract is injected into a special column that is part of the chromatograph instrument. The column is heated and has a gas flowing through it. Drugs from the urine extract are swept along the column and "stick" to a liquid film on the walls of the column. In this manner, different drugs slow down and separate into discrete plugs (or peaks) of material. As these drugs emerge from the end of the column, they are detected by the instrumentation. By standardizing instrument conditions (i.e., temperature, gas flow, column liquid phase) drugs can be identified based on their retention time, which is the time it takes for the substance to migrate through the column. The retention time of an unknown drug is compared to pure drug standards that are run through the chromatograph.

Gas chromatography is one of the most sensitive and specific techniques available. It is estimated to have a false positive rate of less than .01 percent (Journal of the American Medical Association's Council on Scientific Affairs 1987). The technique is expensive and requires highly trained personnel. It is slow because only one sample can be run at a time, and it is therefore not suitable for large-scale screening. It is an excellent technique for confirming specimens found to test positive by a screening test. A variation of this technique based on similar principles but using liquid instead of gases in the column is high performance liquid chromatography.

4. *Confirmation by Gas Chromatography/Mass Spectrometry.* This method, known by the initials GC/MS, is an advanced adaptation of GC. A mass spectrometer serves as the detector of the substance exiting the column. The mass spectrometer shatters the drug into pieces to form a fragmentation spectrum. The fragmentation spectrum and the

retention time of an unknown drug can be compared to analytic standards. The fragmentation pattern of the drug is like a fingerprint; thus GC/MS is considered to be the absolute standard for identifying drugs. A disadvantage of GC/MS is the time it takes to prepare the specimen for analysis. The equipment required is expensive and requires a highly trained operator. The technique requires a commercial laboratory and does not lend itself to large-scale drug screening programs. While GC/MS can provide the most conclusive information about the presence of a drug, there are a number of possible modes of operation of the equipment that could alter the degree of reliability of the procedure (Hawks 1986).

5. *Comparison of Available Tests.*   Table 2 compares the widely available types of urine tests. The more common immunoassay tests (RIA and EMIT) require no pretreatment of the specimen, have high sensitivity, and require moderately trained staff. Their speed and relative low cost make them especially useful for large-scale screening and monitoring programs. Their major weaknesses are that tests can be confounded by adulterating specimens and that results need to be confirmed by another method in order to rule out cross-reactivity. The confirmation tests, all of which employ some variation of GC, require extensive and time-consuming specimen preparation.

In 1988–89, the U.S. Department of Justice sponsored a study comparing four different tests (RIA, TLC, EMIT, TDx) to GC/MS. Preliminary results indicate that all of the immunoassays have fairly similar rates of false positives and false negatives, although specific tests may perform better for detecting certain drugs.[9] Thin-layer chromatography, however, appears to have a substantially higher rate of false negatives. Based on this and prior research already noted, we would recommend that standard TLC not be used to screen for illicit drugs.[10]

The choice of a test depends on a number of factors, including its cost and turnaround time, the level of sensitivity and specificity required, and the risk or consequences of a false positive or false negative result. Another important characteristic is the degree to which the results are legally defensible in court. The findings of a survey of twenty-five

[9] Personal communication from Christy Visher at the National Institute of Justice on May 18, 1989. Results from this study are expected to be released in late 1990.

[10] We are unaware of any research comparing modified TLC tests with the immunoassays. The information in table 2 suggests, however, that at least for some drugs, RIA and EMIT are more sensitive than the Toxi-lab technique.

TABLE 2
Comparison of Commonly Used Analytic Techniques

Technique*	Pre-analysis Treatment of Sample	Major Instrumentation	Drug Identification	Can Specimen Be Adulterated?	Limits of Sensitivity (µg/mL)	Instrumentation Costs ($)	Confirmation Required	Multiple Drug Analysis at Once	Level of Personal Experience
TLC	Yes	No	Position on plate	No	1	. . .	Yes	Yes	High
Modified Toxi-lab	Yes	No	Response to color reagents' fluorescent pattern	No	.2–5	500	Yes	Yes	Moderate
HPLC with scanning ultraviolet detector	Yes	Yes	Relative retention times; comparison of ultraviolet spectra with standards	No	.02–10	20,000–50,000	No†	Yes	High
Dual-column capillary GC with nitrogen detectors	Yes	Yes	Relative retention times matched in both columns; comparison of peaks with standards	No	.01–10	20,000–50,000	No†	Yes	High

Method			Basis						
Capillary GC/MS	Yes	Yes	Relative retention times; comparison of mass spectra with standards	No	.001–5	20,000–200,000	No	Yes	High
EMIT	No	Yes	Variation in enzyme activity	Yes	.025–5	7,000–100,000	Yes	No	Moderate
RIA	No	Yes	Variation of bound radio-labeled tracer	Yes	.001–10	5,000–100,000	Yes	No	Moderate
Color or spot tests	No	No	Response to color reagents	Yes	.1–10‡	. . .	Yes	No	Moderate

SOURCE.—Journal of the American Medical Association's Council on Scientific Affairs (1987), p. 3111.

NOTE.—μg/mL = micrograms per milliliter; ng/nL = nanograms per nanoliter.

* TLC indicates thin-layer chromatography; modified Toxi-lab, modified thin-layer chromatography; HPLC, high-performance liquid chromatography; GC, gas chromatography; GC/MS, gas chromatography/mass spectrometry; EMIT, enzyme-multiplied immunoassay technique; and RIA, radioimmunoassay.

† Confirmation necessary only if results must meet a forensic challenge.

‡ ng/nL.

345

experts asked about the legal defensibility of specific analytic methods for use in employee testing (Hoyt et al. 1987) appear in table 3. The use of EMIT or RIA confirmed by GC/MS was rated fully defensible against legal challenge. The single technique rated the most defensible was GC/MS. Gas chromatography and all other single tests were rated difficult to defend in a legal proceeding.

6. *Cutoff Levels.*   Users of urine tests must be knowlegeable about each test's cutoff. For example, the EMIT test for marijuana can be purchased with any of three cutoffs (20 ng, 50 ng, or 100 ng). The choice of cutoff will affect how long after use the test will show a positive result and will thereby affect the number of drug users detected. The choice of a cutoff is not straightforward, however. Should the cutoff for an initial screening test be higher or lower than the cutoff for a confirmation test? For example, should a confirmation test performed using GC/MS be considered positive if any amount of drug is found or only if it surpasses some arbitrary higher threshold? While the federal employee drug-testing guidelines do suggest recommended cutoff levels (*Federal Register* 1988), there is still considerable lack of consensus and standardization of these procedures.

How long after use a drug can be detected depends on many factors, including the test cutoff, the chronicity of use, the retention of the drug in the body, and the purity of the drug taken. General guidelines for the approximate duration of detection and limits of sensitivity of urine tests appear in table 4. That some drugs can be detected for weeks after use has important implications for monitoring programs that repeatedly test a person.

Testing by the criminal justice system (and the military) was explicitly exempted from meeting the federal employee drug testing guidelines. The guidelines acknowledged that the characteristics of the offender population and the uses of testing by the criminal justice system were often different from those in the employee population. For example, the consequences of a single false positive test result for a convicted felon being monitored over time may not be as severe as those for a job applicant. The convicted felon would probably be assigned to treatment or an increased rate of testing, while the job applicant might be summarily excluded from further consideration for employment. Thus, when consequences affecting liberty or guilt are not involved, it may be acceptable to require less stringent confirmation testing procedures and cutoff levels for persons being screened or monitored by the

TABLE 3
Legal Defensibility of Methods as Determined by Experts (96 Percent Response)*

	Single-Procedure Methods†					Multiple-Procedure Methods†										
	EMIT	RIA	TLC	GC	GC/MS	EMIT, RIA	EMIT, TLC	EMIT, GC	EMIT, GC/MS	RIA, TLC	RIA, GC	RIA, GC/MS	TLC, EMIT	TLC, RIA	TLC, GC	TLC, GC/MS
Amphetamines	3.9	3.9	3.8	3.4	1.7	3.7	2.6	2.2	1.0	2.7	2.2	1.0	2.8	2.8	2.3	1.2
Barbiturates	4.0	4.0	3.8	3.4	1.7	3.7	2.5	2.1	1.0	2.6	2.1	1.1	2.7	2.7	2.3	1.2
Benzodiazepines	4.0	4.0	3.8	3.5	1.7	3.8	2.5	2.1	1.0	2.6	2.2	1.1	2.7	2.7	2.4	1.2
Cannabinoids	3.9	3.9	3.7	3.6	1.7	3.7	2.6	2.3	1.0	2.7	2.3	1.0	2.7	2.7	2.5	1.2
Cocaine	3.9	3.9	3.7	3.4	1.7	3.6	2.5	2.1	1.0	2.5	2.1	1.0	2.5	2.5	2.3	1.2
Methaqualone	3.9	3.9	3.8	3.4	1.7	3.7	2.5	2.1	1.0	2.5	2.1	1.0	2.5	2.5	2.3	1.2
Opiates	4.0	4.0	3.7	3.5	1.7	3.6	2.5	2.1	1.0	2.6	2.1	1.0	2.7	2.7	2.3	1.2
Phencyclidine (PCP)	3.9	3.9	3.8	3.4	1.7	3.6	2.5	2.1	1.0	2.6	2.1	1.0	2.6	2.6	2.4	.2

SOURCE.—Hoyt et al. (1987), p. 506.

* Defensibility was determined by using a 1–4 scale: 1, fully defensible against legal challenge; 2, somewhat defensible; 3, difficult to defend in legal challenges; 4, unacceptable for legal defense.

† EMIT indicates enzyme multiplied immunoassay technique; RIA, radioimmunoassay; TLC, thin-layer chromatography; GC, gas chromatography; GC/MS, gas chromatography/mass spectrometry. First procedure is a "screen"; second procedure is a "confirmation."

TABLE 4

Approximate Duration of Detectability of Selected Drugs in Urine*

Substance	Duration of Detectability
Amphetamine	48 hours
Methamphetamine	48 hours
Barbiturates:	
Short acting	24 hours
Intermediate acting	48–72 hours
Long acting	7 days or more
Benzodiazepines	3 days (therapeutic dose)
Cocaine metabolites	2–3 days
Methadone	Approximately 3 days
Codeine/morphine	48 hours
Propoxyphene/norpropoxyphene	6–48 hours
Cannabinoids (marijuana):	
Single use	3 days
Moderate use (4 times per week)	4 days
Heavy use (daily smoking)	10 days
Chronic heavy use	21–27 days
Methaqualone	7 days or more
Phencyclidine (PCP)	Approximately 8 days

SOURCE.—Journal of the American Medical Association's Council on Scientific Affairs (1987), p. 3112.

* Interpretation of the duration of detectability must take into account many variables, such as drug metabolism and half-life, subject's physical condition, fluid balance and state of hydration, and route and frequency of ingestion. These are general guidelines only.

criminal justice system. Nonetheless, the courts may simply adopt the prevailing attitudes toward testing reflected in the survey above. Given the ambiguity involved in these decisions, it would be advisable to consult with a toxicologist and an attorney before selecting a testing regimen.

B. Analysis of Hair[11]

For over twenty years, hair samples have been analyzed to detect exposure to metals such as arsenic, mercury, and lead. Applications have been made in the fields of forensic toxicology, environmental toxicology, clinical pathology, and nutrition. The extension of this

[11] This section draws heavily from a comprehensive review of RIA conducted by Harkey and Henderson (1988) for the California Department of Alcohol and Drug Programs.

technology to detecting drugs of abuse has occurred in the past ten years (Baumgartner et al. 1979, 1982; Baumgartner, Jones, and Black 1981),[12] and is only now becoming commercially available.[13]

Drugs may enter the hair by incorporation into the growing hair shaft from the blood that supplies the hair follicle or by absorption of chemicals from the external environment into the developed hair shaft (Harkey and Henderson 1988). Consequently, in addition to drugs that have been self-administered and are in the blood, drugs that come into contact with skin or sweat or are in the air may enter the hair. Thus, people who are present where drugs such as opium, cocaine, or marijuana are being smoked may have the drug in their hair even if they did not take the drug.[14]

Hair can be tested for drugs by dissolving the hair shaft and analyzing the resulting solution or by analyzing the solid hair directly. The procedures for analysis of a solution extracted from hair are analogous to the procedure used for urinalysis. Analysis of the intact hair is rarer and most often conducted by heating the hair sample and analyzing the spectrum of the resulting vapors by mass spectroscopy (Martz 1988). This discussion focuses on the more common solution-based extraction techniques.

Criminal justice applications of hair testing to date have been only exploratory. Most have used RIA, sometimes confirmed by GC/MS. Appropriate assays for particular drugs are still being developed. The drugs that have been most fully explored using radioimmunoassay of hair are the opiates, methadone, cocaine, marijuana, PCP, amphetamines, barbiturates, and benzodiazepines (Harkey and Henderson 1988). Hair strands can be cut into sections and analyzed separately. Segments more distant from the root provide an indication of drug use that occurred weeks or months earlier, depending on rate of hair

---

[12] Hair analysis was actually used to detect drugs in animals far before this time (Goldblum, Goldbaum, and Piper 1954; Harrison, Gray, and Solomon 1974). Research into the detection of drugs in humans by hair analysis has also been conducted in West Germany, Italy, Japan, and Greece.

[13] PoisonLab in San Diego and Psychemedics Corporation in Santa Monica, Calif., offer hair analysis for illicit drugs. Psychemedics has conducted the majority of the testing used in criminal justice research projects.

[14] This problem is similar to the problem of passive inhalation of marijuana that can cause a urine test to be positive. Urine-test manufacturers have circumvented this problem by adjusting test cutoffs to 100 ng/mL where the possibility of a positive test from passive inhalation is highly unlikely. Hair-analysis techniques seek to eliminate this problem by thoroughly washing the hair prior to analysis. The effectiveness of such washing procedures and the possibility of absorption of illicit drugs from the environment are subjects that need extensive research.

growth. Segments close to the root document drug use days earlier. Since hair on the head grows at an average rate of about one-half inch per month, a two-to-three-inch strand would contain a record of the last four to six months of drug usage. It is therefore theoretically possible to compare sections of hair at different distances from the root to determine whether the person has been increasing or decreasing his drug use over time. Much more research is needed, however, to determine the extent to which radioimmunoassay of hair can live up to this promise.

Because it has some marked potential advantages over urinalysis, hair analysis is receiving much attention for use in employee and criminal justice settings. First, hair under some circumstances could be a permanent record of drug use. Analyses of hair specimens from the poet John Keats, taken 100 years earlier, confirmed his use of opiates shortly before his death (Harkey and Henderson 1988). Second, hair samples (thirty to forty strands) may be obtained from persons of either sex, in public, without the violation of privacy that occurs in obtaining an observed urine specimen. Third, detection is difficult to evade, and results may be more difficult to contaminate.[15] Even persons who are given a month's notice of an impending test cannot eliminate the traces of drug left over from prior use. Furthermore, the results cannot be contaminated by drinking fluids. While all body hair could be shaved, this would be readily discovered. Fourth, hair analysis allows for a retest of the person by taking another sample if the results from the original sample are challenged because of claims of contamination or laboratory error. Finally, if future research validates the technique, hair analysis may provide a unique measure of a person's pattern of drug use. By sectioning the hair, it could be determined whether drug use increased or decreased during a period of treatment or probation or parole (the time period available would depend upon the length of the person's hair and its rate of growth).

Hair analysis also has some disadvantages. For situations where the criminal justice system needs to detect drugs used in the last few hours or days, hair analysis is inappropriate. Because hair grows relatively slowly, there is a considerable time lag before drugs become detectable

[15] There is a possibility that treating one's hair with chemicals, dye, or shampoo could thwart the test. If hair analysis becomes more widely adopted, it can be expected that persons will try to develop new chemicals that can interfere with the test. Persons could attempt to reduce or remove the drug from their hair or add contaminants in order to claim that a positive test does not indicate use.

In the hair specimen. However, when knowledge is needed about drug use that extends beyond a few days, hair analysis may be the only available test. Another major disadvantage of hair analysis is that the technique is new and still costly and time consuming. Automated techniques for washing, extraction, and analysis are not yet available. Furthermore, the techniques have not been standardized and are not widely practiced. Finally, a number of questions remain regarding the validity of the technique and its possible applications (Harkey and Henderson 1988) that, for the moment, will probably limit the acceptability of hair testing in legal proceedings.

Any new scientific test requires considerable experimentation and experience to determine its proper use and limits. Because hair testing for drugs of abuse is in its infancy, there are numerous technical questions that have yet to be answered. Some of these issues have serious implications for the eventual feasibility of hair testing for particular questions—such as the amount consumed or when the exposure occurred. For example, little is known about how drugs are deposited in hair and whether the concentration of the drug found in hair is strongly correlated with the dose taken. A number of studies have found that, while hair analysis often detects the drugs of confirmed users, the amount detected does not correlate directly with the person's self-reported use (Baumgartner et al. 1982; Puschel, Thomasch, and Arnold 1983). A study of rats found twice as much drug residue in hair collected from the back as from hair collected from the stomach (Niwaguchi, Suzuki, and Inoue 1983). Studies of humans have found dramatic differences in the concentration of substances (not drugs) in hair samples taken from different areas of the scalp (Cornelius 1973; DeAntonio et al. 1982). It therefore may be important to standardize the location from which hair samples are taken.

Harkey and Henderson (1988) note seven factors that may complicate the interpretation of results from hair analysis. We mention these briefly to raise the important issues that need to be resolved before hair testing can be effectively used by the criminal justice system. Not enough is known about the effects of hair treatments, environmental exposure, or retention of drugs by hair. One study found no difference in nicotine concentrations in the hair of smokers and nonsmokers (Ishiyama, Nagai, and Toshida 1983). Interpretation of sectional analyses of hair may be complicated by a breakdown in the hair structure at the tip that allows for drugs to be more easily absorbed there from the environment; this could lead to overestimates of past drug use. Little is known about the correlation between the dose of the drug and the amount found in hair or the minimal amount of drug use needed to result in the detectable amount in hair.

The ability to conduct a valid sectional analysis of hair depends on the assumptions that external contamination has been eliminated, that there is no movement of drugs along the hair shaft, and that the rate of hair growth is constant and documented for the person being tested. Substantial questions remain regarding these assumptions, however. Other problems yet to be resolved are sampling procedures for choosing hair specimens and the lack of knowledge of how variable hair growth rates may affect the concentration of drugs in the hair. In spite of these unresolved issues, hair analysis has been accepted as evidence in several court cases (Harkey and Henderson 1988).

While there remain many unanswered questions regarding hair analysis, we believe that it may offer the criminal justice system a valuable option for drug testing (Gropper 1988*b;* Wish, Toborg, and Bellassai 1988). With the exception of concerns regarding standardization of techniques, hair-sampling procedures, and external contamination, most of the unresolved technical problems are problems only for attempts to quantify the exact amount of drugs used or to designate the trend of use over time. At present, it would appear that hair analysis could be used to confirm urinalysis test results that have been challenged. A person who claims that his or her urine test was in error or that the specimen was not his or hers could be tested by hair analysis (and confirmed by GC/MS), assuming that the hair is long enough to cover the time period in question. Without a second urine specimen taken at the same time as the challenged specimen, there is no other confirmation technique available.

Table 5, from Harkey and Henderson (1988), compares hair analysis to urinalysis. The possible advantages of hair analysis over urinalysis for testing small numbers of persons are readily apparent. When hair analysis has been validated by other independent researchers[16] and

[16] Researchers are working in this area now. A. M. Baumgartner, the developer of a technique for analysis of hair by radioimmunoassay, has a grant from the National Institute of Justice to compare RIA results with urinalysis tests and self-reports in probationers. Preliminary results indicate that RIA detects more drug use than does urinalysis. An independent researcher, Stephen Magura, delivered "blind" hair samples from twenty-four male patients in a methadone treatment program in New York City to Baumgartner for analysis. Radioimmunoassay of hair correctly detected cocaine use in all eighteen persons who indicated use in the past month and was negative for all persons who denied use. Furthermore, EMIT tests detected cocaine in sixteen of the eighteen persons found positive by RIA. Findings from the complete sample of 131 persons replicate these preliminary results and have been submitted for publication (Magura et al. 1989).

TABLE 5

Comparison of Hair Analysis and Urinalysis

Hair Analysis	Urinalysis
1. Detects long-term drug use, depending on hair length	1. Detects short-term drug use (except for marijuana)
2. Sample collected without embarrassment	2. Sample collection can be intrusive and demeaning
3. Initial identification of sample possible by color and texture	3. Samples can be easily exchanged or substituted
4. Difficult to alter sample to give false negative results	4. Sample can be diluted to give false negative results
5. Difficult to adulterate sample to interfere with test	5. Chemicals can be added to sample to interfere with test
6. Sample can be re-collected if results are questioned	6. Sample collected later is not comparable to original sample
7. Labor-intensive preparation of sample, costly procedure	7. Easily automated, cost-effective procedure
8. Great variability in methods	8. Established methods used
9. Quality control difficult and not yet established	9. Established quality control procedures
10. No external proficiency testing program	10. External proficiency programs available
11. Field applications not established	11. Well-accepted procedure
12. Used primarily for small numbers of samples	12. May easily be used for large numbers of samples
13. Current charges: $60–$65 per drug, $50–$125 for GC/MS confirmation	13. Current charges: $15–$30 for several drugs, confirmation often included

SOURCE.—Harkey and Henderson (1988), p. 67.
NOTE.—GC/MS = gas chromatography/mass spectrometry.

more is understood about the possible environmental contamination of hair, the technique could even be used as an initial screening test for small numbers of detainees. We assume that the high cost of these tests and the lack of standardization and quality control will be overcome. Until the accuracy of sectional analysis of hair for dating drug use is better understood, its use for measuring patterns of drug use over time will remain limited.

III. Applications of Urine Testing

This section reviews recent research regarding criminal justice urine-testing programs. The four parts of this section discuss pretrial testing, postadjudication testing, results from the Drug Use Forecasting project, and testing of juvenile detainees.

A. *Pretrial Testing Programs*

Most of the research findings about the usefulness of urine testing of offenders comes from the Washington, D.C., pretrial-testing program because it is the largest testing program operated by a criminal justice agency.[17] Since 1971, virtually all persons arrested for a criminal offense in the District of Columbia who are brought to the D.C. superior court lockup have been tested soon after arrest.

The District of Columbia is the only jurisdiction in the country with an established program for testing all arrestees for recent drug use by urinalysis. Although the program is technically voluntary, if drug-test results are not available when the pretrial-release decision is made (e.g., because the defendant refused the drug test, was unable to urinate, or was brought to court too late in the day to be tested), the defendant will often be ordered by the bail-setting commissioner to report to the D.C. Pretrial Services Agency for a drug-use evaluation as a condition of release (Toborg and Bellassai 1988*a*).

The District of Columbia program has been the subject of considerable research (DuPont and Kozel 1976; Wish et al. 1981; Toborg and Bellassai 1988*a*; Wish, Toborg, and Bellassai 1988; Toborg et al. 1989). The program was established in 1971 under the management of the Narcotic Treatment Administration, the funding agency for public treatment programs in the District of Columbia. The testing information was originally used primarily to refer arrestees into treatment. In 1984, the D.C. Pretrial Services Agency assumed responsibility for the operation of the program and adopted EMIT tests for all screening and monitoring programs.

The Pretrial Services Agency makes a recommendation to the judge regarding each defendant's suitability for release before trial. The judge weighs the agency's recommendation and other available information about the case and the defendant to decide whether the person will be released until his next court date; the judge may order specific conditions of release. The judge may release a person on his own recognizance or into another's custody, order a bond to be posted, or require the defendant to report to a drug-abuse treatment or urine-monitoring program. The practice of setting release conditions varies considerably across the country. Judges in Washington, D.C., often order special release conditions.

---

[17] Some probation and parole departments do test clients, but usually only persons known or suspected to be abusing drugs. Exceptions are the Federal Bureau of Prisons, which randomly tests inmates, and, in some parts of the country, the Federal Probation System.

Statutes in most jurisdictions allow pretrial detention only if the judge concludes the person will fail to appear in court for subsequent appearances. Some jurisdictions, like the District of Columbia and the entire federal system since the Bail Reform Act of 1984, have a preventive detention statute that permits the judge to take into consideration the defendant's dangerousness. Pretrial release agencies, therefore, must base their pretrial release recommendation to the judge on factors believed to be associated with the risks of failure to appear and pretrial rearrest. Typically, pretrial-release staff interview the defendant soon after arrest about the nature of his ties to the community, such as current employment and stability of residence. The more information that pretrial-release staff can verify demonstrating ties to the community, the greater the likelihood that release will be recommended. The pretrial-release interview is voluntary, but most defendants comply because they know that by cooperating they may improve their chances for release.

The available literature regarding the lifestyles of drug-involved offenders describes users' lack of dependability, their tendency to deceive people, and their high rates of criminal activity. These characteristics would suggest that such persons would be at high risk for failure to appear and pretrial rearrest; however, little research has looked directly at this issue. Scales for assessing risk for failure to appear typically rely on measures of community ties and ignore drug use. This is understandable because, in the absence of systematic urine testing of arrestees, the only measure of drug use available to the court is the voluntary self-report. Some studies have attempted to predict recidivism (not necessarily occurring in the pretrial period) or parole outcomes using the presence of a drug-charge or drug-use history to identify drug users and have found drug use to be statistically related to these outcomes (Williams 1979; Gottfredson and Gottfredson 1986).

Few studies have examined the pretrial behavior of drug users. Roth and Wice (1980) found that drug-use history was related both to pretrial failure to appear and to rearrest in releasees in the District of Columbia. Another study of releasees in Philadelphia found that drug use was associated with pretrial misbehavior (Goldkamp and Gottfredson 1981). The strength of the associations uncovered in these studies was probably attenuated, however, by their reliance on information available from police and court records to identify drug users.

Wish et al. (1981) used urinalysis results from arrestees in Washington, D.C., to examine the relations among drug use and failure to appear and rearrests (not necessarily pretrial). Urinalysis test results from over

60,000 arrestees were merged with information maintained by the prosecutor's office. Persons who tested positive for a drug (usually morphine, the metabolite of heroin) were found to have had a greater number of subsequent arrests than persons who tested negative. Persons charged with violating their conditions of bail were those most likely (out of all persons in the sample) to test positive for drugs. This study, however, was based on urinalysis tests (thin-layer chromatography) that are less sensitive than the immunoassay tests and probably missed many users of heroin and cocaine. Subsequent research, discussed below, has examined the relation of drug-test results to pretrial misconduct using the more sensitive screening tests.

A series of research reports has been written about the District of Columbia pretrial testing program (Toborg and Bellassai 1988a, 1988b; Toborg, Yezer, and Bellassai 1988; Yezer et al. 1988a, 1988b; Toborg et al. 1989). A survey of twenty-five superior court commissioners and trial judges in the D.C. superior court indicated considerable judicial interest in the drug-testing program. The survey was nonquantitative in its approach and obtained much descriptive information. Some judges indicated that, in addition to using the testing program to make pretrial-release decisions and to monitor users during release, they also used the information to make sentencing decisions. Thus, persons who reduced their drug use during pretrial urine monitoring were sometimes viewed as being better candidates for probation than were persons who continued to use drugs (Toborg and Bellassai 1988a, 1988b).

Another report examined whether drug-test results were useful in assessing risks of pretrial misconduct, over and above the other information typically available to the judge for making pretrial-release decisions (Yezer et al. 1988b). The authors found that persons who tested positive for three or more drugs or for PCP had a higher likelihood of pretrial rearrest. Persons who tested positive for cocaine, opiates, or both, had higher risks of failure to appear in court.

Perhaps the most important policy-related study of the District of Columbia program was an experiment in which judges randomly assigned drug-positive defendants to one of three experimental conditions: to treatment, to urine monitoring conducted by the Pretrial Services Agency, or to a control condition in which persons received no treatment or urine monitoring (Yezer et al. 1988a). The experiment was designed to measure whether the relative success of defendants in urine testing was associated with different rates of pretrial misconduct and whether initial assignment into urine testing resulted in lower rates of pretrial misconduct than for persons assigned to the other experimental conditions.

The value of the experiment, however, was limited by some unavoidable confounding of the experimental groups. For example, some judges decided that some persons assigned to the control group should receive urine monitoring. And sanctions were not uniformly applied when defendants repeatedly tested positive or failed to appear for testing during the monitoring program. The researchers were also unable to obtain information about the treatment experience. Thus it was unknown how many persons assigned to treatment actually entered treatment, dropped out, or were placed on a waiting list.

For these reasons, the analyses focused on a comparison of pretrial misconduct in persons who successfully participated in the urine-monitoring program with those who were unsuccessful. Persons who appeared for a total of three or more scheduled testing appointments (not necessarily consecutive appointments) were defined as successful. Persons who dropped out after fewer appointments were labeled as unsuccessful. Compared with unsuccessful participants, successful participants were found to have lower rates of pretrial rearrest (33 percent vs. 16 percent) and of failure to appear (33 percent vs. 17 percent). A secondary analysis of these data also found a smaller but significant reduction in pretrial misconduct in persons who appeared for three or more testings (Visher 1988). Overall, Yezer et al. (1988a) found no significant differences in pretrial misconduct in persons assigned to testing, treatment, or to the control group. They conclude that a urine-monitoring program allows a drug user to signal his low risk for future pretrial misconduct by compliance with the urine-testing program.

While there are many possible benefits from a pretrial drug-monitoring program (Carver 1986; Stewart 1988), it is questionable whether the signaling phenomenon is real or practical. First, research has repeatedly shown that persons who remain in treatment longer have better outcomes than those who drop out (Collins and Allison 1983; Leukefeld and Tims 1988; Anglin and Hser, in this volume). Hence, the improved results of the successful participants in the District of Columbia monitoring program may not be necessarily attributable to the urine testing itself. Any court-ordered program that requires defendants to keep multiple appointments could conceivably differentiate more compliant, law-abiding defendants from resistant persons prone to pretrial misconduct. Furthermore, a signaling device may have little practical utility in large cities, where once the defendant fails to appear for the scheduled testing appointment he may already have absconded and be lost to the system.

New York City has no testing program, and judges have no access to drug-test information for making pretrial-release decisions. Thus, while it was not possible to replicate the District of Columbia pretrial-testing experiment in New York City, it was feasible to collect urine specimens for research purposes only. In 1984, a research study collected 4,847 urine specimens from a sample of males being processed in the Manhattan Central Booking facility (Wish, Cuadrado, and Magura 1988). Criminal justice record information for sample members was obtained from a number of agencies. The study's primary objective was to assess the relation between arrestees' urine test results and pretrial misconduct.

Two sets of analyses using slightly different variables and techniques were conducted (Wish, Cuadrado, and Magura 1988; Smith, Wish, and Jarjoura 1989). Wish, Cuadrado, and Magura (1988) looked at the relation between drug dependence and failure to appear. Drug dependence was defined as testing positive for one or more drugs and indicating in the interview current dependence on a drug or a need for treatment. The rationale for constructing this variable was that the single test could only detect onetime use, and by adding self-reported dependence it would be possible to isolate for analysis those persons most likely to be chronic drug abusers. This approach was intended to simulate an operating testing program that screened persons by a drug test and later assessed level of dependence in those who tested positive.

Persons who tested positive at arrest and who indicated current dependence on a drug had among the highest rates of failure to appear. Multivariate analyses indicated that drug-test information was most associated with failure to appear in persons who had no recent prior arrests or warrants. That is, drug-test information contributed little to assessing risk of failure-to-appear cases where evidence already existed to indicate that arrestees were poor risks for release. Thus, drug-test information is most useful when the information available to the judge is minimal or equivocal.

In another series of analyses, a simple count of nine symptoms of drug abuse was constructed. A person was given one point for each of the following: testing positive for an opiate; testing positive for cocaine; testing positive for PCP; testing positive for methadone; testing positive for both cocaine and an opiate; usually taking cocaine by injection; being dependent on heroin; being dependent on cocaine; and needing

TABLE 6

Number of Symptoms of Drug Abuse as a Predictor of Pretrial Failure to Appear

	No. of Symptoms of Drug Abuse[a]				Total Sample
	0	1–2	3–4	5+	
Percent with failure to appear	32	41	51	54	39*
N	1,083	1,004	305	170	2,562

SOURCE.—Wish, Cuadrado, and Magura (1988), p. 28.

[a] Counts following nine items: tests positive for opiate, tests positive for cocaine, tests positive for PCP, tests positive for methadone, tests positive for both cocaine and opiate, usually takes cocaine by injection, is dependent on heroin at arrest, is dependent on cocaine at arrest, needs drug or alcohol treatment.

* $p \geq .001$, using χ^2 test.

drug or alcohol treatment. Twenty-three percent of the 4,847 tested arrestees and 18 percent of the 2,562 arrestees released pretrial had three or more of these symptoms. As table 6 shows, risk of failure to appear was linearly related to the level of drug abuse. Persons with three or more symptoms constituted 18 percent of the releasees but accounted for 25 percent of all persons who failed to appear. The analysis included all releasees with at least one day of pretrial time free. Additional analyses that controlled for the specific number of free pretrial days indicated that all releasees with less than thirty days of pretrial time had relatively low failure-to-appear rates, regardless of their level of drug abuse. Level of drug abuse increasingly discriminated risk of failure to appear as total time free extended beyond one month (Wish, Cuadrado, and Magura 1988).

A reanalysis and extension of the above findings to pretrial rearrest in arrestees in New York City was also performed (Smith, Wish, and Jarjoura 1989). The results from the initial analysis of the data were based on the sample of arrestees who had some pretrial time free and were therefore conditional on a person's having been released. These analyses are potentially biased if persons who are released differed from those who were not. For example, on average, drug abusers who were released by the judge probably had mitigating characteristics lacking in drug abusers who were retained. It would be more useful if the analyses could apply to all who had continued cases and for whom a pretrial release decision had to be made. To produce estimates that apply to all arrestees for whom a pretrial-release decision must be made, it was necessary to control for potential selection bias that resulted from the release decision. This was the purpose of the reanalysis.

Using advanced multivariate methods (censored probit), analyses were conducted to look at whether the drug-test information was associated with failure to appear or pretrial rearrest. The findings with regard to failure to appear were similar to those of Wish, Cuadrado, and Magura (1988) and showed that persons with multiple positive tests had a higher risk of failure to appear even after controlling for other types of information typically available to the judge at arraignment. One primary difference was that there was no statistical interaction between prior arrests and the test results. That is, drug-test information was associated with failure to appear for persons both with and without recent prior arrests.

Persons who tested positive for multiple drugs had higher risks of both failure to appear and pretrial rearrest. There were also some drug-specific relations. Persons who tested positive for heroin or cocaine had higher risks of failure to appear while those who tested positive for PCP had an elevated risk of rearrest. Interestingly, persons who tested positive for methadone, a synthetic opiate frequently prescribed to addicts in treatment in New York City, had a reduced risk of failure to appear and rearrest. Thus, drug-test results from a specimen obtained soon after arrest were related to risk of pretrial misconduct even after other factors (e.g., arrest charge, prior record, age, and pretrial release agency recommendation) had been controlled.

While statistical models can assess level of risk in a cohort, they can rarely be used to make individual predictions of risk that improve on the base rate (Roth and Wice 1980; Shannon 1985; Gottfredson and Gottfredson 1986). Smith, Wish, and Jarjoura (1989) note that a precise test of the ability of their statistical models to predict an individual's risk of misconduct required a new sample of arrestees. However, when they applied their estimation models to the construction sample to predict each individual's likelihood of pretrial misconduct, the authors found that the models that included drug-test information improved individual prediction of failure to appear, but not of rearrest, over models that excluded the drug-test information.[18]

[18] A preliminary report of analyses using a subset of the data from the New York project (Belenko and Mara-Drita 1988) focused on the failure of drug-test results to predict individual risk of failure to appear in court and concluded that urine testing was not a feasible policy alternative. That report had a number of additional important methodological limitations that were addressed in the final analyses using the complete data base (Smith, Wish, and Jarjoura 1989). Among them were no controls for sample

Findings from the pretrial drug-testing research in New York City and Washington, D.C., agree that drug-test results provide information useful to assessing risk of pretrial misconduct. In both cities, cocaine and heroin were related to an elevated risk of failure to appear, while PCP was related to rearrest.

These findings should not be unexpected to persons knowledgeable about the relations between drug use and criminality. Studies of chronic cocaine and heroin users who are committing street crimes have documented their hectic undisciplined lifestyles (reviewed by Johnson et al. 1985; Inciardi 1986; Wish and Johnson 1986). Such persons are not likely, in general, to keep court appointments or to comply with court orders. The relation of PCP to rearrests is less clear. One study of arrestees in New York City and Washington, D.C., who tested positive for PCP suggests, however, that these persons were young risk takers who were most likely to be charged with robbery (Wish 1986). However, PCP is a major drug problem in Washington, D.C., but much less so in New York City. It is rarely found in the urine of arrestees in other cities.

The types of drugs found in the urine of arrestees vary considerably from city to city. Use of PCP in a city with few users may, for example, denote a more serious drug abuser than does use in Washington, D.C., where PCP is common. For these reasons, the findings from New York City and Washington, D.C., should not be applied directly to other cities. The pretrial-testing program in Washington, D.C., is being replicated in six other sites (Tucson and Phoenix, Arizona; Portland, Oregon; Wilmington, Delaware; Milwaukee, Wisconsin; and Prince Georges County, Maryland). Furthermore, section 7304 of the Anti-Drug Abuse Act of 1988 provided for the establishment, by the director of the Administrative Office of the United States Courts, of a demonstration program of mandatory drug testing of criminal defendants in eight judicial districts. Criminal defendants at the pretrial stage and all convicted felons who are placed on probation or supervised release will be tested. The evaluations and experience from all of these programs will provide needed information about the generalizability of the findings from New York City and Washington, D.C., to other cities.

The findings from the District of Columbia experiment are important because they provide information about useful strategies for arres-

---

selection bias and the use of a binary measure of pretrial time free (none vs. any days free) rather than the actual number of days free or, more preferably, the number of scheduled court appearances.

tees who test positive for drugs at arrest. They show that judges will use systematic test information to specify release conditions. And anecdotal information suggests that many judges feel more confident in releasing drug abusers into the community because they know they will be monitored by the Pretrial Services Agency. That persons who reported for testing at least three times had lower rates of pretrial misbehavior is consistent with studies of surveillance of parole populations (Anglin 1988). Furthermore, there are other benefits to a city from a pretrial drug-testing program that were not studied in the report reviewed. For example, the urine tests in Washington, D.C., helped to document the magnitude of the PCP problem and to lead to an expansion of treatment resources (Carver 1986). Testing can also alert authorities to the availability of clandestine laboratories in an area (National Institute on Drug Abuse 1979).

Many questions remain about the efficacy of urine monitoring as a strategy for pretrial releasees. What is the effectiveness of assigning persons to urine monitoring alone or combined with treatment? The research experiment in the District of Columbia was unable to examine the efficacy of treatment and did not examine precise patterns of test results. For example, do persons who have an improving trend in test results perform as well as those who repeatedly test negative? Should pretrial release conditions depend on the exact nature of the drugs detected? How much urine monitoring or drug treatment is optimal? Answers to these questions should be sought as more cities experiment with pretrial testing.

Finally, there are a number of problems that occur in operating a pretrial-testing program. While one must always be alert to attempts by defendants to alter test results by switching, diluting, or otherwise adulterating specimens, the program in Washington, D.C., has also had at least one instance in which employees were bribed by defendants to alter their test results (*Washington Post* 1988). Finally, there are numerous legal and constitutional issues involved in requiring persons who have not yet been convicted to provide urine specimens and to appear for monitoring (Wish, Toborg, and Bellassai 1988).

While there are many questions to be answered regarding how best to use pretrial test results, we feel that there is ample justification for the introduction of random testing at the pretrial stage. Findings from both New York City and Washington, D.C., have documented a link between drug-test results and pretrial misconduct. In both studies, the predictive value of drug-test information survived stringent statistical

controls far beyond those required for justifying the use of other information at the pretrial decision stage. The predictive contribution of
drug-test information was measured above and beyond the contribution of a person's level of community ties and prior criminal record,
both of which are correlated with drug use. The statistical models,
therefore, intentionally minimized the contribution of drug-test information to predicting risk of pretrial misconduct.

While a determination of the "unique variation" attributable to drug-
test information is of academic interest, we believe that the decision
regarding the utility of pretrial drug testing must be based on a wider
consideration of the impact of testing. Drug use is even more prevalent
in arrestee populations today than in 1984, when these studies of arrestees in New York City and Washington, D.C., were conducted. In
1989, it was not rare to find that more than 60 percent of arrestees in the
largest cities tested positive for drugs. This means that future statistical
studies of drug-test results and pretrial misconduct will necessarily find
less of an association between drug use and pretrial misconduct than
was found in these completed studies. A characteristic that is found in
60 percent of the population will be used to predict a rare event that
may occur in fewer than a third of the population.

The decision whether to adopt pretrial testing should not be mired in
a narrow debate regarding the unique contribution that drug-test information may provide to predicting pretrial misconduct. Rather, the
question should be posed, given all that is known about the link between drug abuse, crime, and associated problems in offenders, Are we
willing to bear the cost of having judges make decisions about whom to
release back into the community and the appropriate level of supervision, without the benefit of objective information about the defendant's
use of illicit drugs?

B. Postadjudication Testing Programs

Some questions about matching defendants to the right monitoring
or treatment program are being addressed in the Drug Testing Tech-
nology/Focused Offender Disposition Program funded by the U.S.
Bureau of Justice Assistance.[19] A new instrument, the Offender Profile
Index (OPI), is being developed to designate the appropriate intervention strategy for drug-involved offenders. The OPI measures severity

[19] Beth Weinman (1989), director of the project at the National Association of State
Alcohol and Drug Abuse Directors, provided these details.

of drug abuse, psychological and behavioral functioning, and criminal history information obtained from both self-reports and criminal justice records.

Beginning in December 1988, defendants sentenced in Birmingham, Phoenix, and Miami were assigned to receive urine monitoring or urine monitoring plus outpatient or residential treatment based on their OPI. Random assignment to control groups is also part of the design. The urine monitoring involves graduated sanctions leading to increasingly restrictive monitoring conditions. An evaluation of the effects of these conditions on drug use and criminal behavior is planned with preliminary findings to be available in 1990.[20]

Intensive supervision probation (ISP) programs have often encompassed urine monitoring. These programs differ from traditional probation programs primarily in the small number of clients assigned to each officer. The aim is to reduce caseloads so that an officer can maintain close surveillance of, and work more closely with, each probationer (Petersilia 1987). A higher number of contacts between the probationer and officer are required, sometimes as many as twenty-five to thirty per month, and some programs include visits to employers or family members. Rehabilitation, job placement, and treatment efforts are also more feasible in ISP programs. The Bureau of Justice Assistance has funded the establishment and assessment of ISP programs for drug offenders in four sites.[21] Unlike prior evaluations of ISP programs, these programs allow the evaluator to assign probationers randomly to the special drug ISP program or to a control non-ISP caseload to determine whether the intensive supervision affects outcomes. Sites differ according to the strategies employed. Among the various components in the programs are electronic monitoring, treatment, and urinalysis.

Although this evaluation is not completed, some findings from an

[20] At a meeting of the project directors from these programs (drug-testing/focused-offender disposition program interim data report meeting, Washington, D.C., July 13, 1989), it was decided that a urine-test result from each research subject must be available at the time the OPI is administered. The program originally obtained a specimen only after the person was assigned to a treatment, based on the OPI results. The researchers quickly learned, however, that many of the persons who had denied a history of drug abuse during the OPI assessment later tested positive. This was further evidence that the sophisticated self-report measures of drug abuse were not practical with an offender population. The new strategy would enable a person to be confronted with his positive urine test if he denied drug use on the OPI and thereby improve classification.

[21] Joan Petersilia of the RAND Corporation is directing this evaluation. State departments of corrections are participating in New Mexico, Georgia, Iowa, and Washington.

ISP program in Contra Costa County in California are available (Murakawa 1988). In January 1987, a special ISP program was established for adult drug offenders and street dealers in Richmond, California. One hundred seventy drug offenders were randomly assigned, one-half to an ISP program and one-half to regular probation caseloads. The program has been described as control oriented.[22] Improved access to residential treatment programs was sought and a Narcotics Anonymous chapter was established in the probation building.

The ISP program's primary means of surveillance was a random drug-testing system that required each probationer to phone in six days a week to determine whether he had to report within twenty-four hours to provide a urine specimen. During the first sixty days of supervision, twelve random tests were required of each probationer. The frequency of testing was then adjusted according to the probationer's progress and level of supervision. One weakness in this program was that the initial screening test was conducted using thin-layer chromatography, a relatively insensitive technique that results in a larger number of false negative test results than other tests.

Descriptive data from the department provide some insight into the effectiveness of the program. The drug offenders were difficult to control, with almost 30 percent of the caseload having outstanding warrants requested by the probation officer at any given time. Seventy-five of the eighty-five probationers assigned to urine testing submitted to testing (five were ineligible because the court did not order testing and five refused to submit and were incarcerated). Seventy-five percent of the tested probationers were positive at one time or another. Over one-half of the positive tests were for cocaine, and twenty-five persons tested positive for cocaine more than three times (the report concludes that twenty-five out of seventy-five or 33 percent of the tested probationers were addicted). Methamphetamine was the next most frequently detected drug (11 percent).

Most of the probationers designated as addicted absconded from the program, were rearrested, incarcerated, and then directed into residential treatment. Twenty-nine percent of the probationers in the program

[22] The description of the program states: "We have operated on the assumption that drug or drug-related offenders on probation are frequently in states of social and emotional instability and that the role of the probation officer is to move these defendants toward community stability and responsibility by control and counseling, drug testing, and drug treatment. If particular probationers are unable or unwilling to be directed towards community stability, then stability by use of sanctions or incarceration would be imposed" (Contra Costa Probation Department 1988).

366 Eric D. Wish and Bernard A. Gropper

participated in residential treatment, but only one has successfully completed treatment (seven were still enrolled at the time of this report). Over one-half of those referred to residential treatment programs left or were terminated for rule violations prior to ninety days.

The report notes that "our local residential treatment programs demonstrated an inability to deal with the uncooperative serious offender drug abuser. For this population, either a state institution or a locked treatment program may be most appropriate" (Murakawa 1988, p. 5). At the time of follow-up, 32 percent of the probationers had been arrested for subsequent offenses. The probation officers identified sixteen probationers (19 percent) as having been deterred from further drug use. The report concludes that "random drug testing works effectively as a surveillance and identification tool. Though not as effective as a deterrent as we had hoped, our data have consistently shown that from 15–20% of probationers are deterred from further drug use by the combination of drug testing, threat of incarceration and counseling" (Murakawa 1988, p. 8). The report also stressed the need to have the right types of treatment programs for hard-core criminal drug abusers.

While the conclusions in Murakawa (1988) are based on descriptive information and subjective assessments of the value of urine testing, they do underscore some of the more important limitations of urine monitoring. First, any urine-monitoring program is going to result in the identification of a large number of serious criminal drug abusers. Many of these persons are likely to abscond and to resist treatment. Specialized treatment programs may be required. Second, success rates are low, and expectations may have to be adjusted accordingly. This department was apparently satisfied with the 20 percent success rate in deterring drug use that they thought they had achieved.

A study of a urinalysis pilot project in ten facilities in Georgia demonstrates another possible limitation of urine monitoring of convicted offenders (Erwin 1985). On-site testing was established in a number of centers. In one site, Gateway, the percentage of persons who tested positive was initially high and then declined sharply. The laboratory technicians performed tests to detect if out-of-range readings on the urine tests were caused by contamination or dilution of specimens. A number of specimens were determined to have been tampered with, and the report concluded that the "Gateway Diversion Center is considered to have a population more sophisticated and street-wise in drug knowledge than residents of other diversion centers. Rather than indicating that testing had a deterrent effect at Gateway, the results suggest that during the latter half of the pilot this population was already finding ways to manipulate results. Not only is there evidence of dilution with salt, but there is also some evidence of a switch in the particular drug used" (Erwin 1985, p. 9). We know of at least one federal probation program that routinely tests the specific gravity of urine specimens to identify specimens that have been diluted (by adding water or drinking huge quantities before the test). There are numerous anecdotes in the literature regarding the great lengths to which users have gone to undermine urinalysis tests (Kaplan 1983; Hoffman 1987). Whenever an offender is aware that a specimen will be given, the possibility of deception must be raised.

C. The Drug Use Forecasting Program

The DUF program was pilot tested in New York City in 1986 (Wish 1987). As part of a research project in 1984, urine samples and a brief interview had been obtained from 4,847 males arrested over a six-month period. This study demonstrated that it was possible to obtain specimens and research interviews voluntarily from arrestees being processed in a large urban booking facility. Upon taking successive random samples of increasing numbers from these 4,847 specimens, it was determined that a sample of 200 of the specimens produced estimates of recent drug use that were virtually identical to using all 4,847.[23] In September 1986, researchers returned to Manhattan Central Booking to obtain specimens and interviews from 200 male arrestees. The percentage of persons who tested positive for opiates, PCP, or methadone was quite similar in 1984 and 1986 (Wish 1987). The dramatic difference occurred for cocaine, however, for which 82 percent tested positive in 1986, compared with 42 percent in 1984. Because of the size of the increase in cocaine use, two new samples of 200 were tested in October and November of 1986 and again more than 80 percent of the tested arrestees were positive for cocaine. This was consistent with news reports of a dramatic rise in crack use in New

---

[23] Subsequent analyses of DUF data verified that sample sizes of 200 produced estimates of drug positives that were close to those obtained using larger samples. Comparisons were made between the DUF sample and all arrestees tested in the District of Columbia during that month as part of the pretrial-testing program. A comparison of DUF results with those from a study of arrestees in New Orleans conducted by staff at the Research Triangle Institute also showed considerable similarity (McCalla and Collins 1989).

York City at this time. These findings demonstrated that a city might gain a valuable epidemiological tool for tracking drug-use trends in offenders by testing a sample of arrestees periodically.

In 1987, the DUF program was expanded to include several large cities across the United States. Priority was given to cities that had a central booking facility where enough arrestees were processed to provide a minimum of 200 male arrestees during a two-week period. The National Institute of Justice provides selected sites with the training and funds needed to obtain and process the data. With the exception of two sites (Portland, Oregon, and Phoenix) that operate their own testing laboratories, all specimens are mailed to one laboratory for analysis. Specimens are tested by EMIT for opiates, cocaine, PCP, marijuana, amphetamines, methadone, barbiturates, Darvon, Valium, and methaqualone. The last four drugs are rarely detected. (Confirmatory tests by GC are conducted for amphetamine positives only.) In 1988, the DUF system was operating in twenty-one cities with up to four additional sites to be added by the end of 1989. In addition to obtaining specimens from 200 male arrestees, in some sites with an adequate number of female arrestees, 100 females are sampled. Several sites (Washington, D.C.; San Diego, California; and Phoenix) plan to obtain samples of juveniles.

Specific sampling rules are followed at each DUF site. The often-chaotic nature of booking facilities does not lend itself to systematic random samples. Persons are approached as they become available during booking, and known sources of sample bias are minimized. Drug Use Forecasting samples are selected so as to limit the number of persons charged with petty offenses or drug offenses. Persons charged with traffic offenses or vagrancy are excluded. Where there is a choice of arrestees, persons are selected by arrest charge in the following order: nondrug felony, nondrug misdemeanor, drug felony, and drug misdemeanor. Because of their small number in most jurisdictions, all female arrestees are approached, regardless of charge. In practice, most persons in the DUF samples are charged with nondrug felony offenses.[24] Because persons charged with drug offenses are under-

---

[24] Repeated analyses have confirmed, however, that persons charged with felony offenses are about equally likely to test positive for drugs as persons charged with misdemeanor offenses. In addition, although persons charged with drug sale or possession are the category most likely to test positive, many of the persons charged with nondrug offenses also test positive. Therefore, even when persons charged with drug offenses are excluded from DUF samples, the percentage of persons that test positive drops by only a few percentage points.

sampled, the DUF estimates are conservative estimates of recent drug use in a jurisdiction. This is not a critical issue, however, as long as data-collection procedures remain the same each quarter because the DUF system is primarily intended to show trends in drug use over time rather than to provide exact estimates of drug use in the arrestee population at any one time.

Drug Use Forecasting results are often misinterpreted as providing evidence for the link between drug use and crime. While there is ample evidence in the literature for this connection (e.g., McGlothlin 1979; Robins 1979; Gandossy et al. 1980; Wish and Johnson 1986; Chaiken and Chaiken, in this volume), DUF urine-test results do not directly bear on this issue. A positive urine test can indicate only that the person probably used the drug in the twenty-four to forty-eight hours prior to providing the specimen (in the case of opiates, cocaine, amphetamines, methadone) or within the past month (in the case of PCP or marijuana). The drug use actually may have occurred prior to the crime, after the crime, before arrest, or even after arrest while in detention. The test therefore indicates nothing about whether the need for drugs was a motive for the crime. In addition, the test results say nothing about whether the arrestee was a chronic user or a casual experimenter. The results do indicate the types of drugs recently used by arrestees in a jurisdiction and changes in use trends.

Another limitation pertains to the self-reported interview information obtained as part of DUF. Persons are asked questions about their prior use and dependence on specific drugs, their means of administration, and their participation in treatment programs. Questions are also asked about whether fear of AIDS has influenced their needle-sharing behaviors. The answers to these questions, while internally consistent, are probably underestimates of these behaviors in this population. Prior research has shown that arrestees underreport illicit behaviors in a DUF-type interview but that the information that is disclosed tends to be valid (Wish 1988a).

Table 7 shows the positive urine-test results for the data available at the time of writing for all DUF sites that have tested male arrestees at least once. In each city, more than one-half of the males tested were positive for one or more drugs. Cocaine was the most prevalent drug in more than half of the cities sampled. The prevalence of recent drug use detected here overshadows the estimates of recent drug use found in national surveys of the general population or of students (Johnston et al. 1988; National Institute on Drug Abuse 1989). Only samples of per-

TABLE 7
Percentage of Male Arrestees Testing Positive for Drugs

City (Sample Size), Date of Test	Any Drug Including MJ	Any Drug Excluding MJ	Cocaine	MJ	Opiates	PCP	Amphs
Los Angeles (N = 289), 7/88	73	65	55	28	15	6	5
San Diego (N = 252), 7/88	83	73	38	55	20	4	39
Portland (N = 210), 8/88	76	62	48	48	14	0	19
Phoenix (N = 251), 4/88	66	42	31	46	6	. . .*	10
San Antonio (N = 206), 8/88	63	38	27	44	18	0	3
Dallas (N = 236), 6/88	72	59	53	44	8	. . .*	6
Omaha (N = 94), 7/88	57	27	20	45	1	0	7
Houston (N = 204), 4/88	69	57	54	45	4	0	1
Kansas City (N = 128), 11/88	54	44	41	19	2	2	2
St. Louis (N = 245), 10/88	56	47	38	16	6	9	0
Birmingham (N = 146), 7/88	75	53	51	45	5	0	. . .*
Indianapolis (N = 130), 6/88	54	23	15	42	4	0	0
Detroit (N = 167), 6/88	66	51	45	38	13	. . .*	0
Cleveland (N = 212), 11/88	68	58	52	26	4	4	0
New Orleans (N = 241), 7/88	73	58	53	54	8	6	0
Chicago (N = 227), 7/88	85	67	59	62	22	10	. . .*
Philadelphia (N = 274), 8/88	79	74	70	34	10	. . .*	. . .*
Fort Lauderdale (N = 193), 8/88	62	45	42	42	5	0	0
Miami (N = 182), 8/88	75	66	64	32	1	0	0
Washington, D.C. (N = 675), 5/88	. . .†	63	55	. . .†	17	30	1
New York (N = 257), 6/88	90	86	83	36	27	3	. . .*

SOURCE.—National Institute of Justice (1988).

NOTE.—MJ = marijuana; Amphs = amphetamines; PCP = phencyclidine. Test dates are given by month and year.

* Less than 1 percent.

† Data obtained from Washington, D.C., Pretrial Testing Program, which does not test for marijuana.

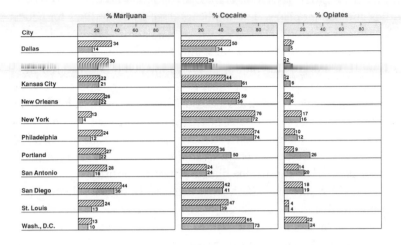

FIG. 2.—Marijuana, cocaine, and opiate use: percent of male and female arrestees testing positive. Source.—National Institute of Justice (1989).

sons enrolled in drug-abuse treatment programs would be expected to have higher rates of positive urine tests. Even Birmingham, Alabama, a relatively small city, had a high proportion of drug-positive tests. Considerable geographical variation occurs in the results. For example, PCP is primarily found in Washington, D.C., where it has a long history of use in the local culture. Amphetamines, usually methamphetamines or speed, are found largely on the West Coast. Drug injectors in these cities are likely to report having injected amphetamines, as well as cocaine and heroin. Marijuana, while prevalent, is found less frequently than cocaine in many cities, even though marijuana can be detected over much longer periods of time. The DUF results clearly document that massive drug use exists in the arrestee population in large cities.

Consistent with other research (Goldstein 1979; Inciardi 1986; Wish and Johnson 1986; Sanchez and Johnson 1987), female arrestees were found to be likely to be drug users (Wish, O'Neil, and Baldau 1990). As figure 2 indicates, females in some cities are even more likely than males to be positive for heroin or cocaine but less likely to be positive for marijuana. Females are more likely to report injecting drugs and therefore are at higher risk of contracting and transmitting the HIV virus. Finally, it appears that white females, although a small proportion of all females arrested, are more likely than other females to be injecting drugs and using opiates. The implications of these findings for educating arrestees about the risks of needle sharing and AIDS were discussed in an earlier report (Wish, O'Neil, and Baldau 1990).

Drug Use Forecasting findings have confirmed other research showing that drug users commit a variety of offenses. While persons charged with sale or possession of drugs are consistently those most likely to test positive for a drug, persons charged with other offenses are only somewhat less likely to test positive (National Institute of Justice 1988). Furthermore, whether a person is charged with a felony or a misdemeanor is unrelated to his likelihood of testing positive.

The DUF results have been used extensively by participating jurisdictions to document the levels of drug use among offenders. Participants in the National Institute on Drug Abuse's Community Epidemiology Work Group increasingly present DUF results when characterizing their state's drug trends (Community Epidemiological Work Group 1988). The results are also often used to bolster applications for federal and local anti-drug-abuse funds and grants. Drug Use Forecasting results in Phoenix were instrumental in influencing the passage of legislation in Arizona requiring pretrial drug testing and were a precipitant in San Diego for the establishment of a task force on drugs. Reliance on DUF results is expected to grow as more cities join the system and establish trend information.

D. Juvenile Drug Testing

The onset of illicit drug use, especially of marijuana and PCP, typically begins in early adolescence.[25] Injection of and dependence on drugs like heroin and cocaine tend to occur in the late teens. If those arrested youths who are using illicit drugs could be identified, it might be possible to intervene and thereby alter their likely progression to serious drug-abuse problems. In October 1986, the D.C. Pretrial Services Agency expanded its adult testing program to include testing of juvenile arrestees (persons under age eighteen).[26] The judges use the test results to set pretrial release conditions for the juveniles and to order follow-up monitoring for juveniles, pending adjudication. Juveniles may be sent to urine surveillance, drug-treatment programs, or both. Drug testing may also continue postadjudication, during probation or as part of a consent decree.

[25] More deviant youths who are arrested might be expected to initiate drug use even earlier. Adult arrestees interviewed as part of DUF frequently had median ages at onset of marijuana or PCP use before age fifteen.

[26] Details of the program have been supplied by Jay Carver (1989), director of the D.C. Pretrial Services Agency, and by Kathy Reade Boyer (1989), the project director.

Two groups of juveniles are tested. The first group consists of persons charged with serious offenses that require them to be detained pending arraignment and others whom the police believe should be detained. These youths are held overnight and tested in the morning in the court lockup. The second group consists of juveniles who are allowed to go home and return within forty-eight hours for testing. During the first year of the program, 4,182 youths were tested (Boyer and McCauley 1988). Of these, 35 percent tested positive for cocaine, marijuana, opiates, or PCP. The most often-detected drug was PCP, which appeared in 27 percent of the cases. This, of course, would be found only in Washington, D.C., which has a unique problem with PCP. Cocaine and marijuana were each found in 14 percent of those tested. Less than 1 percent tested positive for opiates. In the year-and-a-half that juveniles have been tested, the percentage testing positive for cocaine has tripled, from 8 percent in January 1987 to 25 percent in September 1988.[27] Females tended to be more likely to test positive than did males.

Figure 3 provides insight into the onset of frequent drug use (sufficient to make the person test positive at arrest) in a juvenile arrestee population (Boyer and McCauley 1988). No positive test results indicating drug use were found in persons below age eleven. Between 6 percent and 9 percent of those from ages eleven to thirteen tested positive. Beginning with age fourteen, there is a steady rise in the likelihood that a juvenile will test positive, rising from 17 percent at fourteen to 40 percent by age seventeen. Prevention programs may, therefore, have to start as early as age eleven. The results have also consistently shown that youths detained overnight are much more likely to test positive for drugs than are the youths released to the community with an order to appear for testing within forty-eight hours.[28] Thus, detained youths, those charged with serious offenses or viewed as dangerous by the police, are more likely to be recent drug

---

[27] Statistics from the general youth population put in perspective the prevalence of drug use in the detainee population. The national survey of high school seniors in 1986 found that 13 percent reported using cocaine at least once in the past year (Johnston, O'Malley, and Bachman 1988). The test results from juvenile detainees indicate that over 20 percent used cocaine within the past three days. The lower estimates from the student survey are probably caused by a number of factors, including use of self-reports to measure drug use, omission of youths who have dropped out of school, and differences in the level of deviance in the populations measured.

[28] One might suspect that the community-release youths would have an opportunity to abstain from drugs during the forty-eight hours and therefore would be less likely to test positive. However, both PCP and marijuana, drugs frequently found in juveniles, tend to be eliminated slowly from the body and may be detected weeks after use.

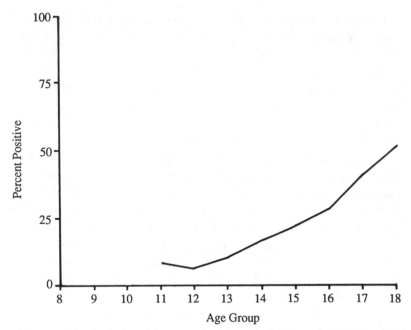

FIG. 3.—Juvenile drug use by age group measured by initial test in 1987 ($N = 4,182$ tests). Source.—Boyer and McCauley (1988, p. 8).

users. These results are consistent with those from a study of juveniles in Tampa, Florida, indicating that youths who test positive for drugs are likely to have worse criminal records than youths who do not test positive (Dembo et al. 1988, 1989).

The National Institute of Justice has funded Toborg Associates, Inc., to conduct an experiment designed to compare the relative efficacy of several drug-testing strategies with juveniles tested by the District of Columbia program. Youths are being randomly assigned to different drug-testing conditions, including weekly scheduled surveillance, random testing twice a month, referral to treatment with random testing once a month, and a control group. In addition, some youths who originally test negative are assigned to receive random testing one time each month. Measures of program outcome include the number of positive retests and rearrests. Results are expected in 1990.

One other research project examines the relation of juvenile urine-test results to prior and subsequent criminal behavior. Dembo and colleagues (Dembo, Washburn, Wish, Schmeidler, et al. 1987; Dembo, Washburn, Wish, Yeung, et al. 1987) began voluntary testing of youths entering the Tampa-based juvenile detention center in November 1985

(Dembo 1988). Their studies of male and female detainees have also found high rates of recent drug use in youths. Fifty-two percent of the sixty-six youths tested in November 1985 tested positive for marijuana. The youths who tested positive for cannabinoids had more than two times the number of prior nondrug felony referrals (mostly burglary, auto theft, and grand larceny) than did those youths who tested negative. A positive test for marijuana in youths may be the same type of indicator of high-rate criminal behavior in youths that a positive test for cocaine or heroin is for adults. The small number of youths who were recent users of cocaine also had more extensive criminal records. Statistically significant relations were found between illicit drug use and other childhood problems, including physical abuse, sexual victimization, and psychological adjustment (Dembo et al. 1988). Dembo et al. (1989) are completing follow-up studies of these youths that will provide more information regarding the subsequent drug use and crime in this cohort of juvenile detainees.

These findings highlight the potential usefulness that drug tests could have with the juvenile detainee population. It may be far easier to intervene with a youth who has a growing problem with marijuana than it is with the older adult who has already developed problems with drug injection and dependence. Thus, in addition to providing epidemiological information about recent drug use in crime-prone juveniles, a testing program may provide a tool for differentiating and treating those youths most likely to become the violent predators of tomorrow.

IV. Legal and Ethical Issues Involved in Drug Testing

This section addresses some of the important ethical and legal issues raised by drug testing and surveillance programs. A complete discussion of the legal and ethical issues involved would require a separate volume. One discussion of these issues as they relate to testing of probationers and parolees is available (del Carmen and Sorensen 1988), but the case law regarding drug testing is sizable and growing rapidly. The following review is, accordingly, neither exhaustive in coverage nor authoritative in tone (or aim); it is instead intended to illustrate a number of the major ethical and legal issues raised in drug testing in the criminal justice system. Cases challenging President Reagan's Executive Order 12564 requiring each executive agency to establish drug testing for employees in sensitive positions are just beginning to reach the Supreme Court.[29] These decisions, while concerned with federal employees, may affect testing in other contexts.

A. *Ethical Concerns*

Obtaining a urine specimen can be an intrusive procedure. There is ample anecdotal evidence of the great lengths that people will go to avoid detection by urinalysis. Persons who have advance warning of testing have designed ingenious mechanical devices to enable them to substitute clean urine for their own. They may also attempt to dilute their specimens with water or to add a substance that will contaminate the test. It is critical to observe carefully the voiding of urine and the handling of the specimens taken from criminal justice detainees, who may feel a special need to avoid detection.

The decision whether this invasion of privacy is acceptable is generally determined by the court's weighing of the burden of this intrusion on personal privacy against the state's need to test. One analogy might be the use of "strip searches" for weapons and contraband; arrestees may be strip searched to uncover concealed weapons because of the possible danger to others. However, should an arrestee whose guilt or innocence has not yet been determined be required to submit to urine testing? Obtaining a specimen from detainees in the criminal justice system is probably not much more intrusive than other routine behaviors expected of arrestees. Criminal justice detainees generally are housed under conditions of, at best, limited privacy. Detention facilities often have plumbing facilities in full view of guards and others so that the prisoner is never out of sight. This potential intrusion of testing must be weighed against the potential cost to the community if a judge releases a person without knowledge of his drug-abuse pattern.

Another ethical question concerns the use of test information: is providing the specimen to be voluntary? If so, should there be an informed-consent procedure so that the person understands the rights that he may be giving up by providing a specimen? The voluntary

---

[29] Two cases challenging the constitutionality of drug testing have been before the court. The first (*Skinner v. Railway Labor Executives Association*, no. 87–1555, 1987), brought by rail employees, sought to determine the legality of a program that requires urine and blood samples of train workers involved in accidents. The second case (*National Treasury Employees Union v. William von Raab*, no. 86–1879, 1986) challenged the right of the government to require testing of new Customs Service employees and those seeking promotions to jobs that involve the carrying of a weapon, fighting drugs, or dealing with classified material. The court upheld the right of the government to require drug testing in both cases.

urine specimens obtained by staff of the D.C. Pretrial Services Agency
are primarily used to set pretrial-release conditions. However, the statute governing the use of information collected by this agency allows the
information to be subpoenaed to impeach a witness's testimony. In one
case (*Jones v. United States*, 548 A.2d 35 [D.C. 1988]), a defendant
testified during his trial that he had no experience with cocaine and
therefore was not sure that the material he had "found on the street"
was cocaine. The prosecutor subpoenaed the defendant's pretrial test
result, which was positive for cocaine, in order to impeach his testimony. Should the arrestee have been told that by providing a urine
specimen he might be giving the prosecutor information that could be
used against him if he testified in his defense? Should the arrestee's
attorney be consulted before he agrees to provide a specimen? Furthermore, how far should a positive test result follow a person? Should a
person be labeled a drug user on the basis of a single test result that
could be referred to at all subsequent proceedings? The answers to
questions like these will probably depend on which stage of criminal
justice system processing the person is in. Ethical concerns are greatest
when testing persons at the pretrial stage before guilt has been determined (Wish, Toborg, and Bellassai 1988). It is conceivable that a
person arrested for a nondrug offense could test positive at arrest, be
assigned to urine monitoring, and, on testing positive repeatedly, receive greater penalties for violating his release conditions than he would
have received for his original charge at arrest. The ethical problems are
arguably less when testing probationers and parolees, however, because these persons have been convicted of a crime and are released to
the community with a number of conditions, including abstinence from
illicit drug abuse. Probation and parole officers typically already have
the authority to order drug testing. Ethical issues like these must be
debated and decided before a testing program is established.

B. Legal Issues

A growing body of case law examines drug testing inside and outside
the criminal justice system. Constitutional issues often concern Fourth
Amendment protections against illegal searches and seizures and Fourteenth Amendment due process rights. We discuss each of these issues
below.

Is it proper for the government to order random drug testing in the
absence of reasons to suspect a person of using? It is argued by civil
libertarians that the intrusiveness and invasion of privacy costs are too

great to justify the testing of persons at random, in the absence of clear indication that drug use will be found. "Federal and state courts that have recently considered mandatory drug testing requirements imposed by government authority have held them to be unreasonable and therefore unconstitutional if they were not based on a standard of *individualized suspicion*" (Adler 1986).

The courts have sustained mandatory testing, however, when there have been unique institutional requirements. For example, tests for jockeys have been upheld in the context of regulation of the racetrack industry and efforts at reduction of criminal influences in it (*Shoemaker v. Handel*, 479 U.S. 986 [1986]), for prison inmates for security needs (*Storms v. Coughlin*, 600 F. Supp. 1214 [1984]), and in the military (*Committee for G.I. Rights v. Callaway*, 370 F. Supp. 934 [1974]).

The right of the criminal justice system to order random testing of all persons in a given class (arrestees, probationers, or parolees) has yet to be determined. Most of the legal challenges have been directed toward testing of employee populations, among whom drug use tends to be relatively rare. The DUF information showing that more than one-half of all arrestees in the largest cities test positive for drugs may be sufficient to establish that the likelihood of drug use among all criminal justice detainees is sufficient to permit random drug testing. The established link in the research literature between crime rates and frequent drug use also argues for drug testing in order to protect society.

Due process considerations under the Fourteenth Amendment concern the rights of a person to a fair testing procedure. This means that the validity of the tests used and the procedures for conducting tests and recording test results must be reliable. Some decisions have explicitly outlined the proper chain of custody procedures to follow (*Wykoff v. Resig*, 613 F. Supp. 1504 [1985]).

The validity of urine tests is often measured in court by what is known as the Frye test. Scientific evidence, including test results, is considered valid if it has received "general scientific acceptance" (*Frye v. United States*, 293 F. 1013 [1923]). Court decisions regarding test validity tend to vary from jurisdiction to jurisdiction. Some courts have ruled that an unconfirmed EMIT test is sufficiently reliable to serve as a basis for punitive actions (*Smith v. State*, 250 Ga. 438, 298 S.E. 2d 482 [1983]; *Jensen v. Lick*, 589 F. Supp. 35 [1984]). Others have ruled that an EMIT test must be confirmed by a second EMIT test (*Peranzo v. Coughlin*, 608 F. Supp. 1504 [1985]) or by an alternative method (*Kane v. Fair*, 33 Cr. L. 2492 [1983]; *Higgs v. Wilson*, 616 F. Supp. 226 [1985];

Johnson v. Walton, No. 561–84 Rm [1985]) The EMIT tests have been most widely used to screen for drugs, and a considerable case law exists for this technology. The District of Columbia Court of Appeals reviewed the scientific validity of the EMIT test and gave it a broad endorsement: "We therefore rely primarily on a trial court decision from our own jurisdiction, based on expert scientific evidence in a record with which we are familiar and in which we have confidence because of the thoroughness with which counsel tried the case and the judge evaluated the evidence. We rely secondarily on, and thus confirm our judgment by reference to, judicial opinions from other jurisdictions which have reached the same result. We conclude that EMIT test results are presumptively reliable and thus generally admissible into evidence in every case" (*Jones v. U.S.*, 548 A.2d 35 [D.C. 1988]).

New screening tests are at a disadvantage in court challenges until their specific technology has been sufficiently used to convince the court that it has received general scientific acceptance. Radioimmunoassay of hair, for example, will probably require considerable comparisons with EMIT and GC/MS results and use by a larger number of scientists before the technique will be accepted in court.

Court decisions regarding the validity of urine tests tend to be overly general. Decisions sometimes imply that a particular technique is appropriate without regard to the drug being detected. While a single or second EMIT test may be valid proof of cocaine use, that standard may not be appropriate for the EMIT test for amphetamines. Because the amphetamine test may cross-react with other over-the-counter drugs, a confirmation technique that can differentiate these types of drugs, like gas chromatography or GC/MS, is more appropriate. The current situation of widely differing testing standards and procedures across the country should be replaced by acceptable scientific guidelines tailored to the needs of the criminal justice system.

V. Future Research Possibilities

The development of testing technology is in many respects a simpler task than the job of responsibly using the tests. The temptation exists to think that the tests themselves somehow provide an answer to the drug-crime problem rather than to see them merely as a means for measuring and uncovering drug use. In this section we discuss some of the research and policy issues that need to be addressed if the criminal justice system is to use drug tests responsibly and effectively.

What Does a Positive Test Result Mean? We need to know what a positive test result indicates about a person's drug use and criminality. Some research has looked at the relation between drug-test results at arrest and pretrial misconduct. However, we know little about how a positive test result relates to behavior on probation or parole. Furthermore, we know virtually nothing about how a positive test result relates to a person's likelihood of drug dependence. For example, what proportion of persons who test positive for a particular drug are casual experimental users rather than chronic abusers? Can we develop strategies for estimating a person's risk of serious drug abuse and crime on the basis of drug-test results, criminal record, and personal characteristics? How do persons who test positive for use of two or more drugs differ from those who test positive for only one drug? How does the type of drug detected affect all of these issues?

What Treatment Strategies Are Effective for Drug Users?   With the introduction of drug testing by the criminal justice system, many more drug users will be identified than ever before. Yet we know relatively little about strategies to reduce their drug use. What type of treatment is most effective for what type of user? What percentage of persons assigned to urine monitoring can we expect to remain in the program and have successful outcomes? Does urine monitoring alone produce reductions in drug use and crime and, if so, for what types of users? Can urine monitoring deter others from using drugs? How should a urine-monitoring program be operated? How frequently should we test, and what types of actions should we take for positive test results? Can we test juvenile detainees and prevent their progression to greater drug abuse?

Evaluating Hair Analysis.   Earlier, we discussed a number of unresolved questions regarding hair-analysis techniques. They need to be tested by many independent researchers. Controlled comparisons should be made between self-reports of drug use, urinalysis, and hair analysis. We need to understand the limits of hair analysis. Can environmental contamination be eliminated? How accurate is sectional analysis? What methods will offenders develop to thwart the test? Can the cost and turnaround time be reduced?

Standardization of Procedures.   Uniform guidelines for the use of drug tests by the criminal justice system need to be developed. The competence of testing laboratories varies greatly, and high rates of false negative results appear to be the norm (Davis et al. 1988). A national proficiency testing and training program should be established to promote the responsible use of drug tests. Model legislation should be be required to facilitate and control drug testing of criminal justice detainees and convicted offenders.

Development of Portable Tests.   The development of small portable screening tests could make drug testing much more practical for the criminal justice system. Test manufacturers have already developed some disposable, very rapid assays for drugs of abuse. For example, one manufacturer has developed a small portable test (on a card about 2 inches × 6 inches) that can detect a single drug (or drug class) in about three minutes. These tests are being tried out in the criminal justice system. With them, a parole or probation officer can quickly test a suspected drug user during a routine home or office visit. Pilot studies of the use of these portable tests (e.g., On-Track) suggest that they affect rates of confession of drug use in excess of 90 percent (Henderson 1989). Tests might even be conducted at the point of arrest, as is the case with Breathalyzers for a drunk-driving arrest. While it is expected that other portable urine tests will be developed in the future, additional research is needed to determine the most effective ways for criminal justice staff to use them.

Refinement of National Estimates of Drug Use.   We noted earlier that the rates of drug use found in arrestees in DUF programs are many times higher than those found in the national surveys of the general population. We need to know more about the nature of these differences. Would the estimates of drug use in the household or high school surveys be closer to those from arrestees if drug use were measured by urine tests rather than self-reports? Should a multimethod strategy (self-report, urine test, hair test) be adopted for measuring drug use? Are arrestees more likely to be using drugs than other persons from the same neighborhood and socioeconomic class? How can the estimates of drug use in arrestees be incorporated in national estimates of drug use? The answers to such questions would enable us to place arrestee drug use in a larger societal perspective and to improve the measurement of national drug-use trends so that more effective policy options can be pursued.

Policy.   A major concern that is raised by administrators faced with the decision whether to introduce drug testing into the criminal justice system is the lack of law enforcement and treatment resources to address drug problems in the large group of abusers who will be identified. These problems take on added urgency in the light of the president's recommendation (White House 1989) that states be required to adopt drug-testing programs for arrestees, prisoners, parolees, and those released on bail (compliance would be required to remain eligible to receive federal criminal justice funds). Some persons have suggested that placing the criminal drug abuser into a drug-abuse treatment program (accompanied by urine surveillance) is less expensive than long-term incarceration and will reduce recidivism, jail overcrowding, and drug abuse (American Correctional Association 1979; Wexler, Lipton, and Johnson 1988). However, the costs of testing programs and of expanding treatment resources are viewed by many city officials as insurmountable problems. There is a critical need for cost-benefit analyses of the potential long-term savings to be achieved by identifying and treating criminal drug abusers so that policymakers can make rational decisions about drug testing.

REFERENCES

Adler, A. R. 1986. Testimony before the Subcommittee on Human Resources, Committee on Post Office and Civil Service. U.S. House of Representatives, September 25.

American Correctional Association. 1979. *Drug Abuse Testing: Successful Models for Treatment and Control in Correctional Programs.* Washington, D.C.: American Correctional Association.

Anderson, T. E. 1985. "Laboratory Evaluation of the Los Angeles Police Department's Drugged Driver Detection Procedures." Research notes. Washington, D.C.: U.S. Department of Transportation, National Highway Transportation Safety Administration.

Anglin, D. 1988. "The Efficacy of Civil Commitment in Treating Narcotic Addiction." In *Compulsory Treatment of Drug Abuse: Research and Clinical Practice,* edited by C. G. Leukefeld and F. M. Tims. National Institute on Drug Abuse Research Monograph no. 86. Rockville, Md.: U.S. Department of Health and Human Services, National Institute on Drug Abuse.

Anglin, M. D., and Y. Hser. In this volume. "Treatment of Drug Abuse."

Bachman, J. G., L. D. Johnston, and P. M. O'Malley. 1986. *Monitoring the Future: Questionnaire Responses from the Nation's High School Seniors.* Ann Arbor: University of Michigan.

Ball, J. C., L. Rosen, J. A. Flueck, and D. N. Nurco. 1981. "The Criminality of Heroin Addicts When Addicted and Off Opiates." In *The Drugs-Crime Connection,* edited by J. A. Inciardi. Beverly Hills, Calif.: Sage.

Baumgartner, A. M., P. F. Jones, W. A. Baumgartner, and C. T. Black. 1979. "Radioimmunoassay of Hair for Determining Opiate-Abuse Histories." *Journal of Nuclear Medicine* 20:748–52.

Baumgartner, A. M., P. F. Jones, and O. T. Black. 1901. "Detection of Phencyclidine in Hair." *Journal of Forensic Science* 26:576–81.

Baumgartner, A. M., C. T. Black, P. F. Jones, and W. H. Blahd. 1982. "Radioimmunoassay of Cocaine in Hair: Concise Communication." *Journal of Nuclear Medicine* 23:790–92.

Belenko, S., and I. Mara-Drita. 1988. "Drug Use and Pretrial Misconduct: The Utility of Pre-arraignment Drug Tests as a Predictor of Failure-to-Appear." Unpublished manuscript. New York: Criminal Justice Agency.

Blanke, R. V. 1986. "Accuracy in Urinalysis." In *Urine Testing for Drugs of Abuse*, edited by R. L. Hawks and C. N. Chiang. Rockville, Md.: U.S. Department of Health and Human Services, National Institute on Drug Abuse.

Bonito, A. J., D. N. Nurco, and J. W. Shaffer. 1976. "The Veridicality of Addicts' Self-Reports in Social Research." *International Journal of Addictions* 11(5):719–24.

Boyer, K. R. 1989. Personal communication with authors, March.

Boyer, K. R., and M. McCauley. 1988. "1987 Juvenile Drug Use Trends and Findings." Report. Washington, D.C.: D.C. Pretrial Services Agency.

Bray, R. M., M. E. Marsden, L. L. Guess, S. C. Wheeless, D. K. Pate, G. H. Duntemann, and V. G. Iannacchione. 1988. "1988 Worldwide Survey of Alcohol and Non-medical Drug Use among Military Personnel." Technical Report no. 4000/06-03FR. Research Triangle Park, N.C.: Research Triangle Institute.

Bureau of Justice Assistance. 1988a. *Treatment Alternatives to Street Crime.* Washington, D.C.: Bureau of Justice Assistance.

———. 1988b. *Urinalysis as Part of a Treatment Alternatives to Street Crime (TASC) Program.* Washington, D.C.: Bureau of Justice Assistance.

———. 1989. *Drug Recognition Program.* Washington, D.C.: Bureau of Justice Assistance.

Carver, J. A. 1986. "Drugs and Crime: Controlling Use and Reducing Risk through Testing." *NIJ Reports.* Washington, D.C.: U.S. Department of Justice, National Institute of Justice.

———. 1989. Personal communication with authors, March.

Chaiken, J. M., and M. R. Chaiken. In this volume. "Drugs and Predatory Crime."

Chang, J. Y. 1987. "Drug Testing and Interpretation of Results." *PHARM-CHEM Newsletter* 16(1):1–12.

Cohen, S. 1986. "The Military Worldwide Surveys: Deterrent Effects of Urine Testing on Drug Use." *Drug Abuse & Alcoholism Newsletter* 15(9):1–3.

Collins, J. J. 1986. "The Relationship of Problem Drinking to Individual Offending Sequences." In *Criminal Careers and "Career Criminals,"* vol. 2, edited by A. Blumstein, J. Cohen, J. A. Roth, and C. Visher. Washington, D.C.: National Academy Press.

Collins, J. J., and M. Allison. 1983. "Legal Coercion and Retention in Drug Abuse Treatment." *Hospital Community Psychiatry* 14(12):1145–49.

Community Epidemiology Work Group. 1988. *Epidemiologic Trends in Drug Abuse*, Proceedings. Washington, D.C.: U.S. Department of Health and Human Services, National Institute on Drug Abuse, December.

Compton, R. P. 1986. *Field Evaluation of the Los Angeles Police Department Drug Detection Procedures*. Report no. DOT HS-807-012. Washington, D.C.: National Highway Transportation Safety Administration, Department of Transportation.

Contra Costa Probation Department. 1988. "Department memo." Martinez, Calif.: Contra Costa Probation Department.

Cornelius, R. 1973. "Neutron Activation Analysis of Hair: Failure of a Mission." *Journal of Radioanalysis Chemistry* 15:305–16.

Davis, K. H., R. L. Hawks, and R. V. Blanke. 1988. "Assessment of Laboratory Quality in Urine Drug Testing: A Proficiency Testing Pilot Study." *Journal of the American Medical Association* 260(12):1749–54.

del Carmen, R. V., and J. R. Sorensen. 1988. "Legal Issues in Drug Testing Probationers and Parolees." *Federal Probation* 52(4):19–27.

DeAntonio, S. M., S. A. Katz, D. M. Scheiner, and J. D. Wood. 1982. "Anatomically-related Variations in Trace-Metal Concentrations in Hair." *Clinical Chemistry* 28:2411–13.

Dembo, R. 1988. *Overview of Drug Use and Delinquency among Youth*. Washington, D.C.: American Correctional Association.

Dembo, R., M. Washburn, E. D. Wish, J. Schmeidler, A. Getreu, B. Estrellita, L. Williams, and W. R. Blount. 1987. "Further Examination of the Association between Heavy Marijuana Use and Crime among Youths Entering a Juvenile Detention Center." *Journal of Psychoactive Drugs* 19:361–72.

Dembo, R., M. Washburn, E. D. Wish, H. Yeung, A. Getreu, E. Berry, and W. Blount. 1987. "Heavy Marijuana Use and Crime among Youths Entering a Juvenile Detention Center." *Journal of Psychoactive Drugs* 19:47–56.

Dembo, R., L. Williams, B. Estrellita, A. Getreu, M. Washburn, E. D. Wish, J. Schmeidler, and M. Dertke. 1988. "The Relationship between Physical and Sexual Abuse and Illicit Drug Use: A Replication among a New Sample of Youths Entering a Juvenile Detention Center." *International Journal of the Addictions* 23(11):1101–23.

Dembo, R., L. Williams, E. D. Wish, and J. Schmeidler. 1989. *Urine Testing of Juvenile Detainees: A Tool for Identifying Youths at High Risk of Future Drug Use and Delinquency*. Executive summary. Washington, D.C.: U.S. Department of Justice, National Institute of Justice.

DuPont, R. L. 1977. "Operation Trip-Wire: A New Proposal Focused on Criminal Heroin Addicts." Speech before the Federal Bar Association Convention, Washington, D.C., October.

DuPont, R. L., and N. J. Kozel. 1976. "Heroin Use and Crime." Paper presented at the annual meeting of the American Psychiatric Association, Miami Beach, Fla., May.

Erwin, B. S. 1985. "Evaluation of Urinalysis Pilot Project." Unpublished report. Atlanta: Department of Offender Rehabilitation, Office of Evaluation.

Federal Register. 1988. Untitled article. 53(69):11983.

Forst, B., and E. D. Wish. 1983. "Drug Use and Crime: Providing a Missing Link." In *Violent Crime in America*, edited by K. R. Feinberg. Washington, D.C.: National Policy Exchange.

Gandossy, R. P., J. R. Williams, J. Cohen, and H. J. Harwood. 1980. *Drugs and Crime: A Survey and Analysis of the Literature*. Washington, D.C.: U.S. Department of Justice, National Institute of Justice.

Goldblum, R. W., L. R. Goldbaum, and W. N. Piper. 1954. "Barbiturate Concentrations in the Skin and Hair of Guinea Pigs." *Journal of Investigative Dermatology* 22:121–28.

Goldkamp, J., and M. R. Gottfredson. 1981. *Bail Decisionmaking: A Study of Policy Guidelines*. Washington, D.C.: National Institute of Corrections.

Goldstein, P. 1979. *Prostitution and Drugs*. Lexington, Mass.: Lexington.

Gottfredson, S. D., and D. M. Gottfredson. 1986. "Accuracy of Prediction Models." In *Criminal Careers and "Career Criminals,"* vol. 2, edited by A. Blumstein, J. Cohen, J. A. Roth, and C. Visher. Washington, D.C.: National Academy Press.

Gropper, B. A. 1985. "Probing the Links between Drugs and Crime." *Research in Brief*. Washington, D.C.: U.S. Department of Justice, National Institute of Justice.

————. 1987*a*. "Drug Detection through Hair Analysis: Developing Future Capabilities." In *Controlling Drug Abuse and Crime: A Research Update*, edited by M. G. Graham. Washington, D.C.: U.S. Department of Justice, National Institute of Justice.

————. 1987*b*. "Advancing the State of the Art in Drug Testing." Paper presented at the annual meeting of the American Society of Criminology, San Francisco, November.

————. 1988*a*. "Drug Detection: Developing New Approaches for Criminal Justice Questions." Paper presented at the annual meeting of the Academy of Criminal Justice Sciences, San Francisco, April.

————. 1988*b*. "Drug Testing and Hair Analysis." Paper presented at the National Alliance of State Drug Enforcement Agencies Conference, Jackson Hole, Wyo., May.

Hall, F. 1988. "On the Lookout for New and Future Street Drugs: Update on Designer Drugs and Controlled Substance Analogs." Unpublished manuscript. Miami: Up Front Drug Information Center.

Hansen, H. J., S. P. Caudill, and D. J. Boone. 1985. "Crisis in Drug Testing: Results of a CDC Blind Study." *Journal of the American Medical Association* 253:2382–87.

Harkey, M. R., and G. L. Henderson. 1988. "Hair Analysis for Drugs of Abuse: A Critical Review of the Technology." Final report submitted to the California Department of Alcohol and Drug Programs, Sacramento.

Harrell, A. V. 1985. "Validation of Self-Report: The Research Record." In *Self-Report Methods of Estimating Drug Use*, edited by B. A. Rouse, N. Kozel, and L. Richards. National Institute on Drug Abuse Research Monograph no. 57. Rockville, Md.: U.S. Department of Health and Human Services, National Institute on Drug Abuse.

Harrison, W. H., R. M. Gray, and L. M. Solomon. 1974. "Incorporation of D-Amphetamine into Pigmented Guinea Pig Hair." *British Journal of Dermatology* 91:415–18.

Hawks, R. L. 1986. "Analytic Methodology." In *Urine Testing for Drugs of Abuse*, edited by R. L. Hawks and C. N. Chiang. National Institute on Drug Abuse Research Monograph no. 73. Rockville, Md.: U.S. Department of Health and Human Services, National Institute on Drug Abuse.

Hawks, R. L., and C. N. Chiang, eds. 1986. *Urine Testing for Drugs of Abuse*. National Institute on Drug Abuse Research Monograph no. 73. Rockville, Md.: U.S. Department of Health and Human Services, National Institute on Drug Abuse.

Henderson, A. 1989. "Remarks." Comment presented at the fourteenth annual training institute of the American Probation and Parole Association, Milwaukee, August.

Hoffman, A. 1987. *Steal This Urine Test*. New York: Penguin.

Hoyt, D. W., R. F. Finnigan, T. Nee, T. F. Shults, and T. J. Butler. 1987. "Drug Testing in the Workplace—Are Methods Legally Defensible?" *Journal of the American Medical Association* 258(4):504–9.

Inciardi, J. A. 1986. *The War on Drugs*. Palo Alto, Calif.: Mayfield.

Ishiyama, I., T. Nagai, and S. Toshida. 1983. "Detection of Basic Drugs (Methamphetamine, Antidepressants and Nicotine) from Human Hair." *Journal of Forensic Science* 28:380–85.

Jaffe, J. H. 1973. "The Pitfalls of Promulgating Policy." *Pharmacologist* 15(1):53–59.

Johnson, B. D., P. Goldstein, E. Preble, J. Schmeidler, D. S. Lipton, B. Spunt, and T. Miller. 1985. *Taking Care of Business: The Economics of Crime by Heroin Users*. Lexington, Mass.: Lexington.

Johnston, L. D., P. M. O'Malley, and J. G. Bachman. 1988. *Illicit Drug Use, Smoking, and Drinking by America's High School Students, College Students and Young Adults 1975–87*. Rockville, Md.: U.S. Department of Health and Human Services, National Institute on Drug Abuse.

Joseph, H. 1970. "A Probation Department Treats Heroin Addicts." *Federal Probation* 34(2):35–39.

Journal of the American Medical Association's Council on Scientific Affairs. 1987. "Scientific Issues in Drug Testing." *Journal of the American Medical Association* 257(22):3110–14.

Kaplan, J. 1983. *The Hardest Drug: Heroin and Drug Policy*. Chicago: University of Chicago Press.

Kleiman, M. 1986. "Data and Analysis Requirements for Policy toward Drug Enforcement and Organized Crime." In *America's Habit: Drug Abuse, Drug Trafficking, and Organized Crime*, edited by the President's Commission on Organized Crime. Washington, D.C.: U.S. Government Printing Office.

Leukefeld, C. G., and F. M. Tims. 1988. "Compulsory Treatment: A Review of Findings." In *Compulsory Treatment of Drug Abuse: Research and Clinical Practice*, edited by C. G. Leukefeld and F. M. Tims. National Institute on Drug Abuse Research Monograph no. 86. Rockville, Md.: U.S. Department of Health and Human Services, National Institute on Drug Abuse.

McCalla, M. F., and J. J. Collins. 1989. "Patterns of Drug Use among Male Arrestees in Three Urban Areas." Mimeographed. Research Triangle Park, N.C.: Research Triangle Institute.

McGlothlin, W. H. 1979. "Drugs and Crime." In *Handbook on Drug Abuse*, edited by R. L. Dupont, A. Goldstein, and J. O'Donnell. Rockville, Md.: U.S. Department of Health and Human Services, National Institute on Drug Abuse.

McGlothlin, W. H., M. D. Anglin, and B. D. Wilson. 1977. *An Evaluation of the California Civil Addict Program*. National Institute on Drug Abuse Research Monograph Series. Rockville, Md.: National Institute on Drug Abuse.

Magura, S., R. C. Freeman, Q. Siddiqi, and D. S. Lipton. 1989. "The Validity of Radioimmunoassay of Hair for Detecting Cocaine and Heroin Use among Addicts." Unpublished manuscript. New York: Narcotic and Drug Research, Inc.

Magura, S., D. Goldsmith, C. Casriel, P. J. Goldstein, and D. S. Lipton. 1987. "The Validity of Methadone Clients' Self-reported Drug Use." *International Journal of the Addictions* 22(8):727–49.

Manili, B. A., E. F. Connors III, D. W. Stephens, and J. R. Stedman. 1987. *Police Drug Testing*. Issues and Practices series. Washington, D.C.: U.S. Department of Justice, National Institute of Justice.

Martz, R. M. 1988. "The Identification of Cocaine in Hair by GC/MS and MS/MS." *Crime Laboratory Digest* 15(3):67–73.

Miike, L., and M. Hewitt. 1988. "Accuracy and Validity of Urine Drug Testing." *University of Kansas Law Review* 36(4):641–81.

Morgan, J. P. 1984. "Problems of Mass Screening of Misused Drugs." *Journal of Psychoactive Drugs* 16(4):305–17.

Murakawa, Y. 1988. Internal memorandum, July 29. Washington, D.C.: U.S. Department of Justice, Bureau of Justice Assistance.

Nadelmann, E. 1988. "The Great Drug Debate: I. The Case for Legislation." *Public Interest* 92:3–31.

National Institute of Justice. 1988. *Drug Use Forecasting*. Washington, D.C.: U.S. Department of Justice, National Institute of Justice.

———. 1989. *Drug Use Forecasting, First Quarter 1989*. Washington, D.C.: U.S. Department of Justice, National Institute of Justice.

National Institute on Drug Abuse. 1979. *Monitoring Drug Use in the Community through a Jail Urine Screening Program*. U.S. Department of Health and Human Services, National Institute on Drug Abuse. Washington, D.C.: U.S. Government Printing Office.

———. 1988a. *Data from the Drug Abuse Warning Network (DAWN)*. Ser. 1, no. 7. Rockville, Md.: U.S. Department of Health and Human Services, National Institute on Drug Abuse.

———. 1988b. *Development and Implementation of a Probability Sample Design for the Drug Abuse Warning Network (DAWN)*. Rockville, Md.: U.S. Department of Health and Human Services, National Institute on Drug Abuse.

———. 1989. *National Household Survey on Drug Abuse: Population Estimates*

1988. Rockville, Md.: U.S. Department of Health and Human Services, National Institute on Drug Abuse.

Niwaguchi T., S. Suzuki, and T. Inoue. 1983. "Determination of Methamphetamine in Hair after Single and Repeated Administration to Rats." *Archives of Toxicology* 52:157–64.

Nurco, D. N. 1979. "Etiological Aspects of Drug Abuse." In *Handbook on Drug Abuse,* edited by R. L. DuPont, A. Goldstein, and J. O'Donnell. Rockville, Md.: U.S. Department of Health and Human Services, National Institute on Drug Abuse.

O'Malley, P., W. H. McGlothlin, and H. Ginzburg. 1977. "Measurement Content." In *Conducting Followup Research on Drug Treatment Programs,* edited by L. D. Johnston, D. N. Nurco, and L. N. Robins. U.S. Department of Health, Education, and Welfare Publication no. (ADM) 78-487. Washington, D.C.: U.S. Government Printing Office.

Petersilia, J. 1987. *Expanding Options for Criminal Sentencing.* Santa Monica, Calif.: RAND.

Puschel, K., P. Thomasch, and W. Arnold. 1983. "Opiate Levels in Hair." *Forensic Science International* 21:181–86.

Reuter, P. 1988. "The Great Drug Debate: III. Can the Borders Be Sealed?" *Public Interest* 92:51–65.

Reuter, P., G. Crawford, and J. Cave. 1988. *Sealing the Borders.* Santa Monica, Calif.: RAND.

Robins, L. N. 1974. *The Vietnam Drug User Returns.* Special Action Office Monograph, ser. A, no. 2. Rockville, Md.: U.S. Department of Health and Human Services, National Institute on Drug Abuse.

———. 1979. "Addict Careers." In *Handbook on Drug Abuse,* edited by R. L. DuPont, A. Goldstein, and J. O'Donnell. Rockville, Md.: U.S. Department of Health and Human Services, National Institute on Drug Abuse.

Robins, L. N., J. E. Helzer, M. Hesselbrock, and E. D. Wish. 1980. "Vietnam Veterans Three Years after Vietnam: How Our Study Changed Our View of Heroin." In *Yearbook of Substance Abuse,* edited by L. Brill and C. Winick. New York: Human Sciences Press.

Robins, L. N., and E. D. Wish. 1977. "Development of Childhood Deviance: A Study of 223 Urban Black Men from Birth to 18." In *Child Psychiatry Treatment and Research,* edited by M. F. McMillian and S. Henao. New York: Brunner/Mazel.

Roth, J. A., and P. B. Wice. 1980. *Pretrial Release and Misconduct in the District of Columbia.* Washington, D.C.: Institute for Law and Social Research.

Sanchez, J. E., and B. D. Johnson. 1987. "Women and the Drugs-Crime Connection: Crime Rates among Drug Abusing Women at Rikers Island." *Journal of Psychoactive Drugs* 19(2):205–16.

Sexton, T. R., and U. Zilz. 1988. "On the Wisdom of Mandatory Drug Testing." *Journal of Policy Analysis and Management* 7(3):542–47.

Shannon, L. W. 1985. "Risk Assessment versus Real Prediction: The Prediction Problem and Public Trust." *Journal of Quantitative Criminology* 1(1):159–90.

Smith, D. A., F. D. Wish, and G. R. Jarjoura. 1989. "Drug Use and Pretrial Misconduct in New York City." *Journal of Quantitative Criminology* 5:101–26.

Spolar, C. 1988. "Testing the Limits: Detecting Drugs in the Workplace." *Washington Post* (December 4, 5, 6), three-part series.

Stewart, J. K. 1988. "Quid pro Quo: Stay Drug-free and Stay on Release." *George Washington Law Review* 57(1):68–76.

Toborg, M., and J. P. Bellassai. 1986. "The Washington, D.C. Urine Testing Program for Arrestees and Defendants Awaiting Trial: A Summary of Interim Findings." Paper presented at the National Institute of Justice Conference on "Drugs and Crime: Detecting Use and Reducing Risk," Washington, D.C., June.

———. 1988*a*. *Background and Description of the Urine Testing Program.* Monograph no. 1 of the Study Assessment of Pretrial Urine Testing in the District of Columbia. Washington, D.C.: Toborg Associates for the National Institute of Justice.

———. 1988*b*. *The Views of Judicial Officers.* Monograph no. 3 of the Study Assessment of Pretrial Urine Testing in the District of Columbia. Washington, D.C.: Toborg Associates for the National Institute of Justice.

Toborg, M. A., J. P. Bellassai, A. M. J. Yezer, and R. P. Trost. 1989. *Assessment of Pretrial Urine Testing in the District of Columbia.* Summary report. Washington, D.C.: U.S. Department of Justice, National Institute of Justice.

Toborg, M. A., A. M. J. Yezer, and J. P. Bellassai. 1988. *Analysis of Drug Use in Arrestees.* Monograph no. 4 of the Study Assessment of Pretrial Urine Testing in the District of Columbia. Washington, D.C.: Toborg Associates for the National Institute of Justice.

University of Michigan. 1989. Press release, February 28. Ann Arbor: University of Michigan.

Visher, C. A. 1988. *Assessment of Pretrial Urine Testing in the District of Columbia: A Reanalysis.* Washington, D.C.: U.S. Department of Justice, National Institute of Justice.

———. 1989. Personal communication with authors, May 18.

Washington Post. 1988. "Bribery Accusations Probed in D.C. Drug Screening Unit." *Washington Post*, July 12.

Weinman, B. 1989. Personal communication with authors, July 13.

Wexler, H. K., D. S. Lipton, and B. D. Johnson. 1988. "A Criminal Justice System Strategy for Treating Cocaine-Heroin Abusing Offenders in Custody." *Issues and Practices.* Washington, D.C.: National Institute of Justice.

White House. 1989. *National Drug Control Strategy.* Washington, D.C.: U.S. Government Printing Office.

Willette, R. E. 1986. "Drug Testing Programs." In *Urine Testing for Drugs of Abuse,* edited by R. L. Hawks and C. N. Chiang. Rockville, Md.: U.S. Department of Health and Human Services, National Institute on Drug Abuse.

Williams, K. 1979. *The Scope and Prediction of Recidivism.* Washington, D.C.: Institute for Law and Social Research.

Wish, E. D. 1986. "PCP and Crime: Just Another Illicit Drug?" Paper presented at the National Institute on Drug Abuse Technical Review Meeting on PCP, Rockville, Md., May.

———. 1987. "Drug Use Forecasting: New York 1984–86." *Research in Action.* Washington, D.C.: National Institute of Justice, U.S. Department of Justice.

———. 1988a. "Urine Testing of Criminals: What Are We Waiting For?" *Journal of Policy Analysis and Management* 7:551–54.

———. 1988b. "Identifying Drug Abusing Criminals." In *Compulsory Treatment of Drug Abuse: Research and Clinical Practice*, edited by C. G. Leukefeld and F. M. Tims. National Institute on Drug Abuse Research Monograph no. 86. Washington, D.C.: U.S. Department of Health and Human Services, National Institute on Drug Abuse.

Wish, E. D., E. Brady, and M. Cuadrado. 1986. "Urine Testing of Arrestees: Findings from Manhattan." Paper presented at the National Institute of Justice Conference on "Drugs and Crime: Detecting Use and Reducing Risk," Washington, D.C., June.

Wish, E. D., E. Brady, M. Cuadrado, and L. Alvarado. 1985. "Female Arrestees: The Most Serious Drug Abusers?" Paper presented at the annual meeting of the American Society of Criminology, San Diego, November.

Wish, E. D., M. Chedekel, E. Brady, and M. Cuadrado. 1985. "Comparison of the Use of Thin-Layer Chromatography and EMIT for Detecting Recent Drug Use by Arrestees." Paper presented at the annual meeting of the American Academy of Forensic Studies, Las Vegas, February.

Wish, E. D., M. Cuadrado, and S. Magura. 1988. "Drug Abuse as a Predictor of Pretrial Failure-to-Appear in Arrestees in Manhattan." Final report submitted to U.S. Department of Justice, National Institute of Justice, January.

Wish, E. D., M. Cuadrado, and J. Martorana. 1986. "Estimates of Drug Use in Intensive Supervision Probationers: Results from a Pilot Study." *Federal Probation* 50(4):4–16.

Wish, E. D., and B. D. Johnson. 1986. "The Impact of Substance Abuse on Criminal Careers." In *Criminal Careers and "Career Criminals,"* vol. 2, edited by A. Blumstein, J. Cohen, J. A. Roth, and C. A. Visher. Washington, D.C.: National Academy Press.

Wish, E. D., K. A. Klumpp, A. H. Moorer, E. Brady, and K. M. Williams. 1981. "An Analysis of Drugs and Crime among Arrestees in the District of Columbia." Executive Summary. Washington, D.C.: U.S. Department of Justice, National Institute of Justice.

Wish, E. D., and J. O'Neil. 1990. "Cocaine Use in Arrestees: Refining Measures of National Trends by Sampling the Criminal Population." Research Monograph. Rockville, Md.: U.S. Department of Health and Human Services, National Institute on Drug Abuse.

Wish, E. D., J. O'Neil, and V. Baldau. 1990. "Lost Opportunity to Combat AIDS: Drug Abusers in the Criminal Justice System." In *AIDS and Intravenous Drug Use: Future Directions for Community-based Prevention Research*, edited by C. G. Leukefeld, R. J. Battjes, and Z. Amsel. National Institute on Drug

Abuse Research Monograph no. #3. Rockville, Md.: U.S. Department of Health and Human Services, National Institute on Drug Abuse.

Wish, E. D., M. Toborg, and J. Bellassai. 1988. "Identifying Drug Users and Monitoring Them during Conditional Release." National Institute of Justice Briefing Paper. Washington, D.C.: U.S. Department of Justice, National Institute of Justice.

Yezer, A. M. J., R. P. Trost, M. A. Toborg, J. P. Bellassai, and C. Quintos. 1988a. "Periodic Urine Testing as a Signalling Device for Pretrial Release Risk." Monograph no. 5 of the Study Assessment of Pretrial Urine Testing in the District of Columbia. Washington, D.C.: Toborg Associates for the National Institute of Justice.

———. 1988b. "The Efficacy of Using Urine Testing Results in Risk Classification of Arrestees." Monograph no. 6 of the Study Assessment of Pretrial Urine Testing in the District of Columbia. Washington, D.C.: Toborg Associates for the National Institute of Justice.

M. Douglas Anglin and Yih-Ing Hser

Treatment of Drug Abuse

ABSTRACT

The major drug-treatment modalities—methadone maintenance, therapeutic communities, outpatient drug-free programs, and some criminal justice system-based treatments such as civil commitment—have all been shown to be successful by most outcome criteria. Programs with flexible policies, goals, and philosophies produce better results than inflexible programs, especially when they adopt combinations of treatment components that are suited to individual clients' problems and needs. Patients' lengths of time in treatment are highly correlated with positive outcomes, but dropout rates are high for most modalities. Clients entering treatment under legal coercion do as well by most outcome criteria as volunteer clients and may stay in treatment longer. The evidence on treatment effectiveness suggests a social policy of expanded treatment capacities and options and increased attention to adequate implementation of treatment programs.

The adverse social consequences of illicit drug use have led to allocation of substantial public resources for drug treatment in the last two decades. Governmental policies have sought to contain the spread of drug use to new populations and to break the link between illicit drug use and criminal behavior in order to reduce overall crime rates (Jaffe 1979; Graham 1987; Newman 1987). Traditional criminal justice system approaches to curtailing the drug supply have not achieved much success in curbing drug use (Anglin 1988a). Treatment of the drug user can

M. Douglas Anglin is adjunct associate professor and Yih-Ing Hser is adjunct assistant professor at the Neuropsychiatric Institute of the University of California, Los Angeles. Preparation of this essay was supported in part by the National Institute on Drug Abuse (grants DA00139 and DA05544) and the National Institute of Justice (grant 87-IJ-CX-042). Special thanks are due B. Perrochet and L. Shishino for their assistance.

reduce or eliminate drug use and thereby reduce the user's criminal activity (McGlothlin, Anglin, and Wilson 1978; Anglin and Speckart 1986, 1988; Anglin and Hser 1987; Ball et al. 1987; Harwood et al. 1988; Hubbard et al. 1989). A greater social investment in treatment may be the most cost-effective way to achieve these public policy goals.

This essay examines evidence of drug-treatment effectiveness, especially in relation to crime control. The analysis addresses issues of how well treatment programs meet both individual and social needs, what effects the commonly available treatment modalities generally produce, and what client and program characteristics are associated with different outcomes.

The treatment research examined comes mostly from studies published since 1980. Studies of heroin addicts predominate because of the clear link to crime and because of the accumulation of relevant studies (Ball et al. 1981; Cooper et al. 1983; Nurco et al. 1984; Tims and Ludford 1984; Speckart and Anglin 1986a, 1986b). Cocaine treatment studies, though fewer in number, are considered because of the drug's widespread use and its serious social consequences. Other abused drugs have been infrequently studied, and few treatment outcome findings are available for assessment.

There is no simple cure for drug dependence. Once drug dependence has developed, it can persist as a chronic condition, and relapse is often the rule. Biological, sociocultural, economic, and psychological factors all contribute to drug abuse. The treatment of drug abuse is thus not a simple medical issue but involves a wide spectrum of social considerations. Complications of treating abusers of a primary drug type include alcohol abuse, polydrug use, psychiatric disorders, criminal involvement, and social adversities such as unemployment and homelessness.

The majority of clients in most treatment programs have traditionally been opiate abusers. Cocaine abuse has, however, become one of the nation's major drug problems and receives increasing public and research attention (Adams et al. 1987). Although much is known about opiate addiction processes and patterns, adequate data on the long-term processes and consequences of cocaine abuse have yet to be collected. The empirically supported association of drug use and criminal behavior has been confined mainly to opiates, but findings relating criminality to use of other drugs, especially cocaine, are increasingly reported (Goldstein, Norman, and Spunt 1982; Johnson et al. 1985; Nurco et al. 1988).

A variety of treatment approaches is used in six modalities. Methadone maintenance has become a dominant modality for the treatment of opiate addicts and has often been evaluated. Methadone maintenance programs substitute a licit opiate, methadone, under controlled conditions, for illicit opiates such as heroin. Therapeutic communities provide a controlled residential environment with intensive personality-restructuring efforts. Therapeutic communities have typically been used for heroin addicts but are increasingly being used for other drugs and, after methadone maintenance, have been the most frequently evaluated modality. Because they are noncontroversial and low in cost, outpatient drug-free programs providing drug education and counseling have increased considerably in number; however, there have been few evaluations of their effectiveness. Detoxification programs are concerned with the medical management of drug withdrawal. If not used in combination with other treatment, detoxification programs have shown minimal long-term therapeutic effects, but they often have limited short-term effects and are a "gateway" to other, more intensive treatments.

Evaluation studies concern mostly opiate users in methadone maintenance. However, findings for other drug dependencies and other modalities are typically consistent with those reported for methadone maintenance. The findings summarized in this essay are based on evaluations that are restricted to treatment programs operated in accordance with current protocols. Small-scale research projects, however, have demonstrated that substantial improvement is possible in all modalities and programs. Furthermore, mixed-modality programs have shown promise in bettering outcomes but have not been implemented except in isolated circumstances (Sorenson et al. 1987).

Most modalities have been shown to achieve demonstrable success whether assessed in terms of drug-use and crime-reduction criteria or in terms of the principal aims of the specific treatment modality. However, relapse to drug use and dependence is common. Efforts to identify factors that consistently predict posttreatment abstinence or relapse patterns have not produced definitive findings. The effectiveness of treatment has been shown to be related to a variety of client characteristics and to a variety of treatment-program characteristics. Little progress has been made in classifying drug users to identify what kinds of users will benefit most from particular kinds of programs (Rounsaville 1989).

All major treatment modalities can be shown to have some positive effects on clients in terms of drug use, criminality, employment, and other aspects of social functioning. Programs with flexible policies and a case-management approach that includes provision of social and psychological services are often found to be more effective than programs with more rigid approaches. Vocational rehabilitation and other special social interventions are valuable over the short run for clients with these needs, but continued long-term benefits have not been demonstrated.

For most types of programs, time spent in treatment increases the likelihood of positive long-term outcomes. Dropout rates are high, however, for all modalities except some methadone maintenance programs. A significant proportion of those seeking treatment do not stay in treatment, especially in therapeutic communities and outpatient drug-free programs, for more than a few weeks. Clients entering treatment under legal coercion do as well as those without such pressures and have been reported to remain in programs for longer periods of time than clients entering without legal compulsion.

Relations between patient characteristics and outcomes generally explain only a small amount of the variation within treatment-outcome results. An intact marriage, a job, a shorter history of drug use, low levels of psychiatric dysfunctioning, and a history of little or no criminality are associated with better outcomes in most programs. Demographic characteristics such as sex, race or ethnicity, and education are related to the likelihood that an individual will enter treatment but are only moderately useful in predicting treatment outcomes. Older age at treatment admission has consistently been found to be positively associated with better treatment outcome.

Program characteristics are often significant determinants of outcome. Although the effects of program characteristics are seldom evaluated quantitatively, most clinical observers believe that substantial differences in outcome can be attributed to program policies and protocols, the quality of therapeutic staff and program management, the breadth of services provided, and general staff and patient morale.

The rest of this essay presents the evidence on which the preceding generalizations are based. First, in Section I, we describe the history and current extent of treatment in the United States. In Section II, we examine a number of methodological problems that characterize drug-treatment research and outline the evaluation framework that we use in this essay. Section III contains a detailed description of program characteristics, major treatment goals, and evaluation results for each major treatment modality. Significant correlates and covariates of treatment outcomes are discussed in Section IV. Conclusions and policy implications are discussed in Section V.

I. An Overview of Drug Abuse Treatment

The four major treatment modalities are outpatient methadone maintenance for narcotics addicts, detoxification, therapeutic communities, and outpatient drug-free programs. A smaller number of other modalities and treatment environments exists, but these four account for more than 90 percent of all clients in treatment as of 1987 (National Association of State Alcohol and Drug Abuse Directors [NASADAD] 1988). Given the historical concern with heroin use, it is not surprising that two of these (methadone maintenance and one form of detoxification using methadone) are oriented exclusively to the opiate-dependent client. Therapeutic community programs have been applied to non-opiate users, even though the approach originally grew out of the experiences of opiate users seeking a community-based strategy of achieving long-term abstinence. Only the outpatient drug-free programs were developed without specific reference to the opiate users (Brown 1984). Detailed descriptions of these modalities and evaluation results are presented in Section III.

Drug-treatment facilities became available in the United States in the early twentieth century in response to the dramatic increase in the number of heroin addicts in federal prisons as a result of the criminalization of opiate use. Federal public health service hospitals for addiction treatment were opened in Lexington, Kentucky, in 1935 and Fort Worth, Texas, in 1938. Long-term evaluations of the effectiveness of treatment at these hospitals were not reported until the 1960s (O'Donnell 1969). The samples studied frequently included persons who were addicted to opiates as a result of medical treatment (or self treatment) for health problems or for alcoholism. Many admissions were placements of individuals under criminal prosecution.

Drug abuse treatment resources were scarce before the major drug-abuse epidemics that began in the mid-1960s. Only heroin addicts received treatment, and that treatment was available only at the two Public Health Service hospitals and at a few scattered therapeutic-community programs. Treatment for problems with other illicit substances was handled in traditional medical or mental health facilities or by the criminal justice system.

This picture changed dramatically from 1962 to 1972. The social upheaval associated with the Vietnam War and the epidemic increase in the use of hallucinogenics and other drugs produced a strong social reaction not only toward traditional criminal justice sanctions but also toward drug abuse prevention and treatment needs of an increasing number of citizens using an increasing variety of drugs.

One treatment approach developed during this decade was linked to the criminal justice system: legally mandated treatment for offenders dependent on narcotics. The first major compulsory treatment program was the California Civil Addict Program, established in 1961. The program was administered through the department of corrections and was primarily a program of diversion from prison sentences, although provisions were made for involuntary (noncriminal) commitments (Anglin and Hser 1990). In 1966, a similar program was established in New York but was short lived and produced considerable controversy, in part because it was administered through a mental health bureaucracy that was unaccustomed to dealing with drug-dependent populations.

The federal government instituted a civil commitment program under the Narcotic Addict Rehabilitation Act of 1966. This effort was also short lived and controversial (Anglin and Hser 1990). Federal funds were provided, however, for numerous demonstration treatment programs for the postincarceration aftercare of offenders, from which grew today's extended network of community drug-treatment programs.

Also during the late 1960s and extending until the late 1970s, a number of state prisons and several federal prisons established drug rehabilitation programs. These programs were typically derived from a therapeutic-community model, called the Aesklepieian model, that was developed by the staff of the U.S. federal prison in Marion, Illinois, in 1969. However, most of these programs ended by the early 1980s (Camp and Camp 1989).

In the mid-1960s, Dole and Nyswander demonstrated that serious, long-term opiate addiction can be treated with a daily oral dose of methadone (Dole and Nyswander 1965; Dole, Nyswander, and Warner 1968). Their findings led to widespread establishment of methadone maintenance programs. The number of methadone maintenance clinics increased rapidly between 1970 and 1973, and methadone maintenance became the major modality for the treatment of narcotic addiction in the United States (Lowinson and Millman 1979).

Medical or psychiatric hospital programs provided the predominant forms of community-based drug treatment during the period from 1930 through much of the 1960s. Therapeutic communities for drug abusers emerged in the 1950s and were based on residential programs for psychiatric patients in which treatment and residential management were shared responsibilities of patients and staff. Therapeutic communities for addicts, however, evolved outside of existing service delivery systems, often with some antipathy toward them. Later, however, the often dramatic results for some therapeutic-community residents caught the public interest, and by the mid-1980s therapeutic communities for drug abuse had evolved into a well-established network of over 500 residential programs across the United States (DeLeon 1985).

The vast increase in drug use in the late 1960s, continuing into the 1980s, produced a demand for treatment for increasingly broad categories of drug-dependent individuals. As a consequence, drug-free outpatient programs were developed to serve the nontraditional, nonopiate addict client at a much lower cost than residential care. Concurrent with the increase of outpatient drug-free programs, self-help or mutual support groups evolved from the twelve-step philosophy of Alcoholics Anonymous. Unlike outpatient drug-free programs, these programs are rarely affiliated with established social service agencies but are sustained by the predominantly volunteer activities of those who are themselves recovering from drug dependence.

Despite the burgeoning number of treatment programs—which often have quite different populations and philosophies—the major modalities, to be described later, remained few in number. (More comprehensive descriptions of the types of programs available are described in Sells [1974] and Sells and Simpson [1976].)

A. Contemporary Treatment in the United States

The number of treatment facilities for drug dependence in the United States is not well documented. Information is available primarily for treatment units and programs that receive at least some funds from federal, state, or local agencies. Only limited data are available about private clinics. Even less information is available concerning the appeal and effectiveness of self-help approaches such as Narcotics Anonymous and Cocaine Anonymous. Evaluation results from the available literature are shaped by the nature of the programs evaluated.

Furthermore, findings are based on publicly funded programs and, because lower socioeconomic individuals are disproportionately served by publicly funded institutions, the findings' generalizability is thereby limited.

The National Association of State Alcohol and Drug Abuse Directors has collected annual information on clients and on treatment and prevention services from fifty state alcohol and drug abuse agencies since 1984. Although a significant number of programs do not report, the data represent the majority of programs receiving public funds. The 1988 report shows that, in fiscal year 1987, among those programs that voluntarily submitted data, a total of 6,632 alcohol- and/or drug-treatment units received state funds (NASADAD 1988). Of these, 1,428 were drug-treatment units and 3,109 were combined alcohol- and drug-treatment units. Focusing on drug treatment only, there were 450,553 drug client admissions. Distributions of these admissions by modality and environment are presented in table 1. A majority of admissions (237,728, or 53 percent) are to drug-free programs in outpatient settings. Whites constitute the largest proportion (48 percent) of admissions, and twice as many men are admitted as women. The largest number of admissions is people between twenty-five and thirty-four years of age.

Heroin has long been the primary drug of abuse for the majority of people admitted to treatment programs (Tims and Ludford 1984). However, over the three years from 1985 to 1987, cocaine admissions more than doubled. By 1987, cocaine abusers ranked second in treatment admissions and first in emergency room visits (National Institute on Drug Abuse 1988), and their numbers continue to increase rapidly. Other types of drugs—including marijuana, phencyclidine (PCP), and amphetamines—have received less attention in treatment evaluations because of the small number of treatment programs for them and, in the case of PCP, its late arrival on the drug scene and its predominance as a major drug of abuse in only some areas (e.g., Washington, D.C.). Intravenous users of heroin and cocaine are drawing more attention than ever before from researchers and from society as a whole because of the associated high risk of transmitting the AIDS virus. Some states provide data to NASADAD on the total number of intravenous (IV) drug abusers. In 1987, the highest estimated numbers of IV drug abusers were in New York (260,000), California (220,000), and Texas (180,700).

TABLE 1

Drug Client Admissions to Publicly Funded Treatment Services in 1987

A. Admissions by Type of Environment and Type of Modality

Modality/Environment	Hospital		Residential		Outpatient		Total	
	N	%	N	%	N	%	N	%
Detoxification	11,291	2.51	23,308	5.17	32,338	7.18	66,937	14.86
Maintenance	188	.04	931	.21	42,436	9.43	43,605	9.68
Drug free	18,505	4.11	57,669	12.80	237,728	52.76	313,902	69.67
Total	29,984	6.66	81,908	18.18	312,552	69.37	450,553	94.21

B. Admissions by Age and Sex

Age/Sex	Men		Women		Total	
	N	%	N	%	N	%
Under 18	36,588	8.12	24,839	5.51	61,427	13.63
18–20	21,631	4.80	9,381	2.08	31,012	6.88
21–24	34,944	7.76	17,610	3.91	52,554	11.66
25–34	94,439	20.96	49,392	10.96	143,831	31.92
35–44	37,766	8.38	15,547	3.45	53,313	11.83
45 +	33,506	7.44	15,534	3.45	49,040	10.88
Total	258,874	57.46	132,303	29.36	450,553	86.80*

SOURCE.—*State Resources and Services for Alcohol and Drug Abuse Problems, FY87* (National Association of State Alcohol and Drug Abuse Directors 1988); data are included for only those treatment units that received some funds administered by the state drug agency during fiscal year 1987.

* Percentages are calculated based on total admission of 450,553. Due to missing or unreported information, total percentages do not add up to 100.

Polydrug use, "simultaneous or sequential use of more than one psychoactive drug for nonmedical purposes" (Wesson and Smith 1979, p. 151), has also become common in recent years. Despite widespread concern about polydrug use, its patterns and consequences, and the questions of whether and how it differs from traditional heroin dependence have not yet been thoroughly examined. Treatment facilities also have been slow to adjust to this changing drug-use pattern, and the effectiveness of treatment when multiple drugs are involved has not been adequately evaluated.

B. Models of Addiction

The development of an effective treatment program for drug abusers requires a comprehensive assessment of both causes and consequences of drug abuse. Unfortunately, drug-use etiology is still poorly understood beyond the general realization that it is a complex, multiply determined behavior influenced by genetic, psychobiological, sociocultural, and environmental factors (Lettieri, Sayers, and Pearson 1980). While many addiction models have been presented, no single one has been generally accepted. As a result, treatment efforts that have been applied have been primarily based on a wide variety of ideas about what might be effective and on the accumulated experience of practitioners, typically with little input from research findings (Allison and Hubbard 1985).

Nonetheless, social policy for intervening with drug use, the focus and choice of specific treatment programs, and most evaluation research are more or less influenced by some implicit model or models of addiction. For example, the *moral model* attributes drug abuse to moral weakness. Intervention under this model usually consists of punishment, incarceration, or moral education. A major public and law-enforcement view of drug abuse conforms to the perspectives of the moral model. By contrast, most treatment-oriented interventions emphasize medical or therapeutic/behavioral management rather than punishment. Methadone maintenance and detoxification programs are examples of this latter approach and reflect a *disease model* perspective emphasizing medication. The *self-medication hypothesis* views addiction as secondary to an underlying psychiatric illness such as depression, attention deficit disorder, or schizophrenia, which the patient may be trying to treat by use of drugs (Khantzian et al. 1984). The *behavioral model* views addiction as a pattern of maladaptive, learned habits that are modifiable by cognitive and behavioral techniques (Marlatt and

Gordon 1985). Most drug-free treatment programs adopt these last two concepts and emphasize psychotherapy or behavioral management accordingly.

Most evaluators choose outcome measures based on their beliefs many of which fall within these four models—about why addiction occurs and what treatment should accomplish. Some maintain that addiction demoralizes character but that the solution is to seek a medical cure. Others assert that unless complete abstinence from all drugs can be achieved, treatment is essentially a failure. The framework we adopt in measuring treatment efficacy, to be described in detail in a later section, reflects a rejection of the moral/legal model in favor of a combination of the medical and behavioral models of drug dependence. We believe such a perspective encompasses the majority of underlying causes of drug dependence, relates to a more flexible spectrum of treatment strategies, and addresses the multiple aspects of drug dependence of concern to most individuals and society.

C. Treatment Components

Most treatment programs usually provide a combination of service components besides their modality-specific treatment. Since the availability and delivery of treatment components within a given modality may enhance or detract from overall outcomes, a brief overview of major components is useful to structure the findings to be presented.

Drug counseling is the primary support service provided to clients in most drug treatment programs and is common across all modalities. Drug counseling focuses on assisting the client in practical problem solving for day-to-day living and is, of course, limited to the period of treatment duration (Hubbard et al. 1983). However, drug counseling does not typically address social, vocational, or other personal needs of clients. Clients' legal problems, acute crises, and appropriate referrals to outside agencies are often beyond the scope of many counselors (Stark 1989).

Drug education contributes to the client's understanding of the biological, familial, psychological, and social factors that contribute to drug dependence. Drug education provides general information on these matters and may demonstrate how they apply to personal circumstances. Successful educational efforts may reduce resistance to programming, lower attrition rates, and decrease anxiety, especially if the client is informed that uncomfortable subjective experiences are transient and "normal" during recovery. Education components may be linked to drug counseling in some modalities, especially outpatient drug-free programs.

Pharmacotherapy interventions with serious drug dependence typically involve a period of detoxification for the purposes of medically managing drug withdrawal symptoms and providing adequate care during stabilization. Considerable attention has been paid to discovering the treatment applications of various medications. Small chemical trials of such agents as desiprimine and bromocriptine have been used to treat depression associated with dysfunctional levels of cocaine use (Dackis and Gold 1985). For heroin addiction, long-term use of narcotic antagonists such as naltrexone or clonidine have been used to "block" the effects of self-administered narcotics (Charney et al. 1981; Charney, Heninger, and Kleber 1986; O'Brian and Woody 1989). Methadone substitution for illicit opiate dependence is perhaps the most lengthy pharmacotherapy applied in drug treatment.

Psychotherapy components can vary widely depending on a program's theoretical approaches, procedural applications, and the client's assessed needs. The unit of the intervention may be the client, the client and his or her spouse, or the family. Group counseling is common both because of its lower cost and because the group interaction is considered therapeutic of itself. This component is most often found in privately funded inpatient and outpatient programs, but may be available in publicly funded programs also.

Educational and vocational services are useful to the vast majority of clients because of serious familial, educational, employment, and legal problems. Education and the development of job skills may help maintain the treatment gains of reduced drug use and criminality. Although these services are rarely provided in most treatment settings, residential programs emphasize them as an important component of client resocialization.

Urine testing provides one objective measure of compliance with the treatment goals of reducing primary drug use and identifying drug use other than that of the primary drug of dependence. Such testing is a common component of all modalities. Most clinicians and counselors value urine testing for its clinical uses in detecting drug use and potential relapse. In addition, urine testing has public relations value by demonstrating treatment programs' ability to maintain adequate control over their clients.

Relapse-prevention training can be used to insulate the carefully cultivated attitudes, skills, and intentions derived from the treatment process against the corrosive influences that may exist in the personal circumstances and immediate communities of the user. Relapse-prevention training assists program staff and clients to identify situations and events that foster relapse, to recognize the signs and symptoms associated with relapse, and to practice techniques that help to interrupt relapse progression (Marlatt and Gordon 1985). Residential and long-term outpatient programs are most likely to emphasize relapse prevention.

Social and community support assists recovery from drug dependence during treatment and after discharge (Hawkins and Catalano 1985). Self-help or mutual support organizations like Alcoholics Anonymous, Narcotics Anonymous, and Cocaine Anonymous can be immensely helpful. Nearly all programs make a special effort to link clients to these groups. For more dysfunctional drug users, such as the psychiatrically impaired or the homeless, sheltered environments may be a useful treatment component. Group homes may also be helpful, either as an adjunct to concurrent outpatient treatment or as an intermediate step from residential care to community care.

These services vary from program to program, even within the same modality, and currently their provision is at low levels because of insufficient treatment funding, overburdened programs, and inadequately trained staff. Only 10 percent of clients surveyed in the Treatment Outcome Prospective Study reported receiving services other than medical and psychological services during their first two months in treatment (Hubbard et al. 1983). Fewer than 50 percent of drug programs maintained a budget for vocational development and fewer than 20 percent reported having a staff member responsible for providing vocational counseling (Hubbard and Harwood 1981).

The unique contribution of these services to outcomes has not been broadly evaluated. In part, this is because, for many drug-dependent clients, only a few services are helpful, desired, or delivered, while for other clients many ancillary efforts are requested or needed to derive maximum benefit from treatment. In addition, some services, such as psychotherapy or pharmacotherapy, require trained professionals to administer. The cost and limited availability of adequately trained professionals often restrict the provision of such services in drug abuse treatment. The typical drug-treatment program makes efforts to distribute its social service resources to those clients most in need or most likely to respond. While perhaps meeting a human need, this method of distributing a broad range of clients across treatment components in a nonsystematic manner limits the generalizations that can be drawn (see Sec. IV*B*).

Understanding that treatment components are diversely aggregated into programs—and that programs in the aggregate comprise the treatment system—provides a structure that helps clarify the complexities of assessing treatment outcomes. In Sections II and III, we turn to the evaluation issues and findings in an attempt to determine the overall efficacy of treatment and to disentangle, where sufficient evidence exists, the contributions of such factors as modality, environment, and components.

II. Evaluation Issues

Considerable effort has been devoted to evaluation of treatment programs initiated since the early 1970s. These studies vary in scope and methodology and often produce inconsistent and carefully qualified results. The interpretation of such findings is complicated by considerations that often lead to inconsistent measures of effectiveness. Prominent among those considerations are the heterogeneous nature of the drug-dependent population, the relapsing nature of dependence, the difficulty of conducting experimentally controlled studies, nonspecifiable and often intangible treatment components, and the interactions among these considerations. As a consequence of those methodological difficulties, results from evaluation studies cannot be properly interpreted without an understanding of adequate research designs, appropriate statistical approaches, and practical outcome measures.

A. *Research Design and Statistical Analysis*

The interpretation of data from any research is constrained by the study design. Several types of research design have been used in drug-treatment evaluations, and their strengths and weaknesses are described below. Types of statistical analysis that are appropriate to the relevant design are then discussed.

Studies based on an experimental design with random assignment to comparison groups yield the most unambiguous results. There have been few implementations of such designs (Bale et al. 1980), and these have produced limited information (Hall 1984). One constraint has been the ethical problems associated with withholding treatment from the control group (DeLeon 1984). Even if random assignment to modalities is implemented, attrition from treatment is usually high and differs between groups so that the remaining samples are too small or too unrepresentative to validate conclusions (Hall 1984).

As an alternative, treatment evaluations have often used variations of a pre- and posttreatment design in which treatment outcomes are assessed by comparing levels of selected behaviors (such as drug use, crime, and employment) before, during, and after treatment. The rationale is that treatment effects should be demonstrable if change after treatment is observed using an individual's own pretreatment behavior for comparison. Many studies used this design in the 1960s and 1970s, with the general conclusion that significant reductions in problem behaviors occurred as a result of treatment. By the end of the 1970s, however, it had become generally recognized that pre- and posttreatment studies were subject to serious methodological shortcomings. Because the pretreatment period was almost invariably characterized by abnormally high levels of drug use, crime, or both, "improvement" might be no more than regression toward the mean in a later period, particularly when the pretreatment period was short. Consequently, on methodological grounds, many treatment-outcome results have been seriously questioned (McGlothlin, Anglin, and Wilson 1978; McGlothlin and Anglin 1979; Hser, Anglin, and Chou 1988). The following research designs have been developed in response to such criticisms.

On- and off-treatment comparisons, a modification of the pre- and posttreatment design, use a longer pretreatment period extending at least three to five years prior to treatment. The postadmission period is divided into two aggregate subperiods, time on treatment and time off treatment (Hser, Anglin, and Chou 1988). This method combines all periods of the addiction career when the subject is actively involved in treatment, aggregating the measures of narcotics use, criminality, employment, and other relevant behaviors during those periods into summary statistics. These summary measures are then compared with their comparable measures aggregated from all periods of the postadmission addiction career when the subject is not in treatment. Most of these statistical comparisons yield positive treatment-outcome results, although to a lesser degree than do comparisons of pre- and posttreatment differences measured in the short term, and the results are much less equivocal in terms of true treatment effects. However, for such analyses to be possible, longitudinal research designs obtaining data for long periods before and after treatment are necessary.

The lack of an appropriate comparison group still severely constrains the interpretations derived from the on- and off-treatment approach. In the absence of a control group, it is difficult to determine whether unanticipated bias occurred in selecting the subjects for study, and whether the resulting experimental group is sufficiently representative for generalizations to be made about the outcome findings. Furthermore, without comparison groups, behavioral changes during and after treatment that result from the passage of time may wrongly be attributed to program activities.

Some natural experiments that take advantage of policy differences or program changes have been able to compare differential outcomes in comparable groups. McGlothlin and his associates (McGlothlin, Anglin, and Wilson 1977; McGlothlin and Anglin 1981a, 1981b; Anglin et al. 1982) completed several major evaluations of this type that demonstrated overall treatment efficacy. (See table 2, part A, for research results on methadone maintenance programs by McGlothlin and Anglin [1981a].) For example, one evaluation of the California civil commitment program compared experiences of an experimental group that received the planned commitment and treatment period (averaging five years), with a second group of subjects who were discharged after minimal exposure to the program (averaging a few months) because of legal errors that occurred during the commitment process (McGlothlin, Anglin, and Wilson 1977) (see table 2, part B). The pretreatment characteristics of the two groups were similar and the group selection resulted from relatively random legal errors; thus differences between groups in the follow-up period (averaging twelve years) could reasonably be attributed to the civil commitment program.

A study with a similar design investigated the effects of involuntary termination of methadone maintenance when a Bakersfield, California, clinic was closed by local officials (McGlothlin and Anglin 1979, 1981b) (table 2, part C). A matched comparison group was constituted from clients in a comparable Tulare, California, clinic where no such policy change was imposed. Again, pretreatment characteristics were similar for the two groups, and differences between them after the closure could reasonably be attributed to the policy change.

The research design, the nature of the data, and the hypotheses under consideration require statistical analyses that yield insightful information while minimizing experimental and nonexperimental biases. Most research data obtained in drug-treatment evaluation have been analyzed only at the descriptive and comparative level. Researchers have, however, increasingly realized the importance of using mul-

univariate statistical methods to assess the importance and the interactions of contributing factors simultaneously. Although correlation and regression methods are useful for certain types of data analysis, a number of more sophisticated statistical models provide useful and more in-depth information. For example, repeated measures analysis of variance is applicable when a within-subject design (e.g., pre- and posttreatment or on- and off-treatment comparisons) is used (Hser, Anglin, and Chou 1988). Survival analysis can be applied for analyses of the time course of the outcome (Anglin and Fisher 1987; Fisher and Anglin 1987; Hser, Anglin, and Liu 1990). A class of techniques based on probability theories such as loglinear modeling (Bishop, Fienberg, and Holland 1975; Anglin et al. 1986), event-history analysis (Coleman 1981; Yamaguchi and Kandel 1985), or Markov modeling (Wickens 1982; Hser 1986) are useful when outcome variables are categorical. Finally, if multiple measures of the same underlying "latent construct" are available over time, structural equation modeling can be applied to assessment of complex interactions among latent constructs for causal hypotheses testing (Speckart and Anglin 1986b; Hser, Chou, and Anglin 1990).

In the absence of adequate experimental designs, the use of multiple methods and replications across independent cohort samples should be common practice to test the consistency of results (Brecht, Hser, and Anglin 1990).

Drug-treatment evaluations have become more sophisticated in recent years both in appreciation of the strengths and weaknesses of alternate research designs and in the use of statistical tools for data analyses. Even if design and data analysis choices are well informed, the findings of evaluations are necessarily shaped by the outcome measures that are used. Here, too, recent evaluation research has made major advances over past practice.

B. Evaluation Measures

The simplest treatment goal has traditionally been to cause the drug abuser to stop using drugs. From a public policy perspective, however, drug abuse is associated with a variety of social problems including crime reduction, prison management, and the spread of AIDS (Ball and Corty 1988).

In examining the effectiveness of treatment, it is important that evaluations employ outcome measures that encompass a variety of behaviors. Several outcome categories are important: cessation or de-

TABLE 2
Treatment Outcomes by Major Evaluation Studies

Part A

Author(s) and Publication Date	Sample Sources and Descriptions	Comparison Time Periods	Treatment Modality	Time Periods	Major Results			
					Arrest Rate (per person year)	Incarceration (% time)	Daily Narcotics Use (% time)	Crime Days (per person/year)
McGlothlin and Anglin (1981a)	297 males first admitted to MM during years 1971–73, and then interviewed 1978–79	D to M vs. M to I	MM program policy differences (Program A and B: high dose with flexible termination; Program C: low dose/strict termination policy)	Program A:				
				D to M	1.86	39	70	96
				M to I	.78	13	14	24
				Program B:				
				D to M	2.03	28	73	131
				M to I	.96	17	19	36
				Program C:				
				D to M	2.43	33	71	100
				M to I	1.72	22	37	70

Part B

Author(s) and Publication Date	Sample Sources and Descriptions	Comparison Time Periods	Treatment Modality		Arrests/Person Year			Incarceration (% Total Elapsed Time)	Daily Narcotics Use (% Nonincarcerated Time)	Employment (% Nonincarcerated Time)	Property Crime (% Nonincarcerated Time)
					Drug Charges	Non-drug Charges	Violations (Parole or Probation)				
McGlothlin, Anglin, and Wilson (1977)	581 male first admissions in 1962–64; interviewed in 1974–75	Period I = first narcotic use to CC; Period II = CC to (CC + 7 years); Period III = (CC + 7 years) to time of interview	California Civil Addict Program								
				Treatment group							
				Period I	.83	1.15	.12	20.7	52.8	50.3	47.2
				Period II	.53	.80	.67	50.5	31.0	61.5	28.6
				Period III	.70	.72	.16	24.5	20.9	61.1	21.0
				Control group							
				Period I	1.06	1.13	.10	23.2	54.5	44.8	49.8
				Period II	.95	1.18	.31	50.9	47.7	48.8	43.1
				Period III	.67	.90	.32	31.7	28.4	53.0	30.5

				Part C	
				Arrested (%)	Readdicted to Narcotics (%)
McGlothlin and Anglin (1979)	Involuntary termination from Bakersfield MM (N = 94); Comparison group from Tulare (N = 83)	26 months after discharge date for Bakersfield and after a comparable date for Tulare	MM		
				Termination group (N = 94)	73 55
				Comparison group (N = 83)	40 31

Part D

				Percent Time		
				Daily Narcotics Use	Property Crime	Employment
Hser, Anglin, and Chou (1988)	720 MM clients in California (251 Anglo men, 283 Anglo women, 141 Chicano men, and 45 Chicano women) interviewed 1978–81, follow-up period 4–6 years	D to M vs. on MM during M to I vs. off MM during M to I	MM			
				D to M	78.0	32.6	35.9
				M to I: On MM	12.8	11.1	51.6
				Off MM	40.6	18.5	42.5

Part E

				Both Heroin and Crime (%)	Heroin Use Only (%)	Crime Only (%)	No Heroin Use and No Crime (%)
Ball et al. (1987)	617 male 1985 admissions in New York City, Philadelphia, and Baltimore	30 days prior to admission vs. past 30 days at in-treatment follow-up	MM				
				Preadmission: Last addiction period (N = 617)	81.0	13.0	0	0
				Postadmission: New admissions (N = 126)	29.4	37.3	7.9	25.4

411

TABLE 2 (Continued)

Author(s) and Publication Date	Sample Sources and Descriptions	Comparison Time Periods	Treatment Modality	Time Periods	Both Heroin and Crime (%)	Heroin Use Only (%)	Crime Only (%)	No Heroin Use and No Crime (%)
							Major Results	
				Intreatment (.5–4.5 years) (N = 342)	7.6	15.8	11.1	65.5
				Intreatment (over 4.5 years) (N = 149)	4	3.4	9.4	83.2

Part F

Author(s) and Publication Date	Sample Sources and Descriptions	Comparison Time Periods	Treatment Modality	Time Periods	Opiate Use, Days	Employment, Days	Crime Days	Illegal Income Dollars
						Status for the Last 30 Days		
McLellan et al. (1982)	282 male veterans admitted for drug problems during 1978 in Philadelphia	30 days preadmission vs. past 30 days at 6-months post-admission	Aggregate of residential treatment, self-help treatment, and out-patient MM	At admission	12	3	9	394
				At 6-month follow-up	4	11	3	91

Part G

Author(s) and Publication Date	Sample Sources and Descriptions	Comparison Time Periods	Treatment Modality	Time Periods	Arrested (%)	Arrest Rate (per Person/Year)
DeLeon et al. (1979)	202 males who entered Phoenix House program during 1970–71	3 years pre-treatment vs. 3 years post-treatment	TC	3 years pre-treatment	72	.65
				3 years post-treatment	41	.31

Part H

Simpson and Sells (1982)	DARP Admissions 1967–73 (N = 2,099) (black and white males)	Pretreatment vs. 1 year and 3 years post-treatment		Status for Past Year at Admission and at 1 and at 3 Years			
						Criminality*	
				Daily Opiate Use (%)	Employment (%)	Arrested (%)	Incarcerated (%)
			MM (N = 895)				
			Pretreatment	100	66	88	50
			At 1 year	36	67	27	28
			At 3 years	24	N.A.	20	30
			TC (N = 582)				
			Pretreatment	100	63	95	62
			At 1 year	39	72	33	33
			At 3 years	26	N.A.	23	32
			ODF (N = 256)				
			Pretreatment	100	60	87	51
			At 1 year	44	65	34	34
			At 3 years	28	N.A.	22	36
			DT (N = 214)				
			Pretreatment	100	71	83	48
			At 1 year	64	64	38	35
			At 3 years	37	N.A.	25	34
			Intake only (N = 152)				
			Pretreatment	100	65	86	43
			At 1 year	53	54	39	41
			At 3 years	41	N.A.	23	38

Part I

Hubbard et al. (1984)	TOPS admissions between 1979 and 1981, in 10 major cities (follow-up period 3–5 years)	1 year pretreatment vs. 1 year post-treatment	Treatment Retention	Weekly or Daily Heroin Use or Other Narcotics (%)	Depression (%)†	Suicide Thought/ Attempt (%)	Self-Reported Predatory Illegal Acts		Employment (%)
							1–10	11 or More	
		MM	<90 days (N = 386):						
			pretreatment	75.9	25.0	31.9	27.7	14.1	55.5
			posttreatment	44.0	17.6	14.0	16.3	10.9	49.6
			≥90 days (N = 541):						
			pretreatment	78.3	26.8	30.7	19.5	12.8	52.5
			posttreatment	25.3	22.8	12.2	13.3	6.4	40.3

TABLE 2   (Continued)

Author(s) and Publication Date	Sample Sources and Descriptions	Comparison Time Periods	Treatment Modality	Time Periods	Major Results					
					Weekly or Daily Heroin Use or Other Narcotics (%)	Depression (%)†	Suicide Thought/ Attempt (%)	Self-Reported Predatory Illegal Acts		Employment (%)
								1–10	11 or More	
			TC	Treatment Retention						
				<90 days (N = 380):						
				pretreatment	49.3	20.3	42.8	32.6	27.7	60.8
				posttreatment	28.3	17.8	20.5	28.3	14.7	58.2
				≥90 days (N = 340):						
				pretreatment	50.8	17.1	40.8	29.6	30.8	61.2
				posttreatment	17.8	12.9	15.1	19.8	9.7	66.7
			ODF	<90 days (N = 553):						
				pretreatment	27.7	12.2	51.0	27.7	10.6	69.2
				posttreatment	17.7	13.7	24.8	18.1	7.1	67.8
				≥90 days (N = 292):						
				pretreatment	23.6	19.4	46.6	24.4	9.4	69.2
				posttreatment	10.7	12.3	22.2	13.3	5.7	70.8

Part J

Author(s) and Publication Date	Sample Sources and Descriptions	Comparison Time Periods	Treatment Modality	Time Periods	Weekly or Daily	
					Heroin Use (%)	Cocaine Use (%)
Hubbard et al. (1988)	TOPS admissions between 1979 and 1981, in 10 major cities (follow-up period 3–5 years)	1 year pre-treatment *vs.* 1 year post-treatment	MM	Treatment Retention		
				<90 days (N = 264):		
				pretreatment	65.0	30.2
				posttreatment	31.2	19.3

414

		Daily Opiate Use	
TC	≥90 days (N = 579): pretreatment	63.5	26.4
	posttreatment	16.7	17.5
	<90 days (N = 373): pretreatment	30.5	29.4
	posttreatment	16.8	19.1
ODF	≥90 days (N = 339): pretreatment	30.9	27.6
	posttreatment	11.5	15.5
	<90 days (N = 506): pretreatment	11.5	17.0
	posttreatment	9.1	10.8
	≥90 days (N = 322): pretreatment	8.6	12.8
	posttreatment	4.9	8.1

Part K

Simpson et al. (1986)	DARP Admissions (N = 405) (black and white heroin-addicted males)	Pretreatment vs. 1, 2, 3, 6, and 12 years posttreatment	Aggregate of MM+TC+ODF +DT+ intake only

Status for Past Year at Admission and at 1, 2, 3, 6, and 12 Years

	Daily Opiate Use (%)	Employment (%)	Criminality*	
			Arrested (%)	Incarcerated (%)
Pretreatment	100	67	87	71
1 year	47	64	31	33
2 years	34	71	21	33
3 years	28	73	21	30
6 years	25	77	22	30
12 years	26	72	13	29

NOTE.—MM = methadone maintenance; D = date of first daily use; M = date of initial entry into MM; I = date of interview; CC = civil commitment admission; TC = therapeutic community; ODF = outpatient drug free; DT = detoxification.
* For pretreatment criminality, arrest and incarceration was for lifetime criminality at admission.
† Based on an aggregate of depression indicators.

415

creased use of the primary drug of dependence or other drugs; decreased levels of illegal activities such as drug trafficking, property crime, or prostitution; increased employment and decreased reliance on social service agencies; improved social and family functioning; improved psychological functioning; and decreased mortality and improved physical health. Some researchers use the increased retention of clients in treatment as an outcome measure (Hall 1984).

Modern evaluations thus measure more outcomes than the traditional standard of how many patients become drug free after treatment. Treatment effectiveness should be evaluated on the basis of whether the behaviors of drug abusers, measured at determined time intervals, have changed for the better.

III. Treatment Outcomes

Because treatment modalities have been evaluated more often than treatment components, we first examine the major modalities. These treatment modalities share some goals, but their objectives often vary. Drug-treatment programs are conducted under correctional auspices and under health care system auspices. Programs in correctional systems are generally described as compulsory or involuntary, and those in the medical health care system as voluntary, even though the majority of individuals entering these programs do so under some degree of life stress. This section reviews evaluation results for the four major modalities for drug use and crime. Table 2 summarizes major evaluation studies and related outcomes.

Evaluations of major programs and modalities have been conducted both as individual program assessments and as parts of large-scale multimodality studies. The latter include nationally oriented data bases such as the Drug Abuse Reporting Program (DARP) and the Treatment Outcome Prospective Study (TOPS). The Drug Abuse Reporting Program contains client information on 44,000 clients entering fifty-two treatment agencies from 1969 to 1973. Several major follow-ups were conducted at one year, three years, six years, and twelve years following DARP treatment. As a successor to DARP, the TOPS study included 11,750 clients who entered forty-one drug-treatment programs in ten cities nationwide during 1979 to 1981. Follow-ups of subsamples have been undertaken, ranging from three to sixty months after termination of treatment (Hubbard et al. 1989).

Where modality-specific outcome results were obtained from large-scale multimodality evaluations, we report only data for that modality.

There is great variability among programs within each major modality. Nonetheless, each modality has distinct characteristics and goals. We begin each part of our review of results by describing common characteristics. Comparisons between modality outcomes are provided at the end of this section.

A. Community-based Drug Treatment

The major treatment approaches have been methadone maintenance, therapeutic community, outpatient drug free, and detoxification. All of these programs operate in community settings. Detoxification from heroin and other drugs has also been used as an initial phase of treatment in therapeutic-community and outpatient drug-free programs.

1. *Methadone Maintenance.*   Federal regulations define maintenance as treatment in which methadone is administered to a drug-dependent individual at relatively stable dosage levels for a period in excess of twenty-one days as an oral substitute for heroin or other morphine-like drugs (U.S. Department of Health and Human Services 1980). Under federal guidelines, clients must have a documented addiction history and must have received some type of previous treatment. Since methadone itself is addictive, clients can often be maintained in the program as long as desired if program rules are followed and if funding is maintained. However, some jurisdictions have terminated or provided only limited-duration public funding. In these areas, clients must pay the full cost of treatment. Most programs are in outpatient settings. Most programs include explicit rules for behavior (with suspension often being a consequence of infractions), mandatory counseling sessions, routine urine testing, and medications taken under direct supervision. Amounts of counseling, dosage levels, and retention policies vary from program to program (Sells and Simpson 1976; Ball et al. 1986).

In general, methadone maintenance is intended for patients who have already attempted drug-free forms of treatment and for whom there is little or no expectation that they will be able to function normally without chemotherapeutic support (Dole and Nyswander 1965). Treatment goals typically do not require complete opiate abstinence but include rehabilitation or improvement in other aspects of social functioning so as to promote a return to conforming and productive community living.

Methadone maintenance programs have been extensively evaluated. Positive outcomes have been obtained in most studies, including

DARP, TOPS, and other individual program evaluations. Several recent reviews (Cooper et al. 1983; Tims and Ludford 1984; Senay 1985) conclude that the evidence consistently shows significant decreases in both opioid use and in criminality and improvements in general health for many addicts when they are in methadone maintenance treatment. Even when addicts are discharged from treatment, some sustained improvement is still observable, although to a lesser degree than when compared to concurrent treatment effects (Hser, Anglin, and Chou 1988). For example, Anglin and his colleagues (Anglin and McGlothlin 1984, 1985; Hser, Anglin, and Chou 1988) have shown that the percentage of nonincarcerated time during which addicts engaged in daily narcotics use decreased from about 70 percent (averaging across several studies) when not in methadone maintenance treatment to about 12 percent when in treatment (see table 2, part D), and the percentage of nonincarcerated time abstinent from narcotics increased from about 12 percent to about 26 percent. Likewise, property crime involvement decreased from about 18 percent of nonincarcerated time when not in treatment to about 11 percent during treatment. (These rates are measured by percentages of time engaging in the designated activity during periods when the subject is in treatment or out of treatment.)

Many evaluations demonstrate the effectiveness of methadone maintenance in reducing criminality. Maddux and Desmond (1979) studied the association between community crime rates and the rates of institutional and methadone maintenance treatment in the San Antonio, Texas, area. They found that community crime rates decreased as treatment rates increased; when cutbacks forced the premature discharge of patients, community crime rates increased. Ball et al. (1987) examined six programs in New York City, Philadelphia, and Baltimore (see table 2, part E). Methadone maintenance was found to be effective for the 617 subjects studied in reducing illicit drug use and crime during treatment. The reduction in criminality was dramatic; the average 307 days per person per year in which drug trafficking and property crimes were committed during the addiction period prior to treatment was reduced to eighteen to twenty-four crime days per person per year when in treatment after six months. Similar findings have been reported by McLellan et al. (1982) at Philadelphia Veterans Administration Medical Centers (see table 2, part F), by Burt Associates (1977) in New York City and Washington, D.C., and by Anglin and McGlothlin (1984) in Southern California, among many others.

These results are striking evidence of the positive effects of drug treatment. Unfortunately, the absence of control groups from these studies makes a strict quantification of the positive results impossible. For example, some degree of improvement may result not from treatment effects but from the passage of time, aging, or maturation. However, results from several natural experiments are available that investigate the effects of the termination of entire treatment programs (McGlothlin and Anglin 1981*b*), and the substitution of fee-for-service methadone programs for those supported by public funds (Anglin et al. 1989).

Research on the effects of involuntary termination of methadone maintenance was made possible when a Bakersfield, California, clinic was closed by local officials (McGlothlin and Anglin 1981*b*). A two-year follow-up compared behavior of the ninety-four methadone clients discharged from the Bakersfield clinic with a matched sample of eighty-three clients obtained from the Tulare, California, clinic where no such policy was enforced. Of the terminated clients, 55 percent became readdicted to heroin compared with 31 percent of the Tulare sample, and the arrest and incarceration rates were approximately double that for the comparison sample.

A similar policy change occurred in San Diego, although, unlike the Bakersfield clinic closure where no alternative programs were established, San Diego allowed private methadone maintenance providers to open clinics. For those who transferred to private methadone maintenance after the closure of a clinic, few differences were observed compared to a matched sample of clients in continuing public clinics in nearby counties (Anglin et al. 1989). Major adverse effects, however, were found for clients unable or unwilling to transfer to private programs: higher crime and drug-dealing rates, more contact with the criminal justice system, and higher rates of illicit drug use.

Methadone maintenance has been and remains controversial. Major issues include detoxification from methadone as a treatment goal, dosage effects, take-home policies, and street diversion. Because dosage effects and take-home policies are unique to methadone maintenance programs, relevant evaluation results are described at some length below.

Several studies suggest that dosage level may be significantly related to treatment outcome. In the original methadone maintenance trials, Dole and Nyswander (1965; Dole, Nyswander, and Warner 1968) employed dosages that were generally at least 100 milligrams/day. Many of the investigations published in the early 1970s suggested that lower dosages in the range of 40 to 50 milligrams could be employed for most patients (Goldstein and Judson 1973). Most of these later studies did not include a follow-up evaluation and focused only on treatment retention and opiate abuse. Seldom did they include criminal involvement as one of the outcome measures.

Craig (1980) studied 322 methadone maintenance clients maintained at an average daily dose of 30 milligrams and found a high dropout rate. Only 17 percent of the sample was still in the program by the end of the sixth month, and this fell to 10 percent at the end of one year. Reductions of heroin use (65 percent) and arrest rate (96 percent) occurred for clients retained one year. Those dropping out within thirty days did as poorly one year later as they had done one year before treatment. This study suggests that low-dose methadone can obtain success rates similar to those reported in other methadone studies using higher doses but at the cost of retaining fewer clients in treatment. McGlothlin and Anglin (1981a) and Fisher and Anglin (1987) compared three methadone maintenance programs, two of which used high doses (a mean stabilization dose of 82–95 milligrams), while the third used low doses (i.e., a mean of 43 milligrams) and a relatively strict policy with respect to involuntary termination for program violations. For the two high-dose programs, retention was much longer than for the low-dose program (two years after treatment entry, approximately 40 and 70 percent of clients remained in the two high-dose programs, while only 20 percent remained in the low-dose program); during the six- to seven-year period from program entry to interview, the clients from the two high-dose programs had significantly fewer arrests and less incarceration, narcotic addiction, and self-reported criminal behavior than did the clients in the low-dose program. These benefits persisted until the time of interview and were present whether the client was on or off methadone (see table 2, part A).

Hargreaves has concluded that "there is persuasive evidence that 100 mg is superior to 50 mg during the first five to ten months of maintenance for an important subgroup (10 percent to 30 percent) of patients; regulations that discourage individualized dosing are inappropriate" (1983, pp. 56–57). Therefore, the appropriate regulatory stance about dosage should also take into account individual differences in dose requirements (Brown, Watters, and Iglehart 1982). However, little is known about optimal matching between patient characteristics and dosage.

Little work on the effects of take-home policies has been reported.

Stitzer (1977) studied the use of take-home privileges as a reinforcement for attendance at counseling sessions. She found that attendance increased significantly above the levels observed during periods when take-home privileges were not contingent on attendance. Likewise, Milby (1978) and Stitzer, Bigelow, and Gross (1989) concluded that methadone take-home privileges can be powerful reinforcers of rehabilitative behaviors.

2. *Therapeutic Communities.*   Therapeutic communities are residential facilities in which treatment involves personality restructuring within a highly structured environment and focuses on development of social relationships. Examples include the early Synanon program and successors like Daytop Village (Biase 1981), Phoenix House, and Gateway House (DeLeon 1985). The treatment does not include any chemical agents except when medically or psychiatrically prescribed. The primary treatment approach includes encounter group therapy, tutorial learning sessions, remedial and formal education classes, residential job duties, and, in later stages, conventional occupations for live-in/work-out clients (Sells 1974). This therapy involves a highly demanding, twenty-four-hour-a-day social setting, with patient involvement in certain aspects of program government and group pressures to socialize the individual into accepting more adaptive attitudes and patterns of productive behavior. The optimal residential stay varies between programs, but traditional therapeutic communities require at least fifteen months in residence. However, some therapeutic communities have incorporated shorter periods of stay from six to twelve months based on clients' needs and progress (DeLeon 1985). Success is defined as a change to a lifestyle that is drug free, economically productive, and free from antisocial behavior.

Both DARP and TOPS and other reviews of evaluations of therapeutic communities have shown significant improvements in immediate and long-term outcomes (DeLeon 1984). Drug use and criminality declined while measures of prosocial behavior such as employment and school involvement increased (Romond, Forrest, and Kleber 1975; Aron and Daily 1976; Pin, Martine, and Walsh 1976; Holland 1978, 1983; Wilson 1978; Wilson and Mandelbrote 1978; DeLeon et al. 1979; Pompi, Shreiner, and McKey 1979; Brook and Whitehead 1980; Barr and Antes 1981; DeLeon 1984). "Time in program" has been identified as a powerful predictor of favorable outcome (Holland 1978; Wilson and Mandelbrote 1978; DeLeon and Rosenthal 1979, 1989; Barr and Antes 1981; Coombs 1981; DeLeon 1984). However, the likelihood of retention is difficult to predict from client characteristics. No studies have yielded contrary results, although the magnitude of the changes varies; several with positive findings failed to observe time-in-program differences (Brook and Whitehead 1980).

Evaluations of therapeutic-community clients in particular programs are best represented by DeLeon's research on Phoenix House (DeLeon, Skodol, and Rosenthal 1973; DeLeon 1983*a*, 1983*b*). The Phoenix House program in New York City is the nation's largest therapeutic-community drug-free treatment system. The program treats all types of substance abuse, although 80 percent of clients have been heroin addicts. Evaluations of immediate and long-term outcomes of clients show significant improvement compared to pretreatment status (e.g., DeLeon et al. 1979 and table 2, part G). Drug use and criminality declined while measures of social behavior increased (see DeLeon 1984). Studies examining differences between clients who complete treatment and those who drop out indicate that the graduates were significantly better than dropouts in all measures of outcome.

3. *Outpatient Drug-free Treatment.*   This type of program includes a wide variety of outpatient nonmaintenance programs. In the early 1970s, outpatient drug-free programs were mainly for youthful nonopiate users. Subsequently, almost as many opiate addicts have entered outpatient drug-free programs as methadone maintenance programs. Whether programs are oriented toward the treatment of opiates or nonopiates, the same services are typically provided. Treatment regimes usually do not include any chemical agent or medication, but prescription drugs are used as an adjunct to treatment or to treat medical problems. Temporary use of drugs such as tranquilizers for psychiatric disorders is permissible. The primary treatment approach employs outpatient services relying on counseling and training in social skills. The outpatient drug-free programs vary widely, ranging from highly demanding daytime therapeutic communities to relaxed programs of recreational activities. The planned duration usually is short, and referral is made to community agencies for health, mental health, educational, vocational, legal, housing, financial, family, and other required services. This treatment emphasizes abstinence from both licit and illicit drugs with attention paid to life circumstances that foster drug use.

Evaluations based on DARP data generally indicate that outpatient drug-free programs are less effective in retention but in longer-term outcomes are as effective as methadone maintenance or therapeutic communities (Kleber and Slobetz 1979; Simpson and Sells 1982) (see also table 2, part H). However, the favorable results for outpatient drug-free programs are restricted to "nonaddicts," clients who used opioids less than daily, usually in conjunction with other drugs, or who used only nonopioids.

Among the three modalities that TOPS compared (detoxification was dropped from any comparison because of the apparent temporary effects), outpatient drug-free clients were most likely to leave treatment in the first one (21 percent) to four weeks (36 percent) (Hubbard et al. 1984). By three months in treatment, more than 60 percent had dropped out, transferred, or completed treatment. Outpatient drug-free clients were also the least successful in reducing their drug use. About a third of those classified as more than minimal users at admission had continued or increased use after three months in treatment, although 45 percent of users reported a large reduction in use. Outpatient drug-free programs were also not successful at reducing crime among clients; about one in four clients who had reported an illegal act before treatment continued involvement in illegal activities (see table 2, part I).

4. *Detoxification.*   This modality provides a short-term use of licit drugs (such as antidepressants, methadone, or buprenophine) that focuses on withdrawal from illicit drugs and the medical management of symptoms. Other than referrals to other treatment services, detoxification usually provides no subsequent therapeutic services. Most detoxification programs focus on narcotics dependence and use methadone to establish a staged withdrawal, typically over twenty-one days (but longer periods are allowed under current federal regulation). Research findings are available only for opioid detoxification and we limit our discussion to this specific form (Wilson, Elms, and Tompson 1975; Maddux and Desmond 1980; Simpson and Sells 1982).

The primary objective of opioid detoxification treatment is to provide symptomatic relief from the opioid abstinence syndrome while physical dependence on opioids is being eliminated. Methadone is the only opioid drug currently approved for treating opiate dependence and is the detoxification agent routinely employed. The patient is first stabilized on a dose of methadone sufficient to prevent withdrawal symptoms and is then detoxified by stepwise reductions in the daily dose.

No evaluation data document the long-term effectiveness of detoxification (see a review article by Lipton and Maranda [1982]).

However, this treatment is effective in reducing drug use temporarily and there is a demand for it. Senay (1984) pointed out that, from a clinical point of view, detoxification programs are needed to treat emerging episodes, reduce the length and severity of "runs," and attract addicts into the treatment system generally.

B. Criminal Justice System-based Drug Treatment

Drug use among individuals within the criminal justice system is extensive. Results from the National Institute of Justice's Drug Use Forecasting project (Wish and Gropper, in this volume) conducted in a number of major cities have shown that urine tests of arrestees indicate high rates of illicit drug use. Illicit drugs are detected in the urine of 40–90 percent of arrestees, depending on the city. As would be expected, these high levels are also present in probation and correctional samples. Studies of prison inmates indicate that from 40–80 percent report serious substance abuse histories (Petersilia, Greenwood, and Lavin 1978; Innes 1988).

Programs of criminal diversion, correctional drug education and treatment, and probation and parole supervision designed for the drug abuser have been developed. Typically, such programs are short-lived—developed under one administration and terminated under subsequent ones. Interest in such programs developed in the early 1970s; most ended by the late 1970s (Lipton, Martinson, and Wilks 1975; Camp and Camp 1989).

Because of high rates of recidivism and criminal justice system overcrowding and the shift away from a rehabilitative philosophy in corrections, programs for drug-abusing offenders have languished in the 1980s until fairly recently. In the 1960s, several states established programs of civil commitment for the treatment of drug-abusing offenders. In 1987, correctional drug-treatment programs were instituted based on the therapeutic-community approach. Outcome studies for programs other than civil commitment, however, have been infrequent, and some programs have been so recently developed that evaluation information is sparse.

1. *Civil Commitment Programs.*   Civil commitment represents one of the early efforts at enforced treatment to control narcotics addiction and provide rehabilitation services for the drug-abusing offender. The federal Public Health Service hospitals in Fort Worth and Lexington are among the earliest examples (Maddux 1988). Beginning in the 1960s, three major civil commitment programs were established in the

United States: the California Civil Addict Program, the New York Civil Commitment Program, and programs under the federal Narcotic Addict Rehabilitation Act. The commitment procedures were similar for these programs and were straightforward, any individual found by medical examination to be addicted to drugs, usually heroin, could be committed to the programs. In practice, however, the majority of those committed had been arrested for property crimes or for drug trafficking and were diverted from conventional criminal processing. These programs typically had two phases: a period of incarceration followed by a period on parole or monitored release in the community. Offenders could be reincarcerated for further treatment for infractions of program and parole regulations. During both the incarceration and parole phases, the objectives of intervention were reductions in drug use and criminal behavior. A secondary focus was often vocational training.

The rationales and enabling legislation for these programs were quite similar, but their implementation and outcomes were substantially different (McGlothlin and Anglin 1990). The New York Civil Commitment Program and the federal Narcotic Addict Rehabilitation Act program were implemented under burdensome procedures, producing management problems which contributed in part to the lack of demonstrable success of these programs (Brill and Winick 1990; Mandell 1990). The California Civil Addict Program achieved better results.

The Civil Addict Program was administered by the California Department of Corrections, which employed both rehabilitation professionals and correctional staff. Because of reasonably effective monitoring by urine testing, any return to compulsive patterns of narcotics use could be identified soon after relapse and a proper intervention effected (often including a short "dry out" incarceration).

Although program results were not spectacular, outcomes at the time were as good as or better than those of other interventions for drug dependence. To some extent, overall outcomes were better because the program could be imposed on any identified addict at any time, and participants thus included many antisocial addicts not likely to enter the few available community-treatment programs. These latter programs attracted only less antisocial addicts, typically later in their addiction careers.

Two evaluations of the Civil Addict Program illustrate the effectiveness of properly implemented civil commitment programs. Using a natural experiment design, McGlothlin, Anglin, and Wilson (1977) compared addicts admitted to the program and subsequently released into the community under supervision with addicts admitted to the program and discharged after a short time because of legal errors in the commitment proceedings. During the five years that constituted the average commitment period, when under supervision in the community, the program group reduced their daily narcotics use by 21.0 percent, while the discharged group reduced their daily use by only 6.8 percent. Furthermore, the program group reported that their criminal activities were reduced by 18.6 percent while the discharged group reported a reduction of 6.7 percent.

A later analysis by Anglin and McGlothlin (1984) examined only the program group and identified three subsamples according to drug use and treatment status at the time of the interview, some twelve years after admission to the program: a "maturing-out" sample (Winick 1962), a "subsequent-treatment" sample, and a "chronic-street-addict" sample. The maturing-out sample (approximately 40 percent of the program group) had steadily reduced daily narcotic consumption when in the community during the average five-year commitment period and did not resume addicted use after discharge. At the time of the interview, subjects in this sample occasionally used narcotics, but few were addicted.

The subsequent-treatment sample, approximately 30 percent of the program group, showed a large decrease (approximately 20 to 25 percent) in daily drug use during the community phase of the commitment period. After discharge, however, without the program's structured supervision, addicted use rapidly increased. Three years after discharge, addicted use by this group had reached precommitment levels. Addicted use continued at that resumed level until the group subsequently reentered long-term treatment, this time with methadone maintenance.

The chronic-street-addict sample, approximately 30 percent of the program group, showed a moderate reduction (7–10 percent) in daily narcotic use during the community phase of the commitment period. After discharge, addicted-use levels exceeded that reported in the precommitment period, and were still high in the year preceding the interview; for that year, the chronic street addicts described themselves as being addicted 55 percent of their nonincarcerated time, as compared to approximately 4 percent for the maturing-out sample and 8 percent for the subsequent-treatment (methadone maintenance) sample.

These studies have two important findings. First, civil commitment reduced daily narcotic use and associated property crime by program participants to one-third the levels displayed by similar addicts who were not in the program. Second, while the program's effects differed across three types of addicts, narcotic use and crime were suppressed in all three groups. The program was generally effective in reducing demand for heroin.

2. *Corrections-based Therapeutic Community Models.* Many criminal justice system personnel believe that rehabilitative efforts aimed at substance-abusing offenders are relatively ineffective (Lipton, Martinson, and Wilks 1975; Carter and Klein 1976). Significant research results, however, indicate that correctional drug-treatment programs can have a substantial effect on the behavior of chronic drug-abusing offenders (McGlothlin, Anglin, and Wilson 1977; Gendreau and Ross 1987). Evidence for these conclusions comes from outcome research on community-based therapeutic communities, which has shown effective results with clients having extensive criminal histories (Sells and Simpson 1976; DeLeon et al. 1979; DeLeon 1984), and a study comparing outcomes for drug-abusing offenders in several prison-based programs to those for both men and women who received no treatment (Wexler, Lipton, and Foster 1985).

The results from this last study compare outcomes for clients in treatments based on therapeutic-community models and psychological counseling treatment with outcomes for drug users admitted to a waiting list but not admitted to a program. The average age for men and women entering these programs was approximately thirty-three. About 50 percent were black and 25 percent Hispanic. Approximately 20 percent had less than an eighth grade education, and all groups were roughly equivalent in terms of criminal history. Intermediate results showed that men and women in the therapeutic-community programs participated significantly longer than men and women in counseling treatment, both while in prison and afterwards. Twenty-seven percent of the male therapeutic-community participants were arrested during the follow-up period, compared to 40 percent of those receiving counseling only and those receiving no treatment. For women, 18 percent of the therapeutic-community participants were arrested during follow-up, compared to 29 percent of the counseling treatment group, and 24 percent of the no treatment group.

As has been found in community-based studies, participants in the therapeutic-community programs for longer periods had significantly better outcomes. Those participating for nine to twelve months had a mean time to arrest of eighteen months compared to thirteen months for those participating from six to nine months, twelve months for those participating three to six months, and eight and one-half months for those leaving treatment before three months. Similarly, those participating for nine to twelve months received positive parole discharges nearly 80 percent of the time, compared to 60 percent for the six-to-nine-month group and the three-to-six-month group; those dropping out prior to three months had only 50 percent positive parole discharges. Similar findings have been reported for the Cornerstone program, a corrections-based therapeutic community within the Oregon State Department of Corrections (Field 1985).

Comparable corrections-based therapeutic-community models have been implemented at local levels. One example is a program conducted by Amity, Inc., in the Pima County, Arizona, jail. Although evaluation results have not yet been reported, both corrections and treatment staff believe the program has had a significant effect on postdischarge behavior of participants (Hecht and Arbiter 1989).

C. Criminal Justice and Community-based Treatment

The relations between drug use and crime and the inability of the criminal justice system to provide adequate treatment for drug-abusing offenders, combined with the encouraging evaluation results for community-based treatment programs, have led to the development of coordinated programs in many states to refer drug-abusing offenders to community-based treatment in lieu of prosecution or probation revocation. One such program, called Treatment Alternatives to Street Crime (TASC), was initiated in 1972 and in 1988 was in operation in eighteen states (Cook et al. 1988). Under TASC auspices, community-based treatment is made available for drug-dependent individuals who otherwise might become progressively more involved with the criminal justice system. To motivate drug offenders to enter and remain in treatment, TASC employs diversionary dispositions like deferred prosecution, creative community sentencing, and pretrial intervention. When arrested, the suspect may be evaluated by a diagnostic unit and held pending transfer to a treatment program. Case-management principles are used to promote compliance with both criminal justice system and treatment expectations. Dropping out of treatment or other noncompliance is treated by the courts as a violation of the conditions of release.

Evaluations of the impact of TASC and other diversion programs have been limited. However, most TASC programs are believed to have performed the treatment outreach function successfully: for example, Sells (1983) reports that 50 percent of the referrals entered treatment for the first time. Although no detailed supportive data are available, some independent local evaluations have concluded that local TASC programs effectively intervened with clients to reduce drug abuse and criminal activity (Cook et al. 1988). No solid data base or data collection mechanism is in place for long-term evaluations of TASC and its effects on drug-related crime or on the activities of the criminal justice system.

The only available evaluations on the impact of TASC or similar programs are based on the TOPS study (Collins and Allison 1983; Hubbard et al. 1988) (see table 2, parts I and J). These studies compared criminal justice system involved clients (in TASC and under other forms of justice system supervision) to voluntary drug-treatment clients in terms of demographic characteristics, treatment retention, treatment progress, and predatory behavior in the year following treatment termination. Criminal justice system referred clients were more likely to be male, nonwhite, younger, and to have previous criminal justice system involvement in the year before treatment than were volunteers. TASC clients improved as much as voluntary clients with regard to drug use, employment, and criminal behavior during the first six months of treatment. TASC clients also tended to remain in both residential and outpatient drug-free treatment modalities six to seven weeks longer than did the clients under other criminal justice system referrals or voluntary clients—a finding usually associated with better treatment outcomes. The monitoring functions of TASC seem to have encouraged this longer treatment participation.

D. Overall Effectiveness: Comparisons among Modalities

Despite the impressive positive outcomes reported by most drug-abuse treatment evaluations, basic questions remain as to whether such improvements would have occurred otherwise due to maturation, regression to the mean, or other nontreatment influences. Random-assignment experimental research addressing this issue is unavailable, but a few studies using matched comparison groups have been reported. Results from these studies attest to the general effectiveness of drug treatment. For example, McLellan et al. (1982) compared a treatment group to patients who had dropped out of treatment after matching pretreatment characteristics of the two groups. The results showed significantly better posttreatment results in employment, drug use, legal status, and psychological functioning in the treatment group. Hunt, Lipton, and Spunt (1984) focused on the effect of treatment on the relations between drug use and criminal activity by comparing methadone maintenance clients with narcotics users who were not in treatment. Methadone maintenance clients were less involved in criminal activity, particularly in more serious crimes such as robbery, burglary, or dealing drugs.

Little systematic knowledge is available on matching of drug abusers to particular treatments best suited to their individual needs. Clients' self-selection into different modalities makes direct outcome comparisons among treatments difficult, and research results often need careful qualification. However, there are some studies using an experimental design that attempted to resolve this issue, though with limited success. Some limited comparative results are also available from DARP and TOPS.

Bale et al. (1980) reported a treatment evaluation comparison between methadone maintenance and three therapeutic communities using an experimental design. Five hundred eighty-five heroin-addicted male military veterans were randomly assigned to methadone maintenance or to one of three therapeutic communities after a five-day detoxification program. Subjects were followed up at six months and at one year. Data were collected on drug use, criminal behavior, work, and school attendance. However, only 108 of the subjects accepted the random assignment and spent as long as one week or more in their assigned program. Most subjects dropped out early in treatment, especially from the therapeutic communities. Less than 50 percent of the clients remained in the programs two months after admission.

There were no outcome differences between the combined therapeutic-community group and the methadone maintenance group at either follow-up. Because of the high dropout rate, the outcome differences were virtually uninterpretable. Furthermore, the extent to which differences at outcome can be attributed to the effects of either treatment is limited because subjects chose to enter and leave various treatment modalities subsequent to the random assignment required by the study design. However, the subjects who remained in a therapeutic community longer than fifty days did consistently better than the methadone maintenance group at a one-year follow-up.

The multimodality nature of DARP and TOPS allows some limited comparisons among modalities despite the considerable self-selection of the client to any particular modality. The DARP research contrasted treatment outcomes for methadone maintenance, therapeutic communities, outpatient drug-free programs, and detoxification against an intake-only group of subjects who were eligible for and admitted to a waiting list, but who did not subsequently enter treatment. The DARP studies showed that actual retention in treatment for all DARP clients was shorter overall than most clients anticipated at entry. The median time in treatment was over twelve months in methadone maintenance, between three and four months in therapeutic communities and outpatient drug-free programs, and less than two weeks in detoxification.

Behavioral changes related to drug use, criminal involvement, and employment in the first one to three years after treatment were consistently better for clients in methadone maintenance, therapeutic communities, and outpatient drug-free programs than for those in the detoxification and intake-only groups. However, the outcome differences among the three effective treatments were not significant. Table 2 reports data on a variety of outcomes. For example, in the first year after DARP treatment, 27 percent of the methadone maintenance clients, 28 percent of those in therapeutic communities, and 24 percent of those in outpatient drug-free programs used no illicit drugs and had no arrests or time in jail or prison, compared with 15 percent of the detoxification clients and 14 percent of the intake-only group (Simpson 1984). The DARP studies also found that clients who remained in treatment longer and who demonstrated more favorable performance during treatment tended to have more favorable posttreatment outcomes. There also appeared to be a minimum time in treatment for any favorable results: clients in methadone maintenance, therapeutic communities, and outpatient drug-free programs who remained less than three months had relatively poor outcomes, comparable with those in detoxification programs, regardless of the reason for termination. Differences for the addict samples among all modalities diminished over the twelve-year follow-up; this is understandable because of the operation of subsequent influences (Simpson et al. 1986) (see table 2, part K for specific findings).

Evaluation results from TOPS contrast the three major modalities and generally support the DARP findings. Dropout rates were high across all drug-treatment modalities (Hubbard et al. 1984) (table 2, part I). At three months in treatment, less than 40 percent of the outpatient drug-free clients remained in treatment (36 percent dropped out by the first month). The comparative retention figure for methadone maintenance was 65 percent; for residential clients, 44 percent. Outcomes reported by clients at follow-up indicated that during the first three months in treatment more than 95 percent of retained residential clients and 80 percent of methadone maintenance clients reported reduced use of their primary drug. Outpatient drug-free clients were least successful in reducing their drug use; only about 45 percent reported a large reduction in use. Client self-reports indicate that some degree of serious drug use continued during treatment, and in some cases it went undetected by program staff in each of these modalities.

Illegal predatory activity was common in the pretreatment period among all clients in the TOPS study but was most frequent among residential clients. During the first three months in treatment, about 70 percent of the retained methadone and outpatient drug-free clients who had committed predatory acts before treatment reported cessation of this behavior during treatment. As would be expected in a restricted environment, the reports of such behavior for residential clients plummeted. Of residential clients who had pretreatment involvement in such activity, 97 percent reported cessation during treatment. Those who reported such activity were not detected by program staff and typically victimized the program, other clients, or the public in rare, unsupervised moments.

As can be seen in table 2, parts I–J, the posttreatment outcomes measured in the year after terminating treatment showed major improvement in drug use and criminal activities for all modalities, although the improvement was smaller than that which occurred during the treatment program. Those clients who remained in treatment longer (at least three months) appeared to have more positive outcomes. The greatest posttreatment reduction in illegal predatory activity occurred for residential clients. While 60 percent reported at least one predatory act in the year before TOPS treatment, only one-third reported such activity in the year after treatment. Smaller decreases in illegal activity were reported for methadone maintenance and outpatient drug-free clients. About 5–10 percent of the clients in all modalities continued to commit a high number of predatory crimes after discharge.

Evidence from numerous sources over two decades demonstrates that drug-treatment programs can reduce both drug use and criminality among their clients. Much more needs to be learned about the comparative effectiveness of different modalities and about classification of drug abusers to match them with the treatment regime most likely to help them. The following section surveys current knowledge about the correlates of successful treatment outcomes.

IV. Correlational Covariates of Treatment Outcome

The major modalities can reduce drug use and crime during treatment, and, to a lesser degree, after treatment discharge. However, drug-treatment clients often will not accept assignments to particular treatments, and consequently different modalities attract different client groups. As a consequence, comparisons between modalities are necessarily restricted because no two modalities necessarily have similar client populations.

In this section, we examine correlates and covariates of positive treatment outcomes across modalities in terms of patient characteristics and treatment characteristics (Sells 1974). Ideally, some combinations of these characteristics will eventually identify optimal matches between treatment types and client types.

A. Client Characteristics

Studies examining the differential responsiveness to treatment by patient characteristics have not clearly established their effects. Factors that have received most attention have been demographics, criminal record, drug-use history, and psychopathology. Evidence is inconclusive or contradictory about the demographic characteristics other than, perhaps, age. However, addicts who have a more stable family background, an intact marriage, a job, a history of minimal criminality, less evidence of alcohol or polydrug abuse, and less severe psychiatric disorders are more likely to achieve a better outcome in most programs.

1. *Demographics.* Differential treatment responsiveness by gender and ethnicity has been found to be significant by some studies (Dale and Dale 1973; Cohen et al. 1980; DeLeon and Jainchill 1981), but not by others (Greene and Ryser 1978; Rosenthal et al. 1979; Marsh and Simpson 1986). Some studies also found significant sex and race interactions (Savage and Simpson 1980; Anglin et al. 1988). Most studies showing differences attributed their findings to clients' pretreatment characteristics. For example, most studies showing race differences found that whites showed greater behavioral changes than blacks as a result of treatment, but that those differences were themselves a function of community, social, and economic variables. Anglin et al. (1988) also found that treatment was generally less successful for Chicanos, particularly for Chicano females, than for whites partly because of the fewer economic opportunities generally available to Chicanos. However, DeLeon and Jainchill (1981) found, with Phoenix House clients,

that favorable outcome and improvement rates (measured by no crime and either no opioid use or no use of a nonopioid primary drug) for seventy-four female clients were consistently higher after two years than those for 214 males, when differences in pretreatment status were controlled. Studies showing race and sex interactions usually claim worse outcomes for minority women; in comparison with white men and women, the least favorable outcomes were found for black females by Savage and Simpson (1980) and Chicano females by Anglin et al. (1988).

In most studies, however, sex and race factors usually do not predict posttreatment narcotics use. These variables seem more often associated with entry into treatment for narcotic addiction (Des Jarlais et al. 1983).

No study has successfully identified any predictor that is significantly associated with positive outcomes for different ethnic groups. One consistent factor for women, however, is a partner's support (Eldred and Washington 1976; Tucker 1979; Nurco, Wegner, and Stephenson 1982). Eldred and Washington (1976) and Tucker (1979) reported that over 70 percent of successful women and men had the support of their partners during their treatment periods. Clients who reported that their partners had influenced them to enter treatment remained in treatment significantly longer than those whose partners did not provide encouragement—a mean of 49.6 months versus 28.2. Also, women who were least responsive to treatment were intensively involved in criminal activities (Weipert, D'Orban, and Bewley 1976), or lived with, and hence were primarily supported by, male addicts (Eldred and Washington 1976).

Questions remain as to whether different ethnic and sex groups have different treatment needs and, if they do, what those needs are or how they might influence the treatment process and outcome. Some studies have shown that increased services relating to children, health, and legal status result in increased client participation and increased effectiveness for women clients (Naierman et al. 1979; Marsh 1982). In addition, Finnegan (1972) found that a comprehensive program for pregnant addicts resulted in lower mortality rates among infants. While there has been a call for attention to ethnic concerns in treatment programming (McMearn 1971; Freudenberger 1975; Espada 1979), there is a virtual absence of studies to support or oppose the development of culturally sensitive programming.

Client age contributes to the prediction of posttreatment narcotics use in many studies (Des Jarlais et al. 1983). In general, older age predicts longer treatment retention or completion, decreased drug use, decreased crime, decreased readmission, and composite success (De-Leon, Holland, and Rosenthal 1972; Rounsaville et al. 1982). Most studies report that patients younger than twenty-five are significantly more likely to leave treatment prematurely than are older patients. The importance attributed to age is largely connected to Winick's (1962) suggestion that addicts "mature out" of their interest in drug use, particularly in relation to the length of the addiction career and the increasingly serious consequences of continuing drug use (Anglin et al. 1986).

2. *Behavioral Factors.* Using multidimensional assessments of multiple outcomes of 123 opiate addicts followed for six months after admission, Rounsaville et al. (1982) found that outcome is predicted with relative accuracy by previous patterns in the behavior being examined. For example, previous work history predicts employment during the follow-up period, history of imprisonments and antisocial personality predicts illegal activity, pretreatment duration of opiate addiction predicts illicit drug use, and initial psychiatric symptom level and depressive diagnosis predict symptom status at follow-up. No single predictor was significantly related to all of the outcome measures. Other studies have consistently shown that clients with more criminal involvement before treatment have the poorest outcomes (Simpson and Sells 1982; Simpson et al. 1986; Hubbard et al. 1984). Other negative prognoses include alcohol use (Stimmel, Cohen, and Hanbury 1978; Stimmel et al. 1982; Roszell, Calsyn, and Chaney 1986; Bickel, Marion, and Lowinson 1987; Corty and Ball 1987), polydrug use (Marcovici et al. 1980; Hubbard et al. 1988), unemployment (Rounsaville et al. 1982; Hubbard et al. 1989), and dual diagnoses (McLellan et al. 1984; Brizer et al. 1985; Kleber 1986; Corty and Ball 1987). Among these factors, psychopathology has been studied most extensively and has been identified as influential in treatment outcomes and is discussed in more detail below.

Research has accumulated that shows a high degree of psychopathology displayed by drug addicts. McLellan and his colleagues (Woody et al. 1981; McLellan et al. 1983) in Philadelphia demonstrated the importance of psychopathology in relation to treatment outcomes. They reported that the severity of psychological problems at admission is a powerful predictor of several outcome criteria, such as illicit drug use, criminal activity, social productivity, and psychological adjustment, when these are measured six months after entry into treatment.

B. Program Factors

Several program components and characteristics have been shown to be generally beneficial when appropriately implemented. Notable components are psychotherapy, urine testing, and legal coercion. For example, a recent study by Joe, Simpson, and Sells (1989) of 590 methadone maintenance clients from the TOPS evaluation confirmed that a higher methadone dosage level, more frequent urine testing, and more frequent dosage take-home privileges were correlated with longer treatment retention and lower relapse rates. Important program characteristics include treatment philosophy, program policies, qualifications of staff, and other quality-of-care aspects.

1. *Psychotherapy.* Since 1970, most studies of psychotherapy with addicts have been done with methadone-treated patients. In eight studies reviewed by O'Brian et al. (1984), opiate-dependent patients were randomly assigned to psychotherapy or to a treatment control condition, usually drug counseling. Six of the studies (75 percent) showed a better outcome for clients in the psychotherapy condition than those in the control condition.

Studies by researchers in Philadelphia and New Haven, Connecticut, have evaluated controlled psychotherapy. The Philadelphia study, based on 110 male veterans, indicated that the addition of psychotherapy to drug counseling may help narcotics addicts. The results were derived from six-month follow-ups measured by an addiction-severity index (McLellan et al. 1980, 1984; Woody et al. 1983). The overall conclusion was that psychotherapy can be helpful for opiate-dependent patients.

A similar study in New Haven, however, did not find a treatment effect (Rounsaville et al. 1983). The study evaluated short-term interpersonal psychotherapy—a brief psychodynamic therapy—for methadone clients with apparent psychiatric disorders. The subjects were seventy-two clients diagnosed as having concurrent psychiatric disorders, such as anxiety or depression. Clients doing poorly in treatment or having significant psychopathology were especially encouraged to attend. Treatment was available for six months. The multiple outcome measures included treatment attrition, number of urine positives for illegal drugs, number of arrests, psychiatric symptomatology, personal and social functioning, and attainment of individual goals. Attrition was high in both groups; only 38 percent of the psychotherapy group and 54 percent of the control group completed the program. The outcome results indicated few differences between the two groups.

The contrast between outcomes of the two studies suggests that the recruiting and implementation strategies of Woody et al. (1983) should be considered in designing additional treatment trials. These strategies include induction of a broad range of clients early in treatment and the integration of drug-treatment and psychotherapy staff.

2. *Urine Testing.* Monitoring of illicit drug use by urinalysis has been a common practice in most drug-treatment programs and in the criminal justice system supervised programs for known drug-using offenders (see Wish and Gropper, in this volume). Whether such monitoring affects treatment outcomes has not been thoroughly studied, although considerable evidence points to its effectiveness when linked to sanctions applied to those who test positive (McGlothlin, Anglin, and Wilson 1977). The few available treatment studies mostly found that urine testing, in the context of the overall treatment, does not improve program outcomes. Goldstein, Horns, and Hansteen (1977) examined whether on-site testing in a full-service program with immediate feedback of results might have some therapeutic value. They concluded that the on-site urinalysis had no therapeutic advantage over the usual off-site testing.

Havassay and Hall (1981) conducted a large-scale test of the effectiveness of urine monitoring as a deterrent to illicit drug use among methadone maintenance clients. Subjects were randomly assigned to monitored and unmonitored groups. Monitored subjects continued to provide urine specimens once a week for one year; unmonitored subjects did not. All other aspects of treatment remained the same. Surprise urine collections of both groups were conducted at four and eight months after the study began. These data showed that slightly more drug-free urine specimens were produced by the urine-monitored group. However, no significant difference in the proportion of drug-free specimens was found between the groups at either time. The study concluded that urine monitoring was not an important component in the context of methadone maintenance treatment, given the cost, time, and staff necessary to implement urine monitoring and the negligible reduction in drug use.

In contrast, McGlothlin, Anglin, and Wilson (1977) found that urine testing in criminal justice system settings rather than in community-treatment settings, and in combination with intensive legal or other supervision with sanctions for detected drug use, was more effective than supervision without testing in reducing daily narcotics use and criminal activity by the narcotics addicts admitted to the California

Civil Addict Program. This finding has been replicated in later work with methadone maintenance admissions (Anglin, Deschenes, and Speckart 1987).

3. *Legal Coercion.*   Drug-dependent individuals enter treatment programs for a variety of reasons. Some have "burned out" or can no longer support their drug use as effectively as they once did. Some have an intact social support system of nonuser relatives and friends who encourage their entry into treatment, and others develop health problems that preclude continued use. Many, however, are brought into contact with the criminal justice system because of their use of drugs or related criminality. Many users apprehended for illegal activities are encouraged or coerced to enter community-treatment programs. Drug-using offenders are often required to enter treatment via court-ordered diversion or probation. The criminal justice system may also formally and informally motivate treatment entry by threat of probation or parole sanctions or suggestions by supervising officials.

Some writers argue that little benefit can be derived when a client is forced into treatment (Bullington, Sprowls, and Phillips 1978; Klein 1979; Newman 1983). Others argue that few chronic addicts would enter treatment without such external motivation, and that legal coercion is as appropriate a motivation for treatment entry as any other.

Some evidence suggests that the criminal justice system consequences that can result from failure to meet treatment program conditions may lead to more socially acceptable behavior than that which is produced by treatment alone (Allen 1959; Cohen 1979; Salmon and Salmon 1983; Orsagh and Marsden 1985). Those who contend that a purely voluntary treatment system would not attract a significant number of addicts also argue that controlling addiction benefits society as a whole; that is, the judicial system should coerce addicts into treatment to safeguard the interests and well-being of the community (Anglin 1988*b*; Hubbard et al. 1988; Anglin and Hser 1990).

Research on the performance and outcomes for addicts coerced into treatment, however, has not produced consistent findings. In a review of the literature, McGlothlin (1979) concluded that, despite less favorable preadmission characteristics, legally coerced clients benefited from treatment as much as other clients, and their addiction-related behaviors markedly improved after entry into treatment. Further support for this finding is derived from two studies of methadone maintenance clients that divided subjects into those entering treatment under no, moderate, or high legal coercion (Anglin, Brecht, and Maddahian 1990;

Anglin and Hser 1990). All three groups decreased addicted heroin use markedly during treatment (one-fifth of the pretreatment level) and sustained the improvement, although to a lesser degree, after treatment discharge (one half of the pretreatment level). Other evidence suggests that coercion brings addicts into their first treatment episode earlier in the addiction career than otherwise might have occurred and that they are retained in treatment longer (Collins and Allison 1983). In contrast, there are some reports that criminal justice system clients are less motivated than noncoerced clients to conform to treatment-program requirements, are more likely to continue their drug use and associated behaviors, and are more difficult for treatment staff to deal with (McGlothlin 1979). Such inconsistent findings may result from the different measures used to assess treatment effectiveness in the case of criminal justice system referred clients.

The majority of findings, including those from the best-designed studies, however, generally support the proposition that a collaborative relation between the criminal justice system and community-treatment delivery systems produces, at an aggregate level, enhanced treatment outcomes.

4. *Retention.*   Time in treatment (retention) and type of discharge are program characteristics that have been consistently related, after controlling for individual client characteristics, to client status at follow-up. These characteristics are valuable measures of a program's ability to maintain client contact and enhance prospects for a therapeutic relationship that facilitates positive treatment outcomes. With few exceptions, most studies on the length of treatment find that longer treatment retention is associated with reduced drug use and crime and increased employment (McGlothlin and Anglin 1979; Simpson 1979, 1981). Simpson's study of DARP data also suggests that a minimum duration in treatment is necessary for effective treatment. Treatments lasting less than ninety days appear to be of limited benefit, regardless of the treatment involved. Beyond ninety days, however, treatment outcome improves in direct relation to the length of time spent in treatment. These findings are consistent with results from studies of therapeutic-community programs in the community by DeLeon et al. (1979; DeLeon and Schwartz 1984), therapeutic-community programs in correctional settings (Wexler, Lipton, and Foster 1985), and methadone maintenance programs (Ball et al. 1987).

Interpretations of these results are, however, complicated by the likely selective termination of patients with poorer prognoses (Maddux and Bowden 1972). For example, Baekland and Lundwall (1975), in their critical review of the literature, concluded that "remainers" are likely to be a more stable group initially, and this may make better treatment outcomes likelier. They had higher rates of pretreatment employment, fewer total arrests, and were slightly older than the drop-outs. Furthermore, follow-up studies often show some degree of improvement in minimal treatment or untreated groups as a function of the passage of time (Burt Associates 1977).

Since programs can exert influence only when patients are enrolled, retention has been viewed as an important goal of all treatments. Determinants of retention in treatment have not been thoroughly studied. There is, however, some evidence to suggest that those who exhibit greater psychological disturbance, particularly depression, are more likely to leave treatment prematurely (Wexler and DeLeon 1977; Steer 1980; Woody et al. 1981; McLellan et al. 1989).

Several demographic variables have been found to be predictors of retention. In general, it appears that clients who are black, unmarried, polydrug abusers, unemployed, or who have longer conviction records are likelier to drop out of treatment (Steer 1980). Sansone (1980) found lower retention rates for women, Hispanics, and other nonblack minorities and suggested that treatment programs be modified to serve the needs of these low-retention subgroups more effectively. DeLeon (1987), however, claimed that correlates between clients' demographic characteristics and retention have been weak, while motivation, perception, and the client's readiness appear more relevant to retention. Sansone also found slightly higher retention for clients on readmission (compared with first admission), regardless of age, sex, or racial background. Collins and Allison (1983) reported that drug abusers who were legally coerced into treatment stay longer. McFarlain et al. (1977) found that retention was positively related to legal pressure but only in the initial phases of treatment. They also reported finding no relation between retention and either age or race.

Programs with a flexible dosage policy were found to be associated with greater retention in treatment (McGlothlin and Anglin 1981a; Brown, Watters, and Iglehart 1982). Programs making use of flexible strategies retained clients an average of about nine months longer than those programs making use of any other dosage policy.

Other research suggests that a broad definition of retention may be needed. Simpson et al. (1978) report that 39 percent of methadone maintenance clients and about one-fourth of the outpatient drug-free clients returned to treatment within a year. This raises the question of whether, for many drug abusers, repeated exposure to treatment is more effective than one episode (McLellan and Druley 1977). In this respect, the total time in treatment may be more important, when accrued across treatment episodes, than retention in a single program.

5. *Program Policies and Staffing.* The philosophies and policies of providers of treatment services are more diverse than the program modalities, components, and approaches that are applied by those providers. Of all the aspects of treatment structure, program policy and its execution by staff are perhaps the least quantifiable (and least studied) in terms of their effects on treatment outcomes (Sells and Simpson 1976). Nevertheless, clinical impressions by many observers concur that disparate outcomes are often a function of providers' policies and staff's manners of implementing those policies. Different outcomes are noted even when comparing programs that are virtually identical in their components and structure (Ball 1989).

Limited evaluation data describe the influence of program policies and staff implementation. In a study of three methadone maintenance programs in Southern California (McGlothlin and Anglin 1981a; Fisher and Anglin 1987, discussed in Sec. III), two programs with similar dosage levels and flexible policies with respect to client management, discharge for program infractions, and degree of supportive counseling had better retention times, a primary indicator of treatment effectiveness, than did the third, less flexible, program. Of the two flexible programs, the program with a more adaptive policy on client infractions retained 77 percent admissions for two years, while the program with a more punitive orientation retained 42 percent. The third program, with the least flexible policies (and mean dosage level about one-half of the other two), retained only about 25 percent of admissions after two years. These differences could not be explained by pretreatment differences among the three programs in the races or ages of the male samples studied.

Outcomes within therapeutic communities also vary considerably. DeLeon (1985) reported three-month and six-month retention rates for seven therapeutic-community programs in which the highest rates were 46 percent and 35 percent and the lowest were 23 percent and 18 percent. Reasons reported by those leaving treatment prematurely included program factors such as conflicts with staff and differing views of treatment. DeLeon concluded that improved outcomes were influenced by the relations between the overall treatment environment and specific treatment elements. However, he noted that the effects on outcomes of variations in character in therapeutic communities have been only indirectly inferred, and he proposes that more program-based research be undertaken to make explicit the relations between treatment environments and outcomes.

The connection between staff characteristics and treatment efficacy was noted by Joe, Simpson, and Sells (1989). Positive outcomes were associated with higher professional quality of the staff involved in diagnosing clients at admission and in designing treatment plans.

John Ball (1989), in his study of six methadone maintenance programs in three East Coast cities, has presented similar findings. Outcomes showed wide variation in methadone maintenance programs of similar design. Results were partially attributable to intangible factors of program "personality" which were affected by staff attitudes and approaches. Ball's study included confidential interviews with program personnel from which emerged a relation between program "morale" and treatment effectiveness. The dynamic relationships among staff, clients, and program structures must be more completely examined in order to make the evaluation of this aspect of treatment more meaningful.

V. Conclusions and Implications

Research on drug abuse treatment demonstrates significant declines in drug use and criminal behavior by drug-dependent clients as a result of treatment (Cooper et al. 1983; Tims and Ludford 1984), although we lack adequate data to enable optimal matching of treatments to individual drug abusers. The conclusions we derived in this essay from the review of evidence are summarized in the introduction, but it may be helpful to recapitulate those findings that pertain to social policy implications and the future direction of drug abuse treatment.

Four structural program features are of greatest importance in designing and implementing treatments. First, the period of intervention must be lengthy since drug dependence (especially in regard to heroin and cocaine) is typically a chronically relapsing condition. Except in a minority of cases, several rounds of treatment (possibly including several different modalities), aftercare, and relapse may be expected, and it is not unreasonable to assume that years of structured intervention will be necessary to control, reduce, or eliminate drug dependence in any given individual.

Second, programs must initially provide a significant level of structure—such as a residential stay in a controlled setting or very close monitoring in an outpatient setting — so that the user can be detoxified from illicit drugs and thoroughly assessed, after which an individual program plan can be instituted. The initial period of close control should be followed by a carefully structured program of further treatment and subsequent aftercare. Objective monitoring for drug use by urine testing may enhance outcomes by diminishing the likelihood of relapse. Even in programs with strong supportive services, when such monitoring may not obtain direct effects, drug testing can provide clinically useful information for treatment staff (Joe, Simpson, and Hubbard 1989). Other ancillary interventions—such as psychiatric care, psychological services, or job training—that encourage retention in treatment and in community aftercare and that prevent relapse should be effected on an individual basis.

Third, effective programs are flexible; no absolute mandates should determine client management. Some level of continued or substitute drug use may be expected from the majority of those in community programs, whether under criminal justice system auspices or not (McGlothlin, Anglin, and Wilson 1977; Anglin and McGlothlin 1985). Intermittent drug use that does not seriously disrupt the individual's program plan should be dealt with on an individual basis in the context of the addict's overall adjustment. Any detected readdiction, however, requires immediate program reactions such as, in the case of heroin use, placement either in a residential setting for detoxification or in a methadone maintenance or naltrexone blocking program.

Finally, any intervention program must undergo regular evaluation to determine its level of effectiveness and to determine whether changing characteristics of clients require compensatory changes in the program. Program staff and policies must be kept current with developments in the treatment of drug dependence so that suitable new methods can be adopted and staff adequately trained in their utilization.

Empirical assessments of the need for treatment in drug-dependent groups suggest the desirability of increases in treatment services and options, and in legally coerced treatment for criminal justice system-identified drug users. Expanded treatment capacities will produce benefits to society and allow clients who need or desire treatment to benefit more readily from such services. Evaluation findings also suggest that a complementary system of other rehabilitation services will achieve additional beneficial treatment effects. Conversely, because of the present climate of restricted treatment availability, resistance by some drug users to entering treatment, and regional variations in determining client eligibility, current treatment populations do not adequately represent the full range of drug-dependent individuals. Furthermore, little information exists about the potentially inhibiting effects of program waiting lists and required client-paid fees that discourage some individuals with dependence problems from entering treatment. The cumulative effect of these "selective filtering" processes may result in inflated estimates of the potential aggregate benefits of treatment. Thus should treatment capacity expand to include a larger segment of the drug-dependent population, the degree of favorable outcomes may decline in the short term.

Treatment components that seem especially important include a determination of psychiatric severity and provision of appropriate psychotherapy, attention to polydrug-use problems (D'Amanda 1983) to assure early detection and thus early intervention, and increased provision of ancillary services (Ball et al. 1987; Wermuth, Brummett, and Sorenson 1987). Provision of legitimate economic opportunities is important so that clients in treatment do not need to remain enmeshed in the drug-abuse subculture of drug trafficking, property crime, or related activities to meet their economic needs. This is especially important for disadvantaged groups, particularly for women with responsibility for child rearing. Finally, for criminal justice system identified drug users, legal sanctions coupled with treatment services should be applied to control drug use and crime among this population more effectively.

Although the above suggestions are amply supported by research findings and have been known within the field for a long time (Sells 1974), their implementation has been difficult. Treatment programs exist in the context of competition for resources with other social programs, the need for adequately trained staff, and perhaps most important, a history of shifting and unstable funding.

The use of public resources for drug treatment remains controversial. To some, it seems inappropriate to provide services to what is considered a criminal population. Perhaps more important, however, is that inflated expectations established in the 1960s and 1970s regarding drug-treatment effectiveness have not been fulfilled; clients in treatment often continue to use narcotics and other drugs and to remain involved in other aspects of the addiction lifestyle (Ausubel 1983). Thus a pervasive public disappointment with drug treatment has emerged, despite extensive positive findings. In addition, funding constraints and a reduced public interest in the social rehabilitation of deviant individuals have curtailed public money dedicated to drug treatment.

The consequences include longer waiting lists for subsidized treatment slots and an increase in fee-for-service drug programs, particularly for methadone maintenance and cocaine treatment. Unfortunately, disrupted treatment progress is often the result when clients are responsible for fees but are unable to meet payment schedules. A costly alternative is "revolving door" admissions to short-term publicly funded programs, such as methadone detoxification, that effectively result in low-level extended treatment. In addition, other public service agencies, hospital emergency room services, and criminal justice system resources are used more heavily by addicts when they are not in treatment (McGlothlin and Anglin 1981*b*). The argument that social costs for the treatment of drug dependence should not be borne by the public—an argument that contributed to public program terminations and extensive restrictions that have considerably reduced the number of accessible treatment slots—may be misconceived. Costs paid from government resources may simply be shifted from drug-treatment programs to other government-funded programs.

A major objective of drug treatment is to reduce the individual and social costs of drug abuse, and treatment programs have been shown capable of accomplishing these goals (Harwood et al. 1988). However, it is important to determine more precisely the extent to which private and social costs of drug abuse are attenuated by treatment. Private costs include such things as labor productivity, health consequences, and reduced life span. Social costs include drug-related crime and crime-enforcement activities and publicly borne medical costs. The reduction in these costs constitutes a large measure of the benefit of drug abuse treatment and prevention programs and provides the rationale for their support by public funds.

Despite the need to define all relevant costs, some major costs of drug abuse are almost impossible to quantify. For example, it is difficult to place a dollar value on the benefit to society of reducing the public's fear of being victimized by drug users who have turned to robbery and burglary to finance their dependence. However, if a framework can be established for determining only those costs that can be easily quantified, the resulting estimates (see the Appendix) will conservatively understate the true benefits associated with treatment effectiveness. The overall approach promoted within this framework also mandates a conservative result—when there is ambiguity about numbers to utilize or assumptions to make—because measures are chosen to yield a minimum estimate of the effectiveness of the programs under consideration.

In the early 1980s, social concerns with cocaine- and crack-related crime and HIV infection in intravenous drug users began to promote greater public funding for treatment. However, many obstacles to enhancing the treatment system persist that increased funding will not necessarily solve: few or no widespread outreach efforts exist to induce drug abusers to come into treatment voluntarily; qualified and willing staff are in short supply; and neighborhoods are resistant to the placement of treatment programs because of mistrust and suspicion toward clients.

What is needed now, besides adequate funding, is a cogent strategy to upgrade our present treatment system at all levels with concentrated efforts to implement treatment elements acknowledged to be effective. A more rapid incorporation into the established treatment protocols of new elements emerging from ongoing research is also needed. Furthermore, methods of keeping program staff and policies current with developments in the treatment of drug dependence must be enhanced so that the lag between knowledge and implementation can be minimized.

A more integrated treatment system would increase the percentage of identified users who will cease using drugs in each year after intervention. Combating the chronic relapsing nature of narcotics and cocaine dependence requires consistent and persistent long-term efforts. These efforts must be applied within a system of flexible treatment structures that are appropriate to individual client characteristics so that the level of dysfunctional drug use and the duration of drug dependence are minimized. Treatment approaches that operate on these precepts have the potential to effect lasting and satisfying amelioration of the multifaceted problem of drug abuse.

APPENDIX

Benefits of Drug Abuse Treatment

Reduced Costs to the Drug Abuser
1. Reduced medical expenditures on drug-related illness
2. Increased school or labor productivity and, thus, increased earnings

Reduced Costs to Third Parties
1. Reduction in the amount of property stolen by drug abusers to support their habits

2. Reduced private costs of crime prevention measures to deter and detect such thefts (e.g., alarms, locks, guards, etc.)
3. Reduced anxiety and fear stemming from the possibility of victimization
4. Reduced levels of abuse, anxiety, and other emotional and physical harm imposed on the children, parents, and spouses of drug abusers

Reduced Costs to Taxpayers
1. Reduced public expenditures for police, courts, and corrections to detect and process drug violations
2. Reduced public expenditures for police, courts, and corrections to detect and process property crimes committed by drug users
3. Reduced public expenditures to treat drug-related illnesses, including overdoses, hepatitis, and AIDS
4. Reduced welfare payments made to drug users and their families
5. Reduced loss of tax revenues because of lower productivity and reduced labor-market participation by drug users

REFERENCES

Adams, E. H., J. C. Gfroerer, B. A. Rouse, and N. J. Kozel. 1987. "Trends in Prevalence and Consequences of Cocaine Use." *Advances in Alcohol and Substance Abuse* 6:49–71.

Allen, F. 1959. "Criminal Justice, Legal Values, and the Rehabilitative Ideal." *Journal of Criminal Law, Criminology and Police Science* 50:226–32.

Allison, M., and R. L. Hubbard. 1985. "Drug Abuse Treatment Process: A Review of the Literature." *International Journal of the Addictions* 20(9):1321–45.

Anglin, M. D., ed. 1988a. Special Issue. "A Social Policy Analysis of Compulsory Treatment for Opiate Dependence." *Journal of Drug Issues*, vol. 18, no. 4.

———. 1988b. "The Efficacy of Civil Commitment in Treating Narcotics Addiction." *Journal of Drug Issues* 18:527–46.

Anglin, M. D., M. W. Booth, T. M. Ryan, and Y. Hser. 1988. "Ethnic Differences in Narcotics Addiction. II. Chicano and Anglo Addiction Career Patterns." *International Journal of the Addictions* 23:1011–27.

Anglin, M. D., M. L. Brecht, and E. Maddahian. 1990. "Pre-treatment Characteristics and Treatment Performance of Legally Coerced versus Voluntary Methadone Maintenance Admissions." *Criminology* 27:537–57.

Anglin, M. D., M. L. Brecht, A. Woodward, and D. G. Bonett. 1986. "An Empirical Study of Maturing Out: Conditional Factors." *International Journal of the Addictions* 21(2):233–46.

Anglin, M. D., E. P. Deschenes, and G. Speckart. 1987. "The Effect of Legal Supervision on Narcotic Addiction and Criminal Behavior." Paper presented at the annual meeting of the American Society of Criminology, Montreal, November.

Anglin, M. D., and D. G. Fisher. 1987. "Survival Analysis in Drug Program Evaluation: Part II. Partitioning Treatment Effects." *International Journal of the Addictions* 22(4):377–87.

Anglin, M. D., and Y. Hser. 1987. "Addicted Women and Crime." *Criminology* 25:359–97.

———. 1990. "Legal Coercion and Drug Abuse Treatment: Research Findings and Social Policy Implications." In *Handbook of Drug Control in the United States*, edited by J. Inciardi. Westport, Conn.: Greenwood (forthcoming).

Anglin, M. D., and W. H. McGlothlin. 1984. "Outcome of Narcotic Addict Treatment in California." In *Drug Abuse Treatment Evaluation: Strategies, Progress, and Prospects*, edited by F. M. Tims and J. P. Ludford. National Institute on Drug Abuse Research Monograph no. 51. Rockville, Md.: U.S. Department of Health and Human Services, National Institute on Drug Abuse.

———. 1985. "Methadone Maintenance in California: A Decade's Experience." In *Yearbook of Substance Use and Abuse*, edited by L. Brill and C. Winick. New York: Human Sciences Press.

Anglin, M. D., W. H. McGlothlin, G. R. Speckart, and T. M. Ryan. 1982. "Shutting Off Methadone: The Closure of the San Diego Methadone Maintenance Program." Final report (grant no. DA02577). Rockville, Md.: National Institute on Drug Abuse.

Anglin, M. D., and G. Speckart. 1986. "Narcotics Use, Property Crime and Dealing: Structural Dynamics across the Addiction Career." *Journal of Quantitative Criminology* 2(4):355–75.

———. 1988. "Narcotics Use and Crime: A Multisample, Multimethod Analysis." *Criminology* 26:197–233.

Anglin, M. D., G. R. Speckart, M. W. Booth, and T. M. Ryan. 1989. "Consequences and Costs of Shutting Off Methadone." *Addictive Behaviors* 14:307–26.

Aron, W. S., and D. W. Daily. 1976. "Graduates and Splittees from Therapeutic Community Drug Treatment Programs: A Comparison." *International Journal of the Addictions* 11(5):1–18.

Ausubel, D. 1983. "Methadone Maintenance Treatment: The Other Side of the Coin." *International Journal of the Addictions* 18:851–62.

Baekland, F., and L. Lundwall. 1975. "Dropping out of Treatment: A Critical Review." *Psychological Bulletin* 82(5):738–83.

Bale, R. N., W. W. Van Stone, J. M. Kuldau, T. J. M. Engelsing, R. M. Elashoff, and V. P. Zarcone. 1980. "Therapeutic Communities vs. Methadone Maintenance: A Prospective Controlled Study of Narcotic Addiction Treatment." *Archives of General Psychiatry* 37:179–93.

Ball, J. C. 1989. Personal communication. Addiction Research Center, National Institute on Drug Abuse, Baltimore, Md., September.

Ball, J. C., and E. Corty. 1988. "Basic Issues Pertaining to the Effectiveness of Methadone Maintenance Treatment." In *Compulsory Treatment of Drug Abuse:*

Research and Clinical Practice, edited by C. G. Leukefeld and F. M. Tims. National Institute on Drug Abuse Research Monograph no. 86. Rockville, Md.: U.S. Department of Health and Human Services, National Institute on Drug Abuse.

Ball, J. C., E. Corty, H. R. Bond, and A. Tommasello. 1987. "The Reduction of Intravenous Heroin Use, Non-opiate Abuse and Crime during Methadone Maintenance Treatment—Further Findings." Paper presented at the annual meeting of the Committee on Problems of Drug Dependency, Philadelphia, June.

Ball, J. C., E. Corty, S. P. Petroski, H. Bond, and A. Tommasello. 1986. "Medical Services Provided to 2,394 Patients at Methadone Programs in Three States." *Journal of Substance Abuse Treatment* 3:203–9.

Ball, J. C., L. Rosen, J. A. Flueck, and D. N. Nurco. 1981. "The Criminality of Heroin Addicts When Addicted and When off Opiates." In *The Drugs-Crime Connection*, edited by J. A. Inciardi. Beverly Hills, Calif.: Sage.

Barr, H., and D. Antes. 1981. "Factors Related to Recovery and Relapse in Follow-up." Final Report of Project Activities. Grant no. 1-H81-DA-01864. Rockville, Md.: National Institute on Drug Abuse.

Biase, D. V. 1981. "Daytop Miniversity: Advancement in Drug-free Therapeutic Community Treatment." Evaluation Report no. 1-H81-DA-01911-01A1. Rockville, Md.: National Institute on Drug Abuse.

Bickel, W. K., I. Marion, and J. H. Lowinson. 1987. "The Treatment of Alcoholic Methadone Patients: A Review." *Journal of Substance Abuse Treatment* 4:15–19.

Bishop, Y. M., S. E. Fienberg, and P. W. Holland. 1975. *Discrete Multivariate Analysis: Theory and Practice*. Cambridge, Mass.: MIT Press.

Brecht, M. L., Y. Hser, and M. D. Anglin. 1990. "A Multimethod Assessment of Social Intervention Effects on Narcotics Use and Property Crime." *International Journal of the Addictions* (forthcoming).

Brill, L., and C. Winick. 1990. "The New York Civil Commitment Program." In *The Compulsory Treatment of Opiate Dependence*, edited by W. H. McGlothlin and M. D. Anglin. New York: Haworth (forthcoming).

Brizer, D. A., N. Hartman, J. Sweeney, and R. B. Millman. 1985. "Effect of Methadone plus Neuroleptics on Treatment-resistant Chronic Paranoid Schizophrenia." *American Journal of Psychiatry* 142:1106–7.

Brook, R. C., and I. C. Whitehead. 1980. *Drug-free Therapeutic Community*. New York: Human Sciences Press.

Brown, B. S. 1984. "Treatment of Non-opiate Dependency: Issues and Outcomes." In *Research Advances in Alcohol and Drug Problems*, vol. 8, edited by R. G. Smart, F. B. Glaser, Y. Israel, H. Kalant, R. E. Popham, and W. Schmidt. New York: Plenum.

Brown, B. S., J. K. Watters, and A. S. Iglehart. 1982. "Methadone Maintenance Dosage Levels and Program Retention." *American Journal of Drug and Alcohol Abuse* 9(2):129–39.

Bullington, B. J., D. K. Sprowls, and M. Phillips. 1978. "A Critique of Diversionary Juvenile Justice." *Crime and Delinquency* 24:59–71.

Burt Associates, Inc. 1977. *Drug Treatment in New York City and Washington, D.C.: Follow-up Studies*. Washington, D.C.: U.S. Government Printing Office.

Camp, G. M., and C. G. Camp. 1989. *Building on Prior Experiences: Therapeutic Communities in Prisons*. South Salem, N.Y.: Criminal Justice Institute.

Carter, R. M., and M. W. Klein, eds. 1976. *Back on the Street*. Englewood Cliffs, N.J.: Prentice-Hall.

Charney, D. S., G. R. Heninger, and H. D. Kleber. 1986. "The Combined Use of Clonidine and Naltrexone as a Rapid, Safe, and Effective Treatment of Abrupt Withdrawal from Methadone." *American Journal of Psychiatry* 143:831–37.

Charney, D. S., D. E. Sternberg, H. D. Kleber, G. R. Heninger, and D. E. Redmond, Jr. 1981. "The Clinical Use of Clonidine in Abrupt Withdrawal from Methadone." *Archives of General Psychiatry* 38:1273–77.

Cohen, S. 1979. "The Punitive City: Notes on the Dispersal of Society Control." *Contemporary Crisis* 3:339–63.

Cohen, S., R. E. Garey, A. Evans, and N. Wilchinsky. 1980. "Treatment of Heroin Addicts: Is the Client-Therapist Relationship Important?" *International Journal of the Addictions* 15:207–14.

Coleman, J. S. 1981. *Longitudinal Data Analysis*. New York: Basic.

Collins, J. J., and M. Allison. 1983. "Legal Coercion and Retention in Drug Abuse Treatment." *Hospital Community Psychiatry* 34:1145–49.

Cook, L. Foster, B. A. Weinman, et al. 1988. "Treatment Alternatives to Street Crime." In *Compulsory Treatment of Drug Abuse: Research and Clinical Practice*, edited by C. G. Leukefeld and F. M. Tims. National Institute on Drug Abuse Monograph no. 86. Rockville, Md.: U.S. Department of Health and Human Services, National Institute on Drug Abuse.

Coombs, R. H. 1981. "Back on the Streets: Therapeutic Communities' Impact upon Drug Abusers." *American Journal of Alcohol Abuse* 8(2):185–201.

Cooper, J. R., F. Altman, B. S. Brown, and D. Czechowicz, eds. 1983. *Research on the Treatment of Narcotics Addiction: State of the Art*. National Institute on Drug Abuse Research Monograph no. (ADM) 83-1281. Rockville, Md.: U.S. Department of Health and Human Services, National Institute on Drug Abuse.

Corty, E., and J. C. Ball. 1987. "Admissions to Methadone Maintenance: Comparisons between Programs and Implications for Treatment." *Journal of Substance Abuse Treatment* 4:181–87.

Craig, R. J. 1980. "Effectiveness of Low-Dose Methadone Maintenance for the Treatment of Inner City Heroin Addicts." *International Journal of the Addictions* 15(5):701–10.

Dackis, C. A., and M. S. Gold. 1985. "Bromocriptine as a Treatment of Cocaine Abuse." *Lancet* 1985:1151–52.

Dale, R. T., and F. R. Dale. 1973. "The Use of Methadone in a Representative Group of Heroin Addicts." *International Journal of the Addictions* 8:293–308.

D'Amanda, C. D. 1983. "Program Policies and Procedures Associated with Treatment Outcome." In *Research on the Treatment of Narcotic Addiction: State of the Art*, edited by J. R. Cooper, F. Altman, B. S. Brown, and D. Czechowicz. Rockville, Md.: U.S. Department of Health and Human Services, National Institute on Drug Abuse.

DeLeon, G. 1983*a*. *The T.C.: Predicting Retention and Follow-up Status*. Final Report no. 1-R01-DA-02741-01A1. Washington, D.C.: National Institute on Drug Abuse.

————. 1983*b*. "Phoenix House 1981: Admissions and Retention." Unpublished manuscript. New York: Phoenix House Foundation.

————. 1984. "Program-based Evaluation Research in Therapeutic Communities." In *Drug Abuse Treatment Evaluation: Strategies, Progress, and Prospects*, edited by F. M. Tims and J. P. Ludford. National Institute on Drug Abuse Research Monograph no. 51. Rockville, Md.: U.S. Department of Health and Human Services, National Institute on Drug Abuse.

————. 1985. "The Therapeutic Community: Status and Evolution." *International Journal of the Addictions* 20:823–44.

————. 1987. "Alcohol Use among Drug Abusers: Treatment Outcomes in a Therapeutic Community." *Alcoholism Clinical and Experimental Research* 11(5):430–36.

DeLeon, G., M. P. A. Andrews, H. K. Wexler, J. Jaffe, and M. S. Rosenthal. 1979. "Therapeutic Community Dropouts: Criminal Behavior Five Years after Treatment." *American Journal of Drug and Alcohol Abuse* 6:253–71.

DeLeon, G., S. Holland, and M. S. Rosenthal. 1972. "Phoenix House: Criminal Activity of Dropouts." *Journal of the American Medical Association* 222:686–89.

DeLeon, G., and N. Jainchill. 1981. "Male and Female Drug Abusers: Social and Psychological Status Two Years after Treatment in a Therapeutic Community." *American Journal of Drug and Alcohol Abuse* 8:465–97.

DeLeon, G., and M. S. Rosenthal. 1979. "Therapeutic Communities." In *Handbook on Drug Abuse*, edited by R. DuPont, A. Goldstein, and J. O'Donnell. Washington, D.C.: U.S. Government Printing Office.

————. 1989. "Treatment in Residential Therapeutic Communities." In *Treatments of Psychiatric Disorders: A Task Force Report of the American Psychiatric Association*, vol. 2, edited by H. Kleber. Washington, D.C.: American Psychiatric Association.

DeLeon, G., and S. Schwartz. 1984. "The Therapeutic Community: What Are the Retention Rates?" *Journal of Drug and Alcohol Abuse* 10:267–84.

DeLeon, G., A. Skodol, and M. S. Rosenthal. 1973. "The Phoenix Therapeutic Community for Drug Addicts: Changes in Psychopathological Signs." *Archives of General Psychiatry* 23:131–35.

Des Jarlais, C. D., H. Joseph, V. P. Dole, and J. Schmeidler. 1983. "Predicting Post-treatment Narcotic Use among Patients Terminating from Methadone Maintenance." *Advances in Alcohol and Substance Abuse* 2(1):57–68.

Dole, V. P., and M. E. Nyswander. 1965. "A Medical Treatment of Diacetylmorphine (Heroin) Addiction." *Journal of the American Medical Association* 193:646–50.

Dole, V. P., M. E. Nyswander, and A. Warner. 1968. "Successful Treatment of 750 Criminal Addicts." *Journal of the American Medical Association* 206(2):2708–11.

Eldred, C., and M. N. Washington. 1976. "Interpersonal Relationships in Heroin Use by Men and Women and Their Role in Treatment Outcome." *International Journal of the Addictions* 11:117–30.

Espada, F. 1979. "The Drug Industry and the 'Minority' Communities: Time for Change." In *Handbook on Drug Abuse*, edited by R. L. DuPont, A. Goldstein, and J. O'Donnell. Washington, D.C.: U.S. Government Printing Office.

Field, G. 1985. "The Cornerstone Program: A Client Outcome Study." *Federal Probation* 49:50–55.

Finnegan, L. P. 1972. "Comprehensive Care of Pregnant Addicts and Its Effect on Maternal and Infant Outcome." *Contemporary Drug Problems* 1(4):795–809.

Fisher, D. G., and M. D. Anglin. 1987. "Survival Analysis in Drug Program Evaluation: Part I. Overall Program Effectiveness." *International Journal of the Addictions* 22(2):115–34.

Freudenberger, H. J. 1975. "The Dynamics and Treatment of the Young Drug Abusers in an Hispanic Therapeutic Community." *Journal of Psychedelic Drugs* 7(3):273–80.

Gendreau, P., and R. R. Ross. 1987. "Revivification of Rehabilitation: Evidence from the 1980s." *Justice Quarterly* 4(3):359–407.

Goldstein, A., and B. A. Judson. 1973. "Efficacy and Side Effects of Three Widely Different Methadone Doses." In *Proceedings of the Fifth National Conference on Methadone Maintenance*, edited by the National Institute of Justice. Washington, D.C.: U.S. Government Printing Office.

Goldstein, A., W. H. Horns, and R. W. Hansteen. 1977. "Is On-Site Urine Testing of Therapeutic Value in a Methadone Treatment Program?" *International Journal of the Addictions* 12(6):717–28.

Goldstein, A., R. Norman, and B. Spunt. 1982. "Habitual Criminal Activity and Patterns of Drug Use." Paper presented at the annual meeting of the American Society of Criminology, Toronto, November.

Graham, M. G. 1987. "Controlling Drug Abuse and Crime: A Research Update." *NIJ Reports*. Washington, D.C.: U.S. Department of Justice, National Institute of Justice.

Greene, B. T., and P. E. Ryser. 1978. "Impact of Sex on Length of Time Spent in Treatment and Treatment Success." *American Journal of Drug and Alcohol Abuse* 5:97–105.

Hall, S. M. 1984. "Clinical Trials in Drug Treatment: Methodology." In *Drug Abuse Treatment Evaluation: Strategies, Progress, and Prospects*, edited by F. M. Tims and J. P. Ludford. National Institute on Drug Abuse Research Monograph no. 51. Rockville, Md.: U.S. Department of Health and Human Services, National Institute on Drug Abuse.

Hargreaves, W. A. 1983. "Methadone Dose and Duration for Maintenance Treatment." In *Research on the Treatment of Narcotic Addiction: State of the Art*, edited by J. R. Cooper, F. Altman, B. S. Brown, and D. Czechowicz. National Institute on Drug Abuse Research Monograph no. (ADM) 83-

1281. Rockville, Md.: U.S. Department of Health and Human Services, National Institute on Drug Abuse.

Harwood, H. J., R. L. Hubbard, J. J. Collins, and J. V. Rachal. 1988. "The Costs of Crime and the Benefits of Drug Abuse Treatment: A Cost-Benefit Analysis Using TOPS Data." In *Compulsory Treatment of Drug Abuse: Research and Clinical Practice*, edited by C. G. Leukefeld and F. M. Tims. National Institute on Drug Abuse Research Monograph no. 86. Rockville, Md.: U.S. Department of Health and Human Services, National Institute on Drug Abuse.

Havassay, B., and S. Hall. 1981. "Efficacy of Urine Monitoring in Methadone Maintenance." *American Journal of Psychiatry* 138:1497–1500.

Hawkins, J. D., and R. F. Catalano, Jr. 1985. "Aftercare in Drug Abuse Treatment." *International Journal of the Addictions* 20(6–7):917–45.

Hecht, F. R., and N. Arbiter. 1989. "The Amity Jail Project." Unpublished manuscript. Tuscon, Ariz.: Amity.

Holland, S. 1978. "Gateway Houses: Effectiveness of Treatment on Criminal Behavior." *International Journal of the Addictions* 13:369–81.

———. 1983. "Evaluating Community Based Treatment Programs: A Model for Strengthening Inferences about Effectiveness." *International Journal of Therapeutic Community* 4:285–306.

Hser, Y. 1986. "The Effects of Study and Test in Relation to Spacing: A Markov Model Analysis of Alternative Interpretations." Ph.D. dissertation, University of California, Los Angeles, Department of Psychology.

Hser, Y., M. D. Anglin, and C. Chou. 1988. "Evaluation of Drug Abuse Treatment: A Repeated Measure Design Assessing Methadone Maintenance." *Evaluation Review* 12(5):547–70.

Hser, Y., M. D. Anglin, and Y. Liu. 1990. "A Survival Analysis of Gender and Ethnic Differences in Methadone Maintenance Treatment Responsiveness." *International Journal of the Addictions* (forthcoming).

Hser, Y., C. Chou, and M. D. Anglin. 1990. "The Criminality of Female Narcotics Addicts: A Causal Modeling Approach." *Journal of Quantitative Criminology* (forthcoming).

Hubbard, R. L., M. Allison, R. M. Bray, S. G. Craddock, J. V. Rachal, and H. M. Ginzburg. 1983. "An Overview of Client Characteristics, Treatment Services, and During-Treatment Outcomes for Outpatient Prospective Study (TOPS)." In *Research on the Treatment of Narcotic Addiction: State of the Art*, edited by J. R. Cooper, F. Altman, B. S. Brown, and D. Czechowicz. National Institute on Drug Abuse Research Monograph no. (ADM) 83-1281. Rockville, Md.: U.S. Department of Health and Human Services, National Institute on Drug Abuse.

Hubbard, R. L., and H. J. Harwood. 1981. "Employment Related Series in Drug Treatment Programs. Treatment Research Report." Department of Health and Human Services Report no. (ADM) 81-1144. Rockville, Md.: National Institute on Drug Abuse.

Hubbard, R. L., M. E. Marsden, E. Cavanaugh, J. V. Rachal, and H. M. Ginzburg. 1988. "Role of Drug-Abuse Treatment in Limiting the Spread of AIDS." *Review of Infectious Disease* 10(2):377–84.

Hubbard, R. L., M. E. Marsden, J. V. Rachal, H. J. Harwood, E. R. Cavanaugh, and H. M. Ginzburg. 1989. *Drug Abuse Treatment: A National Study of Effectiveness.* Chapel Hill: University of North Carolina Press.

Hubbard, R. L., J. V. Rachal, S. G. Craddock, and E. R. Cavanaugh. 1984. "Treatment Outcome Prospective Study (TOPS): Client Characteristics and Behaviors before, during, and after Treatment." In *Drug Abuse Treatment Evaluation: Strategies, Progress, and Prospects,* edited by F. M. Tims and J. P. Ludford. National Institute on Drug Abuse Research Monograph no. 51. Rockville, Md.: U.S. Department of Health and Human Services, National Institute on Drug Abuse.

Hunt, D. E., D. S. Lipton, and B. Spunt. 1984. "Patterns of Criminal Activity among Methadone Clients and Current Narcotics Users Not in Treatment." *Journal of Drug Issues* 14(4):687–702.

Innes, C. A. 1988. *Drug Use and Crime.* Washington, D.C.: U.S. Department of Justice, Bureau of Justice Statistics.

Jaffe, J. H. 1979. "The Swinging Pendulum: The Treatment of Drug Users in America." In *Handbook on Drug Abuse,* edited by R. L. DuPont, A. Goldstein, and J. O'Donnell. Washington, D.C.: U.S. Government Printing Office.

Joe, G. W., D. D. Simpson, and R. L. Hubbard. 1989. "Unmet Service Needs in Methadone Maintenance." *International Journal of the Addictions* (forthcoming).

Joe, G. W., D. D. Simpson, and S. B. Sells. 1989. "Aspects of Treatment Process and Opioid Use during Methadone Maintenance." *American Journal of Drug Abuse* (forthcoming).

Johnson, B. D., P. Goldstein, E. Preble, J. Schmeidler, D. S. Lipton, B. Spunt, and T. Miller. 1985. *Taking Care of Business: The Economics of Crime by Heroin Abusers.* Lexington, Mass.: Lexington.

Khantzian, E. J., F. H. Gawin, C. Riordan, and H. D. Kleber. 1984. "Methylphenidate Treatment of Cocaine Dependence: A Preliminary Report." *Journal of Substance Abuse Treatment* 1:107–12.

Kleber, H. D. 1986. "The Use of Psychotropic Drugs in the Treatment of Compulsive Opiate Abusers: The Rationale for Their Use." *Advances in Alcohol and Substance Abuse* 5(1–2):103–19.

Kleber, H. D., and F. Slobetz. 1979. "Outpatient Drug-free Treatment." In *Handbook on Drug Abuse,* edited by R. L. DuPont, A. Goldstein, and J. O'Donnell. Washington, D.C.: U.S. Government Printing Office.

Klein, M. W. 1979. "Deinstitutionalization and Diversion of Juvenile Offenders: A Litany of Impediments." In *Crime and Justice: An Annual Review of Research,* vol. 1, edited by Norval Morris and Michael Tonry. Chicago: University of Chicago Press.

Lettieri, D. J., M. Sayers, and H. M. Pearson. 1980. *Theories on Drug Abuse: Selected Contemporary Perspectives.* Washington, D.C.: U.S. Government Printing Office.

Lipton, D. S., and M. J. Maranda. 1982. "Detoxification from Heroin Dependency: An Overview of Method and Effectiveness." *Advances in Alcohol and Substance Abuse* 2(1):31–55.

Lipton, D. S., R. Martinson, and J. Wilks. 1975. *The Effectiveness of Correctional Treatment: A Survey of Treatment Evaluation Studies.* New York: Praeger.

Lowinson, J. H., and R. B. Millman. 1979. "Clinical Aspects of Methadone Maintenance Treatment." In *Handbook on Drug Abuse*, edited by R. L. DuPont, A. Goldstein, and J. O'Donnell. Washington, D.C.: U.S. Government Printing Office.

McFarlain, R. A., G. H. Cohen, J. Yoder, and L. Guidry. 1977. "Psychological Test and Demographic Variables Associated with Retention of Narcotics Addicts in Treatment." *International Journal of the Addictions* 12(23):399–410.

McGlothlin, W. H. 1979. "Drugs and Crime." In *Handbook on Drug Abuse*, edited by R. L. DuPont, A. Goldstein, and J. O'Donnell. Washington, D.C.: U.S. Government Printing Office.

McGlothlin, W. H., and M. D. Anglin. 1979. "Effects of Closing the Bakersfield Methadone Clinic." In *Problems of Drug Dependence*, edited by Louis S. Harris. National Institute on Drug Abuse Research Monograph no. 47. Rockville, Md.: U.S. Department of Health and Human Services, National Institute on Drug Abuse.

———. 1981a. "Long-Term Follow-up of Clients of High- and Low-Dose Methadone Programs." *Archives of General Psychiatry* 38:1055–63.

———. 1981b. "Shutting Off Methadone: Costs and Benefits." *Archives of General Psychiatry* 38:885–92.

———, eds. 1990. *The Compulsory Treatment of Opiate Dependence.* New York: Haworth (forthcoming).

McGlothlin, W. H., M. D. Anglin, and B. D. Wilson. 1977. *An Evaluation of the California Civil Addict Program.* Rockville, Md.: National Institute on Drug Abuse.

———. 1978. "Narcotic Addiction and Crime." *Criminology* 16(3):293–315.

McLellan, A. T., and K. A. Druley. 1977. "Responsiveness to Treatment in Court-referred vs. Voluntary Drug Abuse Patients." *Hospital Community Psychiatry* 28:238–41.

McLellan, A. T., L. Luborsky, C. P. O'Brian, G. E. Woody, and K. A. Druley. 1982. "Is Treatment for Substance Abuse Effective?" *Journal of the American Medical Association* 247:1423–28.

McLellan, A. T., L. Luborsky, G. E. Woody, and C. P. O'Brian. 1980. "An Improved Diagnostic Evaluation Instrument for Substance Abuse Patients: The Addiction Severity Index." *Journal of Nervous and Mental Disease* 168:26–33.

McLellan, A. T., L. Luborsky, G. E. Woody, C. P. O'Brian, and K. A. Druley. 1983. "Predicting Response to Alcohol and Drug Abuse Treatments: Role of Psychiatric Severity." *Archives of General Psychiatry* 40:620–25.

McLellan, A. T., G. E. Woody, B. Evans, and C. P. O'Brian. 1989. "Methadone vs. Therapeutic Community in the Treatment of Mixed Abusers: Role of Psychiatric Symptoms." *Annals of New York Academy of Sciences* (forthcoming).

McLellan, A. T., A. R. Childress, J. Griffith, and G. E. Woody. 1984. "The Psychiatrically Severe Drug Abuse Patient: Methadone Maintenance or

Therapeutic Community?" *American Journal of Drug and Alcohol Abuse* 10(1):77–95.

McMearn, J. H. 1971. "Racial Perspectives on the Heroin Problem." *Journal of Psychedelic Drugs* 4:91–94.

Maddux, J. F. 1988. "Clinical Experience with Civil Commitment." In *Compulsory Treatment of Drug Abuse: Research and Clinical Practice*, edited by C. G. Leukefeld and F. M. Tims. National Institute on Drug Abuse Research Monograph no. 86. Rockville, Md.: U.S. Department of Health and Human Services, National Institute on Drug Abuse.

Maddux, J. F., and C. L. Bowden. 1972. "Critique of Success with Methadone Maintenance." *American Journal of Psychiatry* 129:440–46.

Maddux, J. F., and D. P. Desmond. 1979. "Crime and Drug Use Behavior: An Areal Analysis." *Criminology* 19:281–302.

———. 1980. "Outpatient Methadone Withdrawal for Heroin Dependence." *American Journal of Drug and Alcohol Abuse* 7:323–33.

Mandell, W. 1990. "Evaluation of the Federal Civil Commitment Program for Narcotics Addicts." In *The Compulsory Treatment of Opiate Dependence*, edited by W. H. McGlothlin and M. D. Anglin. New York: Haworth.

Marcovici, M. A., T. McLellan, C. P. O'Brian, and J. Rosenzweig. 1980. "Risk for Alcoholism and Methadone Treatment: A Longitudinal Study." *Journal of Nervous and Mental Disease* 168(9):556–58.

Marlatt, G. A., and J. R. Gordon, eds. 1985. *Relapse Prevention.* New York: Guilford.

Marsh, J. C. 1982. "Public Issues and Private Problems: Women and Drug Use." *Journal of Social Issues* 38(2):153–65.

Marsh, K. L., and D. D. Simpson. 1986. "Sex Differences in Opioid Addiction Careers." *American Journal of Drug and Alcohol Abuse* 12(4):309–29.

Milby, J. B. 1978. "Take-Home Methadone: Contingency Effects on Drug-Seeking and Productivity of Narcotic Addicts." *Addictive Behavior* 3:215–20.

Naierman, N., B. Savage, B. Haskins, J. Lear, H. Chase, K. Marvell, and R. Lamothe. 1979. "Sex Discrimination in Health and Human Services." Unpublished manuscript. Cambridge, Mass.: Abt Associates.

National Association of State Alcohol and Drug Abuse Directors. 1988. "State Resources and Services Related to Alcohol and Drug Abuse Problems, Fiscal Year 1987." Report to the National Institute on Alcohol and Alcoholism and the National Institute on Drug Abuse. Rockville, Md.: U.S. Department of Health and Human Services, National Institute on Drug Abuse.

National Institute on Drug Abuse. 1988. *Data from the Drug Abuse Warning Network (DAWN).* Series 1, no. 7. Rockville, Md.: U.S. Department of Health and Human Services, National Institute on Drug Abuse.

Newman, R. C. 1983. "Diversion of Addicts from the Criminal Justice System in Treatment." Paper presented at the National Conference of Standards, Ethics, and Practice, New York.

———. 1987. "Methadone Treatment: Defining and Evaluating Success." *New England Journal of Medicine* 317(7):447–50.

Nurco, D. N., T. W. Kinlock, T. E. Hanlon, and J. C. Ball. 1988. "Nonnarcotic Drug Use over an Addiction Career—a Study of Heroin Addicts in
Baltimore and New York City." *Comprehensive Psychiatry* 29(5):450–59.

Nurco, D. N., J. W. Shaffer, J. C. Ball, and T. W. Kinlock. 1984. "Trends in
the Commission of Crime among Narcotic Addicts over Successive Periods
of Addiction and Nonaddiction." *American Journal of Drug and Alcohol Abuse*
10(4):481–89.

Nurco, D. N., N. Wegner, and F. Stephenson. 1982. "Female Narcotic Addicts: Changing Profiles." *Journal of Addictive Health* 3:62–105.

O'Brian, C. P., A. R. Childress, A. T. McLellan, J. Ternes, and R. N.
Ehrman. 1984. "Use of Naltrexone to Extinguish Opioid-conditioned Responses." *Journal of Clinical Psychiatry* 45:53.

O'Brian, C. P., and G. E. Woody. 1989. "Antagonist Treatment: Naltrexone."
In *Treatments of Psychiatric Disorders: A Task Force Report of the American Psychi-
atric Association*, vol. 2, edited by H. Kleber. Washington, D.C.: American
Psychiatric Association.

O'Donnell, J. A. 1969. "Narcotic Addiction and Crime." *Social Problems*
13:374–85.

Orsagh, T., and M. E. Marsden. 1985. "What Works When: Rational-Choice
Theory and Offender Rehabilitation." *Journal of Criminal Justice* 13:269–77.

Petersilia, J., P. W. Greenwood, and M. Lavin. 1978. *Criminal Careers of
Habitual Felons*. Washington, D.C.: U.S. Government Printing Office.

Pin, E. J., J. M. Martine, and J. F. Walsh. 1976. "A Follow-up Study of 300
Ex-Clients of a Drug-free Narcotic Treatment Program in New York City."
American Journal of Drug and Alcohol Abuse 3:397–407.

Pompi, K. F., S. C. Shreiner, and J. L. McKey. 1979. *Abraxas: A First Look at
Outcomes*. Pittsburgh, Pa.: Abraxas Foundation.

Romond, A. M., C. K. Forrest, and H. D. Kleber. 1975. "Follow-up of
Participants in a Drug Dependence Therapeutic Community." *Archives of
General Psychiatry* 32:369–74.

Rosenthal, B. J., M. J. Savory, B. T. Greene, and W. H. Spillane. 1979.
"Drug Treatment Outcomes: Is Sex a Factor?" *International Journal of the
Addictions* 14(1):45–62.

Roszell, D. K., D. A. Calsyn, and E. F. Chaney. 1986. "Alcohol Use and
Psychopathology in Opioid Addicts on Methadone Maintenance." *American
Journal of Drug and Alcohol Abuse* 12:269–78.

Rounsaville, B. J. 1989. "Clinical Assessment of Drug Abusers." In *Treatments
of Psychiatric Disorders: A Task Force Report of the American Psychiatric Association*, vol. 2, edited by H. Kleber. Washington, D.C.: American Psychiatric
Association.

Rounsaville, B. J., W. Glazer, C. H. Wilber, M. M. Weissman, and H. D.
Kleber. 1983. "Short-Term Interpersonal Psychotherapy in Methadone
Maintained Opiate Addicts." *Archives of General Psychiatry* 40:629–36.

Rounsaville, B. J., T. Tierney, K. Crits-Christoph, M. M. Weissman, and H.
D. Kleber. 1982. "Predictors of Outcome in Treatment of Opiate Addicts:
Evidence for the Multidimensional Nature of Addicts' Problems." *Com-
prehensive Psychiatry* 23(5):462–78.

Salmon, R. W., and R. J. Salmon. 1983. "The Role of Coercion in Rehabilitation of Drug Abusers." *International Journal of the Addictions* 18(1):9–21.

Sansone, J. 1980. "Retention Patterns in a Therapeutic Community for the Treatment of Drug Abuse." *International Journal of the Addictions* 15(5):711–36.

Savage, L. J., and D. D. Simpson. 1980. "Posttreatment of Sex and Ethnic Groups Treated in Methadone Maintenance during 1969–1972." *Journal of Psychedelic Drugs* 12(1):55–64.

Sells, S. B., ed. 1974. *Evaluation of Treatment*, vols. 1 and 2. Cambridge, Mass.: Ballinger.

———. 1983. "Treatment and Rehabilitation." In *Encyclopedia of Crime and Justice*, vol. 2, edited by S. H. Kadish. New York: Free Press.

Sells, S. B., and D. D. Simpson, eds. 1976. *The Effectiveness of Drug Abuse Treatment*, vols. 3–5. Cambridge, Mass.: Ballinger

Senay, E. C. 1984. "Clinical Implications of Drug Abuse Treatment Outcome Research." In *Drug Abuse Treatment Evaluation: Strategies, Progress, and Prospects*, edited by F. M. Tims and J. P. Ludford. National Institute on Drug Abuse Research Monograph no. 51. Rockville, Md.: U.S. Department of Health and Human Services, National Institute on Drug Abuse.

———. 1985. "Methadone Maintenance Treatment." *International Journal of the Addictions* 20(6–7):803–21.

Simpson, D. D. 1979. "The Relation of Time Spent in Drug Abuse Treatment to Posttreatment Outcome." *American Journal of Psychiatry* 136(11):1449–53.

———. 1981. "Treatment for Drug Abuse: Follow-up Outcomes and Length of Time Spent." *Archives of General Psychiatry* 38:875–80.

———. 1984. "National Treatment System Evaluation Based on the Drug Abuse Reporting Program (DARP) Follow-up Research." In *Drug Abuse Treatment Evaluation: Strategies, Progress, and Prospects*, edited by F. M. Tims and J. Ludford. National Institute on Drug Abuse Research Monograph no. 51. Rockville, Md.: U.S. Department of Health and Human Services, National Institute on Drug Abuse.

Simpson, D. D., G. W. Joe, W. E. K. Lehman, and S. B. Sells. 1986. "Addiction Careers: Etiology, Treatment, and 12-Year Follow-up Outcomes." *Journal of Drug Issues* 16(1):107–21.

Simpson, D. D., L. J. Savage, M. R. Lloyd, and S. B. Sells. 1978. "Evaluation of Drug Abuse Treatments Based on the First Year after DARP: National Follow-up Study of Admissions to Drug Abuse Treatments in the DARP during 1969–1972." National Institute on Drug Abuse Research Monograph no. (ADM) 78-701. Rockville, Md.: U.S. Department of Health and Human Services, National Institute on Drug Abuse.

Simpson, D. D., and S. B. Sells. 1982. "Evaluation of Drug Treatment Effectiveness: Summary of the DARP Follow-up Research." National Institute on Drug Abuse Treatment Research Report. Washington, D.C.: U.S. Government Printing Office.

Sorenson, J. L., A. P. Acampora, M. Trier, and M. Gold. 1987. "From Maintenance to Abstinence in a Therapeutic Community: Follow-up Outcomes." *Journal of Psychoactive Drugs* 19:345–51.

Speckart, G. R., and M. D. Anglin. 1986a. "Narcotics and Crime: A Causal Modeling Approach." *Journal of Quantitative Criminology* 2:3–28.

———. 1986b. "Narcotics Use and Crime: An Overview of Recent Research Advances." *Contemporary Drug Problems* 13:741–69.

Stark, M. J. 1989. "A Psychoeducational Approach to Methadone Maintenance Treatment." *Journal of Substance Abuse Treatment* 6:169–81.

Steer, R. A. 1980. "Psychosocial Correlates of Retention in Methadone Maintenance." *International Journal of the Addictions* 15(7):1003–9.

Stimmel, B., M. Cohen, and R. Hanbury. 1978. "Alcoholism and Polydrug Abuse in Persons on Methadone Maintenance." *Annals of New York Academy of Sciences* 311:99–180.

Stimmel, B., R. Hanbury, V. Sturiano, D. Korts, G. Jackson, and M. Cohen. 1982. "Alcoholism as a Risk Factor in Methadone Maintenance: A Randomized Controlled Trial." *American Journal of Medicine* 73:631–36.

Stitzer, M. 1977. "Medication Take-Home as a Reinforcer in a Methadone Maintenance Program." *Addictive Behavior* 2(1):9–14.

Stitzer, M., G. E. Bigelow, and J. Gross. 1989. "Behavioral Treatment of Drug Abuse." In *Treatments of Psychiatric Disorders: A Task Force Report of the American Psychiatric Association*, vol. 2, edited by H. Kleber. Washington, D.C.: American Psychiatric Association.

Tims, F. M., and J. P. Ludford, eds. 1984. *Drug Abuse Treatment Evaluation: Strategies, Progress, and Prospects*. National Institute on Drug Abuse Research Monograph no. 51. Rockville, Md.: U.S. Department of Health and Human Services, National Institute on Drug Abuse.

Tucker, M. B. 1979. "A Descriptive and Comparative Analysis of the Social Support Structure of Heroin-addicted Women." In *Addicted Women: Family Dynamics, Self-Perceptions and Support Systems*. Rockville, Md.: Department of Health, Education, and Welfare, Alcohol, Drug Abuse, and Mental Health Administration.

U.S. Department of Health and Human Services. Alcohol, Drug Abuse, and Mental Health Administration and Food and Drug Administration. 1980. "Methadone for Treating Narcotic Addicts: Joint Revision of Conditions for Use." *Federal Register* 45(184), pt. 3.

Weipert, G. D., P. T. D'Orban, and T. H. Bewley. 1976. "Delinquency by Opiate Addicts Treated at Two London Clinics." *British Journal of Addictions* 11:1–18.

Wermuth, L., S. Brummett, and J. L. Sorenson. 1987. "Bridges and Barriers to Recovery: Clinical Observations from an Opiate-Recovery Project." *Journal of Substance Abuse Treatment* 4:189–96.

Wesson, D. R., and D. E. Smith. 1979. "Treatment of the Polydrug Abuser." In *Handbook on Drug Abuse*, edited by R. L. DuPont, A. Goldstein, and J. O'Donnell. Washington, D.C.: U.S. Government Printing Office.

Wexler, H. K., and G. DeLeon. 1977. "The Therapeutic Community: Multivariate Prediction of Retention." *American Journal of Drug and Alcohol Abuse* 4(2):145–51.

Wexler, H. K., D. S. Lipton, and K. Foster. 1985. "Outcome Evaluation of a Prison Therapeutic Community for Substance Abuse Treatment: Preliminary Results." Paper presented at the annual meeting of the American Society of Criminology, San Diego, November.

Wickens, T. D. 1982. *Models for Behavior: Stochastic Processes in Psychology*. San Francisco: Freeman.

Wilson, B. K., R. R. Elms, and C. P. Tompson. 1975. "Outpatient vs. Hospital Methadone Detoxification: Experimental Comparison." *International Journal of the Addictions* 10:13–21.

Wilson, S. R. 1978. "The Effect of Treatment in a Therapeutic Community on Intravenous Drug Abuse." *Journal of the Addictions* 73:407–11.

Wilson, S. R., and B. M. Mandelbrote. 1978. "The Relationship between Duration of Treatment in a Therapeutic Community for Drug Abusers and Subsequent Criminality." *Journal of Medical Psychology* 132:487–91.

Winick, C. S. 1962. "Maturing Out of Narcotic Addiction." *Bulletin on Narcotics* 14:1–7.

Wish, E., and B. Gropper. In this volume. "Drug Testing by the Criminal Justice System: Methods, Research, and Applications."

Woody, G. E., L. Luborsky, A. T. McLellan, C. P. O'Brian, A. T. Beck, J. Blaine, I. Herman, and A. Hole. 1983. "Psychotherapy for Opiate Addicts: Does It Help?" *Archives of General Psychiatry* 40:1639–45.

Woody, G. E., C. P. O'Brian, A. T. McLellan, and J. Mintz. 1981. "Psychotherapy for Opiate Addiction: Some Preliminary Results." *Annals of New York Academy of Sciences* 362:91–100.

Yamaguchi, K., and D. B. Kandel. 1985. "Dynamic Relationships between Premarital Cohabitation and Illicit Drug Use: An Event-History Analysis of Role Selection and Role Socialization." *American Sociological Review* 50:530–46.

Gilbert J. Botvin

Substance Abuse Prevention: Theory, Practice, and Effectiveness

ABSTRACT

Interventions developed to reduce or prevent substance use have taken many forms, including school-based prevention/education programs, mass media campaigns, youth clubs and activities designed as alternatives to substance use, and community-based movements. Evaluation studies indicate that these interventions have frequently increased knowledge and awareness and have occasionally had an impact on attitudes and other drug-related variables. However, rarely have any of these interventions had an impact on substance-use behavior. A major exception is a class of school-based primary prevention approaches that focus on the key psychosocial factors promoting adolescent substance use. These approaches include either resistance-skills training alone or in combination with life-skills training. Although the evolution of these programs is an encouraging development in a field replete with failures, the extant empirical and theoretical literature suggests the need for a comprehensive prevention strategy that combines school-based interventions with those affecting the family, social institutions, and the larger community. Considerably more research is needed both to develop effective prevention components for such a comprehensive approach and to determine the most appropriate combination of components.

Tobacco, alcohol, and drug abuse have been a source of concern to schools, community organizations, health professionals, and law enforcement agencies for more than two decades. During that time, a concerted effort has been made by individuals and agencies in both the

Gilbert J. Botvin is associate professor and director of the Laboratory of Health Behavior Research, Department of Public Health, Cornell University Medical College.

public and private sectors to reduce the trends that began in the psychedelic 1960s and continued, almost unabated, to the end of the 1970s and beginning of the 1980s.

Although declines in the use of some psychoactive substances have been observed since the early 1980s, substance use has continued at unacceptably high levels. There is also reason to believe that the declines observed in recent years in the use of most drugs may be leveling off (U.S. Public Health Service 1986). The "Monitoring the Future" surveys of high school seniors, a major source of data concerning substance-abuse trends among adolescents, found that current use of sixteen types of drugs was virtually unchanged or slightly increased in the class of 1985 compared with that of 1984. Furthermore, the use of cocaine increased significantly during the same time period. In addition to long-standing concerns over the deleterious health, legal, and pharmacological effects associated with substance abuse, new urgency now exists for the development of effective prevention strategies because of the role played by IV drug use in the transmission of AIDS.

During the past two decades, substance use appears to have become a part of the normal rites of passage for many American youth. To some extent this is encouraged by the accepting, if not supportive, attitudes commonly portrayed in the popular media. Commentators in both the print and electronic media make frequent reference to the "casual" or "recreational" use of drugs, implying rather tolerant societal attitudes toward the use of many psychoactive substances. The use of drugs is frequently glorified in movies and TV shows. The net effect is to provide youth with negative role models and communicate the message that drug use, or at least certain patterns of drug use, is acceptable if not even desirable.

Unfortunately, experimentation and the casual use of most psychoactive substances all too often end in regular patterns of use, characterized by both psychological and physical dependence. Not only does the use of tobacco, alcohol, and illicit drugs pose immediate problems to the health, educational development, and social functioning of adolescents, but the early use of these substances has also been linked with problems later in adulthood.

A variety of intervention approaches have been developed and tested over the years in an effort to reduce substance use/abuse among adolescents. The treatment of substance-abuse problems has proven to be both difficult and expensive. Even the most effective treatment modalities typically produce only modest results, and treatment gains are often lost due to high rates of recidivism. Therapists are confronted by a disorder that more often than not proves to be refractory to change, by patients whose knowledge of drugs may be daunting to even the most experienced practitioner, and by a pathogenic environment that does its best to undermine any progress made by the patient through the ubiquity of drugs and a social network promoting drug use.

Consequently, it is no wonder that the prospect of developing a preventive approach to substance abuse has been so appealing. However, the development of effective prevention strategies has proven to be far more difficult than was initially imagined. School-based tobacco, alcohol, and drug education programs as well as public information programs have sought to deter substance use by increasing adolescents' awareness of the adverse consequences of using these substances. Although this kind of strategy has proliferated for more than two decades, results indicate quite clearly that these approaches are not effective.

More recently, researchers have developed and tested substance-abuse prevention programs that differ from conventional programs in several important ways. First, these newer approaches are based on a more complete understanding of the causes of substance abuse among adolescents, with particular emphasis being placed on the importance of psychosocial factors. Second, these approaches are based on well-accepted theories of human behavior. Third, they utilize well-tested intervention techniques. And, fourth, evaluation studies testing these approaches have emphasized methodological rigor and have employed increasingly sophisticated research designs.

The purpose of this essay is to provide an overview of the evolving field of substance-abuse prevention. Section I briefly examines two major approaches to substance-abuse prevention: supply reduction and demand reduction. Section II discusses the present nature and extent of the substance-abuse problem. A summary of what is known of the causes of substance use and abuse and a description of the most common approaches to prevention and education are presented in Section III. A major focus of this essay is on the description and evaluation of a "new generation" of substance-abuse prevention programs that places primary emphasis on the psychosocial factors believed to be responsible for the initiation of tobacco, alcohol, and drug abuse. Section IV discusses psychosocial approaches, Section V looks at the role of the mass media, and Section VI examines community-based approaches. Conclusions drawn from this body of work and directions for future research are offered in Section VII.

I. Conceptualizing Prevention

In the area of substance-abuse prevention, two major categories of prevention approaches exist: supply-reduction approaches and demand-reduction approaches. Each encompasses a different aspect of prevention, and each has substantially different operational implications.

A. Supply/Demand Reduction

The supply-reduction model is based on the fundamental assumption that substance use can be controlled by simply controlling the supply (i.e., availability). If it were possible to control completely the availability of any drug, use could undoubtedly be controlled. This has been the driving force behind legislation and the activities of law enforcement agencies, particularly with respect to the interdiction of drugs by governmental agencies such as the DEA on the federal level. However, while logically compelling, supply-reduction efforts have consistently been demonstrated to be at best, partial solutions to drug-abuse problems.

The other general category of prevention activities comes under the rubric of demand reduction. The purpose of demand-reduction approaches, not unlike the purpose of supply-reduction approaches, is deceptive in its simplicity: reductions in substance use/abuse can be achieved through strategies that affect the demand side of the equation. Demand-reduction efforts are conceptualized as those that attempt to dissuade, discourage, or deter individuals from either using drugs or desiring to use drugs. Consequently, this category includes prevention, education, and treatment programs. However, demand-reduction approaches have also proven to be more intuitively appealing than effective. This essay focuses on prevention and education approaches, which represent a subset of demand-reduction activities.

B. Primary Prevention

The notion of prevention means different things to different people. Indeed, the term "prevention" has been used rather imprecisely over the years. Many of the programs that exist under the umbrella of substance-abuse prevention concern screening and early intervention. Although obviously important, programs of this kind are not covered because the focus of this essay is on primary prevention.

Consistent with usage in the field of public health, primary prevention interventions are designed to reach individuals before they have developed a specific disorder or disease. As such, strategies will be discussed that are targeted at a general population or individuals who, for the most part, have not yet begun using tobacco, alcohol, or other drugs. The goal of these approaches is to prevent substance use/abuse by intervening upon individual and/or environmental factors viewed as promoting or supporting this type of health-compromising behavior.

II. The Foundation of Prevention: Etiology

Before discussing approaches to substance abuse prevention, some of the factors associated with the initiation and maintenance of tobacco, alcohol, and drug abuse will be briefly summarized. This will not only help provide a context for understanding existing substance-abuse prevention programs but should also provide a means of evaluating the appropriateness of specific prevention strategies. Moreover, a general understanding of etiologic issues should also be useful in developing a prescription for prevention models of optimal effectiveness.

Logically one would expect that the development of effective prevention strategies presupposes an understanding of the fundamental determinants of substance abuse in our society. What "causes" substance abuse? Why do some individuals begin using one or more psychoactive substances while others do not? Furthermore, it is necessary to pinpoint as accurately as possible the time of onset with respect to the most widely used substances and the surrounding critical period in order to determine the most appropriate point of intervention. When does substance use begin? Is there a "critical period" during which individuals are at the highest risk? When should preventive interventions be implemented?

It is also important to understand the developmental progression of substance use/abuse both for particular substances and across an array of psychoactive substances. What is known about the sequence of experimentation and subsequent progression to addictive patterns of use? Is there a logical progression that involves a predictable developmental sequence from some substances to others? Are the early stages of substance use characterized by the use of particular substances?

A. Determinants

A common belief is that individuals begin using drugs because they are not sufficiently cognizant of the adverse consequences (i.e., the dangers) of using them. Implicit in that belief is the notion that individuals, once apprised of the hazards of substance use, will be dissuaded from becoming involved with tobacco, alcohol, or drugs. To what extent is substance abuse largely the result of insufficient knowledge? Is it essentially a moral issue? Is it simply a matter of availability? Perhaps if the penalties were more severe and meted out with greater precision and immediacy, individuals would recognize that the legal risks outweigh any potential benefits of using drugs. Is there a necessary and sufficient condition that leads inexorably to substance use/abuse?

Considerable research has been conducted over the years in an effort to learn more about the causes of tobacco, alcohol, and drug abuse. An extensive literature has developed concerning the antecedents and correlates of substance use/abuse. Much of the earlier evidence was based on retrospective studies. Although suggestive, these studies have generally been criticized by reviewers on methodological grounds. Data have also been collected from a number of cross-sectional studies and a limited number of longitudinal studies.

The evidence that exists in the extant literature indicates that the initiation and early stages of substance use are promoted by a complex array of cognitive, attitudinal, social, personality, pharmacological, and developmental factors (e.g., Braucht et al. 1973; Ray 1974; Jessor 1976; Wechsler 1976; Blum and Richards 1979; Meyer and Mirin 1979). By far, the strongest factors associated with substance use/abuse concern both the behavior and attitudes of significant others such as parents, older siblings, and friends. Individuals who have family members or friends who are substance users have a significantly increased risk of becoming substance users themselves.

Another type of social influence that has received surprisingly little attention by researchers involves the portrayal of substance use in the popular media as something that is an important part of popularity, sophistication, success, sex appeal, and good times. Both the modeling of substance-use behavior by media personalities and the messages communicated are powerful sources of influence that promote and support substance use.

Many studies have found evidence of a relationship between a variety of individual characteristics and substance-use status. This includes psychological characteristics, health knowledge, attitudes, and normative expectations. Substance use has been found to be associated with low self-esteem, low self-confidence, low self-satisfaction, a greater need for social approval, low social confidence, high anxiety, low assertiveness, greater impulsivity, greater rebelliousness, lower personal control, low self-efficacy, and an impatience to acquire adult status.

Although clearly not the only factor promoting substance use, individuals who are unaware of the adverse consequences of tobacco, alcohol, and drug use, as well as those who have positive attitudes toward substance use, have been found to be more likely to become substance users than those with either greater knowledge or more negative attitudes toward substance use. Closely related to substance-use attitudes are normative expectations. Individuals who perceive substance use to be widespread and view it as "normal" behavior for people such as themselves are more likely to engage in it.

Tobacco, alcohol, and other substances that are commonly abused have complex pharmacological effects. Although the pharmacology of these substances varies considerably, virtually all of them produce effects that are highly reinforcing. Many substances are dependency producing, so that individuals who are quietly seduced into using drugs for social reasons find that they are engaged in a behavior that their body has come to "need." For most of these substances, tolerance develops quickly, requiring ever larger dosages and increased frequency of use. Moreover, failure to keep pace with the ever-escalating demands of one's body for these substances produces dysphoric feelings and physical withdrawal symptoms.

An often-stated reason for using drugs is what has been referred to in the clinical literature as the self-medication hypothesis (Millman and Botvin 1983). According to this hypothesis, individuals with a specific psychiatric condition (e.g., anxiety, depression) may use particular substances as a way of alleviating these conditions. Presumably, during the course of experimentation with a variety of substances, these individuals discover that certain substances make them feel better. For example, highly anxious individuals who may find that alcohol or other substances with depressant qualities help them to feel better will engage in substance use as a way of regulating their feelings of anxiety.

Because substance use has been found to be highly associated with a variety of health-compromising or problem behaviors, there is reason to believe that drug use is part of a general syndrome characterized by a particular lifestyle pattern and value orientation (Jessor 1982). First, individuals who use one substance are also more likely to use others. Not only is it the case that there is a predictable and well-ordered sequence of experimentation and use leading from some substances to others, but it is also the case that most individuals who are substance abusers use more than one substance. Second, individuals who smoke, drink, or use drugs also tend to get lower grades in school, are not generally involved in adult-sanctioned activities such as sports and clubs, and are also more likely than nonusers to exhibit antisocial patterns of behavior including lying, stealing, and cheating (Jessor, Collins, and Jessor 1972; Demone 1973; Wechsler and Thum 1973). Finally, substance use has also been found to be related to premature sexual activity, truancy, and delinquency.

The finding that different types of problem behaviors are part of a general syndrome or collection of highly associated behaviors suggests that they may have the same or at least highly similar *causes*. To the extent that this is true, it would have rather significant implications for the development of preventive interventions. If prevention programs are sufficiently comprehensive and effectively target the underlying determinants of several theoretically and empirically related problem behaviors, it may be possible to develop interventions that target several of these behaviors at the same time, obviating the need for developing separate interventions for each specific problem area (Swisher 1979; Botvin 1982). This would not only increase the efficiency of prevention programs but also would greatly increase the likelihood of their utilization.

B. Time of Onset

Considerable variability exists concerning both the time of onset for specific substances and the transition from experimental use to increasingly regular use. For most individuals, experimentation with one or more psychoactive substances occurs during the adolescent years. Initial use of the so-called gateway substances of tobacco, alcohol, and marijuana typically takes place during the early adolescent years.

Substance use, particularly in its early stages, is a social behavior. Consequently, it is not surprising that first use and early experimentation generally occur within the context of social situations. Because of the predominantly social nature of substance use, a number of researchers have hypothesized that substance use may serve as a major focal point for social interaction and may provide individuals with a sense of group identity (Becker 1967; Jessor 1976).

Since the 1960s, some degree of experimentation with tobacco, alcohol, or drugs has become commonplace in contemporary American society. This is particularly true with respect to tobacco, alcohol, and marijuana. Not surprisingly, these gateway substances also are among the most prevalent in our society. Although many individuals may discontinue substance use after a relatively brief period of experimentation, the initial period of use, for some individuals, eventually results in the development of both psychological and physiological dependence.

As substance use increases in both frequency and amount, individuals also begin using these substances in a more solitary fashion. This shift from "social use" (e.g., social drinking) to a mixed social/solitary pattern of use signals the transition from casual use to a more dependent pattern of use leading to progressively greater substance-use involvement. Social and psychological factors are generally viewed as the primary forces promoting the initiation of substance use.

However, pharmacological factors become increasingly important in reinforcing and maintaining more regular patterns of use (Ray 1974; Meyer and Mirin 1979). Consequently, the significance of this shift from an exclusively social pattern of use to a mixed social/solitary pattern suggests a fundamental change from psychosocial motivations to those tied more directly to the intrinsic pharmacological effects associated with use of particular substances.

C. Developmental Progression

Implicit in the notion of gateway substances is a recognition of a developmental progression leading from some substances to others. However, the notion of gateway substances has sparked a good deal of controversy over the years because acceptance of the idea of a developmental progression of substance use brings with it, by implication, the notion of determinism—conjuring up images of an inevitable progression from one substance to another in a manner that suggests little or no control.

Although many substance users may *not* progress from one type of substance use to another, or may even discontinue use entirely after a short time, data from several sources indicate that experimentation with one substance frequently does lead to experimentation with others in a logical and generally predictable progression (Hamburg, Braemer, and Jahnke 1975; Kandel 1978; Loeber and Le Blanc 1990). Most individuals begin by using alcohol and tobacco, progressing later to the use of marijuana. It is interesting that this developmental progression corresponds exactly to the prevalence of these substances in our society, with alcohol being the most widely used, followed by tobacco, which is followed by marijuana. For some individuals this progression may lead to the use of depressants, stimulants, and hallucinogens.

It should be pointed out in this context, however, that the use of one substance does not *necessarily* lead to the use of other substances. In other words, it does not mean that individuals who, for example, use marijuana will necessarily proceed to the use of other illicit substances.

Rather, the likelihood of progressing from one point in the developmental sequence to another can best be understood in probabilistic terms, that is, an individual's risk of moving to greater involvement with drugs increases at each step in the developmental progression.

This information has a great deal of significance for the focus and timing of preventive interventions. Interventions targeted at the use of substances at the very beginning of this developmental progression would have the potential not only of preventing the use of a particular gateway substance but also of reducing or even eliminating altogether the risk of using other substances further along the progression.

D. Adolescence as a Time of Risk

In order to develop effective substance-abuse programs targeted at adolescents, it is necessary to give adequate consideration to the developmental tasks, issues, changes, and pressures motivating adolescent behavior. Virtually all psychology textbooks characterize adolescence as a time of "storm and stress," a period of great physical and psychological change. It is well known that during the adolescent years, individuals will typically experiment with a wide range of behaviors and life-style patterns. This is all part of the natural process of separating from parents, developing a sense of autonomy and independence, establishing a personal identity, and acquiring the skills necessary for functioning effectively in an adult world.

Quite ironically, many of the developmental changes that are necessary prerequisites for becoming healthy adults also increase adolescents' risk of smoking, drinking, or using drugs. In an effort to protect adolescents from potentially damaging behaviors, society has determined that these behaviors should be proscribed for children and adolescents while being widely viewed as acceptable for adults (i.e., they are age-graded). This has traditionally been the case for smoking and drinking. Thus, adolescents who are impatient to assume adult roles and to appear more grown-up may engage in these behaviors as a way of laying claim to adult status. Or both age-graded and illicit behaviors may be engaged in because they provide adolescents with a means of establishing solidarity with a particular reference group, rebelling against parental authority, or establishing their own individual identity.

Part of the natural course of psychosocial development during the adolescent years is the development of autonomy and independence and a decreased reliance on parents. These changes tend to be manifested as a decline in parental influence that begins during the early childhood years and continues well into the adolescent years. This decline in parental influence is accompanied by a corresponding increase in the influence of peers (Utech and Hoving 1969). An increased reliance on the peer group may not only further weaken parental influence with respect to lifestyle issues but may also facilitate the promotion of substance use among individuals who are members of peer groups that hold various supportive attitudes toward substance use.

Significant cognitive changes also take place at precisely the same time. These changes ultimately affect how adolescents view the world and how they think. In contrast to the preadolescent's "concrete operational" mode of thinking, which is characteristically rigid, literal, and grounded in the "here and now," adolescent thought is more relative, abstract, and hypothetical (Piaget 1962). In general, this enables adolescents to conceive of a wide range of possibilities and logical alternatives, to accept deviations from established rules, and to recognize the frequently irrational and sometimes inconsistent nature of adult behavior.

These changes in the manner in which adolescents think may serve to undermine previously acquired knowledge relating to the potential risks of smoking, drinking, or using drugs. For example, the "formal operational" thinking of the adolescent facilitates the discovery of inconsistencies or logical flaws in arguments being advanced by adults concerning the health risk associated with substance use. Similarly, this new mode of thinking may enable adolescents to formulate counterarguments to antidrug messages, which may in turn permit rationalizations for ignoring potential risk, particularly if substance use is perceived to have social or personal benefits. In fact, given the priority of social issues for adolescents, it has been argued that the perceived social benefits of engaging in substance use may override motivations to avoid behaviors that may jeopardize their health.

Increased dependence on the peer group is typically accompanied by a corresponding rise in conformity behavior. Preschool children are almost totally impervious to conformity pressure (Hartup 1970), but the tendency to conform to group norms increases during middle childhood (Costanzo and Shaw 1966). Conformity needs and conformity behavior increase rapidly during preadolescence and early adolescence and decline steadily from middle to late adolescence (Mussen, Conger, and Kagan 1974). However, despite this general developmental trend toward increased conformity, an individual's susceptibility may vary greatly. Thus, if the values of the peer group should be in conflict with those held by the adolescent, the adolescent's susceptibility to change will, to a large extent, depend on the relative importance of peer acceptance.

Furthermore, differential susceptibility to conformity pressure has been shown to be a function of gender and personality characteristics. Girls tend to be more conforming to peer group pressure than boys (Maccoby and Masters 1970); individuals who are more dependent and anxious (Walters, Marshall, and Shooter 1960) and who have low self-esteem and high social sensitivity (Hartup 1970) tend to be more conforming.

Finally, a common characteristic of adolescents that increases their risk of becoming substance abusers is a sense of immortality and invulnerability. Adolescents tend to overestimate their ability to avoid personally destructive patterns of use, frequently laboring under the illusion that they are in control and can discontinue use at any point if they desire to do so. Adolescent substance users exhibit a remarkable absence of concern about the adverse consequences related to their use of psychoactive substances. This sense of "invulnerability" is particularly evident during the early stages of substance use and may perhaps help explain why adolescents so cavalierly disregard warnings from parents, teachers, and health professionals. Adolescents may gain a true appreciation of the seriousness of their involvement with drugs only after they have made a concerted effort to de-escalate their level of drug use or kick the habit entirely.

E. Toward the Development of Effective Prevention Strategies

Once individuals have become involved with tobacco, alcohol, or drugs to the extent that use occurs on a regular basis and both physical and psychological dependence has developed, the clinical literature indicates that it is extremely difficult to achieve abstinence for any sustained period of time. For adolescents, this may be even more difficult than for adults, since they are still living in the same environment and are still subject to the same intrapsychic pressures that led them originally to become involved with drugs.

Given the attendant risk associated with substance use and the fact that individuals have difficulty quitting once dependency has developed, it is axiomatic that the most propitious approach to the problem of substance abuse is prevention. As a consequence, a number of strategies have been utilized in an effort to reduce the number of youth becoming involved with tobacco, alcohol, or drugs. These strategies fall into five general categories: (1) information-dissemination approaches, which may also include the use of fear or moral appeals; (2) affective-education approaches; (3) alternatives approaches; (4) social resistance-skills approaches; and (5) social resistance-skills training incorporated within broader approaches that emphasize personal and social skills training. These prevention approaches are contrasted in table 1 and are discussed in the following sections.

Since most of the research that has been conducted to determine the

TABLE 1

Overview of Major Preventive Approaches

Approach	Focus	Methods
Information dissemination	Increase knowledge of drugs, their effects, and consequences of use; promote anti-drug-use attitudes	Didactic instruction, discussion, audio/video presentations, displays of substances, posters, pamphlets, school assembly programs
Affective education	Increase self-esteem, responsible decision making, interpersonal growth; generally includes little or no information about drugs	Didactic instruction, discussion, experiential activities, group problem-solving exercises
Alternatives	Increase self-esteem, self-reliance; provide variable alternatives to drug use; reduce boredom and sense of alienation	Organization of youth centers, recreational activities; participation in community-service projects; vocational training
Resistance skills	Increase awareness of social influence to smoke, drink, or use drugs; develop skills for resisting substance-use influences; increase knowledge of immediate negative consequences; establish non-substance-use norms	Class discussion; resistance-skills training; behavioral rehearsal; extended practice via behavioral "homework"; use of same-age or older peer leaders
Personal and social skills training	Increase decision making; personal behavior change; anxiety reduction; communication, social, and assertive skills; application of generic skills to resist substance-use influences	Class discussion; cognitive-behavioral skills training (instruction, demonstration, practice, feedback, reinforcement); extended practice via behavioral "homework"

effectiveness of various approaches to substance-abuse prevention has been with school populations, the greatest attention has been given to school-based approaches. However, attention has also been given to mass media approaches and community-based approaches. This review is not meant to be comprehensive but, rather, illustrative of the kinds of substance-abuse prevention programs that have been conducted to date and their effectiveness. Particular emphasis has been placed on the most promising approaches, based on existing empirical evidence.

III. Traditional Educational Approaches

The five most common types of educational approaches to substance-abuse prevention are described here. The effectiveness of these approaches is assessed with respect to the available evaluation literature.

A. Information Dissemination

The most widely used approach to substance-abuse prevention over the years has been one that relies on the dissemination of factual information. Information-dissemination approaches generally focus on the provision of factual information concerning the nature and pharmacology of specific substances, the ways in which these substances are used, and the adverse consequences of use.

The operating assumption of programs based on the information-dissemination model is the primacy of knowledge. According to this model, individuals who begin using drugs do so because they are not sufficiently aware of the adverse consequences associated with it. This cognitive deficit can be remedied through the provision of the appropriate knowledge. Once individuals have adequate knowledge about tobacco, alcohol, and drugs, it is assumed that they will act in a rational and logical way, that is, they will choose not to use drugs. Similarly, it has been assumed that changes in knowledge will cause changes in attitudes, which, in turn, will lead to the appropriate behavior.

For the most part, the information-dissemination approach sees individuals as essentially passive recipients of factual information. Information-dissemination programs have taken the form of public information campaigns, on the one hand, or school-based programs, on the other. Government agencies, community groups, and voluntary health organizations such as the American Cancer Society or the National Council on Alcoholism have produced millions of pamphlets, leaflets, posters, and public service announcements (PSAs).

School programs have involved the teaching of factual information in drug education classes, school-wide assembly programs featuring guest speakers (frequently policemen or health professionals), and films. Some programs have attempted to involve students more actively in both the organization and administration of these programs. In some programs, student involvement has taken the form of organizing the showing of filmstrips, conducting poster contests, developing antidrug PSAs, or producing antidrug plays and skits. Other programs have recruited older peer leaders to talk with younger students in an attempt to dissuade them from becoming tobacco, alcohol, or drug users. The underlying assumption of this approach is that students would be more receptive to antidrug messages from peers than they would be to similar messages coming from teachers or other authority figures.

B. Fear Arousal

Although conceptually distinct, the fear-arousal approach is actually a variation of the information-dissemination model. In contrast to approaches designed merely to disseminate factual information, some have attempted to emphasize and even dramatize the risks associated with tobacco, alcohol, and drug use. The underlying assumption of these approaches is that evoking fear would be more effective than an objective presentation of factual information. These approaches go a step further than traditional information-dissemination approaches since there is a clear and unambiguous message that drug abuse is dangerous, and those individuals foolish enough to disregard warnings by parents, teachers, and health professionals will be left to suffer the consequences.

A classic example of the fear-arousal approach is embodied in the drunk-driving films shown by schools across the country prior to prom night. A recent variation on this approach, designed to prevent cigarette smoking, has involved the use of antismoking public service announcements from famous people who are dying from smoking-related diseases. One of the most dramatic of these involved Yul Brynner, star of *The King and I*, prior to his death from lung cancer. The piece ends with a postscript noting the date on which he died.

C. Moral Appeals

Another approach to substance-abuse prevention, frequently combined with information dissemination, involves attacking the problem of drug use from a moral perspective. This prevention strategy generally involves "preaching" to students about the evils of smoking, drinking, or using drugs and exhorting them not to engage in those behaviors. Many early prevention efforts relied on this approach, where moral objections to substance use were combined with the advocacy of temperance.

Logically, one would expect individuals who were brought up to believe that smoking, drinking, or using drugs was immoral to be less likely to become substance users. Indeed, research evidence indicates that individuals who are highly religious are less likely to abuse drugs (Jessor and Jessor 1977). While this might argue for instilling religious values or at least strong anti-substance-use beliefs in children from an early age, it is not at all clear that a moral approach would be effective for adolescents or adults who are not religious or who are generally unreceptive to religious or moral appeals.

D. Affective Education

In the mid 1970s, drug education was reconceptualized as a process designed to increase affective skills. The affective-education approach placed less emphasis on the provision of factual information concerning the nature and pharmacology of specific substances or their adverse effects. The main thrust of affective education was the enrichment of the personal and social development of students. As Swisher (1979) observed, this type of prevention program was based on several assumptions. First, substance-abuse prevention programs should aim to develop prevention-oriented decision making concerning the use, by persons of all ages, of any licit or illicit drug. Second, such decisions regarding the personal use of drugs should result in fewer negative consequences for the individual. Third, the most effective way of achieving these goals would be by means of programs designed to increase self-esteem, interpersonal skills, and participation in alternatives. (Although "alternatives" has been included within the category of affective education by some writers, it has been described as an independent approach in the following section for ease of exposition and consistent with the way it has been treated in the prevention literature.)

Consistent with these assumptions, the focus of affective-education programs has been to increase self-understanding and acceptance through activities such as values clarifications and decision making; to improve interpersonal relationships by fostering effective communication, peer counseling, and assertiveness; and to increase students' abilities to fulfill their basic needs through existing social institutions. These approaches are based on a different set of assumptions than the approaches described above, with emphasis being placed on values clarification, teaching responsible decision making, increasing self-esteem and interpersonal skills, and promoting participation in alternatives (Swisher 1979).

Two examples of affective-education programs of this type that are noteworthy because they have been widely disseminated are "Here's Looking at You" and "Me-Me." "Here's Looking at You" was developed to cultivate commitment among young people to responsible ways of dealing with alcohol in their environment. The curriculum focused on building self-esteem, developing interpersonal skills, and learning current facts about alcohol and alcoholism. Each section of the curriculum included introductory discussions, films, work sheets, individual and group activities, and follow-up discussions. The "Me-Me" program targets students from kindergarten to grade 6 and is designed to enhance self-concept, decision-making ability, and drug and alcohol information.

E. Alternatives

One of the earliest responses to the problem of substance abuse was to provide adolescents with positive experiences as an alternative to the experiences reported to be associated with substance abuse. However, as Swisher and Hu (1983) have reported, not all alternatives to drug abuse are created equal. Some alternatives may have the potential for decreasing substance use, some for increasing it. Some alternatives have little theoretical connection to substance abuse, while others may be health-compromising in their own right.

Several different alternatives approaches have been developed and, in some cases, evaluated (Swisher and Hu 1983). The original model for alternatives took the form of establishing youth centers providing a particular unique activity or a set of activities for adolescents in the community (e.g., community service or academic tutoring). The underlying assumption of this approach was that adolescents could be provided with real-life experiences that would be as appealing as substance use and, therefore, involvement in these activities would actually take the place of involvement with substance use. An important focus of this model of alternatives was to alter the affective-cognitive state of an individual. A classic example of the alternatives approach is Outward Bound and similar programs.

Another type of alternatives approach involves attempting to match specific alternatives with an individual's unfulfilled needs. This is an individualized approach that is in contradistinction to merely providing adolescents with the same predetermined activity or group of activities. For example, the desire for physical relaxation or more energy might be satisfied by alternative activities such as athletics, exercise, or hiking. The desire for sensory stimulation might be satisfied through alternatives that enhance sensory awareness, such as learning to appreciate the sensory aspects of music, art, and nature. Interpersonal needs, such as gaining peer acceptance for individuals who are rebelling against authority, might be satisfied through participation in sensitivity training or encounter groups.

When considering the possibility of using alternatives as a prevention strategy, Swisher and Hu (1983) have cautioned that it is important to recognize that some activities have been associated with substance abuse, while others have not. For example, entertainment activities, participation in vocational activities, and participation in social activities have all been found to be associated with more substance use. On the other hand, academic activities, involvement in religious activities, and participation in sports are generally associated with less substance use. Consequently, it is conceivable that some alternatives programs could be counterproductive if the wrong type of activities were selected.

F. Effectiveness of Traditional Approaches

Efforts to demonstrate the effectiveness of prevention programs using the approaches described above have been hindered by the fact that many prevention programs have either failed to include an adequate evaluation component or have neglected to examine program effects with respect to substance-use behavior. For example, in an extensive review of 127 evaluation studies of substance-abuse prevention programs, Schaps et al. (1981) found that only four programs had evaluation components that included an assessment of substance-use behavior and were relatively well designed.

Reviews of the existing empirical evidence concerning the effectiveness of traditional approaches to tobacco, alcohol, and drug-abuse prevention have consistently indicated that these approaches are *not* effective (Richards 1969; Braucht et al. 1973; Goodstadt 1974; Swisher and Hoffman 1975; Berberian et al. 1976; Dorn and Thompson 1976; Kinder, Pape, and Walfish 1980; Schaps et al. 1981, 1984). Although it is beyond the scope of this essay to review all of the studies testing the effectiveness of traditional prevention approaches, tables 2–4 sum-

TABLE 2

Studies Testing Informational Approaches

Investigator(s)	Subjects	Intervention Approach	Evaluation Design	Results
Degnan (1972)	Ninth graders	10 weeks, information based	Pre-post	No significant attitude changes
Richardson et al. (1972)	Fifth graders	10 hours, information based (filmstrips, speakers, discussion)	Pre-post	No significant attitude changes
Weir (1968)	High school students	Not clearly described	Repeated administration of questionnaire	Significant attitude change
Friedman (1973)	Seventh and eighth graders	1 class period/week for 14 weeks; illustrations of drug-related situations and decisions	Pre-post questionnaires	Significant attitude change
O'Rourke and Barr (1974)	High school students	6-month course using New York state curriculum guide	Posttest only	Significant attitude change for males only
Mason (1973)	Eighth and twelfth graders	Information based; length not reported	Pre-post	Increased knowledge; increased drug curiosity and tendency toward increased usage
Rosenblitt and Nagey (1973)	Seventh graders	6 45-minute sessions; information based, presented as reasons for use and nonuse	Pre-post; no control group	Increased knowledge; trend toward increased usage of alcohol and tobacco
Stenmark, Kinder, and Milne (1977)	College undergraduates and pharmacy students	2–4 years college-level pharmacy course work	Pre-post	Pharmacy students had more knowledge and more liberal attitudes toward drugs

SOURCE.—Adapted from Kinder et al. (1980).

TABLE 3

Studies Testing Affective and Alternative Approaches

Investigator(s)	Subjects	Intervention Approach	Evaluation Design	Results
Moskowitz, Schaps, and Malvin (1982)	Third and fourth graders	42 sessions over 2 years; Magic Circle technique designed to increase opportunities to communicate in small groups; implemented by teachers	Pre-post (grade 3); follow-up (1 year)	No difference between those in Magic Circle and controls on variables relating to drug use and variables measuring drug use
Schaps et al. (1984) Moskowitz et al. (1984) Malvin et al. (1984)	Fourth–sixth graders Seventh–ninth graders	Effective Classroom Management (ECM) focuses on general teaching style; incorporation of communication and nonpunitive discipline skills with self-esteem enhancement by teacher; implemented by teachers	Pre-post; 1- and 2-year follow-up	No pattern of effects for ECM was observed for either elementary or junior high school students
Moskowitz et al. (1983)	Fourth–sixth graders	Peer tutoring of curriculum in small groups using Jigsaw technique;	Year 1: pretest (grades 4, 5);	No effects using Jigsaw technique

Study	Subjects	Program	Design	Results
Moskowitz (1985)		implemented by teachers and peers	year 2: pretest (grade 4); post-test (grades 4–6); year 3: post-test (grades 5–6)	Students liked tutoring but disliked weekly meetings; no effects on outcome variables such as self-esteem and school liking
Malvin et al. (1985)	Seventh and eighth graders	12-session training by teachers of peer tutors (cross-age peer tutoring); tutors help younger children 4 times per week for a semester	Pretest; 1- and 2-year follow-up	Students liked daily class sessions and working in store; no effects on outcome variables such as self-esteem and school liking
Malvin et al. (1985)	Seventh and eighth graders	1 period per day for a semester; students work in a "school store" 2–3 times per week	Pretest; 1- and 2-year follow-up	
Schaps et al. (1982) Moskowitz et al. (1984)	Seventh and eighth graders	12 sessions; decision making, goal setting, assertiveness, advertising, social influences, knowledge of drugs; implemented by teachers	Pre-post; 1-year follow-up	Effects only on seventh-grade girls' drug knowledge, perception of poor attitudes; but results disappeared at follow-up; no effects for eighth-grade girls or boys

TABLE 4
Studies Testing Psychosocial Approaches

Investigator(s)	Subjects	Intervention Approach	Evaluation Design	Results
Evans et al. (1978)	Seventh graders	4-session social pressures curriculum using videotapes, small-group discussion, and feedback on smoking rates; peers used in videotapes	Pre-post	Smoking onset rates for initial non-smokers exposed to the social pressures curriculum did not differ from onset rates for subjects exposed to repeated testing and a film on physiological effects of smoking
Evans et al. (1981)	Seventh graders with repeat interventions in grades 8 and 9	Same as above	Pre-post; follow-up (2 years)	Less smoking behavior and fewer intentions to smoke for experimental subjects at end of grades 8 and 9
McAlister, Perry, and Maccoby (1979)	Seventh graders	7-session social pressures curriculum using discussion and role playing; slightly older peers implemented curriculum	Pre-post; follow-up (2 years)	Experimental group reported substantially less smoking following treatment and 1 and 2 years thereafter; substantially lower rates of alcohol and marijuana use were also found 1 year following treatment
Perry, Killen, Telch, et al. (1980)	Tenth graders	4-session social pressures curriculum that identified pressures to smoke, demonstrated immediate physiological effects, and modeled ways to resist pressures	Pre-post	Proportion of experimental group smoking declined by the end of the treatment, whereas comparison-group smoking did not decline

482

Perry et al. (1983)	Tenth graders	3-session social pressures curriculum; implementation by regular classroom teachers versus college students	Pre-post	Experimental treatment was no more effective than two comparison treatments in reducing smoking; no significant difference were found between the two types of instructors
Minnesota Team (Hurd et al. 1980)	Seventh graders	5-session social pressures curriculum; conducted by college students; utilized videotapes, discussion, and role playing; compared personalized videotapes where role models were known to students with nonpersonalized videotapes	Pre-post; follow-up (2 years)	Immediately following treatments, the personalized and nonpersonalized groups reported significantly lower smoking rates than the no-treatment control groups, with no significant difference between the 2 experimental groups; 2 years following treatment, smoking rates for the personalized group were significantly less than the nonpersonalized and control groups, and smoking rates for the latter 2 groups did not differ
Minnesota Team (Arkin et al. 1981)	Seventh graders	4 experimental conditions included (1) social pressures curriculum led by professional health educator with med a supplement, (2) social pressures led by same-age peers with med a supplement, (3) social pressures led by peers without media, and (4) long-term health consequences	Pre-post; follow-up (1 year)	Among initial nonsmokers the long-term consequences curriculum had the most favorable initial results, but 1 year later the peer-led social pressures conditions had lower smoking rates; no differences were found for initial smokers

TABLE 4 (*Continued*)

Investigator(s)	Subjects	Intervention Approach	Evaluation Design	Results
Minnesota Team (Murray et al. 1984)	Seventh graders	Same as above except regular class-room teachers replaced professional health educators	Pre-post; follow-up (1 year)	Among initial nonsmokers, no differences were found among the 4 treatment conditions following treatment; smoking rates for all groups combined were lower than a comparison group receiving standard health curriculum; differences among groups for initial smokers were not significant, although there was a tendency toward higher smoking levels for the teacher-led social pressures curriculum
Best et al. (1984)	Sixth graders	8-session social influence approach, plus decision making; 2 boosters in seventh grade; 1 booster session in eighth grade; health educators	Pre-post; follow-up (2½ years)	Significant effects on cross-sectional prevalence; significant reductions in experimental smokers; significant impact on "high-risk" students for experimental to regular smoking

Study	Population	Intervention	Design	Results
Schinke and Gilchrist (1983)	Sixth graders	8-session social skills curriculum focusing on problem solving, decision making, and social pressures resistance	Pre-post	Substantially lower smoking rates 6 months following treatment for experimental versus no-treatment control group
Gilchrist and Schinke (1983)	Sixth graders	8-session social skills training	Pre-post; follow-up (15 months)	Substantially lower smoking rates 3 and 15 months following treatment for experimental group versus a comparison discussion group and a no-treatment control group
Botvin and Eng (1980); Botvin et al. (1980)	Eighth–tenth graders	10-session life-skills training focusing on communications, decision making, assertion, and social pressures resistance, adult educational specialists as implementers	Pre-post; follow-up (3 months)	Substantially lower onset rates among initial nonsmokers immediately after and 3 months following treatment compared with no-treatment control group
Botvin and Eng (1982)	Seventh graders	12-session life-skills training using slightly older peer leaders	Pre-post; follow-up (1 year)	Lower smoking rates among initial nonsmokers immediately after and 1 year following treatment.
Botvin, Renick, and Baker (1983)	Seventh graders	15-session life-skills training using regular classroom teachers; comparisons were made between intensive (daily session) and prolonged (weekly sessions) format	Pre-post; follow-up (1 year)	Among initial nonsmokers both experimental groups had lower smoking rates immediately after and 1 year following treatment; no differences were found between the 2 scheduling formats immediately following treatment, but smoking rates were lower for the intensive format 1 year later; among initial smokers, no differences were found

485

TABLE 4 (*Continued*)

Investigator(s)	Subjects	Intervention Approach	Evaluation Design	Results
Botvin et al. (1984)	Seventh graders	20-session life-skills training; implementation by older peers versus classroom teachers	Pre-post	Substantially lower substance-use rates immediately following treatment for the peer-led group compared with the teacher-led group and no-treatment control group; rates for the teacher-led group did not differ from the control group
Botvin et al. (1984)	Seventh graders	20-session life-skills training targeting alcohol misuse using classroom teachers	Pre-post; follow-up (6 months)	Significantly lower rates of use, misuse, and drunkenness at 6 months follow-up compared to no-treatment control group
Botvin et al. (1989)	Seventh graders (urban, Hispanic)	15-session life-skills training using classroom teachers	Pre-post	Significantly lower experimental smoking among life-skills training group than no-treatment controls

SOURCE.—Adapted from Battjes (1985).

among the better studies that have been conducted.

Studies testing the effectiveness of programs whose primary strategy was providing factual information have rather consistently demonstrated that they are capable of increasing knowledge and, in some instances, of increasing negative attitudes toward substance use. However, with an even greater degree of consistency, these studies have indicated that informational approaches do not reduce or prevent substance use.

Moreover, these evaluation studies call into question the basic assumption of the information-dissemination model (i.e., that increasing knowledge will result in attitude and behavior change). These studies indicate quite clearly that increased knowledge has virtually no impact on substance use or on intentions to engage in tobacco, alcohol, or drug use in the near future. There is even some evidence that this approach may lead to increased usage, possibly because it may serve to stimulate adolescents' curiosity (Swisher et al. 1971; Mason 1973).

Because fear arousal and moral appeals are typically used in conjunction with informational programs, no evidence exists concerning their independent effects, if any, on substance use. However, since virtually all of the evaluation studies conducted with information-dissemination approaches have not found evidence of prevention effects on behavior, it is unlikely that either of these approaches would yield any effects if used independently.

Considering the complex etiology of substance abuse, it is not surprising that approaches that rely on the provision of factual information are ineffective. Quite clearly, information-dissemination approaches are inadequate because they are too narrow in their focus and are based on an incomplete understanding of the factors promoting substance use/abuse. Although knowledge about the negative consequences of substance use is important, it is only one of many factors considered to play a role in the initiation of substance use among adolescents.

The results of evaluation studies testing the effectiveness of affective-education approaches have been equally discouraging. Although affective-education approaches have, in some instances, been able to demonstrate an impact on one or more of the correlates of substance abuse, they have not been able to affect substance-use behavior. For example, according to a recent review by Kim (1989), the results of studies evaluating the efficacy of "Here's Looking at You" were inconsistent and frequently contradictory. The most consistent results across these evaluations indicate increased alcohol knowledge in the absence of any positive impact on drinking behavior. Similarly, an evaluation study of the "Me-Me" program (Kearney and Hines 1980) conducted with students in grades 2–6 found improvements in self-esteem, decision making, drug knowledge, and attitudes. However, no effects were evident on behavior.

Although the affective-education model has considerable intrinsic appeal, it has been hypothesized that approaches based on this model are not effective because they utilize experiential classroom activities in an effort to teach decision making, increase self-esteem, and improve interpersonal skills, rather than using more appropriate techniques for facilitating skills acquisition (Botvin 1984). Thus, while the affective-education strategy is more comprehensive than approaches based on the information-dissemination model, the lack of effectiveness evident in the research literature may be based, at least in part, on deficiencies relating to the teaching method.

As is the case with affective education, intervention effects have been found with some programs designed to provide alternatives. Unfortunately, no impact has been demonstrated with respect to substance use (Schaps et al. 1981). A number of investigators have noted that individuals who participate in religious activities are less likely to engage in substance use (e.g., Jessor and Jessor 1977). Still, it is unclear to what extent involving individuals in religious activities would actually succeed as a preventive intervention.

IV. Psychosocial Approaches

Substantial progress in the field of substance-abuse prevention has been made during the past few years. The first major breakthrough came in the area of cigarette smoking. Researchers have focused on the prevention of adolescent cigarette smoking for several reasons. First, cigarette smoking is a major risk factor for chronic diseases such as coronary heart disease, cancer, and emphysema. Second, cigarette smoking is the most widespread form of drug dependence in our society. Third, cigarette smoking occurs toward the very beginning of the developmental progression of substance use and, consequently, is generally regarded as a "gateway" substance. More recently, prevention programs initially developed to deter adolescent cigarette smoking have been more broadly applied to the prevention of other substances, most notably to alcohol and marijuana.

As recent reviews (e.g., Flay 1985; Botvin 1986) have indicated, the most promising substance-abuse prevention approaches available today are those that focus primary attention on the psychosocial factors promoting substance-use initiation. These reviews not only highlight the evolution of the newer psychosocial approaches to substance abuse prevention over the past eight years and the various permutations tested, but also clearly demonstrate the growing sophistication and methodological rigor of these studies.

A. Psychological Inoculation

The pioneering work of Evans and his colleagues at the University of Houston toward the end of the 1970s triggered a major departure from traditional approaches to tobacco, alcohol, and drug-abuse prevention. Unlike traditional approaches that focus on information dissemination, fear arousal, or moral suasion, the strategy developed initially by Evans and his colleagues (Evans 1976; Evans et al. 1978) focused on the social and psychological factors believed to be involved in the initiation of cigarette smoking.

Evans's work was strongly influenced by an aspect of persuasive-communications theory referred to as "psychological inoculation" as formulated by McGuire (1964, 1968). The concept of psychological inoculation is analogous to that of inoculation used in traditional preventive medicine. The idea is that if an individual is expected to encounter the cultural analogue of "germs" (i.e., social pressures to adopt health-compromising behavior), then "infection" can be prevented by exposing the individual to a weak dose of those "germs" in a way that facilitates the development of "antibodies" (i.e., skills for resisting pressures toward adoption of unhealthy behaviors).

The application of the concept of psychological inoculation as a smoking-prevention strategy is fairly straightforward. If adolescents are likely to be called "chicken" for refusing to try cigarettes, they can be forewarned of the likelihood of encountering that kind of pressure and provided with the necessary skills for countering it. For example, they can be trained to reply: "If I smoke to prove to you that I'm not a chicken, all I'll really be showing is that I'm afraid not to do what you want me to do. I don't want to smoke; therefore, I'm not going to." If adolescents are likely to see older youth posturing and acting "tough" by smoking, they can be taught to think to themselves: "If they were really tough, they wouldn't have to smoke to prove it."

To accomplish this, Evans developed a series of films designed to increase students' awareness of the various social pressures to smoke that they would be likely to encounter as they progressed through the critical junior high school period in order to "inoculate" them against such pressures. Also included in these films were demonstrations of specific techniques that could be used to effectively resist various pressures to smoke. The prevention strategy developed by Evans also included two other important components. One component involved periodic (biweekly) assessment of students' smoking status by questionnaire along with the collection of saliva samples. The rate of smoking in each classroom was publicly announced as objective data at frequent intervals. The student-feedback component was designed to correct the misperception that cigarette smoking is a highly normative behavior (i.e., that everybody is doing it). Another component included in the intervention developed by Evans involved providing students with health knowledge concerning the immediate physiological effects of cigarette smoking.

In the first major test of a psychosocial prevention strategy, Evans compared students receiving monitoring/feedback with those receiving monitoring/feedback plus inoculation against a control group (Evans et al. 1978). When the students in the two treatment conditions were combined, they had smoking-onset rates that were about 50 percent lower than those observed in the control group. It is disappointing, however, that the inoculation intervention did not produce any additional reduction in smoking onset beyond that produced by the monitoring/feedback intervention.

The inoculation procedure may have been less than optimally effective for several reasons. First, it may be the case that the films were only inattentively viewed by students. Second, because the films were presented by adults working in concert with school authorities, and after viewing these films students participated in teacher-led discussion, the information communicated in these films may have had low credibility with those individuals who were the most likely to begin smoking cigarettes. In other words, the inoculation films may have suffered from low source credibility because they were associated with adult authority figures.

Finally, a strategy involving a combination of material communicated by film, followed by class discussions, may be inadequate because it does not provide students with adequate opportunities for the kind of guided practice that is necessary for promoting skills acquisition (Bandura 1977). Without actual practice, the student participants may have been somewhat reluctant to apply the pressure-resistance tactics demonstrated in the intervention films.

B. Resistance Skills Training

Several variations on the prevention model originally developed by Evans have been tested over the years (e.g., McAlister, Perry, and Maccoby 1979; Hurd et al. 1980; Murray et al. 1980; Perry, Killen, Slinkard, and McAlister 1980; Arkin et al. 1981; Telch et al. 1982; Luepker et al. 1983). Similar to the prevention model developed by Evans, these interventions were designed to increase students' awareness of the various social influences to engage in substance use. A distinctive feature of these prevention models is that they have placed more emphasis on teaching students specific skills for effectively resisting both peer and media pressures to smoke, drink, or use drugs.

The term used in this essay to refer to this type of prevention program is "resistance-skills training" since it captures two distinctive aspects of these programs: (1) the focus on increasing participants' resistance to negative social influences to engage in substance use, and (2) the focus on skills training. They have also been referred to as "social influence" approaches (because they target the social influences promoting substance use) or "refusal skills training" approaches (because a central feature of these programs is that they teach how to say "no" to substance-use offers).

The psychosocial prevention approaches that rely on resistance-skills training are based on a conceptual model that stresses the fundamental importance of social factors in promoting the initiation of substance use among adolescents. These influences come from the family (parents and older siblings), from peers, and from the mass media. Adolescents may be predisposed toward substance use because substance-use behavior is modeled by parents or older siblings, or by the transmission of positive or ambiguous messages concerning the rectitude of substance use. Similarly, individuals who have friends who smoke, drink, or use drugs are more likely to become substance users themselves due to issues relating to modeling and the need for peer acceptance (as well as availability). Finally, on the larger societal level, high-status role models in the mass media may promote substance use, supported by the perception of positive norms and expectations with respect to substance use. Group norms are enforced by both implicit and explicit rules governing behavior as well as perceived desirability. As Bandura (1977) has indicated, all social influences are themselves a product of the interaction between individual learning histories and forces in both the community and the larger society.

On the individual level, influences related to specific behaviors arise from learned expectations and skills regarding those behaviors. Individuals may smoke, for example, because they expect relatively immediate positive outcomes such as increased alertness, relief from anxiety, or enhanced social status. Logically, it would appear reasonable that individuals would choose not to smoke if they did not expect to receive rewarding consequences or if they had the ability to resist specific social pressure to smoke. Expectations and skills are learned both from observation and from direct experience.

Resistance-skills training approaches generally teach students how to recognize situations in which they will have a high likelihood of experiencing peer pressure to smoke, drink, or use drugs so that these high-risk situations can be avoided. In addition, students are taught how to handle situations in which they might experience peer pressure to engage in substance use. Typically, this includes teaching students not only what to say (i.e., the specific content of a refusal message) but also how to deliver it in the most effective way possible.

Another distinctive feature of these programs is the use of peer leaders as program providers. The peer leaders used in these interventions are typically older students (e.g., tenth graders might serve as peer leaders for seventh graders). Peer leaders could also be the same age as the participants and may even be from the same class. The rationale for using peer leaders is that peers generally have higher source credibility with adolescents than do adults. Finally, students are generally provided with the opportunity to observe other students using these skills as well as being provided with the opportunity to practice these skills through the use of role playing in class.

Material has also generally been included in these programs to combat the perception that substance use is widespread (i.e., "everybody's doing it") since research has indicated that adolescents typically overestimate the prevalence of smoking, drinking, and the use of certain drugs (Fishbein 1977). This has been accomplished by simply providing students with the prevalence rates of substance use among their age-mates in terms of national survey data or by conducting classroom or school-wide surveys that are organized and directed by students participating in the program. Finally, these programs typically include a component designed to increase students' awareness of the techniques used by

ages and to teach techniques for formulating counterarguments to the messages utilized by advertisers.

Considerable research has been conducted and published in recent years documenting the effectiveness of these kinds of psychosocial prevention strategies. Although variations exist across studies, a review of these preventive interventions indicates that they are able to reduce the rate of smoking by between 35 and 45 percent after the initial intervention. Similar reductions have been reported for alcohol and marijuana use (McAlister et al. 1980).

Follow-up studies indicate that the positive behavioral effects of these prevention approaches are evident for up to two years after the conclusion of these programs for cigarette smoking (McAlister et al. 1980; Telch et al. 1982; Luepker et al. 1983). Studies testing the application of these prevention strategies to substances such as alcohol and marijuana have only recently been conducted, and therefore data concerning their long-term effectiveness are not yet available.

Most of the research studies conducted with the resistance-skills training approaches have been targeted at junior high school students, generally beginning with seventh graders. Some studies have included students as young as fifth and sixth graders, while other studies have been targeted at high school students. The programs tested have been of varying lengths, ranging from as few as three or four sessions to as many as eleven or twelve sessions conducted over a two-year period. Considerable variation also exists among the individuals responsible for implementing these programs. Some programs have been implemented by college students, others by members of the research project staff, while still others have used classroom teachers to implement the prevention programs.

All of the studies testing resistance-skills training models have demonstrated significant reductions in smoking behavior. Most of these prevention studies have focused primarily on preventing the onset of cigarette smoking—that is, preventing the transition from nonsmoking to smoking. The results reported generally indicate reductions of 33–39 percent in the proportion of individuals beginning to smoke, comparing the proportion of new smokers in the experimental group with that of the control group. Several studies have demonstrated reductions in the overall prevalence of cigarette smoking among the participating students both for experimental smoking (less than one cigarette per week) and for regular smoking (one or more cigarettes per week). In these studies, the impact on the prevalence of regular smoking has ranged from reductions of 43–47 percent. The impact on the prevalence of experimental smoking has been somewhat more variable, ranging from reductions of 29–67 percent.

Follow-up studies have found the presence of program effects for at least two years after the initial posttest; however, these effects do seem to decay over time, suggesting the need for continual intervention throughout junior and perhaps even senior high school.

Investigators have generally not attempted to identify and focus on students who might be considered likely to become substance users/abusers. Thus, for the most part, it is difficult to determine the extent to which these prevention programs might have an impact on those individuals most likely to develop more extensive patterns of substance use. This issue was, however, addressed in a study conducted by Best and his colleagues (Best et al. 1984). In addition to evaluating the effectiveness of the prevention program on all of the students participating in the study, prevention effects were determined for those individuals identified as being the most likely to become cigarette smokers using several social predictors of cigarette smoking (e.g., peer smoking, parent smoking, and sibling smoking). In this case, the prevention program was found to be even more effective for students identified as being at high "social risk" for becoming cigarette smokers than for other students in the sample, producing an 85 percent reduction in the proportion of nonsmokers becoming experimental smokers and a 100 percent reduction in the proportion becoming regular smokers.

Finally, although as a group the resistance-skills training approaches have primarily been evaluated in terms of their impact on cigarette smoking, a study conducted by McAlister and his associates (McAlister et al. 1980) has demonstrated an impact on alcohol and marijuana use as well. In addition, some studies have demonstrated an impact on knowledge (Best et al. 1984) as well as attitudes, beliefs, and social resistance skills (Hops et al. 1989).

No firm conclusions can be drawn at this point concerning which program components are the most or the least important or who are the most effective providers. Many studies have tested social influence approaches that include a public commitment component, yet the results of a study conducted by Hurd and his collaborators (Hurd et al. 1980) suggest that this component may not contribute to the effectiveness of these programs. Most of these programs have used films or videotapes similar to those initially developed by Evans and his colleagues (Evans

et al. 1978). However, it is not yet clear what type of media material is
the most effective or the extent to which it is necessary. Finally, little is
known concerning the optimal age (grade) of intervention, program
length, program structure, or the characteristics of the individuals who
are the most influenced by these programs.

It has generally been assumed that peer leaders play an important
role in the social influence approaches. Indeed, the use of same-age or
older peer leaders is a feature that has been evident in nearly all of the
social influence approaches. In general, evidence supports the use of
peer leaders for this type of prevention strategy (Arkin et al. 1981;
Perry, Killen, Slinkard, and McAlister 1980). Still, one must be aware
that although peer leaders have been used to varying degrees in these
programs, they generally have been used mainly in an ancillary fashion
rather than as primary program implementors. In most of these studies,
the primary providers have been either members of the research project
staff or teachers. Moreover, peer-led programs may not be uniformly
effective for all students. The results of one study suggest that while
boys and girls may be equally affected by social influence programs
when they are conducted by teachers, they may be differentially influenced by peer-led programs—with girls being influenced more by
peer-led programs than boys (Fisher, Armstrong, and de Kler 1983).

C. Personal and Social Skills Training

Research has also been conducted to test the efficacy of broader-
based substance-abuse prevention programs (Botvin and Eng 1980;
Botvin, Eng, and Williams 1980; Schinke and Blythe 1981; Botvin,
Renick, and Baker 1983; Gilchrist and Schinke 1983; Pentz 1983; Botvin, Baker, Botvin, Filazzola, and Millman 1984; Botvin, Baker, Renick, Filazzola, and Botvin 1984; Schinke 1984; Schinke and Gilchrist
1984; Botvin et al. 1985). In addition to including many of the components of the resistance-skills training approaches, a distinguishing feature of these programs is an emphasis on the acquisition of generic
personal and social skills.

These approaches are theoretically rooted largely in social learning
theory (Bandura 1977) and problem behavior theory (Jessor and Jessor
1977). From this perspective, substance abuse is conceptualized as a
socially learned and functional behavior, resulting from the interplay of
social and personal factors. Substance-use behavior, like other types of
behavior, is learned through modeling and reinforcement, which is
influenced by personal factors such as cognitions, attitudes, and beliefs.

The primary distinguishing feature of these approaches is that they typically include components targeting two or more of the following: (1) general problem-solving and decision-making skills (e.g., brainstorming, systematic decision-making techniques); (2) general cognitive skills for resisting interpersonal or media influences (e.g., identifying persuasive advertising appeals, formulating counterarguments); (3) skills for increasing self-control and self-esteem (e.g., self-instruction, self-reinforcement, goal setting, principles of self-change); (4) adaptive coping strategies for relieving stress and anxiety through the use of cognitive coping skills or behavioral relaxation techniques; (5) general interpersonal skills (e.g., initiating social interactions, complimenting, conversational skills); and (6) general assertive skills (e.g., making requests, saying "no," expressing feelings and opinions). These skills are generally taught using a combination of instruction, demonstration, feedback, reinforcement, behavioral rehearsal (practice during class), and extended practice through behavioral homework assignments.

The intent of these programs is to teach the kind of generic skills for coping with life that will have a relatively broad application. This is in contrast to the resistance-skills training approaches that are designed to teach skills with a problem-specific focus. Where appropriate, however, generic skills training programs emphasize the application of these skills to situations directly related to substance use/abuse (e.g., the application of general assertive skills to situations involving peer pressure to smoke, drink, or use drugs). Despite similarities in content, theory, and teaching methods, differences exist in the characteristics of the personal and social skills training prevention programs that have been tested. For example, the target age group, program length, frequency of sessions, providers, and the decision to include booster sessions have varied for each program. Although most of the prevention studies conducted thus far with this approach have focused on seventh graders, some studies have been conducted with sixth graders, while others have been conducted with eighth, ninth, or tenth graders. Program length has ranged from as few as seven sessions to as many as twenty sessions. Some of these prevention programs were conducted at a rate of one class session per week, while others were conducted at a rate of two or more classes per week.

All of the studies conducted so far, with the exception of two (Botvin and Eng 1982; Botvin, Baker, Renick, Filazzola, and Botvin 1984), have used adult primary providers. In some cases, these adults were teachers; in other cases, they were outside health professionals (i.e., project staff members, graduate students, social workers). The majority of the intervention studies have not included booster sessions or involved the implementation of program activities over an extended period of time.

The evaluation studies conducted thus far with the broader personal and social skills training approach have also had major differences in terms of design, objectives, populations, dependent measures, sample size, and length of follow-up. Some of the studies have simply tested the effectiveness of the prevention program when contrasted with a comparison (control) group. Others, however, have been designed so that they could provide information on the content of the prevention program, the scheduling format, the relative effectiveness of peers versus teachers as providers, and the effectiveness of booster sessions.

Some of the studies reviewed were pilot studies involving a small number of students from one or two schools, while others were larger-scale studies involving 800 to 1,000 students from as many as ten schools. These differences make the task of drawing conclusions from a group of studies even more difficult. Still, it is possible to make some general statements about these studies as a whole.

All of the studies testing personal and social skills training approaches have demonstrated significant behavioral effects. Moreover, the magnitude of reported effects has typically been relatively large. In general, these studies have demonstrated that generic skills approaches to substance-abuse prevention can produce reductions in new experimental smoking ranging from 42 to 75 percent. Schinke and Gilchrist (1983) reported a 79 percent reduction in the prevalence of experimental smoking. Data from two studies (Botvin and Eng 1982; Botvin, Renick, and Baker 1983) demonstrated reductions ranging from 56 to 67 percent in the proportion of pretest nonsmokers becoming regular smokers at the one-year follow-up without additional booster sessions. One study (Botvin, Renick, and Baker 1983) reported an 87 percent reduction in the initiation of regular smoking for students who participated in the prevention program in grade 7 and received additional booster sessions in grade 8. Overall, the effects reported thus far have been somewhat greater than those reported in the studies evaluating the efficacy of the psychological inoculation and resistance-skills training approaches.

An issue that has been raised by some reviewers (e.g., Flay 1985) is that the psychosocial prevention programs that have demonstrated an impact on behavior may merely have an impact on the transition from nonuse to experimental use and may not, in the final analysis, prevent or reduce more regular patterns of use. However, evidence does exist indicating that these prevention approaches produce initial reductions in the onset of experimental use, followed later by reductions in regular use. Several studies indicate that the initial reductions in new experimental smoking frequently observed at the end of the prevention program do in fact result in later reductions of an equal magnitude in more regular cigarette smoking, whether this is assessed by a weekly measure of smoking (Botvin and Eng 1982; Botvin, Renick, and Baker 1983; Botvin et al. 1985) or a daily measure (Botvin, Renick, and Baker 1983; Botvin et al. 1985).

Several of these studies indicate that broader-based generic approaches, although generally longer than approaches that focus only on resistance-skills training, may be more efficient since they can have an impact on several related behavioral domains at the same time. Botvin and colleagues reported significant effects for alcohol use (Botvin, Baker, Botvin, Filazzola, and Millman 1984; Botvin, Baker, Renick, Filazzola, and Botvin 1984). Pentz (1983) reported that her intervention program had a positive effect on students' alcohol use and academic performance. Schinke (1984) found that an approach similar to the one used in preventing cigarette smoking was also effective as a strategy for the prevention of teenage pregnancy.

These studies also have provided information concerning the conditions under which this type of prevention approach can be effective. The findings of these studies indicate that generic personal and social skills substance-abuse prevention programs can be effective whether the primary providers are project staff social workers, graduate interns, peer leaders, or classroom teachers. Moreover, these approaches have been found to be effective with rural, suburban, and urban students.

One study (Botvin, Baker, Renick, Filazzola, and Botvin 1984) suggests that a more intensive programming format (several sessions per week) may be more effective than a less intensive format (one session per week) spaced over a longer period of time. Evidence also exists indicating that booster sessions may help maintain and even enhance program effects (Botvin, Renick, and Baker 1983; Botvin et al. 1985).

A major strength of the evaluation studies conducted with the broader personal and social skills training approaches is that they have attempted to measure variables that are hypothesized to mediate the impact of the prevention programs on the behavioral outcome variables. All of these prevention approaches have produced measurable effects on a spectrum of mediating variables in a direction consistent with non–substance use. These include significant changes in knowledge and attitudes, assertiveness, locus of control, social anxiety, self-satisfaction, decision making, and problem solving. Most of these variables were measured by questionnaire, raising some questions about the degree to which specific skills, such as assertiveness, have been enhanced (Biglan and Ary 1985). Notable exceptions are seen in the studies conducted by Schinke and his colleagues (e.g., Schinke and Blythe 1981) and by Pentz (1983). These investigators have utilized behavioral assessment techniques such as taped role-play situations requiring students to demonstrate their skill in handling situations that warrant an assertive response. Through such approaches, a relatively direct assessment of the extent to which students have acquired specific skills can be made.

D. Methodological Issues

Despite the emphasis on evaluation and the high-quality research that has been conducted with the newer psychosocial substance-abuse prevention approaches, recent reviews (Biglan and Ary 1985; Flay 1985; Glasgow and McCaul 1985; Botvin 1986) have identified a number of methodological issues that deserve further consideration by prevention researchers. These issues include the validity of self-report data, the appropriateness of research designs, the unit of assignment, the unit of analysis, the pretest equivalence of experimental groups, and the potential impact of attrition on internal and external validity.

Although many of the earlier studies testing psychosocial prevention strategies have been criticized for shortcomings in one or more of these areas, the more recent studies have become progressively more rigorous as investigators have discovered potential methodological problems and have placed an increasingly greater emphasis on enhancing the internal validity of these studies. For example, recent studies have collected saliva or breath samples prior to collecting self-report data. This procedure (commonly referred to as the "bogus pipeline") has been found to increase self-reports of smoking behavior presumably because students are more likely to give truthful self-reports if they believe that their smoking status can be determined through an analysis of their saliva or breath samples.

It is interesting to note that when the earlier pilot studies are compared with the more recent (and more methodologically rigorous) evaluation studies, the same effects are found for substance-use behavior. This consistency of results across studies is perhaps the most persuasive evidence concerning the efficacy of these prevention approaches, providing considerable cause for optimism.

E. Program Providers

Primary substance-abuse prevention programs have been implemented by a variety of providers. Most of the traditional programs have relied on regular classroom teachers, many of whom are health educators. The use of teachers in most school-based tobacco, alcohol, and drug education programs is not surprising since they are the individuals charged with the responsibility of educating students. The obvious advantage of teachers is that they are readily available, they are part of the school environment, and they have teaching experience. In some school districts, prevention and early intervention programs are implemented by drug counselors.

Frequently, school-based prevention programs have been implemented by outside experts such as health professionals or police officers. The rationale behind the use of nonschool personnel generally is that experts from the community would have higher credibility with students and thus would be more effective. Physicians and nurses have been used to teach students about the health effects and pharmacology of substance use. Policemen have been used to emphasize the social and legal consequences of substance use.

In the case of research projects, interventions have been implemented by project staff members. These individuals generally have a strong commitment to the goals of the research, are highly trained, and usually have prior teaching experience. The advantage of using project staff members as program providers is that it increases the likelihood that the prevention program will be implemented according to the intervention protocol, that is, in a way that is complete and consistent. The obvious disadvantage of using providers of this type is that they are not a regular part of the school environment. School personnel concerned about "turf" issues may feel defensive; this may be manifested as low cooperation or, occasionally, may take the form of active efforts to sabotage the research or demonstration project. In addition, once the project is completed, these individuals will no longer be available to implement the program.

Finally, many programs have included peer leaders as either the primary providers or as adjuncts to the primary provider. The rationale behind the use of peer leaders is similar to that for using outside experts. There is a fundamental assumption that peer leaders have greater credibility with students than do teachers with respect to the information being conveyed. Both older students and students who are the same age as the participants have served as peer leaders.

Peer teaching has become recognized as a highly effective way for stimulating poorly motivated learners (Vriend 1969), and peer teaching teams have been used as a way of efficiently providing more traditional health education to large numbers of elementary school children (McRae and Nelson 1971). Peer counseling, in which young people are trained to help peers seeking advice on how to handle personal problems, has also been successfully applied in several settings (Hamburg and Varenhorst 1972; Alwine 1974).

Since the intent in using peer leaders is to increase program effectiveness by using a more credible provider, it is critically important that programs using peer leaders select peer leaders appropriately in order to reach the students at the greatest risk of smoking, drinking, or using drugs. The students selected as peer leaders are frequently the students receiving the best grades and/or the most popular among the teachers and administration. However, these students tend not to be well regarded by the high-risk students and consequently may actually have rather low credibility. In selecting peer leaders, it is also important that the peer leaders be good role models, that is, that they not smoke, drink, or use drugs.

A method of recruiting the most appropriate older peer leaders that has worked well in several studies involves using students from a nearby school and enlisting the assistance of a popular teacher. Peer leaders are selected on the basis of their communication skills and judged attractiveness to the kind of young people who are likely to become involved with tobacco, alcohol, or drugs. Frequently, the best peer leaders are students who are responsible but somewhat unconventional.

Advantages and disadvantages have been found for using peer leaders. For example, while they may have greater credibility with adolescents concerning life-style issues such as smoking and drinking than do teachers, peer leaders not surprisingly have been found to lack the teaching and classroom management skills of teachers (Botvin and Eng 1982). Moreover, peer leader programs require considerable effort in terms of training, coordination, scheduling, monitoring, the need for ongoing support to sustain motivation and enthusiasm, and the need to recruit and train replacements necessitated by normal attrition. This is particularly true for programs in which the peer leaders have primary responsibility for conducting the program. Additionally, the use of older peer leaders (i.e., high school students) may present logistical difficulties if they do not attend school within reasonably close proximity to the school of the younger students participating in the program.

Research with the newer psychosocial approaches to substance-abuse prevention have demonstrated that they can be effectively implemented by teachers (Botvin, Renick, and Baker 1983), older peer leaders (McAlister, Perry, and Maccoby 1979; Perry, Killen, Slinkard, and McAlister 1980; Botvin and Eng 1982; Botvin, Baker, Renick, Filazzola, and Botvin 1984), same-age peer leaders (Hurd et al. 1980; Luepker et al. 1983; Murray et al. 1984), and project staff members (Botvin, Eng, and Williams 1980; Schinke and Gilchrist 1983).

A solution to the problem of whom to use as program providers might be to utilize a combination of both teachers and same-age peer leaders. This would capture the best of both while eliminating most of the problems associated with either type of provider. Using this model, teachers would have primary responsibility for implementing the prevention program, thus taking advantage of their teaching experience and classroom management skills. Peer leaders would assist teachers in program implementation with specific formal functions such as serving as discussion leaders, demonstrating refusal skills, and leading role plays. In addition, peer leaders could serve an important informal function as positive role models for the kinds of skills and behavior being taught in the program, particularly with respect to resisting substance-use offers.

V. Mass Media

It has long been recognized that the media are a powerful source of influence shaping attitudes, beliefs, norms, and behavior. Social commentators have criticized the media for a variety of reasons, including their role in promoting tobacco, alcohol, and drug use. Analysis of the entertainment media indicates quite clearly the pervasiveness of drug content in movies, TV and radio shows, magazines, and records (e.g., Winick and Winick 1976).

Magazines are replete with cigarette and alcohol advertisements as well as ads for an ever-expanding array of proprietary drugs. Adolescents watching TV are literally bombarded with ads promoting alcoholic beverages and proprietary drugs. By contrast, the net effect of public service announcements (PSAs) designed to prevent substance use, which typically run during times of low viewership, can only be characterized as infinitesimal compared with ads promoting tobacco, alcohol, and drug products.

A number of mass media campaigns concerning health promotion and substance-abuse prevention have been developed and implemented. These campaigns have typically taken the form of PSAs. Most mass media campaigns have relied on information-dissemination and/or fear-arousal strategies. As is the case with traditional school-based prevention approaches, most media campaigns have not been adequately evaluated (Flay and Sobel 1983).

However, when evaluated, these campaigns have produced inconsistent effects. Some campaigns have increased knowledge and changed attitudes in the desired direction; others have had no effects; still others have produced negative effects (i.e., have increased substance use). As Flay and Sobel (1983) concluded in their review, "an overwhelming majority of mass media drug abuse prevention programs have failed to change behavior." Still, this is not surprising when one recognizes that most PSA campaigns fail to reach the intended audience.

The one major exception was the counteradvertising campaign mounted against cigarette smoking in the late 1960s in which there was approximately one counteradvertisement for every four or five cigarette ads. It has frequently been said that the effectiveness of that particular PSA campaign was the single most important factor in obtaining the cooperation of the tobacco industry concerning the elimination of cigarette ads on television.

Despite the general absence of effects for substance-abuse prevention mass media campaigns and the paucity of high-quality evaluation research, the possibility remains for the mass media to be a powerful weapon in the war against drug abuse. To do so, however, media campaigns must overcome the deficiencies of past campaigns. It is axiomatic that mass media campaigns must reach their target audience if they are to be effective. That clearly means that PSAs must be aired during "prime time" or other high-viewership periods. Furthermore, media campaigns must de-emphasize the use of information-dissemination and fear-arousal strategies and place greater emphasis on strategies designed to combat the powerful social influences to smoke, drink, or use drugs. Finally, high-quality evaluation research is needed to develop and refine the most effective prevention-oriented mass media campaigns.

VI. Community-based Approaches

The major emphasis of this essay, reflecting current developments in the field of substance-abuse prevention, necessarily has been on school-based prevention and education approaches. Programs targeted at student populations constitute a substantial portion of the prevention efforts initiated in this country over the past several decades. However, community-based approaches, although difficult to evaluate, offer the potential of providing a supportive context for other prevention efforts. It may be difficult to sustain the preventive gains that the newer psychosocial approaches have demonstrated are achievable without affecting the larger social environment of the community.

Several antidrug organizations have been developed in recent years, for example, Students against Drunk Driving (SADD) and Mothers against Drunk Driving (MADD). Moreover, professional associations such as the American Bar Association, the American Medical Association, the American Public Health Association, and the American Psychological Association have all begun taking a greater leadership role in the area of substance-abuse prevention.

A. Parent Groups

A growing force in substance-abuse prevention in recent years is what has come to be called the Parents' Movement. This is essentially a grass-roots movement involving concerned parents from communities throughout the country who have organized themselves into local parent groups. The main function of these groups is to provide support for concerned parents, to provide a mechanism for becoming educated about the problem of drug abuse, to increase the awareness of other parents throughout the community, and to serve as a catalyst for change in their communities.

More recently, many of these local parent groups have come under the umbrella of the National Federation of Parents for Drug-Free Youth (NFP), which was formed in 1980. Its principal objective is to assist in the formation and support of local parent and youth groups across the country that seek to eliminate drug and alcohol use among youth. Parents around the country network to help children understand why they must resist peer pressure to use drugs and alcohol and to offer healthy alternatives. They advocate greater parent involvement in determining the values and environment of their children.

The NFP provides many activities coordinated by its national headquarters and implemented by trained volunteers throughout the counity. They sponsor annual national conferences, distribute public service announcements, and lobby state legislatures and Congress. The NFP has 800 affiliated parent groups.

The NFP umbrella organization networks with existing and new drug-free youth groups. It developed "Reach America," a youth leadership training project designed to help older students educate younger students. This is an effort to reeducate the American public, especially young people, regarding the hazards of drug and alcohol use. The NFP has also developed "Project Graduation Celebration" in conjunction with some business organizations to help students celebrate high school graduation safely.

Despite the energy and enthusiasm of many members of the NFP, it also appears to have encountered difficulties in achieving its stated objectives. A recently completed study, which was conducted by the Office of the Inspector General within the Department of Health and Human Services (April 1988), found that 40 percent of the NFP members were no longer active. Moreover, according to this report, less than one-third of youth surveyed said that their parents were involved. From on-site interviews conducted as part of this study, it appeared that only one or two parents were very active within each local youth program. Sustained parental involvement has been difficult to achieve.

B. Effectiveness of Parent Groups

Although numerous claims have been made in the mass media concerning the effectiveness of parent groups in preventing substance abuse, there has been virtually no effort objectively to evaluate their effectiveness. One exception is a study conducted by Moskowitz (1985) that attempted to evaluate the effects of parent groups on adolescent substance use and its correlates. In this study, two sites where parent groups had been active were selected for study. These sites were selected explicitly because assertions had been made that these parent groups had been particularly successful in positively influencing adolescent substance abuse and its correlates. The evaluation study was conducted in order to determine whether, using archival records, these claims were justified, as well as to increase understanding of how these changes occurred. The selection criteria used for this study were that (1) sites must have a parent group whose goal was to prevent substance abuse among local youth; (2) several individuals with national expertise about parent groups must believe that positive changes had occurred for the youth at that site in terms of substance abuse or its correlates;

(3) community leaders as well as parent group leaders at each site must have attributed any apparent prevention effects to the parent group; and (4) archival data necessary to document the effect of the parent groups must be available for examination.

Nine sites were nominated, with only three sites receiving multiple nominations. Of these, two sites were selected. The parent groups involved at these sites were the Unified Parents of America and the Naples Informed Parents (NIP). Considerable information was available concerning these parent groups because both had been examined in a previous study that had focused on the organization and development of these groups (Associate Consultants 1981; Manett 1983).

According to Moskowitz (1985), these groups are important historically because they are two of the original parent groups. Moreover, both groups have provided technical assistance to incipient parent groups around the country and, due to their apparent success, were featured on an NBC TV "Today" show series on adolescent problems that was broadcast in the early 1980s. The Unified Parents of America had been credited with decreasing alcohol usage and the use of other drugs, truancy, and tardiness as well as with increasing academic achievement test scores and participation in adult-sanctioned extracurricular activities. NIP had also been credited with contributing to positive changes in substance use and academics.

As part of the study, interview schedules were developed and administered to parent group leaders and school personnel. Available archival records were examined with respect to student academic achievement, absenteeism, vandalism, discipline problems (including substance use), and course enrollment. Unfortunately, the available archival records were inadequate to document any of the reported changes in student behavior. In addition, school personnel and parent group leaders had different perceptions of the parents' contribution to changes in school policy and student behavior. Moreover, it was impossible to separate potential parent group effects from other changes occurring concurrently in these communities that may have been the cause of any observed changes. Thus, in this study, the task of objectively documenting the presence of any putative changes relating to substance-abuse prevention was virtually impossible. In order to obtain meaningful data, a more appropriate evaluation design is necessary— one that is conducted prospectively with at least a pretest and posttest for both the treatment community and a comparison community.

G. Comprehensive Community-based Prevention

Although "organizing" a community and raising community consciousness concerning the extent to which drug abuse is a problem requiring attention are important objectives in developing a comprehensive and effective substance-abuse prevention program, they are only the vehicles for initiating the types of changes needed to prevent substance abuse. Unfortunately, once the need for drug-abuse prevention is well recognized in a community, it might not be entirely clear how these communities should proceed once organized. Moreover, controversy may arise concerning the strategies or intervention approaches to utilize in achieving the desired goal of preventing substance abuse. For the most part, communities have continued to rely on substance-abuse prevention approaches that have previously been demonstrated to be ineffective.

An excellent example of a comprehensive community-based substance-abuse prevention approach is that embodied in Project STAR (Students Taught Awareness and Resistance). This ambitious community-based prevention program involves the fifteen contiguous communities making up the greater Kansas City metropolitan area. The project relies on matched funding from a private sector business (Marion Laboratories, a pharmaceutical company recognized for its financial success and commitment to civic service in the Kansas City area), a nonprofit foundation (the Kauffman Foundation), and a federal agency (National Institute on Drug Abuse). The project nicely integrates a community service project with a formal research project (Pentz et al. 1986). The project is being conducted by an on-site Kansas City team in collaboration with researchers at USC who are serving a dual function as intervention developers and project evaluators.

Project STAR is a theory-based community approach that relies on state-of-the-art primary prevention strategies. The intervention strategies are based on social learning theory (Bandura 1977) and an integrated model of community organization theory based on Rothman's model of community organization (Rothman, Erlich, and Teresa 1981), Green's system-centered education model (Green 1985), Rogers's innovation-decision process model (Rogers 1983), and Watzlawick's model of planned change (Watzlawick, Weakland, and Fisch 1974). On an empirical level, the intervention strategies utilized in this study are based on recommendations drawn from research on school-based drug abuse prevention and community-based heart disease prevention.

Because the risk for substance-use involvement generally begins during the early adolescent years, the target population for this community-based project are middle school students. Moreover, it is argued that since proximal influences are the most important to target directly, community-based programs for youth should logically be initiated as school programs.

The core of this community-based substance-abuse prevention program is a school-based curriculum designed to teach resistance skills to middle and junior high school students. Over a six-year period, there is a planned expansion from the school-based component to include parent, media, and community program components that involve community organization and health policy interventions. Figure 1 provides the community organization and evaluation strategy derived from Pentz et al.'s (1986) expanded model of community organization that is being followed in Project STAR. This represents an integration of the major theoretical perspectives regarding community organization and provides a practical step-by-step approach that can be followed by those interested in comprehensive community-based prevention.

The intervention is implemented through four channels of program delivery: the school, family, media, and community organization. There are three levels of intervention based on the principles of social learning theory: (1) direct training of youth to promote the acquisition of drug-resistance skills; (2) indirect training of youth by continued provision of program-implementation skills to teachers, parents, and other program implementors; and (3) support for the continued practice of resistance skills through the reinforcement of youth and program implementors. The intervention modalities are designed to increase individual self-efficacy and skills building, the application of resistance skills to specific interpersonal situations involving drug offers or drug availability, and the promotion of drug-abuse norms consistent with lower levels of drug use.

Thus far, this approach has been quite successful on several levels. During the first two years of the project, the school-based component of the program was adopted by 100 percent of the schools in the Kansas City area and 95 percent of the teachers. The analysis of data collected in 1986 with fifty participating junior high schools found that the rate of cigarette smoking among the students in the program was 14 percent, compared to 22 percent in a control group; 4 percent for marijuana use among the program students, compared with 8 percent in a control group; and, for alcohol use, only a modest difference was evi-

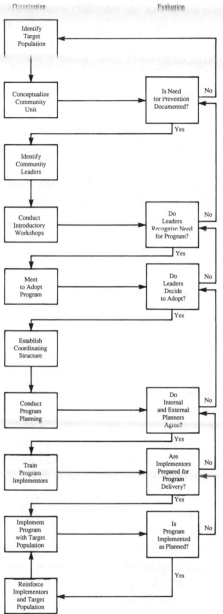

FIG. 1.—Steps to community organization and evaluation

dent, with 10 percent of the students in the program reporting drinking, compared with 13 percent in a control group. Ongoing evaluation is currently under way, so the progress of this project can be followed over the next few years.

VII. Summary and Conclusions

As is clear from the extant literature and the discussion in this essay, a variety of preventive intervention strategies have been developed and implemented in response to the problem of substance abuse in this country. A fundamental problem with most of these interventions is that they have been based on incomplete conceptual models and have failed to target what now appear to be the most important determinants. Furthermore, insufficient attention has generally been paid to evaluation.

At this point, the only prevention approaches that have been demonstrated effectively to reduce substance-use behavior are school-based approaches that focus on the social and psychological factors promoting tobacco, alcohol, and drug abuse. These approaches are based on social learning theory and problem behavior theory. Moreover, they utilize well-tested behavioral intervention techniques to facilitate the acquisition of skills for resisting social influences to engage in substance use. The most promising of these approaches incorporates resistance-skills training within a broader intervention designed to enhance general personal and social competence.

These interventions have generally been implemented with middle or junior high school students in recognition of the critical importance of this period with respect to the initiation of substance use. Furthermore, ongoing intervention activities, at least throughout the early adolescent years, appear to be necessary to maintain the preventive gains achieved by these programs.

Despite the impressive results obtained in studies testing these prevention approaches, it is obvious that more research is clearly needed in several important areas. The studies conducted thus far have involved primarily white, middle-class populations. Little is known concerning the effectiveness of these strategies with other populations (although some studies are currently under way with minority populations). Even within the populations already studied, much more information is needed concerning which kinds of students are affected by these programs. A key question remaining unanswered concerns the efficacy of these programs with high-risk students.

Other issues that require future attention include determining the effectiveness of various types of program providers, the optimal age for intervention, the extent to which school and teacher differences affect program delivery, the impact on other forms of substance use, the relative importance of specific program components, and the extent to which reductions in substance use during early adolescence result in subsequent reductions of substance abuse. Future research is also needed to address several issues related to large-scale dissemination of school-based interventions such as program acceptability, fidelity of implementation, and provider training.

Consideration of the diversity of factors that has been found to be associated with substance use leads to the inescapable conclusion that no single factor is both a necessary and sufficient condition for the initiation of substance use. Adolescent substance use/abuse appears to be the result of the complex interplay of many different factors. Several multivariate models have been posited in order to describe the interrelations among an array of cognitive, attitudinal, social, personality, and behavioral factors. To be optimally effective, preventive interventions must be sufficiently comprehensive to take into account the complex multivariate causation of substance abuse.

A prescription for the type of preventive interventions likely to be optimally effective flows naturally from a consideration of the factors promoting substance use within the framework of social learning theory and problem behavior theory. On one level, substance-use prevention efforts should proceed by eliminating, or at least reducing to the greatest extent possible, environmental influences promoting or facilitating smoking, drinking, and drug use. For example, this would include interventions that were capable of affecting availability, the visibility of negative role models, and social norms.

On another level, preventive interventions should be designed to reduce susceptibility or vulnerability to the various environmental factors promoting substance use. Interventions should also be designed to reduce potential intrapsychic motivations to engage in substance use. For example, individual susceptibility to environmental influences promoting substance use might involve interventions that teach resistance skills and adaptive life skills, alter perceived norms, and increase knowledge of adverse consequences of use.

In order to develop interventions that are comprehensive enough to accomplish these objectives, it is apparent that it will be necessary to go beyond strategies that rely solely on school-based interventions. It will be necessary to determine the most effective uses of the media and the ingredients of effective media campaigns. It will also be necessary to develop the most effective family- and community-based interventions, as well as to learn more about the key ingredients in an effective alternatives program. Finally, it will be necessary to determine the most effective mix of these various preventive interventions in order to maximize their impact.

Notwithstanding the need for further research, there is clearly an immediate need for effective prevention programs. While future research attempts to refine current prevention strategies or develop new ones, it would seem prudent to encourage dissemination of the most promising of the newer psychosocial approaches to substance-abuse prevention. This is particularly important in view of the fact that the most widely utilized school-based prevention programs today are those that rely on intervention strategies that have either been found to be ineffective or to lack any scientifically defensible evidence of their efficacy.

The field of substance-abuse prevention is, no doubt, still in its infancy. However, the past decade has seen the development, for the first time in its history, of interventions that can actually reduce or prevent substance use. Greater emphasis has recently been placed on developing intervention models that are based on firm theoretical and empirical foundations. Research evaluating the efficacy of prevention approaches has become increasingly rigorous, and intervention developers appear to have become more cognizant of the necessity and wisdom of careful and well-designed evaluations. Considerable progress has been made over the past decade; yet, it is manifestly clear that substantial work remains to be done.

REFERENCES

Alwine, G. 1974. "If You Need Love, Come to US—an Overview of a Peer Counseling Program in a Senior High School." *Journal of School Health* 44:463–64.
Arkin, R. M., H. J. Roemhild, C. A. Johnson, R. V. Luepker, and D. M. Murray. 1981. "The Minnesota Smoking Prevention Program: A Seventh Grade Health Curriculum Supplement." *Journal of School Health* 51:616–61.

Associate Consultants. 1981. "State of the Art Report on Concerned Parent Groups." Report submitted to the National Institute on Drug Abuse, Washington, D.C., October 10.

Bandura, A. 1977. *Social Learning Theory.* Englewood Cliffs, N.J.: Prentice-Hall.

Battjes, R. J. 1985. "Prevention of Adolescent Drug Abuse." *International Journal of the Addictions* 20(6–7):1113–34.

Becker, H. S. 1967. "History, Culture, and Subjective Experiences: An Exploration of the Social Basis of Drug Induced Experiences." *Journal of Health and Social Behavior* 8:163–76.

Berberian, R. M., C. Gross, J. Lovejoy, and S. Paparella. 1976. "The Effectiveness of Drug Education Programs: A Critical Review." *Health Education Monographs* 4:377–98.

Best, J. A., B. R. Flay, S. M. J. Towson, L. B. Ryan, C. L. Perry, K. S. Brown, M. W. Kersell, and J. R. d'Avernas. 1984. "Smoking Prevention and the Concept of Risk." *Journal of Applied Social Psychology* 14:257–73.

Biglan, A., and D. V. Ary. 1985. "Current Methodological Issues in Research on Smoking Prevention." In *Prevention Research: Deterring Drug Abuse among Children and Adolescents,* edited by C. Bell and R. Battjes. Washington, D.C.: National Institute on Drug Abuse.

Blum, R., and L. Richards. 1979. "Youthful Drug Use." In *Handbook on Drug Abuse,* edited by R. L. DuPont, A. Goldstein, and J. O'Donnell. Washington, D.C.: U.S. Government Printing Office.

Botvin, G. J. 1982. "Broadening the Focus of Smoking Prevention Strategies." In *Promoting Adolescent Health: A Dialogue on Research and Practice,* edited by T. Coates, A. Petersen, and C. Perry. New York: Academic Press.

———. 1984. "Advances in Substance Abuse Prevention." In *First Triennial Report on Drug Abuse to the U.S. Congress.* Washington, D.C.: U.S. Government Printing Office.

———. 1986. "Substance Abuse Prevention Research: Recent Developments and Future Directions." *Journal of School Health* 56:369–86.

Botvin, G. J., E. Baker, E. M. Botvin, A. D. Filazzola, and R. B. Millman. 1984. "Alcohol Abuse Prevention through the Development of Personal and Social Competence: A Pilot Study." *Journal of Studies on Alcohol* 45:550–52.

Botvin, G. J., E. Baker, A. Filazzola, E. M. Botvin, M. Danilo, and L. Dusenbury. 1985. "A Cognitive-Behavioral Approach to Substance Abuse Prevention: A One Year Follow-up." Paper presented at the ninety-third annual meeting of the American Psychological Association, Los Angeles, August.

Botvin, G. J., E. Baker, N. Renick, A. D. Filazzola, and E. M. Botvin. 1984. "A Cognitive-Behavioral Approach to Substance Abuse Prevention." *Addictive Behaviors* 9:137–47.

Botvin, G. J., L. Dusenbury, E. Baker, and S. James-Ortiz. 1989. "A Skills Training Approach to Smoking Prevention among Hispanic Youth." *Journal of Behavioral Medicine* (forthcoming).

Botvin, G. J., and A. Eng. 1980. "A Comprehensive School-based Smoking Prevention Program." *Journal of School Health* 50:209–13.

————. 1982. "The Efficacy of a Multicomponent Approach to the Prevention of Cigarette Smoking." *Preventive Medicine* 11:199–211.

Botvin, G. J., A. Eng, and C. L. Williams. 1980. "Preventing the Onset of Cigarette Smoking through Life Skills Training." *Journal of Preventive Medicine* 9:135–43.

Botvin, G. J., N. Renick, and E. Baker. 1983. "The Effects of Scheduling Format and Booster Sessions on a Broad Spectrum Psychosocial Approach to Smoking Prevention." *Journal of Behavioral Medicine* 6:359–79.

Braucht, G. N., D. Follingstad, D. Brakish, and K. L. Berry. 1973. "Drug Education: A Review of Goals, Approaches and Effectiveness, and a Paradigm for Evaluation." *Quarterly Journal of Studies on Alcohol* 34:1279–92.

Costanzo, P., and M. Shaw. 1966. "Conformity as a Function of Age Level." *Child Development* 37:967–75.

Degnan, E. J. 1972. "An Exploration into the Relationship between Depression and Positive Attitude toward Drugs in Young Adolescents and an Evaluation of a Drug Education Program." *Dissertation Abstracts* 32(11–B):6614–15.

Demone, H. W. 1973. "The Nonuse and Abuse of Alcohol by the Male Adolescent." In *Proceedings of the Second Annual Alcoholism Conference*, edited by M. Chafetz. Department of Health, Education, and Welfare Publication no. HSM 73–9083. Washington, D.C.: U.S. Government Printing Office.

Dorn, N., and A. Thompson. 1976. "Evaluation of Drug Education in the Longer Term Is Not an Optional Extra." *Community Health* 7:154–61.

Evans, R. I. 1976. "Smoking in Children: Developing a Social Psychological Strategy of Deterrence." *Preventive Medicine* 5:122–27.

Evans, R. I., R. M. Rozelle, S. E. Maxwell, B. E. Rainse, C. A. Dill, and T. J. Guthrie. 1981. "Social Modeling Films to Deter Smoking in Adolescents: Results of a Three-Year Field Investigation." *Journal of Applied Psychology* 66:399–414.

Evans, R. I., R. M. Rozelle, M. B. Mittlemark, W. B. Hansen, A. L. Bane, and J. Havis. 1978. "Deterring the Onset of Smoking in Children: Knowledge of Immediate Physiological Effects and Coping with Peer Pressure, Media Pressure, and Parent Modeling." *Journal of Applied Social Psychology* 8:126–35.

Fishbein, M. 1977. "Consumer Beliefs and Behavior with Respect to Cigarette Smoking: A Critical Analysis of the Public Literature." In *Federal Trade Commission Report to Congress Pursuant to the Public Health Cigarette Smoking Act of 1976*. Washington, D.C.: U.S. Government Printing Office.

Fisher, D. A., B. K. Armstrong, and N. H. de Kler. 1983. "A Randomized-Controlled Trial of Education for Prevention of Smoking in 12-Year-Old Children." Paper presented at the fifth World Conference on Smoking and Health, Winnipeg.

Flay, B. R. 1985. "Psychosocial Approaches to Smoking Prevention: A Review of Findings." *Health Psychology* 4:449–88.

Flay, B. R., and S. Sobel. 1983. "The Role of Mass Media in Preventing Adolescent Substance Abuse." In *Preventing Adolescent Drug Abuse: Intervention Strategies*, edited by T. J. Glynn, C. G. Leukefeld, and J. P. Ludford.

National Institute on Drug Abuse Research Monograph no. 47. Washington, D.C.: Department of Health, Education, and Welfare.

Friedman, S. M. 1973. "A Drug Education Program Emphasizing Affective Approaches and Its Influence upon Intermediate School Student and Teacher Attitudes." *Dissertation Abstracts* 34(5–A):2270.

Gilchrist, L. D., and S. P. Schinke. 1983. "Self-Control Skills for Smoking Prevention." In *Advances in Cancer Control*, edited by P. F. Engstrom and P. Anderson. New York: Liss.

Glasgow, R. E., and K. D. McCaul. 1985. "Life Skills Training Programs for Smoking Prevention: Critique and Directions for Future Research." In *Prevention Research: Deterring Drug Abuse among Children and Adolescents*, edited by C. Bell and R. Battjes. Washington, D.C.: National Institute on Drug Abuse.

Goodstadt, M. S. 1974. "Myths and Methodology in Drug Education: A Critical Review of the Research Evidence." In *Research on Methods and Programs of Drug Education*, edited by M. S. Goodstadt. Toronto: Addiction Research Foundation.

Green, L. W. 1985. *Toward a Healthy Community: Organizing Events for Community Health Promotion*. U.S. Public Health Service, Department of Health and Human Services. Washington, D.C.: U.S. Government Printing Office.

Hamburg, B. A., H. C. Braemer, and W. A. Jahnke. 1975. "Hierarchy of Drug Use in Adolescence: Behavioral and Attitudinal Correlates of Substantial Drug Use." *American Journal of Psychiatry* 132:1155–67.

Hamburg, B. A., and B. B. Varenhorst. 1972. "Peer Counseling in the Secondary Schools: A Community Mental Health Project for Youth." *American Journal of Orthopsychiatry* 42:556–81.

Hartup, W. 1970. "Peer Interaction and Social Organization." In *Carmichael's Manual of Child Psychology*, vol. 2, edited by P. Mussen (3d ed.). New York: Wiley.

Hops, H., W. Weissman, A. Biglan, R. Thompson, C. Faller, and H. H. Severson. 1989. "A Taped Situation Test of Cigarette Refusal Skill among Adolescents." *Behavioral Assessment* (forthcoming).

Hurd, P., C. A. Johnson, T. Pechacek, C. P. Bast, D. Jacobs, and R. Luepker. 1980. "Prevention of Cigarette Smoking in 7th Grade Students." *Journal of Behavioral Medicine* 3:15–28.

Jessor, R. 1976. "Predicting Time of Onset of Marijuana Use: A Developmental Study of High School Youth." In *Predicting Adolescent Drug Abuse: A Review of Issues, Methods and Correlates*, edited by D. J. Lettieri. Department of Health, Education, and Welfare Publication no. ADM 77–299. Washington, D.C.: U.S. Government Printing Office.

———. 1982. "Critical Issues in Research on Adolescent Health Promotion." In *Promoting Adolescent Health: A Dialogue on Research and Practice*, edited by T. Coates, A. Petersen, and C. Perry. New York: Academic Press.

Jessor, R., M. I. Collins, and S. L. Jessor. 1972. "On Becoming a Drinker: Social-Psychological Aspects of an Adolescent Transition." *Annals of the New York Academy of Sciences* 197:199–213.

Jessor, R., and S. L. Jessor. 1977. *Problem Behavior and Psychosocial Development: A Longitudinal Study of Youth*. New York: Academic Press.

Kandel, D. B. 1978. "Convergences in Prospective Longitudinal Surveys of Drug Use in Normal Populations." In *Longitudinal Research on Drug Use: Empirical Findings and Methodological Issues*. Washington, D.C.: Hemisphere.

Kearney, A. L., and M. H. Hines. 1980. "Evaluation of the Effectiveness of a Drug Prevention Education Program." *Journal of Drug Education* 10:127–34.

Kim, S. 1989. "A Short- and Long-Term Evaluation of Here's Looking at You Alcohol Education Program." *Journal of Drug Education* (forthcoming).

Kinder, B., N. Pape, and S. Walfish. 1980. "Drug and Alcohol Education Programs: A Review of Outcome Studies." *International Journal of the Addictions* 51:1035–54.

Loeber, R., and M. Le Blanc. 1990. "Toward a Developmental Criminology." In *Crime and Justice: A Review of Research*, vol. 12, edited by Michael Tonry and Norval Morris. Chicago: University of Chicago Press.

Luepker, R. V., C. A. Johnson, D. M. Murray, and T. F. Pechacek. 1983. "Prevention of Cigarette Smoking: Three Year Follow-up of Educational Programs for Youth." *Journal of Behavioral Medicine* 6:53–61.

McAlister, A., C. L. Perry, J. Killen, L. A. Slinkard, and N. Maccoby. 1980. "Pilot Study of Smoking, Alcohol, and Drug Abuse Prevention." *American Journal of Public Health* 70:719–21.

McAlister, A., C. L. Perry, and N. Maccoby. 1979. "Adolescent Smoking: Onset and Prevention." *Pediatrics* 63:650–58.

Maccoby, E., and J. Masters. 1970. "Attachment and Dependency." In *Carmichael's Manual of Child Psychology*, vol. 2 (3d ed.), edited by P. H. Mussen. New York: Wiley.

McGuire, W. J. 1964. "Inducing Resistance to Persuasion: Some Contemporary Approaches." In *Advances in Experimental Social Psychology*, vol. 1, edited by L. Berkowitz. New York: Academic Press.

———. 1968. "The Nature of Attitudes and Attitude Change." In *Handbook of Social Psychology*, edited by G. Lindzey and E. Aronson. Reading, Mass.: Addison-Wesley.

McRae, C. F., and D. M. Nelson. 1971. "Youth to Youth Communication on Smoking and Health." *Journal of School Health* 41:445–47.

Malvin, J., J. Moskowitz, G. Schaeffer, and E. Schaps. 1984. "Teacher Training in Affective Education of Adolescent Drug Abuse." *American Journal of Drug and Alcohol Abuse* 10(2):223–35.

Malvin, J., J. Moskowitz, E. Schaps, and G. Schaeffer. 1985. "Evaluation of Two School-based Alternatives Programs." *Journal of Alcohol and Drug Education* 30:98–108.

Manett, M. 1983. *Parents, Peers and Pot II: Parents in Action*. Department of Health and Human Services Publication no. ADM 83–1290. Washington, D.C.: U.S. Government Printing Office.

Mason, M. L. 1973. "Drug Education Effects." *Dissertation Abstracts* 34(4–B):418.

Meyer, R. E., and S. M. Mirin. 1979. *The Heroin Stimulus: Implications for a Theory of Addiction*. New York: Plenum.

Millman, R. D., and G. J. Botvin. 1983. "Substance Use, Abuse, and Dependence." In *Developmental-Behavioral Pediatrics*, edited by M. D. Levine, W. B. Carey, A. C. Crocker, and R. T. Gross. Philadelphia: Saunders.

Moskowitz, J. M. 1985. "Evaluating the Effects of Parent Groups on the Correlates of Adolescent Substance Abuse." *Journal of Psychoactive Drugs* 17:(3)173–78.

Moskowitz, J. M., J. Malvin, G. Schaeffer, E. Schaps, and J. Condon. 1983. "Evaluation of a Cooperative Learning Strategy." *American Educational Research Journal* 20:687–96.

Moskowitz, J. M., E. Schaps, and J. H. Malvin. 1982. "Process and Outcome Evaluation in a Primary Prevention: The Magic Circle Program." *Evaluation Review* 6:775–88.

Moskowitz, J. M., E. Schaps, J. Malvin, and G. Schaeffer. 1984. "The Effects of Drug Education at Follow-up." *Journal of Alcohol and Drug Education* 30:45–49.

Murray, D. M., C. A. Johnson, R. V. Luepker, and M. B. Mittlemark. 1984. "The Prevention of Cigarette Smoking in Children: A Comparison of Four Strategies." *Journal of Applied Social Psychology* 14(3):274–88.

Murray, D. M., C. A. Johnson, R. V. Luepker, T. F. Pechacek, and D. R. Jacobs. 1980. "Issues in Smoking Prevention Research." Paper presented at the annual convention of the American Psychological Association, Montreal, September.

Mussen, P., J. Conger, and J. Kagan. 1974. *Child Development and Personality*. 4th ed. New York: Harper & Row.

O'Rourke, T. W., and S. L. Barr. 1974. "Assessment of the Effectiveness of the New York State Drug Curriculum Guide with Respect to Drug Attitudes." *Journal on Drug Education* 4(3):347–56.

Pentz, M. A. 1983. "Prevention of Adolescent Substance Abuse through Social Skill Development." In *Preventing Adolescent Drug Abuse: Intervention Strategies*, edited by T. J. Glynn, C. G. Leukefeld, and J. P. Ludford. National Institute on Drug Abuse Research Monograph no. 47. Washington, D.C.: Department of Health, Education, and Welfare.

———. 1986. "Community Organization and School Liaisons: How to Get Programs Started." *Journal of School Health* 56(9):382–88.

Pentz, M. A., C. Cormack, B. Flay, W. Henson, and C. A. Johnson. 1986. "Balancing Program and Research Integrity in Community Drug Abuse Prevention: Project STAR Approach." *Journal of School Health* 56(9):389–93.

Perry, C., J. Killen, L. A. Slinkard, and A. L. McAlister. 1980. "Peer Teaching and Smoking Prevention among Junior High Students." *Adolescence* 9:277–81.

Perry, C. L., J. Killen, M. Telch, L. A. Slinkard, and B. G. Danaher. 1980. "Modifying Smoking Behavior of Teenagers: A School-based Intervention." *American Journal of Public Health* 70:725–72.

Perry, C. L., M. J. Telch, J. Killen, R. Dass, and N. Maccoby. 1983. "High School Smoking Prevention: The Relative Efficacy of Varied Treatments and Instructors." *Adolescence* 18:562–66.

Piaget, J. 1962. *The Moral Judgment of the Child*. New York: Collier.

Ray, O. S. 1974. *Drugs, Society, and Human Behavior*. St. Louis: Mosby.

Richards, L. G. 1969. "Government Programs and Psychological Principles in Drug Abuse Education." Paper presented at the seventy-seventh annual meeting of American Psychological Association, Washington, D.C.

Richardson, D. W., P. R. Nader, K. J. Rochman, and S. B. Friedman. 1972. "Attitudes of Fifth Grade Students to Illicit Psychoactive Drugs." *Journal of School Health* 42(7):389–91.

Rogers, E. M. 1983. *The Diffusion of Innovations*. New York: Free Press.

Rosenblitt, D. L., and D. A. Nagey. 1973. "The Use of Medical Manpower in a Seventh Grade Drug Education Program." *Journal of Drug Education* 3:39–56.

Rothman, J., J. L. Erlich, and J. G. Teresa. 1981. *Changing Organizations and Community Programs*. Beverly Hills, Calif.: Sage.

Schaps, E., R. D. Bartolo, J. Moskowitz, C. S. Palley, and S. Churgin. 1981. "A Review of 127 Drug Abuse Prevention Program Evaluations." *Journal of Drug Issues* (Winter), pp. 17–43.

Schaps, E., J. Moskowitz, J. Condon, and J. Malvin. 1982. "Process and Outcome Evaluation of a Drug Education Course." *Journal of Drug Education* 12:253–364.

———. 1984. "A Process and Outcome Evaluation of an Affective Teacher Training Prevention Program." *Journal of Alcohol and Drug Education* 29:35–64.

Schinke, S. P. 1984. "Preventing Teenage Pregnancy." In *Progress in Behavior Modification*, vol. 16, edited by M. Hersen, R. M. Eisler, and P. M. Miller. New York: Academic Press.

Schinke, S. P., and B. J. Blythe. 1981. "Cognitive-Behavioral Prevention of Children's Smoking." *Child Behavior Therapy* 3:25–42.

Schinke, S. P., and L. D. Gilchrist. 1983. "Primary Prevention of Tobacco Smoking." *Journal of School Health* 53:416–19.

———. 1984. "Preventing Cigarette Smoking with Youth." *Journal of Primary Prevention* 5:48–56.

Stenmark, D., B. Kinder, and L. Milne. 1977. "Drug-related Attitudes and Knowledge of Pharmacy Students and College Undergraduates." *Journal of the Addictions* 12:153–60.

Swisher, J. D. 1979. "Prevention Issues." In *Handbook on Drug Abuse*, edited by R. L. DuPont, A. Goldstein, and J. O'Donnell. Washington, D.C.: National Institute on Drug Abuse.

Swisher, J. D., J. L. Crawford, R. Goldstein, and M. Yura. 1971. "Drug Education: Pushing or Preventing?" *Peabody Journal of Education* 49:68–75.

Swisher, J. D., and A. Hoffman. 1975. "Information: The Irrelevant Variable in Drug Education." In *Drug Abuse Prevention: Perspectives and Approaches for Educators*, edited by B. W. Corder, R. A. Smith, and J. D. Swisher. Dubuque, Iowa: Brown.

Swisher, J. D., and T. W. Hu. 1983. "Alternatives to Drug Abuse: Some Are and Some Are Not." In *Preventing Adolescent Drug Abuse: Intervention Strategies*, edited by T. J. Glynn, C. G. Leukefeld, and J. P. Ludford. DHHS

Publication no. (ADM) 83–1280. U.S. Public Health Service. National Institute on Drug Abuse.

Telch, M. J., J. D. Killen, A. L. McAlister, C. L. Perry, and N. Maccoby. 1982. "Long-Term Follow-up of a Pilot Project on Smoking Prevention with Adolescents. *Journal of Behavioral Medicine* 5:1–8.

U.S. Public Health Service. 1986. "Drug Abuse and Drug Abuse Research: The Second Triennial Report to Congress from the Secretary." Publication No. ADM 87–1486. Department of Health and Human Services. Washington, D.C.: U.S. Government Printing Office.

Utech, D., and K. L. Hoving. 1969. "Parents and Peers as Competing Influences in the Decisions of Children of Differing Ages." *Journal of Social Psychology* 78:267–74.

Vriend, T. 1969. "High-Performing Inner-City Adolescents Assist Low-Performing Peers in Counseling Groups." *Personnel Guidance Journal* 48:897–904.

Walters, R., W. Marshall, and J. Shooter. 1960. "Anxiety, Isolation, and Susceptibility to Social Influence." *Journal of Personality* 28:518–29.

Watzlawick, F., J. H. Weakland, and R. Fisch. 1974. *Change: Principles of Problem Formation and Problem Resolution*. New York: Norton.

Wechsler, H. 1976. "Alcohol Intoxication and Drug Use among Teenagers." *Journal of Studies in Alcohol* 37:1672–77.

Wechsler, H., and D. Thum. 1973. "Alcohol and Drug Use among Teenagers: A Questionnaire Study." In *Proceedings of the Second Annual Alcoholism Conference*, edited by M. Chafetz. DHEW Publication no. HSM 73–9083. Washington, D.C.: U.S. Government Printing Office.

Weir, W. R. 1968. "A Program of Alcohol Education and Counseling for High School Students With and Without a Family Alcohol Problem." *Dissertation Abstracts* 28(11–A):4454–55.

Winick, C., and M. P. Winick. 1976. "Drug Education and a Content Analysis of Mass Media Dealing with 'Dangerous Drugs' and Alcohol." In *Communication Research and Drug Education*, vol. 4, edited by R. E. Osteman. London: Sage.

James Q. Wilson

Drugs and Crime

The essays in this volume share a common assumption—that the sale and possession of certain drugs, in particular heroin and cocaine, will continue to be illegal. The authors of these essays made that assumption because they were asked to. I do not know whether any of them favor the legalization of these drugs, but I do know that some people who read this book will favor it. It is important, therefore, to be clear as to the arguments for and against legalization. To do so, one must distinguish between the good and bad reasons for controlling the use of drugs.

Some people argue that we must "stamp out" drug abuse in order to reduce crime, break up criminal gangs, and improve public health. But there is no reason to believe that vigorously enforcing the drug laws will achieve any of these goals and many reasons to think that they may make these matters worse.

Consider crime: there is no doubt a strong association between the use of drugs and aggressive behavior, but, as Jeffrey Fagan points out in his essay, it is far from clear that this correlation amounts to a cause. People who become aggressive after drinking alcohol or using cocaine usually turn out to be people who were aggressive before consuming these substances. Personality factors and social setting seem to have a large, perhaps dominant, effect in determining whether getting high will lead to aggression, moody introspection, or quiet gaiety. Heroin seems to induce in its users euphoria, drowsiness, and sexual impo-

James Q. Wilson is a professor in the Graduate School of Management at the University of California, Los Angeles.

tence, but not aggression. There is a good deal of anecdotal evidence suggesting that using phencyclidine (PCP) or amphetamines or smoking crack will cause violent behavior, but so far not much systematic evidence supports this theory.

There is also a strong association between drug use and street crime, and here the research shows that, for at least certain drugs, their use—or more accurately, their purchase—does cause higher rates of income-generating crime. During periods when heroin addicts are using the drug heavily, the rate at which they commit crimes is much higher than it is during periods when they are relatively abstinent. The reason is that the illegality of heroin produces a black market in which price rises to the point where many addicts can only support their habits by theft or prostitution.

Though the search for drugs may cause criminals to increase the rate of their criminality, it is not a desire for drugs that leads people to criminality in the first place. Jan and Marcia Chaiken suggest in this volume that many heavy drug users were committing crimes before they turned to drugs; they began spending money on drugs in part because crime had produced money for them to spend and in part because criminality drew them into a social setting in which drug use was common and expected.

For all these reasons, it is not clear that enforcing the laws against drug use would reduce crime. On the contrary, crime may be caused by such enforcement because it keeps drug prices higher than they would otherwise be.

Or consider criminal gangs: tough law enforcement may break up those criminal enterprises that traffic in drugs, but it may also make such enterprises more skilled, more ruthless, and more dangerous. The more profitable drug sales are, the greater the incentive dealers have to protect their profits by arming themselves against rivals, forcibly maintaining discipline among subordinates, and corrupting or otherwise resisting the criminal justice system. Critics of drug enforcement often compare the effects of our drug laws to those prohibiting the sale of alcohol: any effort to suppress the use of a popular substance will create rich and powerful criminal syndicates.

Or consider public health: injecting drugs, such as heroin or cocaine, can lead to hepatitis or AIDS if contaminated needles are used, and such needles are more likely to be used if the drugs are consumed surreptitiously. Over half the AIDS victims generally contracted the disease through intravenous drug use. Drugs sold illegally are beyond the reach of the pure food and drug laws; as a result, many addicts use heroin that has been "cut," or adulterated, with harmful substances.

When marijuana is grown illegally, it may be produced in fields sprayed by the police with dangerous herbicides or covered by the growers with harmful fertilizers. And even when a drug is free of poisons, its strength is often unknown, so that a user may unwittingly take a fatal overdose. Mislabeling a drug is not a crime to those who sell drugs illegally.

In short, attempting to suppress the use of drugs is costly—very costly. This fact has led many people to call for their legalization, either totally or under some form of government regulation. The readers of this volume may wonder why its authors have spent so much effort exploring the law-enforcement strategies when the "obvious" thing to do is to eliminate all the costs of law enforcement by repealing the laws that are being enforced. The result would be less crime, fewer and weaker gangs, and an opportunity to address the public health problems in a straightforward manner.

But there is another side to the story. Legalizing drugs would also entail costs. Those costs are much more difficult to measure, in part because they are to a large degree moral and in part because we have so little experience with legalized drugs that we cannot be certain how great those costs would be.

The moral reason for attempting to discourage drug use is that the heavy consumption of certain drugs is destructive of human character. These drugs—principally heroin, cocaine, and crack—are, for many people, powerfully reinforcing. The pleasure or oblivion they produce leads many users to devote their lives to seeking pleasure or oblivion and to do so almost regardless of the cost in ordinary human virtues, such as temperance, fidelity, duty, and sympathy. The dignity, autonomy, and productivity of many users, already impaired by other problems, is destroyed.

There are, to be sure, many people who only experiment with drugs or who use them regularly but in a "controlled" way. Citizens—including the contributors to this volume—differ in how seriously they view such use. Some will argue that if users can maintain their moral character while consuming drugs, no social problem exists. Moreover, a national survey suggests that drug use by casual or controlled users has been declining in recent years. The proportion of Americans saying that they currently use any drug has dropped significantly since 1985 (Office of National Drug Control Policy 1989, p. 1). The essays here, however, are primarily concerned with the heavy user of the most dangerous drugs—heroin and cocaine. And for that group, the news is bad. The same survey shows that the proportion of cocaine users who consume it frequently (i.e., weekly or more often) has doubled since 1985 (Office of National Drug Control Policy 1989, p. 3). In this group, the moral costs of drug abuse are undeniable.

But there are some people who deny that society has any obligation to form and sustain the character of its citizenry. Libertarians would leave all adults free to choose their own habits and seek their own destiny so long as their behavior did not cause any direct or palpable harm to others. But most people, however willing they may be to tolerate human eccentricities and support civil liberties, act as if they believed that government, as the agent for society, is responsible for helping instill certain qualities in its citizens. This is one reason (indeed, it was the original reason) for mandatory schooling. We not only want to train children to be useful, we want to train them to be decent. It is the reason that virtually every nation that has been confronted by a sharp increase in addiction to any psychoactive substance, including alcohol, has enacted laws designed to regulate or suppress its use. (The debauch produced by the sudden arrival of gin in eighteenth-century England led to debates not very different from the ones we are having today about cocaine.) Great Britain once allowed physicians to prescribe opiates for addicts. The system worked reasonably well so long as the addicts were middle-class people who had come by their dependence as a consequence of having received painkillers in hospitals. But as soon as oblivion-seeking youth became heroin addicts, Britain ended the prescription system, replacing it at first with a system of controlled dispensation from government clinics and then with a system of substituting methadone for heroin coupled with the stringent enforcement of the laws against the latter.

Even if we were to decide that the government had no responsibility for character formation and should only regulate behavior that hurt other people, we would still have to decide what to do about drug-dependent people because such dependency does in fact hurt other people: a heroin addict dreamily enjoying his euphoria, a crack smoker looking for that next high, a cocaine snorter eager for relief from his depression—these users are not likely to be healthy people, productive workers, good parents, reliable neighbors, attentive students, or safe drivers. Moreover, some people are directly harmed by drugs that they have not freely chosen to use. The babies of drug-dependent women suffer because of their mothers' habits. We all pay for drug abuse in lowered productivity, more accidents, higher insurance premiums, bigger welfare costs, and less effective classrooms.

The question is whether the costs of drug use are likely to be higher when the drug is illegal or when it is legal. In both cases, society must pay the bill. When the drug is illegal, the bill consists of the law-enforcement costs (crime, corruption, extensive and intrusive policing), the welfare costs (poorer health, lost wages, higher unemployment benefits, more aid to families with dependent children, and various treatment and prevention programs), and the moral costs (debased and degraded people). When the drug is legal, the bill will consist primarily of the welfare costs and the moral costs.[1] Which bill will be higher?

The answer chiefly depends on how many people will use the drug under the two scenarios. We have a rough idea of how many people regularly use heroin and cocaine under the present illegal scenario. How many will regularly use it under the legal scenario?

No one knows for certain, but it will almost surely be many more people than now use it. The free-market price of cocaine is probably no more than 5 percent of its present black-market price. The consumption of a widely desired, pleasure-inducing substance will, without question, increase dramatically if the price is cut by 95 percent (Kaplan 1988; Moore, in this volume). But suppose that the government levies taxes on the legal cocaine, either to raise revenue, discourage use, or both. The higher the government sets the tax on, and thus the price of, the drug, the less will be consumed, but the greater the incentive the drug user will have to steal (in order to pay the high price) or to manufacture the drug illegally (in order to undercut the government price). Either way, high taxes get us right back where we started. There is no such thing as an optimal price of cocaine because there is no such thing as an optimal mix of two radically opposed goals—to reduce drug use and to prevent drug-related crime.

Moreover, the true price of the drug is the monetary price plus the difficulty and inconvenience of the search for it and the risk associated with consuming a product of unknown quality. Though drugs are sold openly on the streets of some communities, for most people—especially for novice, middle-class users—they are hard to find and are

---

[1] There will also be law-enforcement costs when the drugs are legal, if we assume—as do most proponents of legalization—that the drugs would not be sold to minors. As we know from our experience with alcohol, it is neither easy nor cheap to keep forbidden things out of youthful hands. Moreover, it is almost inevitable that such drugs would be taxed, partly to pay for the welfare costs associated with their use and partly because "sin taxes" are a politically popular way of raising general revenues. The higher the tax, the greater the incentive to evade it; hence, the government will have to invest in enforcing payment of the tax.

often found only in unattractive and threatening surroundings. Legalizing the drugs, *even if the price is not cut*, will make the drug more attractive by reducing the costs of searching for the product, negotiating a transaction, and running the risk of ingesting a dangerous substance. The combined effect of lowered market prices and lowered transaction costs will be very great.

Just how great cannot be known without trying it. And one cannot try it experimentally, for there is no way of running a meaningful experiment. The increase in drug use that would occur if people in one neighborhood or patients at one clinic were allowed to buy the drug at its market cost can give us no reliable information on how many people would use it if the drug were generally available in all neighborhoods and at any clinic.

The experience of other countries confirms that ease of availability is associated with large increases in use. When Great Britain allowed private physicians to prescribe heroin and young people began to avail themselves of this source, the number of known addicts (many more were unknown to the authorities) increased *thirtyfold* during a fifteen-year period. It was because of this increase that the British government changed the law. After a brief period in the 1970s when the number of known heroin addicts stabilized, a new storm broke. Between 1980 and 1985, the number of newly notified heroin addicts increased *fivefold*. Geoffrey Pearson (1990) estimates that by the mid-1980s Great Britain had some 15,000 registered drug addicts and probably ten times as many unregistered ones; this in a country whose "system" some people once thought should be a model for the United States. The increased availability of heroin in Europe, a continent once generally free of addicts, has been followed by a sharp increase in the number of addicts.

Even if legalization increases the number of addicts, would it not dramatically decrease the number of crimes committed by addicts? Not necessarily. No doubt the average number of crimes *per addict* will fall (few people would have to steal in order to buy drugs at market prices), but the increase in the number of addicts would mean an increase in the number of people leading such deviant lifestyles that occasional crime might be their only (or their preferred) means of support. Thus the *total number* of crimes committed by drug users might not fall at all.

Because we cannot know what our level of drug use would be under a legalized regime (though we can be certain it would be much higher than today) and because people disagree about many of the costs—especially the moral costs—of drug use, the debate over legalization will never be resolved. However, being aware of these issues will help people focus the debate on the right question. That question is this: how can we minimize the sum of the law-enforcement, moral, and welfare costs of drug use? If we want drugs to be illegal, it is because we believe that the very high law-enforcement costs will be offset by lower moral and welfare costs. If we want drugs to be legal, it is because we believe that the higher moral and welfare costs will be offset by the lower law-enforcement costs. In making this choice, we are making an estimate of how large the drug-using population will be in each case, and we are assigning a value to the tangible but real moral costs.[2]

I. Designing a Strategy

Assuming that heroin and cocaine will be illegal because of the moral and welfare costs associated with their use, we want to design a rational control strategy that will minimize those costs for a given level of effort. In doing so, we want to know where the marginal dollar can most effectively be invested.

In answering that question, it is customary, and correct, to distinguish between the demand for drugs and the supply of those drugs. It is also customary, but wrong, to consider demand-reduction strategies as involving prevention, education, and treatment and to think of supply-reduction strategies as involving law enforcement and foreign policy. Demand reducers are the nice guys—teachers, doctors, scientists, publicists; supply reducers are the tough guys—detectives, customs inspectors, and crop eradicators. Much of the debate over the relative budget shares that should go to demand or supply reduction reflects an ideological predisposition to choose either the tender-minded or the tough-minded approach.

There is some truth in this distinction, but not much. Law-enforcement efforts can reduce demand as well as supply. Prevention and education programs can reduce supply as well as demand. The

---

[2] Having stated the issue in what I trust is an evenhanded way, let me be clear about my own views: I believe that the moral and welfare costs of heavy drug use are so large that society should bear the heavy burden of law enforcement, and its associated corruption and criminality, for the sake of keeping the number of people regularly using heroin and crack as small as possible. I also believe that children should not be raised in communities in which heroin and cocaine are sold at the neighborhood drugstore. Obviously, there is some point at which the law-enforcement costs might become too great for the gains they produce, but I do not think we are at that point yet. I set forth my arguments at length in Wilson (1990).

reasons are explained in the essays by Mark Moore, Dana Hunt, and Mark Kleiman and Kerry Smith.

Demand reduction occurs when for any reason drugs become less attractive. If an education or prevention program persuades young people not to seek out drugs, demand is reduced. If the police make it very hard for a first-time or novice user to find a willing seller of drugs, supply is reduced—but so also is demand. The reason is that first-time, novice, or occasional users will abandon the search for drugs if that search is difficult, dangerous, or costly. By the same token, if law enforcement results in the commitment of the user to a mandatory treatment program that the addict would not have voluntarily entered, law enforcement may contribute to demand reduction. Indeed, the chief reason we have laws against possessing (and in some states, using) drugs is to reduce demand. They work—up to a point.

Similarly, if a treatment program successfully eliminates the desire for drugs on the part of a junkie, demand will have been reduced. But if that junkie is also a drug dealer who no longer feels he must deal in order to feed his own habit, then the treatment program has also removed a source of supply. Of course, a reformed supplier may be quickly replaced with an unreformed one, in which case there has been no supply reduction at all. But sometimes the reformed dealer sold to a circle of occasional users who did not know any other "connection"; when their friend/dealer is gone, their drug supply drops.

Drug use, in its early stages, tends to be a social activity occurring among—and often with the encouragement of—friends and associates. Whatever interdicts that network, whether it be a program labeled "prevention," "treatment," or "law enforcement," constitutes demand reduction. Deeply dependent addicts, by contrast, often use drugs in a more individualistic and isolated manner; their demand is much harder to reduce, whether by treatment or law enforcement.

The ambiguity of the distinction between prevention and law enforcement is illustrated by the case of drug testing. There is good evidence that drug testing in the military reduced drug use by curbing demand. Such testing may—no one yet knows for certain—reduce drug demand in civilian occupations. Is drug testing an example of prevention or of law enforcement? If the tests are conducted by doctors in a treatment program, we call it prevention. If they are conducted by probation officers desirous of knowing whether probationers have observed the terms of their freedom, we call it law enforcement. But the tests are identical in the two cases. The consequences for the person tested may also be identical if he is in the treatment program as an alternative to incarceration.

The failure of policymakers to understand that demand reduction is not synonymous with treatment or law enforcement with supply reduction has led them to make funding decisions based on such false identities. The debate over the Omnibus Drug Abuse Act of 1988 was in large measure a debate over whether 50 percent or 60 percent of the federal antidrug budget should be earmarked for prevention, treatment, and education in the belief that these activities, and only these activities, will reduce demand.[3]

The essays in this book try to avoid this artificial distinction. Moore and Kleiman and Smith explain how demand may be reduced somewhat by street-level law enforcement aimed at breaking up vulnerable dealing systems. Eric Wish and Bernard Gropper suggest ways in which random testing for drug use, using either urine or hair samples, may reduce demand. Douglas Anglin and Yih-Ing Hser, in evaluating the effectiveness of drug treatment programs, point out that, the longer drug users spend in such programs, the higher their chances of success. But left to their own devices, users tend to drop out of most programs. Legal coercion can keep these users in programs longer and thus increase their chances of successfully reducing drug use.

II. The Problem

No one should underestimate the difficulty of reducing drug abuse no matter what methods are used. Relatively modest law-enforcement and prevention efforts may be successful with many novice or occasional users, but the persistent heavy user presents a formidable challenge. In the essays by Dana Hunt, Jan and Marcia Chaiken, and Bruce Johnson and his colleagues, we encounter the urban underclass in all its refractory and frightening complexity. Persistent, heavy users have almost every personal and social problem one can imagine: they tend to be poorly schooled, unemployed (except in drug sales), deeply involved in criminality, and lacking any semblance of a normal family life. Some are homeless. They often use many drugs, not just one; if heroin becomes costly or frightening, they shift to barbiturates. They will use amphetamines, PCP, and crack almost interchangeably as circum-

---

[3] The final split was 55 percent for "demand reduction" (by which was meant treatment and education) and 45 percent for "supply reduction" (by which was meant law enforcement).

stances require. They often drink alcohol to excess, alone or in combination with other drugs.

Drug use and crime do not follow one another in some neat sequence; rather, both—as well as many other social pathologies—arise from deeply rooted causes, some symptoms of which appear in early childhood. Casual drug users, like occasional or low-rate lawbreakers, are quite unlike heavy drug users or high-rate offenders. Whether one looks at drugs or crime, the key distinction to make among people involves the *rate* at which misconduct occurs.

The great increases in high-rate users in the United States occurred during three periods. As Bruce Johnson and his colleagues show, heroin became a major problem between 1965 and 1973, so much so that a sizable proportion (though still a minority) of all inner-city blacks and Hispanics who reached the age of eighteen during this period became addicted. This was the "heroin generation." It was followed by a cocaine epidemic in 1975–84. Heroin addicts continued to exist, but the new recruits into the drug culture preferred cocaine to heroin. Unlike heroin before it or crack after it, cocaine snorting was commonplace among many affluent people. Starting around 1984–85, "rock," or crack, appeared—an inexpensive form of cocaine that quickly spread, especially among low-income users. Today, urine testing in jails shows that cocaine, in any of its various forms, is by far the most common drug used by arrestees, more common than opiates (including heroin) by a factor of at least three to one in most large cities. (Washington, D.C., is unusual in having a high proportion of PCP users among its jail population.)

Although heavy drug users typically lead hectic, disorderly, dangerous lives, the organizations that distribute the drugs have become, in many communities, important sources of power, wealth, and social status. The willingness of some crack-distributing gangs to employ violence using automatic weapons is well known.

Given the great appeal of drugs, the disorganized lives of many of their heavy users, and the existence among these users of all manner of social disabilities, no one should suppose that we are capable of achieving, by plan and at any reasonable cost, a dramatic reduction in the extent of current use. We can, perhaps, curb the spread of these drugs to new users and reduce, marginally, their use among some current consumers.

But changes do occur. At one time, heroin seemed to present an insoluble problem, with the number of addicts growing at what appeared to be an exponential rate. Then, in the mid-1970s, that growth slowed and even stopped. Why? We are not certain, but several factors—some planned, some unplanned—were probably involved. Turkey ceased being a source of illegal opium, and France ceased being a haven for illegal heroin laboratories; the temporary—but acute—shortage of heroin drove many addicts into treatment programs. The hazards associated with injecting heroin became so well known as to reduce its use. The glamour associated with heroin use by artists, musicians, and athletes faded as the would-be user began to confront the sorry reality of the typical user—poor, homeless, diseased, wretched. The availability of a heroin substitute—methadone—helped many addicts end their dependence on heroin with its cycle of euphoric highs followed by painful and frightening lows and brought them into a long-term relationship with counselors who helped them lead better lives. It is possible that similar forces will some day stop the growth of cocaine and crack. But that day is not yet here.

III. Reducing the Supply

In his essay, Mark Moore evaluates the likely effect of present and additional efforts to reduce the importation of dangerous drugs. His conclusion is that, while it is desirable to interdict smuggling networks and eradicate crops, we should not expect much gain from even sharply increased efforts along these lines. It is a view shared by many top federal law-enforcement officials.

The reasons are well understood. Eradicating opium poppy and coca crops overseas is difficult to do because such fields can be developed in regions where there is either no effective government at all or one that is hostile, or at best indifferent, to U.S. interests in these matters. There were large, albeit temporary, gains from reducing the Turkish poppy crop in the early 1970s, but Turkey is a nation with an effective government sympathetic to U.S. concerns and prepared to invest in alternative programs (e.g., poppy cultivation methods that greatly reduced the likelihood of an illegal diversion of the product to heroin traffickers). No government at all exists in the Golden Triangle of Southeast Asia; no friendly government exists in Iran; a friendly government does exist in Colombia, but with respect to the drug trade, it was until 1989 barely a government at all: its key officials are regularly exposed to the terror of murderous gangs and the hostility of coca farmers. Mexico is, at the highest levels, committed to reducing the drug trade, but the central authorities find it difficult to impose great costs on their own population (by, e.g., suppressing poppy cultivation) when they confront corrupt local officials and a public unsympathetic to American demands when it is American demand for drugs that has fueled the drug trade in the first place.

Interdicting drug shipments as they cross the U.S. border is desirable and politically essential, but the effect of even major increases in such interdiction is likely to be small. That is because low-volume, high-profit drugs, such as cocaine and heroin, can enter the United States by so many diverse routes and in such easily concealed bundles that even a very large increase in successful interdiction will capture only a small proportion of the smuggled drugs. Moreover, smuggling costs account for only a small fraction (perhaps 10 percent) of the final price of cocaine. Low transportation costs and the ease of substituting new routes for discovered routes combine to make interdiction a poor tool with which to raise drug prices and reduce drug supplies. Peter Reuter and his colleagues at RAND (Reuter, Crawford, and Cave 1988) have estimated that doubling the proportion of drugs intercepted would increase the total cost of getting drugs to the final consumer by only 10 percent. Though these estimates rely on arguable assumptions and imperfect data, there is some clear evidence supporting a pessimistic conclusion: despite substantial increases in antismuggling efforts and massive increases in the amount of cocaine seized, cocaine imports have continued to rise, and its street price has continued to fall during the 1980s (Reuter, Crawford, and Cave 1988).

Even scholars most skeptical of the marginal product of additional investments in crop eradication and smuggling interdiction believe that such efforts must continue at some level. Interdiction has some effect, especially on bulky drugs such as marijuana. It has made a difference, though not a long-lived one, on the availability of heroin. It sends a signal to other nations that the United States is serious about the drug problem. It gives force to our commitment to various international treaties banning drug smuggling. And it responds to popular demands that all parts of the drug-dealing chain confront risks and sanctions (Reuter 1988; Reuter, Crawford, and Cave 1988).

On the international front, Moore argues that immobilizing high-level trafficking networks that operate across national boundaries may be more valuable than going after crops or smugglers. These networks corrupt governments, use violence to defeat competitors, and manipulate large amounts of cash earned from illegal transactions. Breaking up such groups may have some value in reducing drug availability and will certainly be valuable in reducing the power of organized crime.

Mark Moore and Mark Kleiman and Kerry Smith (in this volume) argue that additional money for supply reduction may be more usefully spent on the city streets than overseas or at our borders. Since this is contrary to what many people believe, it is important to understand the reasons. First, the retail markets for drugs are highly localized; if disrupted, not only can the supply of drugs be reduced, but also the demand (at least among those users who are highly sensitive to search costs). Second, the operation of local markets often relies on personal contacts (dealers and users who know each other). Personal contacts can be made more risky, and thus the number of transactions produced by these contacts made fewer if some dealers and users are undercover police officers or "righteous" dealers and users are observed by watchful patrol officers. Third, disrupting local markets can improve the conditions of neighborhood life by reclaiming the streets for honest citizens and emboldening them to assert social control over dealing. Fourth, visible police efforts to reduce local dealing reassure the public that the police have not been corrupted; ignoring local dealing encourages the public to suspect that corruption is the reason.

But if increases in supply-reduction efforts should be directed more at local markets than at international smuggling, what tactic should be used? Kleiman and Smith list five possibilities. While admitting that no one has made a systematic evaluation of any of them, they supply some plausible reasons for thinking that tactics aimed at specific neighborhoods ("focused crackdowns") and at controlling known users who are also predatory criminals or drug sellers are more likely to be helpful than efforts at arresting "Mr. Big" or making citywide dealer arrests ("street sweeps"). Arresting Mr. Big is very costly in law-enforcement resources, and the benefits may not be commensurate since rival Mr. Bigs usually stand ready to take over from the Mr. Big who has gone to jail. (Indeed, many Mr. Bigs are arrested because their competitors have leaked information to the police.) Citywide street sweeps often have too little impact on any one neighborhood to make a difference; Kleiman and Smith compare this tactic to picking up 10 percent of the trash in every city park instead of picking up all the trash in one park. Gang suppression is a more ambiguous case. Sometimes a gang that colonizes a city (e.g., a Jamaican gang that enters a new "market" in Kansas City) brings with it a more sophisticated drug-distribution system, thereby increasing the supply of drugs. But sometimes gangs arise after crack is already abundant; their presence makes street life more dangerous, but their absence would not measurably reduce the amount of crack on those streets.

The uncertainty as to the best local supply-reduction tactic is evident from the variety that exists among the methods now employed in big cities. New York City combines a major effort to catch Mr. Big with heavy reliance on focused crackdowns, such as Operation Pressure Point on the Lower East Side. Detroit tends to emphasize street sweeps. Los Angeles carries out street sweeps and gang suppression efforts, supplemented by a major demand-reduction program involving police officers in the schools—Project DARE.

Kleiman and Smith's support for focused crackdowns is challenged by some who argue that drug dealing and crime are not actually reduced; they are merely displaced to other neighborhoods. No firm answer can be made to this criticism, but Kleiman, Moore, and others (see Sherman 1990) have given us good reasons for thinking that under many circumstances, displacement is a good deal less than 100 percent. Thus, there is a net benefit.

IV. Demand Reduction

I believe that every contributor to this volume agrees that significant reductions in drug abuse will come only from reducing the demand for those drugs. Supply-reduction efforts must continue (and, in the case of heroin, they have had some good results), but the marginal product of further investments in supply reduction is likely to be small, especially at the international level. Bigger reductions may come from well-designed local enforcement efforts, but we have as yet next to no systematic evidence about which efforts produce what effects under what circumstances.

Some enthusiasts for sending the marines to occupy Bolivia may dismiss the scholarly consensus about the importance of demand reduction as springing from the customary softheadedness of intellectuals. Let me say, then, that I know of no serious law-enforcement executive who disagrees with this conclusion. Typically, police officials tell interviewers that they are fighting either a losing war or, at best, a holding action.

There are only two ways of reducing demand: altering the subjective state of potential drug users (through prevention and treatment programs) or altering the objective conditions of potential drug users (by increasing the costs of drug use).

A. *Altering Subjective States*

Everyone agrees we need more prevention and treatment programs. By "prevention" we mean primary prevention—that is, reducing the percentage of young people who use drugs for the first time. By "treatment" we mean reducing the rate at which active drug users continue to use those drugs. The problem is to discover what kinds of prevention and treatment programs work, for what people, and at what cost. This is a good deal harder than the political advocates of prevention and treatment imagine.

1. *Prevention.* Some progress has been made. After many failed efforts and false starts, there is evidence that certain prevention programs may actually reduce the number of young people who begin drug use. Gilbert Botvin's essay reviews the false starts and shows how little we have gained, in terms of lessened drug use, from mass-media campaigns, scare tactics, informational lectures, and the display of role models such as athletes who decry drug use. These efforts have been based on the assumption that drug users are unaware of the bad effects of drugs; once they learn of these effects, they will stop using them.

But ignorance is not what leads some adolescents—the primary target of prevention programs—to become heavy drug users. During their teenage years, people assert their independence from parental authority and begin to conform to the expectations of peers. For most young people, this transfer from family-centered to peer-centered lives occurs with only a few bumps and bruises, including some experiments with drugs. But for some, it takes the form of a wholesale rejection of parental authority and a desire to emulate the behavior of peers who are most defiant of adult standards. Among the characteristics of many of the more defiant and deviant young people are impulsiveness, poor school performance, low self-esteem, and a desire for new experiences. Using drugs is only one way—and usually not the first way—in which deviance is expressed. Heavy drug users also tend to be sexually promiscuous, to smoke and drink (often to excess), and to be truant. Although there is nothing inevitable about the process, it is striking that heavy drug use is typically preceded by "light" drug use (smoking marijuana, swallowing an occasional amphetamine), which in turn is often preceded by smoking cigarettes and drinking alcohol.

To such persons, hearing the facts about drug use is almost irrelevant. Young people, as Botvin notes, have a sense of their own invulnerability and value the opinion of their peers more than the advice of their teachers. Two decades of prevention efforts foundered on the rocks of these stubborn facts.

Then a glimmer of hope appeared from efforts to reduce cigarette smoking. The new strategy was based on teaching junior high school (and in some cases even younger) students how to recognize and cope with peer pressure. It is often called "resistance skills training." A broader version—broader in that it attempts to improve the social competency of the young people—is called "social skills training" (see also Bell and Battjes 1985). The essence of these approaches (though not their full complexity) is captured by the slogan, "learning to say 'no.' " The instructors in these programs are sometimes school teachers, sometimes (as in Los Angeles and a few other cities) police officers, and sometimes other teenagers.

Evaluations of these strategies suggest that they slow the rate at which people begin smoking and reduce the proportion of a given group that ever smokes. But will an approach that reduces smoking also reduce drug use? There is evidence that skills training can reduce alcohol use and may even reduce teenage pregnancy, and there is at least one study (see Botvin, in this volume) that finds a reduction in drug use. Many more carefully evaluated experimental projects will have to be carried out before we can be confident that this psychosocial strategy is truly effective in discouraging drug use, but for the first time there are at least grounds for hope.

2. *Treatment*. The evidence that treatment works is stronger than the evidence that prevention works. Anglin and Hser (in this volume) summarize this evidence; other reviews, already available in the literature, concur with this assessment (Tims and Ludford 1984).

The phrase "treatment can work" does not mean that drug users can be "cured"—that is, that, after the treatment, they will live drug-free lives. Drug dependency cannot be fixed as if it were akin to a broken leg. It is more like a chronic disease that requires long-term management and in which we measure gains, not by the proportion of people who are fully cured, but by the relative improvement in the quality of their lives. There are benefits from treatment even when no cure occurs. Those benefits include a reduction in the *rate* of drug abuse and the personal and social costs associated with it (such as poor health, drug-related crime, and low labor productivity).

There are at least four major kinds of treatment programs. Detoxification involves short-term medical help to end immediate drug use and enable the patient to overcome the pains and hazards of withdrawal. Drug-free outpatient centers rely on counseling and training to help users resist drugs while living in the community. Maintenance programs supply heroin users with a legal opiate, methadone, that when taken orally in stable doses produces no "high" of its own and can block the high produced by heroin. Properly administered, methadone, though addictive, can reduce the craving for heroin and prevent the withdrawal pains associated with ending heroin use "cold turkey." Therapeutic communities (TCs) are residential programs in which drug users are exposed to systematic and continuous efforts to get them to confront their addictive lifestyles and alter their personalities so that they can lead drug-free lives.

All of these programs can reduce drug abuse *if* the patients stay in them. Retention in a program, rather than the characteristics of the programs themselves, appears to be a consistently important factor in explaining success. What, then, explains retention?

The answer to that question is not entirely clear. The characteristics of the drug user explain some of the differences. Anglin and Hser believe therapeutic communities do better with young polydrug users who have poor employment records. These people have the worst problems and the poorest prospects, and so the demanding and all-encompassing nature of a TC is more likely to produce retention than more permissive outpatient programs. Methadone maintenance, by contrast, seems to work better with older addicts who have fewer personal and family problems and are already motivated to seek help. Young polydrug users who are black or Hispanic seem, in some studies, to drop out of programs sooner than persons with different characteristics. But there are practitioners (DeLeon 1984) who believe that there are few, if any, obvious patient characteristics that explain retention (though there may be more subtle psychological states that do explain it).

There is one factor that may affect retention, and that is legal compulsion. Persons who enter community-based treatment programs as a condition of probation or parole, if those conditions are effectively monitored and enforced, tend to stay in programs longer than those who enter without such compulsion. As a consequence, they benefit from the treatment as much as clients who stay in the program without compulsion. The best evidence of this comes from the careful long-term studies of the California Civil Addict Program (CAP) (Anglin 1988). This program, sometimes called "civil commitment," involved sending drug users first to a residential treatment center and then requiring the users, as a condition of release back into the community, to become part of an outpatient service in which their drug use was monitored, and they were supplied with a variety of services.

In evaluating CAP, researchers for several years followed both heroin users whom the courts had put into the mandatory outpatient program and a similar group of users who had also been required to enter it but, because of procedural errors, had been released after a minimal exposure. While in the residential facility, both groups reduced their drug use. After release, those who were required to stay in the CAP outpatient service showed lower rates of drug use than those who were allowed to drop out, a difference that persisted for over a decade. Anglin concluded that "civil commitment has an important and dramatic effect in suppressing daily heroin use by narcotics addicts" (Anglin 1988, p. 11). But scholars studying civil commitment programs in New York and in the federal government found no such effects (Inciardi 1988).

The reason for the different outcomes was the difference in the programs. In California, supervision in the community was close, was done by specially trained parole officers having small case loads, and entailed frequent urine tests to detect drug use. Enforcement was strict: resuming drug use often led to reincarceration. The slogan was "You use, you lose."

In New York and in parts of the federal program, the supervision was less close and done by social workers, testing was less frequently used, and penalties for relapse were less regularly enforced (Anglin 1988; Inciardi 1988; Anglin and Hser 1989). (An exception was that part of the federal civil commitment program administered by the U.S. Bureau of Prisons. It seems to have worked as well as the California program, apparently because the Bureau's personnel, like their California counterparts, were experienced law-enforcement professionals.)

Much of the research on drug treatment has focused on programs that enroll heroin users. We know much less about how to treat cocaine or crack users. And one treatment program—methadone maintenance—has almost no relevance for cocaine. Methadone is useful because it prevents the withdrawal pains that follow a cessation in heroin consumption. But stopping cocaine use, while it can induce a deep emotional depression, does not produce withdrawal pains. There cannot be a cocaine version of methadone.

That does not mean that there can be no chemical treatment for cocaine and crack users. There are, in fact, several exciting leads about the value of giving cocaine abusers drugs that are used to treat depression, epilepsy, and Parkinson's disease.[4] The use of these medications has arisen out of basic research that has begun to identify the way in which drugs affect the brain cells.

Addiction, after all, is a disease of the brain. Different kinds of drugs affect the brain differently. Cocaine seems to interfere with the way in which one brain cell communicates with another. Though the actual processes are far more complex (and less well understood) than this lay summary will imply, the key mechanism seems to involve a neurotransmitter called dopamine (and possibly others as well). A neurotransmitter is a chemical messenger that is especially important in certain brain cells found in those parts of the brain (such as the ventral tegmental area) that produce pleasurable sensations. When the brain is operating normally, dopamine is released by one cell to "turn on" an adjacent cell; then the dopamine is carried back to the first cell to await another signal and the adjacent cell "turns off." Cocaine apparently blocks this return flow, probably by interfering with the transporter molecules. The result is that excess dopamine continues to excite the adjacent cell, leading the cocaine user to experience a prolonged period of intense pleasure (Ritz et al. 1987; Gawin and Ellinwood 1988; Koob and Bloom 1988). The brain tells us we are having a wonderful time even when we are just sitting in a chair. The moderating tendencies in normal brain chemistry are upset.

As more is learned about this basic neurochemical process, we will learn more about how other benign drugs can be used to block the ability of cocaine to upset the regular dopamine transport system. We may also learn why some people are more likely than others to use cocaine in an uncontrolled manner (Kozel and Adams 1985).

In all the political debate about how best to mount (and pay for) a drug-control program, not much is heard about neurochemistry and neurobiology. Yet these disciplines are the ones that will probably

---

[4] These drugs include desipramine, bromocriptine, carbamazepine, imipramine, and buprenorphine, among others. No chemical is likely to be a "magic bullet" that will "cure" drug dependency, if for no other reason than the fact that cocaine users find the drug so pleasurable that they do not wish to become abstinent. Moreover, many drug-dependent people suffer from a host of other problems. Chemical treatment can, however, help addicts function normally while undergoing other forms of counseling and therapy. In time, basic research may reveal ways of using pharmacology to prevent drug experimentation in the first place.

provide us with the best understanding and the most effective treatments for drug abuse. Funding this basic research ought to be a major federal priority. So far, it is not.

B. Changing Objective Conditions

Changing the subjective state of drug users is obviously the most desirable goal, because people who no longer crave a drug can be left free in the community with fewer risks to themselves and to others. But it is not necessary to change the preferences of people to change their behavior. We understand that when we make racial discrimination illegal: people may continue to have racist attitudes, but they are less likely to commit racist acts because the costs of doing so have gone up. We also understand this when we rely on the criminal justice system to deter crime. Whatever their preferences, would-be criminals must take into account to some degree the costs of crime.

We have already seen how law enforcement can indirectly reduce demand, at least among casual or novice users, by making drugs harder to find and buy. We can also use sanctions directly to reduce demand by making it more risky to be identified as a drug user. This is the potential role of drug testing.

There is no question that drug testing, properly done in the appropriate setting, can reduce drug use. The experience of the armed forces during and since the war in Vietnam provides ample evidence of this. The U.S. Navy's program, summarized in the essay by Wish and Gropper, is the most extensive. The testing is roughly at random, with the average person experiencing three tests per year. Almost 2 million urine samples (each taken under direct observation to eliminate substitution) are examined each year. At the first sign of drug use, the person is brought into a treatment program. If that person tests positive a second time, he or she is ordinarily declared unfit for service and discharged. The navy asserts that, in 1981, 48 percent of all enlisted personnel under the age of twenty-five were users; by the late 1980s, that proportion was less than 5 percent. Other studies are consistent with the view that testing in the military has been a deterrent to drug use.

Testing is now being employed by various courts as a way of helping judges make decisions about whom to release while awaiting trial and as a way of helping control the drug usage of convicted offenders who are on probation or parole. The civil commitment program and its kin, Treatment Alternatives to Street Crime (TASC) (Bureau of Justice

Assistance 1989), are examples of this latter function. We do not yet know, however, whether the mere use of random drug testing as a condition of release, absent any other treatment interventions, will deter drug use, but it ought to be possible to find out. Some efforts along these lines are now underway at various sites around the country. Preliminary results suggest that, as with the civil commitment program, testing alone will not be enough. The most serious abusers have so many problems and so deviant a lifestyle that many may skip the tests. Only testing coupled with sufficient supervision and the willingness of the supervisor to revoke probation or parole and reincarcerate may be sufficient to reduce drug use and attendant criminality.

No one knows whether testing can serve as an effective deterrent in settings less disciplined than the military or less powerful than the criminal justice system. It is not obvious, however, that it has no place in civilian occupations. The penalties of failing a test may be less among civilian workers than among probationers, but the typical civilian drug user probably has a less serious problem than the typical probationer and so might be more easily deterred. Suppose, for example, that drug tests were routinely used to screen people applying for the reinstatement of a driver's license after it had been suspended for driving while intoxicated and for people seeking employment in a wide range of occupations where safety and reliability are of paramount concern. By sharply constricting the range of activities open to frequent drug users, the costs of drug use to all but the most addicted would obviously go up and the disadvantages of entering a treatment program would go down. Under these circumstances, the demand for drugs ought to decline. Moreover, the existence of a widespread testing program would presumably have a tutelary effect: young people would observe that society was serious about drug abuse and thus, perhaps, be less inclined to regard drug use as a pro forma evil—something perfunctorily condemned but actually tolerated. Whether the theory is correct will depend on evidence that no one has yet tried to collect.

I am assuming here that drug tests can be made reliable and inexpensive.[5] That is a large but not unreasonable assumption. More difficult to solve are the ethical and legal issues involved in testing. To some,

---

[5] Wish and Gropper review the evidence on reliability and cost. They suggest that cheap urine tests can be used for screening and more expensive tests for confirming or rejecting initial positive results. The combined probability of both tests being in error (unless the urine sample has been adulterated) is very low. Hair samples are expensive to test (as of now) but are hard to adulterate.

testing is an invasion of privacy and intolerable for that reason. That surely cannot be the case in the military or the criminal justice system where far greater invasions of privacy—and of liberty—are necessary and commonplace. In other, less restrictive settings, privacy is a value that must be balanced against other values, such as public safety. Automobile drivers are exercising state-controlled privileges that can expose them to, among other things, the obligation to stop at police roadblocks and submit to tests for sobriety. Adding tests designed to detect drug use does not clearly invade an established right, especially if the tests can be done in ways that are not intrusive and embarrassing (as may be possible if hair or saliva tests can be made as economical and reliable as the urine tests).

The courts have yet to settle the issues involved in testing, nor can they settle them wisely unless careful real-world experiments are carried out. Ultimately, the courts will probably defer to some degree to popular views: to the extent society makes it clear that reducing the demand for drugs is extremely important, the courts will take that into account in striking a balance between public safety and personal privacy.

V. Conclusions

In reading the essays of this book, I am struck both by what we know and what we do not know. We know drug trafficking is driven by the demand for drugs and that reducing that demand, to the extent that it is feasible and fair to do so, will have a greater effect on the drugs-crime connection than reducing the supply. We know that demand reduction, to be effective, must involve elements of both therapy and coercion; a demand-side strategy cannot be purely a medical, an educational, or a law-enforcement strategy. We know that various treatment programs will help reduce demand—if people can be induced to remain in them. We suspect that some primary prevention programs will work, but we are not certain of this. Neither do we know the kinds of persons for whom they will work, nor for how long.

We do not know as much about reducing cocaine use as we know about reducing heroin use. We do not know what kind of street-level enforcement efforts are most effective in reducing either the demand for or the supply of drugs, though we think that the street is where the principal law-enforcement effort must be made.

Above all, we do not know how to alter the moral climate so that drug use is regarded as loathsome. A large number of young people still try drugs; many, though perhaps somewhat fewer than was once the case, go on to use them regularly. Public officials can and should decry drug use and make clear the moral, as well as the practical, grounds for it being wrong. But government statements are not likely to be as effective in shaping the moral climate as the efforts of neighborhood associations, community groups, and literary and artistic figures. Statements from these sources may not have any direct preventive effect, but their cumulative, long-term effect in shaping the ethos within which standards of personal conduct are defined may be great. There is no way to test that assumption, but there can be little harm in acting as if it were true. One of the advantages of making certain drugs illegal and enforcing the laws against their possession is that these actions reinforce the social condemnation of drug use and the social praise accorded temperate behavior.

I have watched several "wars on drugs" declared over the last three decades. The wars typically begin with the statement that the time for studies is past and the time for action has come. "We know what to do; let's get on with it." In fact, we do not know what to do in any comprehensive way, and the need for research is never more urgent than at the beginning of a "war." That is because every past war has led, after brief gains, to final defeat. And so we condemn another generation to risk.

We certainly know enough to begin, if not a "war," then a reasonable array of programs. In our urgency to get on with what we do know, it is important that we organize some of those efforts—in prevention, treatment, and supply reduction—in a frankly experimental manner so that, before the next war is declared, we will have improved our knowledge of what works. Moreover, some of the most urgently needed research is basic research on such questions as the biological basis of addiction, the ability of chemicals to block the euphoric effects of drugs and thereby reduce the craving for them, the presence or absence of biological markers that will help us identify the individuals most at risk for addictive behavior (Braude and Chao 1986), and the early childhood and familial processes that increase the likelihood of young people allowing their impulsiveness, search for thrills, and desire for independence to lead them into self-destructive behavior.

REFERENCES

Anglin, M. Douglas. 1988. "The Efficacy of Civil Commitment in Treating Narcotic Addiction." In *Compulsory Treatment of Drug Abuse: Research and Clinical Practice*, edited by Carl G. Leukefeld and Frank M. Tims. National Institute on Drug Abuse Research Monograph no. 86. Rockville, Md.: Department of Health and Human Services, National Institute on Drug Abuse.

Anglin, M. Douglas, and Yih-Ing Hser. 1989. "Legal Coercion and Drug Abuse Treatment: Research Findings and Social Policy Implications." Unpublished manuscript. University of California at Los Angeles, Drug Abuse Research Group, March.

————. In this volume. "Treatment of Drug Abuse."

Bell, Catherine S., and Robert Battjes, eds. 1985. *Prevention Research: Deterring Drug Abuse among Children and Adolescents*. National Institute on Drug Abuse Research Monograph no. 63. Rockville, Md.: Department of Health and Human Services, National Institute on Drug Abuse.

Botvin, Gilbert J. In this volume. "Substance Abuse Prevention: Theory, Practice, and Effectiveness."

Braude, Monique C., and Helen M. Chao, eds. 1986. *Genetic and Biological Markers in Drug Abuse and Alcoholism*. National Institute on Drug Abuse Research Monograph no. 66. Rockville, Md.: Department of Health and Human Services, National Institute on Drug Abuse.

Bureau of Justice Assistance. 1989. *Treatment Alternatives to Street Crime (TASC): Resource Manual*. Washington, D.C.: U.S. Department of Justice, Bureau of Justice Assistance.

Chaiken, Jan M., and Marcia R. Chaiken. In this volume. "Drugs and Predatory Crime."

DeLeon, George. 1984. "Program-based Evaluation Research in Therapeutic Communities." In *Drug Abuse Treatment Evaluation: Strategies, Progress, and Prospects*, edited by Frank M. Tims and Jacqueline P. Ludford. National Institute on Drug Abuse Research Monograph no. 51. Rockville, Md.: Department of Health and Human Services, National Institute on Drug Abuse.

Fagan, Jeffrey A. In this volume. "Intoxication and Aggression."

Gawin, Frank H., and H. Ellinwood. 1988. "Cocaine and Other Stimulants: Actions, Abuse, and Treatment." *New England Journal of Medicine* 318:1173–82.

Hunt, Dana. In this volume. "Drugs and Consensual Crime: Drug Dealing and Prostitution."

Inciardi, James A. 1988. "Some Considerations on the Clinical Efficacy of Compulsory Treatment: Reviewing the New York Experience." In *Compulsory Treatment and Drug Abuse: Research and Clinical Practice*, edited by Carl G. Leukefeld and Frank M. Tims. National Institute on Drug Abuse Research Monograph no. 86. Rockville, Md.: Department of Health and Human Services, National Institute on Drug Abuse.

Johnson, Bruce D., Terry Williams, Kojo A. Dei, and Harry Sanabria. In this volume. "Drug Abuse in the Inner City: Impact on Hard Drug Users and the Community."

Kaplan, John. 1988. "Taking Drugs Seriously." *Public Interest* 92:32–50.

Kleiman, Mark A. R., and Kerry D. Smith. In this volume. "State and Local Drug Enforcement: In Search of a Strategy."

Koob, George F., and Floyd E. Bloom. 1988. "Cellular and Molecular Mechanisms of Drug Dependence." *Science* 242:715–23.

Kozel, Nicholas J., and Edgar H. Adams, eds. 1985. *Cocaine Use in America: Epidemiological and Clinical Perspectives*. National Institute on Drug Abuse Research Monograph no. 61. Rockville, Md.: Department of Health and Human Services, National Institute on Drug Abuse.

Moore, Mark H. In this volume. "Supply Reduction and Drug Law Enforcement."

Office of National Drug Control Policy. 1989. *National Drug Control Strategy*. Washington, D.C.: U.S. Government Printing Office.

Pearson, Geoffrey. 1990. "Drug Control Policies in Britain: Continuity and Change." In *Crime and Justice: A Review of Research*, vol. 14, edited by Michael Tonry and Norval Morris. Chicago: University of Chicago Press (forthcoming).

Reuter, Peter. 1988. "Can the Borders Be Sealed?" *Public Interest* 92:51–65.

Reuter, Peter, Gordon Crawford, and Jonathan Cave. 1988. *Sealing the Borders: The Effects of Increased Military Participation in Drug Interdiction*. Report no. R-3594-USDP. Santa Monica, Calif.: RAND.

Ritz, Mary C., R. L. Lamb, Steven R. Goldberg, and Michael J. Kuhar. 1987. "Cocaine Receptors on Dopamine Transporters Are Related to Self-Administration of Cocaine." *Science* 237:1219–23.

Sherman, Lawrence. 1990. "Police Crackdowns: Initial and Residual Deterrence." In *Crime and Justice: A Review of Research*, vol. 12, edited by Michael Tonry and Norval Morris. Chicago: University of Chicago Press.

Tims, Frank M., and Jacqueline P. Ludford, eds. 1984. *Drug Abuse Treatment Evaluation: Strategies, Progress, and Prospects*. National Institute on Drug Abuse Research Monograph no. 51. Rockville, Md.: Department of Health and Human Services, National Institute on Drug Abuse.

Wilson, James Q. 1990. "Against the Legalization of Drugs." *Commentary* 89:21–28.

Wish, Eric D., and Bernard A. Gropper. In this volume. "Drug Testing by the Criminal Justice System: Methods, Research, and Applications."

Author Index

Subject Index

Abstinence, 93, 94, 103, 278, 395, 397, 403, 417, 422, 423
Aesklepieian model, 398
Aggregate crime rates, 222, 234
AIDS, 49, 51, 52–53, 55, 56, 72, 107, 315, 328, 337, 369, 390, 400, 409, 447, 453, 462, 522
Alcoholism and crime, 241–320; belligerent drinking, 271, 272; binge drinking, 277, 285; malevolence assumption, 294; states of drunkenness, 294
Anomie theory, 274
Anti-Drug Abuse Act of 1988, 361

Bail Reform Act of 1984, 355
Berry v. District of Columbia, 323
Black market, 117
Bloods, 20, 21, 90, 91, 92. *See also* Gangs
Blood tests, 50, 337
Boys' clubs, 92
Breathalyzer, 336
Buy-and-bust techniques, 21, 104

California Civil Addict Program (CAP), 329, 398, 410, 425, 437–38, 537–38
California Department of Alcohol and Drug Programs, 348
Cambridge-Somerville Youth Study, 262
Caveat emptor philosophy, 187

Censored probit, 360
Chambers Brothers, 83
Client Oriented Data Acquisition Process (CODAP), 128
Cocaine: crack generation (1985–present), 16–17, 69, 173, 530; freebase (freebasing), 9, 15, 16, 17, 28, 29, 33; rock, 16, 21, 69; selling, 17–18; snorting, 12, 15, 28, 29, 34; speedball, 15; on street level, 23–26; rise of use in inner city, 15–16, 40
CODAP, 128
Cognitive impairment, 291–92
Committee for G.I. Rights v. Calloway, 378
Common cause theory, 288
Competition paradigm, 264, 265, 266, 267, 268, 269, 293. *See also* Competitive reaction paradigm
Competitive reaction paradigm, 244
Consequences of drug use/dealing for the inner city, 39–55; declines in economic well being, 43–49, 56; family and kinship ties, 53–55, 56; hard drugs and crime, 41–43, 56; morbidity and mortality, 49–53; rehabilitation difficulties, 48–49; rise and economic importance for the criminal underclass, 40–41
Cornerstone program, 428, 452
Correction agencies (officials), 70, 87
CRASH, 91, 99